The Dictionary of GAMBLING & GAMING

by

Thomas L. Clark

LH

LEXIK HOUSE Publishers
Cold Spring, New York

Library of Congress Cataloging in Publication Data

Clark, Thomas L.
The Dictionary of Gambling & Gaming

87-082866

ISBN: 0-936368-06-3

First Edition

Manufactured in the United States of America

Typesetter: J & M Graphic Concepts, Inc.
Printer: Hamilton Printing Company

TABLE OF CONTENTS

FOREWORD

The language of gambling and gaming has been a subject of lexicographic interest since at least the seventeenth century, when "B. E., Gent." published "A New Dictionary of the Terms Ancient and Modern of the Canting Crew"—that is, the English underworld of beggars, thieves, cheats, and, inevitably, practitioners of the arts of skill and chance. These arts must have existed and been practiced at least as long ago as the discovery that the ankle-bone of a sheep (talus), a cube-like piece, could easily be cast, and could serve to show, from whichever side fell upward, the dictates of chance—or, in divination, the sense of a Power behind.

Since mankind is notoriously a talking animal, as well as a gambling animal, the language of games, incantatory, imprecatory, or merely practical, has been elaborated to a high degree. And because, in gaming, the same objects must be handled and the same actions performed repeatedly, two developments have come in the language: certain standard terms have evolved, those most often and officially used; and with them a vigorous outgrowth of by-forms, variants, or alternatives that avoid repetition and lighten formality. Thus in the very first entry, *A,* the alternatives or variants *able, age, edge, eldest hand,* and *under the gun* show players exercising individual freedom and avoiding cliche.

The present *Dictionary of Gambling and Gaming* is a bold original attempt to cover the terminology, past and present, practiced on the American scene. As the author, Professor Thomas Clark, indicates, its main reason for being is that there was a need. Its production in Nevada, a state historically and presently interested in gambling and gaming, is in part fortuitous, but obviously a valuable circumstance.

Tom Clark, as I must call him from long acquaintance and admiration, came to my attention first as the man who made forty-three field records in Ohio for the *Dictionary of American Regional English.* He learned well the value—indeed, the necessity—of getting his data not only from printed sources, but directly from living people who use the language as it is practiced—in its varieties and valid forms. Such experience, knowledge, and method are evident throughout this book: it is sound in background scholarship, true to present use, and presented with professional style. To all logophiles and aleators it will offer lively reading. I predict a warm reception for it and a space on one's most reachable bookshelf.

Frederic G. Cassidy
Chief Editor, *DARE*

INTRODUCTION

A dictionary is a continuing project, interrupted occasionally by printing the material and sharing it with people. People, in this case, are language scholars, gamers, gamblers, and people who study gaming, such as sociologists, psychologists, anthropologists, historians. In fact, nearly everyone who happens onto a term used in gaming and gambling, whether in literature or on a national news telecast will find something of interest here.

Every dictionary has a special scope and purpose. Sometimes the aim is to list all the words in a language, itself an impossible task, because every living language changes constantly, just as people change and society changes in focus, progress, and emphasis. At other times, the aim is to list special parts of the vocabulary of a language, such as regional dialects, slang, the vocabulary of this or that occupation or profession. This dictionary falls into the latter category.

This dictionary provides explanations for words, terms, and phrases that people encounter wherever gambling takes place. Because gambling is pervasive in our society, cutting across social boundaries and levels of language, the words, terms, and phrases defined here include slang, professional jargon, the argot of the underworld, and every level of usage from the most formal to the colloquial. This is not to say, however, that every term ever found in a gambling or gaming situation is included. Philip B. Gove could have been speaking for all dictionary makers when he remarked in the preface to *Webster's Third New International Dictionary*, "The number of words available is always far in excess of and for a one-volume dictionary many times the number that can possibly be included." (p. 7a.)

The primary reason for producing any dictionary must be that it fulfills a need. But the lexicographer who undertakes a true dictionary, as opposed to a glossary or a simple alphabetical listing of words, must also hope to add something to the art and science of the discipline, to its methodology or to lexicology generally. I would not presume to compare the work here to contributions by such language scholars as Frederic Cassidy or Clarence Barnhart, two who taught me so much, or to Nathanial Bailey, Samuel Johnson, C. T. Onions, Phillip Gove, or any lexicographers of that rank. Yet, this dictionary, while meeting the basic need for which it was designed, also represents attempts to add to the art of making specialized dictionaries.

Some lexicographic features of this dictionary have been used in other dictionaries, but they have not been collectively used in the manner found here. The scope of the dictionary includes a modified use of *historical principles,* comparisons with other dictionaries, illustrative quotations, inclusion of oral and fugitive sources, and glosses of difficult or rare terms found within the illustrative quotations. Each of these five points can be more fully discussed.

On the Concept "Historical Principles" in Dictionaries of Sub-cultures*

Every lexicographer who begins the task of making a dictionary must assess the scope of the collection. We can rarely hope to include everything we would like included; nor can we certainly include everything our critics swear we should have included. Not even the makers of the *Oxford English Dictionary* could hope to assay the entire corpus of English. Consequently, every lexicographer begins the labor by setting out a list of guiding principles for

* From *Dictionaries: Journal of the Dictionary Society of North America,* No. 2-3 (1980-81), pp. 1-6. By permission of Richard W. Bailey, editor. Author Thomas L. Clark.

the size of the collection, the items to be included, the methods for acquisition of citations. Additionally, there must be rules for listing headwords, pronunciations, cross-references.

Early on, the lexicographer must decide whether or not to follow historical principles in creating the dictionary. In those collections of words which, for the most part, sit above the salt, the traditional guidelines of historical principles are fairly firm: list the earliest and latest occurrences, along with citations which reflect a change in the history, form, or sense of the word.

But when a lexicographer is dealing with words which sit below the salt, the problems of what constitutes historical principles become intractable, most interesting. David W. Maurer was one of the great students of those words which have no pedigree. He observed that collecting the language of a sub-culture outside the technical, scientific, professional, or occupational sub-cultures is a chancy business at best. "The continuity of any sub-culture," he said, "is heavily dependent on keeping a significant part of the usage exclusive, since the subculture loses its identity once its language is adopted by the dominant culture."

Obviously, then, an attempt to record the lexicon of particular sub-cultures will result in the necessity for finding unpublished citations. Determining the history of individual words will not be so difficult, because many words used in sub-cultures have a long and documented history. Rather, the lexicographer will spend more time puzzling over the later development in the meanings of words.

In compiling a dictionary of terms peculiar to subcultures outside of the technical or scientific fields, the lexicographer encounters more neosemanticisms than neologisms. New words rarely are created. More often, standard English words are given metaphoric extension or undergo some other form of semantic shift. By way of example, here is a portion of an interview of a member of the gambling sub-culture. This interview was taken for data collection relative to [this project]. The interviewee ("informant" is not a word used in interviewing members of certain sub-cultures) is a person who makes a living as a player of a specialized form of poker. The interviewer is learning how to play Hold 'em, also known as Texas Hold 'em or Hold Me Darling.

> In Hold 'em, two hole cards are dealt face down to each player. The player on the button acts as dealer, even though the house dealer actually shuffles and deals the cards. The play rotates to the left. The first player is usually the blind, though some games have a double-blind or an overblind. The next player must call the player in the blind or fold. Since there is a live blind opening, more action may develop. The house dealer then burns and turns the flop. The flop is three cards face up on the board. All players use these community cards, plus their hole cards, to bet the next round. If you're sitting there with aces wired and the flop comes, say, ace, ace, rag, then you've got the immortals . . . that's what they call the nuts. With a lock like that, you start jamming the pot, though a good player would sandbag that hand. Anyway, after that betting round, the dealer makes the turn, that is, the fourth street card. After another betting round, the dealer turns the river card. Then they check, bet, or call and maybe raise. Each player uses the best five cards to make a hand. That is, he uses any of the five community cards on deck and his hole cards to show. The dealer takes the rake at the end . . . unless it's a snatch game, of course.

In this sample, no neologisms occur, but I think you will agree that a number of terms could use further explication. The "blind" mentioned near the beginning of the passage refers to the first player to the left of the dealer (designated by the button), who must bet a specified amount to start the pot. Since this player bets before seeing any cards, he is "in the blind." The metaphoric extension is clear. What is not clear, however, is whether or not a semantic shift can be classified as a neosemanticism. Since all Hold 'em players, indeed, all professional poker players know what a blind is, how new or old must the shifted semantic sense be to consider it a neosemanticism?

It just so happens that "blind" as a poker term dates to 1850 in the *DA*, and to 1857 in the *OED Supplement*. Table I illustrates a number of the terms from the preceding passage as cross-checked with major historical dictionaries and *Webster's Third International Dictionary* (W3). . . .

Until very recently, terms like *holdem, flop, fourth street, river card, wired, rags, immortals, nuts, jamming the pot* did not appear in print with the special poker senses. Consequently, they could not be listed in a collection based on historical principles—if the term *historical principles* is restricted to its traditional meaning. This problem has been recognized by other lexicographers. Mitford M. Mathews, in the preface to *A Dictionary of Americanisms on Historical Principles* (p. v.) said, "the number of terms included might easily have been greater had it not been for the rigid exclusion of those which, at the time of

TABLE I: CROSS-CHECKING TERMS IN MAJOR DICTIONARIES

HOLDEM (var. hold em, hold 'em, Texas Hold 'em, hold me darling)

	OED	Supp.	DAE	DA	W3
1. blind	n	1872	1857	1850	y
2. burn	n	nH	n	n	nH
3. button	n	nH	n	n	n
4. check	nH	nH	n	nH	y
5. double blind	nH	nH	n	n	n
6. flop	n	n	n	n	n
7. fold	nH	nH	n	n	y
8. fourth street	n	n	n	n	n
9. holdem	n	n	n	n	n
10. immortals	n	n	n	n	y
11. jamming(the pot)	n	n	n	n	n
12. lock	nH	nH	n	n	n
13. nuts	n	n	n	n	n
14. overblind	n	n	n	n	n
15. rags	n	n	n	n	y
16. river card	n	n	n	n	n
17. sandbag	n	nH	n	n	y
18. snatch game	n	nH	n	n	n
19. turn (card)	nH	n	nH	n	nH
20. wired	n	n	n	n	n

n = no gambling sense entered
nH = no gambling sense as used in Hold 'em
y = gambling sense as used in Hold 'em and other poker games
year = earliest citation of poker sense

going to press, *no printed evidence was on hand*." (emphasis added) Similarly, in *A Dictionary of Canadianisms on Historical Principles*, Walter S. Avis used only dated evidence from printed sources, after the fashion of the *OED, DAE,* and *DA*. Then he said (p. xii), "To follow this tradition, however, is to accept certain restrictions, for it precludes the entering of terms for which there is only oral evidence and of others for which the printed evidence is fragmentary or otherwise inadequate." However, a dictionary is a historical documentation of the words in the language at a given moment in time. Because of this, the lexicographer has the duty to record the existence of words to whatever extent is possible.

The question finally comes down to this: what, exactly, constitutes *historical principles* in the making of dictionaries?

Samuel Johnson, of course, used citations from earlier writers. He had hoped that each quotation might show not only the existence of a word, but also provide some efficacious sentiment or moral truth. In his preface, however, he voiced the lament we have heard so often: due to space limitations, some of the citations would merely posit the existence of a word. Later in the century, John Horne Tooke described his theories of etymology, and Charles Richardson, following Tooke's suggestions with a disciple's zeal, used illustrative quotations almost exclusively in his dictionary of 1836-37. From the earliest days, lexicographers, though not always following the practice, have recognized the importance of context to the citation of a word. More recently, Clarence Barnhart offered words of wisdom in describing a golden mean for illustrative citations:

> . . . abbreviated evidence shows the occurrence of a word, but often fails to show the word's distinctive use, quality or cultural status. Expanded contexts are of special importance in historical dictionaries since the lexicographer is trying to throw light on the living vocabulary of another time: it is as useful to know the context in which the word is used as it is to know its meaning and grammatical function or position in a sentence.[2]

The number of historical principles and their refinement grew slowly as the state of the art in British and North American English lexicography developed. In 1962, Hans Aarsleff clearly established that the statement of historical principles Sir James Murray used in the 1933 Preface to the *OED* was taken, nearly word-for-word, from a translation of Franz Passow's 1819 work, *Handworterbuch der Griechischen Sprache.*[3] The prose statement made by Murray outlines general principles which, though slightly modified by lexicographers since, have become ironclad rules for historical dictionaries. I have translated these principles into a list, which has not been done before. A list is easier to work with, and we always find it easier to add to a list than to a delicately written prose statement.

Here is the list of historical principles set forth by Sir James Murray in the 1933 Preface to the *Oxford English Dictionary* (pp. iv, v).

I. Show the source of each English word
   A. Show when it entered the language
   B. Show how it became English
   C. Show its shape (spelling, form)
   D. Show its original meaning
   E. Show its development of form
   F. Show its progress in meaning
   G. Show which uses have become obsolete
   H. Show which uses survive
   I. Show new uses by process and date
II. Illustrate each word with quotations
   A. List the first known occurrence of the word
   B. List the most recent occurrence of the word
   C. List occurrences which reflect important historical changes in the word
III. Treat the etymology of each word
   A. List historical facts for each word
   B. Use the latest methods and findings from modern philological science

Lexicographers working in English in North America have modified this list, expanded it, reduced it as their work demanded. Dean Richard Chenevix Trench, as early as 1857, had supplied the overall guiding principle: he defined the lexicographer as historian, not standard bearer of the language.[4] This principle has been followed by nearly all lexicographers, from Murray to Phillip Gove editing *Webster's Third New International Dictionary*. The tradition has been well established. Lexicographers follow the footsteps of their spiritual ancestors, but make the most of current methods, as admonished in III b, above.

In the *Dictionary of Bahamian English*, editor John A. Holm said that for guidelines, "we turned to the *Dictionary of Jamaican English*, as Cassidy and Le Page had turned to the principles of the *Dictionary of American English* before them, which in turn followed the historical principles of the *Oxford English Dictionary*." Holm goes on to state that even the *DJE* guidelines were slightly modified by him to allow inclusion of more types of words collected by oral methods.

The use of historical principles calls for the use of dated, printed citations. But these principles were established for a general vocabulary at a time when print was still the main means for storing information. In recent years, the advent of audio tape, video tape, computer storage in various forms of tape and disks has made available to the lexicographer an increased volume of both general and sub-culture vocabulary. In addition, oral histories are being collected in every state and province. Many of these oral histories are rich sources of information for little-known or uncollected words. Coupled with the excellent example of using oral and diary information, as firmly established by the *Dictionary of American Regional English*, the concept of historical principles can be expanded somewhat, in order to utilize "the latest methods and findings from modern philological science," to use Murray's phase.

No longer can only the printed word be used as the basis for historical evidence or citation. Modern technology has extended the collection of material beyond the book to microfilm, to typescript, to a variety of methods for storing information. It happened that the Early English Text Society was established to widely distribute rare books for the purpose of collecting citations. We must remember that the EETS also published manuscripts that had been handwritten. Today, oral histories are often maintained only in typescript, even tape, and copies are distributed by microform. This practice might have been adopted by the EETS, had the technology been available. Frederic Cassidy recognized the problem in 1973, while reviewing the *American Dialect Dictionary*. One great fault he found in that work was that, "the dependence is too heavy on printed sources."[5] Cassidy made sure that *DARE* would not suffer the same fault. He sent fieldworkers into every corner of the country to collect citations orally. Like *DARE*, the *Dictionary of Gambling and Gaming* utilizes both printed and oral sources, as well as unpublished manuscripts, diaries, and oral histories.

As every lexicographer builds on the traditions and principles of those scholars of yesterday, so too the expansion of the concept of historical principles to include non-printed historical information is a way of building on tradition, not violating it.

Thus, to Murray's 1933 statement, we must add these three statements:

A. Utilize all historical records, including interviews and oral histories
B. Use citations long enough to demonstrate meaning *in situ*
C. Cross-index with earlier dictionaries based on historical principles

NOTES

1. David W. Maurer, "Culture, Sub-culture, and Lexicography," *Lexicography in English*, Raven I. McDavid and Audrey Duckert, eds. Annals of the New York Academy of Sciences, vol. 211, 1973, p. 185.

2. Clarence L. Barnhart, "American Lexicography, 1945–1973," *American Speech*, 53 (1978), p. 84.

3. "The Early History of the *Oxford English Dictionary," Bulletin of the New York Public Library*, 66 (1962), p. 432. Actually, according to Aarsleff, the principles had been mentioned by Passow seven years earlier, in 1812. Aarsleff provides the German version, along with a translation which is very close to words used by Murray in his Romanes Lecture of 1900, "The Evolution of English Lexicography," Oxford: Clarendon Press, pp. 45–46. The same passage reappeared in the Preface to the *OED* in 1933. Cf. Ronald A. Wells, *Dictionaries and the Authoritarian Tradition,* Janua Linguarum, Series Practica 196: The Hague; Mouton, 1973, p. 28.

4. Richard Chenevix Trench, "On Some Deficiencies in Our English Dictionaries," *Transactions of the Philological Society* (1857), p. 4.

5. Quoted in Barnhart, p. 91.

REFERENCES

Aarsleff, Hans. "The Early History of the *Oxford English Dictionary." Bulletin of the New York Public Library,* 66 (1962), 417–439.

Avis, Walter S., ed. *Dictionary of Canadianisms on Historical Principles*. Toronto: Gage, 1967.

Barnhart, Clarence L. "American Lexicography, 1945–1973." *American Speech*, 53 (1978), 83–140.

Cassidy, Frederic C. and R.B. LePage, eds. *Dictionary of Jamaican English*. Cambridge: Cambridge University Press, 1967.

Craigie, William A. and James R. Hulbert, eds. *A Dictionary of American English on Historical Principles*. Chicago: The University of Chicago Press, 1938–44.

Holm, John A. *Dictionary of Bahamian English*. Cold Spring, New York: Lexik House Publishers 1982.

Mathews, Mitford M., ed. *A Dictionary of Americanisms on Historical Principles*. Chicago: The University of Chicago Press, 1951.

Maurer, David W. "Culture, Sub-culture, and Lexicography." *Lexicography in English*, Raven I. McDavid, Jr. and Audrey Duckert, eds. Annals of the New York Academy of Sciences, 211 (1973), 83–87.

McDavid, Raven I. Jr. and Audrey R. Duckert, eds. *Lexicography in English*. New York: New York Academy of Sciences Annals 211, 1973.

Murray, James A.H. et al., eds. *A New English Dictionary on Historical Principles*. Oxford: Oxford University Press, 1933.

Murray, James A.H. *The Evolution of English Lexicography*. Oxford: Clarendon Press, 1900.

Trench, Richard Chenevix. "On Some Deficiencies in Our English Dictionaries." *Trans actions of the Philological Society* (1857), 3–8.

Wells, Ronald A. *Dictionaries and the Authoritarian Tradition*. Janua Linguarum, Series Practica 196. The Hague: Mouton, 1973.

* * * *

Use of Historical Dictionaries

Although this work is not strictly a dictionary on historical principles, many of the principles used in works such as the *Dictionary of Americanisms on Historical Principles* have been incorporated.

In keeping with the spirit of historical principles, the lexicon listed here has been compared to the main historical dictionaries of record: *Oxford English Dictionary (OED)* and Supplements I–IV, *Dictionary of American English on Historical Principles (DAE),* and *Dictionary of Americanisms on Historical Principles (DA).* Other dictionaries have been consulted for special purposes relating to some of the lexicon, including *Dictionary of American Regional English (DARE), Dictionary of American Slang (DAS), Dictionary of Slang and Unconventional English (DSUE), The Barnhart Dictionary of New English Since 1963 (BDNE I), The Second Barnhart Dictionary of New English (BDNE II),* and *The Barnhart Dictionary Companion* (quarterly) (*BDC*) and *Webster's Third New International Dictionary (W3).* Other dictionaries have been occasionally consulted and references to those works appear as necessary.

References to terms found in the major historical dictionaries of record (*OED, DAE,* and *DA*), appear at the end of each definition, along with the date of the first occurrence of a term with a gambling or gaming sense as found in those works.

Illustrative Quotations

Citations for many of the terms (that is, quotations from printed or oral sources in which the term occurs) are included in the entries. These citations often predate the terms as found in the historical dictionaries. Lexicographers frequently have pointed out that finding citations earlier than those listed in the *OED* has become nearly a monotonous game. Two reasons account for the large number of earlier citations found in this dictionary. First, the scope of the *OED* required that many specialized books dealing with gambling be ignored in searching the general vocabulary. Second, the volunteer readers who provided quotations for this work have been diligent in utilizing the sources available for this study. The citations used are not necessarily the earliest quotations in which a term is to be found. Often, such a quotation merely posits the existence of the word without providing information about its meaning or showing its use in context. Because of this practice, the earliest date from one or more of the historical dictionaries is provided. Readers concerned with the historical features of a term can be referred to the various sources to determine dates of usage. The citations have been selected to show the term in context. This principle, to show the word in use rather than simply to posit the existence of the term, will help to clarify the sense of the word for the general reader.

A large number of the words found here exist only in the oral tradition of professional gamblers. Often, the terms appear in print only in recent publications. Because much more has been written about gambling for the general populace only in recent years, many of the citations to be found here are of recent origin or from oral collecting.

Not all terms have been provided with illustrative quotations. In many cases, such illustrations are unnecessary. In a few cases, no suitable illustrative quotations have been found that meet the criteria for demonstrating usage. An attempt has been made to provide citations for very old terms or those considered rare or obsolete. However, determining obsolescence is chancy. For example, *age,* "the first person to the left of the dealer," is listed as old-fashioned by *DARE* and declared obsolete by one writer in 1964. But the term was used in print as recently as 1949, and is found more than once in the oral interviews. And *william* "any banknote, or *bill,*" is labeled obsolete by *DAS,* but is found in contemporary use in 1983 in the oral collection.

Printed and Oral Sources

The two major sources for citations are the Gaming Collection in the Dickinson Library at the University of Nevada, Las Vegas, and field interviews. The Gaming Collection contains more than seven thousand books, diaries, typescripts, and miscellanea. The collection is the largest available and for this reason, not because Las Vegas is a large center for gambling, the main work on the dictionary was conducted here.

I have also incorporated one of the best features of the *Dictionary of American Regional English* by including citations from oral sources and fugitive sources: interviews, oral histories and fieldwork. I have incorporated a few quotations from Mead Data Central's *Nexis,* an electronic database.

Respondents for field interviews included professional gamblers, dealers, and management and cage personnel from casinos. The bulk of the interviews were conducted by me, between 1971 and 1987, and by Thomas Martinet, from 1983 onward. Martinet's years of experience as dealer, boxman, owner of a school for dealers, and associate of professional gamers allowed him access to language information that would not otherwise have been collectable by anyone outside of the business. Many of the terms used by contemporary gamblers and gamers exist only in oral form. Because gambling is endemic in the land, conducting fieldwork in a single city could be limiting. But the restrictions of traveling outside Nevada for field interviews was greatly vitiated by the fact that most professional gamblers visit Las Vegas from time to time, and the language of such gamblers is common to the social group, not confined to a region.

Glosses within Citations

The fifth feature contributing to innovation in this dictionary is the addition of glosses within citations. Many of the quotations are extensive, the more effectively to show the word in context. And many of the quotations are from early sources. Consequently, several terms in a quotation may be found elsewhere in the volume. To save the reader the trouble caused by having to flip pages back and forth, a word or two of explanation can be found in the citation, immediately after those words that might cause problems for the reader. Including glosses in this fashion lets the reader see words in context in a way not often possible, given the space restrictions common to dictionaries. And because of space restrictions, some of the longer quotations have been entered under a single entry. The reader is referred to that entry from different places in the lexicon. The disadvantage of having to turn to a single long quotation is offset by the fact that the long quotation consulted will yield a number of terms common to the same topic. The quotations at *hazard* and *basset* serve as examples.

"Gambling & Gaming"
The Title of this Dictionary

The words *Gambling* and *Gaming* are used in the title because the two terms are closely intertwined historically and semantically. The following excerpt is from my article "Gaming and/or Gambling: You pays your money . . .," *Verbatim*, volume X, number 4, Spring, 1984, by permission of the editor, Laurence Urdang.

> Las Vegas bills itself as "The Gaming Capital of the World." Yet people who arrive in town expect to "gamble" by playing "games" or "gambling games." My understanding, after working with these materials for more than five years, is that state officialdom, when hoping to sound professional and clinical, uses the term *gaming* as having an ameliorative sense. By contrast, then, the assumption, would be that *gambling* has a pejorative connotation. This article examines some of the connotations in these terms from the stand-point of people committed to the industry of playing while paying and from the standpoint of other people equally committed to abolishing this (nearly) most ancient vice.

In the extreme views, *gaming* is a pastime for sportsmen, persons of gentility: genteel folk out for a lark may frolic and sport by taking chances on winning or losing some money, neither much nor little. *Gambling,* on the other hand, carries a note of desperation, a sense of wantonness, not a pastime but an obsession, risking high amounts on generally losing propositions; it is an activity for wastrels who dissipate estates and fortunes while carousing with all manner of strumpets and consorting with other riotous low-livers. Actually, the distinctions between *gaming* and *gambling* lie somewhere between these extremes. Indeed, for some people, the terms are synonymous.

The members of the Nevada State Legislature first legalized gambling in Assembly Bill number 98 in 1931. The prologue to the bill reads, "An Act concerning slot machines, *gambling games,* and gambling devices" [emphasis mine]. The bill goes on to list specific games played for money and to prescribe licensing fees for such wagering activities, along with a description of the premises where persons may risk money. The index to those statutes of 1931 carries only the listing *Gambling and Gambling Devices.* By 1939, someone in officialdom sensed the nuances between terms. The index for that year lists *Gambling—see Gaming*, and amendments to the 1931 bill are listed under the latter heading. Interestingly, the marginal notes placed alongside each bill and amendment use the term *gambling*.

By 1941 (the state legislature meets only every two years), the index for statutes was back to listing all such bills and amendments under the heading of *Gambling*, a practice that remained in effect even through the 1959 session, when the Nevada Gaming Commission and the State Gaming Control Board were established. In fact, the index for 1959 lists all bills and amendments under *Gambling*, while the entries under *Gaming* list only the two new regulatory boards. In 1967, the indexer for the Nevada Revised Statutes used *see Gambling* for all references to gaming. And so it has remained until today. That the indexer for these official papers has some latitude in description is demonstrated by the fact that the famous (or infamous) "Black Book," a listing of persons "to be excluded or ejected from licensed *gaming* establishments" [emphasis mine] is referenced in the index but not in the amendment that established that famous and seldom-seen document.

It appears that the term *gambling* is used generally within the state to refer to any activity relative to wagering, while the term *gaming* is used in all official references. Today, Chapter 463 of the Nevada Revised Statutes is titled "Licensing and Control of Gaming," and the first definition offered in the chapter is "Short Title: Nevada Gaming Control Act." The definitions go on to explain that *game* and *gambling game* have the same meaning and that *gaming* and *gambling* have the same definition.

A short tour through historical dictionaries brings to light some of the more interesting aspects of the cohesive vocabulary associated with the two terms. First stop: the *Oxford English Dictionary* and *Supplements.*

Game was, from the first, connected to pleasant associations. From the first appearance, in *Beowulf,* on through the 16th century, associations with game are "glee, pleasance, joy, play, mirth." By the 15th century, the connotation could be quite different, as the cruel aspect of *game* begins to make its appearance. In the late 16th century, the sense of *game* could designate an object of ridicule, a laughingstock.

On the other hand, from its earliest appearances, *gamble* was related to vices and foul practice. The relationship to dissipation and to cheating were close and constant through the years. In places where gambling took place, the excesses were such that writers of the times (from about 1815) described them as "gambling hells."

The apparent derivative, *gambling,* antedates *gamble*. The *OED* records that in the 18th century the term was regarded as slang. It probably came about as a dialect survival from Middle English *gamene-n.* The rare 16th- and 17-century *gameling* implies a verb, **gamel*, which is unattested. Progressive partial homorganic assimilation could easily account for the intrusive *b* that showed up in later spellings, though the *OED* does not make such a speculation. In the sense of "wagering on the outcome of games," *gaming* does not carry the pejorative senses of *gambling*, though the latter term is often used as part of the definition.

A Dictionary of American English on Historical Principles (DAE) lists older citations for *gaming* than for *gambling*. Those 17-century citations from Virginia and Plymouth, as might be expected, given the tenor of the time, link *gaming* to idleness, drunkenness, "excess in apparel," and other ruinous pastimes. The earliest citations in *DAE* for *gambling* date from the

19th century but usually carry similar pejorative comments and "warnings to young men of substance." *A Dictionary of Americanisms on Historical Principles (DA)* does not list *gambling* or *gaming* as discrete entries, which is hardly surprising, given the scope of *DA*. The terms, where found, are listed in attributive senses or as part of open compounds. For many years, then, *gambling* has had to sit below the salt, while *gaming* occupies a position at least even with the salt. Official references to the practice seem to prefer *gaming*. Indeed, the more than seven thousand items dealing with gaming and gambling in the Dickinson Library fall under the rubric of The Gaming Research Center, and I was named to the University Gaming Research Center Committee.

The perspective of the individual is often obvious from the relative frequency with which a term is used. In 1891, John Philip Quinn's *Fools of Fortune* was published by The Anti-Gambling Association in Chicago. Quinn's book is a Victorian tome of warning written in the breathless style and with excruciating detail designed to appeal to those gentlemen who might like "to have been there." In keeping with the tone of the time, the subtitle of Quinn's book is *Gambling and Gamblers; Comprehending a History of the Vice In Ancient and Modern Times, and in Both Hemispheres; and Exposition of Its Alarming Prevalence and Destructive Effects; with an Unreserved and Exhaustive Disclosure of Such Frauds, Tricks and Devices as Are Practiced by "Professional" Gamblers, "Confidence Men" and "Bunko Steerers."* His preface, dated 1890, begins, "Of all the vices which have enslaved mankind, none can reckon among its victims so many as gambling." Throughout his book, Quinn uses *gamble, gambler,* and *gambling* in every reference to evil and vice. Other terms, such as *gamester*, appear only in connection with *sharper* or some other such appellation. *Gaming* is used rarely and in the most neutral statements, such as "one whose instinct for gaming is satisfied with a legitimate business." For Quinn, speculation and risk in the name of legitimate business is gaming, otherwise it is gambling. Elsewhere, Quinn uses *gaming* in clearly marked phrases, idioms, or open compounds, such as *gaming hells*.

Other, more objective treatises have been more likely to use a variety of terms with less cumulatively pejorative force—cumulatively, because a term used once may carry only slight negative connotation but, used frequently, can create a considerable sense of pejoration in the mind of the reader. Herbert Asbury, in *Sucker's Progress* (1938, New York: Dodd, Mead and Company) used *gambling game, banking game, gambler, player, gaming tables, Faro Bank, Faro game,* usually without prejudice or undue emphasis of one term over another.

On occasion, people have found a way out of the terminological dilemma. In 1977, the New Jersey State Legislature passed the Casino Control Act, which was described as a method for controlling "Legalized Games of Chance." The policy body and the enforcement body, corresponding to the Nevada Gaming Commission and the State Gaming Control Board, are named the New Jersey Casino Control Commission and the Division of Gaming Enforcement. In the process of defining terms for the Act, the drafters used interesting variations. "Authorized Game" or "Authorized Gambling Game" is defined by exemplum: "Roulette, baccarat, blackjack, craps, big six wheel, and slot machines." On the other hand, "Game" or "Gambling Game" is a stipulative definition: "Any banking or percentage game located exclusively within the casino, played with cards, dice or any mechanical device or machine for money, property, or any representative of value." And, finally, we are given an operational definition: "'Gaming' or 'Gambling'—The dealing, operating, carrying on, conducting, maintaining or exposing for pay any game." We can ignore the style in which the definitions are written. We can even ignore the fact that the definitions exclude, legally, electronic gambling devices by referring only to "mechanical" machines.

By restricting the meaning of *gaming* to wagering on events, a dictionary of terms has a defined scope of coverage. Yet terms used in gaming events are not automatically excluded from future editions of such a book. Words and phrases from, say, basketball can be collected in the archives; terms like *slam dunk, off the glass, in the paint* are already being collected in the citation file.

* * * *

Inclusions and Exclusions

Terms are included which have to do with any frequent wagering situation, such as *chip, bankroll, bet, wager*.

Also included are:

1. terms used in such card games as baccarat, bridge, faro, poker, twenty-one;
2. terms used in such dice games as backgammon, craps, hazard, bar dice, chuck-a-luck;
3. terms used in group games such as bingo, keno;
4. terms used in reel or wheel games such as slot machines, roulette, wheel of fortune;
5. betting terms from sports such as golf, horseracing;
6. terms used in policy-making or numbers;
7. terms used in sportsbooks and racebooks;
8. terms used in table games that engender frequent wagering, such as dominoes.

The names of games are included only to the extent that the game described provides a number of special terms. Hence, there are long entries at the card game *basset*, at the dice game *hazard*, and some others because those games use many special terms. But the myriad of special forms of poker have not been catalogued. Poker games such as baseball, spit-in-the-ocean, anaconda, lowball, Omaha, southern cross, and other variations share terminology common to all poker games. Consequently, the names of these games have not been included. Many books describing the terms of play for such games are readily available. A few varieties of poker such as *hold 'em* and *razz* use terms specific to those games and have been included.

Terms are *not* included from those games which are generally considered non-wagering games. While some people may wager on the outcome of games of chess or checkers, the games are not widely regarded as having wagering as an integrally interesting part of the play. The same can be said for the many varieties of solitaire, board games such as Monopoly, or children's games such as old maid.

In dealing with terms from horseracing, golf, baseball, football and other sports, it is necessary to distinguish those terms which have a relationship to the betting process from those terms which do not. With horseracing, for example, the bettor would not necessarily be concerned about the nicknames for types of feed, various tools used for grooming, or most medical terminology. But those things that directly affect the outcome of a race will affect the bettor and are therefore included. Such terms will include descriptions of horses around the starting gate, such as *bad actor*. Other terms have a relationship to the running of a race, such as whether a horse has the habit of nicking its fetlock or whether the horse needs blinders.

The terms relating to horse racing are of three types: first are those terms which have no relationship to the wagering process—*stable, tack, feed*—and are left out; second are those terms which obviously have a relationship to betting—*morning line, exacta, totalizator, daily double*—and are included; third are those terms which require judgment on the part of the editor for inclusion or exclusion—*bug, apprentice, silks, also eligible, fetlock, back heel*.

In the same fashion, bettors who play golf will be concerned about terms like *medal play, scratch shooter, nassau*. But the nicknames for various irons would not be necessary here.

Generally speaking, unless the equipment used has a bearing on the outcome of a wager, it is not included. Casino gaming tables determine the method of play and have a bearing on the outcome of wagers, since the main reason for their construction is wagering. So terms like *apron, felt, drop box, rack, rail, cushion* and other descriptions of casino furniture are included.

Nicknames and slang terms for chips and checks are included. But many general slang terms for money, such as *kale, cabbage, lettuce, dough, do-re-mi, buck*, are excluded. Those slang terms widely used in wagering situations, such as *bankroll* and its abbreviation *BR*, are included, along with *big nickel, California C-note, baby grand*, and *quarter* (meaning twenty-five dollars).

Some terms borrowed from foreign languages have a long life in English because of the games in which they occur. French terms in baccarat, roulette, and chemin-de-fer serve as examples. Such terms as *a cheval* and *banco* are included if they occur with regularity among English-speaking players.

Format of Entries

A systematic sequence is used for each entry, though not every entry contains each of the features listed. For example, pronunciations are not supplied for all terms, because the bulk of the terms are found in the general vocabulary, and thus treated in standard general dictionaries. The part of speech labels are used for nearly all entries. Often there is no recorded pronunciation of two-word combinations in order to determine the distinction between open compounds and phrases. Just as *White House*, the residence of the president of the United States, has a primary stress on the first syllable, so too does *ace count*. But *ace deuce* is stressed on the second syllable. Many terms, such as *able whacket*, have not been recorded on tape, and consequently the position of primary stress is uncertain. Such terms are tendered on the basis of usage in context. The usual sequence of features within entries follows:

1. Headword, in **heavy boldface**.
2. Part of speech, in *italics*.
3. Pronunciations, using a modified IPA key, within virgules: /.../
4. Source language if borrowed from another language solely as a gaming term: *Spanish*.
5. Variants in spelling, writing or form, in SMALL CAPITALS if separately entered, in **small boldface** if not separately entered.
6. Definition number, when the headword has multiple meanings: **1.** ... **2.** ... **3.**
7. Definition.
8. Restrictive label, when usage deserves special brief notation: *Obsolete, Rare, Facetious use*, etc.
9. Near synomyms or terms where related information is given: "See also" followed by SMALL CAPITALS.
10. Related terms where a comparison reveals an important contrast: "Compare" followed by SMALL CAPITALS.
11. Source reference to a quotation provided in the dictionary: date, short title, page (if applicable).
12. Illustrative or explanatory quotation.
13. Necessary glosses with the quotation, in brackets.
14. Date of first occurrence from historical dictionaries or other resource materials, in brackets: [...].
15. Etymological remarks, in brackets.
16. Editor's comments, explanatory notes, and subsidiary glosses, explained in a usage note preceded by:→.

Variant Forms of the main entry.

able whacket or **able wacket,** *n.* A stinging blow, usually administered to the forearm of the loser of a wager.
[1788 *DSUE,* 1834 *DARE:* obsolete, from a sailor's card game.]

Quotations from oral interviews and field work.

Ajax, *n.* Also called FOAMY CLEANSER. In hold'em poker, an ace and a jack as the first two cards dealt to a player.
1981 Golad *Oral Coll.* A player sits there hour after hour with only two cards to look at, so the different combinations get names . . . foamy cleanser is a spinoff of *Ajax,* ace and jack.

Pronunciations based upon IPA adapted to American English.

barbooth, /bɑr'bu:t/, *n.* Also spelled **barboot, barbudi, barbuti.** /bɑr'bu:t *or* bɑr'bu: di:/ A dice game in which both player and shooter have an equal chance to win.
1981 Clark *Oral Coll. Barboot* is a fast, two dice game played by a lot of old Jewish and Greek immigrants. You can bet with the shooter or the fader and it's a dead even game, except the cutter takes five percent of the win for a house vig.

Currency Note showing obsolescence with a label and a usage note.

blackleg, *n.* A cardsharp, especially in faro. *Obsolete.*
[1771 *OED, DSUE*]
→Used mainly around 1850, eventually meaning any swindler.

Grammatical Label expanded to show syntactic restriction.

calipers, *n. pl. Plural in form, but singular in use.* Dice that are true to required dimensions by one ten thousandths of an inch. Compare CANDY STORE DICE.
[(1950) 1981 Maurer *Lang. of the Underworld* 183]
[Transferred sense from the calipers used for measurement]

Etymolotical Note indicating processes or origins.

carolina, *n.* Also called **carolina nina** or **niner from caroliner** or **nina from carolina.** A cast of the number nine in dice games. Compare NINA.
[1950 Morehead *Culbertson* 599]
→The words "Carolina" and "nine" must always rhyme.

Usage Note explaining special features of structure.

case, *v.* In the phrases:
case the deck, In twenty-one, to mentally record each card played in order to shift betting strategy to take advantage of favorable odds. See also CARD COUNTING.
[1961 Scarne *Complete Guide* 675]
case the rack, In a casino, to count the amount of money represented in the chip container on a gaming table. Pit bosses are adept at being able to instantly determine the number and denominations of chips on the table without disrupting play.
[1975 Clark *Oral Coll*]

Citation of oral or written source material.

Quotation showing earliest evidence.

check, *n.* A chip; a counter used at table games to represent money.
1843 Green *Exposure* 59. The man that plays this game [faro] has to go to great expense; he has to produce, sir, a fine silver box worth, perhaps, one hundred dollars; and then he has to supply

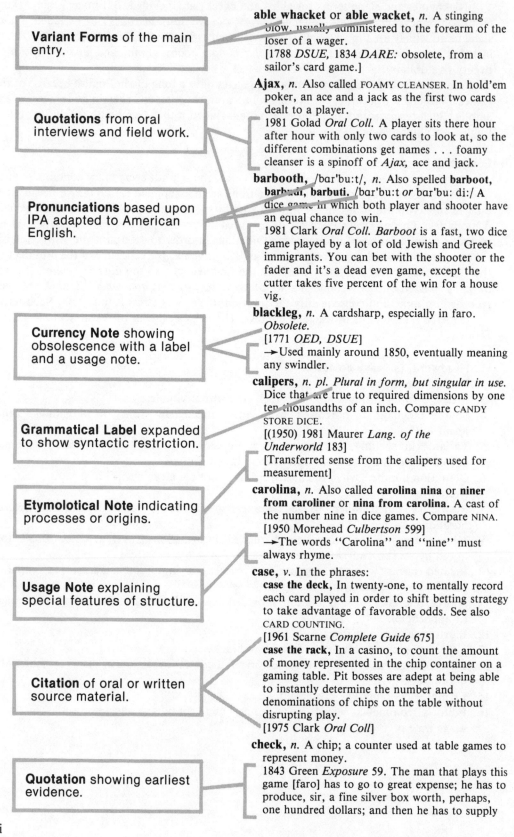

himself with a number of ivory pieces, turned round like a dollar; some of them colored red, with various figures on them, and some of them white, without any coloring, except perhaps around the edge: and these *checks,* as they are called, will cost, probably, two hundred dollars. 1868 Trumps *Pocket Hoyle* 204. The stakes usually consist of counters or *checks,* made of ivory, representing different sums; they are purchased of the banker and are redeemed by him at the option of the holder.
[1845 *DA, DAE, OEDS*]
→*Check* is used exclusively by professional gamblers and those working in legalized gaming. *Chip* is used by the general public, and by those in professional gambling when speaking with non-professionals.

check, *v.* **1.** In poker, to make no additional wager when acting as the first bettor, but to reserve the right to bet at a later time in the hand.
[1949 Coffin *Secrets* 174]
2. In the phrase:
check blind, In poker, to refrain from wagering as the first bettor before picking up the dealt cards. The player who *checks blind* may bet, call, or raise the wager at a later time during the same betting round.
[1968 Wallace *Poker* 212]

field, *n.* **1.** On a bank craps table, a section of the layout for betting that the next number rolled will be the number 2, 3, 4, 9, 10, 11, or 12.
[(1950) 1981 Maurer *Lang. of the Underworld* 185]
2. The horses entered in a specific race.
[1955 Hillis *Pari-Mutuel Betting* 114]
[Compare 1806-7 *OED,* those who are to take part in the sport, hunting]
3. All the competitors in a race except the favorite. [1742 *OEDS*]
4. In keno, a group of numbers selected as a unit on a WAY TICKET, that is, a ticket with combinations of groups of numbers selected by the player.
[ca. 1961 *Hotel Coll*]

hand-betting terminal, *n. phr.* A portable computer terminal used for placing wagers. See also TELEBET. Compare OFF-TRACK BETTING, HANDBOOK.
1987 *New Scientist* 8/20:27. The Royal Hong Kong Jockey **(Club) is developing a *hand-betting*** *terminal* that will allow punters to place bets from anywhere in the territory simply by plugging the terminal into a telelphone line.

longshot, *n.* **1.** In horse racing, an entry with little chance of winning. See also DARK HORSE and OUTSIDER. [1867 *OEDS*]
2. A bet with a remote chance of winning but, if it does win, paying many times the amount of the original wager.
[1968 Thackrey *Nick the Greek* 241]
[1869 *DSUE*]

Quotations from printed sources of historical importance.

Usage Note describing special restrictions of application.

Idiomatic Phrases or **Particle Constructions** set apart from text of entries.

Grammatical Labels identifying: *n., v., n. phr., v. phr., adj., adv., prep., conj.,* etc.

Evidence from historical dictionaries and glossaries.

Cross-references to related or contrasting entries with SMALL CAPITALS.

Quotations from current publications.

Multiple Definitions from one entry clearly distinguished.

Acknowledgements

Many people have been involved in this project during the several years of its compilation. In the early stages of this project, Walter Schlager helped overcome my reticence at taking on such a project, explaining that one function of a lexicographer is to catalog the vocabulary important to a region or activity. Early citation readers were Maffy W. Forrester and Donald T. Clark. Elaine Resnick helped set up the initial citation file.

Two people played a large role in the project. Judith Shively entered thousands of citations into the computer and checked many of the terms against the historical dictionaries. Thomas Martinet entered much of the material into the computer and conducted much of the fieldwork for oral citations. Their yeoman contributions were recognized in 1983 when both were named Presidential Honorary Members in the American Dialect Society by A. Murray Kinloch, president.

Thomas C. Wright, Dean of the College of Arts and Letters, University of Nevada, Las Vegas, supported this project as both scholar and dean. He also found additional funding for research trips made to Texas and Washington, D.C. Funding was also provided for research by the University Research Council, University of Nevada, Las Vegas, for the summer of 1984. The Council's support is gratefully acknowledged. Support was provided also by National Endowment for the Humanities Travel to Collections Grant #RY-20366-84 during the fall semester of my 1984-85 sabbatical. I also thank the Sabbatical Leave Committee of the University of Nevada, Las Vegas, for recognizing the value of this project by granting a leave at a time when many demands were being made for few available sabbaticals.

Byrne Gebhardt wrote the initial programs for sorting and merging files on the mainframe computer. Susan Jarvis, curator of the Gaming Collection at the James Dickinson Library, was instrumental in locating early sources for citations. She and her staff at Special Collections, especially Elizabeth Patrick and Christine Marin, were generous with their time and patience.

Frederic G. Cassidy, the lexicographer's father figure, and his staff at the headquarters for the *Dictionary of American Regional English* at the University of Wisconsin, were most generous with time, information, and working space during the summer of 1984. Will Lindauer and Joan Hall were especially helpful during my stay at Madison.

Many other people served as readers and resource persons: Elizabeth Johnson, Brad Golad on hold 'em poker, Howard Schwartz of Gambler's Book Club, Chuck Hickey, Della Press on panguingue, Thomas Dyer, Brighde Mullins, Robin Feigelman, and Dana Rivers.

The chores of checking each entry against the historical dictionaries was conducted by Dawit Shiferaw, Karen Holm, Sam Bosler, Janice Hanes, and Rene Kruleski. The bibliography was initially typed by Wendy Woyski.

Laurence Urdang is an exacting taskmaster. He took me in hand as I was moving into the stage of providing definitions. I count him as a tutor *par excellence*. Every page of the manuscript that came under his hand benefitted from his years of experience in lexicography. For me, at least, he was also lexicologist.

Jeanne Wilson Clark was supportive and wifely in the extreme during the years this project was underway. Toward the end, she was more than supportive and sat by my side for hours rechecking citation sources and dates. She has indeed learned about "harmless drudgery." Our children (Tim, Helen-Margaret, and Kristin) behaved themselves relatively well through the ordeal and for that I thank them. They were teenagers (or less) when the project started, and are now adults. They have a special view of the rigors of scholarship.

David K. Barnhart of Lexik House Publishers has been a close friend since the first evening we met at an American Names Society banquet a generation ago. Thank you, David.

Publisher's Acknowledgements

Linguistic Consultants:	Edward G. Fichtner (Queens College, CUNY)
	John R. Costello (New York University)
Editorial Consultants:	Gail Greet Hannah
	Charlotte R. Morrill
	Geraldine S. Baldwin
	Rev. Cyprian H. Murray O.F.M., Cap.
Editorial Assistants:	Peter J. Zurita PMP Editorial & Production
	Denise A. Miceli
Typesetting:	J&M Graphic Concepts, Inc.
Printer:	Hamilton Printing Company

ABBREVIATIONS

a	ante, in *Oxford English Dictionary* citations
adj.	adjective
adv.	adverb
BDC	*Barnhart Dictionary Companion*
BDNE I	*Barnhart Dictionary of New English*
BDNE II	*Second Barnhart Dictionary of New English*
c	circa, in *Oxford English Dictionary* citations
Cent. Dict.	*Century Dictionary*
ca.	circa
Coll	collection
DA	*Dictionary of Americanisms*
DAE	*Dictionary of American English*
DARE	*Dictionary of American Regional English*
DAS	*Dictionary of American Slang*
DSUE	*Dictionary of Slang and Unconventional English*
ety.	etymology
n.	noun
n.c.	no city
n.d.	no date
n.p.	no page
OED	*Oxford English Dictionary*
OEDS	*Oxford English Dictionary Supplement* (1972-1986)
OEDS 1933	*Oxford English Dictionary Supplement* (1933 edition)
p.	page
part.	participle
phr.	phrase
prep.	preposition
pseud.	pseudonym
v.	verb
var.	variant
W3	*Webster's Third New International Dictionary of English*

References to authors, titles of books, newspapers, and magazines are found after the letter z.

PRONUNCIATION KEY*

Stress: ˈ primary and secondary ˌ as in ˈdik ʃəˌner i:

Consonants: Most consonant symbols in this key have their customary values of English orthography except the following seven special symbols:

ʃ	sh	in *shore*
tʃ	ch	in *chore*
θ	th	in *thin*
ð	th	in *then*
ŋ	ng	in *bring*
ʒ	s	in *measure*
	si	in *decision*
dʒ	j	in *joy*

Vowels and diphtongs:

æ	a	in *bat*
ɑ	o	in *hot* (U.S.)
ɑr	ar	in *bar*
ɑ:	a	in *father*
ɑi	i	in *bite*
ɑu	ou	in *bout*
e	e	in *bet*
er	ar	in *bare*
ei	a	in *hate*
i	i	in *bit*
ir	eer	in *beer*
i:	ee	in *beet*
ɔ	o	in *hot* (Brit.)
ɔr	oar	in *board*
ɔ:	aw	in *awl*
ou	oa	in *boat*
u:	oo	in *boot*
u	oo	in *hook*
ə	u	in *but, butt*
	u	in *minus*
ər	er	in *herd*

Foreign Language Sounds: Foreign words are shown with symbols as they appear above with the following exceptions:

a	a	in French *masse*
œ	eu	in French *beurre*
x	ch	in German *Bach*
Y	u	in French *tu*
~		nasal vowels in French and Portuguese

*This key is adapted from *The Barnhart Dictionary of New English* (1973).

A

A, *n.* Also ABLE, AGE, EDGE, ELDEST HAND, UNDER THE GUN. **1.** At a poker table, the first position to the left of the dealer.
1949 Coffin *Fortune* 4. Player *A* sits nearest to the left of the poker dealer, B sits next left, and so on clockwise around the table.
2. Abbreviation for ACE.
[1950 Morehead *Culbertson* 589]
3. Also **AA.** The top grade of greyhound racers.
[1968 Bechele *Greyhound Racing* 95]

abandon the deal, *v. phr.* To discontinue the play of a hand in a card game and reshuffle the cards for a fresh deal, usually done when cards are misdealt or a foul has been committed by the dealer, as by neglecting to have the pack cut before the deal.
[1950 Morehead *Culbertson* 589]

abc, *n.* Also **A.B.C.** In poker games such as razz and high-low split, the first three cards dealt, when the ranks are ace, 2, 3.
[1978 Brunson *How I Made* 522]

abc straight, *n.* In poker, five cards in consecutive order from the ace to the 5. See also LITTLE WHEEL.
[1971 Livingston *Poker Strategy* 213]

able, *n.* Also called the AGE. At a poker table, the first position to the left of the dealer. See also FIRST BASE.
[1949 Coffin *Fortune* 172]

able whacket or **able wacket,** *n.* A stinging blow, usually administered to the forearm of the loser of a wager.
[1788 *DSUE,* 1834 *DARE:* obsolete, from a sailor's card game.]

above, *n.* **1.** The gross amount of earnings from a licensed casino or a legal bookmaking operation.
1977 *Nev Int Ctrl.* Accounting procedures shall demonstrate source income for all earnings of the *above* and all expenditures before the below ['net income'].
2. Same as ABOVE THE LINE.

aboveboard, *adv.* Honestly and without guile, as in dealing cards without deception.
[1616 *OED*]

above the line, *prep. phr.* In card games such as bridge, the place on the scoresheet for marking premiums; the score for honors and penalties. Sometimes shortened to ABOVE.
[1953 Crawford *Consistent Winner*]

absolute, *n.* A declaration to win 82 points at trump, or 62 points at no trump.
[1950 Morehead *Culbertson* 598]

A-B, Y-Z, *n.* In card games like whist, the method for designating partners.
1949 Coffin *Fortune* 4. Early bridge books lettered players *A* & *B* as partners against *Y* & *Z.*
→ Now replaced by N(ORTH)-S(OUTH), E(AST)-W(EST).

"A" card, *n.* A certificate issued by a law-enforcement agency indicating security clearance for a casino employee. See also 50 CARD and SHERIFF'S CARD.
1963 Taylor *Las Vegas* 100. No inside man can work on the Strip without the county's "50" card, or downtown without the city's "A" card, signifying clearance.
1983 Clark *Oral Coll.* We used to call a work permit an *A card,* but since Metro was formed [Las Vegas Metropolitan Police, combining city and county police], we just call it and the fifty card a sheriff's card.

acceptance, *n.* **1.** The approving of a horse by track officials for participation in a race.
[1923 *OEDS*]
2. The stage at which the owners of entries in a horse race accept the conditions of the race or withdraw their entry.

accommodation arrest, *n. phr.* A raid on an illegal gambling establishment which is arranged through collusion between the arresting officer and the operator of the establishment. The purpose of the raid is to make a public demonstration of a crackdown on illegal gambling while allowing protected gamblers to flourish.
[1961 Scarne *Complete Guide* 671]

accommodez-moi, *v. French.* In help me neighbor, to request cards from the player on the right.
[1950 Morehead *Culbertson* 589]

according to Hoyle, *adv. phr.* An appeal to authority; said when a player wishes to lend the air of authenticity to a pronouncement about the rules of a game.
[1971 Livingston *Poker Strategy* 213]
[1906 *OEDS,* late 19c *DSUE*]

accumulator, *n.* **1.** *British.* The winnings of one bet on a subsequent event; a parlay wager.
[1923 *OEDS*]

2. *British.* A person who makes a parlay bet. [1889 *OEDS*]

ace, *n.* **1.** Also called a BULLET. A playing card with a single pip on the face. The value of the card varies: in poker, the ace may count for lowest or highest value; in twenty-one, the ace counts for one or eleven points, as declared by the player. [1533 *OED*]
2. A single pip on a die.
1714 Lucas *Memoirs* 68. But if the Caster throw Ames-Ace [2] or Deuce *Ace* [3], then all he has staked be lost.
[1566 *OED*; Compare AMBS-ACE]

ace-and-picture countdown, *n. phr.* In twenty-one, a system for remembering which cards have been played and which cards have not yet been dealt.
[1968 Thackrey *Gambling Secrets* 118]

ace-count, *n.* In twenty-one, a strategy for keeping track of which cards have been played and which cards have not yet been dealt.
[1973 Friedman *Casino Games* 30]

ace-deuce, *v.* To sustain a heavy loss; to die. See CRAP OUT.
[1987 Golad *Oral Coll*]

ace-deuce standoff, *n. phr.* In craps, an initial roll of three pips, which neither wins nor loses for the house or the player. See BAR ROLL.
[1974 Scarne *Dice* 112]
→ Most American casinos now feature a standoff for the number 12, which makes the wager more advantageous for the player.

ace-high, *n.* A poker hand in which the ranking card is an ace; the value of the hand ranks below a hand with a pair.
[1878 *DA, OEDS*]

ace-high flush, *n. phr.* A poker hand in which all five cards are of the same suit, not in sequence, one of which is the ace. See also ROYAL FLUSH.
[1978 Brunson *How I Made* 531]

ace-high straight, *n. phr.* In poker, a hand with five sequenced cards, not of the same suit: 10, jack, queen, king, ace.
[1961 *Hotel Coll*]

ace-high straight flush, *n. phr.* Same as ROYAL FLUSH.
[1970 Clark *Oral Coll*]

ace in the hole, *n. phr.* **1.** In stud poker, a card dealt face-down to a player.
[1922 *DA*]
2. In casino twenty-one, an announcement by the dealer when he has an ace face down and an up card worth ten points.
[1974 Clark *Oral Coll*]

ace in the pot, *n. phr.* A two-dice game in which a player, on throwing a roll with a single pip on one of the dice, must add an amount of money to the pot which equals the amount already there.
[1950 Morehead *Culbertson* 589]

ace kicker, *n. phr.* In draw poker, a single ace held with a pair of another denomination at the time of the draw. The player asks for two cards, hoping the opposition will assume the player is holding three of a kind.
[1968 Adams *Western Words*]

ace out, *v. phr.* To win a poker hand by bluffing an opponent while holding an ace-high hand or other relatively worthless hand; hence, to win by any deception.
[1983 Martinez *Gambling Scene* 185]

aces, *n. pl.* **1.** In casino, a count of one point for each ace won during the hand.
[1950 Morehead *Culbertson* 589]
2. In poker, a hand with two aces.
[1970 Clark *Oral Coll*]
3. Short for a bar game called ACES TO THE CENTER, DEUCES TO THE LEFT, FIVES TO THE RIGHT.
[1974 Scarne *Dice* 365]

aces and spaces, *n. phr.* In poker, a hand containing a pair of aces and three worthless cards.
[1981 Golad *Oral Coll*]

aces center, *n. phr.* Short for ACES TO THE CENTER, DEUCES TO THE LEFT, FIVES TO THE RIGHT, a bar game.
[1974 Scarne *Dice* 365]

aces full, *n. phr.* Also called ACES OVER. In poker, a hand with three aces and a smaller pair; a full house. [1849 *DA*]

aces over, *n. phr.* Same as ACES FULL.
[1961 *Hotel Coll*]

aces to the center, deuces to the left, fives to the right, *n.* A bar game requiring the use of five dice, in which each die showing one, two, or five pips is removed from the player's next cast.
[1974 Scarne *Dice* 365]

aces up, *n. phr.* In poker, a hand with one pair of aces and another pair.
[1953 Crawford *Consistent Winner*]

aces wild, *n. phr.* **1.** In poker, an announcement that an ace may have any value the holder of it declares. [ca. 1961 *Hotel Coll*]
2. In bar-dice games, an announcement that a die with a single pip can assume the value of any other die.
[1971 Smith *Games They Play*]

ace to the five, *n. phr.* A statement made among lowball poker players, indicating that a straight will not disqualify a hand. See also DEUCE TO SEVEN.
[1981 Jenkins *Johnny Moss* 155]

ace up the sleeve, *n. phr.* A statement indicating that a card sharper may be using a deceptive move or trick to cheat an opponent.
[1967 *DAS*]

acey-deucey, *n.* **1.** In backgammon, a variation, popular among sailors, for beginning the game by entering all the pieces from the bar rather

than using the standard layout.
[1971 McQuaid *Gambler's Digest* 298]
2. In hold 'em poker, an ace and deuce dealt to a player as the first two cards of the hand.
[1981 Golad *Oral Coll*]
3. In horseracing, a riding style in which the right stirrup is higher than the left.
[1978 Ainslie *Encyclopedia* 283]
4. In craps, a roll with three pips showing.
[1983 Martinet *Oral Coll*]

a cheval, *n. French.* In roulette, a bet placed on two numbers next to one another on the layout.
1891 *Monte Carlo* 197. You can place your money upon the line dividing the two numbers (*a cheval,* it is called), and if either of them win, your stake is returned you with 17 times the same amount.

acorn, *n.* Among craps dealers, a term for a player who tips well. See also GEORGE.
1984 Martinet *Oral Coll.* We used to call a good tipper an *acorn,* but that is rarely heard anymore.

across, *n.* In bank craps, a type of place bet in which the player bets all of the place numbers (4, 5, 6, 8, 9, 10) except the point.
[1961 *Hotel Coll*]

across, *v.* In bank craps, to make a bet on all the place numbers (4, 5, 6, 8, 9, 10) except the point the shooter must roll in order to win.
1983 Martinet *Oral Coll.* He's fifty-four *acrossing.* ['He is making a bet of fifty-four dollars on the place numbers.']

across the board, *prep. phr.* In horseracing or jai alai, bets of win, place, and show on a single entry. [1950 *OEDS*]

across the card, *prep. phr.* In horseracing, multiple bets, made through bookmakers, on races at different tracks.
[1974 Ewart *Flatracing* 147]

action, *n.* The activity of wagering on the outcome of events such as card or dice games, horseraces, and sports contests; gambling activity in general.
[1953 Fairfield *Las Vegas*]

action spot, n. The space on a gambling table layout where the wager is placed by the bettor.
[1968 Wallace *Poker* 209]

active player, *n. phr.* **1.** In poker, a player who is in competition for the pot.
[1964 Reese and Watkins *Secrets* 137]
2. In baccarat: **a.** the player with the largest bet against the house.
b. the player who represents all persons betting against the bank during the deal of cards.
[1964 Wykes *Illustrated Guide* 326]

actors, *n. pl.* In mah jongg, the suit of characters.
[1950 Morehead *Culbertson* 589]

actual odds, *n. phr.* In pari-mutuel betting, the odds for various entries in an event as determined by the money wagered on the different entries at the mutuel windows. The numbers change continually until the beginning of the event.
1955 Hillis *Pari Mutuel* 116. *Actual odds.* These are the odds that result from the actual cash paid in at the mutuel windows for tickets on the various entrants. They change constantly until post time, i.e., until the starting bell rings. The changes are flashed to the tote board. The odds are given on the tote board only for win. Moreover, they are only approximate but close enough for betting purposes. The actual exact final or post time odds are computed between post time and pay off time. At which latter time they are given on the tote board for all horses which closed in the money.

actual, *n.* **the actual.** Money, especially cash.
[1961 *DSUE*]

actuary, *n.* The oddsmaker for a bookmaking operation.
[1971 McQuaid *Gambler's Digest* 298]

Ada from Decatur, *n. phr.* Also EIGHTER FROM DECATUR. In craps, the roll of eight on the dice.
[(1950) 1981 Maurer *Lang. of the Underworld* 181]
[Rhyming slang]

Ada Ross the stable hoss, *n. phr.* Also shortened to **Ada Ross.** Same as ADA FROM DECATUR.
[1968 Adams *Western Words*]
[Rhyming slang]

added money race, *n. phr.* Also shortened to **added money.** A horse race in which track officials add money, usually the starting fees, to the purse. [1880 *OEDS*]

added starter, *n. phr.* A horse added to the field on the day of the race.
[1983 Martinez *Gambling Scene* 185]

add'em up lowball, *n.* A form of draw poker in which the hand with the lowest total point count wins the pot.
[1968 Wallace *Poker* 209]

adjust the stick, *v. phr.* Also CALIBRATE THE STICK. A facetious order given to a craps dealer by a boxman when the dice are not paying off for the players.
[1983 Martinet *Oral Coll*]

adjusted score, *n. phr.* In duplicate bridge, a score determined by the referee.
[1950 Morehead *Culbertson* 589]

advantage, *n.* A technique for cheating, especially at cards.
1865 Evans *Gamblers Win* 3. The reader will bear in mind that this is strictly a book of *advantages,* and therefore deals but slightly with the rules of square ['honest'] playing, which can be found in almost any book.

advantage card, *n. phr.* A card marked on the back with an identifying symbol.

1843 Green *Exposure* 15. The term *advantage,* as found in many places in this work, signifies cards that are known by the back; or cards that are prepared in the factory, so that the gambler may know them . . . and if the cards are not *advantage cards,* a gambler will so mark them, that he will know the cards by his own marks.
1859 Green *Gam Tricks* 46. If they should be *advantage cards,* he can tell by the back when you draw it out.

advantage player, *n. phr.* A person who cheats, usually by using altered cards or dice.
[1890 Quinn *Fools of Fortune* 196]

advantage tool, *n. phr.* A device used for cheating, usually an altered card, altered die, or a mechanical device for hiding a card or cards. See also HOLDOUT[1].
[1938 Asbury *Sucker's Progress* 63]

adversary, *n.* The opponent in a two-handed game.
[1950 Morehead *Culbertson* 589]

advertise, *v.* To make a bluff which is designed to be detected by one's adversary. The strategy of such a movement is to feign a bluff at a future time, thus catching an adversary unaware.
[1949 Coffin *Fortune* 172]

affranchir, *v. French.* In trump games, to establish a suit which will allow the player to take several tricks in a row.
[1950 Morehead *Culbertson* 589]

African dominoes, *n. phr. Plural in form but usually singular in use.* Dice; the game of craps.
[1919 *DARE,* where it is labeled *jocular*; 1922 *DA*]
→ Used facetiously because it is popularly thought of as a favorite game of blacks.

African golf, *n. phr.* Same as AFRICAN DOMINOES.
[1920 *DA*]

African golfer, *n. phr.* One who plays AFRICAN DOMINOES.
[1963 Drazazgo *Wheels* 319]

Africans, *n. pl.* In a casino, black chips worth one hundred dollars each.
[1983 Martinet *Oral Coll*]

against the house, *adv. phr.* Also shortened to **against. 1.** In games such as baccarat, describing betting on the player's hand rather than the bank's hand.
2. In bank craps, describing betting on the do pass area of the table layout rather than on the don't pass area.
[1972 Kofoed *Meanderings* 204]
→ In reality, the casino keeps a percentage of all wagers, therefore the player is always betting "against the house."

against the shooter, *adv. phr.* In bank craps, describing a bet on the don't pass line.
[1961 *Hotel Coll*]
→ In using the term, players often add a comment to the effect that they are betting "with the house," though such a wager is of less advantage to the player than to the house.

a-game, *n.* In a casino or a poker room, the table or game that features the highest stakes. See also Z-GAME.
[1949 Coffin *Fortune* 172]

age, *n.* Also called, ABLE, EDGE, ELDEST HAND.
1. At a card table, the first player to the left of the dealer. Abbreviated: A
1844 (1883) Shields *Life of S. Prentis* 334. You can't expect me to take a hand in this game when he . . . 'holds two bullets and a bragger and has the *age* of me to boot.'
1866 *American Card Player* 133. *Age.* See quote at ELDEST HAND.
1949 Coffin *Fortune* 169. Before the deal, the nearest player to the left of the dealer, known as the *age,* puts up a partial bet of one chip, the blind, and the second player to the left of the dealer, known as the straddler, puts up a partial bet of two chips, the straddle.
1964 Reese and Watkins *Secrets* 137. *Age.* An obsolete term meaning the player on the left of the dealer. Also known as the Edge.
[1844 *DA, DARE;* 1882 *OEDS*]
2. The cardplayer, usually in poker, with the right to make the final bet of the hand.
1891 Maitland *Amer. Slang Dict. Age,* or Edge, The player next to the dealer holds the "age" and is not compelled to bet until all the players have signified their intentions.
[1844 *DAE, DARE: DARE* lists the term as "old fashioned"]

aged, *adj.* In horseracing, pertaining to a horse more than six years old.
[1974 Ewart *Flatracing* 147]

agent, *n.* **1.** A representative who lures customers to gamble at his establishment. See also ROPER.
2. A confederate in a cheating scheme.
[1961 Scarne *Complete Guide* 671]
3. A person who accepts bets for a bookmaker.
1983 Martinez *Gambling Scene* 185. *Agents*—Individuals who accept bets for bookmakers.
4. In horse racing, a person who represents the jockey in dealings with horse owners.
[1981 Passer *Winning Big* 234]

ahead, *adv.* Pertaining to increased holdings of money as a result of winning bets.
[1961 *Hotel Coll*]

air, *v.* In horse racing, to win over one's opponents with ease.
[(1951) 1981 Maurer *Lang. of the Underworld* 201]

air bandit, *n.* A person skilled in cheating at a variety of games.
1969 Herwitz *You Can Win* 112. A few years ago a news item appeared in a Nevada paper which stated that some *"air bandits"* were apprehended in Las Vegas with 100 pairs of crooked dice, slot machine tools, card cheating equipment, and even burglary tools!

airing, *n.* The running of a horse in a race which the owner has no interest in winning.
[1961 *DSUE*]

Ajax, *n.* Also called FOAMY CLEANSER. In hold'em poker, an ace and a jack as the first two cards dealt to a player.
1981 Golad *Oral Coll.* A player sits there hour after hour with only two cards to look at, so the different combinations get names . . . foamy cleanser is a spinoff of *Ajax,* ace and jack.

Alameda straight, *n.* **1.** In a game of bar dice, a roll in which no two dice of the five rolled have the same number of pips showing; a worthless roll.
[1971 Smith *Games* 103]
2. In poker, a sequence of cards with one number missing, and therefore valueless. For example, a hand with the cards 5, 6, 7, 9, 10. Because the eight is missing, the hand has no value.
[1981 Golad *Oral Coll*]

Alaska hand, *n.* Also called KING CRAB. In hold'em poker, a king and a 3 dealt as the first two cards to a player.
1981 Golad *Oral Coll.* A player sits there hour after hour with only two cards to look at, so the different combinations get names . . . A king crab is a king and a three. The crab part is from the three in craps. You also hear it called an *Alaska hand,* that's where king crab are found.

Albany lead, *n.* In whist, a card played to announce a hand with four trumps and three cards in each of the other suits.
[1950 Morehead *Culbertson* 590]

aleator, *n.* An accomplished dice player.
1976 Figgis *Gamblers Handbook* 127. Tables can usually accommodate a stickman (in control of the dice), three crap dealers who handle the chips, one opposite the stickman and the other two at either end of the table, and up to about 12 *aleators* (the classical word for keen dice players). The right of the *aleators* to do the shooting passes clockwise round the table.

alembert, *n.* **the alembert.** A system of money management that requires adding one unit to a bet after a win, and subtracting one unit from the basic bet after a loss.
[1971 McQuaid *Gambler's Digest* 298]

alien, *n.* **1.** A gambling operator from another city or state.
[1931 *Las Vegas Review-Journal* 3/5; 1]
2. A chip or check from another casino.
[1983 Martinet *Oral Coll*]

alien card, *n. phr.* A card that does not belong in the pack being used.
[1949 Coffin *Fortune* 172]

alive card, *n. phr.* An undealt card; a card that is playable.
[1968 Wallace *Poker* 209]
[Perhaps from confusion with the indefinite article in "a LIVE CARD."]

all alone, *adj. phr.* Noting a horse that is ahead of the pack by several lengths.
[(1951) 1981 Maurer *Lang. of the Underworld* 201]

all black, *adj. phr.* In poker, noting a spade or club flush.
[1981 Golad *Oral Coll*]

all blue, *adj. phr.* In poker, noting a spade or club flush. Compare ALL GREEN. and ALL PINK and ALL RED.
1981 Golad *Oral Coll.* We don't say *all blue* or all green or all pink to refer to flushes; those are tourist terms.
→Not used by professional card players.

all clear, *n. phr.* In horseracing, a signal given by raising a blue flag after the jockeys have weighed in prior to a race, indicating that no objections have been made.
1974 Ewart *Flatracing* 147. *All clear* is given by hoisting a blue flag on the number-board after jockeys have weighed in. A red flag with white E signifies an objection or stewards [sic] enquiry.

all day, *adj. phr.* In bank craps, indicating that a bet made on a hardway number is a wager that continues until the number is rolled or until a 7 is rolled, as distinguished from a single-roll wager.
1983 Martinet *Oral Coll.* When you tell the dealer you're making an *all day* bet, that means it's a standard hardway bet rather than a one-roll proposition bet. They are both hardway bets, but the payoff odds are different, lower for the *all day* bet.

all down, *adj. phr.* **1.** In bank craps, an announcement by the stickman that the dice are being rolled, therefore, that bets should be made.
[1983 Martinez *Gambling Scene* 186]
2. In bank craps, an oral request by a player that the dealer remove and return all his bets from the layout.
[1975 Clark *Oral Coll*]

alley craps, *n. phr.* A casual or pick-up craps game not formally organized; a spontaneous craps game. See also ARMY CRAPS and BLANKET CRAPS and CRAPS.
[1977 Cahill *Recollections* 323]

all fours, *n. pl. Plural in form, but singular in use.* A popular eighteenth century card game, which later became *high, low, jack, and the game.*
1843 Green *Exposure* 236. The game of *all fours* is played by two persons with an entire pack of cards. It derives its name from the four chances therein; for each of what a point is scored, viz: High—the highest trump out; Low—the lowest trump out; Jack—the knave of trumps; Game—the majority of pips reckoned for the following cards, as the players may have in their respective tricks, namely: for an ace, four; for a king, three; for a queen, two; a knave, one; and ten for a ten.
[1707 *OED, DAE*]

all green, *adj. phr.* In poker, noting a heart or diamond flush.
1981 Golad *Oral Coll.* We don't say all blue or *all green* or all pink to refer to flushes; those are tourist terms.
→*All green* is not used by professional card players.

all he left was his fingerprints, *n. clause.* In bank craps, a standard response to a dealer's query about lack of tips left by a big winner. See also EMPTY SACKS AND WAGON TRACKS.
1983 Martinet *Oral Coll.* I came off break and asked what happened to the high roller. I got *"All he left was his fingerprints,"* which is a standard response meaning the guy left no tokes ['tips'], but took the money and ran.

all in, *adj. phr.* In table stakes poker, an announcement by a player that he has placed all his money in the pot and will play only for the amount in the pot at that time.
[1973 Preston *Play Poker* 166]

all jokes and no tokes, *n. phr.* In bank craps, a dealer's statement about a lively game in which he is not receiving any tips or bets placed for him by players.
1983 Martinet *Oral Coll.* When I come onto a game, I want to know how the tokes ['tips'] are running. When I hear *all jokes and no tokes,* I know that everybody is having a good time but the dealers.

all night board, *n. phr.* In bingo parlors, a bingo card used for an entire session of games.
[1961 *Hotel Coll*]

all out, *adj. phr.* In horseracing, noting a horse that has been pushed to its limit. Compare DRIVE and EXTEND.
1889 Ellangowan *Sporting Anecdotes* 336. *All out.*—With nothing left *in* him. "He won, but he was *all out* to win" (i.e. fully extended) we say of a horse who has just pulled through.

allowance race *n.* Also shortened to **allowance.** A horse-race in which the amount of weight carried by the horse depends on its recent performances.
[1955 Hillis *Pari-Mutuel Betting* 112]

all pink *adj. phr.* In poker, noting a heart or diamond flush.
1981 Golad *Oral Coll.* We don't say all blue or all green or *all pink* to refer to flushes; those are tourist terms.
→Not used by professional card players.

all rooters and no shooters, *n. phr.* In bank craps, a comment by the stickman when no players at the table will roll the dice.
1983 Martinet *Oral Coll.* When players keep passing the dice, the stick will say "all rooters and no shooters" to force someone into picking up the dice and keep the game rolling.

all set with a bet, *adj. phr.* In bank craps, an announcement by the stickman that the dice are ready to be rolled. See also ALL DOWN.
1983 Martinet *Oral Coll.* The stickman yells *"all set with a bet"* so that the players will know the dice are coming and they had better keep their hands off the layout.

all the tough guys, *n. phr.* Also **all the toughies.** In bank craps, an announcement that a player wishes to make proposition bets on all HARDWAYS. Compare EASY WAYS.
1983 Martinet *Oral Coll.* When somebody wants all the hardways, the dealer will tell the stickman to give him *all the tough guys.* The odds always are that seven or the easy ways will come first.

all the trumps, *n. phr.* In games like whist, a declaration by the bidder of an intention to win all cards of the trump suit.
[1950 Morehead *Culbertson* 590]

all the way, *n. phr.* In horseracing, a comment noting that a winning horse led throughout the race.
[1961 *Hotel Coll*]

all ties stand off, *n. clause* In baccarat, an announcement that the bank and the players have tied so there is no win or loss. See also PUSH.
[1970 *Baccarat*]

all you need is a buck and a truck, *n. clause* In bank craps, a comment by the stickman that the players are winning heavily.
1983 Martinet *Oral Coll.* The stickman will tell someone passing by the craps table to jump onto the game when the dice are running hot. He'll say, *"All you need is a buck and a truck,"* and you can make some bucks if the run lasts a while.

all you need is an arm and an eye, *n. clause* In bank craps, a comment by the stickman that a prospective player can squeeze into a crowded table.
1983 Martinet *Oral Coll.* All you have to be able to do is stick your bet onto the layout and watch it, no matter how crowded the table. That's why the stickman will call to a watcher, *"All you need is an an arm and an eye."* You don't have to hug the rail to be a player.

almost left, *adj. phr.* Noting a horse that breaks slowly from the gate. Compare LEFT.
[1961 *Hotel Coll*]

almost up, *adj. phr.* Noting a horse that fails to win in the last stride before the finish line. Compare DRIVE and EXTEND.
[1983 Martinez *Gambling Scene* 186]

alone, *adj.* **1.** In euchre, noting a bid by a player to play out a hand without assistance from his partner.
[1950 Morehead *Culbertson* 590]
2. In dice, gambling against the house, especially when a cheat is working without a confederate.
[(1950) 1981 Maurer *Lang. of the Underworld* 181]

alone player, *n. phr.* A cardsharp working without a partner and without the collusion of other players.
[1961 *Hotel Coll*]

also eligible, *n. phr.* A horse that is available for a race if one of the horses scheduled to run is scratched.
[1955 Hillis *Pari-Mutuel Betting* 118]

also ran, *n. phr.* A horse that won no money in a race; a horse that placed no better than fourth position in a race.
[1908 *OEDS*]

alternate straight, *n. phr.* Also called DUTCH STRAIGHT and SKIP STRAIGHT and SKIPPER. In poker, a hand in which the cards skip every second number, as 2-4-6-8-10. Among some poker players, an alternate straight beats THREE OF A KIND, but loses to a normal STRAIGHT.
[1949 Coffin *Fortune* 137]

aluminum plate, *n. phr.* In horseracing, the light racing shoe worn by horses. A common reference among horse-racing enthusiasts is to horses that do not do well as being barely **worth aluminum plate,** much less gold plate (winners' purses).
[1981 Passer *Winning Big* 228]

a. m., *n.* **the a. m.** Also called the MORNING LINE. The earliest announcement of odds on the horses for a particular race.
[1955 Hillis *Pari-Mutuel Betting* 88]

ambs-ace, *n.* Also **ames-ace** or **ambsace.** In hazard, two ones on a pair of dice. See also SNAKE EYES.
See quote at HAZARD: 1680 Cotton *Complete Gamester.*
[*OED* lists a number of spelling variants: *ambes as,* 1297; *ambez as,* 1300; *amys ase,* 1400; *ambes aas,* 1430; *Ames-ace,* 1601; *Aumes-ace,* 1611; *Aums Ace,* 1658; *Alms-Aces,* 1680; *Am's Ace,* 1721; *ame's-ace,* 1731; *ambs-ace* since 1870, alongside *ambsace.*]

American Airlines, *n.* In hold 'em poker, the ace of hearts and the ace of diamonds when dealt as the first two cards to a player.
1981 Golad *Oral Coll.* A player sits there hour after hour with only two cards to look at, so the different combinations get names . . . the red aces are called *American Airlines.*

American wheel, *n.* A roulette wheel with slots marked 0 and 00 in addition to the numbers "1" through "36". See also EUROPEAN WHEEL.
[1964 Lemmel *Gambling* 185]

anchor man, *n.* Also shortened to **anchor.** In twenty-one, the player to the right of the dealer, who is the last to act on the hand before the dealer and is therefore considered highly important to the success or failure of the other players.
[1961 Scarne *Complete Guide* 671]
[Compare 1958 *OEDS*, meaning "television or radio-show host"]

angle, *n.* An idea, scheme, or method for cheating; a deception to facilitate winning a bet; a device used to ensure the winning of a bet.
[1950 Morehead *Culbertson* 590]

animated cubes, *n. phr.* Dice *Facetious use; rare.*
[1961 *Hotel Coll*]

ankle boot, *n.* A rubber or leather protective covering for the fetlock of a racehorse. Compare ANKLE CUTTER.
[1981 Passer *Winning Big* 227]

ankle cutter, *n.* A horse known for nicking or cutting its fetlock with the opposing hoof while racing. The lack of an ANKLE BOOT on such an animal will cause a significant change in the betting at a horserace.
[1978 Ainslie *Encyclopedia* 283]

announce, *v.* In high-low poker, to declare whether a player will play for high hand, low hand, or both high and low hands. Compare SHOOT THE MOON.
[1950 Morehead *Culbertson* 590]

announced bet, *n. phr.* An amount declared to be a wager before a player actually puts down his money; oral wager. See also CALL BET.
[1971 Livingston *Poker Strategy* 213]

ante, *n.* The amount of money put into a pot before beginning the deal of a new hand at poker. Compare POOL.
1830 Anon *Hoyle's Improved* 154. The person on the left of the dealer then puts into the pool any sum he pleases, which is called the *ante.*
1866 *American Card Player* 131. An *"ante"* or stake is deposited in the centre of the table by the dealer; this is called the Pool or Pot.
[1838 *DA, DAE, OEDS*]

ante, *v.* To add a stake to the POT before beginning a card hand.
[1845 *DA, OEDS;* 1854 *DAE*]

ante up, *v. phr.* A request, usually by the dealer in a poker game, for all players to deposit the required amount of money into the POT before the hand is dealt.
[1845 *DA;* 1861 *DAE, OEDS*]

any craps, *n.* Also shortened to **any.** In bank craps, a proposition bet that the next dice roll will yield number two, three, or twelve.
[1963 Taylor *Las Vegas* 78]

any raffle, *n.* In chuck-a-luck, a proposition bet that the next dice roll will yield three of a kind.
[1964 Wykes *Illustrated Guide* 326]

any seven, *n.* In bank craps, a proposition bet that the next dice roll will yield number seven.
[1963 Taylor *Las Vegas* 78]

apartment house, *n.* In games with DICE CUPS, two or more dice stacked on one another after a cast.
[1971 Smith *Games* 103]

apprentice, *n.* In horse racing, a jockey with less than one year of experience.
[1974 Ewart *Flatracing* 148]

apprentice allowance, *n.* In horse racing, a weight concession for a horse carrying a jockey with less than one year of experience. See also BUG.
[1955 Hillis *Pari-Mutuel Betting* 112]

approach bid, *n.* In games such as bridge, a bid designed to inform one's partner about cards held in the hand. See also ASKING BID.
[1929 *OEDS*]

apron, *n.* **1.** A cloth band worn around the waist by casino dealers, which usually bears the name of the casino and is designed to prevent easy access to the pockets of the dealer. See also SUB.
[1961 *Hotel Coll*]
2. The area of a table LAYOUT, as at craps or twenty-one, outside of the betting area, along the perimeter of the table.
[1977 Anness *Dummy Up*]

apron girl, *n.* A female employee of a casino who converts currency to coin for slot-machine players. See also CHANGE GIRL and SLOT ATTENDANT.
[1953 Lewis *Sagebrush Casinos* 79]

Arkansas flush, *n.* In poker, a worthless hand consisting of four cards of one suit and one card of another suit, not in sequence; a FOUR-FLUSH.
[1978 Larson *Vocabulary* 97]

armchair ride, *n. phr.* In horse racing, a particularly easy win for a horse. Compare ALL ALONE.
[1978 Ainslie *Encyclopedia* 283]

army craps, *n. pl.* A craps game in which the person shooting the dice acts as banker, accepting bets from the other players. Compare CRAPS. See also BANK CRAPS, BLANKET CRAPS, CASINO CRAPS, STAG CRAPS.
[1984 Martinet *Oral Coll*]

army marbles, *n. pl.* Dice.
[1963 Drazazgo *Wheels* 319]

army roll, *n.* A controlled cast of the dice on a soft surface.
[1963 Drazazgo *Wheels* 319]

around the bend, *n. phr.* Said of a horse racing on an oval track, just before the horse enters the STRETCH. Compare CLUBHOUSE TURN and FAR TURN.
[1983 Martinez *Gambling Scene* 186]

around the corner straight, *n. phr.* In poker, a card sequence which goes up to ace, then to deuce, e.g., queen, king, ace, 2, 3. Among some players, the hand ranks above any other straight, but below a flush.
[1963 Steig *Common Sense* 181]

around the park, *n. phr.* **1.** In horse racing, a race run over the entire course.
[(1951) 1981 Maurer *Lang. of the Underworld* 202]
2. In horse racing, a morning workout for a horse consisting of one lap around an oval track.
[1983 Martinez *Gambling Scene* 186]
[(1951) 1981 Maurer *Lang. of the Underworld* 202]

around the wheel, *n. phr.* Also called a WHIRL BET or WHEEL. In the game of craps, a proposition bet that number 2, 3, 7, 11, or 12 will appear on the next roll of dice.
[1982 Young *Oral Coll*]

around the world, *n. phr.* In keno, a bet using all eight corners of the keno ticket: numbers 1, 10, 31, 40, 41, 50, 71, and 80.
[1969 Herwitz *Yes You Can* 73]

artist, *n.* Also called a CARD MECHANIC. A person skilled at dealing cards dishonestly.
[1938 Asbury *Sucker's Progress* 14]

artist in coloring, *n. phr.* Also called a PAINTER. A person skilled in marking the backs of playing cards. Compare COSMETICS.
[1890 Quinn *Fools of Fortune* 230]

ascot, *n.* A system betting pattern used by some gamblers in the eighteenth century. See also MONEY MANAGEMENT.
[1971 McQuaid *Gambler's Digest* 298]

asking bid, *n. phr.* In games like bridge, a bid by a player designed to request information about the cards in his partner's hand.
[1936 *OEDS*]

ass-english, *n.* While rolling dice, the various contortions of the body or snapping of the fingers in an attempt to control the dice after they have been thrown.
[(1950) 1981 Maurer *Lang. of the Underworld* 181]

assigned bettor, *n. phr.* In poker, the player who is first to bet in a round.
[1949 Coffin *Fortune* 172]

assist, *v.* In games like bridge, to continue bidding until one's partner settles on trump.
[1950 Morehead *Culbertson* 591]

assist, *n.* In euchre, an announcement by the dealer's partner of the ability to win three tricks.
[1878 *OEDS*]

astragals, *n. pl.* Dice.
[1850 *OED,* ultimately from *astragalus,* the ball of the ankle joint from a sheep, once used as a die.]

at home in the going, *adj. phr.* Noting a horse racing on a track well suited to its style and temperament.
[(1951) 1981 Maurer *Lang. of the Underworld* 202]

at the post, *adj. phr.* Noting a horse in the starting gate, awaiting the signal from the starter to begin the race.
[(1951) 1981 Maurer *Lang. of the Underworld* 202]

au carre, *n. French.* In roulette, the placement of a wager at the intersection of four numbers on the LAYOUT.
1891 *Monte Carlo* 198. Or you can place your money upon the point of intersection of four squares (*au carre,* it is called), and if either of those four numbers comes out, you are paid 8 times the amount of the stake and the stake is returned.

auction, *v.* In chemin-de-fer, to sell the bank to another player.
[1976 Crawford *Consistent Winner*]

auction, *n.* Any card game in which the players bid for the privilege of naming trump, as in *auction bridge.* [1903 *OEDS*]

auction pool, *n.* The total sum realized when the names of horses in a race, or entrants in other contests, are sold by auction. Bidders holding the names of the highest finishers share portions of the pool. See also CALCUTTA.
[1913 *OEDS*]

audition, *v.* In a casino, to give a trial demonstration as a dealer.
[1977 *Gambling Times* Feb: 27]

audition, *n.* In a casino, the demonstration of dealing skills given by a job applicant. In casino *auditions,* the demonstration is given at a table with actual casino patrons. [1961 *Hotel Coll*]

a volente, *n. French.* In chemin-de-fer, an option given to the player to draw another card when the total of the first two cards equals five.
[1976 Figgis *Gambler's Handbook* 121]

award card, *n.* Same as AWARD SCHEDULE.
[1951 *Nevada Gaming Regulations* 155]

award schedule, *n.* Also called AWARD CARD or PAYOUT SCHEDULE. **1.** A record of all payouts by the casino, normally kept in the casino cage.
[1982 Martin *Casino Management*]
2. In a casino, a posted listing of the amounts that can be won on wagers at various games in the casino.
[1974 Clark *Oral Coll*]

ax, *n.* The percentage of a wager or pot, usually from poker games, retained by the gambling establishment as a cost of overhead.
[1961 Scarne *Complete Guide* 672]

B

B, *n.* **1.** Abbreviation for BAKER. In poker, the second player to the left of the dealer. Compare A, C, D, E, F, G, H.
[1949 Coffin *Secrets* 173]
2. Abbreviation for BLINKERS.
[(1951) 1981 Maurer *Lang. of the Underworld* 202]
→This abbreviation is used mostly in the RACING FORM to designate entrants that will be wearing blinkers.

babies, *n. pl.* **1.** Dice.
[1974 Scarne *Dice* 255]
2. Undesired cards of small denominations, such as two through six.
[1973 Preston *Play Poker* 166]

baby, *n.* **1.** In horse racing, a two year old horse during the first quarter of the year.
[1978 Ainslie *Complete Guide* 283]
2. In card games such as razz or high-low split poker, a desired card with a denomination of five or less.
[1978 Brunson *How I Made* 522]

baby grand, *n.* Five hundred dollars.
[1963 Drazazgo *Wheels* 319]

baby needs new shoes, *n. phr.* Also **baby needs a new pair of shoes.** A shout by an excited craps shooter desiring a win.
1979 Clark *Oral Coll.* Whenever you hear somebody yell *"baby needs a new pair of shoes,"* some regular players will pull down place bets. They think a loss might be coming.

baby race, *n.* In horse racing, a race for two year old horses, usually a dash of four furlongs or less. See also MAIDEN RACE.
[1971 McQuaid *Gambler's Digest* 298]

baccarat, *n.* Also spelled **baccara.** A game at cards played for money between a banker and several bettors, in which the object is to draw at least two cards and come closest to a specific number of points, usually eight or nine, without exceeding the determined number. Compare TWENTY-ONE.
[1866 *OED*]

back, *v.* **1.** To place a wager on a horse, sports team, boxer or other contestant.
[1697 *OED*]
2. In the phrases and particle constructions:
back down, To lower the odds on a horse because of a large amount of wagering on that horse.
[(1951) 1981 Maurer *Lang of the Underworld* 202]
back in, 1. In poker, to bet after having checked.
[1949 Coffin *Secrets* 172]
2. In poker, to win a hand with a fortunate draw of cards making the hand more powerful than normally might be expected. [1973 Clark *Oral Coll*]

back up, 1. Of a horse, to lose the lead for want of stamina.
[(1951) 1981 Maurer *Lang. of the Underworld* 202]
2. Of a jockey, to slow a horse in order for it to regain its proper stride.
[(1951) 1981 Maurer *Lang. of the Underworld* 202]
back up the dice, At a bank craps table as an order given to the stickman, to move the dice counter-clockwise because a player was not given an opportunity to be the shooter. The dice normally pass in a clockwise direction.
[1983 Martinet *Oral Coll*]

backboard, *n.* On a bank craps table, the quilted and cushioned board at either end of the table which the dice are to be bounced against to ensure an honest roll.
[ca. 1961 *Hotel Coll*]

backboard control shot, *n. phr.* A controlled dice throw in which both dice are held between the thumb and forefinger, thrown to land at the juncture of the table and the backboard so they will not roll or turn. See also WHIP SHOT.
[1974 Scarne *Dice* 262]

back door, *n.* In poker, the act of drawing a better hand than expected. Compare AMERICAN AIRLINES, FLOP, FOURTH STREET, HOLE, RIVER CARD.
1980 Golad *Oral Coll.* One of the frustrating things [in playing hold 'em poker] is when somebody comes in the *back door.* I had American Airlines ['red aces'] in the hole and another ace on the flop. I could draw out to a full or four of a kind. The best the guy across from me could do was a straight. But fourth street was a four and the river card was a four. He had fours in the hole and *back doored* me [won with four of a kind, rather than losing with a straight].

back door, *v. phr.* In poker, to draw for one hand and instead receive a better hand than the one desired. See the quotation for BACK DOOR, *n. phr.*

backed up, *adj. phr.* In stud poker, pertaining to a pair in the first two cards dealt to a player. See also BACK TO BACK and WIRED.
[1968 Wallace *Poker* 209]

back end, *n.* **1.** In illegal bookmaking operations, a place where the paperwork can be handled for street bookmakers.
2. The last two months of a horse racing season.
[1983 Martinet *Oral Coll*]

back-ender, *n.* A horse entered in saddle races late in the season.
[ca. 1889 *DSUE*]

back end man, *n. phr.* The member of an illegal bookmaking operation who coordinates the betting slips and payouts for the street bookmakers.
[1983 Martinet *Oral Coll*]

backer, *n.* A person who finances a gambler; a supporter, especially one who wagers on a contestant or event.
[1850 *OED*]

back game, *n.* In backgammon, a strategy to delay moving pieces from the opponent's home table, the aim being to send one of the opponent's pieces to the rail, then prevent the piece from being brought back into the game before moving most of one's own pieces into the home table. Compare HOME TABLE, INNER TABLE, RAIL.
[1974 Scarne *Dice* 322]

backgammon, *n.* **1.** A board game in which players roll dice to move stones, or pieces, around the board which is marked with 24 points, often involving betting on the roll of the dice. The object of the game is to be the first player to remove all one's fifteen pieces. See also BEAR OFF and BLOCK.
[1645 *DAE, OED*]
2. Also written **back-gammon.** In backgammon, a win achieved by a player who removes all of his pieces before his opponent has moved all his pieces from the side of the board opposite his own. The win usually counts as a triple score. Compare GAMMON. See also HITS.
1860 Crawley *Backgammon* 58. If the winner has borne off all his men before the loser has carried his men out of his adversary's table, it is a *"back-gammon"* and usually held equivalent to three hits or games.
[1883 *OED*]

backgammon bet, *n.* In golf, an opportunity for a player to double the wager on the hole if he has at least a fifteen foot putt before he can win.
[1971 McQuaid *Gambler's Digest* 299]
[From the DOUBLING CUBE used in backgammon.]

back in, *adj. phr.* **1.** In poker, returning to active betting after passing during the betting round.
[1963 Steig *Common Sense* 811]
2. In bridge, pertaining to the act of bidding after having passed.
[1950 Morehead *Culbertson* 591]

backline, *n.* In bank craps: **1.** the DON'T PASS line on a craps layout.
[1973 Binion *Recollections*]
2. A player's term for a PLACE BET or the area on the layout where place bets are positioned by the dealer.
1984 Martinet *Oral Coll.* Players will mistakenly use the term *backline* when they mean place bet. They will say, "what does it cost to bet the *backline*?"

backline odds, *n. phr.* In bank craps, odds that are layed rather than taken; the laying of odds for a bet against the shooter. See also LAY ODDS and TAKE ODDS.
[1974 Scarne *Dice* 460]

back of the house, *n. phr.* The area of a casino which has the kitchens, housekeeping

departments, coin weighing room, counting area, offices, and so on.
[ca. 1961 *Hotel Coll*]

back peek, *n.* Same as HEEL PEEK.
[ca. 1961 *Hotel Coll*]

backraise, *n.* In a poker game where the number of raises is limited, a small raise made by a player to prevent a larger raise by a later player.
[1949 Coffin *Secrets* 173]

backseat, *n.* In poker, any of the fourth through seventh seats to the left of the dealer.
[1973 Preston *Play Poker* 166]

backstretch, *n.* On an oval race track, the straight section of the course opposite the stands; the far side of the track. Compare HOMESTRETCH.
[1868 *DAE*]

back to back, *adj. phr.* **1.** Pertaining to two consecutive wins or losses.
[1983 Martinez *Gambling Scene* 187]
2. In stud poker, referring to two cards of the same denomination: the card dealt face down, and the first card dealt face up. See also BACKED UP and WIRED.
[1949 Coffin *Secrets* 172]
3. In the game of craps, pertaining to consecutive rolls of the dice yielding the same number.
[1983 Martinet *Oral Coll*]
4. Also abbreviated BB. In sports books and concerning two consecutive wagers, pertaining to a second wager made before the result of the first wager is known.
[1973 Clark *Oral Coll*]

backup, *adj.* In horse racing, pertaining to place and show bets in addition to a bet to win.
[1983 Martinez *Gambling Scene* 187]

back wheel, *n.* In horse racing, a method for wagering on the daily double which requires making combination bets of a horse in the first race with each horse in the second race.
[1981 Passer *Winning Big* 240]

bad actor, *n.* Also called a BAD STARTER. A horse that is fractious and nervous at the post.
[1978 Ainslie *Complete Guide* 284]

badger, *n.* A horse purchased in order to get track privileges for the owner.
[1978 Ainslie *Complete Guide* 283]

bad rack, *n.* A list of casino patrons with poor credit ratings.
[1974 Friedman *Casino Management* 66]

bad seven, *n.* Also called ROUGH SEVEN. In low-ball poker, a hand with cards of the denomination of 7 and 6, along with three cards of lower denomination, such as 4, 3, 2.
[1971 Livingston *Poker Strategy* 213]

bad starter, *n.* Same as BAD ACTOR.
[(1951) 1981 Maurer *Lang of the Underworld* 202]

bag, *v.* To cheat a casino through collusion between a house employee and a player.
[1963 Drazazgo *Wheels* 319]

baggage, *n.* **1.** Also called LUMBER. A person who observes gamblers in action but does not play.
[(1950) 1981 Maurer *Lang of the Underworld* 181]
2. A member of a cheating ring who fails to pay his own way by his winnings.
[(1950) 1981 Maurer *Lang. of the Underworld* 181]

bag-job, *n.* An instance of collusion between a house employee and a player.
[(1950) 1981 Maurer *Lang. of the Underworld* 181]

bagman, *n.* A person who delivers money from illegal gambling operations to a superior or delivers bribe money to government officials.
[1963 Drazazgo *Wheels* 319]
[1952 *DAS*]

bait, *v.* In poker, to make a small bet, hoping to encourage a large raise from an opponent.
[1949 Coffin *Secrets* 172]

baker, *n.* Also abbreviated B. In poker, the second position to the left of the dealer.
[1949 Coffin *Secrets* 172]

balanced hand, *n.* In games like bridge, a hand which contains no SINGLETONS or VOIDS.
[1953 Crawford *Consistent Winner]*

balance the books, *v. phr.* In bookmaking, to place wagers with other bookmakers when one horse or team has been heavily bet.
1979 Clark *Oral Coll.* The line on the Jets didn't move fast enough, so I wound up with too much bet on one side. I had to lay off some of the action so I wouldn't get stung. That's called balancing the books. You have to *balance the books* so you don't get caught too heavily on one side.

balance-top, *n.* A crooked dealing box used in faro which allows the dealer to select two cards at will.
1843 Green *Exposure* 198. This box is what the dealers call a *balance-top.* The top is set on two springs at the ends of the box, the ends being set about the eighth of an inch higher than the rest of the box; so that they are always acting comparatively fair, unless borne down, and then the front rises. This top is not fastened on with screws but with a pivet [sic] and the screws which appear to hold it are flase, as the pivet holds it. In the lid of this box, is a groove, and the spring works into the groove, and when the box is borne down the mouth opens sufficiently for two cards to advance; but unless it is borne down, the spring is strong enough to prevent more than one from coming out.
→See the entry CHEATING BOX for a list of such devices.

balking cards, *n. phr.* In cribbage, the two cards selected by each player to be placed in the CRIB. See also KITTY and WIDOW.
[1950 Morehead *Culbertson* 592]

ball, *n.* A composite of cathartics given a race horse, usually the day before a race.
[(1951) 1981 Maurer *Lang. of the Underworld* 202]

ball-cornered dice, *n. phr.* Also called ROLLERS. Dice with one or more corners rounded to reduce the chances of rolling a particular number.
[1974 Scarne *Dice* 243]

ball team, *n.* Also called BASEBALL TEAM. A group of cheaters who work in the casino they victimize.
[1983 Martinet *Oral Coll*]

bamboos, *n. pl.* In mah jongg, one of the three suits of tiles having nine ranks.
[1950 Morehead *Culbertson* 592]

banco¹, *n. French.* In baccarat and chemin de fer, an announcement by a player that he wishes to make a bet equal to the entire bank.
[1789 *OEDS*]

banco², *n.* Same as BUNCO.
[American Spanish: see quote at BUNCO]

banco skin, *n.* A dice cheating scheme that flourished in the 1880s in which a victim could bet on a number already rolled but still covered by the dice cup.
[1938 Asbury *Sucker's Progress* 57]

banco suivi, *n. French.* In baccarat, the act of placing a wager with the bank rather than against it, especially after a loss on the players' side.
[1964 Wykes *Illustrated Guide* 326]

banger, *n.* In keno, the punch used to make holes in the DRAW TICKETS. The keno dealers use such tickets as an overlay on tickets presented by customers to determine winners.
[1978 Alexander *Glossary* 1]

bang into, *v.* Of a casino dealer, to place a taller stack of chips next to the stack bet by the player, then remove the excess from the taller stack, leaving a stack equal in value to the original bet. Compare BUMP INTO and CUT INTO.
[1983 Martinet *Oral Coll*]

bang up, *v.* In a casino, to close a table, allowing only the players already present at the table to stay.
[1961 Scarne *Complete Guide* 672]

bangle, *n.* Also spelled **bingo.** In golf, the second part of a bet called BINGLE, BANGLE, BONGO, the winner of which is the player whose ball is closest to the hole after all players have reached the green.
[1971 McQuaid *Gambler's Digest* 299]

bangtail, *n.* Also written **bang-tail. 1.** A horse's tail that is cropped horizontally to end in a flat, blunt fashion.
[1870 *OED*]
2. A racehorse with a bluntly cropped tail.
[1921 *OEDS*]

bang-tail, *adj.* Also **bang-tailed.** Pertaining to a thoroughbred's tail, folded and bound short when the race course is muddy.
[1978 Ainslie *Complete Guide* 284]
[1861 *OED,* as *bang-tailed*]

bank, *n.* **1.** In baccarat, one betting area on the layout. The other betting area is labeled PLAYER.
2. Also called TABLE INVENTORY or TABLE LOAD. In a casino, the initial amount of money in the racks when the table is opened for play.
[1780 *OED,* 1835 *DAE*]
3. The amount of money available to a player or dealer. [1720 *OED*]
4. In a policy or numbers game, the place where all the money collected is kept and from which winnings are distributed.
[1963 Drazazgo *Wheels* 319]

bank a game, *v. phr.* **1.** In a casino, to open a table or begin a new game.
[1826 *OED*]
2. For an illegal game, to supply the necessary funds needed to operate the game.
[ca. 1961 *Hotel Coll*]

bank craps, *n.* Often called CASINO CRAPS or **banking craps.** A craps game in which all wagers, both for and against the dice, are covered by the house. The house operates the game, establishes all rules, and handles all wagers. On the other hand, in ALLEY, ARMY, or BLANKET CRAPS, the players arrange all bets among themselves, though the operator of the game may choose to handle certain wagers.
[(1950) 1981 Maurer *Lang of the Underworld* 181]

banker, *n.* **1.** In games like faro, twenty-one, and baccarat, the person who conducts the game, deals the cards and controls the collection and payment of wagers.
1843 Green *Exposure* 30. The *banker* [in faro] is the person who keeps the table . . . In twenty-one, the deal, in the first place, is immensely advantageous; the dealer is the *banker*, and the last to decide his own hand; that is, every player around the table must draw cards, and complete their hands before the dealer does his own hand, and in so drawing, half, or even more of them, may overdraw, and will have to pay the *banker,* before his own hand is decided. The *banker* has much in his favor without trying to cheat; and the professional gambler, who, with all his arts and intrigues, sits down to deal this game, will, in all probability, win on an average seven times, where he loses once; and still the ordinary player will have no room to suspect fraud, as he cannot detect it with his eyes, and if he should partially discover, or intimate that he thinks some manoeuvre was not according to his notions of propriety, the dealer will, with the strongest protestations of honesty, quell his fears, and

instantly practice another to cheat on him.
[1806 *DAE;* 1826 *OED*]
2. In baccarat, the title given to the player who draws the cards for the BANK HAND.
[1968 Thackrey *Nick the Greek*]
3. A card game in which the dealer creates several packets on the table, face down. The player wagers that the card on the bottom of the pile selected will rank higher than the bottom card on the dealer's pile.
[1891 *OEDS*]

banker's card, *n. phr.* In faro, the first card of a pair dealt, which wins for all persons betting on the banker's side rather than the players' side.
1868 Trumps *Pocket Hoyle* 205. A Ten appears, the first card dealt—this is the *banker's card,* and he wins all the money which may have been placed upon it.
→Players could make the same bet by placing a copper button atop the bet, signalling that they wish to bet with the banker rather than against the banker.

bank hand, *n.* In baccarat, one of the two hands dealt. The other hand is called the PLAYER'S HAND.
[1970 *Baccarat, Facts*]

bank hand bet box, *n. phr.* In baccarat, the area on the table layout in which all money bet with the bank is placed. Money bet against the bank is placed in the PLAYER HAND BET BOX.
[ca. 1961 *Hotel Coll*]

bankroll, *n.* Also abbreviated BR. The amount of money a player begins with that will be devoted to wagering.
[1973 Binion *Recollections* 33]
[1887, *DA* was first to record this word in the more general sense of any roll of bank notes]
→Among professional players, the *bankroll* rarely equals the total amount available to the player.

bankroll, *v.* To finance a game or player.
[1974 Scarne *Dice* 57]

bar, *n.* **1.** In backgammon, the center dividing wall on the board, separating the INNER TABLE from the OUTER TABLE. Captured pieces are placed on the *bar* until returned to play by an appropriate roll of the dice.
[1971 McQuaid *Gambler's Digest* 299]
2. In bank craps, the DON'T PASS line; the BACK LINE.
1984 Martinet *Oral Coll.* The term *bar* is used by some players to refer to the back line or the don't pass. We [dealers] don't use the word that way.
3. Also called BARR DICE. A false or loaded die that prevents certain numbers from being rolled. *Obsolete.* [1545 *OED*]

bar a bet, *v. phr.* In faro, to announce that a particular bet on the layout is not to be included during the upcoming turn.
1868 Trumps *Pocket Hoyle* 207. *To Bar a Bet.*—A player having a bet upon a card, and wishing to bar it for a turn, must say to the dealer, "I bar this bet for the turn," pointing to it, in which case, it can neither lose nor win.

bar a point, *v. phr.* In dice, to announce that a combination which would normally win for the shooter, will in fact lose on this turn.
[(1950) 1981 Maurer *Lang. of the Underworld* 181]

barbara hutton, *n.* Also called NICKELS AND DIMES. In hold 'em poker, two cards with the denomination of the numbers five and ten when dealt as the first two, or hole, cards to a player.
1981 Golad *Oral Coll.* A player sits there hour after hour with only two cards to look at, so the different combinations get names . . . a five and a ten is called a barbara hutton.
[So called after the dime-store heiress.]

barber pole, *n.* A stack of chips of different denominations, hence of different colors, mixed together. Compare DIRTY STACK.
[ca. 1961 *Hotel Coll*]

bar bet, *n.* **1.** Any of a variety of wagers designed to win drinks in public rooms or saloons.
[1963 Drazazgo *Wheels* 320]
2. In dice, a bet that a particular combination will not win. See also BAR A POINT.
[(1950) 1981 Maurer *Lang. of the Underworld* 181]
→Among dice players *bar bet* is use especially in hustlers' language.

barbooth, /bɑr'bu:t/, *n.* Also spelled **barboot, barbudi, barbuti.** /bɑr'bu:t *or* bɑr'bu: di:/ A dice game in which both player and shooter have an equal chance to win.
1981 Clark *Oral Coll. Barboot* is a fast, two dice game played by a lot of old Jewish and Greek immigrants. You can bet with the shooter or the fader and it's a dead even game, except the cutter takes five percent of the win for a house vig.

bardot it, *v. phr.* More commonly, BRIDGE IT. In bank craps, to stack the flat bet and the lay bet in a pyramid shape on the don't pass line when both payoffs are the same amount and color.
1984 Martinet *Oral Coll.* . . . somebody lays odds on a don't bet, and the boxman or somebody will say *bardot it.* You hear that only once in awhile. It comes from "bridge it." Say the point is four and a flat bet on the don't is fifteen bucks. So the player lays six reds [$5 chips] and the dealer stacks three chips against the flat bet and places three chips on top, between the two stacks.
[From the pronunciation of the command "Bridge it!" and reference to actress Bridget Bardot]
→Occasional use among dealers and boxmen.

barefoot, *adj.* In bank craps, pertaining to a bet on the pass line on which no odds are taken.
1983 Martinet *Oral Coll.* If a flat bet is left on

the pass line without odds after the point has been made, we say that it's *barefoot.* The dealer will ask if you want feet [odds] on it.

barker, *n.* In bank craps, the STICKMAN.
[1983 Martinet *Oral Coll*]

barn, *n.* In poker, a FULL HOUSE, three cards of one rank and two of another.
[1968 Wallace *Poker* 209]

barney, *n.* A sporting event, the outcome of which is influenced by dishonest scheming, as in a fixed horse race or boxing match.
[1865 *OED,* labeled obsolete; 1938 *DAS,* 1877 *DSUE*]

bar-point, *n.* In backgammon, the first space in the OUTER TABLE; just past the vertical bar, moving forward around the board.
1860 Crawley *Backgammon* 51. On the other side of the division that separates the table into two halves, the first point is called the *bar-point.*
[1743 *OEDS,* as *barr*]

barr dice, *n.* Dice shaved in such a fashion as to prevent a particular number from appearing as often as it might. See also FLAT DICE. Compare CALIPERS and LOADED DICE.
1726 Wilson *Art and Mystery* 32. As there are three sorts of Flatt Dice, such as Quatre-Trois, Six-Ace, and Cinq-Deux, so there are the same sorts of *Barr Dice.* The Difference is this: That as a Pair of Flatt Six-Aces commonly come up oftener than any other Seven, so a Pair of Barr Six-Aces seldom or never come up because the Six-Ace falls away from the Center towards each corner, that the Die will not easily lie upon that point.
[1753 *OED;* as *barred dice* 1532 *OED*]

barred, *adj.* In bank craps, pertaining to a number (usually two, three or twelve) declared to be a standoff or push when it occurs on the first cast. Most commonly, a *barred* roll applies to those who bet against the dice. This standoff, or bar, provides the percentage of the house profit.
[1950 Morehead *Culbertson* 591]

bar roll, *n.* In craps, a number which counts as a tie for certain bets on the first cast of the dice.
1982 Clark *Oral Coll.* In Vegas casinos the number twelve is a *bar roll.* When that comes on the first roll it's a push for the don't [pass line].

bar the roll, *v. phr.* To declare a throw of the dice void. [1673 *OED*]

base, *n.* **1.** In casino twenty-one, a player's position at the table.
[ca. 1961 *Hotel Coll*]
2. In bank craps, one of two dealers' positions flanking the BOXMAN.
[1983 Martinet *Oral Coll*]

baseball bum, *n.* In craps, the roll of the number nine on the dice.
[1949 Blanche *You Can't Win* 23]

baseball team, *n.* Also called BALL TEAM. A cheating ring made up of casino employees.
[1983 Martinet *Oral Coll*]

base count, *n.* **1.** In card games such as samba and canasta, the total of bonus points.
[1953 Crawford *Consistent Winner*]
2. In card games like bridge and pinochle, the estimate of the worth of the hand based on the distribution and ranks of the cards in the hand.
[1950 Morehead *Culbertson* 592]

base dealer, *n.* Also called CELLAR DEALER or SUBWAY DEALER. A person skilled at dealing from the bottom of the deck.
[1977 Carroll *Playboy's Illustrated* 44]

base value, *n.* In bridge, the point count for an odd trick.
[1950 Morehead *Culbertson* 592]

basic line, *n.* In horse racing, the initial odds on a horse determined by a standard handicapping pattern.
[1976 Figgis *Gambler's Handbook* 234]

basket bet, *n.* Also shortened to **basket.** In roulette, the numbers zero, double zero, and two on the table layout for an AMERICAN WHEEL.
[1983 Martinet *Oral Coll*]

basset, *n.* A popular card game of the late seventeenth and early eighteenth centuries, similar to faro. See also COUCH, CROUPERE, MASSE, PAY, PAROLI, and PUNTER.
1714 Lucas *Memoirs* 229. He also play'd very well at *Basset,* in which Game these Terms are to be observ'd. Talliere, which is he that keeps the Bank, who lays down a Sum of Money before all those that play, to answer every winning Card that shall appear in his Course of Dealing, Croupere, who is one that is assistant to the Talliere, and stands by to supervise the losing Cards; that when there is a considerable Company at Play, he may not lose by overlooking any thing that might turn to his Profit. Punter, a Term for every one of the Gamesters that play. Fasse, the first Card that is turn'd up by the Talliere, belonging to the whole Pack, by which he gains half the Value of the Money that is laid down upon every Card of that sort by the Punters. Couch is a Term for the first Money that every Punter puts upon each Card, every one that plays having a Book of 13 several Cards before him, upon which he may lay his Money, more or less, according to his Fancy. Paroli is, when having won the Couch or first Stake, and having a mind to go on to get a Sept-ed-le-va, you crook the corner of your Card, letting your Money Lie without being paid the Value of it by the Talliere. Masse is when you have won the Couch, or first Stake, and will venture more Money upon the same Card, which is only pursuant to the Discretion of the Punter, who knows or ought to know the great Advantages the Talliere has, and therefore should be subtle enough to make the best of his own Game. Pay is when the Punter has won the Couch or first Stake, whether a Shilling, Crown, Guinea, or whatever he lays down upon his Card; and being fearful to make the Paroli, leaves off; for by

going the Pay, if the Card turns up wrong he loses nothing, having won the Couch before, but if by this Adventure Fortune favours him, he wins double the Money that he Stakes. Alpiew is much the same thing as the Paroli, and like that Term us'd when a Couch is won, by turning up or crooking the corner of the winning Card. Sep-et-le-va is the first great Chance that shews the Advantages of this Game; as for example, if the Punter has won the Couch, and then makes a Paroli, by crooking the Corner of his Card, and going on to a second Chance, his winning Card turns up again, it comes to Sep-et-le-va, which is 7 times as much as he laid down upon his Card.
[1645 *OED*]

basto, *n. Spanish.* In the card game ombre or quadrille, the ace of clubs.
See quote at SPADILLO: 1680 Cotton *Compleat Gamester.*
[1675 *OED*]

bat, *n.* In horse racing, the whip carried by a jockey. [1935 *DAS*]

bay and a gray, *n. phr.* In poker, a bet of a red chip and a white chip, for a total of six dollars. A six dollar bet is common in cardrooms where, after an initial bet of three dollars, all following bets and raises are in six-dollar increments.
[1978 Larson *Vocabulary* 159]
[In horse racing, a bay is a reddish-brown horse with a dark mane and tail. A red chip often has black markings around the edge.]

BB, *n.* Abbreviation for BACK TO BACK. In sports books, a second wager made before the result of the first wager is known; two consecutive wagers.
[1973 Clark *Oral Coll*]

beagle, *n.* A race horse. *Derogatory use.* See also DOG.
[1983 Martinez *Gambling Scene* 188]

bean, *n.* **1.** A poker chip, usually valued at one dollar. [1903 *DA*]
2. One dollar.
[Compare 1811 *OEDS*, meaning "a coin"]

beard, *n.* A person who makes bets for another. The use of a *beard* to disguise the source of a wager is common when a player wishes to bet a large sum of money, but does not want the bookmaker to know that the bets are from a single source.
1985 *Las Vegas Sun*, 2/7:1B. [Someone] will contact bookmakers and *'beards'* (people who place bets for others) and instruct them on how to place certain bets for the group.

bear, *v.* In the particle constructions:
bear in, In horse racing, to run toward the inside rail.
[(1951) 1981 Maurer *Lang. of the Underworld* 203]
bear off, bore off, borne off. In backgammon, to remove pieces from the board after moving all one's pieces into the home table. The player who *bears off,* or removes all his pieces first is the winner.
1860 Crawley *Backgammon* 57. It is the business of each player to bear his men; that is, to take them off the board. For every number thrown, a man is removed from the corresponding point, until the whole are *borne off* . . . In *bearing off,* doublets have the same power as in the moves.
[1562 *OED*]
bear out, In horse racing, to run toward the outside rail; to run wide on a turn.
[1955 Hillis *Pari-Mutuel Betting* 112]

beat, *v.* In the phrases:
beat the board, In stud poker, to have the best hand showing on the table before the final betting round.
[1963 Steig *Common Sense* 181]
beat the favorite, To pick a LONGSHOT to win.
[(1951) 1981 Maurer *Lang. of the Underworld* 203]
beat the gate, In horse racing, to get a split second lead on the other horses at the start of a race.
[1983 Martinez *Gambling Scene* 188]
beat the house, To win in a casino.
[1974 Scarne *Dice* 254]
beat the price, To place a wager with a bookmaker at better odds than those generally offered by other bookmakers.
[(1951) 1981 Maurer *Lang of the Underworld* 203]

beaten length, *n. phr.* In horse racing, the distance behind the leader that a losing horse runs, measured in terms of time: one-fifth of one second equals one length.
[1955 Hillis *Pari-Mutuel Betting* 112]

bed roll, *n.* A controlled throw of the dice on a soft surface. See also BLANKET ROLL.
[1963 Drazazgo *Wheels* 320]

beetle, *n.* A race horse. *Derogatory in use.*
[1934 *DAS*]

beg, *v.* In such games as all fours (high, low, jack and the game), OLD SLEDGE, and SEVEN UP, to excercise a request for additional cards, a privilege allowed only to the player at the dealer's left.
1836 Eidrah *Hoyle Famil* 63. *Beg,* is when the non-dealer, not liking his cards, says "I *beg,*" the dealer must give him three more cards from the pack, and take three to himself; or suffer him to add one point to his game. Three cards are usually thrown out in lieu of the three taken in.
1866 *American Card Player* 121. *Begging* is when the elder hand, disliking his cards, uses his privilege, and says, "I beg;" in which case the dealer must either suffer his adversary to score one point, saying "Take one," or give each three cards more from the pack, and then turn up the next card, the seventh, for trumps.
[1793 *OEDS*]

beggar, *n.* In poker games other than lowball, a hand with no card higher than a ten.
[1937 *DSUE*]

beginner's luck, *n. phr.* The condition of a player, usually a novice, who wins in spite of violating acceptable betting practices.
[1897 *OEDS*]

behind the line odds, *n. phr.* Also shortened to **behind the line.** In bank craps, the actual or true odds on a FLAT BET placed on the PASS LINE.
[1983 Martinez *Gambling Scene* 186]

behind the log *v. phr.* In the phrase to **play behind the log.** In poker, to bet conservatively, even though ahead in winnings.
[1971 Livingston *Poker Strategy* 213]

behind the sink, *prep. phr.* Having lost all of one's money.
[(1950) 1981 Maurer *Lang. of the Underworld* 181]
[Perhaps a corruption of BEHIND THE SIX.]

behind the six, *prep. phr.* Having lost all of one's money.
[1943 Maurer *Argot*]
[From faro in which the money drawer is behind the number six card. When all of a player's money has been lost, it is "behind the six," and a player will say he is *behind the six.*]

bela, *n.* Also spelled **bella.** In the games of alsos and klaberjas, the king and queen of trump when held by one player.
[1950 Morehead *Culbertson* 593]

belly-buster straight, *n.* Same as BELLY HIT.
[1978 Brunson *How I Made* 523]

belly hit, *n.* Also called GUT SHOT. In poker, a successful draw to fill an inside straight.
[1968 Wallace *Poker* 210]

belly stripper, *n.* A card shaved or trimmed on the long side to make the card narrower. See also STRIPPER.
[1943 MacDougall *Danger* 124]

below, *n.* The net income of a licensed gaming operation after operating costs have been deducted.
1977 *Nev Int Ctrl.* Accounting procedures shall demonstrate source income for all earnings of the above [gross income] and all expenditures before the *below.*

below, *adj.* Pertaining to earnings not reported to state gaming control regulators; of skimmed profits.
[1961 Scarne *Complete Guide* 672]

below the line, *prep. phr.* In bridge, the area of the score sheet for recording the scores for contracts.
[1953 Crawford *Consistent Winner*]

bend, *v.* To mark a card by slightly folding or creasing it.
[1983 Martinez *Gambling Scene* 188]

bent, *n.* A card which has been bowed so that it is easily located by the person who is to cut the cards.
1680 Cotton *Compleat Gamester* 94. The *bent* is a Card bended in play which you cut.

best bet, *n.* **1.** In horse racing, a handicapper's selection published in the racing form.
[(1951) 1981 Maurer *Lang. of the Underworld* 203]
2. In bank craps, the number six or eight, when taken with true odds; generally, the wagers offered that have the lowest house advantage.
[1961 Scarne *Complete Guide* 672]

best bower, *n.* In certain trump games, the joker, when it is ranked as the highest trump card.
[1950 Morehead *Culbertson* 593]
[From German *bauer,* jack or knave.]

bet, *n.* **1.** A wager or stake, usually between two parties, on the outcome of an event.
[1460 *OED,* 1852 *DAE*]

bet, *v.* **1.** To wager or stake a prize, usually between two parties, on the outcome of an event.
[1597 *OED*]
2. In the phrases and particle constructions:
bet blind, In poker, to make a wager before looking at the cards.
[1949 Coffin *Secrets* 172]
bet both ways, In bank craps, to bet on the PASS and the DON'T PASS at the same time, a common practice in some betting systems. After a point has been established, the player can then take or lay odds at will.
[(1950) 1981 Maurer *Lang. of the Underworld* 182]
→Especially found in those casinos offering double, triple, or up to ten times the normal odds wager.
bet down, In horse racing, to force the odds on a horse lower than initially posted (i.e., below the MORNING LINE) by wagering a large amount of money on the horse.
[1982 *Today's Racing Digest* 15]
bet even stakes, To bet the same amount on every hand during the course of a game such as faro or twenty-one.
1868 Trumps *Pocket Hoyle* 208. *Betting even stakes* is when the player constantly bets the same amount.
bet into (someone), In poker, to make a large wager prior to another player who is suspected of having a stronger hand, usually for purposes of bluffing.
[1963 Steig *Common Sense* 182]
bet on muscle, To place a bet without supplying the money for the wager; to bet on credit. See also CALL BET.
[(1950) 1981 Maurer *Lang. of the Underworld* 203]
bet or fold, Same as BET OR GET.
[ca. 1961 *Hotel Coll*]
bet or get, Also **bet or drop.** In poker, to make a wager or retire from the hand, an expression of impatience made to a player who hesitates during his turn to act.
[1968 Wallace *Poker* 210]
bet out of turn, In poker, to put one's money

into the pot before those players with a prior right have acted.
1979 Clark *Oral Coll.* One of the tricks used by some amateurs is to *bet out of turn* if they want somebody ahead of them to call or at least not raise, or if they want it to look like they are going to call, but then make a raise when it finally gets around to their turn. Sometimes if a person raises after they have bet out of turn, they may take their money back and fold. Sometimes betting out of turn is an honest mistake, but usually it's a cheap trick.
bet right, 1. In bank craps, to wager that the person shooting the dice will make a pass; to wager on the PASS LINE. Compare BET WRONG.
[ca. 1961 *Hotel Coll*]
2. To wager the proper amounts in order to receive the correct odds payoff.
[1983 Martinet *Oral Coll*]
bet the dog, In the card game red dog, to wager an amount equal to the pot.
[1971 Smith *Games* 103]
bet the farm or **bet the ranch,** To wager one's entire stake on one hand.
[1983 Martinet *Oral Coll*]
bet the jockey, In horse racing, to make a wager based on the past performance of the jockey rather than the past performance of a horse.
[1975 Clark *Oral Coll*]
bet the limit, To wager the maximum amount allowed by the person conducting the game. See also HOUSE LIMIT.
[1961 Scarne *Complete Guide* 672]
bet the pot, In no-limit poker, to wager an amount equal to the total amount already in the betting pool.
[1949 Coffin *Secrets* 173]
bet wrong, In bank craps, to wager that the person shooting the dice will not make a pass; to bet on the DON'T PASS line. Compare BET RIGHT.
[ca. 1961 *Hotel Coll*]

bet back, *n.* A special wager in a casino, in which a player is allowed to place a bet and receives true odds. If the player wins, he must wager the original amount and his winnings on another bet on which he receives the regular, or house, odds.
1983 Martinet *Oral Coll.* You don't much see a *bet back* anymore. It was a special bet you could take with the house. In roulette, for example, you could bet a number and get true odds of thirty-eight to one rather than the house odds of thirty-six to one. If you won you had to put the entire amount on another bet. But this time you got house odds rather than true odds.

bet box, *n.* In baccarat, the area on the table layout on which bets for the player or bank are placed. See also BANK HAND BET BOX.
[ca. 1961 *Hotel Coll*]

bet card, *n.* Also called CASE CARD or CASE. In faro, the fourth card of a particular denomination.
1868 Trumps *Pocket Hoyle* 208. When three cards of one denomination are out, the one remaining in the box is called the *bet,* case, or single *card.*
[1909 *OEDS*]

betting forecast, *n. phr.* In horse racing, a prediction by a racing agency as to the probable opening odds on horses for a race.
[1974 Ewart *Flatracing* 148]

betting interval, *n. phr.* In card games like twenty-one and poker, the period of time during which an individual player has an opportunity to make a wager or retire from the hand.
[1949 Coffin *Secrets* 173]

betting procedure, *n. phr.* The routine of planned money management by a frequent player.
[1971 McQuaid *Gambler's Digest* 299]

betting slip, *n.* In a casino, the written memorandum recording the amount wagered by an individual or on a table.
[ca. 1961 *Hotel Coll*]

betting ticket, *n.* A serially numbered form used in casinos and sports books to record the date and amount wagered.
[1978 Alexander *Glossary* 2]

bettor, *n.* A person who wagers on the outcome of gaming events.
[1894 *DAE*]

beveled suction shapes, *n. pl.* Sometimes shortened to **beveled shapes.** Also called BEVELS. Dice that have been slightly rounded on one face of each die.
[1974 Scarne *Dice* 238]

bevels, *n. pl.* Short for BEVELED SUCTION SHAPES.
[1961 Scarne *Complete Guide* 672]

B-game, *n.* The second highest stake game in a casino or cardroom.
[1949 Coffin *Secrets* 173]

bicycle, *n.* Also called LITTLE WHEEL or WHEEL. In lowball poker, a sequence of cards from the ace to five.
[1953 Crawford *Consistent Winner*]

bid, *v.* **1.** In card games like bridge and whist, to announce an intention to win a specified number of tricks. See also BID, *n.* (def. 2).
[1880 *OEDS*]
2. In high-low poker, to declare an intention to win the high hand, the low hand, or both the high and low hands. See also BID, *n.* (def. 2).
[1949 Coffin *Secrets* 173]

bid, *n.* **1.** In games like bridge and whist, a declaration of intention to win a specified number of tricks.
[1880 *OEDS*]
2. In high-low poker, the declaration of an intention to win half the pot with the highest hand, or to win half the pot with the lowest hand, or to win the entire pot with both high and low hands.
[1949 Coffin *Secrets* 173]

bidder, *n.* In games such as bridge and whist, the player who offers to win a specified number of tricks. [1880 *OEDS*]

bidding, *n.* In auction card games, the period during which offers and counteroffers of contracts are made.
[1880 *OEDS*]

big apple, *n.* Especially **the Big Apple.** Horse racing which features strong competition, good tracks, and expensive PURSES for the winners, especially New York racing.
[(1951) 1981 Maurer *Lang. of the Underworld* 203]

big casino, *n.* In the card game casino, the ten of diamonds. [1950 Morehead *Culbertson* 594]

big cat, *n.* Also called BIG TIGER. In poker, a hand with various cards ranging in denomination from king to eight, with no pair or flush. Compare BIG DOG. [1949 Coffin *Secrets* 173]

big dick, *n.* In craps, a cast of the dice resulting in showing ten pips upward; the point ten.
[1949 Blanche *You Can't Win* 23]
[Perhaps from French *dix,* ten]

big dick from (Battle Creek, Boston, etc.) *n. phr.* Same as BIG DICK.
[(1950) 1981 Maurer *Lang. of the Underworld* 182]

big digger, *n.* The ace of spades.
[ca. 1937 *DSUE*]

big dog, *n.* In poker, a hand with various cards ranging in denomination from ace to nine, with no pair or flush. Compare BIG CAT.
[1949 Coffin *Secrets* 173]

big draw, *n.* In poker, a hand in the final betting round that has a good chance to win the pot.
[1978 Brunson *How I Made* 524]

big drop, *n.* Also called DROP. The headquarters of a numbers ring or policy game.
[1961 Scarne *Complete Guide* 673]

big duke, *n.* In poker, especially in hold 'em, a strong hand; potentially, a winning hand.
[1981 Golad *Oral Coll*]

big eight, *n.* In bank craps, a place on the table layout to place a wager that the number eight will be rolled before the number seven.
[1950 Morehead *Culbertson* 594]

big figure, *n.* In faro, the area on the layout containing the jack, queen, and king.
1868 Trumps *Pocket Hoyle* 203. The King, Queen, and Jack are called "the *Big Figure.*"

big full, *n.* In poker, the highest possible FULL HOUSE, three aces and two kings. See also UNDERFULL.
[1978 Brunson *How I Made* 524]

big game, *n.* A dice or card game with high stakes being wagered.
[1974 Scarne *Dice* 151]

big general, *n.* In a bar dice game, five dice of the same denomination when they appear on the first roll. This cast is often considered an automatic winner.
[1974 Scarne *Dice* 370]

big hand, *n.* A specially arranged packet of cards; a STACKED DECK.
1859 Green *Gam Tricks* 21. *Big hand*—This is a hand that is stocked [stacked], and is put up very often in playing for fun, in order to get bets on it, as it is much more easy to stock [when playing for small stakes].

big Joe from Boston, *n. phr.* Also called BIG DICK. In craps, the roll of ten.
[1968 Adams *Western Words*]

big mitt, *n.* The name of a swindle at stud poker, using a stacked deck. The victim is dealt a high hand, the cheater deals himself a higher hand.
[1901 *OED,* 1903 *DA*]

big natural, *n.* In craps, the number eleven on the first, or COME OUT ROLL.
[1968 Adams *Western Words]*

big nickel, *n.* Five hundred dollars.
[ca. 1961 *Hotel Coll*]

big one, *n.* One thousand dollars.
[1968 Thackrey *Nick the Greek* 238]

big order, *n.* A large wager handled by a bookmaker.
[ca. 1961 *Hotel Coll*]

big plunger, *n.* A person who gambles for large stakes; a HIGH ROLLER. See also BP.
[1978 *Gambling Times*]

big poker, *n. phr.* A high stakes poker game; NO-LIMIT poker, a TABLE STAKES poker game, or a POT-LIMIT poker game.
[1949 Coffin *Secrets* 173]

big Q, *n.* In dog races, jai alai, and horse racing, a bet on the first two finishers in two races, though not necessarily in the correct sequence. See also QUINELLA.
[1968 Buchele *Greyhound Racing* 95]

big red, *n.* In bank craps, the space on the layout for a proposition bet that the next roll will yield the number seven.
[1973 Clark *Oral Coll*]

big six, *n.* **1.** In bank craps, a space on the layout for betting that the number six will appear on a roll before the number seven appears.
[1949 Blanche *You Can't Win* 23]
2. Short for BIG SIX WHEEL.
[1953 Lewis *Sagebrush Casinos* 193]

big six wheel, *n. phr.* A vertical standing WHEEL OF FORTUNE with fifty-four positions, and, originally, six different available wagers.
[1968 Thackrey *Nick the Greek* 164]

big slick, *n.* Also called SANTA BARBARA. In hold 'em poker, an ace and a king when they are the first two cards dealt to a player.
1981 Golad *Oral Coll.* A player sits there hour after hour with only two cards to look at, so the different combinations get names . . . an ace and a king are a Santa Barbara. The older term for

that is *big slick,* but a few years ago there was an oil spill off the coast and the California players started calling it Santa Barbara. You hear that in Vegas and Texas, too.

big square, *n.* In faro, the area of the table layout with the ace, two, queen, and king.
[1890 Quinn *Fools of Fortune* 194]

big table, *n.* In dice, a gaming table where a BIG GAME is played, especially where the table LIMIT is high.
[(1950) 1981 Maurer *Lang. of the Underworld* 182]

big tiger, *Same as BIG CAT.*
[1949 Coffin Secrets 173]

bike, *n.* Same as BICYCLE.
[1978 Brunson *How I Made* 524]

bilk, *n.* A person who cheats at cards.
[1717 *OEDS,* 1790 *DAE*]

Bill Daley, *n.* See ON THE BILL DALEY.
[1941 *DAS*]

bingle, bangle, bungo, *n. phr.* Also spelled **bingo, bango, bongo.** A golfing wager in which the first player to reach the green in regulation play wins the BINGLE portion of the wager, the person closest to the flag wins the BANGLE, and the person who drops his putt first, playing in regular sequence, wins the BUNGO portion of the wager. See also BLITZ and GREENIES.
[1971 McQuaid *Gambler's Digest* 299]

bingo, *interj.* The winner's cry in the game of the same name.
[1964 Wykes *Illustrated Guide* 326]
[1927 *OEDS*]

bingo, *n.* A game which resembles LOTTO by using BINGO NUMBERS and a BINGO CARD, often in a BINGO PARLOR or to raise money for charity.
[1936 *DA*]

bingo blower, *n.* The glass cylinder which contains the seventy-five balls used in calling a bingo game.
[1953 Lewis *Sagebrush Casinos* 94]

bingo card, *n.* A card with twenty-four numbers printed on a five-by-five grid (the center square is blank) used in playing bingo.
[1978 Harrah *Recollections* 58]

bingo hall, *n.* Same as BINGO PARLOR.
[1964 *OEDS*]

bingo numbers, *n. pl.* The lightweight balls used in a bingo game. Each ball carries a letter and a number corresponding to spaces on the bingo card. Numbers one through fifteen are prefixed with the letter B, numbers sixteen through thirty are prefixed with the letter I, numbers thirty-one through forty-five are prefixed with the letter N, numbers forty-six through sixty are prefixed with the letter G, and numbers sixty-one through seventy-five are prefixed with the letter O.
[1976 Figgis *Gambler's Handbook* 132]

bingo parlor, *n.* A large room in which the game of bingo may be played, such as separate space in a casino, a church hall or basement or annex, or a dedicated building on an Indian reservation.
[1978 Harrah *Recollections* 60]

bingo war, *n.* Competition for the same patrons by the owners or operators of neighboring bingo parlors.
[1978 Harrah *Recollections* 73]

binocle, *n.* variant of PINOCHLE.
[1950 Morehead *Culbertson* 594]

bird, *n.* A twenty-five cent chip.
[1974 Scarne *Dice* 461]

birdcage, *n.* **1.** The metal basket, closed on all sides, used to scramble the three dice used in CHUCK-A-LUCK.
2. Another name for CHUCK-A-LUCK.
[1938 Asbury *Sucker's Progress* 57]

bird dog, *n.* A person who guides players to illegal gambling locations.
[1949 Coffin *Secrets* 173]

bitch, *n.* In playing cards, a queen of any suit.
[ca. 1900 *DAS*]

BJ, *n.* In a casino, the letters on the DROP BOX beneath a twenty-one table.
[1979 Newman *Dealer's Special* 12]

black, *n.* **1.** Short for BLACK CHECK, a one hundred dollar chip.
[1977 Anness *Dummy Up*]
2. In roulette, a color on the table layout for making an EVEN-MONEY bet that the ball will land on a black number rather than a red number.
[ca. 1961 *Hotel Coll*]

black and whites, *n. phr. Plural in form but singular in use.* The uniform worn by casino dealers, normally, a white shirt and black slacks or skirt.
[ca. 1961 *Hotel Coll*]

black book, *n.* Also written **blackbook.** Also called the LIST OF EXCLUDED PERSONS. In Nevada gaming, the state-maintained list of undesirable people who must be excluded from gambling establishments by the owners.
[ca. 1961 *Hotel Coll*]
[Compare 1592 *OED*]

blackbook, *v.* To enter the name of an undesirable individual in the LIST OF EXCLUDED PERSONS, the state-maintained list of undesirable people who must be excluded from gambling establishments by the owners.
[1963 Taylor *Las Vegas* 4]

black box, *n.* In twenty-one, a small calculator popular during the 1960s dedicated to calculating odds of various card combinations.
[1965 Wilson *The Casino*]

black check, *n.* Also called **black chip.** In a casino, a one-hundred dollar chip.
[1979 Hughes *Dealing*]

blackjack, *n.* **1.** Also called TWENTY-ONE. A card game in which a player attempts to draw cards

totalling twenty-one points, without exceeding that number. [1910 *OEDS*]
2. Also called SNAPPER. In twenty-one, two cards dealt to a player consisting of an ace and a ten through king of any suit.
[1951 Jones *Wilbur Clark's* 2]
3. In hearts, the jack of spades, which counts ten points against the person taking it. In another version of hearts, the queen of spades serves the same function and counts thirteen points against the player taking it, unless the player also captures all thirteen cards of the heart suit.
[1950 Morehead *Culbertson* 594]

blackjack dealer, *n.* In a casino, a person who deals the game of twenty-one.
[ca. 1961 *Hotel Coll*]

blackleg, *n.* A cardsharp, especially in faro. *Obsolete.*
[1771 *OED, DSUE*]
→ Used mainly around 1850, eventually meaning any swindler.

blackout, *n.* **1.** In bingo, a game in which all the numbers on the card must be called in order to win.
[1953 Woon *The Why, How, and Where*]
2. An electrical failure on a slot machine. A *blackout* is often programmed into a slot machine, designed to shut the machine down when a payout is required that exceeds the amount of money available for a jackpot.
[1977 Cahill *Recollections* 581]

blackwood convention, *n.* In bridge, a system of bidding used to reach a slam contract.
[1953 Crawford *Consistent Winner* 2]

blank, *n.* **1.** In dominoes, a tile with no pips on the face. [1950 Morehead *Culbertson* 595]
2. In hold 'em poker, a card of no value which is dealt fifth or sixth during a hand.
[1978 Brunson *How I Made* 524]

blank suit, *n.* In trump games, a hand without any cards of one particular suit.
[1953 Crawford *Consistent Winner* 2]

blanket craps, *n.* Also called ARMY CRAPS. An illegal craps game; a FLOATING CRAPS game.
[1977 Cahill *Recollections* 323]

blanket finish, *n.* In horse racing, a race in which two or more horses reach the finish line together.
[1955 Hillis *Pari-Mutuel Betting* 112]

blanket roll, *n.* Also called SOFT-PAD ROLL. A controlled cast of the dice on a soft surface. Compare PAD ROLL.
[(1950) 1981 Maurer *Lang. of the Underworld* 182]

blaze, *n.* **1.** A face card.
2. A hand with five face cards. In some poker games, the hand has special significance and may win in certain conditions.
1830 Anon *Hoyle's Improved* 138. *Blaze* is five face or court cards.
1887 Keller *Poker* 17. The *blaze* is another hand that is occasionally played in Draw Poker. It consists of five court cards, and when played beats two pairs. It is the most contemptible of all poker innovations and has become almost obsolete.
[1866 *DA;* 1880 *OEDS;* 1887 *DAE*]

blaze full, *n.* In poker, a FULL HOUSE comprised of face cards, for example, three kings and two queens.
[1968 Wallace *Poker* 210]

blazing, *n.* The marking of cards by scratching the backs with a pin or thumbnail.
[1938 Asbury *Sucker's Progress* 37]

bleacher bettor, *n.* **1.** A baseball fan who makes wagers on any of a variety of events during a game, such as which team will make the first error or which player will get the first hit.
2. Anyone who will wager on any observable event, not restricted to sporting events.
[1971 McQuaid *Gambler's Digest* 300]

bleed, *v.* **1.** To lose a large amount of money by gambling. [1668 *OED*]
2. To slowly but steadily extract money from a game or a player.
[1680 *OED*; 1875 *DAE*]

bleeder, *n.* **1.** Also called SWEATER (def. 2). In casinos, an executive such as a pitboss or floorman who agonizes and frets about money lost by the establishment.
[1974 Friedman *Casino Management* 46]
2. A player or bettor who complains about losses in a whining fashion.
[1968 Wallace *Poker* 210]
3. In horse racing, a horse prone to nasal hemorrhage during or after a workout or race.
[(1951) 1981 Maurer *Lang. of the Underworld* 204]
4. In boxing, a fighter prone to being easily cut.
[1973 Clark *Oral Coll*]

blind, *n.* **1.** In poker, a bet required of the first (and sometimes the second) player to the left of the dealer before the player may pick up the cards. See also AGE, DOUBLE BLIND, and STRADDLE.
1843 Green *Exposure* 108. The next was obliged to put up a half, the next one dollar, the next two dollars, the fifth four dollars, and Mr. Winall, the dealer, had to put up eight dollars, and the deal was finished. As Mr. Consequence sat first on the dealer's left, he had first to say whether he would go the *blind* or not; he, with an air of great consequence, answered, "Yes;" and much to the surprise of all, he added, "I will go a hundred besides." It took him fifteen dollars and seventy-five cents to go the *blind,* and his extra bet made his share of the stake one hundred and fifteen dollars and seventy-five cents which was all counted and put up by him.
1866 *American Card Player* 133. The eldest hand has the privilege of making a bet before he raises his cards; this bet is usually limited to a few chips, and is called "going *blind.*" The *blind* may be doubled by the player to the left of the eldest hand.

1949 Coffin *Fortune* 169. Before the deal, the nearest player to the left of the dealer, known as the age, puts up a partial bet of one chip, the *blind,* and the second player to the left of the dealer, known as the straddler, puts up a partial bet of two chips, the straddle.
1950 Morehead *Culbertson's Hoyle* 71. Whether or not there was an ante before the deal, at the conclusion of the deal the player at dealer's left (called the age, or the *blind*), without looking at his hand, must make an opening bet of one chip.
[1850 *DA*; 1857 *DAE*; 1872 *OEDS*]
2. Also called WIDOW. In games like cribbage or euchre, a packet of cards set aside for later play.
[1950 Morehead *Culbertson* 595]
3. In cards, a cheating move entailing a false shuffle and control of certain cards.
[1983 Martinez *Gambling Scene* 189]

blind bet, *n.* **1.** Same as BLIND (def. 1).
[1961 Scarne *Complete Guide* 627]
2. In bookmaking, a small or unusual wager made by a player who intends to deter notice from a larger bet placed.
[1964 Wykes *Illustrated Guide* 326]

blind cinch, *n.* In cinch, a small packet of cards dealt to each player, not to be looked at or used until after the auction.
[1950 Morehead *Culbertson* 595]

blind hand, *n.* In poker games featuring a BLIND-BET provision, the first position to the left of the the dealer.
[1871 *OEDS;* 1882 *OED, DA, DAE*]

blind hookey, *n.* A procedure in which each player draws a single card from the pack to determine who shall deal. The dealing is done by the person drawing the highest card.
[1840 *OEDS*]

blind lead, *n.* **1.** In poker games featuring a BLIND-BET provision, the initial bet by the first person to the left of the dealer, made before the player is allowed to look at his cards.
[1872 *DA*]
2. In trump games, a card placed face up on the table before any other cards are shown.
[1950 Morehead *Culbertson* 595]

blind money, *n.* In poker games featuring a BLIND-BET provision, the amount of the required wager by the first person to the left of the dealer, made before the player is allowed to look at his cards.
[1882 *OEDS*]

blind poker, *n.* A poker game featuring the provision of a BLIND BET by the first player to the left of the dealer.
[1871 *DAE, OEDS;* 1882 *DA*]

blind shuffle, *n.* A procedure for appearing to mix a pack of cards while maintaining a STACKED DECK.
[1968 Wallace *Poker* 210]

blind spot, *n.* **1.** In roulette, the third column on the layout. So called because the third column is to the extreme left of the dealer, while the wheel is at his right.
[1973 Clark *Oral Coll*]
2. In bank craps, the FIELD betting area on the layout. The field is directly in front of the dealer, but sometimes overlooked in the busy activity of paying bets on the pass line, which is just beyond the field.
[1983 Martinet *Oral Coll*]

blind switch, *n.* In horse racing, a position behind one horse and between another horse and the rail. A horse cannot move out in front from such a position and is said to be IN THE POCKET.
[1978 Ainslie *Complete Guide* 284]
[From a switch, i.e., trail, without an outlet.]

blind tiger, *n.* In poker, a requirement that the second player to the left of the dealer double the bet made by the first player to the left of the dealer (the BLIND) before looking at his cards.
[1963 Steig *Common Sense* 182]

blinkers, *n. pl.* Screens attached to a horse's briddle to direct its vision forward.
[(1951) 1981 Maurer *Lang. of the Underworld* 204]
→ *Blinkers* are useful in preventing a horse from being distracted as by the rail or another horse running next to it. OED cites the use of the term in non-racing contexts from 1789.

blister, *v.* To mark the backs of playing cards with a sharp pointed device, such as a pin.
[1935 Newman *Esquire's Book* 53]

blitz, *n.* A wager at golf in which points are scored for the longest drive, the first ball on the green, and the longest putt. See also BINGLE, BANGLE, BUNGO.
[1971 McQuaid *Gambler's Digest* 300]

block, *n.* **1.** In backgammon, a position on the board with two or more stones, or pieces. The opponent may not occupy that position. See also BLOCKED POINT and STONE.
[1950 Morehead *Culbertson* 595]
2. In panguingui, the wooden piece against which the cards rest while being dealt.

block, *v.* **1.** In card games, to prevent another player from winning by retaining a high ranking card needed by that player to win.
[1844 *DA*]
2. In trump games, to prevent another player from leading a card from a particular suit.
[1885 *OEDS*]
3. In the phrases:
block a suit, In card games like bridge, to prevent another player from playing a particular suit.
[1950 Morehead *Culbertson* 595]
block the dice, To arrange a pair of dice so that each pair of faces shows seven pips. Used in making controlled shots.
[1963 Drazazgo *Wheels* 320]

blocked point, *n.* In backgammon, same as a BLOCK.

[1976 Figgis *Gambler's Handbook* 68]

blocker, *n.* In a casino, an accomplice who assists a SLOT CHEATER by shielding the cheater's activities from security guards and closed-circuit television cameras.
1984 Martinet *Oral Coll.* A slot cheat needs *blockers* to cover the activity. He can drill a machine in thirty seconds or less and set a jackpot, but the blocker shields him and distracts the security guard, if necessary.

block game, *n.* In backgammon, a strategy for preventing an opponent from taking his pieces from the board or bearing off. See also BEAR OFF.
[1974 Scarne *Dice* 322]

blocking, *n.* In trump games, the preventing of another player from playing a particular suit.
[1898 *OEDS*]

block-out work, *n.* The marking of the backs of cards by covering part of the design with india ink, similar to the BLOCK SYSTEM.
[1961 Scarne *Complete Guide* 673]

block system, *n.* **1.** A method for marking cards on the back by adding to the design with india ink, similar to BLOCK-OUT WORK.
[ca. 1961 *Hotel Coll*]
2. In poker, a method of play in which the dealer antes for all the players rather than waiting for each player to place the appropriate amount into the pot.
[1949 Coffin *Secrets* 173]

bloomer, *n.* A race horse that runs better in the morning workout than in the race.
[(1951) 1981 Maurer *Lang. of the Underworld* 204]

blot, *n.* In backgammon, a single piece on a point, which is vulnerable to attack by the opposing player's pieces.
1860 Crawley *Backgammon* 53 If during these forward marches one man be left on a point, it is called a *blot.*
[1598 *OED*]

blow, *v.* **1.** To lose money by gambling, especially rapidly or foolishly.
[1874 *OEDS,* 1889 *DA*]
2. Especially of a victim in dice gambling, to detect cheating.
[(1950) 1981 Maurer *Lang. of the Underworld* 182]
3. In the phrases:
blow back, 1. In poker, to raise a bet, especially after having called or checked, or after an opponent has raised a bet. See also CALL, CHECK, and RAISE.
[1968 Wallace *Poker* 210]
2. To continue to gamble until all winnings have been lost.
[1983 Martinet *Oral Coll*]
blow the whistle, To inform the police of the location of an illegal gambling operation.
[1948 *DAS,* compare 1934 *OEDS*]
blow out, In horse racing: **1.** To slacken gradually the pace of a horse following a strenuous workout.
[(1951) 1981 Maurer *Lang. of the Underworld* 204]
2. Of a horse, to train.
[(1951) 1981 Maurer *Lang. of the Underworld* 204]

blower, *n.* In keno, the clear plastic sphere that mixes the numbered balls and forces twenty of them randomly into tubes, or RABBIT EARS, where they may be read.
[1979 Hilton Hotel *Procedures* 5]

blow out, *n.* A brief exercise for a race horse, either before a race or after a strenuous workout.
[1971 McQuaid *Gambler's Digest* 300]

blue, *adj.* In poker, pertaining to black pipped cards, especially spades. See quote at ALL BLUE.
[1890 *DA*]

blue, *n.* A particular denomination of gambling chips, often five dollars.
[1973 Clark *Oral Coll*]

Blue Peter, *n.* In whist, a request to a partner for a lower trump than the one played.
1860 Pardon *Handbook* 22. *Blue Peter*—A signal for trumps, allowable in modern play. This term is used when a high card is unnecessarily played in place of one of lower denomination, as a ten for a seven.
[1803 *OED* under *peter*]

bluff, *n.* Another name for POKER.
1866 *American Card Player* 130. Success in playing the game of Poker (or *Bluff,* as it is sometimes called) depends rather upon luck and energy than skill.
[1838 *DA;* 1845 *DAE;* 1848 *OED*]

bluff, *v.* **1.** To misrepresent one's hand, making opponents think the hand is more valuable or less valuable than it actually is.
1859 Green *Gam Tricks* 77. The gambler, under these circumstances, will *bluff,* (which means in the gambling phrase betting on small worthless cards) only when his hand is better; and frequently, in order to set his victim to *bluffing,* he will, by stocking, palming, &c., deal him three aces and a pair of kings, while he himself gets four tens or jacks.
[1845 *DA*; 1879 *DAE*]
2. In the phrase:
bluff off, In poker, to represent one's hand as very strong.
1866 *American Card Player* 134. *Bluffing off.*—When a player with a weak hand bets so high he makes his opponents believe he has a very strong hand, and they are deterred from "seeing" him, or "going better." He thus gets the pool, and "*bluffs* them *off.*"
[1845 *DA, DAE;* 1871 *OED*]

board, *n.* **1.** A playing surface for card and dice games. See quote at HAZARD: 1680 Cotton

Compleat Gamester.
[1680 *OED*]
2. In card games, the amount of money on the table wagered for a certain hand; the POT.
[1848 *DA;* 1852 *DAE*]
3. Also called the WALL. In bank craps, the vertical padded cushion at either end of a craps table.
[1983 Martinez *Gambling Scene* 190]
4. A playing card.
[*DAS, DSUE*]
→The word is considered old-fashioned and is now used only facetiously.
5. A faro layout, usually made of felt, with the figures of the thirteen cards, usually ace through king of spades, painted on the surface.
[1890 Quinn *Fools of Fortune* 194]
6. A playing surface for backgammon, divided into an INNER TABLE and an OUTER TABLE.
[1974 Scarne *Dice* 318]

boardman, *n.* The person who posts the race results in a bookmaking parlor. See also TICKERMAN.
[(1951) 1981 Maurer *Lang. of the Underworld* 204]

boaston, *n.* In boston (similar to bridge), the act of winning five or more tricks.
[1836 Eidrah *Hoyle Famil* 31]
[1805 *OED*; 1821 *DAE;* both sources list *boston* only]

boat race, *n.* Also called a FIXED RACE. A dishonest horserace in which the winner is preselected. [1956 *DAS*]

bobtail, *n.* In poker, a four card flush or straight. Compare LITTLE BOBTAIL.
1865 Evans *Gamblers Win* 49. After the deal, if he sees, at any time while giving the players their draft, a [marked] card on top which will match his pair or a four flush . . . he deals from under it till he comes to himself, when he draws this card to his four flush, or "*bobtail.*"
[1873 *DA;* 1875 *OEDS;* 1887 *DAE*]

bolt, *v.* **1.** In brag, to drop from active participation in the hand and relinquish one's cards.
1830 Anon *Hoyle's Improved* 154. . . . if his cards are bad, he may *bolt,* that is, throw up his cards, and forfeit his interest in the pool for that deal.
2. In racing horses, to lose stride, falter, or swerve to one side or the other.
[1820 *OED*]

bone, *n.* **1.** A piece or TILE in a set of dominoes.
[1950 Morehead *Culbertson* 591]
2. bones, *pl.* A set of dominoes.
[1976 Figgis *Gambler's Handbook* 78]
3. Usually, **bones,** *pl.* a die or dice.
[1887 *DAS*]
4. A white colored CHIP or CHECK, worth one dollar.
[1964 Reese and Watkins *Secrets* 138]

boneyard, *n.* In dominoes, the TILES remaining in the pot after each player has drawn the required number to begin play.
[1950 Morehead *Culbertson* 596]

bongo, *n.* Also spelled BUNGO. A bet in golf won by the player who successfully makes the longest putt.
[1973 Clark *Oral Coll*]

bonnet, *v.* **1.** To lure a victim into a crooked card or dice game. *Obsolete.*
[1833 *OED*]
2. To put a coat or blanket over a dealer's head, then steal the money from the table.
[1938 Asbury *Sucker's Progress*]
→In the 1850s, a gang of toughs would "*bonnet* the dealer" by throwing a blanket over the dealer's head and stealing his money in the confusion. By 1900 *bonneting* meant "to cheat using any deception.".

bonnet, *n.* The employee of a gambling establishment who plays with house money, encouraging visitors to the establishment to join the game. See also HOUSE MONEY (def. 1).
1889 Ellangowan *Sporting Anecdotes* 113. In the places I have named the play was perfectly fair, so there was no occasion for the presence of sham players, '*bonnets,*' as they were called, who acted as decoys.
[1860 *OED*]

bonus, *n.* In poker, a premium or prize paid to a player holding certain cards. Among some players, for example, a player exacts a designated tribute (perhaps five dollars) from the other players if he shows a royal flush.
[1964 Reese and Watkins *Secrets* 138]

bonus jackpot, *n. phr.* In slot machine play, the amount of money paid when a multiple-coin machine yields a jackpot and the player has put the maximum number of coins allowed into the machine before pulling the handle or pressing a button to begin play.
[1973 Clark *Oral Coll*]

bonus payment, *n. phr.* In slot machine play, money or merchandise added by the owner for certain JACKPOTS, designed to increase play on a machine.
[1972 Kofoed *Meanderings* 201]

book, *n.* **1.** A record of wagers made with different people.
[1856 *OED*; originally kept in a memorandum *book*]
2. Generally, a wager on the outcome of a horserace.
1887 Proctor *Chance* 97. All that answers my present purpose is to indicate the nature of the '*book*' which the gentlemanly Dallison succeeds in making for himself and his equally gentlemanly friend on the strength of the 'tip' given by the latter.
3. A person who makes wagers with several different people; a professional bettor.
[1862 *OED*]

4. In poker, a draw of three cards.
[1949 Coffin *Secrets* 173]
5. In bridge, the number of tricks required to win a hand.
[1953 Crawford *Consistent Winner* 2]
6. In whist, the first six tricks taken by either party.
[1953 Crawford *Consistent Winner*]
7. In horse racing, a jockey's riding schedule.
[1978 Ainslie *Complete Guide* 285]

book, *v.* **1.** To accept wagers on the outcome of a sports or similarly uncertain event.
[1812 *OED*]
2. In the phrase:
book the action, In sports books, to accept a wager on a sporting event.
[1977 Anness *Dummy Up*]

bookie, *n.* **1.** Short for BOOKMAKER.
[1885 *OEDS,* 1909 *DAS*]
2. Short for BOOKIE JOINT.
[(1951) 1981 Maurer *Lang. of the Underworld* 204]

bookie joint, *n.* Same as HANDBOOK.
[(1951) 1981 Maurer *Lang. of the Underworld* 204]

booking odds, *n. pl.* The betting odds offered by a bookmaker when different from TRACK ODDS.
[(1951) 1981 Maurer *Lang. of the Underworld* 204]

bookmaker, *n.* Also written **book-maker.** A person who takes several bets on an event, trying to balance the various amounts so that the number of wins equals the number of losses.
1868 Laing-Meason *Turf Frauds* 111. These persons are *"bookmakers."* Their trade is to attend every race of importance run in this country . . . and to make money by betting—by "bookmaking"—not upon the way in which one horse beats the speed or the stamina of another horse, but by careful calculations, and making the result of betting upon one event cover that of another.
1887 Proctor *Chance* 115. *Bookmakers*—that is, men who make a series of bets upon several or all of the horses engaged in a race—naturally seek to give less favorable terms than the known chances of the different horses engaged would suffice to warrant.
[1862 *OED*]

bookmaking, *n.* Also written **book-making.** The activity of taking or making wagers on the outcome of sporting events such as horse racing or team sports. See quote at BOOKMAKER.
[1868 Laing-Mason *Turf Frauds* 111]
[1824 *OEDS*]

booster, *n.* Also called a CAPPER. A cardsharp's confederate; a decoy who directs victims to a dishonest card game. See also ROPER.
[1968 Adams *Western Words*]

boot, *v.* **1.** In horse racing, to kick a horse in the sides with the heels while racing.
[(1951) 1981 Maurer *Lang. of the Underworld* 204]
2. Among horse racing observers, to cheer for a horse as it comes down the stretch. Common in the phrase, **"boot it** (the horse) **home."**
[1973 Clark *Oral Coll.* Earliest published citation 1983 Martinez *Gambling Scene* 186]

borderline bid, *n. phr.* In bridge, a bid on a hand that barely meets the minimum requirement for bidding a contract.
[1953 Crawford *Consistent Winner* 2]

border work, *n.* The marking of cards by applying india ink along the edges.
[1968 Wallace *Poker* 210]

borrow, *v.* In panguingue, to place cards from earlier melds back into the deck during play.
[1950 Morehead *Culbertson* 596]

both ends against the middle, *n. phr.* **1.** A method for trimming the edges of faro cards for purposes of cheating.
[1938 *DA* under *end*]
2. A reply made by faro players to observers who ask what they are betting. *Facetious use.*
[1943 Maurer *Argot*]

bottom deal, *n.* The act of distributing cards from the bottom of the deck; a cheating move.
[1890 Quinn *Fools of Fortune* 270]

bottom dealer, *n.* Also called BASE DEALER, CELLAR DEALER, SUBWAY DEALER. A person who cheats by distributing cards from the bottom of the deck rather than the top.
[1961 Scarne *Complete Guide* 673]

bottom layout, *n.* In monte, the two cards from the bottom of the deck which are placed face up on the table to begin the wagering process.
[1938 Asbury *Sucker's Progress* 53]

bottom stock, *n.* A small packet of cards arranged in a predetermined order which is placed on the bottom of the deck and dealt at will. Compare TOP STOCK.
1865 Evans *Gamblers Win* 20. The *Bottom Stock* . . . is done by putting the pair up as in the top stock, and placing them on the bottom of the pack.

bounce, *n.* In the prep. phr. **on the bounce**. Also called HOP. The next cast of the dice. The term is used when a bettor makes a one-roll wager, or PROPOSITION BET.
[1983 Martinet *Oral Coll*]

bounce shot, *n.* The act of casting dice with a spinning or sliding motion to prevent them from rolling or turning.
[ca. 1961 *Hotel Coll*]

boveries, *n. Plural in form, but singular in use.* In a variation of backgammon, the act of having one piece in the eleventh position of one's own table and one piece in the eleventh position of the opponent's table.
1680 Cotton *Complete Gamester* 114. *Boveries* is when you have a man in the eleventh point of

your own tables, and another in the same point of your Adversaries directly answering.

bower, *n.* **1.** In trump games, the jack of trump.
[1830 *DA,* 1844 *DAE,* 1858 *OEDS*]
2. A joker in a deck of cards. See also RIGHT BOWER and LEFT BOWER.
[German *bauer*]

bowl, *n.* **1.** In bank craps, the dish or cup in which extra dice are kept. The *bowl* contains several dice which are offered to the shooter by the stickman. The shooter chooses two dice, and the rest are returned to the *bowl* which sits in front of the stickman.
[ca. 1961 *Hotel Coll*]
2. Also called WHEEL WELL. In roulette, the hollowed portion of the table in which the wheel rests.
[1961 Scarne *Complete Guide* 672]

box, *n.* **1.** A container for holding and shaking dice before a cast.
[1753 *OED*]
2. In twenty-one, a position on the table layout for placing a wager.
[ca. 1961 *Hotel Coll*]
3. Same as LINE. In gin rummy, a point bonus for winning a hand.
1950 Morehead *Culbertson* 33. Each player then adds to his score 25 points for each hand he has won (called a line or *box*).
4. In faro, a shuffled deck which is ready for dealing.
[1950 Morehead *Culbertson* 596]
5. Short for DROP BOX. In a casino, the container attached to the underside of a gaming table into which the dealer places money which has been exchanged for chips. See also TOKE BOX.
[1621 *OED*]
6. In greyhound racing, the enclosure from which the dogs begin the race.
[1968 Buchele *Greyhound Racing* 95]
7. Short for DEALING BOX in games like twenty-one and faro.
[1973 Clark *Oral Coll*]
8. In bank craps, the position occupied by the person overseeing the game; the position for the BOXMAN.
[1938 Asbury *Sucker's Progress* 41]

box, *v.* **1.** In faro, to prepare a deck of cards for honest dealing.
[1950 Morehead *Culbertson* 596]
2. In twenty-one, to square the deck before beginning the deal, making sure that all four sides of the deck are even.
[1978 Clark *Oral Coll*]
3. In horse or dog racing, to make a combination bet of two or three numbers, listing the different orders of finish in the race.
[1981 Passer *Winning Big* 237]
4. In the phrases and particle construction:
box numbers, In dice, to bet that the shooter will not make the POINT.
[(1950) 1981 Maurer *Lang. of the Underworld* 183]
box up, In bank craps, to put all the dice into a bowl for mixing after which they are dumped from the bowl and offered to the SHOOTER, who selects two for his cast.
[(1950)1981 Maurer *Lang. of the Underworld* 183]

boxcars, *n. pl.* Plural in form, but singlar in use. In craps, a cast of two sixes with a pair of dice. Compare BOXES.
[1949 Blanche *You Can't Win* 23]

boxed, *adj.* **1.** In LIAR DICE, pertaining to a losing position regardless of the course of action taken.
[1971 Smith *Games* 103]
2. In horse racing, pertaining to a horse running behind another horse and blocked from passing it because of the rail or another horse running alongside.
[1979 Clark *Oral Coll*]

boxed card, *n.* A card facing the wrong direction in a deck; a card accidentally turned face up in a pack in which the rest of the cards are face down.
[1968 Wallace *Poker* 211]

boxes, *n. pl.* Plural in form, but singular in use. In craps, a cast of the number eight, four pips on each die; a HARD EIGHT. Compare BOXCARS.
[1983 Martinet *Oral Coll*]

box hand, *n.* A condition in which a card player wins three consecutive hands and must therefore pay a set sum of money to the operator of the game. The money paid is passed through an aperture in the table and into a box fastened beneath the table. *Obsolete.*
[1833 *OED*]

boxing the dice, *n. phr.* A method for turning a dice box directly over on a table so that the number pips facing down before the toss land face up on the table.
1859 Green *Gam Tricks* 111. In landing [the dice] on the table there is a difficulty, if thrown boldly, for, as is the usual method, they naturally turn over, and the intended effect would be lost; by what is called *boxing the dice,* that is, merely turning the box, mouth downwards, on the table, and raising it up after the dice are landed—it is secured with little chance of detection.

boxman, *n.* Also written **box man. 1.** In bank craps, an employee responsible for supervising all money transactions, table play, and table security.
[1953 Fairfield *Las Vegas* 15]
2. Originally called a BOX-KEEPER. In illegal gambling establishments, a representative of the owner who watches over a gambling game.
[1693 *OED*]

box meter, *n.* Also called DROP METER. A counting device in a slot machine that records the number of coins played.
[1978 Alexander *Glossary* 2]

box money, *n.* The percentage of money wagered at a gambling table that is kept by the operator of the game. See also RAKE.
[1833 *OED*]

box number, *n.* In bank craps, any of the spaces at the back of the table layout marked with the point numbers 4, 5, 6, 8, 9, and 10.
[(1950) 1981 Maurer *Lang. of the Underworld* 182]

box shot, *n.* Also called GREEK SHOT. A controlled cast of the dice from a cup. Compare BOXING THE DICE.
[(1950) 1981 Maurer *Lang. of the Underworld* 183]

boy, *n.* A jack or knave in playing cards. See also COWBOY.
[1968 Wallace *Poker* 211]

BP, *n.* Abbreviation for BIG PLUNGER or *big player.* See also HIGH ROLLER.
[1973 Clark *Oral Coll*]

BR, *n.* Abbreviation for BANKROLL.
[1978 Brunson *How I Made* 523]

brace, *v.* **1.** In faro, to punch small holes in cards for cheating purposes.
2. In the phrase:
brace a game, To operate a dishonest gambling game, usually at cards.
[1890 Quinn *Fools of Fortune* 184]

brace box, *n.* In faro, a dealing box which facilitates cheating.
1902 Andrews *Artifice* 18. By roughening the faces of some of the cards they will hold together, and are more easily retained while shuffling. Faro cards, used in connection with a certain form of *"brace" box,* are treated in this manner.
[1908 *DA, OEDS*]

brace dealer, *n.* A card sharp; a card cheat.
[1890 Quinn *Fools of Fortune* 196]

brace game, *n.* Around 1850, a dishonest faro game. By 1900, *brace game* came to mean any dishonest card game.
[1875 *DA, DAE, OEDS*]

brace house, *n.* Also called BRACE ROOM. An establishment devoted to dishonest gambling. *Obsolete.*
[1938 Asbury *Sucker's Progress* 184]
→In use especially around 1850.

brace room, *n.* Same as BRACE HOUSE.
[1938 Asbury *Sucker's Progress* 182]

brace work, *n.* Also called LINE WORK. The markings placed on the backs of cards by dishonest players, which are often obvious and spurned by CARD SHARPS.
[ca. 1961 *Hotel Coll*]

brag, *n.* A popular card game of the eighteenth century which had features similar to the later game of poker, in that the bluff is important to the play.
1714 Lucas *Memoirs* 112. He plays very well at *Brag,* which Game being the main Thing by which the second Stake is to be won by the Ingenuity of its Management, it takes from thence its Name; for you are to endeavour to impose upon the Judgment of the rest that play, and particularly on the Person that chiefly offers to oppose you, by boasting of Cards in your Hand, that are better than his or hers that plays against you. Thus it is to be observ'd, that the witty ordering of this Brag is the most pleasant part of this Game; for those, that by fashioning their Looks and Gestures, can give a proper Air to their Actions, as will so deceive an unskilfull Antagonist, that sometimes a pair of Treys or Deuces, in such a Hand, with the Advantage of his compos'd Countenance, and subtle Manner of over-awing the other, shall out-brag a much greater Pair, and win the Stakes.
[1734 *OED*; 1835 *DA*; 1845 *DAE*]

brag, *v.* To challenge an opponent with a wager in the game of BRAG.
1866 *American Card Player* 134 *Brag*—Betting for the pool.
[1835 *DA;* 1846 *DAE*]

bragger, *n.* In brag, a jack or a nine. See also WILD CARD.
1830 Anon *Hoyle's Improved* 154. This game is played with an entire pack of cards, which rank as at Whist, except the knaves and nines, which are called *braggers,* and rank the same as any cards they may be held with.
[1807 *DA, DAE, OEDS*]

break, *v.* **1.** Also called BUST. In twenty-one, to exceed the card count total of twenty-one points.
[1973 Friedman *Casino Games* 29]
2. In gin rummy, to cast off a card which forms part of a combination.
[1953 Crawford *Consistent Winner* 2]
3. In harness racing, to begin running after a pace or trot; to change gait or lose a level stride.
[1839 *DA, OEDS*; 1868 *DAE*]
4. In greyhound and horse racing, to start the race from the box or gate.
[1955 Hillis *Pari-Mutuel Betting* 112]
5. In the phrases or particle constructions:
break a game, 1. To bring a game to a finish by winning most or all of the money at the table.
[(1950) 1981 Maurer *Lang. of the Underworld* 183]
2. In a casino, to relieve a dealer at a table.
[1977 Anness *Dummy Up*]
break a maiden, Of a horse or jockey, to win a race for the first time, not necessarily in the horse's MAIDEN RACE.
[(1951) 1981 Maurer *Lang. of the Underworld* 204]
[Metaphoric extension from breaking the hymen (maidenhead)]
break down, Of a racehorse, to become unable to race because of an injury.
[1978 Ainslie *Complete Guide* 285]
break down a bet, In casino dealing, to separate

a stack of chips of various colors into separate stacks, each of a single denomination.
[ca. 1961 *Hotel Coll*]
break down a game, In a casino, to close a table.
[1983 Martinet *Oral Coll*]
→Usually done early in the morning or when several tables have one or two players each. The DEALER, PIT BOSS, and security guard return the game to impress and secure the CHIP RACK. The dealer brushes the table and, in some casinos, places a cover over the layout.
break even, 1. To win as much as one has lost.
[1938 Asbury *Sucker's Progress* 15]
[Compare 1914 *OEDS*, meaning "to balance gains and losses"]
2. In faro, to bet that a card of a particular rank will win or lose an even number of times during the deal.
[1909 *OEDS*, in *Century Dict. Supplement*]
break gait, Of horses in harness racing, to run, cantor, or gallop rather than trot or pace.
[1971 McQuaid *Gambler's Digest* 301]
break in, 1. In casinos, to train as a dealer.
[1979 Newman *Dealer's Special* 7]
2. Of race horses, to veer toward the rail at the beginning of a race.
[1899 *DA*]
break off, In faro, to lose on a specific card after two or more wins on that same card.
[1943 Maurer *Argot*]
break out, Of a race horse, to veer to the right near the beginning of a race.
[1983 Martinez *Gambling Scene* 191]
break the bank, In a casino, to win all the chips on one table; to exhaust the quota of money allotted to one table by the bank.
[1672 *OED*]
→The popular notion that winning all of the money in a casino is the same as *breaking the bank* is mistaken. As applies to casinos, the bank is the amount of money (in chips) allotted to a table at the beginning of a shift. The popular concept of bankruptcy is attested in *OED*, 1612-15.
break the deck, To shuffle a deck of cards.
[1965 Wilson *Casino* 15]
break the table, In a casino, to win all the money at a table, thereby forcing management to restock the table with chips. See also BREAK THE BANK.
[1983 Martinet *Oral Coll*]

break, *n.* **1.** The start of a horse or dog race.
[1968 Buchele *Greyhound Racing* 95]
2. Usually plural, in the expression **the breaks.** Fortuitous events; good or bad luck; unexpected good fortune.
[1949 Coffin *Secrets* 191]

breakage, *n.* The odd amount of cents left when a winning bet is rounded down to the nearest unit.
[1968 Thackrey *Nick the Greek* 219]
→In parimutuel betting, the amount on a win might be lowered to the nearest tenth, for example $2.80 instead of the actual $2.84 that the odds might require. In a casino, a win of $2.37 might be rounded down to $2.25 or even $2.00.

breaker, *n.* **1.** In harness racing, a horse that breaks gait or loses stride.
[1868 *DA, OEDS*]
2. breakers, *pl.* Also called OPENERS. In draw poker, the minimum cards, usually a pair of jacks, required to begin the first betting round.
[1949 Coffin *Secrets* 173]

break in, *n.* In casinos, a new dealer; a trainee.
→Used adjectivally in phrases such as *break-in store, break-in house, break-in joint, break-in jobber* to refer to establishments which make a practice of hiring novice dealers.

breaking hand, *n.* In twenty-one, two cards totaling twelve through sixteen points. So called because a single card may put the total point count over twenty-one.
[1982 Martin *Casino Management* 12]

breastworks, *n. Plural in form, but singular in use.* Also called a VEST HOLD-OUT. A device bound around the chest used to hide cards until the wearer wishes to use them.
[1938 Asbury *Sucker's Progress* 66]

breather, *n.* **1.** In poker, an opportunity to CHECK without having to put money into the POT.
[1950 Morehead *Culbertson* 597]
2. In horse racing, a short period before the end of a race in which a jockey will allow the horse to relax. Usually done when the horse is an easy winner or the horse is far behind the leaders and has no chance to place among the winners.
[1901 *OEDS*]

breeder, *n.* The owner of a dam or bitch, especially at the time of foaling or whelping.
[1531 *OED,* 1856 *DAE*]

breef, *n.* Another spelling of BRIEF.
[1680 *OED*]

breeze, *v.* **1.** Of a racehorse, to run easily and swiftly without urging by the jockey.
[(1951) 1981 Maurer *Lang. of the Underworld* 205]
2. In the particle construction:
breeze in, To win a race without great effort.
[1949 *DAS*]

brelan, *n.* Also spelled **brelen.** *French.* Three cards of the same denomination.
[1950 Morehead *Culbertson* 597]

brelen carre, *n. French.* Four cards of the same denomination.
[1968 Wallace *Poker* 211]

brick, *n.* A die shaved on one face, designed to land with that face downward.
[(1950) 1981 Maurer *Lang. of the Underworld* 183]

bridge, *n.* **1.** A card bent in such a fashion as to be recognized by the person making the cut, indicating that the cards are to be cut at that place.

1859 Green *Gam Tricks* 101. The *bridge* is a card slightly curved. By introducing it carelessly into the pack, and shuffling them, it can be cut at pleasure.
1888 Kunard *Card Tricks* 174. The *Bridge* is a card slightly curved, and is used by conjurors as well as sharpers, with the object of having a particular card cut.
[1859 *OED*]
2. In the card game of euchre, the condition in which one team has scored four points while the opponents have scored only one.
1887 Keller *Euchre* 22. When one side has made four points, and the other has made but one, the condition of the game is called "the *bridge*."

Bridge. This card game, descended from WHIST or WHISK, is played with a DECK of 52 cards by two TEAMS, North and South against East and West, often abbreviated N-S, E-W. In whist, this scheme is called A-B, Y-Z. The players each receive 13 cards from the DEALER. In BIDDING to name TRUMPS, the teams BID with TRUMP SIGNALS or other CUE BIDS for SUPPORT based on the DEFENSIVE STRENGTH and the OFFENSIVE STRENGTH of their respective HANDS at the OPENING BID. The players REBID with RAISES according to a CONVENTION, such as the HEART CONVENTION of the BLACKWOOD CONVENTION, in order to ESTABLISH A SUIT in a CONTINUOUS BID resulting in a CONTRACT. HEARTS, and SPADES (the HIGH SUIT), and NO TRUMP are MAJOR SUITS; DIAMONDS and CLUBS are MINOR SUITS. The highest bid is for a GRAND SLAM which means that the BIDDER intends to win every TRICK. To bid a LITTLE SLAM (or SMALL SLAM) requires the partners to make a contract for all but one of the 13 tricks. A player may choose to PASS, while the winner BUYS THE CONTRACT and becomes the DECLARER. The DECLARATION in the ROUNDS of BIDDING is central to the game. The MAKER names the TRUMP SUIT, usually the LONG SUIT, or DECLARES that he chooses NO TRUMP determined by the POINT COUNT in SHORT SUITS. An UNBALANCED HAND has a SINGLETON in one suit and a VOID in another, while a BALANCED HAND has neither. The other suits are PLAIN SUITS. The strategies of BIDDING and REBIDDING may involve a FORCING BID or FORCING PASS in contrast to a FREE BID or FREE PASS. If one's opponents suspect an OVERBID they use a DEFENSIVE BID to DOUBLE. In response one may REDOUBLE, especially if one started with an UNDERBID. In the ROTATION of play the DECLARER LEADS and the first player of the opposing side then should FOLLOW SUIT. But he RENEGES if he chooses not to follow the suit of the OPENING LEAD. Playing the wrong card in an attempt to RUFF may result in having to RENOUNCE or REVOKE or RENEGE.

A player may FINESSE or FORCE another into playing a particular card with an ECHO or PETER, or with a SMOTHER PLAY. Or, a player may BLOCK A SUIT or CLEAR A SUIT.

The PARTNER to an OPENING LEAD is the DUMMY whose cards are laid face upward and played by the winner of the contract.

QUICK TRICKS may be estimated without a LAYDOWN. One may UNDERPLAY, UNDERTRICK, or UNDERTRUMP to TAKE THE LEAD as play progresses which is easy with a PIANOLA HAND.

A SCORECARD or TALLY is kept to determine the outcome of each game in a SESSION. Winning the first game means a TEAM is VULNERABLE and a RUBBER GAME, or MATCH GAME, settles the outcome. POINTS are determined before the bidding. The DECLARERS are assessed PENALTIES for failing to MAKE THE CONTRACT. HONORS improve one's score and are taken ABOVE THE LINE on the SCORE SHEET.

bridge bet, *n.* Also called a CONTRACT BET.
[1971 McQuaid *Gambler's Digest* 301]

bridge it, *v. phr.* Also called BARDOT IT. In bank craps, to stack the FLAT BET and the LAY BET in a pyramid shape on the DON'T PASS LINE when both payoffs are of the same amount and color.
1984 Martinet *Oral Coll.* . . . somebody lays odds on a don't bet, and the boxman or somebody will say bardot it. You hear that only once in a while. It comes from *"bridge it."* Say the point is four and a flat bet on the don't is fifteen bucks. So the player lays six reds [$5 chips] and the dealer stacks three chips against the flat bet and places three chips on top, between the two stacks.

bridge-jumper, *n.* In horse racing, a bettor who wagers on the favorite horses to run second.
[1978 Ainslie *Complete Guide* 285]

brief, *n.* Also spelled BREEF. A playing card trimmed on the edges to make it narrower or shorter than the rest of the pack. *Obsolete.*
1680 Cotton *Compleat Gamester* 94. The *Breef* in cutting is very advantageous to him that cuts, and it is thus done; the Cheat provides beforehand a Pack of Cards, whereof some are broader than others.
1714 Lucas *Memoirs* 114. But the cleanest rooking Way is by the *Breef;* that is, take a Pack of Cards and open them, then take out all the Honours, that is to say, the four Aces, Kings, Queens and Knaves, then take the rest and cut a little from the Edges of them all alike, by which Means the Honours will be broader than the rest; so that when your Adversary cuts to you, you are certain of an Honour; when you cut to your Adversary, cut at the Ends, and then it is a Chance if you cut him an Honour, because the Cards at the Ends are all of a Length; thus you may make *Breefs* End-ways, as well as Sideways.
[1680 *OED*]

brief, *adj.* Also BREEF. Of a card which is a different size from the rest of the pack, either lengthwise or sideways.
1746 Wilson *Art and Mystery* 95. Of *Breef* Cards there are two sorts; one is a Card longer than the rest, the other is a Card Broader than the rest.

brilliant, *n.* In pachter, the six of diamonds.
[1950 Morehead *Culbertson* 597]

bring down (a specified bet), *v. phr.* Also called TAKE DOWN. In bank craps, to request the dealer to remove one's PLACE BETS.
[1983 Martinet *Oral Coll*]

brisque, *n.* In bezique, each ace or ten taken in the tricks.
1866 *American Card Player* 115. The last trick having been made, each player counts the Aces and Tens which are in the tricks he has taken; these Aces and Tens are called *brisques.* For each *brisque* the holder scores ten points.
[1861 *OED* under *bezique;* 1870 *OEDS*]

bristle dice, *n.* Dice with hog bristles or small pins inserted to protrude slightly at the corners and thus hinder the roll of certain numbers. *Obsolete.*
1680 Cotton *Compleat Gamester* 9. . . .*Bristle-Dice,* which are fitted for their purpose by sticking a Hogs-bristle so in the corners, or otherwise in the Dice, that they shall run high or low as they please, this bristle must be strong and short, by which means the bristle bending, it will not lie on that side, but will be tript over.
[1532 *OED*]

broad, *n.* **1.** A playing card. *Obsolete.*
[1812 *OED*]
2. In playing cards, a queen of any suit.
[1973 Clark *Oral Coll*]

broad-pitcher, *n.* **1.** A dealer of three-card monte.
[1938 Asbury *Sucker's Progress* 205]
2. Also called **broadsman.** Same as CARD SHARP.
[1860 *OEDS*, as *broadsman*]

broad-tosser, *n.* Also called a THROWER. Same as a BROAD-PITCHER.
[1968 Adams *Western Words*]

broadway, *n.* In hold 'em poker, a sequence of five consecutive cards, from ten to ace; an ACE-HIGH STRAIGHT.
[1981 Gold *Oral Coll*]

broke money, *n.* A small amount of money given to a player who has lost all his money, intended to pay his transportation from the gaming establishment.
[(1950) 1981 Maurer *Lang. of the Underworld* 183]

broken fall, *n.* In hold 'em poker, the third, fourth, and fifth card dealt (the FLOP), from which a player cannot make a straight.
[1978 Brunson *How I Made* 525]

brush, *v.* **1.** Among casino twenty-one players, to scrape the cards on the table surface to indicate a request for another card from the dealer.
[1971 McQuaid *Gambler's Digest* 301]
2. Among racehorses, to move quickly ahead of the other horses after the first pole.
[1867 *OED*]

brushman, *n.* In casinos, an employee who stands near the entrance of a poker pit and invites passersby to enter and play. Other duties include assisting dealers by supplying chips and fresh cards, and keeping tables clean. See also ROPER.
[1979 Hilton Hotel *Procedures* 3]
[The act of brushing the felt table covers with a soft brush gave rise to the term.]

BS, *n.* In a casino, an abbreviation for the BIG SIX WHEEL or table.
[ca. 1961 *Hotel Coll*]

bubble, *n.* A person who is cheated or duped. *Obsolete.* [1668 *OED*]

bubble, *v.* To cheat or defraud a person. *Obsolete.* [1675 *OED*]

bubbleable, *adj.* Capable of being cheated or defrauded. *Obsolete.*
[1669 *OED*]

bubble peek, *n.* An action in which a dealer, by squeezing the top card on a pack between his little finger and the heel of his hand, can see the index value of the card before dealing it.
[1973 Clark *Oral Coll*]

buck, *n.* **1.** A marker used to designate the position of a dealer, when a house employee actually deals every hand. In modern casinos, the *buck* is called the BUTTON or PUCK.
1876 Heather *Cards* 59. Instead of an "ante" being put up by each of the players, the first dealer pays to the pool an equivalent amount, and passes "a *buck*"— usually some small article, as a key, or a knife, to the player on his left; when the hand is over, this player "chips" a like amount, and passes "the *buck*" on to the next player.
[1878 *DA*]
[The term appears more commonly in the phrases "*pass the buck*" and "the buck stops here." Originally from *buckhorn knife*, the handles of which served as markers. *Buck* meaning money is probably from *buckskin.*]
2. In poker, anything other than chips placed in the pool as part of a bet, such as papers proving ownership of property. *Obsolete.*
[1865 *OEDS*]

buck, *v.* **1.** To wager or lose money in gambling.
[1851 *DAE, OEDS*]
2. To play at a game of hazard.
[1849 *OEDS*]
3. In the phrases:
buck it, In craps, to repeat the same number on the next roll of the dice.
[1974 Scarne *Dice* 462]
buck the game, In a casino, to bet with the card player or dice shooter and against the house.
[ca. 1961 *Hotel Coll*]
buck the tiger, 1. To play faro.
[1863 *DAE,* 1863 *OED* under "tiger"]
2. More generally, to gamble on any game.
1891 *Monte Carlo* 229. Adolphe Belot, who used to be a great friend of the Monte Carlo Casino people, and has written so many books concerning this infamous establishment, under

the guise of flimsy novels, that he was always suspected of being in the pay of the corporation, had made quite a study of the various ways of *"bucking the tiger;"* in spite of which it appears that most of the profits he realized out of the bank, by his literary efforts, were carefully collected back into the fold, by means of his inveterate fondness for gambling.
[So called because a picture of a tiger usually adorned the layout or the cards used in faro.]

bucket-shop, *n.* An establishment for illegal wagering on sporting events or the stockmarket. *Obsolete.*
1889 Ellangowan *Sporting Anecdotes* 281. A *"bucket-shop"* is a stockbroker's office which is frequented by and kept for the convenience of "punters." Such institutions are almost invariably owned by what are called "outside brokers," an industrious and enterprising class of practitioners, who have, however, no more connection with the Stock Exchange than they have with the Vatican.
[1880 *DA,* 1882 *OED,* 1887 *DAE*]

buddy poker, *n.* A poker game in which two people play as partners.
[1968 Wallace *Poker* 211]
→ The term does not imply collusion or cheating.

bug, *n.* **1.** A mechanical device for holding a card and is usually attached to the underside of the card table.
1865 Evans *Gamblers Win* 36. The best arrangement for holding out [a card] . . . is with an instrument called the *bug*. This consists of an English awl, with a smooth broad head on the butt, and a piece of watch coil brazed on to the side so that it runs as far as the point, and curls over. The point is pushed into the under side of the table, just the width of a card from the edge, and the watch coil snaps up against the bottom of the leaf.
[1889 *DA*]
2. The joker in a deck of playing cards. In some poker games, the *bug* is added to the pack to make a fifty-three card deck. The card may then represent a designated value to assist in straights or flushes as a WILD CARD.
[1949 Coffin *Secrets* 173]
3. An apprentice jockey. Such a jockey is given an additional weight allowance on the horse he rides, and the fact is indicated by an asterisk next to the jockey's name in the program.
[1955 Hillis *Pari-Mutuel Betting* 112]
4. A thoroughbred that has never won a race. [*DAS*]
5. the bug. Same as NUMBERS.
[1983 Martinet *Oral Coll*]

builders, *n. pl.* In backgammon, several pieces, or stones, in a player's outer table which give him an advantage over his opponent.
[1950 Morehead *Culbertson* 598]

buildup, *n.* The gaining of the confidence of a victim before cheating. See also GRIFTER.
1961 Scarne *Guide* 477. The dream of every carnival grifter has always been to have a *build-up* or angle that will stir up a player's emotions to such a degree that he wants to keep betting and increasing the size of his bets until he goes flat broke.
1971 McQuaid *Gambler's Digest* 274. There were plenty of gullible people around, but you had to find one who could put up some money. And sometimes after you'd spent time and money in the *buildup,* he got frightened away before you could take him for a big killing.
[1927 *DA*]

bulking, *n.* The act of distracting another player from observing a cheating move. See also BLOCKER.
1726 Wilson *Art and Mystery* 71. When he has occasion to draw a Card, he either treads upon the Croupe's Toes, or makes a private Signal to the Puffs; so one of them readily puts his hand cross the Table, in which time the Card is drawn and the Mischief done . . . The Cant Name on this Occasion is *Bulking,* so frequently practis'd.

bull, *n.* **1.** Short for BULLET. An ace in playing cards.
[1949 Coffin *Secrets* 173]
2. Also called a BULLDOZER. In poker, a player who bets aggressively, bluffs often, and raises the bets frequently.
[1949 Coffin *Secrets* 173]

bull, *v.* **1.** To cheat, especially in an overbearing or pushy manner.
[1532 *OED*]
2. In the phrase:
bull the game, In poker, to play aggressively, bet and raise frequently, and bluff often.
[1968 Wallace *Poker* 211]

bulldozer, *n.* See BULL (def. 2).

bullet, *n.* Also called a BULL. In playing cards, the ace.
[1807 *DA, DAE, OED*]

bullfrog, *v.* In bank craps, to make a PROPOSITION BET that will be resolved on the next roll of the dice.
1983 Martinet *Oral Coll.* Sometimes a player wants to make a hop bet and he will throw out a check and say "give me a hard eight, *bullfrogging*" or just "hard eight, *bullfrog* it."
[Suggested by the noun form of a single-roll proposition bet, a HOP.]

bull ring, *n.* A small oval track for racing horses.
[1968 Ainslie *Complete Guide* 445]

bumblepuppy, *n.* A weak, inexperienced, or careless card player.
[1884 *OED,* as humourous use for an inexperienced whist player.]

bum move, *n.* a clumsy, inept cheating move.
[(1950) 1981 Maurer *Lang. of the Underworld* 183]

bump, *v.* **1.** In poker, to increase the amount of the previous bet.
[1935 *DAS*]
2. In the phrase:
bump into, Among casino dealers, to set a larger stack of chips against a winning stack, then remove the excess so that both stacks are the same size. See also BANG INTO and THUMB CUT.
[1977 Anness *Dummy Up*]

bumper, *n.* In whist, a RUBBER won in two games.
[1934 *DAS*]

bunch, *v.* **1.** To gather the cards for shuffling after a hand has been played.
[1949 Coffin *Secrets* 174]
2. To request a new deal in the game of all fours.
1866 *American Card Player* 124. In some coteries privilege is granted to the dealer and eldest hand to *bunch* the cards, i.e., to have a fresh deal provided they mutually agree to do so, after the latter has begged, and the cards have been run by the former; and sometimes, instead of *bunching* the cards, they mutually agree to run them, three more all around, and turn up a new trump.

bunch, *n.* A pack of playing cards. *Obsolete.*
[1563 **OED**]

bunching, *n.* A betting system in roulette in which a player bets on six numbers and the zero.
[1953 Woon *The Why, How, and Where* 44]

bunco, *n.* Also BANCO, BUNKO. A cheating scheme; a swindle; a scam.
1938 Asbury *Sucker's Progress* 57. Although this so called gambling game, under its original name of Eight-Dice Cloth, was played in England during the eighteenth century, it was unknown in the United States until about 1855, when it was introduced into San Francisco by a crooked gambler who made various changes in the method of play and christened it *Banco.* After a few years this was corrupted in *Bunco,* sometimes spelled *Bunko,* and in time *Bunco* came to be a general term applied to all swindling and confidence games, while the sharpers who practiced them were called *Bunco* men.
[1872 *DAE, DA, OEDS,* probably from American Spanish *banca* a card game]

bunco, *v.* to cheat; swindle.
[1892 *DAE, OEDS*]

bunco-cards, *n.* A marked deck of cards. See also MARK, *v.* (def. 1). Compare STACKED DECK.
[1950 Morehead *Culbertson* 598]

bunco squad, *n.* A unit within a police force charged with combating swindling and fraud.
1985, Jim Murray, *Los Angeles Times,* 6/9: 1. Listen. When a guy on the Celtics wearing No. 33 misses 11 jump shots from the top of the key, when he throws up a cement block from the foul line, when he passes the ball like it was a flat iron, when he misses a technical foul shot, for crying out loud, what you have is one of the most outrageous impersonations of our day. A swindle. A fraud. Something for the bunco squad.
[1976 *US News & World Report* 52]

bunco-steerer, *n.* Also spelled BUNKO-STEERER. A person who leads unwary victims to dishonest games; an accomplice for a swindler, especially a cardsharp. See also ROPER and SHILL.
[1888 *OEDS*]

bunco-steering, *n.* Also spelled BUNKO-STEERING. The act of swindling.
[1892 *DAE, DA*]

bundle, *n.* A large sum of money, especially as used for betting.
[1905 *DAS*]

bundle, *v.* To wager a large sum of money on a betting proposition.
[1922 *OEDS*]

bungo, *n.* Also spelled BONGO. A bet in golf won by the player who successfully makes the longest putt.
[1971 McQuaid *Gambler's Digest* 299]

bunko, *n.* Also BANCO, BUNCO. **1.** A cheating scheme; a swindle; a scam.
1890 Quinn *Fools of Fortune* 326. It is doubtful whether there is a man, woman, or child in the United States, who has been in the habit of reading the daily press, who has not heard of *"Bunko,"* and does not have a vague sort of idea that it is a gigantic scheme for swindling.
[1875 *DAE*; 1875 *OEDS,* in *bunko-steering*]
2. A cheat; swindler.
[1884 *DA*]

bunko, *v.* To cheat; swindle.
[1875 *DAE, OEDS*]

bunko artist, *n.* Also spelled **bunco artist.** A swindler or confidence man; a cheater.
1953 Lewis *Sagebrush* 72. In the Nevada gaming rooms a battle of wits is continuously being waged between the owners and their staffs and a numerous crew of *bunko artists* bent on getting the best of the house by whatever means their imaginations can conjure up.
[1945 *DAS;* 1946 *DA,* as *bunco artist*]

bunko-steerer, *n.* Also spelled BUNCO-STEERER. A person who leads unwary victims to dishonest games; an accomplice for a swindler, especially a cardsharp. See also ROPER and SHILL.
[1875 *DAE*, DA, OEDS]

bunko-steering, *n.* The act of swindling.
[1875 *DAE, DA, OEDS*]

buried card, *n. phr.* A playing card inserted at random into a deck.
[1949 Coffin *Secrets* 174]

burn, *v.* **1.** In twenty-one, to remove the top card from the deck before beginning play; generally to remove a card from play.
[1949 Coffin *Secrets* 174]

2. To lose a large amount of money by gambling.
[1983 Martinet *Oral Coll*]
3. In the phrase:
burn the dice, In dice, to halt the dice while they are rolling. See also NO BET.
[(1950) 1981 Maurer *Lang. of the Underworld* 183]
➛Usually restricted to grabbing the dice if its is evident they will not reach the cushion or if a bet is placed while the dice are rolling. Sometimes, in non-casino play another player will seek to change the shooter's luck with this move.

burn and turn, *n. phr.* In hold 'em poker, the practice of removing the top card from the pack before dealing the first, third, sixth, and seventh cards. See also BURN CARD and BURNT CARD.
[1978 Brunson *How I Made* 525]

burn card, *n.* In poker or twenty-one, the top card on the deck, set aside before dealing the rest of the pack.
[1968 Wallace *Poker* 211]

burnt card, *n.* In twenty-one, the top card from the deck which is placed on the bottom before the deal begins.
1868 Trumps *Pocket Hoyle.* After the dealer has shuffled and cut the pack, he must, before dealing, take the top card and place it on the bottom of the pack, back outwards. This is called the *burnt card.*

burst, *v.* In blackjack, to exceed the count of twenty one.
1865 Evans *Gamblers Win* 68. This [strategy], of course, is to deceive the dealer into the belief that the player is standing on nineteen or twenty, and thus induce him to draw till he *"bursts."*
➛Now regularly BUST, *v.*

bury, *v.* **1.** To place used cards at random places in the pack.
[1953 Crawford *Consistent Winner* 2]
2. To remove a card from the top of the pack before dealing. See also BURN (def. 2).
[1983 Martinet *Oral Coll*]

business, *n.* **1.** The movements or actions of a card manipulator, designed to draw attention away from the pack of cards.
[1925 *OEDS*]
2. The manipulation of cards.
[1973 Clark *Oral Coll*]

bust, *n.* **1.** In blackjack, a hand that exceeds a point count of twenty-one.
[1953 Crawford *Consistent Winner* 2]
2. Any worthless hand at cards.
[1932 *OEDS*]

bust, *v.* 1. In blackjack, to fail to draw desired cards and finish with a worthless hand. Compare BURST. [1939 *OEDS*]
2. In the phrase:
bust in or **bust out,** To switch loaded dice into and out of a game.
[(1950) 1981 Maurer *Lang. of the Underworld* 183]

busted flush, *n.* In draw poker, the holding of four cards in one suit and one card of another suit after the draw.
[1934 *OEDS*]

buster brown, *n.* Loaded or gaffed dice.
[1963 Drazazgo *Wheels* 321]
➛A request by an accomplice to introduce such dice into a game is often phrased, **"Where's Buster Brown?"**

busters, *n. pl.* Loaded or gaffed dice.
[(1950) 1981 Maurer *Lang. of the Underworld* 183]

bust out dealer, *n. phr.* Same as **bust-out man.**
[1982 Martin *Introduction* 24]

bust-out joint, *n.* A gambling establishment in which large scale cheating takes place.
[1953 *DAS*]

bust-out man, *n.* A dice or card dealer who is a skillful cheater when required to be so. See also MECHANIC.
[(1950) 1981 Maurer *Lang. of the Underworld* 183]

bustouts, *n. pl.* Dice that have been misspotted so as to roll the number seven more often than other numbers. Usually, such a die will have two fives or two twos on it. See also TOPS.
[[1939 Macdougall *Gambler's Don't*]

busy card, *n.* In poker, a drawn card that completes a flush or straight.
[1949 Coffin *Secrets* 174]

butter and eggs, *n.* Same as NUMBERS.
[1973 Clark *Oral Coll*]

button, *n.* **1.** In poker, the marker or puck that is placed in front of the designated dealer when the game has one person who actually shuffles and deals each hand without taking part in the play. Compare BUCK.
[1976 Sklansky *Hold'em Poker* 4]
2. In bank craps, a marker or puck measuring about three inches across that is placed on the layout number corresponding to the shooter's point.
[1983 Martinez *Gambling Scene* 192]
3. In bank craps, a small token placed atop a player's bet when the player requests a wager out of the ordinary. For example, a bet on a HARDWAY number (4, 6, 8, 10) is usually active, or WORKING, on the first, or COMEOUT ROLL of the shooter. If a player does not want his bet to remain active during that roll of the dice, he will tell the dealer, who then places a *button* atop the wager to distinguish it from all others that are active for that roll. Compare BUY BUTTON.
[1983 Martinet *Oral Coll*]

buy, *v.* In the phrases:
buy a card, In poker, to place enough money into the pot to receive a card or cards.
[1973 Clark *Oral Coll*]
buy a pot, In poker, to win a pot with a mediocre hand by betting a large sum of money, thereby bluffing the other players.

[1949 Coffin *Secrets* 174]
buy the board, Same as BUY THE RACK. To make a large variety of wagers on a horse or dog race.
[1968 Buchele *Greyhound Racing* 95]
buy the contract, In games like bridge or whist, to win the right to name trump by bidding highest in that suit or in no trump.
[1950 Morehead *Culbertson* 598]
buy the rack, See BUY THE BOARD.
[1978 Ainslie *Complete Guide* 285]

buy bet, *n.* In bank craps, a type of wager placed on one of six numbers (4, 5, 6, 8, 9, 10) for which the player normally pays the house a percentage of the bet for the transaction.
[1964 Lemmel *Gambling* 59]

buy button, *n.* In bank craps, a small marker placed atop a BUY BET to distinguish it from a COME BET or PLACE BET. Compare BUTTON.
[1973 Friedman *Casino Games* 81]

buy-in, *n.* The amount of money exchanged for chips before beginning play in a card or dice game.
[1968 Wallace *Poker* 211]

buy off slip, *n.* A record of the money paid out for a jackpot on a slot machine, when the amount paid to the player exceeds the amount released by the machine.
[1977 Nevada Gaming Control *Internal Control* 19]

buzzer, *n.* In horse racing, a small electrical device used to shock a horse into a sudden burst of speed.
[1981 Passer *Winning Big* 227]

by, *prep.* As in BY A NOSE, BY A NECK, BY A LENGTH. An expression indicating the distance by which a horse won a race.
[1983 Martinez *Gambling Scene* 192]

by bet, *n.* A side bet; a wager on some aspect of an event other than the main one. *Obsolete.* See also BLEACHER BETTOR.
1803 Lewis *Journals* 59. The Comdts horse lost the main race, but won by six inches the *by betts,* the odds generally given against him in the *by betts* was 12 feet.
[1627 *OED,* 1803 *DAE*]

bye, *n.* In tournaments, a round that a player is excused from, due to an odd number of players in that round.
[1883 *OED*]

by me or **bye me,** *prep. phr.* An expression used by draw poker players to indicate that they cannot open the betting with the cards they hold. Often a player is required to hold at least a pair of jacks in order for the betting to begin.
[1949 Coffin *Secrets* 174]

C

C, *n.* **1.** Abbreviation for CHARLIE. In poker, the third player to the left of the dealer. Compare A, B, D, E, F, G, H.
[1949 Coffin *Secrets* 174]
2. Abbreviation for CRAPS, as **a.** the letter on the DROP BOX beneath the craps table. **b.** an abbreviation for ANY CRAPS, a proposition bet that the next cast of the dice will lose for the shooter.
[ca. 1961 *Hotel Coll*]

cackle, *v.* Especially **cackle the dice.** To hold the dice tightly for a controlled roll while clicking them together in such a fashion as to make others believe the dice are being shaken freely. Compare BARR DICE.
[(1950) 1981 Maurer *Lang. of the Underworld* 183]

cage, *n.* **1.** Also called the CASINO CAGE. In a casino, a centralized enclosure where the records of transactions are kept, money is counted and exchanged for chips.
[1974 Friedman *Casino Management* 15]
2. In faro, a rack with thirteen wires, one corresponding to each card denomination, and four buttons on each wire, corresponding to the four cards of each denomination. The *cage* is used to tally cards as they are played.
[1968 Adams *Western Words*]

cage credit, *n.* In a casino, a condition allowing players to sign credit slips, or markers, for cash or chips.
[1978 Alexander *Glossary* 2]

calamity jane, *n.* In poker, the queen of spades.
[1950 Morehead *Culbertson* 598]
[Compare (1876) 1930 *OEDS,* meaning "a doomsayer"]

Calcutta, *n.* In tournament golf, an auction of the teams before the final, sometimes only, round. The money collected in the auction is shared by the bidders who purchased the top finishers. See also AUCTION POOL.
1984 Jimmy K *Wager at Golf* 28. A *Calcutta* is a process whereby you purchase yours or someone else's team. . . . The *Calcutta* is

usually based on the last day of a tournament. . . . After the bidding is complete, the teams have the right to purchase half of their team from the highest bidder, if the bidder so wishes. After the auction, the money is collected and counted. When play is completed, the monies are divided among the top places.

calibrate the stick, *v. phr.* Same as ADJUST THE STICK. [1983 Martinet *Oral Coll*]

California bet, *n.* Also shortened **California.** In bank craps, simultaneous place bets on the numbers 4, 5, 6, 8, 9, and 10. When one of the numbers wins, the player takes the winnings and leaves the original bet on the number.
1978 Clark *Oral Coll.* There's another bet called the *California bet.* On this one you place all the numbers, and take down the win instead of pressing. The trouble is that on a long hand [several consecutive wins] you could make a bundle, but if you play tight you just barely break even. It's a dumb bet, but a lot of tourists use it because there's a lot of action, but they scare easy and don't shoot the moon.
[(1950) 1981 Maurer *Lang. of the Underworld* 183]

California bible, *n.* Also called a CALIFORNIA PRAYER BOOK. A deck of cards.
[n.d. *DAS*]

California blackjack, *n.* In casino twenty-one, an ace and a nine. Compare PUSH and DOUBLE DOWN.
1982 Martinet *Oral Coll.* We call an ace-nine a California blackjack. About half the time you just get a push [tie with the dealer]. But you would be surprised how many people will double down when the dealer has a ten showing.
→ This is used facetiously; an ace and a nine adds up to a count of twenty.

California C-note, *n.* A ten dollar bill.
[1983 Martinet *Oral Coll*]
→ This is used facetiously; a *C-note* is a one hundred dollar bill.

California fourteens, *n.* Misspotted dice in which one die has two facets with five pips, the other die has two facets with two pips. The combination of pips is a sum of fourteen. See also DOOR POPS, EASTERN TOPS, HORSES, SOFT ROLLS, TAT, TOPS AND BOTTOMS. Compare CALIPERS.
1967 Goffman *Interaction* 150. Among the types of unsporting dice are misspotted ones variously called tops and bottoms, horses, tees, tats, soft rolls, *California fourteens,* door pops, Eastern tops, etc. These dice do not have a different number on each of the six sides, and allow a player to bet on an outcome that is not among the possibilities and therefore rather unlikely to occur.

California prayer book, *n.* Same as CALIFORNIA BIBLE. A deck of cards.
[1852 *DAE*]

calipers, *n. pl. Plural in form, but singular in use.* Dice that are true to required dimensions by one ten-thousandths of an inch. Compare CANDY STORE DICE.
[(1950) 1981 Maurer *Lang. of the Underworld* 183]
[Transferred sense from the calipers used for measurement]

call, *v.* 1. To ask for a card.
[1680 *OED*]
2. In trump games, to ask for a card of trump. [1746 *OED*]
3. In poker, to equal the wager of the previous bettors and ask for a show of the cards.
1866 *American Card Player* 134. *Call.*—To call a show of hands, is for the player whose *say* is last to deposit in the pool the same ante bet by any preceding player, and demand that the hands be shown.
[1833 *OED*]
4. In bingo and keno, to announce the numbers as they are drawn from a pool of all the numbers available.
[1977 Nevada Gaming *Internal Control* 28]
5. In horse racing, to announce the positions of the horses at various stages of the race. The track recorder notes the position of each horse at those stages in the race.
[(1951) 1981 Maurer *Lang. of the Underworld* 205]
6. In bridge, to make a bid, to pass, or to declare a suit as trump.
[1953 Crawford *Consistent Winner* 2]
7. In bank craps, to announce the number after each roll of the dice.
[1983 Martinet *Oral Coll*]
8. In the phrases:

call all bets, In poker, to increase the amount of betting while one is consistently losing. See also CHASE.
[1978 Silberstang *Winning Poker* 140]

call a raise cold, Also shortened to CALL COLD. In poker, to put an amount into the pot equalling a previous bet and previous raise.
1981 Golad *Oral Coll.* Unless you have the nuts [unbeatable hand], you don't want to *call a raise cold.* You can't read the player ahead of you and he may have a lock [the best hand]. So you have to worry about the player who made the bet as well as the player who made the raise. That's walking into two strong hands.

call cold, Same as CALL A RAISE COLD.
[1978 Brunson *How I Made* 527]

call solo, In six-bid solo, to declare an intention to win all the points in a hand.
[1950 Morehead *Culbertson* 599]

call the turn or **call the last turn both ways,** In faro, to bet on the order in which the last two cards for the player will appear.
1868 Trumps *Pocket Hoyle* 205. When there is but one turn left in the box, the player has

the privilege of "calling the last turn," that is, of guessing the order in which the cards will appear, and if he calls it correctly, he receives four times the amount of his stake. [1889 *DA* under "turn"]

call bet, *n.* A wager made without using money or chips.
1973 Clark *Oral Coll.* A *call bet* in a casino is usually restricted to known players, and if the bet loses, the player immediately supplies the amount of the wager to the dealer. *Call bets* are normally made while a player is reaching for more money, but wants to keep the game moving while getting his money out.
[1971 Livingston *Poker Strategy* 215]

caller, *n.* **1.** In poker, the player who matches a previous bet.
[1973 Clark *Oral Coll*]
2. The announcer at a racetrack, bingo parlor, or keno lounge.
[(1951) 1981 Maurer *Lang. of the Underworld* 205]

call for insurance, *n. phr.* In casino twenty-one, an announcement made by the dealer when the dealer has an ace face up after the first two cards are dealt. The player may then bet an amount of one-half the original wager; if the dealer then turns over a twenty-one, the player is paid two to one for the second wager; if the dealer does not have twenty-one points, the second, or reduced, wager is lost.
[ca. 1961 *Hotel Coll*]

calling station, *n.* Also called a TELEPHONE BOOTH. In poker, a player who will call nearly any bet. Such a player is difficult to bluff and therefore unwelcome in most games.

callman, *n.* In baccarat, the employee of the casino who is responsible for the control of the cards, or SHOE. He asks for the cards to be dealt and announces the numbers for the banker and players.
[1968 Wallace *Poker* 211]

calls, *n. pl.* In horse racing, the poles on an oval track at which the positions of the horses are announced for the track recorder.
[1977 Carroll *Playboy's Illustrated* 191]

call solo, *n.* In six-bid solo, the declaration of an intention to win all the points in a hand.
[1950 Morehead *Culbertson* 599]

can, *n.* **1.** In faro, a metal dealing box. The *can* was often modified into a TELL BOX, that is, a dishonest dealing box.
[1943 Maurer *Argot*]
2. In a casino, the DROP BOX, a container attached beneath the table to receive all money and chips dropped through a slot in the table.
[1983 Martinet *Oral Coll*]

C and E, *n.* Abbreviation for CRAP-ELEVEN. A proposition bet that the next roll of the dice will be a 2, 3, 11, or 12.
[ca. 1961 *Hotel Coll*]

candy store dice, *n. phr.* Same as DRUGSTORE DICE. Imperfect dice not intended for gambling that are mass-produced and not subject to careful measurement. Compare CALIPERS.
[1974 Scarne *Dice* 322]

candy wrapper, *n.* **1.** In a casino cage, a paper band used to hold together bills of high denomination, usually hundred or thousand dollar bills.
[1983 Martinet *Oral Coll*]
2. A one-hundred dollar bill.
[1983 Martinet *Oral Coll*]
[So called because it is sometimes used, rolled into a tube, to sniff cocaine, or "nose candy."]

cane, *n.* Also called the STICK. In bank craps, the wicker, rattan, hickory, or bamboo rake used by the dealer to move the dice.
[(1950) 1981 Maurer *Lang. of the Underworld* 183]

canoe, *n.* In roulette, the numbered slot on the wheel in which the ball comes to rest.
[1961 Scarne *Complete Guide* 674]

cantaloups, *n. pl.,* Dice altered with weights, designed to roll only the numbers 4, 5, or 6. See also SNOWBALLS. Compare BUST IN and CALIPERS.
1983 Martinet *Oral Coll.* Those loads are *cantaloups.* You can't roll a deuce, trey, or any number above six. You don't want to bust them in [switch] too often.

cap, *n.* A chip of a different denomination atop a stack of chips which are the same denomination.
[1977 Anness *Dummy Up*]

cap, *v.* **1.** To place a chip of a different denomination atop a stack of chips which are the same denomination.
[ca. 1961 *Hotel Coll*]
2. In twenty-one and craps, to add a chip or chips to a bet after the cards have been dealt or the dice have been cast.
[1983 Martinet *Oral Coll*]
3. Among casino dealers, to place winnings atop a bet rather than alongside. Such action is considered a grave error because there is no way to determine the amount of the original bet if a dealer pays too many or too few chips.
[1973 Clark *Oral Coll*]

capet, *n.* Also spelled **capot.** In the card game piquet, the act of winning all the cards.
1680 Cotton *Compleat Gamester* 62. He that wins more than his own Cards reckons Ten, but he that wins all the Cards reckons Forty, and this is called a *Capet.*
[1651 *OED*]

capital saddle, *n.* In numbers, the picking of two of the first three numbers drawn. Compare SADDLE. [1938 *DA* under *saddle*]

capped die, *n.* Usually **capped dice,** *pl.* Also called **cap dice. 1.** A die that has been treated on one face to prevent its landing with a particular face down. Compare BARR DICE.
[ca. 1961 *Hotel Coll*]

2. A die that has been altered to make it bounce in a more lively fashion.
[(1950) 1981 Maurer *Lang. of the Underworld* 183]

capped loaded missouts, *n.* Dice bored and filled with lead to cause certain numbers to be rolled more often than others. Compare LOADED DICE.
[1983 Martinez *Gambling Scene* 193]

capper, *n.* A cardsharp's confederate; a decoy who directs victims to a dishonest card game. See also ROPER.
[1853 *DA,* 1870 *DAE,* 1871 *OEDS*]

capping liquid, *n. phr.* A sticky substance applied to the face of a die to make the die land with that face down.
[1974 Scarne *Dice* 261]

captain hicks, *n.* Also called SISTER HICKS. In craps, the number 6.
[1983 Martinez *Gambling Scene* 193]
[Rhyming slang]

captain sharp, *n.* A cheater or swindler. Compare SHARP. *Obsolete.*
[1690 *OED*]

card, *n.* **1.** One of a set of small rectangular pieces of stiff paper or plastic with a regular design on one side and a designated value on the other. The set, or PACK is used in playing games of skill and chance. The most widely used pack, or DECK of *cards* is divided into four designs, or SUITS, called CLUBS, DIAMONDS, HEARTS, and SPADES. The thirteen *cards* of each suit are identified in sequence with numbers, or PIPS on the face of each, from the number one to the count of ten, and three figured, or FACE CARDS designated JACK (or KNAVE), QUEEN, and KING.
[1400 *OED*]
2. In many sporting events such as horse racing or boxing, a list of participants.
[1903 *OEDS*]
3. A playing title in dominoes.
[1664 *OED*]

card cheat, *n.* A player of card games who manipulates or marks cards to steal money from others by dishonest means. Compare CARD SHARK or CARDSHARP.
[1859 *OED*]

card-coney-catching, *n. phr.* Also spelled **card-cony-catching.** The cheating or swindling of victims at cards by a CARDSHARP. *Obsolete.*
[1592 *OED*]

card count, *n.* In games like twenty-one and gin rummy, the total numeric value of cards held in a hand.
[1982 Martin *Introduction* 12]

card counter, *n.* In twenty-one, a player who keeps a mental tally of every card played, and bets large sums when the odds are greatly in his favor. Pit bosses watch for wide variations in the betting patterns of players and eject those they suspect of CARD COUNTING.
[1970 *Baccarat, The Facts*]

card counting, *n. phr.* In twenty-one, a process of mentally recording the cards played in order to change a betting pattern or strategy. See also CASE THE DECK.
[ca. 1961 *Hotel Coll*]

card-dauber, *n.* A person who marks the backs of cards with india ink or aniline pencil for purposes of cheating. Compare COSMETICS.
[1965 Fraiken *Inside Nevada* 75]

card down, *n. phr.* In casinos, a statement made to a pit boss by a dealer when a card is dropped from the table. Dealers are not allowed to bend over and leave the chip rack exposed, therefore a pit boss must retrieve anything a dealer drops.
[1977 Anness *Dummy Up*]

carder, *n.* A person who plays at card games, especially a professional gambler. Compare DICER.
[1530 *OED*]

card for the bank, *n. phr.* In baccarat, a statement made by the employee in charge of the game when the rules require that a card be dealt for the BANK HAND.
[1977 Anness *Dummy Up*]

card for the players, *n. phr.* In baccarat, a statement made by the employee in charge of the game when the rules require that a card be drawn for the hand representing all the players.
[1977 Anness *Dummy Up*]

card-holder, *n.* **1.** A wooden, plastic, or cardboard case for keeping a pack of cards.
2. A servant who holds the cards for a patron at a game. *Obsolete.*
[1659 *OED*]

card-hustler, *n.* Also called CARD SHARP. A person who cheats at card playing.
[1971 McQuaid *Gambler's Digest* 302]

carding, *n.* **1.** The art or skill of playing at cards; the act of card playing.
[1495 *OED*]
2. In poker, the noting of exposed cards during the play of a hand and the using of the information to change betting strategy. Compare CARD COUNTER.
[1964 Reese and Watkins *Secrets* 138]

card mechanic, *n.* A person adept at manipulating cards for the purpose of cheating others. See also CARD SHARK and CARD SHARP.
[1961 Scarne *Complete Guide* 675]

card mob, *n.* Two or more cheaters working in collusion to cheat at a card game. Compare DICE MOB and MONTE MOB.
[1961 Scarne *Complete Guide* 675]

card-money, *n.* Money held by a gambler to be used at playing card games.
[1760 *OED*]

card mucker, *n.* **1.** In panguingue, an employee of the establishment who deals the cards and

does not play the game.
[1973 Clark *Oral Coll*]
2. In twenty-one, a cheater who switches cards into and out of a game.
[1965 Fraiken *Inside Nevada* 75]

card play, *n.* The participation in gambling games using cards. Compare CARDING.
[1577 *OED*]

card player, *n.* One who participates in card games. Compare CARDER and DICE-PLAYER.
[1589 *OED*]

card punch, *n.* A tool for making indentations in the backs of playing cards for purposes of cheating.
[1890 Quinn *Fools of Fortune* 204]

cardroom, *n.* An establishment or an area in a building devoted to card playing.
[1760 *OEDS,* 1802 *DAE,* 1876 *OED*]

cardroom license, *n.* A certificate of approval from a municipality or a state allowing an operator to conduct a specified number of particular card games, usually forms of poker.
[1981 Jenkins *Johnny Moss* 182]

cards, *n. pl.* **1.** In baccarat, an announcement by the person conducting the game indicating that the person acting on behalf of the bank is to deal cards from the shoe.
[ca. 1961 *Hotel Coll*]
2. In casino, a score of three points won by the player winning more than twenty-seven cards.
[1950 Morehead *Culbertson* 599]
3. In the clause:
the cards speak for themselves, In poker, a statement made by a player indicating that the value of a hand is determined by the cards being shown, not by the player holding the hand.
[1968 Wallace *Poker* 211]

card sense, *n.* An ability to play card games well; a knowledge of probabilities in card games, especially in poker.
[1930 *OEDS*]

card shark, *n.* Also written **cardshark.** A person who manipulates or marks cards for purposes of cheating; a cheater at card games, especially one skilled at false dealing. See also CARD MECHANIC. Compare DICE SHARK.
1973 Clark *Oral Coll.* In the 1950's we used the term *card shark.* I didn't know until years later that card sharp was an older term.
[n.d., *DAS*; Compare SHARK (def. 2), 1600 *OED*]

card sharp or **cardsharp,** *n.* Also called CARD SHARK. A person who manipulates or marks cards for the purposes of cheating; a cheater at card games, especially one skilled at false dealing.
[1884 *DAE, DA, OEDS*]

cardsharper, *n.* Also written **card-sharper.** A CARD SHARP. *Rare.*
[1859 *OED,* 1884 *DA, DAE*]

card-sharping, *n.* Also written **cardsharping.** The practice of cheating in card games.
[1870 *OED*]

card table, *n.* A table designed for playing cards. Different styles of tables are used for playing bridge, poker, baccarat, and twenty-one.
[1713 *OED,* 1767 *DAE*]

carolina, *n.* Also called **carolina nina** or **niner from caroliner** or **nina from carolina.** A cast of the number nine in dice games. Compare NINA.
[1950 Morehead *Culbertson* 599]
→The words "Carolina" and "nine" must always rhyme.

carousel, *n.* **1.** In a casino, a slot machine with a jackpot payout that increases as more coins are played; a slot machine with a PROGRESSIVE JACKPOT.
[1973 Clark *Oral Coll*]
2. In a casino, a group of slot machines that take the same denomination of coin arranged on a circular or oval platform. See also CAROUSEL ATTENDANT.
[1973 Clark *Oral Coll*]

carousel attendant, *n.* In a casino, an employee in charge of a group of slot machines. The employee changes bills to coins for patrons, announces large payouts and calls a mechanic if a slot machine fails to operate correctly.
[1973 Clark *Oral Coll*]

carpet joint, *n.* Also called a RUG JOINT. A plush or luxurious casino which offers a wide variety of betting opportunities, entertainment, and food. See also SAWDUST JOINT.
[1961 Scarne *Complete Guide* 675]

carryover, *n.* **1.** In golf, a bet not resolved on a hole that continues on to the next hole or until won by a player.
2. Among casino dealers who share tips, an amount of money too small to be divided evenly and therefore held over and added to the tips the following day. Compare TOKE.
1984 Martinet *Oral Coll.* The dealers in the twenty-one pit split tokes. If there is a small amount left over that can't be split, that's a *carryover. Carryovers* are added to the next day's tokes.

carte blanche, *n. French.* A hand in playing cards that contains no FACE, or COURT cards.
[1820 *OED*]

cartwheel, *n.* A silver dollar or a metal gaming token worth one dollar.
[1855 *DA, DAE;* 1867 *OED*]

carve up scores, *v.* To discuss past games or hands, especially large wins at poker.
[1973 Clark *Oral Coll*]

case, *n.* **1.** Short for CASE CARD. The last of four cards of one denomination still undealt. Compare CAT-HARP.
1843 Green *Exposure* 210. When there are five cards in the box [in faro], one *case* (odd card)

and two doubles (such as two fours and two sevens), this is called the "double cat-harp;" when these cards are in, one odd and one doublet—it is called "single-cat-harp." [1856 *OED, DAE, DA*]
2. In faro, the folding box that holds the cards during the deal. Compare SHOE.
[1968 Adams *Western Words*]

case, *v.* In the phrases:
case the deck, In twenty-one, to mentally record each card played in order to shift betting strategy to take advantage of favorable odds. See also CARD COUNTING.
[1961 Scarne *Complete Guide* 675]
case the rack, In a casino, to count the amount of money represented in the chip container on a gaming table. Pit bosses are adept at being able to instantly determine the number and denominations of chips on the table without disrupting play.
[1975 Clark *Oral Coll*]

case bet, *n.* The final wager by a gambler who has lost his stake.
[1983 Martinet *Oral Coll*]

case card, *n.* Same as CASE (def. 1). The fourth card of the denomination that is yet undealt. 1868 Trumps *Pocket Hoyle* 208. When three cards of one denomination are out, the one remaining in the box is called the bet, *case,* or single *card.* [1856 *DAE*]

case-keeper, *n.* Also called the CASE MAN or CUE KEEPER. The assistant to a faro dealer who records the denomination of each card as it is dealt from the CASE RACK.
1868 Trumps *Pocket Hoyle* 207. *Case-Keeper.*—The person who marks game on the cue-box.
[1867 *DA, OEDS,* 1903 *OEDS*]

case man, *n.* Same as CASE KEEPER.
[1968 Thackrey *Nick the Greek* 128]

case money, *n.* A gambler's last bit of money, used for making a final wager in a game. See also CASE BET and CASE NOTE.
[1974 Scarne *Dice* 463]

case note, *n.* A gambler's last bill, usually a one dollar bill.
[(1950) 1981 Maurer *Lang. of the Underworld* 183]

caser, *n.* Also called a CARD COUNTER. In twenty-one, a player adept at remembering every card played.
1983 Martinet *Oral Coll.* A good *caser* can track every card played in a six-deck shoe. When the cards left in the shoe are mostly tens, he will jump in with big bets to take advantage of the odds.

case rack, *n.* In faro, a rectangular device with thirteen wires, each wire holding four buttons, representing the four suits of the thirteen denominations. On this abacus, the CASE-KEEPER records each card as it is dealt, so that the players know how many cards of each denominations are yet undealt.
[1943 Maurer *Argot*]

cash, *v.* **1.** In trump games, to lead with cards from an established suit in order to win several tricks in a row.
[1934 *OEDS*]
2. In the particle constructions:
cash in, Also called CASH OUT. To exchange chips for money and withdraw from a gambling game.
[1896 *DA, OEDS*; 1899 *DAE*]
cash out, Same as CASH IN.
[1949 Coffin *Secrets* 174]

cash point, *n.* In casino, the score awarded for an ace or a CASINO (the ten of diamonds or the two of spades).
[1950 Morehead *Culbertson* 599]

casino, *n.* **1.** A building or large room devoted to gambling games or wagering on a variety of events. Compare CARDROOM.
[1851 *OEDS*]
2. Also spelled **cassino.** In the game of that name, the ten of diamonds or the two of spades, also known respectively as the BIG CASINO or GREAT CASINO and LITTLE CASINO or SMALL CASINO. [1792 *OED*]

casino cage, *n.* Also called the CAGE (def. 1). The secured area in a gaming establishment where records of transactions, money, and chips are kept.
[1979 Hilton Hotel *Procedures* 24]

casino cage bank, *n. phr.* **1.** The inventory of all chips currently in use in various sections of the gaming establishent. See also FLOAT.
[1982 Martin *Introduction*]
2. The moneys available in a casino for cash and chip transactions.
[1973 Clark *Oral Coll*]

casino cage cashier, *n. phr.* **1.** A casino employee, usually an accountant, in charge of recording all transactions relating to money, chips, and credit for the various departments in the casino (craps tables, twenty-one pits, slot machines) and for patrons of the casino.
[1979 Hilton Hotel *Procedures* 22]
2. Also called **casino cashier.** Generally, any employee working with money exchange and records of transactions in a casino. Often called a CASINO CLERK.
[1978 Alexander *Glossary*]

casino clerk, *n.* A casino employee who works in the cage under the supervision of the CASINO CAGE CASHIER.
[1979 Newman *Dealer's Special* 6]

casino craps, *n.* A dice game of BANK CRAPS in which players wager against the establishment, or house, as opposed to making wagers with other players in the game. See also ARMY CRAPS and FADE CRAPS.
[1970 *Baccarat, The Facts*]

casino dice, *n.* Also called TRUE DICE. Dice made

to specification which are accurate to within one ten-thousandths of an inch. Compare CALIPERS and CANDY STORE DICE or DRUGSTORE DICE
[1974 Scarne *Dice* 23]

casino entertainment tax, *n. phr.* In Nevada, a special tax levied on all forms of entertainment (music, dancing, shows, boxing matches, tennis exhibitions, bowling tournaments) that take place on the premises of a casino.
[1963 *Nevada Revised Statutes* IV, 5]

casino gambling, *n.* Legal, licensed, and regulated gambling. Usually contrasted with unlicensed or unregulated and consequently illegal gambling.
[1978 Harrah *Recollections* 13]

casino gaming industry, *n.* All of the activities related to legalized gambling and the operation of legal gambling establishments.
[1978 Harrah *Recollections* 6]

casino host, *n.* Also called a GREETER. An employee in a casino, usually a well-known gambler or former sports star, who roams the casino in a public relations capacity, greeting regular players and arranging for credit, complimentary drinks, meals, and entertainment.
[ca. 1961 *Hotel Coll*]

casino manager, *n.* In a combination hotel and casino, the employee responsible for the daily operation of all activities related to gambling. Sometimes the *casino manager* is also ultimately responsible for the operation of the entire resort. Some resorts use a variety of managers: food and beverage manager; manager of front-desk operations; director of entertainment; personnel manager, and so on. See also SHIFT BOSS and CASINO OPERATOR.
[1961 Scarne *Complete Guide* 675]

Casino Operations. Where CASINO GAMBLING is legal it is licensed, usually by a GAMING COMMISSION under state authority, such as by the NEVADA GAMING CONTROL ACT. CASINO OPERATORS are licensed through a GAMING PERMIT which may be a RESTRICTED LICENSE. DEALERS and other casino employees need a SHERIFF'S CARD to work on the LAS VEGAS STRIP.

There are all manner of GAMING HOUSES, from RUG JOINTS (also called CARPET JOINTS) to SAWDUST JOINTS to HELLS or JUICE JOINTS which are special kinds of CLIP JOINTS. Most STORES are RIGHT JOINTS, at least in GLITTER GULCH.

Within a big casino there are public areas such as a CARDROOM or a PIT, such as the DICE PIT, or the BINGO PARLOR. Some offer KENO LOUNGES. GAMING ROOMS are also found in hotels. The GAMING OPERATION has a BACK OF THE HOUSE where there is a COIN ROOM, COUNT ROOM, DEALER'S ROOM and MAIN BANK. CHIPS are exchanged for the customer's cash at the CAGE, or CHANGE BOOTH, or by a CHANGE PERSON. Security is provided by TINS and with the EYE-IN-THE-SKY in the CATWALK.

JUNKETEERS are directed to offer EXECUTIVE PACKAGES to PREFERRED CUSTOMERS who are usually HIGH-ROLLERS, in the form of RFB COMPS, or they may COMP them in some other fashion. GREETERS are often hired to act as CASINO HOSTS, offering CREDIT LINES, FREE PLAY, and otherwise given the POWER OF THE PENCIL.

A CASINO OPERATOR may hire a CASINO MANAGER to supervise the SHIFT BOSSES who, in turn, oversee the responsibilities of the PIT BOSSES and FLOORMEN. The latter watch over the DEALERS, such as: CROUPIERS for roulette or faro, CALLMEN in baccarat, KENO WRITERS for lottery, HEARSE-DRIVERS in faro, MUCKERS in panguingue or roulette, TWENTY-ONE DEALERS, and in craps: CRAPS DEALERS, BOXMEN and LADDERMEN.

KENO RUNNERS, CHECK RUNNERS, APRON GRILS, and SLOT MECHANICS further assist the smooth operation for PACKAGE TOURISTS, OUTSIDE GAMBLERS, ALIENS, RIM CUSTOMERS, PREMIUM CUSTOMERS, even the GRIND CUSTOMERS. The people in SLOT BOOTHS, as well as CHECKERS, CASHIERS, CREDIT MANAGERS, CUTTERS, the COUNT TEAM, and those responsible for the WEIGH COUNT keep money flowing.

This necessitates detailed records at every turn, including: FILL SLIPS, PIT FILL RECORDS, GAMING CREDIT INSTRUMENTS (such as ISSUE SLIPS, MARKERS, CREDIT SLIPS, RIM CARDS, or other IOUS), the corresponding PAYMENT SLIPS, or BUY OFF SLIPS, INSIDE TICKETS, KENO TICKETS, OUTSIDE TICKETS, SLOT COUNT SHEETS, SLOT THEORETICAL CALCULATION SHEETS, MASTER GAME REPORTS, the STIFF SHEETS, and TABLE INVENTORY FORMS.

All of these are necessary because of taxes such as the CASINO ENTERTAINMENT TAX and a TABLE TAX. And there are all manner of overhead expenses, from payments to LUGGERS who bring in gamblers and to PLUGGERS or PAID SHILLS who entice them to play; to COLLECTORS who take a percentage of the unpaid debts which they collect; to LEAKAGE from SKIPPERS and BUNKO ARTISTS. NONPRODUCERS and CARD COUNTERS in particular can BREAK THE TABLE which adds to the cost of doing business. Notorious cheaters may wind up in the BLACKBOOK or LIST OF EXCLUDED PERSONS. When BETTORS lose all their money they may be given BROKE MONEY, also called WALKING MONEY, or they may be extended a COURTESY PLAY, also called a SEVEN-ELEVEN.

casino operator, *n.* A person who runs a gaming house. The *casino operator* usually owns a percentage of the establishment and shares with other casino owners who may not be concerned with the regular daily operation, but who also own a percentage of the establishment.
[1953 Lewis *Sagebrush Casinos* 39]

cast, *n.* A throw of dice.
[1509 *OED*]

cast, *v.* To throw dice, either from a dicebox or from the hand.
[1458 *OED*]

caster, *n.* In hazard, the person who throws the dice. *Rare.* See quote at HAZARD: 1680 Cotton *Complete Gamester*
[1669 *OED*]
→The term has been replaced by ROLLER (def. 2), SHOOTER, or THROWER (def. 2).

casting box, Same as DICE BOX. *Obsolete.*
[1616 *OED*]

cat, *n.* 1. Also CAT-HARP. In faro, an event in which two of the last three cards in the deal have the same value, that is, are paired.
1868 Trumps *Pocket Hoyle* 207. When the last turn consists of two cards of the same denomination, and one other card, as two Tens and a King, it is called a *cat.*
2. Short for **a.** BIG CAT, five cards, not of the same suit, between 8 and king, without a pair, or **b.** LITTLE CAT, five cards, not of the same suit, between 3 and 8, without a pair.

catalog man, *n.* A would-be cheater who acquires information only from mail-order catalogs, books, or articles. *Derogatory.*
1945 Scarne *Dice.* The cheat whose only knowledge of the art and craft of cheating was obtained from a study of the catalog and the writers and gambling exposure lecturers who glean their information from the same source and who are unable to separate the sucker items from the smart stuff are known among the boys as *catalog men*, a highly derogatory term.

catbird seat, *n.* In poker, the last position to the left of the dealer.
[1981 Golad *Oral Coll*]
[Compare 1942 *OEDS*, meaning "a superior or advantageous position"]

catch, *n.* **1.** In keno, a number selected by a player that is drawn by the announcer, or CALLER, of the game.
[ca. 1961 *Hotel Coll*]
2. In poker, a desired or valuable card.
[1949 Coffin *Secrets* 174]

catch, *v.* **1.** In keno, to match a chosen number on a ticket with the same number as called by the announcer, or CALLER.
[1973 Friedman *Casino Games* 101]
2. In poker, to draw a desired card, especially toward the end of a hand; such as for completing an INSIDE STRAIGHT.
[1949 Coffin *Secrets* 174]
3. In the phrase:
catch a point, In craps, to establish a number (4, 5, 6, 8, 9, or 10) on the first roll by a shooter.
[1973 Binion *Recollections* 8]

catcher, *n.* An accomplice to a dice cheat, who retrieves the loaded dice and substitutes honest dice after the cheater has won.
[1938 Asbury *Sucker's Progress* 58]

cat-harp, *n.* Also spelled **cat hop. 1.** In faro, two cards of the same denomination, along with a single card of another denomination, as the last cards undealt. Sometimes the term refers to five cards rather than three; in such a case, the five cards consist of two doublets and a fifth card of another denomination. See also DOUBLE-CAT-HARP and SINGLE-CAT-HARP.
1843 Green *Exposure* 210. When there are five cards in the box [in faro], one *case* (odd card) and two doubles (such as two fours and two sevens), this is called the "double cat-harp;" when these cards are in, one odd and one doublet—it is called "single-cat-harp."
2. Short for BIG CAT or LITTLE CAT.

cats and dogs, *n.* In poker, a variation in which special hands are accorded values in the ranking of winning combinations.
[1971 Livingston *Poker Strategy* 215]

catwalk, *n.* In a casino, the overhead observation platform above the tables and behind two-way mirrors. See also EYE-IN-THE-SKY.
1985 Clark *Oral Coll.* The *catwalks* are narrow platforms behind one-way mirrors above the tables in the casino, where security [guards] could monitor play. But now just about all the casinos use video cameras and closed-circuit TV systems.

cellar dealer, *n.* Also called BASE DEALER or BOTTOM DEALER or SUBWAY DEALER. A card cheat who distributes cards from the bottom of the deck. Compare BOTTOM STOCK.
[1962 Garcia *Marked Cards* 154]

center bet, *n.* **1.** Also called **center money.** In army craps, the wager placed by the person shooting the dice. Other players may bet against all or part of the shooter's stake.
[(1950) 1981 Maurer *Lang. of the Underworld* 183]
2. In bank craps, a reference to any proposition bet that the next roll of the dice will result in a specified number. The area in the center of the layout contains spaces for hardway bets, and the numbers 2, 3, 7, 11, and 12.
[1982 Clark *Oral Coll*]

century, *n.* Also called a C-NOTE. A one-hundred dollar bill.
[1839 *DA*, 1859 *OEDS*]

C-game, *n.* In poker rooms, any low-stake game in the room, usually the third highest stakes table.
[1949 Coffin *Secrets* 174]

chain dice, *n.* A pair of cheating dice connected with wire, designed to roll a particular configuration of numbers more often than others. Compare LINKED DICE. *Obsolete.*
1726 Wilson *Art and Mystery* 33. *Chain* or Link'd Dice [are] so called from their being made fast together so nicely, with a Horse-hair or Wire stain'd to the Colour of the Ivory, that it is difficult to discover it at any little distance from you, more especially by Candlelight.

chalk, *adj.* Of or pertaining to an almost certain winner. In combinations: **chalk bettor** or **chalk eater** or **chalk player** is a person who wagers only

on the horses or dogs with low odds or a high probability of winning, while a **chalk horse** is a strong favorite to win; in poker, a **chalk hand** is a LOCK, a certain winner.
[1955 Hillis *Pari-Mutuel Betting* 112]

chance, *n.* **1.** An opportunity to win a bet.
2. In hazard, the number which the shooter must roll to win; equivalent to the point in craps. See quote at HAZARD: 1680 Cotton *Complete Gamester.* [1386 *OED*]

change, *v.* To exchange money for chips at a gaming table.
1843 Green *Exposure* 64. On the following day the Doctor "opened" for them, and T. *"changed"* (that is, took checks) to the amount of a hundred dollars, and commenced playing.

change booth, n. In a casino, an elevated platform from which a slot machine attendant exchanges bills and coins for patrons. Compare CAROUSEL (def. 2).
[ca. 1961 *Hotel Coll*]

change girl, *n.* Also called a CHANGE PERSON. In a casino, a roving employee, usually a woman, in the slot machine area who exchanges the paper money of patrons for coins, a supply of which are carried in an apron with large pockets; an APRON GIRL. See also SLOT ATTENDANT.
[1953 Lewis *Sagebrush Casinos* 171]

change-in, *n.* In poker, the amount of money required to buy enough chips to join a game. See also BUY-IN.
[1949 Coffin *Secrets* 174]

change person, *n.* In a casino, a roving employee, either male or female, in the slot machine area who exchanges the paper money of patrons for coins, a supply of which are carried in an apron with large pockets. See also SLOT ATTENDANT. Compare APRON GIRL and CHANGE GIRL.
[1979 Hilton Hotel *Procedures* 4]

change space, *n.* On a twenty-one table, the area of the layout in front of the dealer where money is exchanged for chips.
[ca. 1961 *Hotel Coll*]

charlie, *n.* Abbreviated as C. In poker, the third position to the left of the dealer.
[1949 Coffin *Secrets* 174]

chart, *n.* In horse racing, the published statistics on past races, and the horses and jokeys who participated.
[1955 Hillis *Pari-Mutuel Betting* 113]

chase, *v.* In poker, to remain in a game against better hands; to bet recklessly while hoping to recover losses.
[1949 Coffin *Secrets* 174]

cheat, *v.* To use deception or any device or gaffed cards or dice to achieve an advantage over other players. [1532 *OED*]

cheat, *n.* Same as a CHEATER.
[1968 Adams *Western Words*]
[*a*1559 (?), 1664 *OED*]

cheater, *n.* A player who violates the rules of a game or uses devices to win by any dishonest means.
[1532 *OED,* labeled *obsolete*]

cheaters, *n.* A deck of marked cards.
[*DAS;* 1968 Adams *Western Words*]

cheater's bar, *n.* In slot machines, a metal flange attached to the reels inside the machine that prevents a RHYTHM PLAYER from developing a pattern, as by paying in coins at a rate that keeps the third reel moving until the player stops it at a configuration for a payout.
[1968 Thackrey *Nick the Greek* 173]

cheating box, *n.* Usually in faro, any one of a wide variety of devices designed to hold cards for dishonest dealing. See also: COFFEE MILL, CRANK-BOX, DEALING BRACE, END SQUEEZE, HORSE BOX, JIMMIED-UP BOX, LEVER MOVEMENT, NEEDLE SQUEEZE, SAND TELL BOX, SCREW BOX, SNAKE BOX, SNAKE TELL BOX, TELL BOX, TONGUE-TELL, TOP-SIGHT TELL. Compare SHOE.
[1938 Asbury *Sucker's Progress* 12]

check, *n.* A chip; a counter used at table games to represent money.
1843 Green *Exposure* 59. The man that plays this game [faro] has to go to great expense; he has to produce, sir, a fine silver box worth, perhaps, one hundred dollars; and then he has to supply himself with a number of ivory pieces, turned round like a dollar; some of them colored red, with various figures on them, and some of them white, without any coloring, except perhaps around the edge: and these *checks,* as they are called, will cost, probably, two hundred dollars.
1868 Trumps *Pocket Hoyle* 204. The stakes usually consist of counters or *checks,* made of ivory, representing different sums; they are purchased of the banker and are redeemed by him at the option of the holder.
[1845 *DA, DAE, OEDS*]
→ *Check* is used exclusively by professional gamblers and those working in legalized gaming. *Chip* is used by the general public, and by those in professional gambling when speaking with non-professionals.

check, *v.* **1.** In poker, to make no additional wager when acting as the first bettor, but to reserve the right to bet at a later time in the hand.
[1949 Coffin *Secrets* 174]
2. In the phrase:
check blind, In poker, to refrain from wagering as the first bettor before picking up the dealt cards. The player who *checks blind* may bet, call, or raise the wager at a later time during the same betting round.
[1968 Wallace *Poker* 212]

check change, *n. phr.* In a casino, an announcement made by a dealer to a pit boss while exchanging chips of one denomination for chips of another, usually lower, denomination. See also COLOR UP.
[ca. 1961 *Hotel Coll*]

check cop, *n.* A sticky substance put on the palm of the hand to facilitate stealing a chip from the top of a stack.
[1961 Scarne *Complete Guide* 675]

check copper, *n.* Also called a CHIP COPPER. A person who steals chips from the table, either from the pot or from other players.
[ca. 1961 *Hotel Coll*]

check down, *n.* In a casino, a statement made by a dealer to a pit boss when a chip has dropped from the table. The dealer is not allowed to bend over while standing or sitting in position, so the pit boss must retrieve the dropped chip.
[1977 Anness *Dummy Up*]

checker, *n.* **1.** In a casino, an employee who verifies a large payout at keno or on a slot machine.
[ca. 1961 *Hotel Coll*]
2. In an illegal gambling establishment, an employee who verifies the number of patrons brought to the establishment by persons who recruit such patrons. The recruiters, called LUGGERS or ROPERS, are paid a certain amount of money for each patron they bring to the establishment.
[(1950) 1981 Maurer *Lang. of the Underworld* 183]

checkers bet, *n.* In golf, a doubled wager after a loss. When a player loses a hole, he may request an opportunity to bet for twice the amount on the next hole.
[1971 McQuaid *Gambler's Digest* 302]
[From the "jump" in checkers.]

check jacket envelope, *n. phr.* In a casino cage, the folder in which a personal check has been returned to the casino from the bank, containing all information about the credit of the individual whose name appears on the check, and about any of the bank's attempts to recover the money represented.
[1978 Alexander *Glossary* 3]

check rack, *n.* Same as a CHIP RACK. On a casino table, a grooved or slotted tray for holding chips and keeping them separate by denomination.
[1890 Quinn *Fools of Fortune* 194]

check-rack, *v.* To refuse to pay a player because the bank has no money or because a player is suspected of cheating.
[1968 Adams *Western Words*]

check-raise, *v.* In poker, to refrain from betting as the first player to act, then to raise the amount wagered when given the opportunity to call or bet again.
[1968 Wallace *Poker* 212]

check run, *n.* **1.** In a casino, a trip from the cage to a table with more chips.
[1979 Newman *Dealer's Special* 11]
2. A trip to various casinos to redeem chips. An employee is sent to other casinos to exchange chips from one casino used at the tables of another. [1983 Martinet *Oral Coll*]

check runner, *n.* A casino employee, usually a security guard, who carries chips from the casino cage to a table or to another casino.
[1979 Newman *Dealer's Special* 11]

chemin de fer, *n.* Also spelled **chemine de fer.** A game similar to baccarat, but differing in the manner of wagering. In BACCARAT, the gaming establishment constitutes the BANK, or entity covering all wagers and charging a commission to players who bet with the bank rather than against it; in *chemin de fer,* one of the players acts as the banker until he has lost his stake or sells the bank.
[1891 *OEDS;* French *railway,* supposedly from the speed of the game.]

chicoree, *n.* In ombre, a hazard or potential loss by holding either three or four false MATADORS.
[1950 Morehead *Culbertson* 601]

chinese, *adj.* Of or pertaining to any bizarre variant of an established game. For example, cutting the cards into several parts instead of two might be referred to as a "*chinese* cut."
[1950 Morehead *Culbertson* 601]

Chinese lottery, *n.* Another name for KENO. The earliest version of keno in the American West utilized eighty Chinese characters on the playing slips and was played primarily by Chinese laborers from San Francisco to Rock Springs, Wyoming.
[1977 Cahill *Recollections* 581]

chink ink, *n.* India ink used by cheaters for marking the backs of playing cards.
[1968 Wallace *Poker* 212]

chip, *n.* **1.** A CHECK, TOKEN, or COUNTER used to represent money. At one time, *chips* were made of ivory or bone, but are now commonly made of composition or plastic.
1866 *American Card Player* 134. *Chips.*—Counters representing money, the value of which should be determined by the players at the beginning of the game.
[1856 *DAE;* 1873 *OED*]
→ Professional gamblers more often use the term CHECK.
2. chips, *pl.* In the n. clause:
the chips are down, In poker, a statement made at the end of all betting on a hand, announcing that the hands must be shown and a winner declared.
[1976 Larson *Vocabulary* 97]

chip, *v.* **1.** In poker, to make a wager.
1866 *American Card Player* 134. *Chipping,* or to *Chip,* is synonymous with betting. Thus a player, instead of saying "I bet" may say "I chip" so much. [1876 *DA, DAE*]
2. In the phrases:
chip along, In poker, to bet consistently the smallest amount allowed; to make raises in the smallest amount allowed with the hope of preventing large raises by other players.
[1949 Coffin *Secrets* 174]

chip the pot, In poker, to remove a percentage from each pot to pay for refreshments or to the operator of the establishment.
[1971 Livingston *Poker Strategy* 215]

chip copper, *n.* Same as a CHECK COPPER.
[1971 McQuaid *Gambler's Digest* 302]

chip declaration, *n.* In high-low poker, the announcement of an intention to win half of the pot with a high hand or with a low hand, or to win the entire pot with both the high and the low hand. The intentions of all the players competing for the pot are announced simultaneously, usually by secreting chips in the palm of the hand (one chip to play high, two chips to play low, no chips to play both ways). The players hold their fists above the table and open their hands at an agreed signal.
[1963 Steig *Common Sense* 183]

chip fill, *n.* In a casino, the replenishment of chips at a table. The PIT BOSS signs a form requesting chips from the casino cage, which an employee (a security guard in larger establishments) presents at the cage and then returns with the requested chips. The form, or FILL SLIP is signed by the dealer and the deliverer at the table receiving the chips.
[1979 Hilton Hotel *Procedures* 22]

chip float, *n.* The dollar value of all the chips held by casino patrons. See also FLOAT (def. 1).
[1982 Martin *Introduction* 24]

chip game, *n.* Any of a variety of low-stake games, usually a variation on a WHEEL OF FORTUNE. [1978 Harrah *Recollections* 126]

chip hustler, *n.* Usually at bank craps, a player who stands next to a person making large bets (a HIGH ROLLER) and wheedles chips for proferred advice or steals chips from the players next to him. [1974 Powell *Verbal Dexterity*]

chip rack, *n.* **1.** Same as a CHECK RACK. On a gaming table, the grooved or slotted tray that holds a large number of chips and keeps them separated by denomination.
[1935 *Nevada Gaming Regulations* 156]
2. A grooved tray used for carrying chips.
[1973 Clark *Oral Coll*]

chip run, *n.* Same as a CHECK RUN.
[1973 Clark *Oral Coll*]

chip shuffler, *n.* In a casino, a player who wanders around rattling a handful of chips of a large denomination and seeking favors (such as complimentary rooms, meals, show tickets) from pit bosses. Compare COMP.
[ca. 1961 *Hotel Coll*]

chisel, *v.* To make small bets that have the best probability of success.
[(1950) 1981 Maurer *Lang. of the Underworld* 183]
[Compare 1808 *OED*, meaning "to cheat"]
→This meaning of *chisel* is quite in contrast with the popular slang usage "To cheat, defraud."

chiseler, *n.* In dice, a player who makes only small bets with the best probability of success.
[(1950) 1981 Maurer *Lang. of the Underworld* 183]
[Compare 1918 *OEDS*, meaning "a cheat"]

choice, *n.* The horse favored to win a race.
[1983 Martinez *Gambling Scene* 194]

choice pots, *n.* In poker, an announcement that the dealer will name the particular variant (such as stud, high-low, hold'em) he intends to play for that hand.
[1964 Reese and Watkins *Secrets* 139]

chop, *v.* Of the dice in craps, to make a series of rolls that have no discernible pattern of winning or losing.
1983 Martinet *Oral Coll.* Sometimes you'll stand at a table for a long time while the dice *chop*. . . . When there is no pattern for misses and passes you say the dice are *chopping*.

chopper, *n.* An employee in an illegal gambling establishment who takes a percentage of shooter's winnings for the house. See also CUTTER.
[(1950) 1981 Maurer *Lang. of the Underworld* 184]

choppy, *adj.* Pertaining to a short, uneven stride in a racehorse.
[(1951) 1981 Maurer *Lang. of the Underworld* 206]

chops, *n.* In faro, a progressive betting system in which a player increases his bets on a CASE CARD, the last card of a denomination not yet dealt.
[1943 Maurer *Argot*]

chouse, *n.* **1.** A cheater or swindler. *Obsolete.*
[1610 *OED*]
2. A person who is easily cheated or swindled. *Obsolete.* [1649 *OED*]

chouse, *v.* To cheat, trick, or swindle a victim. *Obsolete.* [1659 *OED*]

chuck, *n.* Short for CHUCK-A-LUCK.
[1974 Scarne *Dice* 314]

chuck-a-luck, *n.* Also spelled **chuck-luck, chucker-luck, chuckle-luck.** Also called BIRDCAGE, SWEATCLOTH, HAZARD. A dice game in which three dice contained in a wire cage are rolled and in which players may make various wagers on the results: triplets, low (eight or under), high (nine or over), a specific number between three and eighteen, and so on.
[1836 *DA, DAE, OEDS*]

chuck cage, *n.* The wire dice container shaped like an hourglass that contains the three dice used in CHUCK-A-LUCK, and which is rotated end-for-end with the pips facing upward being counted.
[1974 Scarne *Dice* 335]

chuck number, *n.* On a CHUCK-A-LUCK layout, any of six spaces (numbered 1 through 6) on which a player may place a wager. The player wins if each of the three dice have that number upward after the roll.
[1964 Wykes *Illustrated Guide* 326]

Church of England, *n.* Same as a CRAP-ELEVEN bet, C AND E bet. In bank craps, a wager that the next number rolled will be a 2, 3, 11, or 12.
[1983 Martinet *Oral Coll*]
[from the literal use, 1534 *OED*]
→Facetious use of the name for the Anglican Church.

chute, *n.* **1.** In a casino, the slot on a gaming table above the DROP BOX where the dealer places bills exchanged for chips.
[1983 Martinet *Oral Coll*]
2. On an oval race track, a straight stretch of track in front of the starting gate, where the horses or dogs may be fully extended before going into the turn.
[(1951) 1981 Maurer *Lang. of the Underworld* 206]

cinch, *n.* A sure, safe, or easy bet to win; a certainty. [1888 *OEDS*]

cinch hand, *n.* Same as LOCK.
[1961 Scarne *Complete Guide* 675]

cinquo primero, *n.* In the card game primero, a sequence of five consecutive cards. Compare SPADILLO.
1714 Lucas *Memoirs* 137. He was a Sharper at Cards, and play'd very well at Primero; in which Game it is to be observ'd, that whoever of the Players has in his Hand *Cinquo Primero,* which is a Sequence of 5 of the best Cards, assisted with Spadillo, which is the Ace of Spades, and counted the best Card, or any other valuable Trump, he is sure to be successful over his Adversary.

claim agent, *n.* Also called CLAIMER. A player who disputes bets and argues that his bet won when it actually did not, or says that a bet made by another player belongs to him.
1978 Clark *Oral Coll.* When the craps table is busy, a *claim agent* will stand next to a player who has a lot of action [several bets] out, and try to grab a winner when the guy with all the action loses track of some of his bets. Or he will dispute bets and try to take what isn't his.

claimer, *n.* **1.** A horse entered in a special race in which all the entrants are for sale.
[1955 Hillis *Pari-Mutuel Betting* 113]
2. Same as CLAIM AGENT.
[1983 Martinet *Oral Coll*]

claiming price, *n.* In horse racing, the price for a horse in a CLAIMING RACE.
[(1951) 1981 Maurer *Lang. of the Underworld* 206]

claiming race, *n. phr.* A horserace in which all the entrants are for sale.
[1955 Hillis *Pari-Mutuel Betting* 113]

class, *n.* **1.** In poker, the rank of a hand in value for claiming the POT, usually in ascending order: HIGH CARD, ONE PAIR, TWO PAIR, THREE OF A KIND, STRAIGHT, FLUSH, FOUR OF A KIND, STRAIGHT FLUSH, ROYAL FLUSH.
[1949 Coffin *Secrets* 157]
2. In racing, the rank of an entry (horse, dog, car driver) among other entrants, usually based on performance in previous races.
[1981 Passer *Winning Big* 157]
[ca. 1850 *DSUE*]

clean dealer, *n.* An efficient card or dice dealer.
1984 Martinet *Oral Coll.* A *clean dealer* is one that deals checks out to the players smoothly and clearly. The payoffs can be read easily by the pit boss.

clean money, *n.* Legally obtained money.
[1978 Skolnick *House of Cards* 4]
→Among managers of casinos, the term is used to indicate that the source of a large bettor's stake is known, and that his money was not obtained illegally.

clean move, *n.* A well-executed cheating maneuver; an adept use of a cheating device or, more commonly, a cleverly concealed misdeal in a card game.
1981 Golad *Oral Coll.* A dealer with *clean moves* doesn't usually show a great deal of expertise in handling cards. He seems to fumble around while he shuffles and deals, but he is dealing out exactly the cards he wants to who he wants.
[(1950) 1981 Maurer *Lang. of the Underworld* 184]

clean out, *v.* **1.** To take all of a person's money in gambling.
2. To lose a BANKROLL.
[1812 *OED*]

clear a suit, *v. phr.* In trump games, to play potentially losing cards on tricks in order to ESTABLISH A SUIT in which all cards led will win tricks.
[1953 Crawford *Consistent Winner* 2]

clearing house, *n.* Same as NUMBERS RACKET.
[(1951) 1981 Maurer *Lang. of the Underworld* 207]

clerk, *n.* A smooth and efficient card dealer. See also CLEAN DEALER.
[1977 Anness *Dummy Up*]

clerk of the scales, *n. phr.* At a racetrack, the official who weighs the jockeys before and after a race.
[1877 *OED* under *scale*]

client, *n.* **1.** Among bookmakers, a person who bets regularly and whose bets are accepted orally, without money exchanging hands.
[1960 Cook *Gambling, Inc.* 270]
2. In horse racing, a person who pays money to TOUTS for information about particular horses or races.
[1978 Ainslie *Complete Guide* 195]

climb, *v.* Of a racehorse, to raise the forelegs abnormally high while running.
[(1951) 1981 Maurer *Lang. of the Underworld* 207]

climber, *n.* A racehorse that runs with the forelegs higher than the rear legs.
[1978 Ainslie *Complete Guide* 286]

clip, *n.* **1.** A device for holding a card up a sleeve or under a table. Compare BUG.
[1968 Adams *Western Words*]
2. In a casino cage, bundled bills held together with paper strips or bands.
1984 Martinet *Oral Coll.* [One casino clerk to another] How much do you have in *clip?* Give me three aces [bundles of one dollar bills] and a bill [one thousand dollars].

clip joint, *n.* An illegal gambling establishment that allows cheaters to flourish.
[1933 *OEDS*]

clock, *v.* To count, especially money: **a.** In a casino, to count all the money on hand in the cage at the beginning and end of a shift.
b. Among poker players, to count the amount of money represented by chips in front of an opponent, especially in TABLE-STAKES games, where the amount of money held by an opponent influences betting patterns.
[1961 Scarne *Complete Guide* 675]

clocker, *n.* In horse racing, a person who times the morning workouts of racehorses and sells the information. [1909 *DA*]

closed card, *n.* In poker, a card dealt face down.
[1953 Crawford *Consistent Winner* 2]

closed game, *n.* In a casino, a table at which no new players are accepted. A player making large bets may request a *closed game,* in which case he is the only patron allowed to play at that table.
[1949 Coffin *Secrets* 175]

closed hand, *n.* In games such as cribbage or draw poker, the dealing of all cards face-down, so that only the holder of each hand may see his own cards.
[1963 Steig *Common Sense* 183]

closed point, *n.* In backgammon, a position occupied by two or more stones or pieces. See also BLOCK (def. 1) and BLOCKED POINT.
[1950 Morehead *Culbertson* 602]

closed poker, *n.* A poker game such as draw, in which all cards are dealt face-down. See also CLOSED HAND.
[1949 Coffin *Secrets* 175]

closer, *n.* A racehorse that sprints well at the end of a race and often passes the leading horse.
[1977 Carroll *Playboy's Illustrated* 191]

close to the vest, *adv. phr.* carefully and cunningly, in cards or dice, where the odds favor the player.
[(1950) 1981 Maurer *Lang. of the Underworld* 184]
[Probably from card playing in which careful players *keep the cards close to the vest*; compare n.d. *DAS*]

clubhouse turn, *n.* The final turn on an oval racetrack, leading into the HOMESTRETCH, or final portion of the race.
[(1951) 1981 Maurer *Lang. of the Underworld* 207]

club poker, *n.* Poker played in a licensed establishment with posted rules and restricted to specific poker games, such as draw and low-ball.
[1968 Wallace *Poker* 212]

clubs, *n. pl.* Also, *plural in form but singular in use.* **1.** One of the four suits in a pack of cards, distinguished by a black trefoil shape for each pip. [1563 *OED*]
2. club, *sing.* a card of this suit.

club stakes, *n.* Established and posted rules for wagering at poker games, normal in licensed gaming houses.
[1949 Coffin *Secrets* 175]

C-note, *n.* Abbreviation for CENTURY. A $100 bill.
[1839 *DA*]

C-note charlie, *n.* A player who uses hundred dollar bills, frequently refusing to use chips. Compare BP and HIGH ROLLER.
[1949 Coffin *Secrets* 175]

coat card, *n.* Also shortened to **coat.** Also spelled **coate.** A king or a queen. Compare FACE CARD and PICTURE CARD.
1680 Cotton *Compleat Gamester* 105. Now if it so happen, that what is turn't up proves an Ace or *Coat-Card,* that is a great advantage to him who won the last trick; for if it be an Ace turn'd up than he reckons five, if a King four, if a Queen three as aforesaid.
[1563 *OED*]
→In regular use until around 1688, then corrupted to COURT CARD, and soon included the KNAVE, or JACK.

coaxer, *n.* In poker, a small raise after an opponent has already raised. The object in making a small raise is to entice the original raiser into raising the bet again, at which point, the player who made the *coaxer* will make a very large raise.
1865 Evans *Gamblers Win* 19. A common thing with first-class players, when they have a high hand, and on betting, some one "raises" them, is to throw in what is called a *"coaxer;"* that is, raising the first "raise" very slightly, in order to get a second one, when they will bet in very heavily.

cock, *v.* In the card game faro, to bet on the same numbered card after a win.
1726 Wilson *Art and Mystery* 62. Some *cock* (or continue) their Card if it wins, others transfer to the losing Card, and many draw a card from their Book every time by chance.

cocked die, *n.* Usually singular, but referred to in the plural, **cocked dice.** A die that comes to rest against an obstruction so that it does not lie flat, but is tilted.
[1949 Blanche *You Can't Win* 23]

cock-eyes, *n. pl.* Three pips turned face up on a pair of dice; in craps, a roll of the number 3.
[1968 Thackrey *Nick the Greek* 95]

cocking, *n.* In the card game faro, a method for doubling a bet after a win.
1843 Green *Exposure* 167. Parolet, sometimes

called *cocking,* is when a punter, being fortunate, chooses to venture both his stake and gains, which he intimates by bending a corner of his card upwards.

cocktail, *n.* A race horse that is not a thoroughbred.
1829 Brown *Turf* 53. Horses, which appear as racers, and are understood not to be thorough-bred, are, in the common language of the turf, denominated *Cocktails.*
[1808 *OED*]
→The more frequent, popular usage meaning "A drink, consisting of spirit mixed with a small quantity of bitters, some sugar, etc." (*OED,* 3) is attested in *DAE, DA* and *OEDS* from 1806 and ascribed first to American usage. The first attestation of a mixed-breed horse is British.

codille, *n. Spanish.* Also spelled **codillio** or **codill.** In the card game ombre, the loss of the game.
1680 Cotton *Compleat Gamester* 72. It is called *Codillio* when the Player is bested, and another wins more Tricks than he.
[1712 *OED*]

coffeehouse, *v.* In poker, to mislead opponents by means of contrived mannerisms and speech.
[1949 Coffin *Secrets* 175]

coffee housing, *n.* In poker, behavior designed to mislead opponents. Compare TELL.
1979 Clark *Oral Coll.* Sometimes hold'em players try different things to hide tells [mannerisms] . . . One way is to act different from your emotions, talk a lot and cut up. But coffee housing only works for a time. After awhile, people start reading your tells that way.
[1953 Crawford *Consistent Winner* 2]

coffee-mill, *n.* In faro, a dishonest dealing box with a crank on top for drawing cards. By manipulating the crank, the dealer may determine the specific card to be dealt from the next three cards at the top of the pack. See also CHEATING BOX.
[1938 Asbury *Sucker's Progress* 12]

cog, *v.* **1.** To throw dice in such a fashion as to cause a designated number to appear face upwards.
[1690 *OED;* The sense "to cheat generally" dates from 1542.]
2. To turn a die with the finger after a cast.
[1950 Morehead *Culbertson* 602]

cogged dice, *n. pl.* Dice that have been altered so that a particular number of pips will come up more often than normal.
1887 Proctor *Chance* 98. Yet every wager by which this result has been obtained, if rightly considered, was as certainly a fraud as a wager laid upon a throw with *cogged dice*. For, what makes wagers on such throws unfair, except the knowledge that with such dice a certain result is more likely than any other?
[1806 *OED*]

cogging, *n.* The act of throwing a die in such a fashion as to cause a specific number to appear face upwards.
1714 Lucas *Memoirs* 83. Shevalier had an excellent knack at *cogging* a Die, and such a command in the throwing, that chalking a Circle on a Table, with its Circumference no bigger than a Shilling, he would at above the distance of 3 Foot throw a Dice exactly into it, which should be either Ace, Deuce, Trey, or what he pleas'd. [1532 *OED*]

coin operated gaming device, *n. phr.* Any mechanical or electronic machine designed to accept coins and to pay coins under certain conditions, especially a slot machine, or pin-ball, video poker, or horserace machine.
[1982 Martin *Introduction* 3]

coin room, *n.* A separate area in a casino cage for weighing and counting coins, and wrapping them in paper tubes. Compare COUNT ROOM and WEIGH.
[1979 Hilton Hotel *Procedures* 2]

cold, *adj.* Of or pertaining to a period of losing bets. See also COLD DICE, COLD HANDS (def. 2, 3), COLD HORSE, and COLD PLAYER.
[(1950) 1981 Maurer *Lang. of the Underworld* 184]

cold bluff, *n.* In poker, a large bet made by a player with a very weak hand. Compare LOCK and TELL.
1980 Clark *Oral Coll.* The strategy behind a *cold bluff* is not necessarily to win that hand by making an outrageous bet. Maybe you want people to see that you have nothing on that hand, so you flash [show the cards]. Later you might be able to pull the same thing when you've got a lock [sure winner]. Or maybe you want to hide a tell [mannerism]. If you fold right after making a *cold bluff,* you can sure cause some raised eyebrows. And that can be useful information for later.

cold call, *n.* In poker, the matching of the amount of money put into the pot by previous bettors who have bet, raised, and re-raised.
[1978 Brunson *How I Made* 527]

cold deck, *n.* **1.** A pack of cards arranged in a specific order, to be used by the dealer who wishes to cheat during one hand.
1859 Green *Gam Tricks* 19. Changing packs, or wringing in *"cold decks,"* is practiced in this game to a great extent, and of course any kind of a hand the person wished is got by this trick.
[1857 *OEDS, DA;* 1868 *DAE*]
2. In poker, a good hand dealt at the beginning of the round so there is no need to draw additional cards.
1889 Farmer *Americanisms* 158. *Cold deck.*—A good hand; *cold* or a *cold deck* in poker phraseology is to get a good hand at first, without the necessity of drawing fresh cards. In thieves' slang it means a prepared pack of cards.
[1889 *DARE*]

cold-deck, *v.* Also written **cold deck.** To introduce a STACKED DECK into a card game. [1884 *OEDS, DARE*]

cold-decker, *n.* A card cheat; one who prepares decks of cards in a specific order for a single deal. [1920 *DA, OEDS*]

cold dice, *n.* In craps, dice that lose for the shooter on several consecutive rolls; dice that are MISSING (not making the point) rather than PASSING (making the point).
[ca. 1961 *Hotel Coll*]

cold game, *n.* A dishonest card or dice game.
[1943 Maurer *Argot*]

cold hand, *n.* **1.** In poker, a hand with cards dealt face up, sometimes without intervening bets.
[1949 Coffin *Secrets* 175]
2. In poker, a weak or worthless hand.
[1981 Golad *Oral Coll*]
3. In bank craps, a series of rolls by one shooter in which none of the players wins much money.
[1983 Martinet *Oral Coll*]

cold horse, *n.* A horse entered in a race that the owner expects not to win.
[1983 Martinez *Gambling Scene* 195]

cold player, *n.* A gambler on a losing streak.
[(1951) 1981 Maurer *Lang. of the Underworld* 207]

cold turkey, *n.* In five-card stud, an instance of two kings (or face cards) dealt at the beginning of the hand, one face down, the other face up.
[1968 Wallace *Poker* 212]

coll, *n.* Also called JOHN or MARK. A victim of professional cheaters; a gull.
See quote at LAMB: 1680 Cotton *Compleat Gamester.* [1674 *OED*]

collector, *n.* **1.** In a poker club, a person who circulates through the room, usually every half hour, to collect a fee from each player on behalf of the club. See also AXE and TIME CUT.
[1968 Wallace *Poker* 212]
2. An agent of a casino who traces players with outstanding debts against the casino and collects money owed in exchange for a percentage of the debt.
[ca. 1961 *Hotel Coll*]

color, *n.* In a casino, chips of denominations larger than one dollar. Chips worth one dollar are usually white, while other denominations are red ($5), green ($25), black ($100) and so on.
[1977 Anness *Dummy Up*]

color, *v.* In the particle construction:
color up, In a casino, to exchange chips of one denomination for chips of a higher denomination. See also COLOR CHANGE and COLOR COMING IN.
[1977 Anness *Dummy Up*]

color change, *n. phr.* In a casino, an announcement by the dealer to the pit boss that a player is exchanging chips of a smaller denomination for chips of a larger denomination. See also CHECK CHANGE and COLOR UP.
[1973 Friedman *Casino Games* 34]

color coming in, *n. clause.* In a casino, an announcement by the DEALER to the PIT BOSS that a player is exchanging chips worth more than one dollar for chips of a still higher denomination. See also COLOR UP.
1978 Clark *Oral Coll.* Some of the things you have to call out to the pit boss, even if he doesn't pay attention to you. *Color coming in* tells the pit boss that a player is turning in a stack of reds [$5 chips] say, and you break them down into greens [$25 chips]. The player doesn't have to lug around a handful of checks and you can keep your rack full of [the denomination most commonly being used at the table].

color for color, *n. phr.* In a casino, an instruction to a dealer to pay the player's bet in the same denominations as those making up the original bet. Compare BARBER POLE.
1978 Clark *Oral Coll.* You might be making pays and coloring up flat bets of three dollars to a red and a white. That's an extreme example. No pit boss would call you on that. But say you have a barber pole [a stack of chips of different denominations and therefore different colors] and the pit boss is standing there. He'll almost always say *"color for color"*. Then you have to break down the stack and cut into it with the same denominations of checks as in the player's stack.

colors, *n. pl.* **1.** A betting system in faro in which a player wagers consistently on red cards, diamonds and hearts.
[1943 Maurer *Argot*]
2. Also called SILKS. In horse racing, the blouse and cap of a jockey, identifying the owner of the horse by color.
[(1951) 1981 Maurer *Lang. of the Underworld* 207]
2. Chips of varying denominations. Because the chips are all the same size, and are usually stacked, colors are used to display the values. In a casino, some normal colors are white ($1), red ($5), green ($25), black ($100). Larger denominations vary in color in different casinos.
[1974 Powell *Verbal Dexterity* 13]

colt, *n.* In horse racing, a horse under five years of age. [1778 *DAE*]

column, *n.* In roulette, one of three rows on a layout containing twelve numbers. Compare DOZEN.
[1964 Wykes *Illustrated Guide* 326]

column bet, *n.* In roulette, a wager on a row of twelve numbers. The usual payment for a win is two to one.
[1961 Scarne *Complete Guide* 675]

combination, *n.* **1.** In cribbage, the point count of all the cards in one hand, determined after playing the hand.

2. In gin rummy, two of three cards required to MELD.
[1958 Fisher *No House Limit* 2]
3. In dice, the numbers which face each other in preparing for a CONTROLLED THROW.
[(1950) 1981 Maurer *Lang. of the Underworld* 184]

combination bet, *n.* **1.** In bank craps, multiple wagers on a single roll of the dice.
[ca. 1961 *Hotel Coll*]
2. Also called a COMBINATION TICKET. In races for dogs and horses, a single wager on one entry to win, place, or show.
[1971 McQuaid *Gambler's Digest* 303]
3. In keno, another name for a COMBINATION TICKET or a WAY TICKET.
[1973 Friedman *Casino Games* 104]

combination strippers, *n. pl.* A deck of cards with some cut shorter and some narrower. See also END STRIPPER and STRIPPER DECK and STRIPPERS.
[ca. 1961 *Hotel Coll*]

combination ticket, *n.* **1.** Also called a WAY TICKET or, sometimes, a COMBINATION BET. In keno, a wager on groups of numbers on the same sheet which are matched with one another for purposes of determining the cost of the ticket and the payment for a winner.
[ca. 1961 *Hotel Coll*]
2. In dog and horse racing, same as a COMBINATION BET.
[1983 Martinez *Gambling Scene* 195]

come, *n.* **1.** Especially in the phrase **on the come.** In poker, a desire or expectation to improve a hand by drawing one or more cards.
1981 Golad *Oral Coll.* A player with a four-flush or a four-card straight has to look at the other bettors. If they know he's betting on the *come,* they will make him pay dearly for that next card.
2. In bank craps, the area on the table layout where a wager is made when a new shooter begins to roll or a new HAND begins. A wager placed there is called a COME BET. See also COME-OUT ROLL.
[1953 Lewis *Sagebrush Casinos* 101]

come, *v.* In the phrases and particle constructions:
come back, In horse racing, to slow down in a race, losing position and allowing other horses to catch up or pass.
[1978 Ainslie *Complete Guide* 286]
[*DSUE*]
come home early, In horse racing, to win a race easily.
[(1951) 1981 Maurer *Lang. of the Underworld* 207]
come in, 1. In poker, to remain in contention for the pot; to CALL a bet.
2. In draw poker, to enter the betting round after another has opened the betting.
1887 Keller *Draw Poker* 23. If he comes in, he must make good the ante and deposit in the pool a sum equal to the raise, if there be any, of the preceding player.
[1887 *DA, DAE*]
come off, In high-low poker, to discard a possible low hand combination in an attempt to draw for high cards. For example, a player holding two aces and a two, three, and four may keep the aces and discard the others.
[1968 Wallace *Poker* 212]

come bet, *n.* In bank craps, a wager that the next roll of the dice will win (numbers 7 or 11) or establish a POINT (numbers 4, 5, 6, 8, 9, or 10) which the shooter will roll again before rolling the number 7. Before establishing a point the numbers 2, 3, or 12 will cause the **come bettor** to lose. After the point is established, a roll of the number 7 will lose the *come bet.*
[(1950) 1981 Maurer *Lang. of the Underworld* 184]

come line, *n.* On a bank craps layout, an area for placing a wager on the next roll of the dice after the shooter has already established a POINT, that is, if the shooter has already rolled the number 4, 5, 6, 8, 9, or 10 and is seeking to roll the same number again before rolling the number 7.
[1973 Binion *Recollections* 7]

come-on, *n.* **1. a.** *Often used attributively.* Among cheaters, the gaining of the confidence of a victim by allowing him to win small bets before taking large bets from him.
[1905 *DA, OEDS*]
b. a swindler. [1905 *DA, OEDS*]
2. Also called an ECHO. In bridge, a signal to a partner to play a particular card or suit.
[1953 Crawford *Consistent Winner* 2]
3. In gin rummy, a discard designed to give false information to the opponent. See also ADVERTISE.
[1953 Crawford *Consistent Winner* 2]

come-out bet, *n.* In bank craps, the first wager of a series of rolls. If the shooter rolls the numbers 2, 3, or 12 on the first roll, the wager is lost; if the shooter rolls the numbers 7 or 11 on the first roll, the wager is won; if any other number (4, 5, 6, 8, 9, or 10) is rolled, then a point is established, and the shooter must again roll that number before rolling the number 7. See also COME BET.
[1961 Scarne *Complete Guide* 676]

come-out roll, *n.* In bank craps, the first cast of dice for a HAND. See also COME-OUT BET.
[1974 Scarne *Dice* 76]

comet, *n.* In stops, a wild card, usually the 9 of diamonds, that has the value of any card declared by the player holding it. See also the CURSE OF SCOTLAND.
[1950 Morehead *Culbertson* 603]

comfort station, *n.* In backgammon, the twelfth point on either side of the board.
[1950 Morehead *Culbertson* 603]

coming out, *n. phr.* In bank craps, an announcement made by the STICKMAN just before

the dice are rolled on a new HAND, intended to inform the players to make their bets and keep their hands above the table, so as not to interfere with the roll. See also FLAT BET.
1978 Clark *Oral Coll.* When the dealer yells "coming out" and taps the stick, all the players know to get their bets down and their hands up. And that is what the announcement is for. But remember, if hands are up, bets are down. Nobody can fiddle the flats [flat bets] if they can't touch them.
[(1950) 1981 Maurer *Lang. of the Underworld* 184]]

coming the change, *n. phr.* Exchanging the deck of cards for a STACKED DECK.
1843 Green *Exposure* 148. And the way this pack, already stocked, is introduced on the table, is as follows (it is called *coming the change*): the dealer will have the stocked pack lying privately in his lap and when the cards they will be using have been cut, and are ready to be dealt, the dealer slips his left hand up to the under edge of the table, as if to receive the pack which is on the table, and which, at the same time, he is drawing to him with his right hand, as if to place it in his left, in which he would hold it to deal from; but in reality he carries his right hand down into his lap, and lodges its contents there, and brings up his left hand over the table, and commences dealing from the stocked [sic] pack.

commission, *n.* **1.** In a SPORTS BOOK or RACE BOOK, a fee charged for taking a wager.
[ca. 1961 *Hotel Coll*]
2. In bank craps and baccarat, a percentage of a bet paid to the house for making certain bets.
[1970 *Baccarat, The Facts*]
3. In cardrooms, a portion of the bets retained by the operator of the game or the house. See also VIGORISH.
[1973 Preston *Play Poker* 166]

commission agent, *n.* Another term for a BOOKMAKER. *Facetious use.*
[1974 Ewart *Flatracing* 149]

commission bet, *n.* **1.** In bank craps, a percentage charged to a player for certain bets, such as a BUY BET or a LAY BET.
[1964 Lemmel *Gambling* 59]
2. In horse racing, a sizeable wager shared by a group of bettors who use an agent to place it as small bets so as not to adversely influence the betting odds.
[(1951) 1981 Maurer *Lang. of the Underworld* 207]

commission marker, *n.* In baccarat, a button or token used by the dealer to indicate a percentage of the wager (usually five percent) that the house collects from the bettors playing and winning on the BANK HAND rather than the PLAYER HAND.
[ca. 1961 *Hotel Coll*]

commission marker box, *n.* In baccarat, an area on the table layout where the dealer places the COMMISSION MARKER for each wager made by each player that wins on the BANK HAND.
[ca. 1961 *Hotel Coll*]

common card, *n.* Also called COMMUNAL CARD and COMMUNITY CARD. A playing card placed face up in the middle of the table for use by all players.
[1949 Coffin *Secrets* 175]

common marriage, *n.* In trump games like bridge, a king and queen of a suit that is not trump.
[1950 Morehead *Culbertson* 603]

common suit, *n.* In trump games like bridge, cards of a suit that is not trump.
[1950 Morehead *Culbertson* 603]

Common Vocabulary. Many words and expressions which we use in our daily lives, from CARD TABLE to "NO DICE!", are shared with or derive from the argot of gamblers and the gaming industry.

"Doing things by the book" is a concept for which people often invoke the phrases: ACCORDING TO HOYLE or the MARQUIS OF QUEENSBERRY, especially in reference to a SQUARE DEAL, a term much popularized in political campaigning and which can be expected when one's adversary has an ACE IN THE HOLE or when someone is using a STACKED DECK (which is not the same as having a FULL DECK).

Very often an undertaking is just a CRAP SHOOT. You may have to BET THE RANCH when the CHIPS ARE DOWN. Or, when you see that you're in a CLIP JOINT, you TAKE YOUR BEST SHOT (even if it's a LONGSHOT) and hope that in the HOMESTRETCH you'll be IN THE MONEY and come in UNDER THE WIRE or, better yet, BREEZE IN and not have to call on your STRONG SUIT or rely upon BEGINNER'S LUCK.

Sometimes you must employ a POKER FACE when you're trying to complete the INSIDE STRAIGHT as a DARK HORSE to FINESSE a HIGH ROLLER to make him FOLD rather than GO THE DISTANCE and force a SHOWDOWN when it might be EVEN MONEY that you HIT THE JACKPOT or GO BUST, especially when your opponent turns out to be a FOUR-FLUSHER. In his DOUBLE DEALING, a SHARK will SWEETEN THE POT or rely upon a SILENT PARTNER to SHORTEN THE ODDS that you will not call his BLUFF.

Everyone wants a PIECE OF THE ACTION when SMART MONEY is ON A ROLL and is likely to SHOOT THE MOON rather than play PENNY-ANTE.

A WELSHER (one who RENEGES or fails to ANTE-UP) is the kind of JOKER who quickly finds himself in a DICEY situation because he hasn't given his adversaries a FAIR SHAKE when the play is for HIGH STAKES.

A HUNCH-PLAYER with no WILD CARDS is usually an ODDS-ON-FAVORITE to try to PARLAY a FULL HOUSE into a SURE THING and, perhaps, BREAK THE BANK unless someone BLOWS THE

WHISTLE because he's caught playing BOTH ENDS AGAINST THE MIDDLE (in which case he may be CLEANED OUT). However, he may be able to BLUFF or to HEDGE HIS BET if he has enough FRONT MONEY.

commoquer, *n.* Earlier spelling of KOMOKER. In panguingue, two cards of the same rank and suit.
[1981 Silverstone *Player's Guide* 138]

communal card, *n.* Same as COMMON CARD.
[1971 Livingston *Poker Strategy* 216]

community card, *n.* Same as COMMON CARD.
[1973 Preston *Play Poker* 167]

comp, *n.* In a casino, a gift given by managers to favored patrons, such as a meal, room, or show reservation. Compare COMPLIMENTARY PLAY, HIGH ROLLER and JUICE.
1977 Cahill *Recollections* 1397. And a part of this is that all, or substantially all, of their expenses are *"comped,"* as the phrase in the industry goes. They're given to them free, just for the purpose of, as the gambler might say, "getting action on their money."
1983 Martinet *Oral Coll.* A high roller can get just about any kind of *comp* he wants. All he has to do is be thick with the man with the pencil [a management person empowered to sign an expense sheet or order services] and his juice [influence] can get the use of a car, room, just about anything.
[1977 *DARE,* n.d. *DAS.* Short for *complimentary* (ticket or pass). Compare 1909 *Dialect Notes* (1914) 4]

comp, *v.* In a casino, to provide favors (free meals, rooms, transportation and so on) for valued patrons.
1983 Martinet *Oral Coll.* You want to *comp* your high rollers so they don't take their business elsewhere. That's why every shift has someone around the joint with the power of the pencil. When somebody with juice [influence] wants something they want it right now.
1978 Stokes *Washington Post* (Nexis). 2/5, B1 Weinburger and Wald also served as the ranking officers of the Nevada Resort Association, Las Vegas casino trade group, which Ritchie now represents as a lobbyist. During trips to Las Vegas, Ritchie was often "comped" by Caesar's management. Ritchie acknowledges accepting free dinners and drinks. "Yes, I was their guest several times," he says, "but I would hope that in view of my 10 years as a prosecutor and an attorney that I couldn't be bought."
[1977 *DARE*]

complete bluff, *n.* In poker, a large bet, especially one that wins the POT, made with a hand that has no value.
[1978 Brunson *How I Made* 527]

complete hand, *n.* In draw poker, a hand in which all five cards contribute to the value of the hand, such as a STRIAGHT, FLUSH, or FULL HOUSE.
[1949 Coffin *Secrets* 175]

completed trick, *n.* In trump games, a round of play to which a player has contributed a card.
[1953 Crawford *Consistent Winner* 2]

complimentary play, *n.* Also called COURTESY PLAY. The act of an owner or executive of a gambling establishment who visits another gambling establishment as a gesture of good will and gambles for a short time. Compare COMP, *n.*
[1974 Scarne *Dice* 464]

concave card, *n.* Also shortened to **concave.** A card trimmed with scissors so that the card is narrow in the middle, wider at the ends. Compare COMBINATION STRIPPERS and CONVEX CARD.
1859 Green *Gam Tricks* 99. All from the eight to the king are cut convex, and all from the deuce to the seven, concave. Thus by cutting the pack in the centre, a convex card is cut; and by taking hold of the cards, in cutting them, at either end of the pack, a *concave card* is secured.
[1825 *OED*]

concave spot, *n.* A pip on a die that is slightly indented and filled with paint, as opposed to a FLUSH SPOT, or a pip painted on the flat surface of the die.
[1974 Scarne *Dice* 23]

concealed hand, *n.* Also shortened to **concealed.**
1. In poker games such as draw, a hand in which the cards are not exposed until the SHOWDOWN, or end of the betting.
[1973 Preston *Play Poker* 167]
2. In meld games such as gin rummy or canasta, a hand in which the cards are not exposed until the player lays all the cards face up at one time to end the hand.
[1953 Crawford *Consistent Winner* 344]

concealed pair, *n.* In seven-card stud, two cards of the same rank dealt face down at the beginning of the hand.
[1978 Brunson *How I Made* 527]

condition, *n.* **1.** In keno, a group of numbers selected in conjunction with another group of numbers on a single ticket.
[1973 Friedman *Casino Games* 107]
2. In panguingue, a group of cards with value. When a player melds such a group, he collects chips immediately from the other players.
[1981 Silverstone *Player's Guide* 138]

conditional, *n.* In banco, a number designated by the operator of the game which requires the player to roll the dice again without removing a wager, or sometimes with an increased wager.
[1890 Quinn *Fools of Fortune* 327]

condition book, *n.* In horse racing, the schedule of a season's races kept by the secretary of the club that owns the racetrack.

[(1951) 1981 Maurer *Lang. of the Underworld* 208]

conditions, *n.* In horse racing, the rules and regulations setting the terms of a race including such things as weight requirements, size of the purse, elegibility of horses for a particular class, and so on.
[1968 Ainslie *Complete Guide* 446]

condone, *v.* In card games such as poker or bridge, to waive a penalty for an irregularity in dealing or play.
[1949 Coffin *Secrets* 175]

confederate, *n.* A member of a cheating ring, especially an accomplice of a CARD CHEAT. See also CAPPER.
[1953 Ralli *Viva Vegas* 94]

contentment, *n.* In ombre, a hazard created by holding five matadors in the same hand.
[1950 Morehead *Culbertson* 603]

continuous bid, *n.* In trump games, the practice of continuing the bidding for a contract until three players PASS, or refuse to make a bid.
[1950 Morehead *Culbertson* 603]

contract, *n.* **1.** In trump games like bridge and whist, the declaration of an intention to win a specified number of tricks, using a particular suit as trump.
[1908 *OEDS*]
2. In high-low poker, a declaration to play a high hand, a low hand, or both a high and a low hand.
[1968 Wallace *Poker* 212]
3. In bank craps, an oral bet declared by a player and honored by the house. The player does not need to produce money unless the bet loses.
[1983 Martinet *Oral Coll*]
4. In bowling, a wager that a player can bowl a line higher than his league average.
[1971 McQuaid *Gambler's Digest* 303]

contract rider, *n.* In horse racing: **1.** a jockey who follows instructions from the owner to lose the race.
[1981 Passer *Winning Big* 234]
2. A jockey who is under contract to ride for a specific stable.
[(1951) 1981 Maurer *Lang. of the Underworld* 208]

control, *n.* **1.** The body of legal restrictions on the operation of gambling establishments.
[1977 Cahill *Recollections* 421]
2. The security system of a casino.
[1981 *Nevada Magazine* 12]

control card, *n.* In trump games like bridge and whist, a card that enables the player holding it to win a trick in a particular suit at a specified point during the play.
[1906 *OEDS*]

controlled shot, *n.* Also called **controlled throw** or **control shot.** A cast of the dice in which the shooter determines the number of pips that will land face upward.
[(1950) 1981 Maurer *Lang. of the Underworld* 184]

controller, *n.* The main runner in a numbers operation, who collects and delivers the money bet with other runners in the organization.
[1961 Scarne *Complete Guide* 676]

convention, *n.* In games like bridge or whist, a standardized signal to a player's partner.
1950 Morehead *Culbertson* 148. A *convention,* in the Bridge sense, is an understanding between partners that a given call will have some definite meaning. (For example, that an opening bid of one no trump will show a hand containing four honor-tricks, rather than some other number.)
[1862 *OEDS*]

conversion, *n.* In a casino, the payment of a winning wager with chips of a different denomination. Compare BUMP INTO. See also COLOR FOR COLOR.
1983 Martinet *Oral Coll.* A dealer normally has to bump into a stack, but he can do a *conversion* on a small stack. Say a player has eight bones [white chips worth $1 each] on a flat bet [a straight bet without odds] and wins. The dealer will leave six aces [dollars] and give him two nickels [five-dollar chips]. That's a partial *conversion.* A complete *conversion* is when the dealer can make a straight exchange of color. If the same player has five nickels out and wins, the dealer will take it and give him two quarters [$25 chips]. That's a total *conversion.*

convex, *n.* A reflector, usually a highly polished coin, placed on the table over which the dealer passes the cards thereby keeping track of opponents' cards.
1865 Evans *Gamblers Win* 39. The *"convex"* is now made in various forms, and has been brought to a high degree of perfection. At first it was a rude affair, consisting simply of a piece of brightly polished silver of a convex form, about the size of a nickel cent.

convex card, *n.* Also shortened to **convex.** A card trimmed with scissors in such a fashion as to make the card taper inward toward the ends, leaving the center of the card wider, the ends narrower. Compare COMBINATION STRIPPERS and CONCAVE CARD.
1859 Green *Gambler's Tricks* 99. All from the eight to the king are cut convex, and all from the deuce to the seven, concave. Thus by cutting the pack in the centre, a *convex card* is cut; and by taking hold of the cards, in cutting them, at either end of the pack, a concave card is secured.
[1873 *OED*]

cooler, *n.* **1.** A prearranged pack of cards; a STACKED DECK.
2. A box or case that holds a prearranged or STACKED DECK of cards.

[1968 Adams *Western Words*]
3. In racing, a horse that does not respond to urging by the jockey.
[(1951) 1981 Maurer *Lang. of the Underworld* 208]

cool-off man, *n.* In a swindle, the person who stays with the victim, talking and sympathizing until he is sure the victim will not call the police.
[1977 Carroll *Playboy's Illustrated* 44]

cooncan, *n.* A game similar to rummy, played with a standard deck from which the 8s, 9s, and 10s have been removed; sometimes dice are added to the play of the game.
[1889 *DARE; DARE* notes spelling variants *conquain, councan*]
[Mexican Spanish *conquian* from *con quien',* "with whom"]

cop, *v.* **1.** To steal chips from a stack being wagered or from a poker pot.
[1961 Scarne *Complete Guide* 676]
2. In the phrases:
cop a mope, Also called **cop a sneak.** To steal away from a place where someone has been cheated; to depart.
[1974 Scarne *Dice* 464]

copper, *v.* In the phrases:
copper a bet, In faro, to place a marker or token (originally a copper penny) atop a wager on a card to indicate a bet with the bank rather than against the bank.
1950 Morehead *Culbertson's Hoyle* 526. A player may *copper* his bet—bet that his card will lose. In this case, he must bet to win or lose; he may not forfeit.
1868 Trumps *Pocket Hoyle* 207. *Coppering a Bet.*—If a player wishes to bet that a card will lose (that is, win for the bank), he indicates this by placing a cent, or whatever may be provided for that purpose, upon the top of his stake. It is called "coppering" because coppers were first used to mark such bets.
[1864 *DA, DAE;* 1892 *OED*]
copper the dice, In dice, to bet the shooter will lose.
[(1950) 1981 Maurer *Lang. of the Underworld* 184]
copper the odds, In faro, to bet that the first, third, fifth (and so on) card will lose, while betting the second, fourth, sixth (and so on) to win.
[1943 Maurer *Argot*]

copper on and copper off, *n. phr.* In faro, a system for moving bets about the layout and cheating the dealer in the process.
[1943 Maurer *Argot*]

corner, *n.* In games like whist and bridge, one point or game of a three-game rubber.
[1825 *OED*]

corner-bend, *n.* A crimp on the corner of a card to distinguish it from others.
1726 Wilson *Art and Mystery* 97. The next [cheating method] is the *Corner-bend,* which is Four Cards turn'd down finely at one corner, a Signal to Cut by.

corner bet, *n.* In roulette, a wager made at the juncture of a block of four numbers.
[1971 McQuaid *Gambler's Digest* 303]

corner flash, *n.* The intentional showing of a corner of the face of a card. The *corner flash* is sometimes used to give information to a confederate at a card table, and sometimes designed to mislead others at a poker table.
[1968 Wallace *Poker* 212]

correct bet, *n.* In bank craps, a wager that is of a size to take proper advantage of the odds offered by the house.
[1983 Martinet *Oral Coll*]

cosmetics, *n. Plural in form but often singular in use.* The markings on the backs of a deck of cards, placed there by the card cheat, usually made with india ink or aniline pencil. See also CUT-OUT and DAUB and PAINT and ROUGE.
[1968 Wallace *Poker* 213]

couch, *n.* In the card game basset, the initial wager placed by a bettor. See also ENJOU. Compare PUNTER.
1714 Lucas *Memoirs* 230. *Couch* is a Term for the first Money that every Punter puts upon each Card, every one that plays having a Book of 13 several Cards before him, upon which he may lay his Money, more or less, according to his Fancy.
[French *couche*]

count, *n.* **1.** In many card games, the value of the number of pips on the cards held in one player's hand.
[1951 Jones *Wilbur Clark's* 2]
2. In a casino, the amount of money or chips in a given place or a given period of time. Depending on the procedure being referred to, the *count* may be the value of the chips in a dealer's RACK, the money in the DROP BOX that is attached to the underside of the table, or the revenue for a shift or a day.
[1977 Anness *Dummy Up*]
3. In card-counting systems used in playing twenty-one, the actual value of the deck at any given point during the play.
[ca. 1961 *Hotel Coll*]

count, *v.* **1.** In twenty-one, to memorize the ranks of all cards played in a hand in order to make large bets when the odds are favorable. See also CARD COUNTING.
[1953 Crawford *Consistent Winner* 344]
2. In the particle construction:
count down, 1. At a casino table, to separate tall stacks of chips into smaller stacks for ease of counting. Compare BANG INTO and CUT INTO.
[1977 Anness *Dummy Up*]
2. In twenty-one, to memorize the values of cards as they are played. See also COUNT, *v.*
[1968 Thackrey *Gambling Secrets* 117]

count card, *n.* In games like twenty-one, a jack, queen, or king of any suit; a FACE CARD; a

COURT CARD.
[1968 Wallace *Poker* 213]

count down, *n.* **1.** At a casino table, the act of separating tall stacks of chips into smaller stacks for ease of counting.
[1977 Anness *Dummy Up*]
2. In twenty-one, the act of memorizing the values of cards as they are played.
[1968 Thackrey *Gambling Secrets* 117]

counter, *n.* **1.** Also called a CARD COUNTER. In twenty-one, a player who memorizes all cards played and changes betting patterns according to the shift in odds.
[1974 Powell *Verbal Dexterity* 4]
2. Also called the MAN and STONE. In board games such as backgammon, a piece moved around the board as determined by the roll of the dice. [1605 *OED*]
3. In card games, a card with a point value different from the face value of the card. In hearts, for example, the queen of spades has a value different from other queens.
[1953 Crawford *Consistent Winner* 334]
4. Also called a CHIP or CHECK. A token representing monetary value used for purposes of wagering. [1579 *OED*]
5. A player who habitually counts his chips, even when he has not used any since he last counted.
6. In craps, a SYSTEMS BETTOR. *Facetious use.* 1985 Martinet *Oral Coll.* Every throw of the dice is a new roll, that is, there can be no prediction of what specific number will be rolled at any given time. But you still see systems players recording every roll, then suddenly placing a bet on occasion. These *counters* are welcome at the table if real bettors have enough room. But most *counters,* they are sometimes called *dice counters,* just take up time and space. They don't win any more or less than other players, that's why calling them *counters* is a joke.

counter game, *n.* Any gambling game such as keno, bingo, or a place such as a SPORTS BOOK, or RACEBOOK that requires patrons to bring their wagers to a window or counter.
[1957 *Nevada Gaming Regulations* 33]

counting device, *n.* A mechanical or electronic recorder in a slot machine that enumerates the number of coins dropped into the slot, the number of times the handle is pulled, and the number of coins paid out. See also DROP METER.
[1978 Alexander *Glossary* 4]

count room, *n.* In a casino, the area where money from the table DROP BOXES is counted. The *count room* is in a separate area from the COIN ROOM, where coins from the slot machines are counted.
[1961 Scarne *Complete Guide* 676]

country straight, *n.* Also called an OPEN-ENDED STRAIGHT. In poker, four consecutively numbered cards which can become a successful straight by drawing the next card higher or the next card lower to become five consecutively numbered cards. Compare INSIDE STRAIGHT.
[1978 Brunson *How I Made* 527]

count team, *n.* In a casino, the group of employees who count the money from each DROP BOX and record the contents of each separately. The *count team* is normally made up of representatives from the cage, accounting department, and an outside spectator from another department in the casino.
[1977 Nevada Gaming Control *Internal*]

coup, *n. French.* **1.** A successful wager.
[1823 Persius *Rouge et Noir* 164]
[(1951) 1981 Maurer *Lang. of the Underworld* 208]
2. In chemine de fer or faro, one completed turn. 1843 Green *Exposure* 166. *Coup,* any two cards dealt alternately to the right or left.

coup, *v.* To win a large bet.
[(1951) 1981 Maurer *Lang. of the Underworld* 208]

court card, *n.* A jack, queen, or king; a FACE CARD.
[1577 *OED* as "coate card"; 1641 *OED* as "court card"; corrupted to and regularly used as *court card* since around 1650]

courtesy play, *n.* Same as COMPLIMENTARY PLAY.
[1953 Lewis *Sagebrush Casinos* 202]

court-skin, *n.* Also called a PAINT-SKIN. A jack, queen, or king; a FACE CARD. *Obsolete.*
[1943 Maurer *Argot*]

cover, *v.* To accept a bet by matching the amount of money proposed by another player.
[1857 *OED*]

cover-all, *n.* In bingo, a game that a player wins when all the numbers on his card have been called by the announcer.
[1973 Clark *Oral Coll*]

covered square, *n.* In bingo, the center square on a bingo card, usually labeled "free square" and covered before the game begins.
[ca. 1961 *Hotel Coll*]

cowboy, *n.* **1.** In cards, a king of any suit.
[1949 Coffin *Secrets* 175]
2. A gambler who bets recklessly and plays fast, sometimes making simple errors.
[(1950) 1981 Maurer *Lang. of the Underworld* 184]

crab, *n.* In hazard, the lowest cast of the dice, two aces. [1768 *OED*]

crabs, *n.* **1.** Also spelled CRAPS (def. 2). In craps, a throw of the numbers 2, 3, or 12.
[1938 Asbury *Sucker's Progress* 40]
2. In playing cards, the three of any suit.
[1981 Golad *Oral Coll*]

crack the nut, *v. phr.* Among professional gamblers and casino managers, to win enough money to meet daily expenses.
[1961 Smith and Noble *Quit Winners* 53]

crackle the dice, *v. phr.* To rattle dice together as though shaking them, while holding at least one

die with a specific face upward. Compare BARR DICE. [ca. 1961 *Hotel Coll*]
[A corruption of CACKLE the dice.]

crank-box, *n.* A dealing box in faro designed to let the dealer select particular cards at will. Compare DEALING BOX and SHOE.
1843 Green *Exposure* 190. This box, which is taken to be so very fair, is as full of deception as any other, and is called the *crank-box*; and when the cards are shut up in it, and the crank turned, they come out one by one until all are out.

crank game, *n.* Any game such as wheel of fortune, roulette, or big six wheel that is resolved after a single event, such as the turning of the wheel or a cast of dice. Such games move quickly and are designed to resolve a wager quickly and simply.
[ca. 1961 *Hotel Coll*]

crank-store, *n.* Also called a GRIND STORE. A gambling establishment with slot machines only, in which no games that require a dealer or other person are played.
[1973 Clark *Oral Coll*]

crap dealer, *n.* In bank craps, an employee who collects losing wagers, pays winners, and announces the numbers as the dice are rolled.
[1961 Scarne *Complete Guide* 672]

crap-eleven, *n.* In bank craps, a PROPOSITION BET that the next roll of the dice will result in the number 2, 3, 11, or 12. Abbreviated as C AND E.
[ca. 1961 *Hotel Coll*]

crap game, *n.* **1.** Same as CRAP SHOOTING (def. 1). [1890 *OEDS*]
2. Any risky undertaking; CRAP SHOOTING (def. 2).
[1930 *OEDS*]

crap hustler, *n.* **1.** The operator of a crap game who offers wagers to players at less than true odds.
[(1950) 1981 Maurer *Lang. of the Underworld* 184]
2. A person who cajoles money from other craps players or brings players to a game and plays with their money, keeping a share of all of the winnings.
[1983 Martinet *Oral Coll*]

crap layout, *n.* In bank craps, the felt playing surface on a table with spaces for the various wagers marked on them. The player wishing to make a particular bet places his money or chips on the appropriately marked space. See also LAYOUT.
[1953 Lewis *Sagebrush Casinos* 11]

crap out, *v.* Also shortened to **crap**. Of the shooter in craps, to cast one of the numbers 2, 3, or 12.
[1891 *DA*, 1909 *OEDS*]
→Players (not dealers) use the term to mean to cast the number 7 when attempting to roll for the second time one of the numbers 4, 5, 6, 8, 9, or 10.

craps, *n. Plural in form but sometimes singular in use.* **1.** In craps, a roll of the numbers 7 or 11.
1890 Quinn *Fools* 277. The numbers 7 and 11 are called "craps."
2. Usually spelled CRABS (def. 1). In craps, a roll 2, 3, or 12. [1890 *OEDS*]
3. a gambling game resembling hazard in which players bet on the roll of dice. See also SHOOT (def. 2). Compare ALLEY CRAPS, ARMY CRAPS, BANK CRAPS, BLANKET CRAPS, CASINO CRAPS, and STAGE CRAPS.
[*OED* records the term *crabs* as early as 1768. The term was taken into French and used as *creps, crebs,* to refer to a form of the game *hazard.* A form of the French game was introduced into New Orleans around 1840, and the date of 1843 is listed as the earliest usage in American English of *craps* by *DA, DAE,* and *OEDS.*]

crap shoot or **crapshoot,** *n.* any risky undertaking; CRAP GAME (def. 2).
[1975 William Flanagan *Business Week* 7/7, 60; but presumed to be much earlier; probably a back formation from CRAP SHOOTING]
→Normally figurative use, compare CRAP SHOOTER (def. 2) and CRAP SHOOTING (def. 2) which show both literal and figurative uses.

crap shooter, *n.* **1.** Also written **crap-shooter** or **crapshooter**. One who plays craps.
[1895 *DAE, DA, OEDS*]
2. Especially **crapshooter**. One who undertakes any risky activity, especially in business or politics.
[1975 William Flanagan *Business Week* 12/29, 117; but presumed to be much earlier]

crap shooting, *n.* Also written **crapshooting** or **crap-shooting. 1.** Playing at a game of craps.
[1885 *OEDS*]
2. The undertaking of any risky activity, especially in business or politics.
[1975 *Chemical Week* 9/25, 40; but presumed to be much earlier]

credit line, *n.* Also shortened to LINE (def. 5). In a casino, the amount of money a player has deposited in the casino cage, or the amount of money the casino manager is willing to advance to a player.
[1983 Martinet *Oral Coll*]

credit play memorandum, *n.* Also called a MARKER. In a casino, a slip that is filled out at a table and signed by the player when the pitboss advances chips to him. The *credit play memorandum* is deposited in the casino cage and returned to the player when the debt is paid. See also RIM CARD and TABLE CARD.
[1957 *Nevada Gaming Regulations* 33]

credit slip, *n.* In a casino, a printed form on which a pit boss and a casino cage employee note a shipment of chips between a table and the cage.
[1957 *Nevada Gaming Regulations* 31]

crib, *n.* **1.** Also called WIDOW. In cribbage, the four cards, two from each player, set aside before beginning play. The *crib* belongs to the dealer, who counts the score of the *crib* after playing the hand.
1680 Cotton *Compleat Gamester* 78. Lastly you look upon your *Crib*, that is the two Cards apiece laid out at first, which is the Dealers.
[1680 *OED*]
2. Short for CRIBBAGE.
[1885 *OED*]
3. A gambling dive; a dissolute house for gambling and prostitution. [1901 *DA*]

cribbage, *n.* A game at cards played by two or four people using a 52-card pack and a board with sixty-one holes for each player or team, on which the score is recorded by using pegs.
[1630 *OED*]

cribbage board, *n.* An oblong board with two rows of sixty-one holes on which players keep score with two sets of pegs, in the game of cribbage. [1785 *OED*]

cribbage cards, *n. pl.* The playing cards used for cribbage. [1769 *OED*]

cribbage player, *n.* A person who plays at cribbage. [1824 *OED*]

cribbage-table, *n.* A specially designed gaming table on which cribbage is played.
[1755 *OED*]

crimp, *n.* A bend made in a playing card so it can be recognized from the back. See also WAVE. Compare CORNER-BEND.
[1961 Scarne *Complete Guide* 676]

crimp, *v.* To bend the corner of a playing card or crease it so that it can later be recognized while face down. See also WAVE.
[1961 Scarne *Complete Guide* 676]

crimp artist, *n.* Also called a **crimper**. A card cheat who bends the corners of certain cards so they may be recognized when face downwards.
[1968 Adams *Western Words*]

crooked-honest system, *n.* Also called CROSSLIFT or CROSSFIRE. In poker, a cheating method in which two players in collusion catch an honest player between them and raise each others' bets until the honest player withdraws from the hand.
[1968 Wallace *Poker* 213]

cross, *n.* The act of cheating a cheater.
[*DAS, DSUE;* 1974 Scarne *Dice* 262]

cross, *v.* **1.** To win against a cheater by cheating him.
[(1950) 1981 Maurer *Lang. of the Underworld* 184]
[*DAS, DSUE*]
2. In the phrase:
cross fill, In a casino, to transfer chips from one gaming table to another without sending chips to or from the cage.
[1982 Martin *Introduction* 3]
→*Cross filling* is illegal in Nevada gambling.

cross colors, *n. pl. Plural in form, singular in use.* In faro, a betting system in which the player switches his bet to the opposite color after two cards of the same color are drawn.
[1943 Maurer *Argot*]

cross fill, *n.* In a casino, the act of transferring chips from one gaming table to another without sending chips to or from the cage.
[1978 Alexander *Glossary* 5]
→It is illegal to use a *cross fill* in the state of Nevada, but not currently illegal in New Jersey.

crossfire, *n.* Same as the CROOKED-HONEST SYSTEM.
1902 Andrews *Artifice* 19. Advantages without dexterity can be taken in almost any card game when two or more players are in collusion. . . . Again, the allies may resort to "*crossfiring,*" by each raising until the other players drop out.

crosslift, *n.* Same as the CROOKED-HONEST SYSTEM. [1968 Wallace *Poker* 213]

crossroader, *n.* A cheater who moves from one gambling establishment to another, looking for opportunities to cheat the house.
[1961 Smith and Noble *Quit Winners* 20]

crossruff, *n.* **1.** In trump games, the alternate trumping of cards of different suits between partners, each leading the suit which the other renounces. [1862 *OED*]
2. An obsolete game at cards.
[1592 *OED*]

crossruff, *v.* In trump games, to lead a card of a suit that a partner has renounced, and having a card from a renounced suit led in turn, enabling each of the partners to alternate in taking tricks.
[1905 *OEDS*]

croupe, *n.* The overseer of a card game, or several games, who watches to prevent errors in the play or in the payoffs.
1726 Wilson *Art and Mystery* 60. *Croupe*—A person to take care no Mistakes are made by the Dealers, either by overlooking the Cards or miscounting the Cash.
[1728 *OED* as *croup*]

croupere, *n. French.* In the card game basset, the banker's assistant, who collects lost bets and pays winning bets. Compare PIT BOSS.
1714 Lucas *Memoirs* 229. . . . *Croupere,* who is one that is assistant to the Talliere [banker], and stands by to supervise the losing Cards; that when there is a considerable Company at Play, he may not lose by over-looking any thing that might turn to his Profit.

croupier, *n.* Also spelled **crouper, croupee, crowpee. 1.** A confederate who stands behind a gambler, giving advice and helping to manage the gambler's bets. *Obsolete.*
[1707 *OED*]
2. An employee of a gaming house who sweeps lost bets from the roulette table, originally by means of a wicker rake.
[1731 *OED*]

3. In a faro game, an assistant to the banker who watches the table to help keep track of several bets.
1843 Green *Exposure* 166. At public tables, the banker, according to the number of punters, has two, three, or more assistants, called *croupiers,* whose business it is to watch the games of the several punters.

crowns, *n. pl.* A fifth suit sometimes added to a standard 52-card pack, making a 65-card pack. Compare EAGLES and FIVE-SUIT PACK.
[1950 Morehead *Culbertson* 604]

crying call, *n.* In poker, the act of equalling the wager of a previous bettor, or CALLING, while complaining about the size of the bet.
[1978 Brunson *How I Made* 528]

cub, *n.* In georgia skin, the dealer's card.
[1981 Jenkins *Johnny Moss*]

cubes, *n. pl.* Dice.
[1890 Quinn *Fools of Fortune* 194]
[n.d. *OED*]

cucumber, *n.* An especially naive or inexperienced gambler.
[1974 Scarne *Dice* 465]

cue bid, *n.* Also written **cue-bid.** In games like bridge and whist, a signal to one's partner indicating a strong suit.
[1932 *OEDS*]

cue-box, *n.* In faro, a miniature layout on which an assistant to the banker records each card as it is played. See also CASE-KEEPER and CUE KEEPER.
1868 Trumps *Pocket Hoyle* 207. Case-Keeper.—The person who marks game on the *cue-box.*
1868 Trumps *Pocket Hoyle* 206. Another mode of keeping the game, common in the Northern States, is by a *"cue-box,"* by which the different stages of the game are correctly noted by one of the players, or by a regular "cue-keeper," who is usually attached to the bank.

cue card, *n.* In faro, a printed sheet with the layout of the faro table printed on it, with which a player can record the cards as they are dealt.
[1892 *DA*]

cue keeper, *n.* In faro, the assistant to the banker who records each card played on a miniature layout designed for that purpose.
1868 Trumps *Pocket Hoyle* 206. Another mode of keeping the game, common in the Northern States, is by a "cue-box," by which the different stages of the game are correctly noted by one of the players, or by a regular *"cue-keeper,"* who is usually attached to the bank.
[1864 *DA*]

cull, *v.* In poker, to cluster a group of cards together and select some for secreting for later use.
[1968 Wallace *Poker* 213]

cup, *n.* A receptacle, often leather covered, used for shaking and throwing dice in certain games. See also DICE CUP.
[(1950) 1981 Maurer *Lang. of the Underworld* 184]

cup and wire worker, *n. phr.* A slot-machine cheat who used a short piece of tubing and a spoon or stiff wire to prop open the payout door of a slot machine and allowing all the coins to drop out. *Obsolete.*
[1941 Fair *Spill the Jackpot* 38]
→No slot machines were built to accommodate the method after the late 1940s.

curfew, *n.* In poker, an agreed-upon time to stop playing.
[1968 Wallace *Poker* 213]

curse of Mexico, *n.* The two of spades.
[1949 Coffin *Secrets* 175]

curse of Scotland, *n.* The nine of diamonds.
1816 Singer *Researches* 271 . . . the nine of diamonds [is called] the *Curse of Scotland* because every ninth monarch of that nation was a bad King to his subjects. I have been told by old people, that this card was so called long before the Rebellion in 1745, and therefore it could not arise from the circumstance of the Duke of Cumberland's sending orders accidentally written upon this card, the night before the battle of Culloden, for General Campbell to give no quarter.
[1710 *DSUE,* 1715 *OED;* perhaps ultimately from the similarity of design of the nine of diamonds and the coat of arms of Sir John Dalrymple (1648-1707), widely held to be responsible for the massacre of the Macdonald clan at Glencoe in 1692, supporter of the Act of Union and councilor to William III of England]

curve, *n.* On a bank-craps table, a corner of the layout on the STICKMAN'S side of the table, as opposed to the hook, a corner on the BOXMAN'S side of the table.
[1983 Martinet *Oral Coll*]

cushion, *n.* On a casino craps table, the quilted wall at either end of the table, against which the dice are rolled, causing the dice to bounce irregularly, thereby reducing opportunities for a CONTROLLED SHOT.
[1983 Martinet *Oral Coll*]

cut, *n.* **1.** The act of dividing a deck of playing cards into two or more packets as part of the process of shuffling, and which are reassembled in reverse order before the dealer distributes the cards. [1598 *OED*]
2. Also called the RAKE. A percentage of or share of money wagered which is turned over to the operator of a game or the establishment in which the game takes place. See also CUT THE POT.
[(1950) 1981 Maurer *Lang. of the Underworld* 184]

cut, *v.* **1.** To divide a deck of playing cards into two or more packets as part of the process of shuffling. The packet from the lower part of the deck is then placed atop the deck before the

dealer distributes the cards.
[1532 *OED*]
2. In the phrases and particle constructions:
cut checks, In a casino, to reform a stack of chips into smaller stacks for ease of counting. Compare BANG INTO and BUMP INTO.
[ca. 1961 *Hotel Coll*]
cut for high card, To lift a small packet from a deck of cards in an attempt to turn up a higher ranked card than an opponent can turn up.
[1971 Livingston *Poker Strategy* 216]
cut in, To join a card game already in progress, such as whist, by taking the place of a player who is retiring from the game. See also CUT OUT.
[1760 *OED*]
cut into, Also, to SIZE. Of a casino dealer, to place a taller stack of chips next to a shorter stack, then remove the excess to leave both stacks the same size. Compare BANG INTO and BUMP INTO.
[1977 Anness *Dummy Up*]
cut out, To retire from a game of cards already in progress, such as whist, in order to allow another player into the game. See also CUT IN.
[1771 *OED*]
cut the action, In sports books, to reduce the amount of betting on a particular event by changing the odds or the SPREAD.
[1968 Thackrey *Nick the Greek* 26]
cut the pot, In poker, to withdraw money from a pot to pay for refreshments or to pay the operator of a game for the use of his facilities. See also RAKE.
[1949 Coffin *Secrets* 175]
cut tokes, In a casino, to divide the tips or gratuities received from patrons among the dealers.
[1977 Anness *Dummy Up*]
cut up a score, Same as CUT UP A TOUCH.
[1961 Scarne *Complete Guide* 676]
cut up a touch, Same as CUT UP A SCORE. To divide money obtained by cheating among the members of a cheating ring.
[ca. 1961 *Hotel Coll*]
cut up jackpots, To reminisce about past games, especially those involving large amounts of money.
[1950 Morehead *Culbertson* 604]

cut card, *n.* Also called a SWEAT CARD. On a casino twenty-one table, a rectangular piece of plastic or a joker used by a patron to divide the cards into two packets. The dealer then places the lower packet atop the upper packet and begins to deal.
[1977 Anness *Dummy Up*]

cut dice, *n. pl.* Dice that have been altered by shaving, drilling, or otherwise physically altering their shape or weight. Compare CUT EDGES.
[1711 *OED*]

cut edges, *n.* Also called BEVELS. Dice that have been shaved along one or more edges so they roll past some numbers more easily than others.
[ca. 1961 *Hotel Coll*]

cut-out, *n.* A card or cards marked by scraping the back or putting bleach spots on the back. See also COSMETICS.
[1961 Scarne *Complete Guide* 676]

cutout work, *n.* Markings placed on cards by scraping away part of the design on the back. See also BLOCKOUT WORK and COSMETICS.
[ca. 1961 *Hotel Coll*]

cutter, *n.* A person in charge of a gambling game whose responsibility is to remove a share of the winnings for the proprietor of the gambling operation. Compare DEAD EVEN and FADER and SHOOTER and VIGORISH.
1981 Clark *Oral Coll.* Barboot is a fast, two-dice game played by a lot of old Jewish and Greek immigrants. You can bet with the shooter or the fader and it's a dead even game, except the *cutter* takes five percent of the win for a house vig.
[(1950) 1981 Maurer *Lang. of the Underworld* 184]

cutting, *n.* The act of dividing a deck of cards into two parts, then placing the bottom packet atop as part of the process of shuffling.
1836 Eidrah *Hoyle Famil* 3. *Cutting* is the next operation, and it consists merely in lifting from the top of the pack a portion of the cards, which must be more than a trick, generally from one-fourth to three-fourths of the pack, and placing that portion under the remainder.
[1532 *OED*]

cutting for the deal, *n. phr.* The act of drawing for highest card or lowest card to determine the player who will deal the cards first. Compare CUT FOR HIGH CARD.
1836 Eidrah *Hoyle Famil* 3. In *cutting for the deal,* each person lifts a few cards from the pack, and shews the undermost card of the parcel he lifted; and whoever shews the lowest card (which is an ace in this case) is entitled to deal. If two have cards equally low, they each drop two or three, and the person then shewing the lowest deals. To save trouble, it is usual in large companies, instead of cutting, to deal one card to each party, and the person getting the lowest is dealer.

D

D, *n.* Also called DOG (def. 2). In poker, the fourth player to the left of the dealer. Compare A, B, C, E, F, G, H.
[1949 Coffin *Secrets* 176]
→Used in written descriptions of poker games, not used orally.

daily double, *n.* Abbreviated DD. Also called SWEET DEEDEE. In dog and horse racing, a pool which can be won by picking the winner of two consecutive races.
[1955 Hillis *Pari-Mutuel Betting* 113]
→At some racetracks, the *daily double* is offered for the first two races. At other tracks, the proposition is offered on the second and third race.

daisy-cutter, *n.* A racehorse.
[1791 *OED*]

dame, *n.* In poker, a name for the queen of any suit.
[1949 Coffin *Secrets* 176]

damnation alley, *n.* In roulette, the column of twelve numbers on the left-hand side of the LAYOUT.
[1979 Newman *Dealer's Special* 69]
[So called because the column is sometimes out of the peripheral vision of the dealer as he watches the wheel, and a player may try to slip a bet onto the layout in that area after the ball falls into a slot.]

dark, *adj.* Of a track during the racing season, noting a day on which no races are run.
[1978 Ainslie *Complete Guide* 287]

dark bet, *n.* In poker, a wager made before looking at the cards; a BLIND BET. See also BLIND (def. 1)
[1968 Wallace *Poker* 213]

darken, *v.* **1.** In draw poker, to bet without looking at the cards drawn, usually a singleton.
[1971 Livingston *Poker Strategy* 216]
2. In cards, to bet on a bluff or a hand that cannot be improved.
[1973 Preston *Play Poker* 167]

dark horse, *n.* A horse not favored to win a race. See also UNDERDOG.
1829 Brown *Turf* 83. Forth's two horses were nothing thought of, particularly Frederick, the winner. He was a *dark horse*, who shed an unpleasant and irksome light upon the visual orbs of the knowing ones by winning the great stake just mentioned.
[1831 *OED*]

dash, *n.* **1.** In horse racing, a race of one heat only, when normal procedures call for two or more heats to determine a winner.
[1881 *DA, OED*]
2. In horse racing, a sprint race of six furlongs or less.
[1971 McQuaid *Gambler's Digest* 304]

daub, *n.* **1.** A paste or fluid used to mark the backs of cards for purposes of cheating. See also COSMETICS and PAINT and ROUGE.
[1949 Coffin *Secrets* 176]
2. A paste put on one face of a die to make the die come to rest on that side at the end of a roll. Compare BARR DICE.
[1973 Binion *Recollections* 6]

daub, *v.* To mark the backs of playing cards with ink or some other fluid. See also COSMETICS.
[ca. 1961 *Hotel Coll*]

dauber, *n.* A card cheat who marks recognizable patterns on the backs of playing cards with ink or some other fluid. Compare CARD-BENDER.
[1953 Fairfield *The Sucker* 15]

DD, *n.* Abbreviation for DAILY DOUBLE.
[1968 Thackrey *Nick the Greek* 228]

dead card, *n.* **1.** In games like poker and twenty-one, a card that has been played or inadvertently exposed.
2. In faro, the first or last card drawn from the box, or an indication that all four cards of a rank have been drawn. See also SODA CARD and HOCK CARD.
[1901 *DA*]

dead even, *adj.* **1.** Of no advantage to betting one side or the other. Compare CUTTER and FADER and SHOOTER.
1981 Clark *Oral Coll.* Barboot is a fast, two-dice game played by a lot of old Jewish and Greek immigrants. You can bet with the shooter or the fader and it's a *dead even* game, except the cutter takes five percent of the win for a house vig.
2. Holding the same amount of a stake that a player began with, after having won and lost over a period of time.

deadfall, *n.* Also written **dead fall** and **dead-fall.** Also called a WOLF TRAP. A gambling establishment in which cheating is common.
[1837 *DA, DAE, OEDS*]

dead fish, *n.* A player who makes small wagers in an attempt to play for a longer period of time.
[1963 Riddle and Hyams *Weekend Gambler* 9]

[He is called such because the odds in honest games are against the player over a long period of time.]

dead hand, *n.* **1.** In card games, a hand made unplayable because of a foul, too many or too few cards dealt, or other misdeal.
[1963 Steig *Common Sense* 183]
2. In poker, in a table-stakes game, an individual's hand made unplayable because the player has bet the last of his money.
[1949 Coffin *Secrets* 176]

dead head, *n.* An observer of a game who cannot play because he has lost all his money.
[(1950) 1981 Maurer *Lang. of the Underworld* 185]

dead heat, *n.* In racing, a tie between two or more entries that reach the finish line simultaneously. Compare PHOTO FINISH.
[1840 *OED*]

dead in the pot, *n. phr.* In poker, any indication that a player still in contention for the pot has no chance to win.
[1973 Preston *Play Poker* 167]

dead man, *n.* In whist, the partner of the winner of the contract. Compare DUMMY.
[1786 *OED*]

dead man's hand, *n.* In poker, a hand with a pair of aces and a pair of eights.
[1909 *Century Dict. Supplement,* at *hand*; 1944 *DA,* so called because it was the hand held by Wild Bill Hickock when he was shot by Jack McCall in the Mann-Lewis saloon in Deadwood, South Dakota on August 2, 1876.]

dead money, *n.* In bank craps, chips or cash left on the LAYOUT, overlooked after a bet has been lost or change has been made.
[1983 Martinet *Oral Coll*]

dead-number dice, *n.* Also called FIRST FLOP DICE. Heavily loaded dice which do not roll easily. Compare BARR DICE.
[1974 Scarne *Dice* 288]

deadpan, *n.* Also written **dead pan** or **dead-pan.** In poker, an expressionless face on a player; a POKER FACE.
[1934 *DAS*; 1933 *OEDS*, 1928 *OEDS* as adjective]

dead spot, *n.* In bank craps, the field area on the layout. See also BLIND SPOT (def. 2).
[1983 Martinet *Oral Coll*]
[So called because dealers sometimes neglect bets on that area in the flurry of paying bets on the pass line.]

dead table, *n.* In a casino, a gaming table that is open and has a dealer standing by, but no players.
1983 Martinet *Oral Coll.* So if no one is playing at a table and the table is open, that's a *dead table.*

deadwood, *n.* Also called TIMBER. In poker, the discard pile; used cards that are out of play.
[1949 Coffin *Secrets* 176]

deal, *v.* **1.** To distribute cards or domino tiles to players at the beginning of a game.
[1529 *OED*]
2. To operate any table game in a casino. A person may *deal* craps or a big-six wheel, in addition to cards.
[(1950) 1981 Maurer *Lang. of the Underworld* 185]
3. In the phrases and particle constructions:
deal from the bottom, To distribute cards from the bottom of the pack, a dishonest activity. Compare BOTTOM DEALER.
[1943 Conboie *Lincoln Slim* 205]
deal off, In poker, to distribute the cards for the last hand of the session.
[1949 Coffin *Secrets* 176]
deal out, In poker or twenty-one, to omit a player from the hand for one round.
[1949 Coffin *Secrets* 176]

deal, *n.* **1.** The distribution of playing cards or dominoes. [1674 *OED*]
2. In a casino, the operation of any of a variety of games, not restricted to card games.
[1973 Clark *Oral Coll*]
3. The interval of time from the beginning of one hand to the beginning of the next; the complete cycle of play for the events in a hand of poker or a hand of craps. *Obsolete.*
[1607 *OED*]
4. In faro, the completed set of twenty-five turns of two cards each, exposing two cards each time. The first and last cards are not used.
1868 Trumps *Pocket Hoyle* 207. The dealer is said to have made a *deal,* when he has dealt out the whole deck.

deal card, *n.* In faro, the card on top of the deck before play begins. See also SODA CARD. Compare DEALER'S CARD.
1843 Green *Exposure* 194. The top card, when the deal is first commenced, is called the *deal card*; this card neither wins nor loses, and on that account is sometimes called the soda card.
[1843 *DA*, under *soda*]

dealer, *n.* The person who conducts a game at cards or dice, or a table game such as BIG-SIX, WHEEL-OF-FORTUNE or ROULETTE.
[1600 *OED*, as "distributor of cards"]

dealer-advantage, *n.* In poker, the favorable odds that come with being the last person to act in the betting process. The player with the *dealer-advantage* may not be the dealer if that person has already retired from the betting, but is the last to wager and can modify his actions after the previous bettors act.
[1968 Wallace *Poker* 213]

dealer's advantage, *n. phr.* Also called DEALER'S EDGE. In twenty-one, reference to the fact that the player may draw and exceed twenty-one points before the dealer draws and exceeds twenty-one points. Although both have losing hands, the player has lost first and loses his wager.
[ca. 1961 *Hotel Coll*]

dealer's card, *n. phr.* In faro, the second card dealt, which wins for the dealer and all those who took a dealer's bet on that card. Compare DEAL CARD and SODA CARD.
1978 Clark *Oral Coll.* The first card is soda, or deal card, and wins for nobody. The second card is *dealer's card* and wins for everybody who bet that way, not just the dealer. The third card is the player's card, and wins for everybody who bet that way, that is, for everybody who had an uncoppered bet on the layout for that card or that figure.

dealer's choice, *n. phr.* A declaration by the dealer as to what game will be played.
[1949 Coffin *Secrets* 176]

dealer's edge, *n. phr.* Same as DEALER'S ADVANTAGE.
[ca. 1961 *Hotel Coll*]

dealer's hitting rule, *n. phr.* In casino twenty-one, a requirement that a dealer must draw a card if the total value of his cards is sixteen or less, and must not draw another card if the total value on his hand is seventeen or more. In some casinos, the dealer must draw a card if his first two cards are a six and an ace, SOFT SEVENTEEN.
[ca. 1961 *Hotel Coll*]

dealer's room, *n. phr.* In a casino, an area, from which patrons are excluded, set aside for dealers who have been relieved from their stations for a short period.
[ca. 1961 *Hotel Coll*]

dealing, *n.* The act of distributing cards to each player in a card game.
1836 Eidrah *Hoyle Famil* 3. *Dealing* is distributing the cards, and is done by giving to each player in succession, from the top of the pack, one, two, or three cards at a time, according to the game played, the dealer beginning with the person on his left hand, and going regularly round.
[1602 *OED*]

dealing box, *n.* In faro and twenty-one, a container from which the cards are dealt. The *dealing box* in faro contains one deck, while the *dealing box* used in twenty-one may contain six or more decks of cards. See also SHOE.
[1938 *DA*]

dean, *n.* An accomplished professional gambler, especially one who can figure odds quickly and accurately. See also PROFESSOR. Compare CARD MECHANIC and CARD SHARP.
[1961 Scarne *Complete Guide* 677]

debone, *v.* To bend a card so that it can be recognized from the back at a later time; to CRIMP a card. Compare CORNER BENDER.
[1968 Wallace *Poker* 213]

decatur, *n.* Short for EIGHTER FROM DECATUR.
[1983 Martinez *Gambling Scene* 98]

decision, *n.* The result or outcome of a match or game; the declaration of a winner in a boxing match, the announcement of the roll of the dice in craps, a heat run to determine the winner after two horses finish in a DEAD HEAT, or the resolution of a dispute in a poker game.
[ca. 1961 *Hotel Coll*]

deck, *n.* A pack of playing cards. In most gambling games in this country, the fifty-two playing cards comprising a *deck* consist of four designs, or SUITS (clubs, diamonds, hearts, spades), with thirteen cards in each, ranging from king, queen, jack, ten, nine, etc., down to ace (one) in rank. See also DENOMINATION.
[1593 *OED,* 1853 *DAE*]

deckhead, *n.* The card turned up for trump in games which require the exposure of another card after players have received their cards.
[1950 Morehead *Culbertson* 606]

declaration, *n.* **1.** In games like bridge and whist, the naming of the trump suit at the end of the bidding. [1905 *OEDS*]
2. In high-low poker, the signal of an intention to play for high hand, low hand, or both high and low hand. The intention is usually signaled by holding chips in the fist (one for high, two for low, none for both high and low). All players in contention then open their hands simultaneously to show their intention.
[1949 Coffin *Secrets* 176]

declare, *v.* **1.** In games like bridge and whist, to announce the trump suit at the end of the bidding. [1905 *OEDS*]
2. In high-low poker, to signal an intention to play for the high hand, the low hand, or both the high and low hands. See DECLARATION (def. 2).
3. To withdraw a horse from a race in which it is entered. See also SCRATCH.
[1847 *OEDS*]

declarer, *n.* In games like bezique and bridge, the player who wins the bidding and plays both his own and his partner's cards.
[1870 *OED*]

declaring out, *n. phr.* In games like bridge and whist, the claiming of enough tricks in unplayed cards to make the contract and then laying the cards face up on the table.
[1950 Morehead *Culbertson* 606]

defender, *n.* In games using partners, such as bridge and whist, an opponent of the DECLARER.
[1953 Crawford *Consistent Winner* 344]

defensive bet, *n. phr.* In poker, a wager designed to limit the size of a potential loss, usually done by raising the bet a small amount to prevent a large raise.
[1968 Wallace *Poker* 213]

defensive bid, *n. phr.* In games like bridge and whist, a bid designed to prevent the opposition from gaining an easy contract and to inform one's partner of the strengths held in the hand.
[1953 Crawford *Consistent Winner* 344]

defensive strength, *n. phr.* In games like bridge and whist, cards with which the opponents of the

maker of the contract can expect to win tricks. Compare TRUMP.
[1953 Crawford *Consistent Winner* 345]

defensive value, *n. phr.* In draw poker, the strength of a hand after the drawing of additional cards fails to improve it.
[1949 Coffin *Secrets* 176]

degenerate, *n.* A player who gambles regularly, usually for small stakes.
[1981 Golad *Oral Coll*]
→Not a pejorative term as one might expect from the use of this term in the common vocabulary.

degout, *n.* In ombre, a hazard created for a player by losing the last game of a party.
[1950 Morehead *Culbertson* 606]

deliver, *v.* To distribute cards to players at the beginning of a hand; to DEAL.
[1979 Newman *Dealer's Special* 7]

delivery, *n.* The act of distributing cards to players at the beginning of a hand; the DEAL.
[1977 Anness *Dummy Up*]

demand bid, *n.* In bridge, a bid that serves as a signal to one's partner to keep the bidding open.
[1953 Crawford *Consistent Winner* 345]

denial bid, *n.* In bridge, a bid that serves as a signal indicating lack of support for the bid made by one's partner.
[1950 Morehead *Culbertson* 606]

denomination, *n.* The rank of a playing card. The value of the playing cards usually increases in value from two upwards, through the ace. Sometimes the ranking begins at one, the ace, and increases in value through the king.
[1949 Coffin *Secrets* 176]

dent, *v.* To mark the back of a card with pressure from the thumbnail or by bending the corner of the card slightly. See also ROUNDING. Compare CORNER-BENDER and COSMETICS.
[1968 Wallace *Poker* 213]

deskman, *n.* In keno, the supervisor who verifies and authorizes the payment of winning tickets, usually those of more than a specified amount, usually $100.
[1978 Alexander *Glossary* 5]

despatchers, *n. pl.* Misspotted dice which usually carry two faces with five pips or two faces with two pips each. Compare BARR DICE.
1859 Green *Gambler's Tricks* 106. The dice called *despatchers* have their number, or pips, varying.
[1798 *OED* as *despatch,* variant of *dispatcher*]

desperate money, *n. phr.* Money that is intended for living expenses, not for gambling. Professional gamblers claim that such money is easily lost because the person plays with impaired judgment in betting strategy and is alternately conservative and reckless. See also SCARED MONEY.
[1978 Silberstang *Winning Poker* 13]

deuce, *n.* **1.** A playing card with two pips. [*OED* lists spelling variants between 1519 and 1775: *deux, dewse, deuis, dewce, deuse, dews, deus, duce. Deuce* has predominated since 1775.]
2. Two dollars.
[(1950) 1981 Maurer *Lang. of the Underworld* 185]
3. A die face with two pips.
[1519 *OED*]
4. A cast of two ones with a pair of dice.
[1651 *OED*]

deuce-ace, *n.* A dice throw resulting in a three, with two pips showing atop one die and one pip showing on the other.
[1481 *OED*]

deuce dealing, *n. phr.* Delivering the second card usually from the bottom of the deck. Compare BOTTOM DEAL.
[1965 Fraiken *Inside Nevada* 69]

deuces wild, *n. phr.* In a number of variations of poker, the rule that each of the four cards with two pips has a value declared by the holder.
[1949 Coffin *Secrets* 176]

device, *n.* **1.** A coin-operated gambling machine; a slot machine.
[1957 *Nevada Gaming Regulations* 4]
2. An appliance or piece of equipment used by a cheater in any of a variety of gambling games. Compare CHEATERS and CHEATER'S BOX.
[1973 Clark *Oral Coll*]

devil's bedposts, *n. phr.* **the devil's bedposts.** In playing cards, the four of clubs.
[1873 *OED*]

devole, *n.* In ombre, the loss of all tricks by the player who contracted to win the game.
[1950 Morehead *Culbertson* 607]

diamonds, *n. pl. Plural in form, but singular in use.* **1.** One of the four suits in a pack of cards distinguished by a four-sided figure (rhombus) for each pip. [1594 *OED*]
2. diamond, *sing.* A card of this suit.
[1820 *OED*]

dice, *n. pl.* **1.** *Plural in form, frequently singular in use.* Also called BONES. Cubes with six faces, each face given a number of one through six pips. Compare DIE.
[1393 *OED*]
2. *Plural in form, but singular in use.* The name given to a variety of games such as hazard or craps.
[1548 *OED,* 1619 *DAE*]
3. *Plural in form, but singular in use.* Short for DICE PIT, the casino area where the craps tables are located.
1984 Martinet *Oral Coll.* People will say, "I work in *dice,*" meaning they work in the dice pit. Just like they will say, "I work in twenty-one, or BJ," meaning the twenty-one pit.

dice, *v.* **1.** To play or gamble with dice.
[1440 *OED*]
2. To lose money or goods by gambling at dice; to gamble away. [1549 *OED*]

Dice. Playing at dice, also called DICING, has been portrayed on the pottery of ancient Greece. The numbered CUBES go by many names. ASTRAGALS is derived from *astragalus*, a name for the upper part of the ankle bone of sheep—a word from Greek *astragalos*. Other names more commonly encountered include: BABIES, BONES, IVORIES, and MARBLES. These are neutral terms which contrast with the names for ANIMATED CUBES which have been modified by DICE SHARKS to produce MIS-SPOTS such as CALIFORNIA FOURTEENS, DESPATCHERS and EASTERN TOPS, or weighted to provide the SHOOTER with LOADS (a popular term for LOADED DICE), or compressed to create distorted SHAPES. Some DICE MECHANICS will employ BARR DICE or FLAT DICE which have been shaved on one side to alter the characteristic ROLL. BEVELED SUCTION SHAPES (BEVELS) or SCOOPED DICE are made by creating one face which is concave. Magnetic filings are used to control ROLLING BONES called ELECTRIC DICE.

GAFFED DICE are not the recourse of the DICE CHEAT who prides himself by being able to SWITCH easily TOPPERS for CALIPERS, so the MARK will not BLOW the scheme. The CONTROLLED SHOT allows the DICE-MAN to execute a PALM HOLDOUT with his COGGED DICE in a COMBINATION until he needs to ROLL THE POINT. Or, he may rely upon FLOATS, REPEATERS or MISSOUTS. Many CASTERS will CRACKLE THE DICE with the GREEK SHOT, HUDSON SHOT, or WHIP SHOT to win by GREEKERY often with ENGLISH imparted to one DIE. Or, they will engage in BOXING THE DICE if a DICE BOX is being used.

Many games depend upon CANDY STORE DICE to regulate the movement of PIECES, STONES, or a MAN. BACKGAMMON is an example of a GAMBLING GAME with a BOARD in which the DOUBLING CUBE is important. CHUCK-A-LUCK uses a BIRDCAGE to scramble the dice. Dice are popular with bar customers who may play LIAR DICE, POKER DICE or ACES TO THE CENTER, DEUCES TO THE LEFT, FIVES TO THE RIGHT. HAZARD has given way to CRAPS as the predominant game of dice in CASINOS, however.

Craps has many varieties of play. BANK CRAPS, also called CASINO CRAPS, is the most common in America. The CRAP DEALER and the STICKMAN administer the game under the supervision of a BOXMAN, FLOORMAN, SHIFT BOSS, and PIT BOSS. The HOUSE BANK covers all the bets unlike OPEN CRAPS where SIDE BETS are characteristic. The BANKER is the SHOOTER in ARMY CRAPS, also known as BLANKET CRAPS. PRIVATE CRAPS depends on side bets for the ACTION among the players.

The HOUSE LIMIT in a casino often determines where CHIPS will be placed on the LAYOUT of the CRAPS TABLE. A BETTOR with a CHIP HUSTLER'S advice may WAGER that the THROWER will CRAP OUT, he may make a PLACE BET on a particular number, a FIELD BET on a range of numbers, or a bet that the CRAP SHOOTER will MAKE A POINT. Regular, not COMBINATION BETS, include a COME BET or PASS LINE BET or a wager on the DON'T PASS LINE. A PROPOSITION BET (or ONE-ROLL BET) may be placed any time during the HAND unless "ALL SET WITH THE BET" is declared by the stickman. "HANDS UP" is the call to warn against DICE BITE. "NO BET" or "NO DICE" announces a LATE BET for which the roll is nullified, and the stickman may BURN THE DICE.

HARDWAY BETS contrast with EASY WAY bets based on the ODDS of various possible WAYS a die can land face-up after it has caromed off the BACKBOARD of the TABLE. "HIT THE BOARDS" is the instruction when a SHORT ROLL fails to bounce off the END RAIL.

There are six ways for two dice to roll a LITTLE NATURAL (7) on a COME-OUT ROLL, and two ways to cast a BIG NATURAL (11). SNAKE EYES can only occur with the single PIP, or ACE, of both dice. BOXCARS, or twelve, requires both sixes, also popularly called GARY COOPER or HIGH-NOON. Two fives face-up are called a TEXAS SUNFLOWER, two fours are called BOXES. And, ADA ROSS THE STABLE HOSS signifies any roll of eight. SIXIE FROM DIXIE identifies a roll of six, NINETY DAYS for a nine.

When a die lands ON THE RAIL it is dubbed a RAIL ROLL. Should it fall to the floor the STICKMAN will express a commonly held superstition among CRAP HUSTLERS: "DIE ON THE FLOOR, SEVEN AT THE DOOR" or "ONE ON THE FLOOR, HIT THE DOOR." When the ACTION is crowded at the DICE TABLE, a DEALER will call out "ALL YOU NEED IS AN ARM AND AN EYE." When a HIGH ROLLER is HOT, the stickman may exclaim: "ALL YOU NEED IS A BUCK AND A TRUCK." To entice RAILBIRDS a SHILL, or HOUSE PLAYER, will be given HOUSE MONEY to gamble with while ACTION is slow. When none of the bettors will become the next SHOOTER he will exclaim: "ALL ROOTERS AND NO SHOOTERS." And, when the players turn out to be ACORNS he calls out "ALL JOKES AND NO TOKES."

Players may cajole COLD DICE with such an expression as: BABY NEEDS NEW SHOES.

The basic GAMING EQUIPMENT for CRAP SHOOTING in CASINO GAMBLING includes a DICE TABLE with a CUSHION, and a DICE BOWL from which several sets of TRUE DICE (or PERFECTS) are poured onto the GREEN BAIZE. The DICE PLAYER (or DICER) picks any two for his THROWS.

dice bite, *n.* In bank craps, a small indentation left on the back of the hand when struck by a thrown die. The corners of casino dice are sharp and sometimes draw blood.
1983 Martinet *Oral Coll.* The stickman shouts, "there's no cure for *dice bite*," as a signal for the players to keep their hands up when the dice are coming out. But you learn in a hurry just how painful a *dice bite* can be. Sometimes it draws blood, those dice are coming so hard and

fast, but it always leaves a painful bruise. If you leave your hand down and get hit, maybe the dice won't bite you, but the shooter sure will.

dice board, *n.* A flat surface without indentations that is used for throwing dice from a cup in various games.
[1844 *OED;* 1586 *OED* as *dicing-board*]

dice bowl, *n.* In bank craps, the dish in front of the boxman containing the dice not in use. After a shooter loses, the stickman pours all the dice from the *dice bowl* and offers them to the new shooter, who selects two.
[1973 Friedman *Casino Games* 44]

dice box, *n.* A cup-shaped container usually made of leather, or wood, or, more recently, plastic, in which dice are shaken and cast in games like backgammon. The notion that dice so shaken in a cup cannot be manipulated or controlled is untrue. [1552 *OED*]

dice-box holdout, *n.* A container for shaking and rolling dice that is modified to allow the user to shift from honest dice to loaded dice at will.
[1974 Scarne *Dice* 256]

dice-cage, *n.* In games like chuck-a-luck, a wire framework, usually shaped like an hourglass, to hold and toss dice.
[1968 Thackrey *Nick the Greek* 167]

dice cheat, *n.* A player who uses loaded or mismarked dice to steal money from gamblers.
[1961 Scarne *Complete Guide* 18]

dice cogging, *n. phr.* **1.** Also called COGGING DICE. The manipulation of dice during or after the cast; the turning of a die with the finger after the dice have been thrown.
2. The making of false dice.
[1852 *OED*]

dice counter, *n.* Same as COUNTER (def. 6).
[1985 Martinet *Oral Coll*]

dice degenerate, *n.* A compulsive or habitual craps player. Usually the *dice degenerate* plays for small stakes in order to stay in the game as long as possible.
[1961 Scarne *Complete Guide* 677]
→The term is not pejorative or denigrating as one might expect from the status of *degenerate* in the common vocabulary.

dice gospeller, *n.* A frequent player at dice games; an itinerant gambler who roams from place to place setting up dice games; a known cheater at dice games. *Obsolete.* Compare DICE CHEAT. [1550 *OED*]

dice hustler, *n.* A professional craps player; an accomplished craps shooter.
[ca. 1961 *Hotel Coll*]
→The term is not pejorative or degrading as one might expect from the connotation associated with *hustler* in common vocabulary.

dice knife edge, *n.* In bank craps, a small square similar to a carpenter's square, used to measure dice suspected of being shaved or rounded.
Compare BARR DICE.
[1983 Martinez *Gambling Scene* 198]

dice maker, *n.* A person who makes, usually true, dice. [1714 *OED*]

dice-man, *n.* Also called a DICE MECHANIC. A person, often a craps dealer, who is an accomplished cheater at dice; a person who can easily switch crooked dice into and out of a game. Compare CARD MECHANIC.
[1871 *OED*]

dice mechanic, *n.* Same as a DICE-MAN.
[1961 Scarne *Complete Guide* 17]

dice mob, *n.* Two or more cheaters working in collusion in a dice game. Compare CARD MOB.
[1961 Scarne *Complete Guide* 677]

dice pit, *n.* In a casino, the area where the craps tables are situated. If there are two or more tables, the area between them, where patrons are not allowed to stand, is the PIT.
[1983 Martinet *Oral Coll*]

dice-play, *n.* The action or playing of gambling games with dice.
[1440 *OED;* 1490 *OED* as *dice-playing*]

dice-player, *n.* A person who gambles at dice games. Compare CARD PLAYER.
[1377 *OED*]

dicer, *n.* Same as a DICE-PLAYER. *Rare.* Compare CARDER.
[1408 *OED* as *dyser.* Later variants: 1460 *dysar;* 1500 *dysour;* 1531 *disars.* Now regularly *dice-player*]

dice shark, *n.* A person who cheats in dice games by manipulating the dice or using loaded or mispotted dice. Compare BARR DICE. See also CARD SHARK.
[1943 Conboie *Lincoln Slim*]

dice switch, *n.* A maneuver replacing honest dice with loaded dice and back again during the course of a dice game. See also DICE-MAN.
[1961 Scarne *Complete Guide* 18]

dice table, *n.* A specially designed felt LAYOUT mounted on a wooden or slate surface surrounded by walls about fourteen inches high, used for playing CRAPS. The interior of the end walls are quilted or corrugated to deflect the dice.
[1983 Martinet *Oral Coll*]

dice-top, *n.* A top for spinning that has a polygonal form with numbers marked on each face. See also TEE-TOTUM.
[1894 *OED*]

dicing, *n.* The action or practice of gambling or playing with dice.
[1456 *OED; OED* lists spelling variants: 1456 *dysyng,* 1535 *dising,* 1550 *diceynge,* 1648 onward *dicing*]

dicing-house, *n.* A building devoted to playing and gambling at dice; generally, a gambling house or den.
[1549 *OED*]

dicing table, *n.* A table with a smooth, flat top, often polished, on which games at dice were played. *Obsolete.* Compare DICE TABLE.
[1571 *OED*]

die, *n.* A cube with a number on each of the six faces. Each face has a number from one through six with no numbers repeated. The 1 is opposite the six, the 2 is opposite the 5, and the 3 is opposite the 4.
[1393 *OED*]
→ The plural form, DICE, is often used for the singular *die.*

die down, *n. phr.* In bank craps, a call by the STICKMAN when a die is thrown over the end of the table.
[1983 Martinet *Oral Coll*]

die on the floor, seven at the door, *n. phr.* Also called ON THE FLOOR, HIT THE DOOR. In bank craps, a phrase often used by players indicating a common belief or superstition that when a die is thrown over the end of the table and out of play, the next roll of the dice will be seven.
[1983 Martinet *Oral Coll*]

dig, *v.* To produce additional money from the pocket for a wager during the playing of a hand. A player may *dig* in poker games which are not limited to TABLE STAKES (the amount of money in front of the player). In casino twenty-one a player may *dig* to DOUBLE DOWN, that is, to turn his first two cards face upward and place an amount equal to his original wager on the table to receive one card. Or, the player may *dig* to take INSURANCE during the course of a hand, that is, to place an amount equal to one-half of his original wager that the dealer does not have twenty-one when an ace is face upward on the dealer's upward-facing card.
[1973 Clark *Oral Coll*]

dildock, *n.* A card cheater who uses a marked or STACKED DECK. Compare CHEATERS.
[1968 Adams *Western Words*]

dime store, *n.* A small gambling establishment, usually filled with slot machines and low limit gambling games; one that caters to casual passersby or tourists and makes no attempt to appeal to professional gamblers or large bettors.
[1953 Lewis *Sagebrush Casinos* 157]

dirty money, *n.* Same as a DIRTY STACK.
[ca. 1961 *Hotel Coll*]

dirty stack, *n.* Also called DIRTY MONEY. In a casino, a stack of chips with different denominations mixed together. Compare BARBER POLE.
[1983 Martinet *Oral Coll*]

discard, *v.* To remove unwanted playing cards from the hand during play.
1866 *American Card Player* 134. *Discard.*—Taking one or more cards from your hand and placing them in the centre of the table, face downwards.
[1591 *OED;* 1857 *DAE*]

discard, *adj.* Of or pertaining to playing cards that have been used in play and are set aside until the pack is reshuffled. In baccarat, twenty-one and other games, the adjective is used with a variety of names for receptacles: **discard bowl** or **discard holder** or **discard rack** or **discard tray.** In other games like poker, no receptacle is present, used cards being placed in a **discard pile.**
[1890 Quinn *Fools of Fortune* 218]

discord, *n.* In ombre, a hazard created by holding four kings.
[1950 Morehead *Culbertson* 607]

discouraging card, *n.* In bridge, a card played to signal one's partner to discontinue leads in one suit and switch to another suit.
[1953 Crawford *Consistent Winner* 345]

dispatchers, *n. pl.* Also spelled **dispatches, despatches.** False dice that may be hollowed, weighted, or misspotted. Compare BARR DICE and LOADED DICE. [1798 *OED*]

disqualify, *v.* In horse racing, to disallow the finishing place of a horse after a race, due to a FOUL, or other broken rule.
[1955 Hillis *Pari-Mutuel Betting* 113]

distance, *n.* **1.** In horse racing, a measurement of length that varies from one track to another, but often 220 to 240 yards. See also FURLONG.
1829 Brown *Turf* 170. Newmarket Courses . . . 240 yards are a *distance.*
2. Generally, a designated length before the finish line, usually marked with a post, that a horse must pass before the winner of a heat crosses the finish line. Failure to make the *distance* disqualifies the horse for subsequent heats.
[1674 *OED;* 1853 *DAE*]
3. In the phrases:
at the distance, In horse racing, referring to a position one furlong (220 yards) from the finishing post.
[1974 Ewart *Flatracing*]
by a distance, In horse racing, a margin of more than 20 lengths.
[1803 *DAE*]

distanced, *past participle.* In horse racing, beaten by a distance, or designated length.
[1674 *OED;* listed as "obsolete in England, but not in the U.S."]

distance elimination rule, *n. phr.* In horse racing, an informal rule of thumb for some bettors by which they decide not to bet on a horse that has not previously run the same distance at the same track.
[1971 McQuaid *Gambler's Digest* 304]

distance-flag, *n.* A flag held by a man or attached to a pole at a designated distance from the finish line on a race course.
[1870 *OED*]

distance-judge, *n.* In horse racing, a man stationed at the distance-post to determine the eligibility, for future heats, of horses reaching that post. [1870 *OED*]

distance-post, *n.* In horse racing, a post, sometimes with a flag attached, set at a specified distance from the finish line or post, used to determine what horses are DISTANCED.
[1809 *OED*]

distance-stand, *n.* In horse racing, a platform or tier of seats erected for spectators at the distance-post. [1870 *OED*]

dix, *n.* **1.** In pinochle, the lowest trump card, the nine.
2. In bezique and sixty-six, the nine of trump.
[1908 *OEDS*; So called because the player who exchanges it for the turned-up trump scores ten points.]

do, *n.* In bank craps, the PASS LINE; a bet that the dice win, or PASS.
[(1950) 1981 Maurer *Lang. of the Underworld* 185]

do bettor, *n.* Also called a FRONT-LINE BETTOR. In bank craps, a player who wagers only on the PASS LINE.
[1974 Scarne *Dice* 113]

doctor, *n.* **1.** An altered die weighted or misspotted to roll a particular number. See also LOADED DICE or SCOOPED DICE. Compare BARR DICE and CASTER and LITTLE DICK FISHER.
1726 Wilson *Art and Mystery* 30. This gives me occasion to say something of little Dick Fisher so often called upon by the Caster, when his Chance is Four or Five; what must be done then? Why you must put in a low Die (called a *Doctor*). [1700 *OED*]
2. A DICE BOX which allows the CASTER to cheat by throwing a preselected number. Compare DICE-BOX HOLDOUT.
1859 Green *Gambler's Tricks* 111. The most destructive box [for throwing dice] is that called the *doctor* . . . Three-fourths of the internal space at the bottom are filled up, leaving only sufficient room in the centre for the dice, placed flat, to fit into, the portion of the box towards the top gradually becoming enlarged, and the sides made smooth. When the dice are once introduced into this box, their position cannot be altered by shaking, and when thrown out carefully on the table they fall in the same way, with the exposed surface underneath.

doctor, *v.* To alter the inside or outside of dice or the backs of playing cards. Compare BARR DICE and COSMETICS and LOADED DICE.
1902 Andrews *Artifice* 16. The usual plan is to mark the standard decks by hand. For the benefit of the unenlightened or curious reader we shall describe the process. It is not at all difficult, and a deck can be *"doctored"* in an hour or so.

dog, *n.* **1.** Short for UNDERDOG. A team, racehorse, or other contest entrant not favored to win.
[1973 Clark *Oral Coll*]
2. Same as D.
[1949 Coffin *Secrets* 176]

dog it, *v. phr.* To continue to make small bets when winning several times in a row.
[1961 Scarne *Complete Guide* 677]

doghouse cut, *n.* The dividing of a pack of playing cards into three parts or more before reassembling the pack and passing it back to the dealer to distribute cards at the beginning of a hand. Compare CUT, *v.*
[1949 Coffin *Secrets* 176]

dog throw, *n.* The lowest, or losing throw, in a dice game. *Rare.* Compare SNAKE-EYES.
[1880 *OED*]

Dolly Parton, *n.* Also called SNAKE EYES. In craps, a roll of two; a single pip on each die. Compare E AND T and ET and JACKSON FIVE.
1983 Martinet *Oral Coll.* . . . What's going on in the world has an influence on craps players. And sometimes there's a little confusion about when people started using some words. A long time before the Jackson Five or Michael Jackson was even born, a Jackson five was a hundred dollars. Five twenties, Jackson's face is on the twenty. But nowadays people assume that it's because of the singers. Maybe some things stay. A Dolly Parton is aces. I've been hearing that for years. And E and T [a proposition bet on the numbers eleven and twelve] became ET after the movie. I don't ever hear E and T anymore.

domino, *n.* **1.** Any one of the (usually) 28 rectangular tiles used in the game of dominoes. One side is blank; the other is divided in half, each end of which may have from zero to six pips on it. [1820 *DAE*]
2. Usually **dominoes.** *Plural in form, but singular in use.* The game played with these rectangular tiles.
[1801 *OED*]

don't, *n.* Short for DON'T PASS LINE.
[(1950) 1981 Maurer *Lang. of the Underworld* 185]

don't bettor, *n.* A player who consistently bets on the DON'T PASS LINE, that is, wagers that the dice will not make the point.
[1982 Martin *Introduction* 15]

don't come, *n.* **1.** In bank craps, a wager that the next roll of the dice will not pass and that, if a point is established, the point will not be made in ensuing rolls.
[(1950) 1981 Maurer *Lang. of the Underworld* 185]
2. An area on a bank craps table layout for placing a bet after the shooter has established a point. The area can be used for a wager only after the person shooting the dice has rolled a number 4, 5, 6, 8, 9, or 10. The *don't come* area then becomes eligible for use on the next roll, considered the first roll of a new hand. That is, the rules for the DON'T PASS LINE are in effect.

See also COME.
[1973 Friedman *Casino Games* 29]

don't pass, *n.* **1.** In bank craps, a type of bet made before a shooter begins to roll the dice which wins if the shooter then rolls the numbers 2 or 3, and loses if the shooter rolls the numbers 7 or 11. In bank craps, the number 12 is often BARRED, or declared a standoff between the house and the *don't pass* bettor. If the shooter rolls the number 4, 5, 6, 8, 9, or 10, that is his POINT. He must then roll the number 7 before repeating his point for the *don't pass* bet to win.
2. Short for DON'T PASS LINE. See also PASS.
[1968 Thackrey *Nick the Greek* 95]

don't pass line, *n. phr.* In bank craps, the area on the table layout for placing DON'T PASS bets.
[(1950) 1981 Maurer *Lang. of the Underworld* 185]

door card, *n.* **1.** In hold 'em poker, the first card dealt to a player.
1982 Clark *Oral Coll.* Door-Card Charlie got his name from his habit of pounding on the first card dealt. That's the *door card* and he was always knocking on the door.
2. In stud poker, the first card dealt face up. In five-card stud, it is the second card dealt; in seven-card stud, the third card dealt.
[1978 Brunson *How I Made* 529]

door pops, *n. pl.* MISMARKED DICE on which one die has six pips on three of the faces and two pips on three faces, the other die has five pips on each face. The only numbers that can be rolled with *door pops* are seven and eleven, which are winning numbers on the first cast in craps. See also DESPATCHERS. Compare BARR DICE and LOADED DICE.
[(1950) 1981 Maurer *Lang. of the Underworld* 185]

dope, *n.* **1.** In horse racing, information about the past performances of a horse's races. Compare RACING FORM.
[1903 *DAE, DA*]
2. Any illegal stimulant given to a racehorse before a race. [1900 *OEDS*]

dope, *v.* **1.** Also **dope out.** In horse racing, to predict the outcome of a race by analyzing information about the past performances of the horses and jockeys entered in the race.
[*DAS,* 1914 *OEDS*]
2. To give a horse an illegal stimulant before a race. [1900 *OEDS*]

doped cards, *n. pl.* Playing cards that have been marked on the back with liquid such as india ink, bleach, or even water. Compare COSMETICS.
[1968 Adams *Western Words*]

dope sheet, *n.* Also called a TIP SHEET or TOUT SHEET. In horse and dog racing, a publication that lists information about the past performances of the entries, often with suggestions for making wagers. See also FORM and RACING FORM.
[1903 *DA, DAE, OEDS*]

double, *n.* **1.** In bridge, a challenge by the opponent of a bidder, announcing a willingness to count twice the penalty value of a failed contract. See also REDOUBLE.
[1903 *OEDS*]
2. In short whist, a game in which one team scores five before the other team scores three; in long whist, a game in which one team scores 10 and the other side scores none.
[1838 *OED*]
3. A domino tile bearing the same number of pips on each half.
[1870 *OED*]

double, *v.* **1.** In poker, to raise the amount wagered by a previous bettor.
[1964 Reese and Watkins *Secrets* 139]
2. In faro, to bet twice on a card of the same denomination.
[1938 Asbury *Sucker's Progress* 9]
3. In games like bridge and whist, to indicate a belief that the opposing team will not achieve the contract they propose by offering to double the value of the hand.
[1953 Crawford *Consistent Winner* 345]
[1894 *OEDS*]
4. In the particle constructions:
double down, In twenty-one, to increase a bet up to the amount of the original bet, and receive a single hit.
[1961 Scarne *Complete Guide* 677]
double through, In poker, to win a pot from two other players, making the profit for a pot twice the size that it would be if opposed by only one other player.
[1973 Preston *Play Poker* 167]
double up, To double the size of a regular bet after a win or a loss. See also PRESS. Compare DOUBLE PROGRESSION and MARTINGALE.
[1971 McQuaid *Gambler's Digest* 305]

double belly buster, *n. phr.* A poker hand that requires two cards to make an INSIDE STRAIGHT. If a player holds, say, a ten, king, and ace, the hand is a *double belly buster* because the two cards required are the jack and queen. Compare BELLY-BUSTER STRAIGHT.
[1978 Brunson *How I Made* 529]

double-blank, *n.* In dominoes, the tile with no pips on either half of the face. See also DOUBLE, *n.* (def. 3).
[1868 *OEDS*]

double bluff, *n.* In poker, an attempt to make an opponent believe a hand is stronger than it is by reraising a raise made by the opponent.
[1968 Wallace *Poker* 214]

double-cat-harp, *n.* In faro, a condition in which five cards are yet undealt, including two pairs. Compare SINGLE-CAT-HARP.
1843 Green *Exposure* 210. When there are five

cards in the box [in faro], one case (odd card) and two doubles (such as two fours and two sevens), this is called the *"double-cat-harp;"* when these cards are in, one odd and one doublet—it is called "single-cat-harp."

double center, *n.* A roulette table with interchangeable wheels, one accurate and true, the other dishonest by being unbalanced, having narrower CANOES, or slots, on some numbers, or by being rigged to cheat in some other fashion.
[1890 Quinn *Fools of Fortune* 250]

double cut, *n.* A method for cutting cards which keeps the top several cards on top after the cut. See also CUT, *n.*
1865 Evans *Gamblers Win* 38. The *double cut* is executed by drawing the middle of the pack out at the end with the middle finger and thumb, and just as they touch the top of the deck, catching the other cards which were on top with the third finger and lower part of the thumb, drawing them out at the end, throwing them on top again.

double dealing, *n.* In poker, a cheating move, giving more cards to a confederate than to other players. Compare MISDEAL.
[ca. 1961 *Hotel Coll*]
[from earlier *a*1589 *OED*, in the general sense: "action marked by duplicity."]

double deck, *n.* In certain games like pinochle and twenty-one, the use of two packs of cards shuffled together as one.
[1977 Anness *Dummy Up*]

double deuce, *n.* A mismarked die on which the face with five pips, opposite the face with two pips, is changed to a face with two pips. The die then has two faces with two pips on each. See also DOUBLE FIVE and MISMARKED DICE and ONE WAY TOPS AND BOTTOMS.
[1961 Scarne *Complete Guide* 677]

double discard, *n.* A cheating move in draw poker whereby a player draws more cards than he needs and substitutes one for a desired card in his hand.
1865 Evans *Gamblers Win* 45. The *Double Discard*—Calling for four cards, he discards the two pair or four flush, and drops them in front of him; lifts the draft with his odd card, and if in the draft there be a card of the same suit as the four flush, or (if the natural hand be two pair) of the same size as either of the pair, he discards four cards again and drops this card on the four first discarded, and, raising it, has either a full hand or a flush.

double down, *n.* In casino twenty-one, a rule allowing a player to increase his bet up to the amount of his original bet, turn his original two cards face up and receive one additional card from the dealer dealt face downward.
1979 Clark *Oral Coll.* The *double down* is common when the player holds two cards totaling ten or eleven points. Sometimes the *double down* is used when the player holds an ace and a low card, and the dealer's faced card is a five or a six.

double-ended straight or **double-end straight,** *n.* Also called an OPEN-END STRAIGHT. In poker, four cards of consecutive rank, as 9, 10, jack, queen. Drawing either an 8 or a king will complete the STRAIGHT.
[1949 Coffin *Secrets* 176]

double event, *n.* In horse racing and jai alai, an earlier term for the DAILY DOUBLE, which bet requires picking the winner of two designated races or games on one betting ticket.
1868 Laing-Meason *Turf Frauds* 120. A *"double event"* bet is to back two named horses to win two named races.

double five, *n.* A mismarked die. The face with two pips, which is opposite the face with five pips, is replaced with five pips, giving the die opposite faces with five pips each. See also DOUBLE DEUCE and MISMARKED DICE and ONE WAY TOPS AND BOTTOMS.
[1961 Scarne *Complete Guide* 677]

double header, *n.* **1.** In poker, a pot that is doubled because a hand is not played, either through misdeal or refusal of players to begin the wagering. The pot then passes to the next hand.
1866 *American Card Player* 134. *Double-Header.*—When all the players "pass," and decline to enter the pool, or where a misdeal occurs, the stakes must be doubled, and the dealer deals again.
2. A coin used for cheating in gambling. The coin has the same figure on both sides.
[1948 *OEDS*]

double ningre, *n.* In romestecq, a hand with two pairs of cards, each pair consisting of two cards of the same denomination.
[1950 Morehead *Culbertson* 608]

double-odd, *n.* In faro, two extra cards placed in the pack by a cheating dealer.
[1943 Maurer *Argot*]

double odds, *n. pl. Plural in form, but singular in use.* In bank craps, a rule allowing a player to wager up to twice the normal odds allowed on a FLAT BET, a regular PASS LINE BET.
[ca. 1961 *Hotel Coll*]

double or nothing, *n. phr.* An expression indicating a proposition that an amount bet and won may be doubled if the person wins a second time or, if that person loses, the amount owed will be nothing.
[1890 Quinn *Fools of Fortune* 287]

double or quits, *n. phr.* An expression indicating that the stake on a particular wager will be doubled or the player will retire from the game, depending on the outcome of the wager.
[1580 *OED*]

double out, *n.* In faro, a wager that the fourth card of a denomination will fall on the same side of the layout as the third card of that denomination.
[1968 Adams *Western Words*]

double pairs royal, *n. phr.* In cribbage, four cards of the same denomination held in one hand or played consecutively on the table.
1824 Anon *Hoyle's* 28. *Double Pairs royal* are four similar cards, and reckon for twelve points, whether in hand or playing.
[1749 *OED*]

double pinochle, *n.* In pinochle, the condition of two queens of spades and two jacks of diamonds being held in the same hand. See also PINOCHLE.
[1971 McQuaid *Gambler's Digest* 304]

double-pop, *n.* In poker, a bet which increases the size of the previous bet, which was itself an increase in size of the bet before.
[1978 Brunson *How I Made* 529]

double progression, *n.* A betting system that requires twice the wager on the next event after a loss. See also MARTINGALE.
[1949 Blanche *You Can't Win* 17]

double quinella, *n.* In horse racing, a bet on four horses, naming their WIN and PLACE positions in two races.
[ca. 1961 *Hotel Coll*]

double rome, *n.* In romestecq, a hand with one pair of aces or kings.
[1950 Morehead *Culbertson* 608]

double run, *n.* In cribbage, a three-card straight, with one rank duplicated, as 6, 7, 8, 8.
[1953 Crawford *Consistent Winner* 345]

double shuffle, *n.* A cheating move at playing cards. A method for appearing to shuffle a deck of cards but without disturbing their original order.
[Compare *DSUE, DAS* which record cheating generally]

double-side dealer, *n.* A casino table with the same layout repeated at both ends of the table which is common to craps tables, less so with roulette tables, and not found on card tables.
[1973 Clark *Oral Coll*]

doublet, *n.* **1.** A roll of two dice in which the same number appears on each die.
1860 Crawley *Backgammon* 55. When *doublets* (that is, two dice with same numbers upwards) are thrown, the player has four moves instead of two; for example, if a deuce doublet (two twos) be thrown, one man may be moved eight points.
[1450 *OED* as *dublettes*]
2. In faro, two cards of the same denomination which appear in a single turn. Compare COUP (def. 2) and PUNTER.
1843 Green *Exposure* 166. *Doublet* is when the punter's card is turned up twice in the same coup; in which case the bank wins half the stake.
3. In dominoes, a tile with the same number of pips at each end. See also DOUBLE BLANK.
[1950 Morehead *Culbertson* 608]

double tenace, *n.* In games like bridge and whist, the ace-queen-10 or ace-jack-10 of a depleted suit, when held by the fourth player to act in a hand. See also TENACE.
[1655 *OED*]

doubleton, *n.* In games like bridge and whist, two cards of the same suit held in one hand. See also SINGLETON. [1906 *OEDS*]

double-zero, *n.* In roulette, the thirty-eighth slot on an AMERICAN WHEEL. See also EUROPEAN WHEEL.
[1968 Thackrey *Nick the Greek* 22]

doubling, *n.* In backgammon, a strategy for increasing the size of a wager by a player who believes he has an advantage.
[1974 Scarne *Dice* 321]

doubling cube, *n.* In backgammon, a six-sided die used to increase the size of the wager when a player believes he holds an advantage. The numbers on the faces of the cube are 2, 4, 8, 16, 32, 64.
[1976 Figgis *Gambler's Handbook* 69]

down, *n.* In bank craps, a statement that certain bets on the layout are to be ignored on the next roll of the dice.
1983 Martinet *Oral Coll.* Somebody with bets on the backline may look at a new shooter and decide he doesn't like the action. He might say, "all bets down," which means he wants his backline bets not to work on the roll . . . *down* means there is no bet for that player's checks on the layout.

down and dirty, *n. phr.* In seven-card stud, said of the last, or seventh, card dealt, which is face down.
[1968 Wallace *Poker* 214]

down-card, *n.* Any playing card dealt face downward. Most common to games like stud poker and hold 'em poker, where some cards are dealt face downward and some cards are dealt face upward. See also DOWN AND DIRTY.
[1963 Steig *Common Sense* 183]

downhills, *n. pl.* Dice altered to result in rolling low numbers. See also DOCTOR and LOADED DICE. Compare BARR DICE.
[1700 *OED*]

down inside, *adv. phr.* In bank craps, an announcement by the STICKMAN that a die has bounced off the table into the PIT. See also DOWN OUTSIDE.
[1973 Clark *Oral Coll*]

down outside, *adv. phr.* In bank craps, an announcement by the STICKMAN that a die has bounced off the table on the players' side.
[1983 Martinet *Oral Coll*]

down the river, *n. phr.* In poker games like seven-card stud and hold 'em poker, the seventh, or last card dealt. Compare DOWN AND DIRTY.

[1949 Coffin *Secrets* 176]

Doyle Brunson, *n.* In hold 'em poker, a hand in which the first two cards are a ten and a two. Compare DEAD MAN'S HAND.
1982 Golad *Oral Coll.* There is a hand of a deuce [and] ten called the *Doyle Brunson* or the *Dolly Brunson.* That's because Texas Dolly [Brunson] won the World Series of Poker two years in a row with it.

dozen, *n.* In roulette, a bet that includes twelve numbers: 1 to 12, 13 to 24, or 25 to 36. Compare COLUMN.
[1964 Wykes *Illustrated Guide* 326]

draft, *n.* Another name for *draw poker;* the draw in draw poker. *Obsolete.*
1865 Evans *Gamblers Win* 43. Draw poker, though played to a considerable extent in the Middle and Eastern States, is more especially a Western game, a little *"Draft,"* being the favorite amusement of the inhabitants of the North and Southwest . . . the beauty of the game being in the *draft.*

drag, *n.* Also called the RAKE. In cardrooms, a percentage of each pot taken for the operator of the establishment.
[1949 Coffin *Secrets* 176]

drag, *v.* **1.** In poker, to take chips from the pot surreptitiously.
[1968 Wallace *Poker* 214]
2. In the particle constructions:
drag down, 1. To remove a recoverable bet from the table.
[1964 Lemmel *Gambling* 188]
2. To pocket winnings while continuing to play smaller bets after a large win.
[(1950) 1981 Maurer *Lang. of the Underworld* 185]

draw, *n.* **1.** Short for DRAW POKER.
[1857 *DA, OEDS*]
2. In card games, the act of requesting additional cards or of taking a card from the stock on the table. [1898 *DA, DAE*]
3. In draw poker, the stage of the game, after the first round of betting, in which players still active in the game may exchange discards for newly dealt cards. [1857 *DAE*]
4. In keno, the procedure of taking twenty numbered balls, one at a time, from the eighty in a common pool. The twenty numbers taken constitute a game.
5. A tie; the outcome of an event which has no winner or loser.
[1836 *DAE,* 1825 *OEDS,* both as attributive]

draw, *v.* **1.** To take a playing card from a pack.
[1622 *OED*]
2. In draw poker, to request replacements for discards.
1866 *American Card Player* 134. *Draw.*—To discard one or more cards, and receive a corresponding number from the dealer.
[1856 *DA;* 1864 *DAE*]
3. In keno, to take twenty numbered balls, one at a time, from the eighty in a common pool. The twenty numbers taken constitute a game.
4. In trump games, to cause a card or particular cards, especially from one suit, to be played out. [1878 *OED*]
5. To withdraw a horse from competing in a race. See also SCRATCH. [1597 *OED*]
6. In the phrases and particle constructions:
draw away, In horse racing, to increase a lead over other horses in a race.
[1971 McQuaid *Gambler's Digest* 305]
draw dead, In poker, especially hold 'em, to stay in contention for the pot and fail to receive a card that improves the hand.
[1981 Golad *Oral Coll*]
draw out, In poker, to achieve the winning hand with the final card dealt to the hand.
[1968 Wallace *Poker* 214]
draw the set, In hold 'em poker, to receive a third card that matches a pair held in the hand.
1981 Golad *Oral Coll.* I sat there with American Airlines [two red aces] and the flop [three community cards placed face up on the table] came ace, rag, rag. I knew it [the pot] was mine when I *drew the set.*
draw to, In draw poker, to request replacements for discards, especially to fulfill a specific hand.
[1882 *DAE*]

draw poker, *n.* See article at POKER.
[1864 *OED*]

draw ticket, *n.* In keno, a sheet with eighty numbers into which holes are punched corresponding to the twenty numbers taken from the common pool of all eighty numbers. The sheet is used to verify winning tickets purchased by patrons.
[1973 Friedman *Casino Games* 100]

dream book, *n.* Especially in numbers games, any of the pamphlets that translate the events of dreams into numbers on which a person might gamble. [1938 *DA*]

drill cards, *v. phr.* In a casino, to punch a hole through a pack of used cards before giving it to a patron who requests a deck used in casino play.
[ca. 1961 *Hotel Coll*]

drive, *v.* **1.** In horse racing, to use the whip on a horse while coming down the stretch to the finish line. Compare EXTEND.
[1955 Hillis *Pari-Mutuel Betting* 114]
2. In the phrase:
drive the hearse, In faro, to keep a record of the cards as they are played; to KEEP CASES. See also CASE-KEEPER.
[1943 Maurer *Argot*]

drive, *adj.* In horse racing, descriptive of the effort to achieve maximum speed while approaching the finish line, especially the rider's use of the whip.
[1971 McQuaid *Gambler's Digest* 305]

drop, *n.* In a gambling establishment, the amount of money taken from players in a given period, such as one shift or one day.
[1957 *Nevada Gaming Regulations* 32]
[The term originally referred to *dropping* money through the slot on a gaming table (compare DROP BOX), but now refers to money collected from any source, including slot machines, keno, bingo, sports books, and so on.]

drop, *v.* **1.** Also, to FOLD. In poker, to retire from a hand rather than continuing to bet and contend for the pot.
[1949 Coffin *Secrets* 177]
2. To lose money gambling.
[n.d. *DAS;* 1971 Livingston *Poker Strategy* 217]
3. In a casino, to place money exchanged for chips into a slot in the table. The money is collected in a box attached to the underside of the table. See also DROP BOX.
[1974 Friedman *Casino Management* 15]

drop box, *n.* **1.** In a casino, the container attached to the underside of the table, used to collect money that is deposited through a slot in the table. Compare HANGER.
[1957 *Nevada Gaming Regulation* 32]
2. In a casino, any container for money: the metal or plastic bucket under the slot machine, the cash drawer in the sports book, and so on.

drop bucket, *n.* A container set in a cabinet below a slot machine to catch any overflow of coins fed into the machine. See also DROP BOX (def. 2).
[1978 Alexander *Glossary* 2]

drop cut, *n.* In a casino, a procedure for paying out a new stack of chips to match a player's stack, in which the new chips held as a large stack in the dealer's hand are released in rapid succession until they match the height of the player's stack, any excess chips being retained with the index finger. See also THUMB-CUT.
1984 Martinet *Oral Coll.* The *drop cut* isn't recommended, because if it isn't executed properly, house money and player's money can get mixed. But people do it. The old-timers do it all the time.

drop meter, *n.* A COUNTING DEVICE in a slot machine that records the number of coins played, the number of times the handle is pulled, and the number of coins paid out.
[1978 Alexander *Glossary* 2]

dropping the pigeon, *n.* See PIGEON DROP.
1843 Green *Exposure* 230. There is another fraud sometimes practiced on men who cannot be enticed into a game at cards, or perhaps are unacquainted with any game; this trick is called *"dropping the pigeon."*
1859 Green *Gam Tricks* 49. . . . they agreed to *drop the pigeon* on him, saying, that they knew he would bet on it. This pigeon is a curiously contrived needle-case, which opens at both ends, but has but one visible opening.
[1817 *DA, DAE*]

drop shot, *n.* A method for throwing dice so that a desired number is face upwards after the cast, in which the shooter picks up the dice with the desired number face upwards, then lofts the dice so they hit the backboard at its junction with the table. One or both dice will not turn over. See also WHIP SHOT. Compare DUMP OVER SHOT.
[(1950) 1981 Maurer *Lang. of the Underworld* 185]

drugstore dice, *n.* Imperfect, mass-produced dice, not intended for gambling, that are not uniform in weight or size. See also CANDY STORE DICE.
[1974 Scarne *Dice* 23]

drummer, *n.* Also **drum.** In poker, a conservative player who makes large bets only when holding a very strong hand.
1981 Clark *Oral Coll.* A *drummer* might be thought of as a person who makes a big deal out of betting big on a very strong hand, like beating a drum to announce his hand. But that isn't it at all. The guy is called a *drummer* because he is tight as a drum and doesn't take chances.

dry, *adj.* Describing or pertaining to a person without money.
[(1950) 1981 Maurer *Lang. of the Underworld* 185]
[Compare, 1552 *OED* meaning "miserly" and labeled obsolete]

duck, *n.* Variant of DEUCE, a playing card with two pips or a die with two pips facing upward after a cast.
[1949 Coffin *Secrets* 177]

duke, *n.* **1.** In poker, a hand of cards; the cards held in the player's hand.
[1968 Wallace *Poker* 214]
2. An oral command by a CARD SHARP to his accomplice, telling the accomplice that a prospective victim is approaching, at which the accomplice suddenly appears to be excited about good fortune in playing against the card sharp.
[1943 MacDougall *Danger* 133]
[The term appears to have originated among pickpockets who signaled one another that a prospective victim was at hand. Compare *duke* (v. def. 3) *DAS;* and *duke* (n. def. 5) ca. 1840 *DSUE*]

dummy, *n.* Also spelled **dumby.** In trump games, the hand of the partner of the person winning the bid. The hand is laid face up on the table and played by the person who won the bid.
1836 Eidrah *Hoyle Famil* 28. One of the party undertakes to play the spare hand, called *Dumby.* The other two of course are partners. The spare hand is laid out on the table by *dumby's* partner, so that all the party may see it, and the game goes on, the cards in *Dumby* being played by his partner.
[1736 *OED* as *dummy,* 1825 as *dumbee,* 1860 as *dumby*]

dummy up, *n. clause.* Often, **dummy up and deal.** In a casino, an oral command given by a

PIT BOSS to a dealer, telling the dealer to stop chatting with the patrons.
[ca. 1961 *Hotel Coll*]

dump, *v.* In the phrase or particle construction: **dump out,** Of a casino dealer, to cheat the house by paying to an accomplice on losing wagers or by paying with chips of a higher denomination than those played.
[ca. 1961 *Hotel Coll*]
dump the bowl, In bank craps, an order from the BOXMAN to the STICKMAN to withdraw from play the dice being used in the game and offer the shooter other dice while the boxman inspects the dice called in. [1983 Martinet *Oral Coll*]

dump over shot, *n.* A method for throwing dice to insure that the faces originally on the bottom land face upward. See also WHIP SHOT. Compare DROP SHOT.
[1974 Scarne *Dice* 256]

dust, *v.* **1.** Of a casino dealer, to clap the hands before leaving the table to show that no chips are held in the palms. The dealer puts the palms together, then turns the open hands palm up and palm down so that overhead cameras or observers can record the fact that the dealer's hands are empty.
[1977 Anness *Dummy Up*]
2. To cheat a victim, usually quickly and completely.
[(1950) 1981 Maurer *Lang. of the Underworld* 185]

dutch straight, *n.* Also called an ALTERNATE STRAIGHT or SKIP STRAIGHT. In poker, a hand in which all the cards are two pips apart in rank, as 2, 4, 6, 8, 10.
[1949 Coffin *Secrets* 177]

E

E, *n.* **1.** Also called EASY. In poker, the fifth player to the left of the dealer. *Rare.* Compare A, B, C, D, F, G, H,
[1949 Coffin *Secrets* 177]
2. Abbreviation for EAST. In bridge, one of the four player positions, the others being NORTH, SOUTH, and WEST.
[1950 Morehead *Culbertson* 610]
[1926 *OEDS*]

each way, *n.* In horse racing, a two-part wager on the same horse to WIN and PLACE. If the horse wins the race, the player wins both wagers. If the horse finishes second, the player wins only the place bet.
[1869 *OEDS*]

eagle-back, *n.* A playing card with a picture of an eagle on the back.
[1880 *DAE, DA*; compare EAGLE 1810 *DA*]

eagles, *n. pl.* **1.** A fifth suit sometimes added to a standard 52-card pack, making a 65-card pack. Now *rare.*
[1944 *DA*]
2. Originally, a brand of playing cards, probably featuring a picture of an eagle on the back of each. By 1880, generalized reference to any of several brands of American-made playing cards, many of which featured pictures of eagles on the back. [1810 *DA*]

E and T, *n.* Also called E.T. Abbreviation for **eleven and twelve.** In craps, a proposition bet that the number eleven or twelve will be thrown with the next roll of the dice.
1983 Martinet *Oral Coll.* . . . What's going on in the world has an influence on craps players. And sometimes there's a little confusion about when people started using some words. A long time before the Jackson Five or Michael Jackson was even born, a Jackson five was a hundred dollars. Five twenties, [Andrew] Jackson's face is on the twenty. But nowadays people assume that it's because of the singers. Maybe some things stay. A Dolly Parton is aces. I've been hearing that for years. And *E and T* [a proposition bet on the numbers eleven and twelve] became ET after the movie. I don't ever hear *E and T* anymore.

ear, *v.* **1.** To bend the corner of a playing card so it can be recognized from the back at a later time.
2. Of casino dealers, to bend the corner of a bill so it does not drop all the way through the slot on the table into the DROP BOX.
[1961 Scarne *Complete Guide* 678]
[Perhaps from *dog ear* 1886 *OED* and *dog's-ear* *a*1659 *OED*]

early foot, *n. phr.* The condition of a racehorse that leaves the gate quickly, then slows. See also EARLY SPEED.
[1955 Hillis *Pari-Mutuel Betting* 114]

early out, *n.* In a casino, the last work break taken at the end of a shift for a dealer. The dealer with an *early out* is allowed to leave the

casino before the other dealers are finished with the shift.
[1977 Anness *Dummy Up*]

early position, *n.* In an eight-handed poker game, the first, second, and third players allowed to act on the hand.
[1978 Brunson *How I Made* 530]

early speed, *n. phr.* Describing a racehorse that leaves the gate quickly and takes the lead. See also EARLY FOOT.
[1955 Hillis *Pari-Mutuel Betting* 114]

earnings, *n.* The amount of money won in purses by a racehorse.
[1981 Passer *Winning Big* 229]
[Compare 1732 *OED,* applying to a worker's pay]

ease, *v.* To rein a racehorse slowly at the end of the race; to gradually slow a horse after it has extended itself.
[1955 Hillis *Pari-Mutuel Betting* 114]

east, *n.* Abbreviated as E. One of the four positions at a bridge table, the others being NORTH, SOUTH, and WEST.
[1926 *OEDS*]

Eastern tops, *n.* MISSPOTTED DICE used for cheating. Compare CALIFORNIA FOURTEENS.
1967 Goffman *Interaction* 150. Among the types of unsporting dice are misspotted ones variously called tops and bottoms, horses, tees, tats, soft rolls, California fourteens, door pops, *Eastern tops,* etc. These dice do not have a different number on each of the six sides, and (as with a two-headed coin) allow a player to bet on an outcome that is not among the possibilities and therefore rather unlikely to occur.

easy, *n.* **1.** In bank craps, short for EASY WAY. The number 4, 6, 8, or 10 rolled in combinations of uneven numbers on each die or without pairs of numbers. For example, a roll of one die with three pips, the other with one (*easy way* four); one die with six pips, the other with four (*easy way* ten), and so on.
2. Abbreviated E. In poker, the fifth position to the left of the dealer. *Rare.*
[1949 Coffin *Secrets* 177]

easy money, *n.* Winnings taken from inexperienced players.
1981 Golad *Oral Coll.* The *easy money,* in playing hold 'em comes mainly from tourists. They are having a good time, bet loosely, and usually don't understand the odds as well as a regular.

easy way, *n.* In bank craps, the number 4, 6, 8, or 10 rolled in combinations of uneven numbers on each die, or without pairs of numbers. For example, a roll of one die with three pips, the other with four (*easy way* four); one die with six pips, the other with four (*easy way* ten), and so on. Compare HARDWAY.
[1961 Scarne *Complete Guide* 678]

echo, *n.* Also called a PETER. In bridge, a signal to a partner, made by playing a higher card of a suit before a lower card. The signal may indicate the number of cards of a suit held or request a specific lead, depending on the partner's agreement. [1899 *OEDS*]

echo, *v.* To indicate to a partner how many cards of one suit are being held, or to request a specific lead by means of a signal.
[1885 *OEDS*]

eclipse, *n.* The act of holding a die against the dice cup during a throw so that the die does not turn or roll over. See TOPPING.
1726 Wilson *Art and Mystery* 36. The *Eclipse* is securing a Die on the outside of the Box sideways; it is much us'd at Passage, and at most as Three Throws, as well as Hazard; to discover which, the Box does not produce the same sound; and observe also, that you will always find one Die near the Place where the Box was stamped, and the other remote.
[1711 *OED*]

edge, *n.* **1.** The advantage in a gambling situation. Compare PERCENTAGE.
1974 Scarne *Dice* 54. He must, in some way, gain an advantage or an *edge* on the law of averages; he must have a slightly better chance to win then the next guy.
1968 Thackrey *Secrets* 46. He's got to have what he'd call a "percentage," or *"edge,"* or he couldn't stay in business. And he gets his *edge* by never paying off at true odds.
1977 Puzo *Inside* 18. It's just that the house percentage or *"Edge"* cannot be beat by an honest player.
2. Also called the AGE or ELDEST HAND. The first position to the left of the dealer in poker games in which an automatic bet is used; the player in this position has an advantage because he is the last to act in the first betting round by virtue of the fact that his first bet was automatic and he is given an opportunity to increase it.
1891 Maitland *Amer. Slang Dict.* Age, or *Edge.* The player next to the dealer holds the "age" and is not compelled to bet until all the players have signified their intentions.
[1891 *DARE,* which suggests the term derives from a phonetic similarity to *age.*]

edge work, *n.* The marks placed on the borders of the backs of playing cards, allowing them to be easily identified by a card cheater. See also COSMETICS and CORNER-BEND.
[(1950) 1981 Maurer *Lang. of the Underworld* 185]

eighter from Decatur, *n.* Same as ADA FROM DECATUR. Also shortened to DECATUR. In craps, the number 8.
[1949 Blanche *You Can't Win* 23]

eighth pole, *n.* On a race track, the green and white post placed one furlong (220 yards) from the finish line. Also called EIGHTH POST.
[1982 *Today's Racing*]

eighth post, *n.* Same as EIGHTH POLE. On a race

track, a pole placed one furlong before the finish line.
[1978 Ainslie *Complete Guide* 288]

eighty kings, *n.* In pinochle, a meld of four kings, one from each suit. Compare FORTY JACKS.
[1953 Crawford *Consistent Winner* 345]

eighty-six, *v.* To eject a patron from a casino for improper behavior or cheating.
[ca. 1961 *Hotel Coll*]
[1968 *BDNE I,* probably rhyming slang for *nix,* used in the jargon of cooks, waiters, etc., to indicate that there is nothing left of an item ordered from the menu; later generalized to apply to a person who is refused service because he is disorderly, cannot pay, etc.]

elder hand, *n.* The first player to the left of the dealer. Compare AGE and EDGE.
1836 Eidrah *Hoyle Famil* 4. *Elder hand* is the person who leads, or plays the first card; and the suit to which the card he plays belongs is called the suit led—in that trick.
[1589 *OED,* 1857 *DA*]

eldest hand, *n.* Also AGE or ABLE. The first position at a card table to the left of the dealer, who is the first to act in bidding or betting. If the game is poker and a BLIND is in use, then the first player to the left of the dealer is the last person to act in the first betting round, which is an advantage. Compare LOO and PAM.
1680 Cotton *Compleat Gamester* 65. The *eldest hand* bids for the stock in hopes of bettering his Game . . . The first or eldest says "I'le vye the Ruff."
1714 Lucas *Memoirs* 223. . . . Lanterloo, in which Game you must note, that he who hath 5 Cards of a Suit in his Hand, Loos all the Gamesters then playing, be they never so many, and sweeps the Board; if there be two Loos, he that is the *eldest Hand* hath the Advantage; but if there be a Loo of Trumps, that takes the advantage from all, except any one hath Pamm, that is the Knave of Clubs, who saves his Loo, and is pair for one Trick out of his Stock.
[1589 *OED;* 1857 *DA, DAE*]

electric dice, *n.* Dice altered with metallic fillings that can be controlled electromagnetically. See also LOADED DICE.
[1961 Scarne *Complete Guide* 678]

elevator, *n.* A cheating move at shuffling cards, in which the dealer offers the pack to the player on the right for the cut, then restores the deck to its original sequence. See also HOP THE CUT.
[1982 Martin *Introduction* 24]

elk river, *n.* In poker, a hand with three tens.
[1968 Adams *Western Words*]

end, *n.* **1.** A share of a cheater's winnings given to an accomplice.
2. Any share of a poker pot or other winnings.
[1926 *DA, OEDS*]

end bet, *n.* In poker, the last wager of an interval; the final round of betting in a hand. After all the cards have been dealt, the players make final bets. Many variations of poker allow special *end bets,* such as the allowance of an extra raise, doubling the previous bet, or making a special side bet.
[1964 Reese and Watkins *Secrets* 139]

end-hole, *n.* In cribbage, the last hole gained before exceeding thirty-one points in a hand. The player who plays last without exceeding thirty-one receives one point. If the card played makes thirty-one points exactly, the player receives two points.
1843 Green *Exposure* 270. *End-hole* is gained by the last player, and reckons for one point when under thirty-one, and for two points when thirty-one. To obtain either of these points is considered a great advantage.
[1796 *OEDS*]

end rail, *n.* Also called the BACKBOARD. On a craps table, the padded and quilted cushion at the end of the table against which the dice are required to bounce.
[1983 Martinet *Oral Coll*]

end squeeze, *n.* In faro, a dealing box designed to allow the dealer to select the next card to be drawn. See also NEEDLE MOVEMENT.
[1890 Quinn *Fools of Fortune* 200]

end stripper, *n.* A playing card that has been shaved on the end to make it shorter. The dealer may then use the card in a variety of cheating moves in cutting and dealing cards. See also BELLY STRIPPER and COMBINATION STRIPPERS.
[1890 Quinn *Fools of Fortune* 197]

English, *n.* Also written **english.** In dice play, any of a variety of sliding or spinning motions of the dice made by throwing them with different flicks of the wrist or hand.
[1869 *DA, DAE, OEDS*]
[Probably from the motion or movement used to cause a twist or spin by striking a cue ball in billiards to the right or left of center.]

English poker, *n.* Any of a number of poker variations that are considered unusual, such as playing stud poker and allowing the players to draw additional cards.
[1950 Morehead *Culbertson* 611]

English shot, *n.* In dice, same as a DROP SHOT.
[(1950) 1981 Maurer *Lang. of the Underworld* 185]

enjou, *n. French.* The stake, or wager; the bet.
1843 Green *Exposure* 166. Couche, or *Enjou,* is the stake.

enter, *v.* In backgammon, to free a captured piece from the BAR by rolling an appropriate number on a die.
1860 Crawley *Backgammon* 55. To *enter* means to throw a number on either of the dice; and the point so numbered must be vacant or blotted on the enemy's table. The captured man may be *entered* or placed there.
[1870 *OED*]

entire, *adj.* Of a male racehorse, not castrated.
[1876 *OED*]

entry, *n.* **1.** A contestant in an athletic or sporting event, as a racehorse, boxer, ball team, a person participating in a poker tournament.
[Compare 1885 *OED,* the list of contestants]
2. In bridge, the transference of the lead to a partner or to DUMMY by playing a specific card.
[1884 *OEDS*]

E.O., *n.* Abbreviation for EVEN-ODD. In roulette, an obsolete table layout that used no numbers, but allowed players to wager only on whether the ball would fall into an even numbered slot or an odd numbered slot.
[1750 *OED*]

establish a line, *v. phr.* **1.** In a sports book, to determine the advantage one team has over another and to subtract points from the favored team for betting purposes. See also LINE and SPREAD.
[1973 Clark *Oral Coll*]
2. In a casino, to determine the amount of credit a patron may be given.
[ca. 1961 *Hotel Coll*]

establish a suit, *v. phr.* In games like bridge, to lead cards in such a fashion that the cards of a particular suit can all be winners after an opponent's cards in that suit have been exhausted.
[1950 Morehead *Culbertson* 611]

E.T, *n.* Same as E AND T.
[1983 Martinet *Oral Coll;* see quote at DOLLY PARTON]

euchre, *n.* Also spelled **uker, yuker, eucre. 1.** A card game played by two, three, or four people using a deck of thirty-two cards.
[1841 *OED*]
2. The act of taking advantage of someone, originally by cheating at cards.
[1880 *OED*]

euchre, *v.* **1.** To play the game of euchre.
[1841 *OED*]
2. To gain advantage over someone, especially by cheating at cards.
[1866 *OED*]
3. In euchre, to fail to win three tricks after naming the trump suit.
1887 Keller *Euchre* 20. If the side which adopts or makes the trump, fails to take three tricks, it is *"euchred,"* and the opposing side scores two.

euchreist, *n.* A person who plays euchre.
[1861 *OED*]

European wheel, *n.* A roulette wheel with thirty-seven slots, numbered 0 to 36. Compare AMERICAN WHEEL.
[1964 Lemmel *Gambling* 188]

even, *n.* In roulette, a wager that the ball will fall into an even-numbered slot, such as 2, 4, 6, 8, and so on. Compare ODD.
[ca. 1961 *Hotel Coll*]

even, *adj.* During or at the conclusion of gambling, having the same amount of money one started with because the losses equaled the gains.
[1973 Clark *Oral Coll*]

even break, *n.* Also called **even chance.** A statistically equal chance that an event will or will not occur. See also EVEN MONEY (def. 2).
1981 Golad *Oral Coll.* There's a big difference between even-money and an *even break.* If you get an *even break,* that means your bet has exactly a fifty percent chance of winning or losing. But if you bet even-money that means you can win the same amount that you bet. But the odds are generally against you, so you have less than an *even break,* less than a fifty-fifty chance to win.
[1911 *OEDS* for *even break;* 1816 *OEDS* for *even chance*]

even money, *n.* **1.** In casino twenty-one, a request by a player who has a count of twenty-one on the first two cards to be paid the amount of his bet before the dealer, who has an ace face upward, looks at the card he has dealt himself face downward.
[1973 Clark *Oral Coll*]
2. The odds on a wager that offer the bettor the chance of winning an amount equal to the bet. Compare EVEN BREAK.
1981 Golad *Oral Coll.* There's a big difference between *even-money* and an even break . . . But if you bet *even-money,* that means you can win the same amount that you bet.
[1891 *OEDS*]

even money transfer, *n.* An exchange of money for chips of equal value.
[1978 Alexander *Glossary* 4]

even-odd, *n.* Same as E.O.
[1950 Morehead *Culbertson* 611]

even roll, *n.* A throw of the dice in such a fashion that they both turn the same number of times. An *even roll* is necessary for making a CONTROLLED SHOT which allows the shooter to turn specific faces of the dice upward before throwing.
[(1950) 1981 Maurer *Lang. of the Underworld* 185]

even-up, *adj.* Pertaining to an event that has an equal opportunity to occur or not occur. See also DEAD EVEN (def. 1).
[1961 Scarne *Complete Guide* 678]

exacta, *n.* A wager at horse racing or jai alai in which the bettor must predict the first and second place winners. Compare DAILY DOUBLE and PERFECTA and QUINELLA.
[1964 *OEDS;* from American Spanish, short for *quiniella exacta,* exact QUINELLA]

executive package, *n.* In a casino, a favored patron who is invited to the casino by the management. Compare COMP and HIGH ROLLER.
1980 Clark *Oral Coll.* An *executive package* is a

high roller or a BP [big plunger] who has his plane fare and room comped in exchange for depositing a large amount of money with the casino cage, then drawing on that money to gamble in the casino.

exposed card, *n.* A playing card that is dealt face upward so all the players may see its value. In some games, exposing a card may invalidate the hand. Compare MISDEAL.
[1949 Coffin *Secrets* 177]

exposed hand, *n.* In bridge, the hand held by the partner of the successful bidder, which is laid face upward on the table for the bidder to play. Compare DUMMY.
[1950 Morehead *Culbertson* 611]

exposed pair, *n.* In stud poker, two cards of equal rank turned face upward in the hand of one player.
[1949 Coffin *Secrets* 177]

extend, *v.* In horse racing, to force a horse to run as fast as it can. Compare DRIVE.
[1856 *OEDS*]

extra board, *n.* In a casino, a list of dealers available to report for duty on short notice.
[1977 Anness *Dummy Up*]

eye-in-the-sky, *n.* Also called a WATCHER. In a casino, a security guard or video camera used to watch games from behind two-way mirrors placed in the ceiling.
[1963 Taylor *Las Vegas* 13]

eyes, *n. pl.* Also called **eyes of Texas** and NEEDLES. In hold 'em poker, a pair of aces, especially as the first two cards dealt to a player.
1981 Golad *Oral Coll.* I picked up my hand and saw those *eyes* staring at me. That's when I decided to stay.
1983 Martinet *Oral Coll. Eyes,* that's what you call a pair of aces dealt to you in hold 'em. Some call them the *eyes of Texas* because so many hold 'em players are from Texas. Or maybe it's because hold 'em started in Texas.

eyes down, *n. clause* An announcement at the beginning of a bingo game made by the caller of the game; hence, the beginning of a bingo game.
[1962 *OEDS*]

F

F, *n.* **1.** Abbreviation for FOX. The sixth player to the left of the dealer. *Rare.* Compare A, B, C, D, E, G, H.
[1949 Coffin *Secrets* 177]
2. In horse racing, **a.** abbreviation for *filly,* a young mare.
[*?a*1400 *OED*]
b. abbreviation for *first at all calls,* of a horse in first place at every CALL (def. 5).
[1955 Hillis *Pari-Mutuel Betting* 88]

face, *n.* The front of a playing card, the side with the value of the card represented.
[*c*1645 *OED*]

face card, *n.* Also called a COURT CARD or COUNT CARD. In playing cards, a jack, queen, or king of any suit. [1826 *OED*]

faced card, *n.* A card mistakenly dealt face up rather than face down. See also MISDEAL.
1836 Eidrah *Hoyle Familiar* 4. *Faced Card* is a card lying in the pack with its face upwards, so as to be seen in dealing, and in most games renders a fresh deal necessary.
[1674 *OED*]

face value, *n.* The rank of a playing card as shown on its face. The thirteen cards in a SUIT rank in value from 2, 3, 4, and so on up to ten, then jack, queen, and king. The ace may count as the lowest card or the highest card, depending on the game.
[1951 Jones *Wilbur Clark's* 2]

fade, *v.* **1.** In craps, to match the amount of money, all or in part, which the dice shooter offers as a wager. In a casino or in bank craps, the operator of the game takes all bets for or against the shooter, collecting from the losers and paying the winners. The players are not allowed to make wagers among themselves, or *fade* one another.
[(1950) 1981 Maurer *Lang. of the Underworld* 185]
[1890 *OEDS*]
2. Of a horse in a race, to tire and fall behind the rest of the horses.
[1971 McQuaid *Gambler's Digest* 305]
[Compare 1900 *OEDS*]

fader, *n.* In dice games like hazard or craps, a person who places a wager equal to the amount bet by the person casting the dice.
[(1950) 1981 Maurer *Lang. of the Underworld* 185]

fading craps, *n.* Also called **fading game.** A craps game in which the SHOOTER acts as the BANKER,

taking bets from the rest of the players.
[1950 Morehead *Culbertson* 612]

fairbank, *v.* To allow a victim to win temporarily before cheating him.
[1961 Scarne *Complete Guide* 678]

fair shake, *n.* In dice games, the act of rattling the dice freely in the hand or in a DICE CUP to insure that all six sides of both dice have an equal opportunity to be rolled face upward.
[ca. 1961 *Hotel Coll*]
[Compare 1830 *DA*]

faked box, *n.* A case, or SHOE, for holding cards to be dealt that is constructed so a dealer may cheat the players. Compare DEALING BOX.
[1890 Quinn *Fools of Fortune* 245]

fall, *n.* **the fall of the cards.** The order in which cards are dealt, originally in stud poker. The term came to represent a fatalistic attitude on the part of poker players generally.
[1885 *OED*]

fall, *v.* In bank craps, to lose a particular proposition bet called a HARDWAY BET. For example, a player may wager that the number 4, 6, 8, or 10 will be rolled as a pair on the dice (two twos, two threes, and so on) before the number is rolled with different numbers on each die (three and one for a total of four, two and four for a total of six, and so on), or before the number seven is rolled. If the hardway bet loses, the wager is said to *fall.*
1983 Martinet *Oral Coll.* When a hardway bet comes easy, the stickman says to the player, "Your hard eight (or whatever hardway the guy is on) *fell.* Do you want it back up?" If the guy wants to bet again, he throws a check to the stickman.

fall guy, *n.* In a cheating ring, a DICE MOB or a CARD MOB, the member of the ring designated by mutual consent of mob members to be arrested if the cheating ring is detected. The *fall guy* carries incriminating evidence or otherwise puts himself in a position to be arrested in place of any other mob member. He is then bailed out of jail by his confederates, and the rest of the mob goes free.
[1983 Martinet *Oral Coll*]
[1912 *OEDS; DAS*]

fall money, *n.* Money set aside by a cheater or swindler or a cheating ring for bail or bribery in case of an arrest.
[1893 *OEDS;* 1900 *DA,* 1901 *DAE*]

false-card, *v.* Also written **false card.** In trump games, to play a card other than the one expected so as to mislead an opponent.
[1589 *OEDS*]

false cut, *v.* To divide a deck of cards into separate packets, then put them back into the original sequence while appearing to change the sequence, as a cheating move at playing cards.
[1953 Crawford *Consistent Winner* 346]

false cut, *n.* The act of dividing the deck of cards into separate packets, then putting them back into the original sequence while appearing to change the sequence, as a cheating move at playing cards. Compare FALSE SHUFFLE.
[1890 Quinn *Fools of Fortune* 225]

false matadors, *n. pl. Plural in form but singular in use.* In ombre, a hand with several high trump cards, but without the SPADILLE, the highest trump card.
[1950 Morehead *Culbertson* 612]

false openers, *n. pl.* In draw poker, a hand that does not meet the requirements for the player holding it to initiate betting.
[1968 Wallace *Poker* 214]

false riffle, *n.* Same as FALSE SHUFFLE. *Rare.*
[1968 Wallace *Poker* 215]

false shuffle, *n.* Also called FALSE RIFFLE. Any of a variety of cheating moves by a dealer who appears to mix the pack of cards but retains the original order of the deck. Compare FALSE CUT.
[1890 Quinn *Fools of Fortune* 219]

false start, *n.* In horse racing, the act of beginning a race prematurely. *Rare* since the development and widespread use of the automated gate.
[1978 Ainslie *Complete Guide* 288]
[n.d. *OED;* 1815 *OEDS*]

falter, *v.* Of a racehorse, to hesitate and lose ground during a race for no apparent reason.
[1603 *OED*]

family of games, *n. phr.* A group of games of similar ancestry or similar rules. The poker family includes card games like stud, draw, hold'em, razz, and also variants of these, such as deuces wild, southern cross, spit-in-the-ocean; the craps family of dice games includes bank craps and blanket craps; the bridge family of card games includes auction and duplicate, and so on with other games.
[1950 Morehead *Culbertson* 612]

family pot, *n.* In poker, a pool for which all or nearly all the players are still competing at the end of the hand.
[1949 Coffin *Secrets* 177]

fan, *v.* To mix a pack of cards; to shuffle a deck of cards.
[1950 Morehead *Culbertson* 612]
[Compare 1785 *OED,* in the sense "to beat"]

fanatique, *n.* In the card game ombre, a hazard created by holding four jacks in one hand.
[1950 Morehead *Culbertson* 612]

fan-tan, *n.* Also written **fantan.** A Chinese gambling game, popular in the western U.S. around the turn of the twentieth century, in which a handful of coins are placed under a bowl, then players bet on the number of coins that will remain when the pile has been divided by four.
[1878 *OED;* originally from Chinese *fan t'an* repeated divisions]

faro, *n.* Also spelled PHARO, PHARAO, **pharoah,** PHARAOH, **pharoan, ferro, farro.** A gambling game at cards, in which the players bet on the order in which certain cards will appear when taken singly from the top of the pack. See also BIG FIGURE and CASE KEEPER and DEALING BOX and GRAND SQUARE and JACK SQUARE and LAYOUT and LITTLE FIGURE and NINE SQUARE and POT and SPADES. See 1938 quotation.
1824 Anon *Hoyle's* 65. The game of *Pharo,* or *faro,* is very similar to Basset, a game formerly much in vogue.
1938 Asbury *Sucker's* 7. In front of the dealers was the dealing box, and the layout, the latter a suit of thirteen cards, usually spades, pasted or painted on a large square of enameled oilcloth. On the left of the dealer was another assistant who manipulated the case-keeper, a small box containing a miniature layout, with four buttons running along a steel rod opposite each card. The buttons were moved along, as on a billiard counter, as the cards were played, so that the players could tell at a glance what cards remained to be dealt. In some houses the progress of the game was also kept by the players on small printed sheets. The use of these sheets, however, was not general.
The cards in the layout were arranged in two parallel rows, with the ace on the dealer's left and the odd card, the seven, on his extreme right. Sufficient space was left between the rows for the players to place their bets. In the row nearest the players were the king, queen and jack, called the "big figure," and the ten nine and eight. In the row nearest the dealer were the ace, deuce and trey, called the "little figure," and the four, five and six. The six, seven and eight were called the "pot." The king, queen, ace and deuce formed the "grand square"; the jack, three, four and ten were the "jack square," and the nine, eight, six and five were the "nine square."
[Variant spellings in *OED:* 1717 *pharaon,* 1739 *pharaoh,* 1782 *pharoan,* 1792 *pharo,* 1797 *faro;* 1815 *DAE,* as *faro*]

Faro. The name of this card game is also spelled PHARO or PHAROH. The more colorful description of play is BUCK THE TIGER. The FARO TABLE is managed by a FARO DEALER who uses a DEALING BOX and money supplied by a FARO BANKER. Gamblers bet upon which rank of card will appear next from the box to be counted as either the DEALER'S CARD or the PLAYER'S CARD in each TURN. Neither the SODA (or DEAL CARD) nor the HOCK count in betting which is why SODA TO HOCK describes the game of twenty-five turns. As the KANGAROO CARD and subsequent cards appear, the CASE-KEEPER (or HEARSE-DRIVER) records them on the CASE RACK so that a bettor may KEEP CASES on his own CUE CARD. A BRACE GAME is often characterized by a CHEATING BOX (sometimes called a COFFEEMILL or a HORSE BOX or a TELL BOX) which allows the BANKER to control the game. All this action is watched over by the LOOKER OUT.

Bettors may COPPER A BET (in a FLAT FOOT), COPPER THE ODDS or PLAY THE CASES by STRINGING ALONG a series of bets with wins and/or losses, such as a SINGLE-OUT or DOUBLE-OUT. An adventurous player may attempt to swindle the FARO BANK when he will use a COPPER ON AND COPPER OFF, or run a HORSEHAIR GAME.

However, if the player can CALL THE TURN the payoff will be four times the bet. When a player loses two bets on a single turn he is WHIPSAWED.

The sequence of cards in a turn is so important to the play that BACKLEGS who TWIST THE TIGER'S TAIL developed names for them long ago: the HANGMAN'S TURN is the jack and king, the MEDICINE TWIN is the queen and nine, while two fives is the PICKPOCKET TURN.

faro bank, *n.* The money, layout, chips, cases, and assistants required to operate a faro game.
[1756 *OED,* 1815 *DAE*]

faro banker, *n.* The person who supplies the bankroll to operate a faro game.
[1798 *OED,* 1858 *DAE*]

faro box, *n.* The DEALING BOX, or SHOE used in a faro game to hold the cards before they are drawn. [1848 *DAE*]

faro dealer, *n.* Also written **faro-dealer.** The operator of a faro game, the person who deals the cards, collects and pays bets, and, unless he has an assistant, KEEPS CASES.
[1856 *DAE, OEDS*]

faro table, *n.* A layout with figures of thirteen cards painted on a felt surface on which players may wager whether cards of a particular rank will appear on the banker space or the player space, which are also painted on the felt.
[*a*1735 *OED,* 1799 *DAE*]

fasse, *n. French.* In basset, the first card turned face upward by the dealer. The dealer takes half of all money wagered on that card rank. See quotation at BASSET.
[1645 *OED*]

fast close, *n.* A burst of speed by a racehorse in the HOME STRETCH. See also DRIVE and EXTEND.
[1971 McQuaid *Gambler's Digest* 305]

fast company, *n.* Seasoned or professional gamblers.
[ca. 1961 *Hotel Coll*]

fast count, *n.* A method for cheating a player by paying a winning bet quickly while holding back part of the winnings then moving rapidly to the next wagering event, whether it be throwing dice, dealing cards, or some other gambling activity.
[ca. 1961 *Hotel Coll*]

fast game, *n.* A poker game in which the players make large bets frequently and quickly.
[1968 Wallace *Poker* 215]

fast player, n. In poker, a player who bets large amounts and raises bets frequently to drive

conservative players from the hand.
[1973 Preston *Play Poker* 167]

fast sevens, *n. pl.* Dice that have been shaved so the number seven appears more frequently than normal. [1974 Scarne *Dice* 236]

fast shuffle, *n.* Also called a DOUBLE SHUFFLE. A cheating move in card dealing in which a dealer appears to mix two packets of cards, but retains the original order by pulling one packet through the other, then replacing the top half on the deck. Compare FALSE CUT.
[1983 Martinet *Oral Coll*]
[*DAS; DSUE*]

fast track, *n.* A racetrack that is dry and hard-packed.
[1955 Hillis *Pari-Mutuel Betting* 114]

fat, *adj.* Pertaining to a gambler or player with a large bankroll.
[(1950) 1981 Maurer *Lang. of the Underworld* 185]
[Compare 17th Century *DSUE*; 1817 *DAE*; c1920 *DAS*; 1928 *OEDS*, in *fat cat*]

fat deck, *n.* In twenty-one, a deck in which a large number of cards worth ten points are undealt after nearly half of the deck has been used.
[1973 Clark *Oral Coll*]

fatten, *v.* Also called FEED or SWEETEN. Especially in the phrases:
fatten the kitty or **fatten the pot,** In poker, to add chips to the pot.
[1949 Coffin *Secrets* 177]
fatten the trick, In pinochle, to play a high-counting card on a trick won by one's partner.
[1950 Morehead *Culbertson* 612]
[Compare 1697 *OEDS*; for figurative use]

fat trick, *n.* In trump games, a packet of cards containing several which count additional points for the person winning the packet.
[1950 Morehead *Culbertson* 612]

favorite, *n.* **1.** A horse, dog, person, or team expected to win an event; the entry in a sporting event with the lowest odds posted for bettors.
[1813 *OED*]
2. Especially in the phrase: **favorite suit.** In ombre or quadrille, the suit that has preference over the others.
[1763 *OEDS*]

feather-edge dice, *n. pl. Plural in form, but singular in use.* Dice that have been physically altered by shaving one or more edges or by beveling the corners so the dice are unlikely to come to rest on certain faces. Compare BARR DICE and LOADED DICE.
[ca. 1961 *Hotel Coll*]

fee-bee, *n.* In dice games, a roll of the number five.
[ca. 1968 Adams *Western Words*]
[Probably corrupted from *phoebe.*]

feed, *v.* Also called FATTEN or SWEETEN. Especially in the phrases: **feed the kitty** or **feed the pot.** In poker, to place chips in the pot.
[1950 Morehead *Culbertson* 612]

feeler, *n.* **1.** In poker, a small wager made to see who will increase the bet.
[Compare 1830 *OED,* a proposal to ascertain the opinions of others]
2. The confederate of a cheater, especially an assistant to a dice cheater, who helps to locate a victim and assess how best to cheat him.
[Compare 1847 *OED,* a scout]
3. A trial of a horse in a race of lesser prestige.
[1883 *OED*]

feet, *n. pl.* In bank craps, an additional wager on a bet already made; the odds taken on a FLAT BET.
1983 Martinet *Oral Coll.* After a player has a point on a come bet, the dealer will move the bet to the top of the layout and ask the player if he wants to put *feet* on it. If the player wants the odds, he puts the right number of checks on the layout and the dealer, not the player, puts the odds on the bet.

fever¹, *n.* An uncontrolled gambling habit.
[(1950) 1981 Maurer *Lang. of the Underworld* 185]

fever², *n.* **1.** The number five on a playing card or die.
[(1950) 1981 Maurer *Lang. of the Underworld* 185]
2. A bill or chip worth five dollars.
[ca. 1961 *Hotel Coll*]
[Probably a corruption of *fiver* 1843 *OEDS,* a five dollar bill]

fido, *n.* In horse racing, a combination bet of twenty wagers made by selecting five horses and combining two or three horses for each wager.
[1974 Ewart *Flatracing* 149]

field, *n.* **1.** On a bank craps table, a section of the layout for betting that the next number rolled will be the number 2, 3, 4, 9, 10, 11, or 12.
[(1950) 1981 Maurer *Lang. of the Underworld* 185]
2. The horses entered in a specific race.
[1955 Hillis *Pari-Mutuel Betting* 114]
[Compare 1806-7 *OED,* those who are to take part in the sport, hunting]
3. All the competitors in a race except the favorite. [1742 *OEDS*]
4. In keno, a group of numbers selected as a unit on a WAY TICKET, that is, a ticket with combinations of groups of numbers selected by the player.
[ca. 1961 *Hotel Coll*]

field bet, *n.* In bank craps, a wager that the next roll of the dice will be the number 2, 3, 4, 9, 10, 11, or 12.
[(1950) 1981 Maurer *Lang. of the Underworld* 185]

field roll, *n.* In bank craps, any roll of the dice that results in the number 2, 3, 4, 9, 10, 11, or 12.
[1974 Powell *Verbal Dexterity* 8]

fifteen, *n.* In cribbage, a score of two cards equaling fifteen pips, which counts two points for the person scoring.
1843 Green *Exposure* 270. Every *fifteen* reckons for two points, whether in hand or playing. In hand they are formed either by two cards, such as five and any tenth card, a six and a nine, a seven and an eight, or by three cards, as a two, a five, and an eight, &c. And in playing thus; if such cards are played as make together fifteen, the two points are to be scored towards the game.
[1674 *OED*]

fifth street, *n.* In stud and hold'em poker, the last card dealt face upward in a hand.
[1976 Sklansky *Hold'em Poker*]

fifty card, *n.* A certificate issued by a law-enforcement agency indicating security clearance for a casino employee. See also "A" CARD and SHERIFF'S CARD
1963 Taylor *Las Vegas* 100. No inside man can work on the Strip without the county's *"50" card*, or downtown without the city's "A" card, signifying clearance.
1983 Clark *Oral Col.* We used to call a work permit an A card, but since Metro was formed [Las Vegas Metropolitan Police, combining city and county police], we just call it and the *fifty card* a sheriff's card.

fifty-fifty, *adj.* Pertaining to an equal chance to win or lose on a bet.
[1974 Scarne *Dice* 52]
[Compare 1913 *OEDS,* 1981 *DA,* generally half-and-half]

fifty-five, *n.* **1.** In primiera, the ace, 7, and 6 of one suit held in the same hand, a scoring combination.
[1950 Morehead *Culbertson* 613]
2. In craps, a roll with ten pips showing.
[1974 Powell *Verbal Dexterity* 8]

fight the tiger, *v. phr.* To gamble at FARO.
[1839 *OED* under "tiger"; 1847 *DA*]
[From the figure of a tiger on many faro layouts.]

figure, *n.* **1.** In playing cards, a jack, queen, or king; a FACE CARD or COURT CARD.
[1950 Morehead *Culbertson* 613]
2. In faro, an area on the layout for betting on multiple cards.
1843 Green *Exposure* 165. It may be played by any number of persons; and each player, or punter, as he is termed, is furnished with a suit of cards denominated a livret, and four other cards which are called *figures;* viz: the first is a plain card, with a blue cross, and is called the little figure, and designates the ace, deuce, and three. The second is a yellow card, and answers for the four, five, and six. The third is a plain card, with a black lozenge in the center; and designates the eight nine and ten. The fourth is a red card, and answers for the king, queen and knave.

fill, *v.* **1.** In poker, to receive cards late in the hand which improve the chances for winning.
1866 *American Card Player* 134. *Filling.*—To match, or strengthen the cards to which you draw.
[1865 *DAE, OEDS;* 1903 *DA*]
2. To place a weight in a die to alter the natural roll. Compare LOADED DICE.
[1974 Scarne *Dice* 218]
3. In a casino, to supply a table with chips from the casino cage.
[1963 Taylor *Las Vegas* 11]

fill, *n.* **1.** The act of drawing cards in poker that improve the hand.
[1963 Taylor *Las Vegas* 11]
[1866 *DA*]
2. Also **fills,** *pl.* The weight placed in a die to alter its natural roll.
[(1950) 1981 Maurer *Lang. of the Underworld* 185]
3. In a casino, the chips sent from the casino cage to replenish a game.

fill slip, *n.* In a casino, a numbered form or receipt on which is recorded the value of chips taken from the casino cage to a gaming table, and which is signed by an employee in the CAGE, the PIT BOSS, and the DEALER at the table to which the chips are delivered.
[1960 Cook *Gambling, Inc.* 300]

filly, *n.* In poker, a FULL HOUSE; three cards of one rank and two cards of another rank.
[1978 Larson *Vocabulary* 98]

fimps, *n. Plural in form, but singular in use.* In craps, a cast of two fives; a HARD ten.
[1968 Adams *Western Words*]

final credit, *n.* Also called FINAL FILL. In a casino, the action of supplying chips to a gaming table at the end of a shift to equal the amount that the table had at the beginning of the shift.
[1982 Martin *Introduction* 24]

final fill, *n.* Same as FINAL CREDIT.
[1978 Alexander *Glossary* 4]

finesse, *n.* In card games like whist or bridge, the attempt to take a trick with a lower card than necessary on the chance that the opponent will not hold a card of greater value or not use it if he does. [1862 *OED*]

finesse, *v.* In card games like whist or bridge, to attempt to take a trick with a lower card than necessary on the chance the opponent will not hold a card of greater value or not use it if he does.
1746 Hoyle *Short Treatise* 68. *Finnessing* means the endeavoring to gain an Advantage by Art and Skill, which consists in this; when a Card is led [by the player on the right] and you have best and third best card of that suit, you judge it best to put your third best Card upon that Lead, and run the Risk of your Adversary's having the second best of it, that if he has it not, which is 2

to 1 against him, you are then sure of gaining a Trick.
[1746 *OED*]

finger, *n.* One of the flat metal bars or rods between the reels of a slot machine that catch the indentations on the reels and stop them from rotating.
[1941 Fair *Spill the Jackpot* 47]

finger bet, *n.* In a casino, a signal to a PIT BOSS that a player wishes to wager a specific amount. The player holds up two or three fingers indicating he wishes to bet two or three hundred dollars. If the pit boss nods, the player need not place the money for the wager on the table layout.
[1974 Friedman *Casino Management* 90]

fingering, *n.* A cheating move in playing cards, made by marking a playing card by bending it slightly. See also CORNER-BEND and CRIMP.
[1978 Larson *Vocabulary* 98]

finger poker, *n.* A poker session in which all players have credit with the banker and collect their winnings or pay their losses at the end of the session.
[1968 Wallace *Poker* 215]

finish, *n.* **1.** Also called **finish line.** The designated ending place of a race.
[1879 *OED*]
2. The position of a horse in relation to the rest of the field, or entries, at the end of a race.
[ca. 1961 *Hotel Coll*]

finish, *v.* To come to the end of a course or race.
[1881 *OED*]

first base, *n.* In twenty-one, the first position to the left of the dealer. See also THIRD BASE.
[1977 Cahill *Recollections* 680]

first break, *n.* In a casino, the initial relief period at the beginning of a shift. Compare EARLY OUT.
1983 Martinet *Oral Coll.* People have different feelings about *first break* because you show up for work and before you even start you have to take a break. Usually, whoever shows up late gets *first break* and they don't like it because they know they won't get early out.

first dozen, *n.* In roulette, a wager on the numbers 1 through 12.
[ca. 1961 *Hotel Coll*]

first flop dice, *n. phr.* Also called DEAD NUMBER DICE. Heavily LOADED DICE that do not roll easily.
[(1950) 1981 Maurer *Lang. of the Underworld* 185]

first jack, *n.* In card games, a method to determine the first person to be the dealer in which one player distributes cards face upward to the other players in turn. The first time a jack is turned up, the player it was dealt to becomes the dealer.
[1949 Coffin *Secrets* 177]

first over, *n.* In horse racing, the first horse to challenge the leader on the outside, away from the rail.
1979 Clark *Oral Coll.* The *first over* comes up on the outside. We say he came overland. If he can pass the pack, he'll take the rail. If he's in the stretch, he won't come all the way over to the rail, but will maintain on a straight line. But he's still called the *first over.*

fish, *n.* Chips or counters used in wagering games.
1836 Eidrah *Hoyle Famil* 31. The players put eight counters or *fish* into the pool, and dealer four additional.
[1728 *OED*]
[French *fiche* chip]

fish, *v.* In the phrase:
fish or cut bait, Among poker players, to not hesitate too long before betting or dropping out of the hand.
[1949 Coffin *Secrets* 177]
[1876 *DAE, DA, DAS*]

fishback, *n.* A deck of cards marked so a cheater can read the cards from the back.
[1968 Adams *Western Words*]
[The *fishback* was a style of playing cards used in the latter part of the eighteenth century, with a scallop design on the back.]

fishhook, *n.* In playing cards, another name for a jack or a seven.
[1968 Wallace *Poker* 209]
[From the resemblance of a 7 or J (for jack) to a fishhook.]

five and dime, *n.* In poker, a hand with a five and a ten and three unmatched cards between.
[1968 Wallace *Poker* 215]

five count, *n.* In twenty-one, a system for counting cards that have been played.
[1973 Clark *Oral Coll*]

five-eighths pole, *n.* In horse racing, the post placed five furlongs before the finish line on a race track.
[1978 Ainslie *Complete Guide* 289]

five fingers, *n.* In the card game of spoil five or five cards, the five of trumps, which is the highest ranking card.
1680 Cotton *Compleat Gamester* 88. The *five fingers* (alias, five of trumps) is the best Card in the Pack; the Ace of Hearts is next to that, and the next is the Ace of Trumps.
[1611 *OED*]

five-number bet, *n. phr.* In roulette, a combination bet on the 0, 00, and the numbers 1, 2, and 3.
[ca. 1961 *Hotel Coll*]

five of a kind, *n. phr.* In poker games that use a WILD CARD, five cards of the same rank.
[1963 Steig *Common Sense* 183]

five-point card, *n. phr.* In canasta, any club or spade with a rank of 7, 6, 5, 4, or a 3, each of which counts for five points to the player holding it.

[1953 Crawford *Consistent Winner* 346]

five-suit pack, *n. phr.* A deck of playing cards with 65 cards rather than the normal 52-card deck with four suits. The extra suit contains thirteen cards of a suit usually called "crowns" or EAGLES.
[1950 Morehead *Culbertson* 613]

fix, *n.* Especially **the fix**. The bribing of an official to ignore an illegal gambling game, the marking of cards, the loading of dice, the bribing of a contestant to lose a race, boxing match, or game.
[1949 Coffin *Secrets* 177]
[Compare 1929 *OEDS*, "a bribe"]

fix, *v.* To insure the outcome of an event by eliminating the element of chance before the event takes place; to mark playing cards, load dice, bribe contestants or officials, and so on.
[1790 *DA* "bribe official"; 1865 *DA* "arrange outcome of a race"; 1881 *DAE* "alter horse to prevent its winning"]

fixed deck, *n.* A pack of playing cards arranged in a particular sequence (STACKED) or marked so the backs of the cards can inform a cheater of the face value of each. Compare COSMETICS.
[1953 Lewis *Sagebrush Casinos* 72]

fixed fight, *n.* A boxing match with a predetermined winner, usually accomplished by bribing or coercing one of the boxers to lose.
[1971 McQuaid *Gambler's Digest* 305]

fixed limit, *n.* In many gambling games, but especially in poker, a predetermined amount of money allowed as a maximum wager. See also TABLE STAKES and NO-LIMIT.
[1968 Wallace *Poker* 215]

fixed race, *n.* In racing, same as a BOAT RACE.
[1931 *DA, OEDS*]

fixer, *n.* A person who arranges dishonest or illegal activities by bribing officials or contestants, or by providing marked or stacked cards or altered dice. Compare COSMETICS and LOADED DICE and STACKED DECK.
[(1950) 1981 Maurer *Lang. of the Underworld* 185]

flag, *v.* To signal a confederate during a cheating move.
[(1950) 1981 Maurer *Lang. of the Underworld* 185]

flash, *v.* In card playing, especially poker, to show a card to another player either purposely or accidentally. Compare FLOP and TELL.
1981 Golad *Oral Coll.* You practice giving false tells and you pick up some other tricks. For example, you can *flash* another player and make it look accidental. Say I'm sitting with a jack-five and the flop comes five, five, three. Maybe I'll *flash* the jack so whoever sees it makes me for a pair of jacks at most, but I've really got trips.

flash cash, *n.* A roll of money used to impress others, especially in an attempt to win favors. Compare C-NOTE and COMP and DRUMMER.
1983 Martinet *Oral Coll.* Guys try to get comps by impressing the pit boss with how much they are worth. They might shuffle checks or use a wad of *flash cash . . . Flash cash* is a roll of bills, usually with a C-note [$100 bill] on the outside and wrapped with a rubber band. They will play with it in an absent-minded fashion while they are putting the rap on the pit boss. Sometimes it's laughable, because anyone with *flash cash* is a drum [stingy person].

flasher, *n.* An attendant at a gaming table. *Obsolete.* [1731 *OED*]

flat, *adj.* **1.** In pan, pertaining to the melding of ten cards. Compare MELD.
1982 Clark *Oral Coll.* To go *flat* or make a *flat* play means that a player melds all ten cards at one time and not the eleventh. It makes everybody sit up and take notice.
2. Usually in the expression FLAT DICE. Of false dice, shaved on one or more sides to make them broad and thin.
[1550 *OED*]
3. In horse racing, pertaining to a course laid out on level ground without hedges or ditches.
[1836 *OED*]

flat, *n.* **1.** A dupe or person easily cheated.
[1762 *OED*]
2. Especially **flats,** *pl.* Same as FLAT DICE.
[1545 *OED*]
3. Usually **flats,** *pl.* A playing card.
[1812 OED]
4. In horse racing, a level course without hedges or ditches. [1836 *OED*]
5. Short for FLAT-RACER, a horse that races on flat ground without jumps or ditches.
[1811 *OED*]

flat bet, *n.* **1.** Also called a STRAIGHT BET. A wager that is paid, when won, with the same amount as bet.
[1973 Friedman *Casino Games* 46]
2. A bet made with another player or observer, not with the banker; a SIDE BET.
[(1950) 1981 Maurer *Lang. of the Underworld* 186]

flat call, *n.* In poker, to match the bet made by an earlier player, without raising the amount; a CALL BET.
[1978 Brunson *How I Made* 531]

flat catcher, n. A person who takes advantage of naive players; a cheater. *Rare.*
[1841 *OED*]

flat dice, *n.* Dice shaved on one face so as to roll a particular number more often than another. Compare BARR DICE.
1726 Wilson *Art and Mystery* 32. As there are three sorts of *Flatt Dice*, such as Quatre-Trois, Six-Ace, and Cinq-Deux, so there are the same sorts of Barr Dice. The Difference is this: That as a Pair of Flatt Six-Aces commonly come up

oftner than any other Seven, so a Pair of Barr Six-Aces seldom or never come up because the Six-Ace falls away from the Center towards each corner, that the Die will not easily lie upon that point.
[1711 *OED*; 1545 *OED* as *flattes*]

flat foot, *n.* In faro, a bet placed on a single card rather than on a combination of cards.
1868 Trumps *Pocket Hoyle* 203. The check "*flat foot*" upon the Ace, is bet upon that card only.

flat gig, *n.* In policy or numbers, a sequence of three numbers, specified in the order in which they will appear.
[1938 Asbury *Sucker's Progresss* 92]

flat joint, *n.* Also called a FLAT STORE. A gambling establishment in which the players are cheated regularly.
[1961 Scarne *Complete Guide* 679]

flat limit, *n.* In poker, a fixed amount of money set for betting and for raising previous bets.
[1968 Wallace *Poker* 215]

flat passers, *n. pl.* Dice shaved on various faces so that the numbers rolled most frequently are 4, 5, 9, and 10, that is to say, passing or winning numbers.
[1961 Scarne *Complete Guide* 679]

flat play, *n.* A method of making a series of wagers of the same amount.
1983 Martinet *Oral Coll.* You can't make any money with the FLAT PLAY. If you sit there putting out the same amount time after time, you'll just get eaten up slowly. You have to ride the game and push hell out your raises when you're in a streak. If somebody on a *flat play* is winning reds [five-dollar chips] regularly and is up fifty or sixty bucks, he should be up three hundred. But just plugging along, he'll eventually go back down and think he was lucky to break even. If he hadn't just used *flat play*, he could quit even a hundred ahead.

flat race, *n.* A horse race run over level ground without jumps, as opposed to hurdle-racing or steeple-chasing.
[1848 *OED*]

flat racer, *n.* A horse trained to race on a level course without jumps.
[1886 *OED*]

flat racing, *n.* Horse racing on a track without jumps or hurdles.
[1886 *OED*]

flats, *n.* **1.** Same as FLAT DICE.
[1545 *OED*]
2. Playing cards.
[1812 *OED*]

flat store, *n.* Same as FLAT JOINT.
[1961 Smith and Noble *Quit Winners* 21]

float, *n.* **1.** Also called CHIP FLOAT. In a casino, the value of all chips held by the players.
[1973 Clark *Oral Coll*]
2. floats, *pl.* Dice hollowed at one corner to change the balance and the frequency of certain numbers being rolled. Such dice float in a bowl of water.
[(1950) 1981 Maurer *Lang. of the Underworld* 186]

floating crap game, *n. phr.* Also shortened to **floating game.** An illegal game, usually craps, that is moved from place to place to avoid detection by the authorities.
[(1950) 1981 Maurer *Lang. of the Underworld* 186]

floorman, *n.* In a casino, the representative of the management who watches over one or more games. The floorman reports to the PIT BOSS or the SHIFT BOSS.
1983 Martinet *Oral Coll.* Working from the bottom up in the pecking order, you have the dealer, then the boxman in craps, then the *floorman* in craps or twenty-one. If you have a big dice pit with several games, then you might have a pit boss in craps. In twenty-one the pit boss has several tables and his *floormen* report to him. He reports to the shift boss. The shift boss may or may not be the casino manager. And the casino manager usually has some points [owns a percentage of the casino] but probably reports to the owner, or the guy fronting for the owners.
[(1950) 1981 Maurer *Lang. of the Underworld* 186]

flop, *n.* **1.** In hold 'em poker, the turning up of three COMMON CARDS in the center of the table, after each player has received two cards face down.
[1968 Wallace *Poker* 215]
2. Also called HOP (def. 1). A single cast of the dice.
[1983 Martinez *Gambling Scene* 202]

flush, *n.* In poker or cribbage, a hand of cards which are all of the same suit.
1843 Green *Exposure* 270. [In cribbage] flush is when all the cards are all of the same suit, and reckons for as many points as cards.
[By extension from the sense of "sated" or "completely filled," 1529 *OED*; 1857 *DAE*]

flushing the john, *v. phr.* Playing the slot machines.
[1979 Newman *Dealer's Special* 32]
[The pun is on *john* as a "victim" and as a "toilet." Pulling the handle on the slot machine after depositing money is likened to putting money into a toilet and pulling the handle.]

flush-spot dice, *n. pl.* Dice with the pips painted on the surface of each face rather than indented, then filled with paint.
[(1950) 1981 Maurer *Lang. of the Underworld* 186]

flush-spots, *n. pl.* Same as FLUSH-SPOT DICE.
[1961 Scarne *Complete Guide* 679]

fluss, *n.* Same as a FLUSH.
[n.d. *OED*]

flux, *n.* Same as a FLUSH.
[1798 *OED*]

fly bet, *n.* Any unusual or unlikely wager.
[1977 Carroll *Playboy's Illustrated* 43]
[Perhaps from the *fly and sugar hustle*, in which a cheater puts out two cubes of sugar, one dosed with DDT, and offers bets on which cube a fly will land on first.]

flyer, *n.* **1.** A racehorse.
[1856 *DAE*]
2. flyers, *Plural in form, but singular in use.* In backgammon, the action of bringing a single piece around the board before one's opponent moves a single piece to the outer table. This requires throwing high scoring dice (usually doublets) at the beginning of the game.
1680 Cotton *Compleat Gamester* 114. *Flyers* is, when you bring a man round the Tables before your Adversary hath got over his first Table, to the effecting of which there is required very high throwing of your side, and very low throwing of his.

flying, *adj.* In poker, pertaining to three cards of the same rank in a FULL HOUSE, that is, a hand with three cards of one rank and two cards of another rank.
1949 Coffin *fortune* 178. Kings *flying* are kings full.

fly the turn, *v. phr.* In greyhound racing, to run wide at a turn on an oval track and thereby lose ground.
[1968 Buchele *Greyhound Racing* 96]

foamy cleanser, *n.* Also called an AJAX. In hold 'em poker, an ace and a jack as the first two cards dealt to a player.
1981 Golad *Oral Coll.* A player sits there hour after hour with only two cards to look at, so the different combinations get names . . . *foamy cleanser* is a spinoff of Ajax, ace and jack.
[From the way the product is advertised: "Ajax, the *foamy cleanser*"]

foil the cut, *v. phr.* To make a cheating move at playing cards, specifically, to return the pack of playing cards to its original sequence after another player has separated the deck into two piles. [1968 Wallace *Poker* 215]

fold, *v.* In poker, to withdraw or retire from a hand.
[1949 Coffin *Secrets* 178]
[Compare 1865 *OED,* meaning "to fold the hands;" or *a*1250 *OED,* meaning "to fail"]

follow suit, *v. phr.* In trump games, to play a card of the same suit as that led, or placed on the table, by the first player.
[1680 *OED,* under "suit"]

fool, *n.* In guimbaude, the jack of diamonds.
[1950 Morehead *Culbertson* 613]

foot, *n.* **1.** In panguingue, the bottom part of the pack of cards that is set aside.
[Compare 1669 *OED*]
2. A good speed by a race horse.
[1737 *OED*]

footing, *n.* The condition (hard, soft, muddy, and so on) of a race track. Compare FAST TRACK.
[(1951) 1981 Maurer *Lang. of the Underworld* 211]

for, *prep.* Expressing a relationship by substitution of two quantities in a wager, by which odds offered by the first bettor are *exchanged* for the wager by the second bettor when the second bettor is the winner. See also TO.
1969 Clark *Oral Coll.* The only admonition I have to offer is to beware of the distinction between to and *for* when you are taking or placing a bet. *To* means you are placing one wager against that of another person, at whatever odds, and the winner will take both bets. For example, if you take either side of a bet at 5 to 1 odds and win, you end up with the six units placed at stake. On the other hand, *for* means that the wager of one person offering odds replaces that of the person taking the bet. Say you put up 1 unit for 5, that is, you take odds of 5 for 1. If you win, the person offering the odds replaces your one unit with his five. So when you win at 5 to 1, you end up with six units, and when you win at 5 *for* 1 you end up with five units.
[Compare *c*1000 *OED*, meaning "in place of;" and *a*1225 *OED*, with the meaning of staking a specific amount or object risked, but does not offer a citation in the sense of replacing the odds offered for a wager by another person.]

force, *v.* **1.** In card games like whist or bridge, to oblige another player to use a particular card by using a specific lead or a conventional signal.
[1746 *OED*]
2. In poker, to increase the amount wagered by a previous player; to RAISE.
[1949 Coffin *Secrets* 178]
3. In the phrases:
force a card, To project a card slightly from the pack, so that, when told to draw a card, the player is likely to pick the projecting card.
1859 Green *Gambler's Tricks* 46. He will sometime *force a card.* This is done by projecting a little some three of four cards that he knows, and has previously looked at. These cards, by projecting a little, are most handy to you, and you will be likely to take one of them.
force the cut, To make a cheating move in playing cards, specifically to divide a deck of cards into two parts at a prearranged card. The cut may be made by the person manipulating the cards or by an accomplice. Compare FUZZ (def. 1). [ca. 1961 *Hotel Coll*]

force, *n.* In card games like bridge and whist, an act of forcing. [1862 *OED*]

force bet *n.* In stud poker, the requirement that the player with the highest-ranking card(s) act first in the betting round.
[1981 Golad *Oral Coll*]

force-in, *n.* In poker, a required bet on the part of the first player to the left of the dealer. The player retains the option to increase, or raise the

bet after the rest of the players have acted in that betting round.
[1968 Wallace *Poker* 215]

forcing, *n.* In trump games, the obliging of a player to use a trump card.
1746 Hoyle *Short Treatise* 68. *Forcing* means the obliging your Partner or your Adversary to trump a Suit of which [suit] he has none.

forcing bid, *n.* In bridge, a demand that one's partner keep the bidding open, normally until the person making a *forcing bid* reaches game or the highest bid.
[1953 Crawford *Consistent Winner* 346]
[1862 *OEDS*]

forcing pass, *n.* In bridge, a bid that requires one's partner to double, or challenge, the bid of an opponent.
[1950 Morehead *Culbertson* 614]

forehand, *adj.* In three-handed card games, designating the person with the privilege to act first in betting. See also ELDEST HAND.
[1892 *OED*]

foreign check, *n.* Also called FOREIGN CHIP. In a casino, a chip from a different casino.
[1979 Hughes *Dealing* 53]

foreign chip, *n.* Same as FOREIGN CHECK.
[1957 *Nevada Gaming Regulations* 33]

foreigners in action, *n. clause* In a casino, a phrase used by a DEALER to announce to the FLOORMAN that chips from another casino are being used at the table.
[1983 Martinet *Oral Coll*]

Foreign Words. Many terms of gambling argot, as in the English vocabulary generally, are borrowed especially from such languages as French and Spanish. ROULETTE is, perhaps, one of the more obvious ones. It has even non-gambling meanings as have such other borrowings as: CARTE BLANCHE, FINESSE, PARLAY, and MATADOR. CHEMIN-DE-FER, JAI ALAI, PELOTA, ROUGE-ET-NOIRE (also called TRENTE ET QUARANTE) and VINGTE-ET-UN are well known names of games which are non-English in origin.

The names for cards from Spanish include: BASTO, CINQUE PRIMERO, MALLILLIO, PEDRO, and SPADILLO. French card names include: BRELAN and BRELAN CARRE, FANATIQUE, PARTIE CARREE, SEPTIET and TIERCE.

A loss may be a CODILLE or GRAND MISERE; a tie may be L'UNE POUR L'AUTRE. A bet may be a PAIX, PAIX PAROLET, or PARLAY.

With dice one may take a PIQUE SHOT. Equipment names include FRIJOLE and PALETTE. While people or jobs include CROUPERE or TAILLEUR.

KIBITZ comes from Yiddish (ultimately from German). While MELD derives directly from German. TREY from French is well established and recognizable as "English". In contrast: ACCOMMODEZ MOI, AU CARRE and BANCO SUIVI appear to retain features which betray their non-English origins.

form, *n.* **1.** In racing, a publication listing all the information about the previous performances of a horse or dog. Same as RACING FORM.
[(1951) 1981 Maurer *Lang. of the Underworld* 211]
2. The physical condition of a horse or dog before a race. [1760 *OED*]
3. The style and speed of a horse or dog while running a race.
[1971 McQuaid *Gambler's Digest* 305]
[Compare 1868 *OED*, meaning "manners, etc.," and 1877 *OED*, meaning "speed, liveliness"]

form player, *n.* A bettor who makes all decisions about which horse or dog to wager on from the published information. Compare DOPE SHEET and RACING FORM.
[1978 Ainslie *Complete Guide* 289]

forty-four, *n.* In alsos, the declaration of an intention to win all four aces.
[1950 Morehead *Culbertson* 614]

forty jacks, *n.* In pinochle, four jacks, one of each suit, held in the same hand. Compare EIGHTY KINGS.
[1953 Crawford *Consistent Winner* 346]

foul hand, *n.* A MISDEAL in draw poker.
1866 *American Card Player* 134. *Foul Hand.*—A hand composed of more or less than five cards.
[1864 *DA, DAE*]

foundation, *n.* In stud poker, the first card dealt to a player. See also DOOR CARD.
[1949 Coffin *Secrets* 178]

four-bluff, *n.* In poker, an attempt to bet high enough to force out players while holding only a FOUR STRAIGHT or FOUR FLUSH.
[1949 Coffin *Secrets* 178]

four-bluffer, *n.* In poker, a player who bets while holding only a FOUR STRAIGHT or FOUR FLUSH.
[1949 Coffin *Secrets* 178]
→Commonly used of a person who bets while holding such a hand after all the cards have been dealt for the hand.

four-flush, *n.* Also written **fourflush.** In poker, a hand with four cards of the same suit and one card from a different suit. In some variations of poker, a *four-flush* ranks higher as a hand than a pair, two cards of the same rank. Compare BOBTAIL.
[1887 *DA, DAE, OEDS*]

four-flush, *v.* Also written **four flush**, but especially as **four-flushing**. In poker, to bluff with four cards of one suit, one card of another; usually a worthless hand.
[1901 *DA*]

four-flusher, *n.* Also written **fourflusher.** Also called **four-card flusher**. In poker, a player who tries to cheat by showing four cards of a flush, hoping to steal the pot without showing a fifth card from a different suit.
[1904 *OEDS*; 1910 *DA, DAE*]

four-number bet, n. In roulette, a bet placed on

four numbers by placing a chip at the intersection of the four numbers.
[1968 Thackrey *Nick the Greek* 157]

four of a kind *n.* Four cards of the same rank, usually in poker.
[1864 *DAE*, under "four"; 1883 *OED*, under "fours"]

four straight, *n.* In poker, a hand with four cards in a sequence and one card not in the sequence. Compare FOUR-FLUSH.
[1983 Martinez *Gambling Scene* 203]
[1887 *DA, DAE*]

fourth street, *n.* In hold 'em poker, the fourth card placed face up in the middle of the table for the third betting round.
[1976 Sklansky *Hold'em Poker*]

four-way sevens, *n.* Dice that are shaved in such a fashion as to roll the number seven more often than any other number. The three configuations for dice to roll the number 7 are 6-1, 5-2, and 4-3. The altered dice make the *fourth way.* Statistically, six configurations for rolling a 7 are possible using two dice: 6-1, 1-6, 5-2 2-5, 4-3, and 3-4. Compare BARR DICE.
[1974 Scarne *Dice* 236]

fox, *n.* Abbreviated F. In poker, the sixth player to the left of the dealer. *Rare.*
[1949 Coffin *Secrets* 177]

fraction, *n.* In horse racing, the elapsed time for one segment of a race.
[1978 Ainslie *Complete Guide* 289]

frame, *n.* In poker, the interval of play between the beginning of the deal and the final betting round; a HAND.
[1961 Scarne *Complete Guide* 679]

freak, *n.* In poker, a joker or WILD CARD.
[1949 Coffin *Secrets* 178]

free bet, *n.* In bank craps, a winning bet that allows the player to take odds on the next bet without providing additional money from his own bankroll.
[ca. 1961 *Hotel Coll*]

free bid, *n.* In bridge, a voluntary bid, one made without constraints of a bidding system.
[1950 Morehead *Culbertson* 615]

free-card, *n.* In poker, a card dealt to each player after a betting round in which no player made a wager. See also FREE RIDE.
[1978 Brunson *How I Made* 532]

free double, *n.* In bridge, a challenge made to the adverse contract offered by an opponent, the winning of which contract would result in a game even if the challenge had not been made.
[1953 Crawford *Consistent Winner* 347]

free double-odds bet, *n. phr.* In craps, a winning wager that allows the player to double the odds on the net wager without risking additional money of his own.
[1961 Scarne *Complete Guide* 680]

free odds, *n.* In craps, a wager that is paid at true odds if won, rather than at house odds, which are less. [ca. 1961 *Hotel Coll*]

free play *n.* In casinos, an advertising promotion that allows a player to make a wager with house money. The notion is that, win or lose, the player is then in the casino and will likely make additional wagers using his own money. Compare COMP.
[1977 *Regulations* 361]

free ride, *n.* In poker, a betting round in which no player makes a bet and all players therefore receive the next card without having to add money to the pot. See also FREE-CARD.
[1949 Coffin *Secrets* 178]

free wheeler, *n.* A poker player who has lost all his money but is allowed to play on credit until he wins a pot. Compare FREEZE-OUT.
[1968 Wallace *Poker* 215]

freeze, *v.* **1.** In draw poker, to refuse the opportunity to discard and replace the rejected cards with new cards. See also PAT HAND.
[1971 Livingston *Poker Strategy* 218]
2. In the phrase:
freeze the pack, In canasta, to place a wild card on the discard pile to prevent an opponent from retrieving the cards below it.
[1953 Crawford *Consistent Winner* 347]

freeze-out, *n.* Also written **freezeout.** Also called **freeze-out poker.** In poker, a table stakes game from which a player must withdraw when all the money he had on the table has been lost.
1880 Blackbridge *Complete Poker* 134. In *freeze-out,* each player exposes an equal amount at the beginning of the game, which cannot be added to from any source other than winnings from other players.
[1855 *DA*, 1856 *OEDS*, 1877 *DAE*]

freezer, *n.* In poker, a small raise of a previous bet in order to stop further raises. See also SHORT CALL.
[1968 Wallace *Poker* 215]

French monte, *n.* Also called THIMBLERIG or THREE-CARD MONTE. A cheating game in which the game operator shows three cards, usually one face or picture card, such as a queen, and two cards of lower rank, such as a seven and an eight. The operator then throws the three cards face down on the table and takes wagers as to which of the three is the face card. The operator substitutes the face card for another card of low rank so that any choice made by the victim will be a losing card.
[1851 *DAE, DA*]

frenchy, *n.* A generally honest professional gambler who cheats occasionally.
[ca. 1961 *Hotel Coll*]

fret, *n.* In roulette, the partition separating one slot on the wheel from another. See also CANOE.
[1961 Scarne *Complete Guide* 680]

friendly game, *n.* A card or dice game, organized

for sociability, at which only small wagers are allowed.
[1949 Coffin *Secrets* 178]

frijole, *n.* Another term for a POKER CHIP. *Rare.*
[1903 *DA*; ultimately from American Spanish *frijole* kidney bean]

frisk room, *n.* An anteroom in an illegal gambling establishment used to search incoming players for weapons.
[(1950) 1981 Maurer *Lang. of the Underworld* 186]

from here to there without a pair, *prep. phr.* In poker, said of a STRAIGHT, a continuous sequence of cards, such as eight, nine, ten, jack, queen.
[1978 Larson *Vocabulary* 98]

from soda to hock, *prep. phr.* From the beginning to the end; in faro, the SODA is the first card dealt, and the HOCK is the last card dealt.
[1968 Adams *Western Words*]

front line, *n.* Same as the PASS LINE. In bank craps, the area on the table layout for making the initial bet before a shooter begins a new sequence of rolls.
[(1950) 1981 Maurer *Lang. of the Underworld* 186]

front-line bettor, *n.* Also called a DO BETTOR. In bank craps, a player who wagers only on the PASS LINE.
[1983 Martinet *Oral Coll*]

front line odds, *n. phr.* In bank craps, the extra wager placed behind the original wager on the PASS LINE after a POINT (of the number 4, 5, 6, 8, 9, 10) has been established by the SHOOTER.
[1961 Scarne *Complete Guide* 680]

front man, *n.* Also shortened to FRONT. A respectable person without a criminal record who acts as an agent for other people, especially as the visible operator or owner of a legal gambling operation.
[1926 *DA*, for *front man*; 1905 *DA, OEDS*, for *front*]

front money, *n.* **1.** In a casino, money deposited by a player with the casino cage and drawn on as needed at the gaming table.
[ca. 1961 *Hotel Coll*]
2. Money lent to a gambler with the understanding that it will be returned after the gambling session.
[1983 Martinet *Oral Coll*]
3. A roll of money used to impress a potential victim of a cheater. Compare FLASH MONEY.
[(1950) 1981 Maurer *Lang. of the Underworld* 186]

front peek, *n.* A cheating move by a card dealer to look at the value of the card on top of the deck, in which the dealer squeezes the deck between the thumb and the little finger so the top card is bowed slightly, allowing him to see its underside corner.
[ca. 1961 *Hotel Coll*]

front runner, *n.* A horse that regularly takes an early lead in a race and sets the pace for the rest of the horses.
[(1951) 1981 Maurer *Lang. of the Underworld* 212]
[Compare 1914 *OEDS*, applied to automobile racing]

front wheel, *n.* In horse racing, a wager on two races in which one horse in the first race is paired with all the horses in the second race. A common wager in betting the DAILY DOUBLE.
[1981 Passer *Winning Big* 240]

full, *adj.* Denoting a poker hand consisting of three cards of one rank, two of another.
[1844 *DA*]

full, *n.* Same as a FULL HOUSE.
[1844 *DA*]

full burn, *n.* Same as a FULL HOUSE. *Rare.*
[1949 Coffin *Secrets* 178]

full boat, *n.* Same as a FULL HOUSE. *Rare.*
[1978 Brunson *How I Made* 533]

full deck, *n.* Also called a FULL PACK. A complete pack of playing cards; an honest pack of cards.
[1887 *DAE*]

full-hand, *n.* Same as a FULL HOUSE. *Rare.*
[1850 *DA*, 1857 *DAE*]

full house, *n.* Also called a FULL BARN or FULL BOAT or FULL HAND. In poker, a hand with three cards of one rank and two of another.
[1887 *OEDS*, 1899 *DAE*, 1903 *DA*]

full odds, *n.* In bank craps, the maximum bet allowed to be added to a wager after the shooter has established a point, that is, has rolled the number 4, 5, 6, 8, 9, or 10, which must be rolled again before the number 7 is rolled.
[ca. 1961 *Hotel Coll*]

full pack, *n.* same as a FULL DECK. *Rare.*
[1950 Morehead *Culbertson* 615]

full pencil, *adj.* Pertaining to a casino executive who has the authority to issue complimentary rooms, drinks, meals, show tickets, transportation, and so on. See also COMP.
[ca. 1961 *Hotel Coll*]

full table, *n.* In a casino, a crowded gaming table, especially a craps table at which so many people are playing that they lean over the people in front to place wagers on the layout.
[(1950) 1981 Maurer *Lang. of the Underworld* 186]

fullum, *n.* Also spelled **fulham, fullan, fullam, fullom.** A die that has been altered either by loading it with a weight or by changing the pips on the facets, for example, by marking two pips on two faces of the die. See also BARR DICE and LOADED DICE.
1714 Lucas *Memoirs* 26. Besides committing all these notorious Cheats, Major Clancy was a very great Sharper at most Games, in which dice are us'd, and to this end he never went without *Fullums* in his Pocket. The high ones would run 4, 5, and 6; the low Fullums 1, 2, and 3, by

drilling the Holes, loading them with Quicksilver and stopping the Holes with Pitch.
[*c*1550 *OED*]

fun pack, *n.* **1.** In a casino, chips in exchange for a one hundred dollar bill that includes two chips worth twenty-five dollars apiece, six chips worth five dollars apiece, and twenty chips worth one dollar apiece. See also VARIETY PACK.
1983 Martinet *Oral Coll.* Some of these guys come in for a short time of entertainment, so they drop a bill [one hundred dollar bill] on the table and ask for a *fun pack* . . . A *fun pack* is two greens, six reds, and twenty aces. It gets called that from the coupon books different joints hand out offering freebies for come-ons: drinks, slot and keno play, that sort of thing. A guy gets a *fun pack* if he's just passing through and gets a feeling for a table for a few minutes. He'll usually place some bets, take odds and the hardways, then let the hand run. On a decent run he'll make a few hundred. If not, so what. The whole thing takes a few minutes, then he's out of there, on to something else.
2. A promotional booklet of coupons given out by casinos that offer patrons free drinks, free play on tables and slot machines, and discounts on food service. Compare COMP.

furlong, *n.* In horse racing, one eighth of a mile, 220 yards. [*c*1333 *OED*]

future book, *n.* The offering of wagers on a sporting event such as a horserace or ball game or boxing match that is to take place several days, weeks, or even months later. During the intervening time, the odds offered for different propositions may change from time to time.
[ca. 1961 *Hotel Coll*]

fuzz, *v.* **1.** To make a cheating move in dealing cards by mixing a pack of cards with an OVERHAND SHUFFLE, a technique for maintaining the original order of the deck. Compare CARD MECHANIC AND FORCE THE CUT.
[1971 McQuaid *Gambler's Digest* 306]
2. Also MILK. In poker, to mix one's own cards during the play of a hand by holding them face down and sliding one card at a time from the top to the bottom. The action is repeated several times in rapid succession.
[1968 Wallace *Poker* 216]

G

G, Abbreviation for GEORGE (def. 2). In poker, the seventh position to the left of the dealer. *Rare.* Compare A, B, C, D, E, F, H.
[1949 Coffin *Secrets* 178]

GA, *n.* Abbreviation for GAMBLERS, ANONYMOUS.
[1983 Gamblers Anonymous, *Sharing,* preface]

gaff, *n.* **1.** A ring with a small projection on the palm side of the band, worn on the finger and used to palm cards. *Obsolete.*
1843 Green *Exposure* 196. For this purpose, the dealer has on the middle finger of his left hand, what is called a *gaff* or spur; this is fastened on by cement made for that purpose. It is about an inch and a quarter in length, and is cemented on the middle joint of the finger just named, and projects out from the part to which it is fastened. About half an inch of the *gaff* does not touch the finger, but lies a little more than the thickness of the back plate from the finger, and is itself just the thickness of two cards, and when he pushes it against the two top cards, it pushes them both out.
[1934 *OEDS*]
2. Any of a variety of cheating devices or methods.
[(1950) 1981 Maurer *Lang. of the Underworld* 186]

gaff, *v.* **1.** To alter cards or dice, or use any trickery or deceit to cheat a victim. Compare BARR DICE and COSMETICS and LOADED DICE and STRIPPERS. [1934 *OEDS*]
2. To gamble. *Obsolete.*
[1828 *OED*]

gaffed dice, *n.* Dice altered by changing the pips on the faces, by shaving the faces or edges, or by drilling holes and inserting weights. See also DOCTOR. Compare BARR DICE and LOADED DICE.
[(1950) 1981 Maurer *Lang. of the Underworld* 186]

gag, *n.* Same as HARDWAY.
[(1950) 1981 Maurer *Lang. of the Underworld* 186]

gag bet, *n.* Same as HARDWAY BET.
[(1950) 1981 Maurer *Lang. of the Underworld* 186]

gallery, *n.* **1.** In poker, onlookers or nonplayers. When a player loses all his money, he may join the *gallery.*
[Compare 1891 *OEDS,* meaning "a group of spectators . . . at a . . . game or sport"]
2. In ecarte, the onlookers who are betting on either player and who may offer suggestions on the play. [1890 *OEDS*]

galloping dominoes, *n. pl.* A slang term for DICE. See AFRICAN DOMINOES. *Facetious use. [(1950) 1981 Maurer Lang. of the Underworld* 186]
[n.d. *DAS*]

gam, *n.* Usually **gams.** Short tor GAMBLER. *Obsolete.* [1875 *DA*]

Gam-Anon, *n.* A support group for compulsive gamblers, not affiliated with GAMBLERS ANONYMOUS but closely associated with that group.
[1983 Gamblers Anonymous, *Sharing*, 85]

Gam-A-Teen, *n.* A self help group designed to assist the children of compulsive gamblers. The group is not affiliated with GAMBLERS ANONYMOUS or GAM-ANON, but is associated with both groups.
[1983 Gamblers Anonymous, *Sharing*, 97]

gamble, *n.* The risk of money or something of value on the outcome of a chance event such as a dice or card game, race, or contest.
[1879 *OED*]

gamble, *v.* **1.** To risk money or something of value on the outcome of a chance event such as a dice or card game, race, or contest.
[1775 *OED*]
2. In the particle construction:
gamble away, To lose by gambling; usually, to lose a large amount by gambling.
[1808 *OED*]

gambler, *n.* **1.** A person who plays at games of chance for money or something of value; a person who takes chances on the outcome of a particular event.
[1747 *OED*]
2. A fraudulent gamester; a cheater. *Rare.*
[1755 *OED*]

gambler's goods, *n. phr.* The paraphernalia of a cheater; a cheater's MARKED CARDS, LOADED DICE, COSMETICS, weights, mirrors, and so on.
[1890 Quinn *Fools of Fortune* 229]

gambler's gun, *n. phr.* A small, short-barreled pistol favored by transient gamblers; a derringer. *Obsolete.*
[1968 Adams *Western Words*]

gambler's point, *n. phr.* **1.** In all fours, the ten of trumps, required for the fourth portion, or "game" of high, low, jack, and the game.
[1950 Morehead *Culbertson* 616]
2. In craps, a reference to the numbers 4 and 10, considered a poor risk by many gamblers. *Facetious use.*
[1983 Martinet *Oral Coll*]

Gamblers Anonymous *n.* An organization founded in 1957 designed to help compulsive gamblers in a fashion similar to the way Alcoholics Anonymous assists compulsive drinkers.
1983 Gamblers Anonymous, *Sharing*, ix. *Gamblers Anonymous* is a voluntary fellowship of compulsive gamblers gathered for the sole purpose of helping themselves and each other to stop gambling.

gamblesome, *adj.* Addicted to gaming. *Obsolete.*
[1884 *OED*]

gamblesomeness, *n.* A great fondness for gaming. *Obsolete.*
[1881 *OED*]

gambling, *n.* The risking of money or something of value on the outcome of a chance event such as a card or dice game, race or contest.
[1784 *OED, DAE*]

gambling, *adj.* **1.** Of or pertaining to risking of money or something of value on the outcome of a chance event such as a card or dice game, race, or contest.
[1726 *OED*; originally pertaining to cheating at gaming.]
2. A common first element or descriptor:
a. For places to gamble, such as *gambling casino.*
[1812 *DA,* gambling *hall;*1 1812 *OED,* gambling *hell;* 1812 *DAE, gambling room*]
b. For legal aspects of wagering: *gambling industry, law, license, licensing law, ordinance, permit, business.*
c. For persons who wager: *gambling junketeer, man, operator, ring, star, type.*
[1726 *OED, gambling fraternity*]

gambling debt, *n.* A debt incurred by gambling on credit and losing.
[1852 *OED*]

gambling game, *n.* A pastime, often involving playing cards or dice, designed or intended primarily for the purpose of wagering or betting.
[1837 *OED*]

gambling table, *n.* Same as GAMING TABLE.
[1852 *DAE, OEDS*]

game, *n.* **1.** Short for GAMBLING GAME.
[*a*1300 *OED*]
2. A contest or diversion involving risk, usually played for money.
[1656 *DAE,* 1746 *OED*]
3. The possession, at the end of a hand, of the number of points required to win the stakes being wagered. [1830 *OED*]
4. In bridge, the gaining of a specific number of points to win a division of a larger contest, as a rubber.
[1973 Clark *Oral Coll*]
5. In all fours (high, low, jack and the *game*), the majority of pips collected during the course of playing the hand.
1836 Eidrah *Hoyle Famil* 63. *Game,* the majority of pips, collected from the tricks taken by the respective players. The cards from which this is obtained are, ace, king, queen, knave, and ten of trumps. The ace reckons for four pips, the king for three, the queen for two, the knave for one, and the ten for ten.
[1830 *OED*]

game, *v.* To stake a wager on the outcome of an event, as at cards or dice; to gamble.
[1529 *OED*]

game count sheet, *n. phr.* In a casino, an accounting form that records the value of the chips on the table when a game or shift begins and ends, as well as the amount of cash in the money container attached to the table. See also STIFF SHEET, PIT REPORT, MASTER GAME REPORT.
[1979 Hilton Hotel *Procedures* 31]

game debt, *n.* Same as GAMBLING DEBT.
[1824 *OED*]

game hole, *n.* Same as END HOLE.
[1870 *OED*]

gamer, *n.* A person knowledgeable about games of chance, as a player or as an operator of gambling games.
[1973 Clark *Oral Coll*]

game starter, *n.* Also called SHILL.
[1970 *Baccarat, The Facts*]

gamester, *n.* Same as a GAMER.
[1553 *OED*]
→Used especially factiously or in reference to programmers of computerized games.

gamestress, *n.* A female gambler knowledgeable about games of chance, as a player or operator of gambling games. *Rare.*
[1651 *OED*]

gamestry, *n.* The practice of gambling. *Obsolete.*
[1579 *OED*]

gaming, *n.* The playing at games of chance for stakes; GAMBLING.
[1501 *OED; OED* lists spelling variants: 1501 *gamyng,* 1510 *gamning,* 1561 *gamenyng,* 1571 onward *gaming;* 1619 *DAE*]

gaming activity, *n.* Involvement in gambling. The term is usually applied to legal gambling practices or involvement.
[1973 Binion *Recollections* 3]

gaming commission, *n.* A state or city agency devoted to regulating legal gambling operations.
[1977 *Regulations* 1]

gaming community, *n.* The aggregate of people involved in gambling as a business, such as casino owners, dealers, managers, players, and state and county agents.
[1977 Cahill *Recollections* 1]

gaming control act, *n. phr.* A state statute that legalizes certain forms of gambling and provides guidelines for the operation and taxation of gambling games.
[1957 *Nevada Gaming*]

gaming control board, *n. phr.* A state or county agency that enforces policies set by the GAMING COMMISSION, investigates allegations of cheating, and provides background information on persons or corporations requesting licensing as operators of gambling establishments.
[1957 *Nevada Gaming*]

gaming credit instrument, *n. phr.* **1.** Another term for MARKER, CREDIT SLIP or IOU.
[1979 Hilton Hotel *Procedures* 29]
2. In a casino, a form for recording amounts of money or chips turned over to a player or a table.
[1979 Hilton Hotel *Procedures* 29]

gaming device, *n.* Any of various items used in the actual determination of a winner or loser in a gambling activity, such as slot machines, playing cards, dice, keno or bingo blower, and so on. The term is used to distinguish these instruments from GAMING EQUIPMENT.
[1957 *Nevada Gaming Regulations* 4]

gaming equipment, *n.* The furnishings and furniture necessary to conduct gambling activity, such as special tables, chip racks, coin-counting machines, accounting forms, and so on. The term is used to distinguish these items from a GAMING DEVICE.
[1961 Scarne *Complete Guide* 17]

gaming gig, *n.* A job as a dealer working in a gambling establishment.
[1979 Newman *Dealer's Special* 7]

gaming graduate, *n.* A person who has taken a course of study in dealing casino games such as craps, twenty-one, roulette, and so on.
[1979 Newman *Dealer's Special* 7]

gaming guide, *n.* A pamphlet provided by a hotel or casino that provides a brief description of each of the gambling games available there.
[1973 Clark *Oral Coll*]

gaming hell, *n.* Also called a HELL. *Obsolete.*
[1890 Quinn *Fools of Fortune* 266]

gaming house, *n.* A gambling establishment; a casino.
[1624 *OED;* 1579 *OED* as *game-house;* 1851 *DAE*]

gaming industry, *n.* The business of providing places and materials for diversion by gaming and gambling, such as the casinos, gaming devices, gaming equipment, personnel, and all accoutrements such as restaurants, lounges, showrooms, etc.
[1972 Kofoed *Meanderings* 5]

gaming license, *n.* A permit issued by a local or state agency for the conduct of a gambling operation. See also GAMING CONTROL BOARD.
[1973 Clark *Oral Coll*]

gaming operation, *n.* A venture devoted to gambling; a casino; a place for participating in gambling activity; a gambling activity.
[1978 Harrah *Recollections* 6]

gaming ordinary, *n.* An establishment devoted to gambling. *Obsolete.*
[1712 *OED*]

gaming permit, *n.* A certificate issued by a local or state agency allowing a person or a group of persons to conduct a gambling operation. See

also GAMING LICENSE. Compare GAMING COMMISSION.
[1931 *Review Journal* 6/6: 1]

gaming room, *n.* A room, usually in a hotel, restaurant, or other place of business, devoted to gambling. [1856 *DAE*]

gaming table, *n.* A table specially designed and built for gaming, constructed to specific dimensions and of a particular shape to accommodate a particular game such as craps, baccarat, roulette, or twenty-one.
[1598 *OED,* 1812 *DAE*]

gammon, *n.* In backgammon, a double score, which is achieved by a player who removes all his pieces before his opponent removes any.
1860 Crawley *Backgammon* 57. If one player has not borne off his first man before the other has borne off his last, he loses a *gammon,* which is equivalent to two games or "hits."
[1735 *OED*]

gano, *n.* In ombre, a card designated as the highest ranking card and therefore allowed to win any trick it is placed on. Compare TRUMP.
[1950 Morehead *Culbertson* 616]

gap, *n.* In poker, a card missing from within a sequence that is required to complete a straight, as 7, 8, 9, jack. The missing card, the 10, is the *gap.*
[1968 Wallace *Poker* 216]

gaper, *n.* Same as a GLEAMER. Compare SHINER.
[1968 Adams *Western Words*]

garbage, *n.* Also called TRASH. In poker, cards that are worthless in the hand; the DISCARDS.
[1968 Wallace *Poker* 216]

garbage pile, *n.* In poker, the DISCARDS, or rejected cards; the stack of cards from players who have retired from the hand.
[1971 Livingston *Poker Strategy* 218]

Gardena miracle, *n.* In poker, the drawing of cards in a very lucky fashion; a draw that seems to defy the laws of probability, such as holding a queen and ten of spades, then drawing the jack, king, and ace of spades for a *royal flush.*
[1978 Brunson *How I Made* 533]
[From *Gardena*, California, which has legal cardrooms devoted to playing draw poker.]

gar hole, *n.* In poker, a place where chips are inaccessible for use. Chips committed to a pot or a *widow* that do not yet belong to anyone are said to be in the *gar hole.*
[1978 Brunson *How I Made* 533]

garreting, *n.* The practice of hiding cards about the upper part of the body. *Obsolete.*
1859 Green *Gambler's Tricks* 100. *Garretting* is so called from the practice of securing the cards either under your hat or behind your head.

Garrison finish, *n.* In horse racing, a win by a horse that trailed through most of the race, then had a sudden burst of speed close to the finish line.
1978 Ainslie *Encycl* 289. *Garrison finish.*—Come from behind in the stretch, in manner of oldtime rider, Snapper Garrison.
[1943 *DA*]

Gary Cooper, *n.* Also shortened to **Coop**. In craps, a roll of the number 12. Compare ADA FROM DECATUR and BOX CARS and DOLLY PARTON
1983 Martinet *Oral Coll.* Some names for dice combination just seem to go on, like Ada from Decatur . . . or *Gary Cooper,* that's a boxcar roll. But people never call it "High Noon," it's always a *Gary Cooper* or sometimes a "Coop."

gate, *n.* **1.** In monte, the top card at the beginning of play.
[1938 Asbury *Sucker's Progress* 53]
2. In horse and greyhound racing, the metal barrier that opens to start the race.
[1955 Hillis *Pari-Mutuel Betting* 115]
3. The money representing ticket sales for a sporting event; the number of attendees at a sporting event.
[1891 *OED*]

gate, *v.* In craps, to stop the dice while they are rolling, voiding the cast.
[(1950) 1981 Maurer *Lang. of the Underworld* 186]

gee-gee, *n.* A race horse. *Obsolete.*
[(1950) 1981 Maurer *Lang. of the Underworld* 212]
[n.d. *DAS*, from the *gee*, 1845 OEDS, meaning "to direct a horse by the call of 'gee'"]

george, *n.* **1.** A patron of a gaming establishment who tips employees freely and generously.
1979 Clark *Oral Coll.* Both men and women are george. It's not a sex thing, george just refers to a good tipper.
2. Abbreviated G. In poker, the seventh player to the left of the dealer.
[1949 Coffin *Secrets* 179]
→Use of the term (def. 2) is restricted to written accounts of poker.

georgette, *n.* A female patron of a gaming establishment who tips employees. Occasional use.
1979 Clark *Oral Coll.* Once in a while you'll hear a dealer refer to a *georgette* who plays a hand for the dealer, or drops a toke. But if she is a pretty heavy player and tokes pretty good, she's usually george. Both men and women are george. It's not a sex thing, george just refers to a good tipper.

get, *v.* In the phrases:
get behind it, To support a cheating move or cooperate with a cheater; to play the role of a disinterested party and vouch for the honesty of a cheating move.
[1961 Scarne *Complete Guide* 680]
get behind the stick, In bank craps, an oral command from the PIT BOSS to a craps dealer to begin a game or to relieve a dealer who is having problems on the table.
[(1950) 1981 Maurer *Lang. of the Underworld* 186]

ghost hand, *n.* In poker, a sequence of cards repeated on a deal following a poor shuffle.
[1968 Wallace *Poker* 216]

giant twist, *n.* In draw poker, a rule allowing a player to discard all five cards and request five new cards from the dealer. See also TWIST.
[1968 Wallace *Poker* 216]

gig, *n.* In policy or numbers, a sequence of the same three numbers regularly selected by a player.
[1847 *DA, DAE*]

gimmick, *n.* A device for secretly manipulating the outcome of a gambling venture. See also GAFF.
[1926 *OEDS,* 1928 DA]

gin, *n.* In gin rummy, a melding of all ten cards at once; the bonus points scored for melding the entire hand at one time.
[1944 *DA*]

ginny up the pasteboard, *v. phr.* Also shortened to **ginny up.** To mark the back of a playing card for purposes of cheating. Compare COSMETICS.
[1968 Adams *Western Words*]

girl, *n.* Also called a LADY or MOP-SQUEEZER. In playing cards, a queen of any suit.
[*DAS*; 1968 Wallace *Poker* 216]

glass-work, *n.* Especially in poker, the using of a mirror or reflective device by a dishonest dealer to read the value of cards as they are dealt face down.
[*DSUE;* 1968 Adams *Western Words*]

glazed card, *n.* In poker, a card that has been sanded slightly to allow the dealer to cheat with it. Compare STRIPPERS.
[1890 Quinn *Fools of Fortune* 223]

gleamer, *n.* Also called a GAPER. A cheating device. In poker, a small mirror, often disguised as a coin, cigarette lighter, or some such object, used by a dishonest dealer for seeing the undersides, or faces, of cards as they are dealt.
[1969 Herwitz *Yes, You Can Win* 113]
→ *Gleamer* is perhaps a variant of GLIMMER.

gleek, *n.* Also spelled **gleeke** or **gleke. 1.** A popular card game of the eighteenth century. See also MOURNIVAL and TIB and TIDDY and TOM and TOWSER and TUMBLER.
1680 Cotton *Complete Gamester* 65. [. . . he] became a great Gamester, especially at *gleek,* which is a Game on the Cards wherein the Ace is called Tib, the Knave Tom, the four of Trumps Tiddy. Tib, the Ace, is fifteen in Hand, and eighteen in Play, because it wins a Trick; Tom, the Knave, is nine; and Tiddy is four; the fifth Towser, the sixth Tumbler, which if in Hand, Towser is 5, and Tumbler 6, and so double if turned up; and the King or Queen of Trumps is three.
[1533 *OED*]
2. In gleek, a hand with three similar face cards.
1680 Cotton *Complete Gamester* 68. A mournival is either all the Aces, the four Kings, Queens, or Knaves, and a *gleek* is three of any of the aforesaid.
[1614 *OED*]

gleeker, *n.* An obsessive player of GLEEK.
[1676 *OED*]

glimmer, *n.* Also called a SHINER. A cheating device in playing cards. In poker, a mirror or polished surface on a coin, cigarette lighter and so on used by a dealer to see the undersides of the cards he is dealing. Compare GLEAMER.
[1983 Martinez *Gambling Scene* 204]

glim worker, *n.* In poker, a dealer who cheats by using a mirror to see the undersides of the cards he is dealing. See also GLASS-WORK.
[1962 Garcia *Marked Cards* 14]

glitter gulch, *n.* The casino area of downtown Las Vegas, Nevada. See also STRIP.
[1953 Lewis *Sagebrush Casinos* 188]

go, *v.* **1.** In cribbage, to announce to the opponent that a player cannot make a play and therefore relinquishes a turn.
1824 Anon *Hoyle's* 31. When the party whose turn it may be to play cannot produce a card that will make 31, or come in under that number, he then says, "*go*", to his antagonist, who thereupon is to play any card he has that will come in to make 31.
[1821 *OED*]
2. To stake a wager on the outcome of an event.
[1605 *OED*; 1831 *DA*; 1846 *OEDS*]
3. To make a call for a specific number of cards or tricks.
[1876 *OEDS*]
4. In the phrases and particle constructions:
go all in, In table-stakes poker, to bet all of one's chips in one hand.
[1949 Coffin *Secrets* 178]
go back, In bridge, to redouble.
1907 Foster *Bridge* 16. If either the eldest hand or the pone doubles, it is the privilege of the player who named the trump to double him again, the usual expression being; 'I *go back*'.
[1907 *OEDS,* labeled *obsolete*]
go banco, In chemin-de-fer, to make a bet equal to the entire amount of money in the bank.
[1976 Figgis *Gambler's Handbook* 121]
go better, In poker, to increase the amount bet by the previous player.
1866 *American Card Player* 134. *Going Better.*— When any player makes a bet, it is the privilege of the next player to the left to raise him, or run over it, that is, to deposit in the pool the amount already bet by his adversary, and make a still higher bet. In such a case it is usual to say: "I see you, and *go* so much *better,*" naming the extra sum bet.
1887 Proctor *Chance* 227. Each player may (in his regular turn only) increase his stake, in which case all who wish to stay must 'see' him—that is, raise their stakes in the same degree, or *go better*—that is, raise the stake further.
[1845 *DAE, OEDS*; 1878 *OED*]

go bust, In twenty-one, to draw cards until the point value in a hand exceeds twenty-one and loses.
[1951 Jones *Wilbur Clark's* 5]

go down, 1. Same as GO RUMMY. In gin rummy, to end a game by showing the cards in one's hand.
[1964 Wykes *Illustrated Guide* 327]
2. In bridge, to fail to fulfill the contract.
[1918 *OEDS*]
3. To reveal the rest of the cards in a hand, as when declaring the ability to win the rest of the tricks in a hand.
[1934 *OEDS*]

go in, 1. In poker, to put money into the pot and remain eligible to win it.
[1882 *DAE, OEDS*]
2. In rummy, to take a group of cards from the discard pile.
[1949 Coffin *Secrets* 179]

go off, In trump games, to lead the first card.
[1879 *OED*]

go off at, In horse racing, to begin a race with particular odds.
1980 Clark *Oral Coll.* He wasn't sure what the horse *went off at* . . . So you don't know if the odds changed [on a horse] just before the race so you ask somebody "What did he *go off at.*"

go on top, In panguingue, to pay a forfeit to the pot for the privilege of passing from the responsibility of being the dealer.
[1950 Morehead *Culbertson* 651]

go out, 1. In games like bridge and rummy, to reach the total number of points or tricks necessary to make the contract or end the game.
2. Of a horse, to be entered in a race.
[n.d. *OED*]

go over, 1. Same as GO BUST. In twenty-one, to exceed the point count of twenty-one and thereby lose.
[1902 *OEDS*]
2. In bridge, to play a higher card than necessary to win a trick.
[1950 Morehead *Culbertson* 617]

go rummy, In gin rummy, to meld the entire hand at one time, thereby ending the game.
[1950 Morehead *Culbertson* 617]

go south, 1. To leave a gambling game or establishment with money gotten dishonestly.
[(1950) 1981 Maurer *Lang. of the Underworld* 186]
2. To pocket winnings during the course of play.
[(1950) 1981 Maurer *Lang. of the Underworld* 186]

go to bat, Same as PUT TO THE PUNISHMENT.
[(1951) 1981 Maurer *Lang. of the Underworld* 214]

go, *n.* In the phrase **the go.** In cribbage, the point nearest thirty-one, when the two players are playing out the hand.
1863 Pardon *Hoyle's* 97. *The Go*—The point nearest thirty-one. If thirty-one exactly be made, the player scores two holes: for the simple "*go,*" one hole; in addition, of course, to any more he may make with his last card.

golden glow, *n.* A type of liquid considered superior for use in marking the backs of playing cards. Compare COSMETICS.
[1968 Wallace *Poker* 216]

golf balls, *n. pl.* Another word for DICE.
[ca. 1961 *Hotel Coll*]
[Perhaps from the term AFRICAN GOLF as another name for craps.]

good man, *n.* **1.** A gambler adept at cheating, especially a card dealer capable of dealing from the bottom of the deck or otherwise manipulating the cards. See also BOTTOM DEALER and CARD MECHANIC.
[1600 *OED*]
2. A gambler with a large bankroll.
[(1950) 1981 Maurer *Lang. of the Underworld* 186]
3. Used ironically as a label for a petty thief or a player who bets small amounts.
[1608 *OED,* with cross reference to "goodfellow"]

goose, *n.* In bingo and keno, the plastic or metal cage that holds all the balls to be drawn for the calling of a game.
[1973 Friedman *Casino Games* 99]

gooseneck, *n.* In bingo and keno, a plastic tube mounted atop a plastic bubble holding all the balls used in a game. A blower beneath the bubble forces balls, one at a time, up the *gooseneck.* See also RABBIT-EARS.
[ca. 1961 *Hotel Coll*]

grand hazard, *n.* Another name for CHUCK-A-LUCK.
[1890 Quinn *Fools of Fortune* 282]

grand misere, *n. French.* Also spelled **grand misery.** In boaston, the act of losing every trick without leading a card.
[1950 Morehead *Culbertson* 591]

grand misere ouvert, *French. n.* In boaston, the act of losing thirteen tricks by declaring the loss and exhibiting the hand before the first card lead.
[1950 Morehead *Culbertson* 591]

grand slam, *n.* The winning of every trick at a hand of bridge. Compare LITTLE SLAM and MINOR SLAM.
1836 Eidrah *Hoyle Famil* 31. *Grand Slam.*—To gain every trick.
[1892 *OED*]
[Originally from the game of boaston.]

grand square, *n.* In faro, the area on the table layout containing the queen, king, ace, and deuce.
[1938 Asbury *Sucker's Progress* 7]

grandstand, *n.* Also written **grand stand.** The main platform for spectators at a racetrack, usually centered at the finish line, with the highest price of admission.
[1841 *OED,* for *grand stand;* 1912 *DAE* for *grandstand*]

grandstand, *v.* To make an ostentatious show of winning or performing some unlikely feat, whether at cards or in a sporting event.
[1973 Clark *Oral Coll*]
[1900 *OEDS*]

grate, *n.* A DICE BOX used for cheating, allowing the person holding the box to look at the numbers on the dice inside the box before inverting it to deposit the dice on the board. See also CRANK BOX and DEALING BOX and SHOE.
1726 Wilson *Art and Mystery* 39. The *Grate* is a Box made with great Ingenuity, and like another, excepting that it hath a Spring at the top, which, when press'd on, causes an Opening that shews you both the Dice; and when you take away your finger, it falls and closes . . . These boxes are become scarce, because the Inventor and Maker is dead.

gravity dice, *n. pl.* Dice that have been loaded with weights. See also LOADS. Compare FLOATS.
[(1950) 1981 Maurer *Lang. of the Underworld* 186]

gray, *n.* A white chip, usually worth one dollar. See also BARBER POLE and BAY AND A GRAY and GREEN.
[*DSUE;* 1983 Martinet *Oral Coll*]

great cassino, *n.* Also BIG CASINO. In the card game CASSINO, the ten of diamonds.
1824 Anon *Hoyle's* 23. *Great Cassino* [is] the ten of diamonds, which reckons for two points.
[1811 *OED*]

great martingale, *n.* Another name for MARTINGALE. A wagering system in which a player doubles the amount of a wager following a loss.
[1971 McQuaid *Gambler's Digest* 307]

grec, *n.* Same as GREEK.
[1950 Morehead *Culbertson* 617]

greek, *n.* Also spelled GREC. **1.** A CARD SHARP; a cheater in card games
[1528 *OED*]
2. Any professional gambler.
[1938 Asbury *Sucker's Progress* 16]

greek bottom, *n.* The second card from the bottom of a deck of playing cards.
[1949 Coffin *Secrets* 179]

greek shot, *n.* In craps, a controlled throw of the dice in which one die is placed atop the other in the toss to prevent the bottom die from turning over.
[(1950) 1981 Maurer *Lang. of the Underworld* 186]

greekery, *n.* The act of cheating at cards or dice.
[1823 *OED*]

Greekery. Man's desire to control his activity extends also to GAMBLING. Consequently, many gamblers seek to influence GAMING so that the ODDS are more on the side of the gambler whether that be the HOUSE or the PLAYER. GREEKERY is one word for manipulating games of chance.

Not all GREEKS and SHARPS engage in outright dishonest gaming. CARD COUNTERS have good memories; many DICE SHARPS control PERFECTS in the WHIP SHOT without chicanery. Many PROFESSIONAL GAMBLERS resort to being SWITCH MEN or DAUBERS or HUSTLERS or GRIFTERS.

The BUNKO ARTIST, however, is often called simply a CHEAT. Most ALONE PLAYERS or DICE MOBS or CARD MOBS are not AIR BANDITS but rely upon a refined specialty. HUSTLING requires CONNING a JOHN with a SCAM into a position where he becomes a SITTING DUCK, especially with the help of a STEERER or SHILL.

Many CARD MECHANICS rely upon MOVES with which they appear to conduct a SQUARE DEAL but, in fact, engage in a FAST SHUFFLE (such as a FALSE CUT, ELEVATOR, DOUBLE CUT, LAS VEGAS RIFFLE, WHOREHOUSE CUT, or OVERHAND SHUFFLE or otherwise trying to FOIL THE CUT) or by DEUCE DEALING, or with a BOTTOM DEAL, DOUBLE SHUFFLE, or an otherwise deliberately engineered MISDEAL. A PEEKER can surreptitiously sneak a glance at the cards with a BUBBLE PEEK or FRONT PEEK, in order to know which ones are about to be dealt and thus deal favorable cards to a confederate as a BOTTOM DEALER or SECOND DEALER or MIDDLE DEALER. To facilitate the PEEK a dealer may employ a GLEAMER, SHINER, or some other GLASS-WORK. This is easier or unnecessary when playing with a STACKED DECK (such as a SVENGALI DECK).

When a dealer needs a WILD CARD he may rely on a VEST HOLDOUT, a TABLE HOLDOUT, a SLEEVE HOLDOUT, some other BUG, or a PALMED CARD. Or he may SLIP THE CARDS or SNAKE THE CARD. Any of which MOVES may involve GARRETING.

A CARD SHARK may rely upon a deck which he has had a chance to DOCTOR, as with COSMETICS or RAISED SPOT WORK or STRIPPING or PIN WORK or STAMPED CARDS in place of a normal RAILROAD BIBLE. SHARKS may also become CRIMP ARTISTS.

A card game which calls for a DEALING BOX may offer an opportunity for a HELLITE to manipulate the dealing with a TELL BOX, BRACE BOX, CRANK-BOX, or other CHEATING BOX (also generally called a FAKED BOX).

A CARD HUSTLER may rely upon WORKING THE TELEGRAPH with THE OFFICE for communicating with the other CARD SHARPERS as they WORK THE BROADS.

DICE MECHANICS may rely on a practiced CONTROLLED SHOT rather than upon GAFFED DICE, BARR DICE, BUSTERS, CAPPED DICE, or LOADED DICE (such as UPHILLS).

The PALM HOLDOUT is usually used to introduce LOADED DICE (such as DEAD-NUMBER DICE) or BEVELS or MIS-SPOTS (such as CALIFORNIA FOURTEENS or FOUR-WAY SEVENS or TRIP DICE), in a MOVE called a PALM SWITCH. If a DICE BOX is required for casting the dice then the DICE SWITCH is called a DICE-BOX HOLDOUT. Other SCAMS utilize a SLICK DICE CUP or a TRIP

BOX. The use of a crude GAFF such as LINKED DICE (also called CHAIN DICE) or BRISTLE DICE are avoided now by cheaters in casino play. PEETIES is one of the preferred GIMMICKS for THROWERS of GAMBLER'S GOODS, such as REPEATERS or DESPATCHERS. DROP SHOTS and DUMP OVER SHOTS and GREEK SHOTS favor this ROLLER.

A dishonest DICE DEALER may resort to being a SHORT-CHANGE ARTIST putting the CHIPS withheld in a SUBMARINE.

A ROBIN-HOOD CHEATER operating as a ROULETTE DEALER may use a SQUEEZE WHEEL to manipulate the outcome of a WHEEL OF FORTUNE or ROULETTE WHEEL by using the SQUEEZE SPINDLE or perhaps JUICE.

JOCKEYS may conspire to prearrange the FINISH of a BOAT RACE, especially with a PULL. Some owners will register one horse and substitute a RINGER. Others will instruct the jockey to ROPE IN his mount, to deliberately RUN OUT OF THE MONEY, setting the stage to LENGTHEN THE ODDS for betting heavily in subsequent races. Crooked trainers may administer drugs such as adrenalin Benzedrine to FIX a race.

PAST POSTERS work as a RING in trying to bet only on SURE THINGS, especially by learning the results of a race before the BOOKIE does and placing a quick bet.

The BUNCO SQUAD is swamped with all manner of schemes by both JOINTS and BOOKMAKERS on the one hand, and GRIFTERS, HUSTLERS, RAIL HAWKS, HEMINGWAYS, SKIMMERS, FRENCHIES, ALONE PLAYERS, TEAMS, and FIXERS on the other. Compare DICE, SHUFFLING, HORSE RACING.

green, *n.* Also called a QUARTER. In a casino, a chip worth twenty-five dollars. Compare BARBER POLE, GRAY.
[ca. 1961 *Hotel Coll*]

green baize, *n.* **1.** The green felt covering of a gaming table. [1843 *OED*]
2. A gaming table.
[1880 *OED*]

green cloth, *n.* **1.** The surface of a gaming table, usually imprinted with a layout for the game.
1891 *Monte Carlo* 223. Systems at Roulette and Trente-et-Quarante, or in other words, the calculation of "probabilities" in those famous games of chance, have not only been conceived and minutely studied by people addicted to that fatal vice—gambling, but have formed the subject of interested and interesting investigations on the part of mathematicians of no mean reputation, whose very last thought would have been to stake one pound, dollar or franc upon the *green cloth.*
[1871 *OED* From the practice of covering gaming tables with green felt or some other green cloth.]
2. A gaming table.
[1891 *OED*]

green game, *n.* In a casino, a table game with a minimum bet requirement of twenty-five dollars.
1983 Martinet *Oral Coll.* There are a lot of red games [five dollar limit] around, but to find *green games* you have to go to the twenty-one pit. You won't find those around here [at the craps pit]. Same with black games, they are in twenty-one.

greenies, *n. pl. Plural in form, but singular in use.* In golf, a wager won by the person whose ball is closest to the pin after the drive on a par three hole. Compare BINGLE, BANGLE, BUNGO.
[1971 McQuaid *Gambler's Digest* 307]

green number, *n.* In roulette, the number zero or double-zero. All other numbers are red or black.
[ca. 1961 *Hotel Coll*]

greeter, *n.* In a casino, an employee usually well-known to regular patrons who circulates through the casino welcoming players. See also CASINO HOST.
1974 Friedman *Management* 114. A few Strip hosts act strictly as "*greeters*" and do not handle credit. These *greeters* roam through the hotel's public facilities, particularly the casino, and single out customers for a personal welcome. Almost every Strip *greeter* is a recognized sports figure who knows the premium casino clientele.

grift, *v.* To cheat or swindle, usually of small amounts of money.
[1925 *OEDS,* 1915, as *grifting; c*1925 *DAS*]

grift, *n.* **1.** A cheater, usually in card or dice games, who steals small amounts on a sporadic basis.
[1974 Scarne *Dice* 203]
2. A scheme or scam used by a cheater.
[ca. 1961 *Hotel Coll*]
[*DAS;* Compare 1914 *OEDS*]

grifter, *n.* A cheater or swindler, especially one that steals small amounts of money by cheating victims, then quickly moving on.
[*c*1925 DAS, 1930 *OEDS*]

grind, *v.* Also **grind away.** To make a profit in a gambling operation slowly and steadily.
[(1950) 1981 Maurer *Lang. of the Underworld* 186]

grind customer, *n.* Also shortened to **grind.** A player who gambles for small stakes. See also PREMIUM CUSTOMER.
[1973 Clark *Oral Coll*]

grind joint, *n.* Also called a GRIND STORE. A gambling operation that caters to small-stakes bettors; a gambling establishment that contains few games requiring dealers, but depends on continual operation of slot machines for profit.
[1978 Skolnick *House of Cards* 40]

grind operation, *n.* A gambling venture, such as a numbers game or establishment with slot machines and low-limit games. The profit comes from a large number of players who make small bets and lose regularly.
[1974 Friedman *Casino Management* 15]

grind store, *n.* Same as a GRIND JOINT.
[1961 Scarne *Complete Guide* 672]

groom-porter, *n.* **1.** An appointee in the English Royal House responsible for overseeing the acquisition of gaming paraphernalia, such as cards and dice, and for serving as a referee in gambling disputes. Abolished during the reign of George III. *Obsolete.*
[1502 *OED*]
2. Also written **grumporters**. Loaded dice. *Obsolete.*
[1687 *OED*]

gross gaming revenue, *n. phr.* In a casino, the total of all money won, less the overhead expenses.
[1978 Alexander *Glossary* 6]

group game, *n.* A gambling game with a large number of participants, such as bingo or keno.
[1961 Scarne *Complete Guide* 681]

group one license, *n.* In Nevada gambling, a state permit authorizing a gambling operation that has a GROSS GAMING REVENUE, or profit, of more than one million dollars annually.
[1957 *Nevada Gaming Regulations* 33]

group two license, *n.* In Nevada gambling, a state permit authorizing a gambling operation that has a GROSS GAMING REVENUE, or profit, of less than one million dollars annually.
[1957 *Nevada Gaming Regulations* 33]

guinguette, *n.* **1.** In ombre, a hazard created by winning a hand without holding an ace of clubs or an ace of spades.
2. In guinguette, the queen of diamonds.
[1950 Morehead *Culbertson* 617]

gun turn, *n.* Also called a PICKPOCKET TURN. In faro, a turn of two fives.
[1943 Maurer *Argot*]

guts, *n.* In draw poker, the lack of a requirement for a hand of a specific value to begin the betting.
[1949 Coffin *Secrets* 179]
[Compare 1893 *OEDS,* meaning "courage"]

gut shot, *n.* Also called a BELLY HIT. In poker, a hand requiring a fifth card within the sequence for a straight, such as nine, ten, jack, king.
[1968 Wallace *Poker* 216]

gyp, *n.* A cheater who uses guile and deception.
[1889 *OED* as "U.S." usage, originally a small-time horse trader]

H

H, *n.* Abbreviation for HOWARD. In poker, the designation for the position of the dealer in an eight-handed game. Compare A, B, C, D, E, F, G.
[1949 Coffin *Secrets* 179]

hair copper, *n.* Same as HORSEHAIR GAME.
[1890 Quinn *Fools of Fortune* 202]

half a yard, *n.* Also called HALF-CENTURY. Fifty dollars.
[ca. 1961 *Hotel Coll*]

half-century, *n.* Same as HALF A YARD.
[1908 *DA;* Compare *century,* 1839 *DA*]

half-mile pole, *n.* The post of an oval racetrack placed four furlongs before the finish line. Compare EIGHTH POLE.
[1978 Ainslie *Complete Guide* 290]

half-pot limit, *n.* In poker, a special stakes limit, forbidding a player to make a bet greater than half the money currently in the pot.
[1949 Coffin *Secrets* 179]

half-stock, *n.* An incomplete deck of playing cards, especially a pack of cards from which one or more have been removed by a cheater. Compare STACKED DECK.
[1890 Quinn *Fools of Fortune* 258]

hand, *n.* **1.** One game in a series of card games.
[1622 *OED*]
2. The cards held by one player during a card game. [1630 *OED*]
3. The person holding a set of cards during a card game. [1589 *OED*]
4. In a craps game, the series of casts by one shooter.
[(1950) 1981 Maurer *Lang. of the Underworld* 186]
5. A unit of measurement equivalent to four inches used to determine the height of a horse from the ground to the top of the withers.
[1664 *OED*]

hand-betting terminal, *n. phr.* A portable computer terminal used for placing wagers. See also TELEBET. Compare OFF-TRACK BETTING, HANDBOOK.
1987 *New Scientist* 8/20:27. The Royal Hong Kong Jockey (Club) is developing a *hand-betting terminal* that will allow punters to place bets from anywhere in the territory simply by plugging the terminal into a telephone line.

handbook, *n.* A place away from a racetrack where bets can be placed on horse races. Compare OFF-TRACK BETTING.
[1894 *DA, DAE, OEDS*]

handicap, *n.* **1. a.** The amount of added weight a horse must carry in a race to equalize the chances for any horse to win.
1786 *OED*; probably from *hand i' cap,* ultimately from *hand in the cap*, probably referring to the drawing of lots]
b. Any restriction placed on an entrant in a contest or match.
[1955 Hillis *Pari-Mutuel Betting* 115]
[1883 *OED*]
2. a. A horse race in which an umpire (HANDICAPPER) decrees what amount of weight a horse shall carry to equalize the chances of any horse winning.
[1786 *OED*]
b. any race or competition in which less efficient contestants are aided or more efficient ones are hindered in order to equalize the chances for anyone winning.
[1875 *OED*]

handicap, *v.* **1.** To determine the amount of added weight to be carried by each horse in a race. [1856 *OED*]
2. To weigh down, hamper, or otherwise penalize a superior competitor in any match or contest, so as to equalize the chances for anyone winning.
[1864 *OED*]
3. To predict the winner of a race based on an analysis of past performance and the competition in the current race. Compare RACING FORM.
[(1951) 1981 Maurer *Lang. of the Underworld* 214]

handicapper, *n.* **1.** A racetrack official who equalizes the chances for each horse to win a race by determining whether each horse is required to carry added weight during the race, and if so, how much.
[1754 *OED*]
2. A horse entered in a race in which handicaps are applied. [1895 *OEDS*]
3. A person who predicts the outcome of races by analyzing the past performances of the entries. Compare RACING FORM.
[ca. 1961 *Hotel Coll*]

handicapping, *n.* **1.** The determining of the amount of added weight that must be carried by a horse during a race to equalize the chances to win for every horse entered.
[1856 *OED,* see *handicap,* v. (def. 4)]
2. The determining of the weight or other restriction upon a superior competitor in any match or contest, so as to equalize the chances for anyone winning.
3. The predicting of the outcome of a race by analyzing the past performance of each entry.
[1971 McQuaid *Gambler's Digest* 307]

hand-in *n.* In a casino, a tip given directly to the dealer rather than being bet for the dealer. Compare TOKE.
1983 Martinet *Oral Coll.* The dealer will normally announce a *hand-in,* because the boxman gets nervous when he sees the dealer's hand go toward the shirt pocket. Most tokes are from bets the players make for the dealers, so *hand-ins,* especially in craps, you have to be careful with.

handle, *n.* In a gambling enterprise, the total amount of money exchanging hands, between the players and the house, in a given period. Compare GATE.
[1957 *Nevada Gaming Regulations* 8]

hand mucker, *n.* In roulette, an assistant to the dealer who collects losing wagers and sorts the chips according to color. Compare MUCKER.
[1982 Martin *Introduction* 5]
2. A panguingue dealer.
[1973 Clark *Oral Coll*]
[From the dealer's actions, continually shuffling cards that have been played and reinserting them in the deck.]

hand-off, *v.* To pass chips to a confederate in a cheating scheme, usually accomplished by a dishonest dealer overpaying an accomplice who acts as a player.
[ca. 1961 *Hotel Coll*]

hand ride, *n.* A horse race in which the jockey does not use a whip; an easy race for a horse. Compare DRIVE and EXTEND.
[1955 Hillis *Pari-Mutuel Betting* 115]

hand ride, *v.* In horse racing: **1.** To lengthen a horse's stride, by causing the horse's head to rise at the beginning of the stride.
[(1951) 1981 Maurer *Lang. of the Underworld* 214]
2. To use the reins and hands to urge a horse on rather than to GO TO BAT.
[(1951) 1981 Muarer *Lang. of the Underworld* 214]

hand signal, *n.* In twenty-one, a sign given by a player, indicating whether he wants another card or wants to stand. Because the noise in a casino may blur spoken commands, three *hand signals* are common in twenty-one: the player may hold the cards and scratch the layout with them to indicate a request for another card; after splitting a pair and making two hands, the player may place the index finger next to the card he wishes another card to accompany; the player may move the hand horizontally above the cards, palm down, to indicate no more cards are to be dealt to the hand.
[ca. 1961 *Hotel Coll*]

hands up, *n. phr.* In bank craps, a call by the stickman to the players to move their hands away from the layout because the cast of the dice is imminent. Compare DICE BITE.
[1983 Martinet *Oral Coll*]

haneton, *n.* In papillon, a bonus score for taking three ranking cards in a trick with a fourth card of a higher rank.
[1950 Morehead *Culbertson* 618]

hanger, *n.* On a casino gaming table, a piece of paper currency that does not go completely through the table slot into the DROP BOX because of a bent corner. The dealer must then make a pause in the game and reinsert the bill.
1982 Clark *Oral Coll.* A pit boss hates to see any slowdown in the action because it costs the house money. He can't do much about slow players, but he can rag on a dealer for slow shuffles, *hangers,* slow pay, or anything like that. . . . A *hanger* is just a bill that doesn't go clear into the drop. The dealer has to stop and shove it in again.

hangman's turn, *n.* In faro, the appearance of a jack and a king in a single turn of the cards.
[1943 Maurer *Argot*]

hard, *adj.* **1.** In twenty-one, of or pertaining to a hand without an ace, or a hand in which the ace counts one point rather than eleven points.
[1953 Crawford *Consistent Winner* 347]
2. In craps, pertaining to the numbers 4, 6, 8, or 10 rolled in pairs of 2, 3, 4, or 5 respectively.
[1973 Clark *Oral Coll*]

hard count, *n.* **1.** In a casino, the total value of coins or chips taken from a slot machine or a table.
[ca. 1961 *Hotel Coll*]
2. In twenty-one, the total number of points in a hand without an ace, or in a hand with an ace that counts for one point rather than eleven points.
[1981 Silverstone *Player's Guide* 140]

hard count drop supervisor, *n. phr.* In a casino, the employee in charge of the coin weighing room.
[1982 *Review Journal* 10/27: 12]

hard drop, *n.* In a casino, the currency and chips contained in the DROP BOX fastened to the underside of a gaming table.
[ca. 1961 *Hotel Coll*]

hard hand, *n.* In twenty-one, a hand held by a player or dealer that contains no aces, or a hand in which any ace counts as one point rather than as eleven points.
[1973 Friedman *Casino Games* 18]

hard money, *n.* In a casino, currency and coin, as opposed to chips. Compare EASY MONEY. See also HARD COUNT.
[1964 Lemmel *Gambling* 6]

hard play, *n.* In poker, the controlled and conservative betting strategy used by a skilled player.
[1953 Fairfield *Las Vegas* 15]

hard rock, *n.* A poker player who is controlled and skilled enough to take few chances during the betting process.
[1961 Scarne *Complete Guide* 681]

hardway, *n.* Also written **hard way**. Also called GAG. In craps, the numbers 4, 6, 8, or 10 rolled in pairs of the numbers 2, 3, 4, or 5 respectively. See also EASY WAY.
[1953 Lewis *Sagebrush Casinos* 101]

hardway bet, *n.* Also written **hard-way bet**. Also called GAG BET. In craps, a wager that the numbers 4, 6, 8, or 10 will be rolled as pairs of 2, 3, 4, or 5, respectively, before the number 7 is rolled or before the numbers 4, 6, 8, or 10 are rolled in combinations other than pairs (such as 3-1, 4-2, 5-1, and so on).
[ca. 1961 *Hotel Coll*]

hardways working, *n. phr.* In bank craps, an announcement by the stickman that bets placed in the section of the table layout for HARDWAY BETS are considered active when the shooter begins a new hand, after a win. Compare COPPER, *v.*
1983 Martinet *Oral Coll.* At the beginning of a hand, the stickman calls out, "hardways working unless called off." More usually, it's just, "hardways working." That means the hardway bets can win or lose on the first roll. A lot of players like to take down hardway bets on the come out. Since the dealers are always hustling to get players to make those bets in the first place, they will just copper the hardways [place a marker on the bet, indicating it is out of play until the marker is removed] if the player wants them down for one roll.

Harlem tennis, *n.* Another name for CRAPS. *Facetious use.* See also AFRICAN GOLF.
[1983 Martinez *Gambling Scene* 205]

harness, *n.* In a casino poker room, the amount of money provided to house employees who play at a table until enough patrons join the game so that it can continue without them.
[1979 Hilton Hotel *Procedures* 4]

Hart, Schaffner, and Marx, *n. phr.* In poker, a hand with three jacks.
[1971 Livingston *Poker Strategy* 218]
[n.d. *DAS;* jocular application of name of well-known men's clothing manufacturer.]

hawk the dice, *v. phr.* In bank craps, an order from the BOXMAN or FLOORMAN to a DEALER to watch the dice at all times to prevent any cheating moves by a player.
[1983 Martinet *Oral Coll*]

hayburner, *n.* A racehorse that does not earn enough money in purses to pay for the feed it eats. *Sometimes used facetiously.*
[1978 Ainslie *Complete Guide* 291]

hazard, *n.* Also spelled **hasard, hasarde. 1.** A dice game, forerunner to craps, popular through the nineteenth century. Compare AMBS-ACE and BOARD and CASTER and CHANCE and NICK.
1680 Cotton *Complete Gamester* 121. This Game of *hazard* has been very fatal to many a good Gentleman, of which it will not be amiss to give one Example, for the better Information of them who are so bewitch'd as to venture their Fortunes on the Turn of the Dice. Suppose seven is the Main, the Caster throws five, and that's his

Chance, and so has five to seven; if the Caster throws his Chance, he wins all the Money was set him, but if he throws seven, which was the Main, he must pay as much Money as is on the Board: If again, seven be the Main, and the Caster throws eleven, that is a Nick, and sweeps away all the Money on the Table; but if he throws a Chance, he must wait which will come first: Lastly, if seven be the Main, and the Caster throws Ames-Ace, Deuce-Ace or twelve, he is out; but if he throws from four to ten, he has a Chance, though they two are accounted the worst Chances on the Dice, as seven is reputed the best and easiest Main to be flung: Thus it is in eight or six, if either of them be the Main, and the Caster throws either four, five, seven, nine, or ten, this is his Chance, which if he throws first he wins, or otherwise he loseth; if he throws twelve to eight, or six to the same Cast with the Main he wins; but if Ames-Ace or Deuce-Ace, to all he loses; or if twelve when the Main is either five or nine. Here note, that nothing nicks five but five, nor nothing nine but nine.
[1300 *OED*]
2. Another name for CHUCK-A-LUCK.
[ca. 1961 *Hotel Coll*]

head, *n.* In panguingue, the front part of the pack of cards, from which cards are dealt by the dealer or drawn by the players.
[1950 Morehead *Culbertson* 618]

head a trick, *v. phr.* In trump games, to play a higher card than any other on a trick.
[1863 *OED*]

head bet, *n.* In policy or numbers, a wager on three numbers in a specific order.
[1961 Scarne *Complete Guide* 681]

head on, *adj.* Same as HEAD TO HEAD.
[1965 Fraiken *Inside Nevada* 29]

heads-up or **head-up,** *adj.* Same as HEAD TO HEAD.
[1981 Golad *Oral Coll*]

head to head, *adj.* Also called HEAD ON, HEADS-UP. In card games, especially poker, (of a player) playing against another player.
[(1950) 1981 Maurer *Lang. of the Underworld* 187]

hearse-driver, *n.* Also CASE-KEEPER. In faro, the employee who records the cards as they are dealt.
[1943 Maurer *Argot*]

heart convention, *n.* In bridge and whist, a challenge to double the risk, made in the third round of bidding, by which a player informs his partner to lead a card from the suit of hearts after the other team has completed the bidding.
[1950 Morehead *Culbertson* 618]

hearts, *n. pl. Plural in form, but singular in use.*
1. One of the four suits in a common deck of playing cards distinguished by a heart-shaped figure for each pip, the others being CLUBS, DIAMONDS, and SPADES.
[1529 *OED*]
2. heart, *sing.* A card of this suit.

heat, *n.* **1.** In horse racing, one trial in a race that has multiple trials to determine a winner.
[*a*1663 *OED*]
2. In a casino, pressure applied to a DEALER by a PIT BOSS in the form of comments and threats. 1979 Clark *Oral Coll. Heat* is pressure from the bosses, not from the players.
[Compare 1928 *OEDS,* meaning "pressure"]

heavy, *adj.* In poker, denoting a POT containing more money than should be there.
[1949 Coffin *Secrets* 179]

heavy-fisted, *adj.* In a poker room, denoting a dealer who removes more money from the pot than required for the house percentage.
[1978 Larson *Vocabulary* 99]

heavy Texas corner, *n. phr.* An altered die with a rounded edge or corner. Compare BARR DICE.
[1974 Scarne *Dice* 74]

heavy track, *n.* A racetrack condition worse than MUDDY. Compare SLOPPY TRACK and MUDDY TRACK.
[(1951) 1981 Maurer *Lang. of the Underworld* 215]

hedge, *v.* Especially in the phrase **hedge one's bets.** To make multiple wagers in an effort to minimize losses.
1868 Laing-Meason *Turf Frauds* 116. . . . thus so arranging his book, that what he will lose to some persons if the horse wins, he will win from others if the horse loses. This is called *"hedging"* or squaring the account in the bookmaker's betting book.
[1672 *OED*]

hedge bet, *n.* Also shortened to **hedge.** A second wager made on an event to prevent the loss of the first wager.
[1968 Wallace *Poker* 216]
[1736 *OED*]

heel, *v.* **1.** In bank craps, to set the top chip on a wager slightly off center, indicating that the player has taken odds on the bet.
[ca. 1961 *Hotel Coll*]
2. In bank craps, on a DON'T PASS bet, to set the stack of chips made on a LAY BET slightly off center from the bottom chip so as to distinguish the lay bet from a flat bet.
[1977 Anness *Dummy Up*]
3. Also in the phrase:
heel a string, In faro, to bet that a particular card will lose for the player on one turn and win on the next turn or turns.
[1943 Maurer *Argot*]

heel, *n.* Also called HEELER. **1.** In faro, a person who bets that a specific card will lose on one turn and win on the next.
[1938 Asbury *Sucker's Progress* 15]
2. In draw poker, a single, high-ranking card, such as an ace or a king that is retained in the hand rather than discarded after the first betting

round. See also KICKER.
[1968 Wallace *Poker* 216]

heeled bet, *n.* In faro, one of a series of wagers, alternating between betting on the dealer and on the player.
[1923 *OEDS, DA*]

heeler, *n.* Same as HEEL (def. 2).
[1949 Coffin *Secrets* 179]

heel peek, *n.* Also called a BACK PEEK. A cheating move in playing cards. An act by a card dealer to see the value of the top card on the deck by squeezing the top of the deck between the little finger and the thumb, bowing the top card upwards in the middle so the value of the card can be seen.
[1982 Martin *Introduction* 27]

hell, *n.* A gambling dive where cheating takes place regularly.
1859 Green *Gambler's Tricks* 112. Unequal dice are used at French and English hazard; and from the difficulty in detecting them, if not made to "work too strong," as the phrase is, are said to be introduced, without much hesitation, at many of the New York *hells.*
[1794 *OED;* 1835 *DAE*]

hellite, *n.* The owner or operator of a gambling house, especially an establishment known to harbor cheaters. *Obsolete.*
[1824 *OED*]

hemingway, *n.* A code name for a fellow cheater, especially at card games.
[1939 MacDougall and Furnas *Gambler's Don't* 73]

hen, *n.* In playing cards, another name for the QUEEN.
[1949 Coffin *Secrets* 179]

hickey, *n.* In dominoes, a side bet on a bid for tricks.
[1981 Jenkins *Johnny Moss* 82]

high, *n.* In all fours (high, low, jack and the game), the ace of trumps.
1836 Eidrah *Hoyle Famil* 63. *High,* the ace of trumps, or next best trump out.
[1680 *OED*]

high, *adj.* **1.** In stud poker, noting the ranking card in a betting round. The player holding the highest ranking card begins the betting for that round. [1887 *OEDS*]
2. In chuck-a-luck, noting the numbers from 11 to 18.
3. Pertaining to gambling for large stakes.
[1828 *OED*]

highball, *n.* A poker game in which the player holding the highest ranking hand wins. Compare LOWBALL.
[1881 *DAE,* 1894 *OED*]

high-belly strippers, *n.* A playing card trimmed or shaved so the ends of the card are narrower than the middle, usually the higher ranking cards in a deck. See also COMBINATION STRIPPERS and LOW-BELLY STRIPPERS.
[1961 Scarne *Complete Guide* 681]

high card, *n.* **1.** The card with the highest rank on the table.
[1973 Binion *Recollections* 13]
2. At the showdown in poker, the card with the highest rank, which wins the pot if no other hand contains a pair or better, or if two hands tie.
[ca. 1961 *Hotel Coll*]

high-card trick, *n.* In bridge, a trick won by the ranking card of the suit led, rather than by a trump card.
[1950 Morehead *Culbertson* 619]

high die, *n.* **1.** A die that has been altered to roll high numbers more often than low numbers. Compare LOW DICE.
[1890 Quinn *Fools of Fortune* 283]
2. In bank craps, a die that bounces up onto the rail circling the table and is therefore out of play.
[1983 Martinet *Oral Coll*]

high-fullam, *n.* A die that has been altered so that the faces with four, five, or six pips will be turned up more often than the faces with one, two, or three pips. See also FULLUM and LOW-FULLAM.
1680 Cotton *Compleat Gamester* 9. This they do by false Dice, as *High-Fullams* 4, 5, 6. Low-Fullams 1, 2, 3.
[1592 *OED* under "fulham"]

high game, *n.* A method for cheating at cards, featuring marks on the backs of certain cards of higher rank. Compare COSMETICS.
[1674 *OED*]

high hand, *n.* At the conclusion of the hand in poker, the player with the highest ranking cards.
[1953 Lewis *Sagebrush Casinos* 38]

high layout, *n.* In faro, a table constructed so the DEALING BOX is flush with the top of the LAYOUT, but holds extra cards so the dealer can cheat by drawing one of two or three secreted cards.
[1943 Maurer *Argot*]

high-low bet, *n.* In bank craps, a wager that the number 2 or 12 will appear on the next roll.
[1963 Steig *Common Sense* 184]

high-low poker, *n.* A variation in poker in which the player with the highest-ranking hand splits the pot with the player holding the lowest-ranking hand.
[ca. 1961 *Hotel Coll*]

high-low ticket, *n.* In keno, a special bet on three groups of four numbers each on the same betting slip. The player hopes to win a small amount of money on one of the groups, while being eligible for a large payoff at very long odds.
[ca. 1961 *Hotel Coll*]

high-noon, *n.* In craps, a roll of twelve. See also GARY COOPER.
[1982 Clark *Oral Coll*]

high-number bet, *n.* In roulette, a wager on the group of numbers from 19 to 36.

[1968 Thackrey *Nick the Greek* 157]
→*High-number bet* is the term used in the U.S. Elsewhere the wager is called PASSE.

high roller, *n.* A gambler who places large bets often. See also BIG PLUNGER and COWBOY and HIGH STAKES.
1985 Hopkins *Suite Life* 32. The term "high roller" is commonly used to describe anyone who bets large amounts of money. However, people in the gambling business give it a narrower meaning, says Tony "Toby" DiCesare, casino manager at the Tropicana Hotel. DiCesare, one of the few executives who will speak openly about the care and feeding of *high rollers,* explains, "A *high roller* might come around only once a year, but he will always bet the limit, whatever the limit is." Most big bettors would more properly be described as "preferred customers," he says. "A preferred customer is a good, steady customer who comes about once a month, gives you perhaps $20,000 worth of action, and will always bet black chips"—the $100 kind—"but not necessarily the limit. Some preferred customers will be *high rollers* also, but you treat either type the same."
[(1881) 1968 *OEDS,* 1892 *DAE,* n.d. *DAS;* Compare *high game* 1828 *OED* and *high play* 1889 *OED*]

high spade, *n.* In stud poker, a side bet won by the person holding the spade of the highest rank in a hand still in play at the completion of the hand.
[1978 Larson *Vocabulary*]

high spade in the hole, *n. phr.* In stud poker, a variation in which the player with the ranking spade in the hole in a hand still in play at the completion of the hand wins half the pot. Compare HIGH-LOW POKER.
[1968 Wallace *Poker* 217]

high stakes, *adj.* Also written **high-stakes.** Noting a game in which large bets are allowed.
[ca. 1961 *Hotel Coll*]

high suit, *n.* In any of several card games, the spade suit. In these games the suits are ranked from low to high, as CLUBS, DIAMONDS, HEARTS, and SPADES.
[1890 Quinn *Fools of Fortune* 209]

hipe, *v.* Also spelled HYPE. To short-change a player, especially by removing a chip from his stack while paying him. See also CHECK COPPER.
[Compare 1926 *OEDS,* as *hype,* meaning "to deceive, especially by false publicity." See also HYPE.]

hippodrome, *n.* A race or athletic event in which a winner has been prearranged; a fix. *Obsolete.*
[1866 *DA,* 1868 *DAE,* n.d. *Century Dict.*]

hippodrome, *v.* To conduct a contest or race in which the result has been prearranged.
[n.d. *OED,* 1868 *DA, DAE; a*1867 *OEDS* and 1886 *Century Dict.* as *hippodroming*]

his heels, *n.* Same as HIS KNOB.
1863 Pardon *Hoyle's* 97. *His Heels*—The knave when turned up. It reckons for two holes, but is only once counted.
1876 Heather *Cards* 89. *His Heels.*—Counts two to the dealer when the turn-up is a knave.
[1796 *OED,* as any knave of trump]

his knob, *n.* Also called HIS HEELS, HIS NIBS, HIS NOB, KNAVE NODDY, NOB, NODDY. In cribbage, the jack of the suit turned up after the cut; it counts one point for the person holding it. If the jack is turned on the cut, the dealer receives two points.
1876 Heather *Cards* 89. *His Knob.*—One point allowed for having the knave of the turn-up suit. It counts whether in hand or crib. Two points to the dealer if turned for trump.

his nibs, *n. pl.* Also clipped to **his nib.** *Sometimes plural in form, but singular in use.* Same as HIS KNOB.
[1973 Clark *Oral Coll*]
[Compare 1812 *OED,* as *his nabs* meaning "a jocular designation of a person"]

his nob, *n.* Same as HIS KNOB.
1863 Pardon *Hoyle's* 97. *His Nob*—The knave of the turned-up suit. In counting, in hand or crib, it marks one point.
[1844 *OED*]

hit, *n.* **1.** Generally, an instance of winning at gambling.
[1960 Cook *Gambling, Inc.* 282]
2. In backgammon, the equivalent of a game, or win.
1860 Crawley *Backgammon* 57. If one player has not borne off his first man before the other has borne off his last, he loses a *gammon,* which is equivalent to two games or "hits." If each player has borne off, it is reduced to a *"hit,"* or game of one. If the winner has borne off all his men before the loser has carried his men out of his adversary's table, it is a "back-gammon," and usually held equivalent to three *hits* or games. [1766 *OED*]
3. In backgammon, the taking of an opponent's single counter, sending it to the bar.
[1778 *OED,* 1847 *DAE*]
4. The drawing of a winning number in policy gambling. [1847 *DAE, DA*]
5. In twenty-one, the act of being dealt another card.
[1982 Martin *Introduction* 13]
6. In dice games like craps and hazard: **a.** the act of rolling the required number on the dice to win.
[(1950) 1981 Maurer *Lang. of the Underworld* 187]

b. hits, *pl.* Same as HIT DICE.
[(1950) 1981 Maurer *Lang. of the Underworld* 187]
7. In keno, the drawing of a number selected by a player on a ticket.
[ca. 1961 *Hotel Coll*]
8. In bingo, the drawing of a number on a

player's board.
[1973 Clark *Oral Coll*]

hit, *v.* **1.** To win money by gambling.
[1960 Cook *Gambling, Inc.* 282]
2. In backgammon, to take an opponent's single piece by landing on the same slot with a piece; to remove an opponent's piece from the spot it occupies.
1860 Crawley *Backgammon* 53. If your antagonist throw a number or two which count (either or both) from a point occupied by his own dice to the place where the unhappy blot is alone in his insecurity, the single man may be taken, and the blot is said to be *hit*—that is, taken prisoner, torn from his position and placed on the bar to wait till he can be entered again.
[1599 *OED*]
3. In twenty-one, a direction to the dealer to deal another card (to a designated hand).
[1968 Adams *Western Words*]
4. In various card and dice games, to win money by drawing a particular card or rolling a specific number on the dice.
[1961 Scarne *Complete Guide* 681]
5. In keno and bingo, to have a number on a keno ticket or a bingo board that is drawn by the operator of the game.
[ca. 1961 *Hotel Coll*]
6. To win a lottery or numbers game.
[1977 Clark *Oral Coll*]
7. In the phrases:
hit a blot, In backgammon, to land on a slot occupied by single counter belonging to the opponent, sending the piece to the bar. Compare HIT, *v.* (def. 2).
[1691 *OED*]
hit a jackpot, To win a large payout on a slot machine. Compare HIT THE JACKPOT.
1986 Clark *Oral Coll.* The difference between the phrases "hit a jackpot" and "hit the jackpot" is a difference in degree of specificity. The distinction is most easily seen in the form of questions. When one player asks another, "Did you hit a jackpot?", the referent is general and refers to winning money on any of the varieties of slot machines. But when one player asks another, "Did you hit the jackpot?", the reference is usually to a specific slot machine or a specific jackpot.
hit a log, In craps, to result in a losing number.
[1983 Martinet *Oral Coll*]
hit and run, To gamble and win quickly, then withdraw from a continuing game as twenty-one or craps.
[1974 Scarne *Dice* 470]
hit a rock or **hit a stump,** In craps, to result in a losing number.
[(1950) 1981 Maurer *Lang. Of the Underworld* 187]
hit it, 1. In craps, to roll the number desired on the dice.
[1983 Martinez *Gambling Scene* 206]
2. In poker, to increase the size of a previous bet; to raise.
[1978 Brunson *How I Made* 534]
3. In twenty-one, a direction to the dealer to deal another card (to a designated hand). Also called HIT ME.
[ca. 1961 *Hotel Coll*]
hit me, Same as HIT IT (def. 3).
[1961 Scarne *Complete Guide* 681]
hit the boards, Also called HIT THE END RAIL. In craps, a command from the stickman to the shooter to roll the dice harder so they hit the cushion at the other end of the table and bounce off to roll freely. If the dice do not hit the back cushion, the shooter may be using a controlled roll of the dice.
[1961 Scarne *Complete Guide* 681]
hit the deck, In draw poker, to take replacement cards after discarding.
[1978 Brunson *How I Made* 534]
hit the end rail, Same as HIT THE BOARDS.
[1983 Martinet *Oral Coll*]
hit the jackpot, To win a specific large payout on a slot machine or to win the payout on a machine, usually a specific machine. See quotation at HIT A JACKPOT.
[1953 Lewis *Sagebrush Casinos* 150]
[1944? *OEDS, DA*, n.d. *DAS*]
hit the kicker, In draw poker, to draw a card that makes a pair with a card that was kept in the hand along with a smaller pair.
[1895 *OED,* under "kicker"]

hit and run, *n. phr.* In a casino, the act of making a single bet, usually at twenty-one, then withdrawing if the bet wins.
[(1950) 1981 Maurer *Lang. of the Underworld* 187]

hit and run artist, *n. phr.* Also called HIT AND RUNNER. A player who joins a continuing game such as poker or twenty-one, then leaves the game after winning some bets in a short period.
1981 Golad *Oral Coll.* Nobody likes a *hit and run artist* who joins a game for a short time then leaves with his winnings. People like that get a reputation, so when they show up at a game, everybody just folds for three or four hands until the jerk leaves. A *hit and run artist* takes money out of the game so the rest of the players are going after short money.

hit and runner, *n. phr.* Same as HIT AND RUN ARTIST.
[1979 Newman *Dealer's Special* 11]

hit dice, *n. pl.* Also called HITS. Dice that have been altered so that the number 7 cannot be rolled.
[1961 Scarne *Complete Guide* 681]

hock card, *n.* Also shortened to **hock.** Also called **hockelty card** and **hocly** and **hockley** and **hoc.**
1. In faro, the last card in the box. See also SODA TO HOCK.
1843 Green *Exposure* 210. Then there is what Mr. Hoyle calls *"hockelty";* this is when the

card on which the bettor is betting is the last card, and the dealer takes all the stakes.
1868 Trumps *Pocket Hoyle* 207. The *Hock,* or *Hockelty Card* is the last card remaining in the box after the deal has been made. When one turn remains to be made, there are three cards in the box, they may be, for example, the Five, Six, and Seven; we will suppose the last turn to be Five, Six, leaving the Seven in the box, which would be called the *hock* card, because, as the game was originally played, the dealer took *"hock,"* that is, all the money which happened to be placed upon that card; the bank, therefore, had a certainty of winning that money, without the possibility of losing it—hence the term *hock,* which means *certainty.*
[1843 *DA, OEDS;* 1859 *DAE;* n.d. *Century Dict., OED*]
2. In faro, the penultimate card dealt. It wins for the dealer. *Obsolete.*
[1843 *OEDS,* at *hockelty*]
1824 Anon *Hoyle's* 66. *Hockley* signifies the last card but one, the chance of which the banker claims, and may refuse to let any punter withdraw a card when eight or less remain to be dealt.
3. In faro, a special bet made on the last turn.
[1898 *DAE, DA*]
4. In the phrase:
in hock, Pertaining to having lost money by gambling. [1859 *DAE, DA*]

hold, *n.* In a gambling establishment, the amount of money won by the house. See also AX and DROP and HANDLE.
[ca. 1961 *Hotel Coll*]

hold, *v.* In the phrases and particle constructions:
hold it up, To simulate a dice throw from a cup while holding one die with the index finger so that it does not rattle in the cup or turn over on the table, but is placed on the table with the desired face upward.
[1974 Scarne *Dice* 33]
hold out, To conceal a playing card or cards for use later in a game.
[1968 Adams *Western Words*]
[1894 *OED*]
hold up, In trump games like whist and bridge, to refrain from playing a high-ranking card on a trick. [1879 *OED*]
hold up a dead table, Of a casino dealer, to stand at an empty table with crossed arms, waiting for patrons.
[1977 Anness *Dummy Up*]

hold check, *n.* In a gambling establishment, a marker, IOU, or check signed by a patron in exchange for cash or chips and retained by the pit boss, floorman, or manager for a specified period.
[1961 Scarne *Complete Guide* 681]

hold count, *n.* A technique once used by slot-machine players who could set a rhythm in mechanical slot machines to align the reels for a payout, in which the reel balancing device in that type of slot machine could be rocked like a pendulum by pulling the handle with a particular rhythm, then a sudden jerk of the handle would lock the slowly spinning reels in place. *Obsolete.* Compare VARIATION TIMER.
[1961 Scarne *Complete Guide* 681]

hold 'em poker, *n.* A popular form of poker. See description in prefatory essay.

holding, *n.* The cards in one player's hand.
[1929 *OEDS*]

holdout, *n.* Also written **hold-out**. Any of a variety of cheating devices employed to conceal a playing card up a sleeve, in a vest, under the table, or elsewhere, until required for play. See also BUG and LIZARD and SPIDER.
1902 Andrews *Artifice* 14. Many mechanical contrivances termed *"hold outs"* have been invented to aid the card player. The simplest form is a steel spring with an awl-like attachment at one end which can be pressed into the underside of almost any table in an instant.
[1893 *OED*]

hold-out, *adj.* Noting a playing card or cards dishonestly retained by a player for later use: **hold-out artist, hold-out device, hold out machine,** or **hold out man.**
[1938 Asbury *Sucker's Progress* 35]

hold up, *n.* In trump games like whist and bridge, the act of refraining from playing a high-ranking card on a trick.
[1945 *OEDS*]

hole, *n.* **1.** In stud poker, the position for the card or cards dealt face down. Hence, the reference to a specific card "in the hole."
[1963 Steig *Common Sense* 184]
2. A position on a gambling table layout for placing a bet.
[1964 Lemmel *Gambling* 113]
3. A number on a craps table layout on which no money was bet when the dice roll results in that number.
1983 Martinet *Oral Coll.* Say the dice roll a six and nobody had bet that number, you say the dice hit the *hole* on the layout, especially when there are bets on the numbers on either side.
4. A stall in the starting gate for a horse race, usually the inside position closest to the rail.
[1978 Ainslie *Complete Guide* 291]

hole-card, *n.* In games like stud and twenty-one, a card dealt face downward to a player.
[1908 *DA, OEDS*]

hollow chip, *n.* A flattened cup made to look like a one-dollar chip that a cheating dealer in a casino can use to cover a chip of a higher denomination, which is passed to a confederate, thus stealing from the house.
[ca. 1961 *Hotel Coll*]

hollows, *n. pl.* Playing cards that have been trimmed or shaved on the long side so they can

be identified by a card cheat. See also STRIPPERS.
[1890 Quinn *Fools of Fortune* 197]

Hollywood, *n.* A scoring system in gin rummy designed to keep the score for three games simultaneously.
[1968 Wallace *Poker* 217]

holy city, *n.* A poker hand, usually a full house, composed of aces and face cards.
[1949 Coffin *Secrets* 179]

home, *n.* **1.** In cribbage, an announcement during a game that a player has maintained an average score for a hand, usually for the crib.
[1877 *OEDS*]
2. The finish line in a race.
3. Also called HOME BASE. Same as INNER TABLE.
1860 Crawley *Backgammon* 51. The board consists of twenty-four points, coloured alternately of different colours, usually blue and red; and that division in which are placed five black men and two white, is called the table or *home* of the white.
[1870 *OED*]

home base, *n.* Same as INNER TABLE. See also HOME TABLE.
[1976 Figgis *Gambler's Handbook* 68]

homestretch, *n.* The straight portion of an oval race track before the finishing line. Compare DRIVE and EXTEND.
[1841 *DA,* 1861 *OED,* 1868 *DAE*]

home table, *n.* In backgammon, the half of the board closest to the player. The *home table* is divided into the INNER TABLE, or HOME BASE, and the OUTER TABLE.
[1974 Scarne *Dice* 318]

honest reader, *n.* Playing cards that have not been marked, trimmed, or altered in any fashion.
[1968 Wallace *Poker* 217]

honor, *n. Especially British* **honour. 1.** In any of a variety of card games, a playing card designated to have special value in scoring or play. Compare TRUMP and WILD CARD.
[1949 Coffin *Secrets* 179]
2. In bridge, points counted in scoring: in trump, any four of the cards from 10 through ace, held in the same hand, counts 100 *honours;* all five counts 150 *honours;* in no-trump bids, all four aces held in the same hand counts 150 *honours.*
[1950 Morehead *Culbertson* 619]
[1909 *OEDS*]
3. In card games like whist, the jack, queen, king, or ace, especially of TRUMP.
1843 Green *Exposure* 146. In whist they stock primarily to get the *honor,* that is, ace, king, queen, and jack, of the suit that is trump.
[1674 *OED*]
4. In ombre and quadrille, the aces of spades and clubs, and the lowest card of the trump suit.
[1878 *OED*]

hook, *n.* **1.** In playing cards, a jack or a 7. See also FISHHOOK.
[1949 Coffin *Secrets* 179]
2. Also called the TWIG. In sports books, the half point assigned to be added to or subtracted from the score of a team for betting purposes. The *hook* prevents tied scores. Compare SPREAD.
1984 Clark *Oral Coll.* Around here, everyone refers to the half point on a spread as the *hook.* I've seen twig used only in sports betting publications.
3. On a craps table, the corner of the layout on the stickman's side of the table.
1983 Martinet *Oral Coll.* The dice flew down the table and knocked over a stack of greens on the pass line and stopped in the *hook* . . . The *hook* is the outside corner on the layout, where the big 6 and 8 are.

hop, *n.* **1.** In craps, a single roll of the dice. See also BULLFROG.
[1973 Friedman *Casino Games* 91]
2. In playing cards, a cheating move that restores the deck to its original order after another player divides, or cuts the deck into two packs. See also ELEVATOR CUT and STEP CUT.
[1961 Scarne *Complete Guide* 681]

hop, *v.* In the phrases:
hop the cut, To restore a deck of cards to their original order with a cheating move, after the deck has been divided into two packets by another player. See also ELEVATOR THE CUT.
[1982 Martin *Introduction* 26]
hop the deck, Same as HOP THE CUT.
[ca. 1961 *Hotel Coll*]

hop bet, *n.* In craps, a proposition bet resolved by the next roll of the dice. Compare BIG RED.
1983 Martinet *Oral Coll.* Superstitious players make a lot of *hop bets.* If a die goes down or hits someone on the hand, someone is sure to make a *hop bet* on big red, that is, that the next roll will be 7.

hopper, *n.* The metal bin inside a slot machine that holds the coins put into the machine, and from which coins are dropped upon winning.
[1957 *Nevada Gaming Regulations* 33]

hopper fill slip, *n. phr.* A document for recording the amount of coins used to replenish a slot machine that has been emptied.
[1978 Alexander *Glossary* 7]

horn bet, *n.* In bank craps, a wager that the next roll will be a 2, 3, 11, or 12, usually requiring the bettor to place at least four times the minimum wager on the bet.
[1973 Friedman *Casino Games* 90]

horn high bet, *n. phr.* A proposition wager that the next roll of the dice will be 2, 3, 11, or 12, for which the bettor places an extra chip on one of the four numbers.
[ca. 1961 *Hotel Coll*]

horse, *n.* **1.** In policy or numbers, a wager that four different, specific numbers will appear somewhere on the list of winning numbers.
[1872 *DA,* 1882 *DAE*]

2. horses, *pl.* Mismarked dice used for cheating. *Obsolete.*
[(1950) 1951 Maurer *Lang. of the Underworld* 187]

horse box, *n.* In faro, a DEALING BOX designed in such a fashion as to allow the dealer to cheat.
[1938 Asbury *Sucker's Progress* 12]

horsehair game, *n.* In faro, a cheating move by which a player places a fine wire or horsehair beneath his chips on the table layout so that if a losing card is turned up by the dealer, a confederate distracts the dealer while the cheater pulls the wire, moving the chips to another card on the layout. *Obsolete.*
1873 Morris *Wanderings* 379. To play the *"horse hair game"* scientifically, required two persons, a full board of players, and many bets on the layout. The manipulator took a position in front of the table and played small, until one of the cards near him became "dead." This card he made his base for operating. His "pal," immediately upon its becoming "dead," placed upon it a couple of stacks of white checks, of about twenty each. The operator places behind these, ten or fifteen red ones, to the bottom one of which is attached the end of a horse-hair, the other end being fastened to one of his vest-buttons. For example, we will say that the "dead," or base card, is the Jack, next to it on the lay-out are the ten and Queen, and four or five of theses cards are still in the dealing box. Should he see one of these cards come winning, while the dealer is making this turn, and all eyes are concentrated on the cards as they fall from the box, he leans gently back in his chair, and as he does so the movement drags the stack of red checks from off the Jack, taking in the winning card behind it.

Horse Racing. The "Sport of Kings", or the TURF RACE, as an organized activity in modern times began in England during the 12th century. Epsom was the site of an early RACECOURSE. In America, STAKES RACES were first established on Hempstead Plain on Long Island (New York) in the 17th century.

RACEGOERS, who may be RAILBIRDS, can WAGER on the outcome of a contest among TROTTERS or PACERS which pull TROTTING SULKIES with DRIVERS. Or, they may choose to follow the PONIES in FLATRACING, in which a JOCKEY rides the horse.

When all horses carry the same weight it is dubbed a SKATE RACE. Some races are HANDICAPPED to account for the differences in PAST PERFORMANCE as determined by a HANDICAPPER employed by the RACE TRACK or by a BOOKIE. Such an ALLOWANCE RACE is called a HANDICAP, while a WEIGHT-FOR-AGE-RACE is more complicated. Only two year olds run in a BABY RACE. However, if there is no record for a horse it receives a STARTER HANDICAP. An inexperienced jockey, or BUG, may be given an APPRENTICE ALLOWANCE until he begins to win races.

Sometimes a race is a CLAIMING RACE which may be organized as a SELLING RACE. When a track hosts a MAIDEN CLAIMING EVENT all the horses are MAIDENS.

A RACING SECRETARY will accept entries for an OVERNIGHT RACE up to a couple of days before a contest.

When the PURSE for a race is increased by adding to it the STARTING FEES it is referred to as an ADDED-MONEY RACE.

If JOCKEYS conspire to throw a competition the result is a BOAT RACE, which one jockey will win with a HAND RIDE.

Some BETTORS place a STRAIGHT BET on a horse to WIN, usually a TWO-DOLLAR BET. Others may prefer to bet ACROSS THE BOARD for one horse to WIN or PLACE or SHOW, which is called a SIX-DOLLAR COMBINE. An EXACTA, PERFECTA, TRIFECTA, and SUPERFECTA are increasingly refined predictions for finishing IN THE MONEY. QUINELLA is like a PERFECTA but without a prediction for order of finish. A DOUBLE QUINELLA further tries the bettor's skill by applying it in two races. A DAILY DOUBLE (also called SWEET DEEDEE from its abbreviation DD) merely requires the prediction of the winner in two successive races, usually designated by the track. A SPLIT CHOICE picks either of two FAVORITES to win, whereas a TWO-HORSE PARLAY involves two horses in separate races.

Many serious bettors follow the ODDS published in the RACING FORM. A BETTING FORECAST suggests probable OPENING ODDS. THE A.M., or MORNING LINE and LATE LINE keep bettors apprised of the ACTUAL ODDS until the POST ODDS are announced at POST TIME.

The TRACK ODDS may differ from odds offered by a BOOKMAKER. But OTB offers the same odds as ON-TRACK BETTING. BOOKMAKING has reacted to OFF-TRACK BETTING with the TELEBET and the HAND-BETTING TERMINAL.

A RACECARD is the guide for the RAILBIRD in selecting his choices for purchasing a WIN TICKET, PLACE TICKET or SHOW TICKET. STOOPERS frequently find TOTE tickets on the floor of the BOOK or GRANDSTAND after they have been discarded by bettors who thought that their SHOW TICKET was on a LOSER after their NAG WON.

The DAILY RACING FORM will guide the FORM PLAYER while a TOTE BOARD (also called the TOTALIZATOR) further assists the PUNTER who is a HUNCH-PLAYER looking for a RIGHT PRICE or CHALK HORSE.

SPORTS BOOKS and legalized PARI-MUTUELS derive their income by keeping a percentage of the bets placed by the bettors. BUCKET-SHOPS (also called LISTSHOPS) often operate by relying upon PROTECTION (or PRO). A TOUT (bettor who is a TIPSTER) or TIP SHEET can often mislead the unsuspecting.

The ODDS MAKER for a RACEBOOK or TRACK sets the conditions upon which PENCILLERS may BOOK THE ACTION of PUNTERS whether or not they are GRIND CUSTOMERS or PLUNGERS.

horseroom, *n.* A bookmaking establishment.
[1983 Martinez *Gambling Scene* 206]
[1956 *DAS*]

host, *n.* In a casino, a representative of the management who greets high-spending patrons, arranges credit checks, and issues complimentary meal and room passes. See also FULL PENCIL and GREETER. Compare COMP.
[ca. 1961 *Hotel Coll*]

hot, *adj.* **1.** Pertaining to a run of good fortune; lucky; descriptive of cards, dice, horses, numbers, and so on, that win money for a gambler. Compare COLD.
[1894 *OED*]
2. Generating heavy betting.
1889 Ellangowan *Sporting Anecdotes* 336. *Hot,* and sometimes Warm.—Backed for a great deal of money. A horse is said "to come *hot*" in the betting when he is suddenly backed for a large amount.

hot sucker, *n.* A card player who gets angry and makes poor judgments about betting.
1982 Golad *Oral Coll.* You try to keep from becoming a *hot sucker,* but it happens to almost everyone at sometime . . . If you make a bad judgment at hold 'em, or more often, if somebody snaps you off down the river [wins a pot by drawing a needed card to make a weak hand strong] you get mad. You're a *hot sucker* and everyone likes that because you make bad bets. If I'm suddenly turning into a *hot sucker* I'll stand up and walk around the room or the table for a hand or so.

hot walker, *n.* In horse racing, a groom who walks a horse after a race until it is cooled down.
[(1951) 1981 Maurer *Lang. of the Underworld* 215]
[n.d. *DAS*]

house, *n.* Also called a STORE or JOINT or SAWDUST JOINT or CARPET JOINT. A gambling establishment. Compare AGAINST THE HOUSE.
[1901 *DA;* compare 1550 *OED,* meaning "an inn, tavern"]

house advantage, *n.* Also called the HOUSE EDGE or HOUSE ODDS or PC. The odds that favor the gambling establishment; the percentage of money gambled that the casino or gambling establishment can expect to keep as a profit.
[1964 Wykes *Illustrated Guide* 327]

house bank, *n.* The money held by a gambling establishment to cover all bets made by patrons in games like baccarat, craps, twenty-one, roulette, and so on. In games with a *house bank,* the players wager AGAINST THE HOUSE rather than against each other, as distinguished from games with a RAKE, in which players wager against each other while the house retains a percentage of the winnings, as with poker played in a casino. Compare TABLE BANK.
[1968 Thackrey *Nick the Greek* 28]

house chips, *n.* In a gambling establishment, chips that are used by employees of the establishment and not sold to patrons.
[ca. 1961 *Hotel Coll*]

house cut, *n.* Also called the RAKE. In a poker room, the percentage of each pot taken for the establishment by the dealer.
[1968 Wallace *Poker* 217]

house edge, *n.* Same as the HOUSE ADVANTAGE.
[ca. 1961 *Hotel Coll*]

house limit, *n.* The maximum bet accepted by a gambling establishment, varying from game to game within an establishment, even from table to table, depending on the game and the table minimum.
[1968 Thackrey *Nick the Greek* 158]

house money, *n.* **1.** Funds belonging to the gambling establishment; the money used to bank games in a casino.
2. The money a player has won from the casino, which he bets in continued play.
[1983 Martinet *Oral Coll*]

house numbers, *n. pl.* In roulette, the spaces on the table layout for 0 and 00.
[ca. 1961 *Hotel Coll*]

[So called because two additional numbers bring the total numbers in the game to thirty-eight, but a single number is paid at thirty-six to one rather than thirty-eight to one, thereby increasing the advantage to the establishment.]

house odds, *n.* Same as HOUSE ADVANTAGE.
[1953 Lewis *Sagebrush Casino* 104]

house percentage, *n.* The odds on a gambling game that favor the gambling establishment; the PAYOFF ODDS that differ from TRUE ODDS.
1980 Clark *Oral Coll.* In roulette, the payoff odds are thirty-six to one. But there are thirty-eight chances every time the wheel spins, so the true odds would be thirty-eight to one. The knotholes [0 and 00] make the *house percentage.*

house player, *n.* Same as SHILL.
[1978 Harrah *Recollections* 55]

house rules, *n. pl.* Regulations governing a game in an establishment, especially variations for special hands or betting practices.
[1968 Wallace *Poker* 217]

house ticket, *n.* In keno, a betting proposition peculiar to an establishment, usually a special price or combination bet not offered at other keno parlors.
[ca. 1961 *Hotel Coll*]

housewives' special, *n.* A bingo session with reduced prices for admission or bingo cards, usually sessions held in the morning or afternoon.
[1951 Woon *The Why, How, and Where* 79]

howard, *n.* Same as H.
[1949 Coffin *Secrets* 179]

Hoyle, Edmond, (1672-1769). Writer of a short treatise on whist, in 1742, he gained a reputation as an arbiter of disputes about rules for games. Compare ACCORDING TO HOYLE.
[1949 Coffin *Secrets* 179]

hudson shot, *n.* A cheating move at dice; a controlled throw of dice designed to keep the same number face up at the finish of the cast as at the beginning. See also WHIP SHOT.
[(1950) 1981 Maurer *Lang. of the Underworld* 187]

humps, *n. pl.* A cheater's playing cards trimmed or shaved on the long edge so that the ends of the cards are wider in the middle, usually applied either to the low cards or to the high cards, such as face cards. See also STRIPPERS.
[1890 Quinn *Fools of Fortune* 197]

hunch-player, *n.* A gambler who bets on impulse rather than using information available about an event.
1978 Clark *Oral Coll.* A *hunch-player* doesn't count the cards left in the deck or look at what other players have showing or look at the past performance of a horse or a team. He just bets on whatever feels good. We like to see *hunch-players* coming, it's an easy living.

hung, *adj.* Noting a horse that slows down for no apparent reason during a race.
[1955 Hillis *Pari-Mutuel Betting* 115]

hush money, *n.* Also called ICE. A bribe paid to a public official to ignore an illegal gambling operation.
[Compare 1709 *OED,* meaning "money paid to prevent disclosure of a crime"]

hustle, *n.* A scheme for swindling; a fraud or deception, especially in a game of skill such as pool, or in a rigged game such as craps. See also GRIFT (def. 2).
1985 Polsky *Hustlers, Beats and Others* 45. At that point [playing at a disadvantage] the hustler should of course refuse to play. There is often a temptation to do otherwise, not only because the hustler is proud of his skill but because action is his lifeblood (which is why he plays other hustlers when he can't find a *hustle*), and there may be no other action around.
[1954 *DAS;* 1963 *OEDS*]

hustle, *v.* To engage in a game with a scheme for swindling one's opponent. See also GRIFT.
[n.d. *DAS*]

hustler, *n.* A swindler or cheat, especially in games of skill such as pool, or in a rigged game such as craps. See also GRIFTER (def. 2).
1985 Polsky *Hustlers, Beats and Others* 42. The best hustler is not necessarily the best player among the *hustlers.* He has to be a very good player, true, but beyond a certain point his playing ability is not nearly so important as his skill at various kinds of *conning.* Also, he has to possess personality traits that make him "rock-like," able to exploit fully his various skills—playing, conning, others—in the face of assorted pressures and temptations not to exploit them fully.
[1825 *OED,* in reference to pickpocks; *c*1930 *DAS;* 1914 *OEDS*]

hustling, *n.* The action of a HUSTLER.
[Compare 1823 *OEDS,* meaning "robbery"]

hype, *v.* Same as HIPE.
[Compare 1926 *OEDS;* but see also 1811 Francis Grose *A Provincial Glossary,* meaning "to hype at one, to make mouths at, or afront one"]

I

I beg, *n. clause.* In seven up or old sledge, words used in requesting three additional cards. If the dealer refuses the request, the player scores a point.
[1793 *OEDS,* under "beg"]

ice, *n.* **1.** Same as HUSH MONEY.
[1948 *OEDS*]
2. A deck of cards prearranged to deal particular hands; a COLD DECK (def. 1).
[1968 Wallace *Poker* 217]

ice-cold, *adj.* **1.** In craps, noting dice that roll few winning numbers.
[(1950) 1981 Maurer *Lang. of the Underworld* 187]
2. Pertaining to ill-fortune; of bad luck in gambling.
[ca. 1961 *Hotel Coll*]

iceman, *n.* The representative of an illegal gambling operation who carries bribes to public officials in return for favors; a BAGMAN.
[1961 Scarne *Complete Guide* 681]

idle card, *n.* In poker, a card that adds no value to the hand, as a spade in a heart-flush hand.
[1949 Coffin *Secrets* 179]

if bet, *n.* The first half of a wager made on two races or games. If the bettor picks the winner of the first race or game, then the money won from that wager is automatically bet on the second race or game. See also PARLAY.
[1956 *DAS,* as *if betting*]

immortals, *n. pl. Plural in form, but singular in use.* Also called NUTS. In poker, especially hold 'em, an unbeatable hand; the highest hand possible at the table, determined after the flop in hold 'em or after three face-up cards in seven card stud. See also LOCK.
[1949 Coffin *Secrets* 179]

imperfect pack, *n.* A deck of playing cards with cards missing or duplicated.
[1949 Coffin *Secrets* 179]

imperial tombee, *n.* In imperial, a bonus score for winning the four highest trump cards.
[1950 Morehead *Culbertson* 620]

impost, *n.* The amount of weight carried by a horse; the weight assigned to a horse by the track handicapper.
[1883 *OED*]

imprison, *v. French.* In games like roulette, to hold a wager for the next betting round.
1891 *Monte Carlo* 196. Let us suppose that we have punted five Napoleons upon the red compartment. The 0 comes out; the bank provisionally *imprisons* our stake—this is a technical word. If we don't care to be imprisoned until the next turn of the wheel is over, we may compromise with the bank by abandoning to it one-half of our stake, and thus rescuing the rest. If we prefer to stay imprisoned, then the next drop of the ball will settle our fate.

imprisoned, *adj. French.* In roulette, noting bets already placed that must wait for the next spin of the wheel to determine a win or loss.
[1968 Thackrey *Nick the Greek* 155]

improve, *v.* In poker, to draw cards that increase the value of the hand.
[1949 Coffin *Secrets* 179]

in, *adv.* In poker, noting eligibility to win a pot by betting the required amount.
[1949 Coffin *Secrets* 179]

in, *prep.* In the phrases:
in the bag, Oral code used by a cheater to inform a confederate that a cheating scam has been initiated, although the victim still holds his money.
[1961 Scarne *Complete Guide* 681]
[Compare 1922 *OEDS,* meaning "certain"]
in the money, In horseracing, a phrase indicating that a horse in a race finished in a high enough order, usually first through fourth, to win a share of the purse. Compare OUT OF THE MONEY.
[1928 *OEDS*]

independence, *n.* In Boston, a declaration of an intention to win more than five tricks.
[1950 Morehead *Culbertson* 620]

index, *n.* **1.** On a playing card, a number from 2 through 10 or a letter (A, K, Q, J) printed in the upper left-hand corner, indicating the value of the card.
2. A mark placed on the back of a playing card by a cheater, indicating the face value of the card. Compare COSMETICS.
[1968 Wallace *Poker* 217]
3. In racing, a number in the FORM SHEET used as a code in determining the record of a horse's performance.
[(1951) 1981 Maurer *Lang. of the Underworld* 216]

index, *v.* To place a mark on the back of a playing card so its value can be recognized by a cheater. Compare MARK, *v.*
[1968 Wallace *Poker* 217]

indicator card, *n.* In twenty-one games, especially those played with multiple decks, a card-sized

piece of plastic or a joker from a deck with a different colored design on the back that is buried toward the bottom of the deck by the dealer. When the dealer reaches that place in dealing, the hand is completed and the deck reshuffled.
[ca. 1961 *Hotel Coll*]

informatory double, *n.* Same as TAKEOUT DOUBLE.
[1953 Crawford *Consistent Winner* 348]

in-meter, *n.* In a slot machine, the counting device that records the number of coins dropped into the machine. Compare JACKPOT METER.
[1977 Nevada Gaming Control *Internal* 25]

in-meter summary, *n.* A form used by the accounting department in casinos to record the number of coins put into each slot machine by players. The form usually records the total number of coins put into the machine, the number of coins paid out, and the number of coins still in the machine and in the drop box.
[1978 Alexander *Glossary* 7]

inner table, *n.* In backgammon, the far quadrant of the board in which all a player's pieces must be before they can begin to be removed. See also HOME TABLE. Compare OUTER TABLE.
1860 Crawley *Backgammon* 52. It must be understood that the points are named alike—ace, deux, &c.—in each table, and that the left-hand division is called the *inner table,* and the right-hand the outer table.
[1870 *OED,* under *table*]

inquiry, *n.* In horse racing, an investigation of matters peculiar to a race, such as a complaint from a jockey or owner about another entry. All wagers on such a race are held until the *inquiry* is complete and a winner has been declared.
[(1951) 1981 Maurer *Lang. of the Underworld* 216]
[Compare c1440 *OED,* meaning "investigation"]

inside, *n.* **1.** On a craps table layout, the betting spaces marked with the numbers 5, 6, 8, or 9 depending upon the POINT a shooter has established. For example, if the shooter's point is 9, the inside numbers will be 5, 6, and 8. See also OUTSIDE.
[1983 Martinet *Oral Coll*]
2. Especially in the phrase **on the inside.** In racing, the position nearest the inner rail on an oval course. See also OUTSIDE. Compare POLE (def. 3).
[Compare 1857 *OEDS,* in the phr. *inside track*]

inside bet, *n.* **1.** In roulette, a combination bet that includes the 0 and 00 spaces; generally, a bet on any number on the layout. See also OUTSIDE BET.
[ca. 1961 *Hotel Coll*]
2. In bank craps, a wager made on a number or numbers closer to the center of the layout (the numbers 4, 5, 6, 8, 9, 10), than the point (the number the shooter must roll before rolling the number 7). For example, if the point is 5 or 9, the *inside* numbers are 6 and 8; if the point is 4 or 10, the *inside* numbers are 5, 6, 8, and 9. See OUTSIDE BET.
[1981 Silverstone *Player's Guide* 140]

inside corner, *n.* In faro, a position on the table layout that allows the player to wager on three cards simultaneously.
[1943 Maurer *Argot*]

inside hand, *n.* On a craps table staffed with two dealers and a stickman and a boxman, the dealers' hands closest to the boxman, who sits between the two dealers at the middle of the table across from the stickman.
[1978 Clark *Oral Coll*]

inside man, *n.* In a casino, an employee with access to the casino cage.
1963 Taylor *Las Vegas* 100. No *inside man* can work on the Strip without the county's "A" card, signifying clearance.

inside rail, *n.* On an oval racecourse, the fence between the track and the infield. Compare INSIDE (def. 2).
[1968 Ainslie *Complete Guide* 49]

inside straight, *n.* In poker, a broken sequence of four cards in which the missing card must be drawn to complete the sequence of five cards, such as a 9, jack, queen, and king for which the 10 must be drawn in order to complete a STRAIGHT. Compare DRAW TO.
[1949 Coffin *Secrets* 179]

inside ticket, *n.* In keno, the original slip, filled out by a player, that is retained by the operator of the keno game and a copy of which is given to the player to be presented to the keno operator, if the player has selected winning numbers.
[1961 Scarne *Complete Guide* 681]

inside track, *n.* On an oval racecourse, the portion of the course close to the rail, which requires less distance to cover than other portions of the course.
[1857 *OEDS,* under "inside"]

inside work, *n.* A weight inside a die to alter the roll of the die. See also GAFF. Compare LOADED DICE.
[(1950) 1981 Maurer *Lang. of the Underworld* 187]

insufficient bid, *n.* In bridge, an improper call, a bid not high enough to follow the previous bid.
[1953 Crawford *Consistent Winner* 348]

insurance, *n.* In twenty-one, an optional wager allowed to a player when the dealer has an ace face upward after dealing the second card to all players in which the player may bet up to half his original wager that the dealer has a twenty-one.
[1953 Crawford *Consistent Winner* 348]

intermission ticket, *n.* In bingo, a special discount card sold for bingo games played for

small amounts during the rest period of a longer session.
[ca. 1961 *Hotel Coll*]

ironclad hand, *n.* Also called IRON DUKE. In poker, a hand of cards that has a very good chance to win the pot. See also IMMORTAL and NUTS and LOCK.
[1950 Morehead *Culbertson* 621]

iron duke, *n.* Same as IRONCLAD HAND.
[1949 Coffin *Secrets* 180]

irons, *n. pl.* Stirrups, especially on a racing saddle.
[1955 Hillis *Pari-Mutuel Betting* 115]
[1894 *OEDS*]

issue slip, *n.* In a casino, the third part of a credit form, or marker, signed by a player in exchange for chips and placed in the DROP BOX at the table of the player so the employees in the casino cage can reconcile the difference in chips advanced to that table with amounts won or lost.
[1978 Alexander *Glossary* 8]

itemer, *n.* A confederate of a CARD SHARP, who generally assists him with signals and by carrying a STACKED DECK.
[1938 Asbury *Sucker's Progress* 35]

iteming, *n.* The using of an accomplice for signals or other assistance in cheating.
[1938 Asbury *Sucker's Progress* 35]

ivories, *n. pl.* **1.** Another word for DICE.
[1830 *OED*, n.d. *DAS*]
2. Another word for white chips, normally worth one dollar each.
[1973 Clark *Oral Coll*]

J

j, *n.* Abbreviation for JACK in playing cards.
[1950 Morehead *Culbertson* 621]

jack, *n.* The lowest valued face card, ranking between a 10 and a queen; the KNAVE.
1680 Cotton *Compleat Gamester* 80. . . . and having six apiece, he turns up a Card which is Trump; if Jack (and that is any Knave) it is one to the Dealer.
1836 Eidrah *Hoyle Famil* 63. *Jack,* the knave of trumps.
[1674-80 *OED*; 1845 *DAE*; Perhaps from all fours, also called high, low, jack and the game]

Jack Benny, *n.* In hold 'em poker, a three and a nine as cards dealt to a player.
1981 Golad *Oral Coll.* When you sit there for hours holding only two cards, pretty soon the combinations get names, and some of the names stick . . . A three and a nine is still called a Jack Benny because he always claimed to be thirty-nine years old.

jackpot, *n.* **1.** Also **jackpots,** *pl. Plural in form, but singular in use.* In draw poker, a pool of money accumulated from the players that increases with each round of cards dealt until one player can open the betting with a pair of jacks or a higher ranked hand.
[1887 *DA, DAE*; 1897 *OED*; 1881 *OEDS*, as *jackpots*]
2. A, usually large, amount of money that can be won on a slot machine, in a lottery, at bingo or keno, or at any game with low odds for the player. Compare HIT THE JACKPOT.
[1941 Fair *Spill the Jackpot!* 48]
3. Also **jackpots,** *pl. Plural in form, but singular in use.* An early name for *draw poker.*
[1887 *DA,* which lists an alternate name, *jacker* as obsolete; 1895 *OED* as *jackpots*]

jackpot meter, *n.* In a slot machine, a counter that records the number of jackpots and the total amount of money paid by the machine. Compare IN-METER.
[1978 Alexander *Glossary* 8]

jackpot payout, *n.* An additional amount of money paid to a winner who wins a jackpot on a slot machine which could not hold the amount of money promised by the establishment for a winning combination. The money is given to the player by an employee of the establishment who verifies the proper configuration of the reels on the machine.
[1957 *Nevada Gaming Regulations* 32]

jackpot payout slip, *n. phr.* In large gambling establishments, a printed form used in the slot machine area to record the total amounts of JACKPOT PAYOUTS by employees.
[1982 Martin *Introduction* 24]

jackpot payout summary, *n. phr.* Same as JACKPOT PAYOUT SLIP.
[1978 Alexander *Glossary* 8]

jacks back, *n.* In draw poker, a variation in which, if no player has a hand with a pair of jacks or higher in rank, the game reverts to LOWBALL, in which the lowest hand wins the pot.
[1949 Coffin *Secrets* 180]

Jackson five, *n.* Five twenty-dollar bills; generally, one hundred dollars. See quotation at E AND T. [1983 Martinet *Oral Coll*]
[From President Andrew Jackson, whose face appears on the twenty-dollar bill]

jacks or better to open, *n. phr.* Sometimes shortened to **jacks or better.** In draw poker, a statement made by the dealer indicating that a player must have a pair of jacks or a hand of higher rank to begin the betting round.
[1887 *DA, DAE,* under *jackpot*]

jack square, *n.* In faro, a betting area on the layout which includes four cards, the jack, the two, the three, and the queen. See quotation at FARO.
1868 Trumps *Pocket Hoyle* 203. The money in the "*Jack square*" includes the Jack, Queen, Two, and Three.

jack stripper, *n.* In playing cards, a jack trimmed or shaved to make it a different size from the rest of the cards, used for cheating. Compare STRIPPERS. [1968 Adams *Western Words*]

jai alai, *n.* A gamed played on a walled court, a hard rubber ball, and a scoop-like wicker racket, between two players, upon which the outcome is the source of wagering. See also PELOTA.
[1910 *OEDS*, from Spanish, from Basque *jai* festival + *alai* merry]

jail, *n.* In horse racing, a thirty-day period after a claiming race, during which time anyone may purchase any horse that ran in the race.
1986 Clark *Oral Coll.* Gentle Margie performed well at Hialeah and will be in *jail* for about two more weeks, in case you are thinking of an investment.

jam, *n.* In horse racing, a group of horses running together in a tight bunch so that no horse can break from the pack to move ahead of the others.
[(1951) 1981 Maurer *Lang. of the Underworld* 216]
[Compare 1806-7 *OED*, 1805 *OEDS*, meaning "a crush, a squeeze"]

jambone, *n.* **1.** In railroad euchre, a variant of play in which one player shows his hand and the other players lay out cards one at a time on a series of TRICKS, or packets of cards.
1887 Keller *Euchre* 23. A *jambone* [is] to play a lone hand with the cards exposed on the table, and to give to the adversary having the lead, the privilege of calling one card from the exposed hand, to the first trick; or if it be the *jambone* player's lead, to allow this same adversary to demand that card shall be led.
[1864 *DA, DAE, OEDS;* 1886 *OED*]
2. In euchre, a condition in which one player declares an intention to win all five tricks without his partner's assistance.
[1950 Morehead *Culbertson* 622]

jamboree, *n.* **1.** In railroad euchre, a hand containing the five highest trump cards.
1887 Keller *Euchre* 45. *Jamboree* is the combination in one hand of the five highest cards in Euchre; viz., the two bowers, ace, king, and queen of trumps. It is not necessary to play a *jamboree* hand, for it is invincible. The mere announcement of the fact that a player holds such a hand is sufficient; and if he claims *jamboree* before a lead is made, and then shows his hand, he is entitled to score sixteen points.
[1864 *DA, DAE;* 1886 *OEDS*]
2. In euchre, the condition of holding the five highest cards in one hand.
[1950 Morehead *Culbertson* 622]

jam the pot, *v. phr.* In poker, to make many large bets during the course of one hand.
[1981 Golad *Oral Coll*]

jam-up game, *n.* A poker session in which several players bet more excessively and more often than usual. Compare JAM THE POT.
[1981 Golad *Oral Coll*]

jass, *n.* Also spelled **jasz.** In klabberjass or clob, the jack of trump, which is also the highest-ranking card in the game.
[1950 Morehead *Culbertson* 622]

J-bird, *n.* Also called J-BOY. Another term for a JACK in playing cards.
[1978 Larson *Vocabulary* 99]

J-boy, Same as J-BIRD.
[1949 Coffin *Secrets* 180]

Jesse James, *n.* In hold 'em poker, a four and a five as the first two cards dealt to a player.
1981 Golad *Oral Coll.* When you sit there for hours holding only two cards, pretty soon the combinations get names, and some of the names stick . . . A four and a five is still called a *Jesse James* because he was supposedly shot with a forty-five.

jimmied-up box, *n.* A faro DEALING BOX, that has been altered for cheating so the dealer can draw a card other than the card on top of the pack.
[1978 Nelson *Gaming* 25]

Jimmy Hicks, *n.* Also called SISTER HICKS. In craps, a roll of the number six on a pair of dice. Compare BOX CARS.
[(1950) 1981 Maurer *Lang. of the Underworld* 187]
[Rhyming slang.]

jink it, *v. phr.* In spoil five, to win three tricks and announce an intention to win all five tricks.
[1887 *OED*]

jock, *n.* Short for JOCKEY.
[1826 *OED;* now also applied to any athlete: 1963 *OEDS, 1968 BDNE I*]

jockey, *n.* **1.** A person who rides a horse during a race.
[1670 *DAE, OED;* ultimately from *a*1529 *OED,* diminutive of *John*]
2. A cheat.
[(1683) 1777 *OED,* in reference to dice]

jockey, *v.* **1.** To ride a race horse in competition.
[1825 *OED*]
2. To cheat.
[1708 *OED*]

jog, *n.* A packet of cards prearranged in a particular order and slipped into a deck of

playing cards for cheating. Compare STACKED DECK.
[1890 Quinn *Fools of Fortune* 220]

jog cut, *n.* A cheating method for cutting a deck of cards so that a confederate keeps certain cards on top of the pack.

jog stock, *n.* A type of STACKED DECK used for cheating in which the upper portion of the pack to be cut is set slightly off center, so that a confederate may cut the deck just above the stacked portion.
1865 Evans *Gamblers Win* 22. To execute it (the *jog stock*), the player will put up a pair as in the top stock, with the necessary number of cards on the top, to make the pair fall to himself; he will then shuffle them once or twice, keeping them on top, and then shuffle and slide a portion of the pack over the hand thus set up, leaving a narrow "jog" or break along the side, between such portion of the pack and the hand stocked. His partner, who sits at his right, will seize the cards on the top of the hand by the ends, with the thumb and middle finger of his right hand, and with the thumb and middle finger of his left hand will seize the hand stocked underneath in the same manner, and drawing them out, place them on top of the others, leaving them as if they had not been cut.

john, *n.* **1.** Another name for a JACK in playing cards. [1968 Wallace *Poker* 218]
2. Also called a MARK. An easy victim for a CARDSHARP; a naive or ignorant player, especially one who is egotistical, pompous, or self-important; a DOG-ROBBER.
[1969 Clark *Oral Coll*]
[n.d. *DAS*, compare *a*1911 *OEDS*, meaning "a client of a prostitute"]

joint, *n.* Also called a STORE. A gambling establishment. See also BUST-OUT JOINT and CARPET JOINT and JUICE JOINT and SAWDUST JOINT.
[1899 *OED*, meaning "a bookmaker's outshop," 1883 *DAE, DA* meaning "a place for illegal gambling"]
→Not necessarily a pejorative term. Originally, a *joint* was an external (thoroughbred racing) bookmaker's outside shop, made of jointed pieces that could be assembled and disassembled quickly at racetracks.

joker, *n.* An extra playing card added to the standard fifty-two card deck. In several games, especially variations of poker, the *joker* is used as a *wild card.* See also LITTLE JOKER.
1887 Keller *Poker* 83. This is the use of the "*joker.*" In playing any form of Poker with this extra card, the player holding it is at liberty to call it anything he pleases, and if by so doing he can make a better Poker hand than his adversaries he must win . . . This innovation, however, has never proved popular, and is, in fact, so foreign to the genus of Poker that I would not have mentioned it at all, had it not been for the desire to cover every phase of the game.
[1885 *DA, DAE, OED*]

Jonah, *n.* **1.** An unlucky gambler; a continual loser suffering from bad luck.
[*a*1885 *OED*; from the biblical story of Jonah, who had the misfortune to be swallowed by a great fish.]
2. A player who seems to bring bad luck to others.
[1949 Coffin *Secrets* 180]
[From Jonah's refusing to go to Nineveh and inciting God's wrath, who sent a storm after the ship, which brought misfortune to Jonah's companions. Compare 1612 *OED*]

Jonah, *v.* In dice, to attempt to control the roll of the dice with cajoling or body movements.
See also BABY NEEDS NEW SHOES and COLD DICE and ENGLISH.
[(1950) 1981 Maurer *Lang. of the Underworld* 187]

jones, *n.* A gambling addict; a person who gambles often and for small stakes. See also DEGENERATE.
[1973 Clark *Oral Coll*]

joy girl, *n.* Also called a LADY or MOPSQUEEZER or WHORE. A queen in a deck of playing cards.
[1973 Clark *Oral Coll*]
[From the common reference to prostitutes as "party girls" or *joy girls.*]

Judge Duffy, *n.* Also called THIRTY DAYS, THIRTY (DIRTY) MILES. In poker, three tens.
1977 Clark *Oral Coll.* Back in the thirties and forties, a common sentence for pleading guilty to illegal gambling was thirty days or thirty dollars. So you kept three tens for fall dough [thirty dollars for paying the fine]. So in poker trip tens was called thirty days or *Judge Duffy.* Actually, you could hear other judge's names, but *Judge Duffy* is always the most common. I don't think anybody knows who Judge Duffy was.

juice, *n.* **1.** Influence and prestige; the power to get favors, ranging from complimentary rooms in a hotel to a job in a casino.
[ca. 1961 *Hotel Coll*]
[Compare 1935 *OEDS*, meaning "political influence"]
2. Electricity or electromagnetic power used in cheating to control loaded dice or a wired roulette wheel.
[1896 *DA, OEDS*, meaning "electricity in general"]
3. Same as VIGORISH.
[1978 Brunson *How I Made* 535]
4. Money acquired by illegal gambling or cheating.
[1956 *DAS*; Compare 1971 *OEDS*]
5. Same as PROTECTION (def. 1b).
[(1950) 1981 Maurer *Lang. of the Underworld* 187]

juice, *v.* **1.** To use influence or money to buy favors or bribe officials.
[ca. 1961 *Hotel Coll*]
2. To use electromagnets to control the roll of loaded dice or a wired roulette wheel.
[1969 Herwitz *Yes, You Can Win* 113]

juice dealer, *n.* An operator of a craps or roulette game in which electricity is used to control the dice or the roulette wheel.
[ca. 1961 *Hotel Coll*]

juice joint, *n.* Also called a WIRE JOINT. A gambling establishment devoted to cheating, especially by means of an electromagnetically controlled dice table or roulette wheel.
[(1950) 1981 Maurer *Lang. of the Underworld* 187]

jump, *n.* **1.** Also called HOP. In craps, the next roll of the dice. See also BULLFROG.
[1983 Martinet *Oral Coll*]
2. In bridge, a bid higher than necessary, usually as a signal to one's partner.
[1927 *OEDS*]

jump *v.* **1.** In bridge, to bid higher than necessary, usually as a signal to one's partner.
[1927 *OEDS*]
2. In the phrase:
jump the cut, To manipulate a deck of playing cards in a cheating move so that the pack only appears to be cut. In actuality, the pack is restored to its original order.
[1968 Adams *Western Words*]

jump bid, *n.* In games like whist or bridge, a raise in the bidding process of more than is necessary.
[1928 *OEDS*]

junior jackpot ticket, *n. phr.* In bingo, a card sold at a reduced rate and with lower amounts paid to winners.
[1961 Scarne *Complete Guide* 682]

junket, *n.* A trip to a gambling resort paid for by the gambling establishment. In exchange for travel, room, and meal costs, the gambler must deposit a specific amount of money at the casino cage and use that money to gamble in the establishment.
1977 Cahill *Recollections* 1396. A *junket,* primarily, as it's been defined many times in attempted regulations, is an entry into the state of Nevada by a group of people who are brought into the state for the primary purpose of inducing people to come to these hotels and to gamble.

junketeer, *n.* Also called JUNKET MASTER. Sometimes called a **junket leader** or a **junket representative.** An individual hired by casino operators to organize junkets.
[1974 Scarne *Dice* 138]

junket master, *n.* Same as JUNKETEER.
[1974 Friedman *Casino Management* 132]

junket player, *n.* Same as EXECUTIVE PACKAGE.
[1982 Martin *Introduction* 24]

K

K, *n.* Abbreviation for KING in a pack of playing cards.
[ca. 1961 *Hotel Coll*]

kangaroo card, *n.* In faro, the first card dealt in a betting system.
[1943 Maurer *Argot*]

k-boy, *n.* A king in a pack of playing cards.
[1949 Coffin *Secrets* 175]
[Perhaps *k*(ing) & (cow)*boy*]

keep cases, *v. phr.* In faro, to record the cards as they are dealt so the players know which cards are left in the dealing box.
[1856 *OEDS*; Compare 1552 *OED, keep amount,* or 1633 *OED, keep book*]

keeper, *n.* The operator of a roulette wheel.
1843 Green *Exposure* 83. For he could not be conversant with these games, and not know, at the same time, that the chances of winning were nearly all on the side of the *keeper* of the wheel, or that he who bets against the wheel can win only when the *keeper* chooses to let him.

keno, *n.* **1.** Also written **keeno** or **kino** or QUINO. Also called CHINESE LOTTERY. A game played with eighty numbered balls. Players mark up to fifteen numbers on a keno ticket, and the operator of the game then draws twenty of the numbered balls to determine any winners. Compare LOTTO.
[1814 *DA, OEDS,* as *keeno;* 1879 *OED;* 1845 *DAE*; adapted from French *quine,* meaning "five winning numbers"]
2. The exclamation made by a keno player when he has winning numbers.
[(1868) 1884 *OEDS,* 1907 *DAE*]

keno ball, *n.* One of eighty consecutively numbered balls used in a keno game.
[ca. 1961 *Hotel Coll*]

keno board, *n.* A large display board mounted on the wall behind the keno desk and in various

places around a casino, on which the twenty numbers drawn for a game are displayed.
[1953 Lewis *Sagebrush Casinos* 98]

keno caller, *n.* The employee of a keno operation who draws the numbered balls and announces the number drawn.
[ca. 1961 *Hotel Coll*]

keno dealer, *n.* Same as KENO CALLER.
[1875 *OEDS*]

keno goose, *n.* Usually shortened to GOOSE. A sphere constructed of wood, plastic or wire that holds the eighty balls used in a keno game. The sphere has a tube attached, through which one ball may pass at a time when the operator is drawing the numbers for the game. Compare RABBIT EARS.
[1887 *DA, DAE*]

kenoist, *n.* The operator of a keno game, especially an illegal one. *Obsolete.*
[1873 *DA*]

keno lounge, *n.* The room or area of a casino in which keno tickets are written and balls are drawn, normally with rows of chairs for the players to sit in during and between games, or races. Compare JOINT.
[ca. 1961 *Hotel Coll*]

keno runner, *n.* In a larger casino, an employee who moves about outside the KENO LOUNGE in the public areas, bars, and restaurants of a casino, collecting tickets and money from players, then delivering the winnings or copies of the tickets to the players.
[ca. 1961 *Hotel Coll*]

keno ticket, *n.* A slip of paper with eighty boxes numbered 1 through 80, on which a player marks from one to fifteen numbers, then turns the slip over to a KENO WRITER, along with the amount of money to be wagered, a copy of which is returned to the player as a receipt. See also INSIDE TICKET. Compare RACE.
[ca. 1961 *Hotel Coll*]

keno writer, *n.* An employee in a KENO LOUNGE who duplicates the KENO TICKET, takes the wager, and pays any winning tickets presented for collection.
[ca. 1961 *Hotel Coll*]

Kentucky stepup, *n.* A cheating method for stacking a deck of playing cards to insure that one player receives winning hands. Compare STACKED DECK
[1982 Martin *Introduction* 24]

key control ledger, *n. phr.* In a casino, a record of the employees who hold keys to secured areas such as the coin room, counting room, DROP BOXES, and so on.
[1978 Alexander *Glossary* 9]

key employee, *n.* An employee of a casino, usually a part-owner, who is empowered to make decisions concerning the disposition of money belonging to the casino.
[1957 *Nevada Gaming Regulations* 4]

keyman, *n.* An employee in the slot machine department of a casino authorized to unlock slot machines; a slot machine mechanic.
[1975 Clark *Oral Coll*]

kibitz, *v.* To watch games, especially card games, and offer unsolicited advice to the players.
[1927 *OEDS;* from Yiddish, ultimately from German *Kiebitz* lapwing, pewit]

kibitzer, *n.* Also called LUMBER or WOOD. A spectator, usually at card games, who watches the play and offers unsolicited advice to the players.
[1927 *OEDS,* 1928 *DA;* from Yiddish *kibitser*]

kick, *v.* **1.** Also BUMP. In poker, to make a bet that is higher than an earlier one; to raise.
[1949 Coffin *Secrets* 180]
2. In craps, to turn the dice with the stick. The stickman will often turn one of the dice before pushing them to the shooter if the number of pips exposed atop the dice is considered unlucky, such as 2, 3, 7, or 12.
[1983 Martinet *Oral Coll*]

kicker, *n.* Also called SIDE CARD. **1.** In draw poker, an extra card kept in the hand in addition to a pair or three of a kind. The strategy is designed to make opponents believe the hand is stronger than it would otherwise appear. The player holding a *kicker* hopes to draw another card of the same denomination.
1979 Clark *Oral Coll.* The term *kicker* comes from the practice of old pro gamblers to "keep something in the kick [pocket]," that is, to keep some money in reserve for future games. A high card held in reserve is half of a good pair.
[1892 *OEDS,* 1902 *DA*]
2. In hold 'em poker, a card held in the hand which does not match one turned face up in the middle of the table.
[1981 Golad *Oral Coll*]

kicker trouble, *n.* In hold 'em poker, the holding of a small unpaired card in a hand, while the higher card in the hand matches one of the cards in the center of the table, especially when an opponent apparently holds a pair of the same rank.
[1978 Brunson *How I Made* 536]

kilter, *n.* Also spelled **kelter. 1.** In poker, a worthless hand consisting of an ace, 3, 5, 7, and 9.
[1968 Wallace *Poker* 218]
2. Any of a variety of odd hands or unusual combination of cards. See also PELTER and DUTCH STRAIGHT and SKEET.
[1895 *OEDS*]

king, *n.* **1.** The highest ranking picture card in a pack of playing cards, in most games the card ranking above a queen, and in some games below the ace.
[1563 *OED*]
2. In keno, a single number marked on a KENO TICKET, usually part of a combination wager

made in keno called a WAY BET.
[1973 Friedman *Casino Games* 116]

king crab, *n.* Also called an ALASKA HAND. In hold 'em poker, a king and a three as the first two cards dealt to a player.
1981 Golad *Oral Coll.* You sit at a game holding those two cards for such a long time that after awhile the combinations get named . . . A *king crab* is a king and a three. The crab part is from the three in craps. You also hear it called an Alaska hand.

king george, *n.* Also called GEORGE. A player in a casino who tips especially well. *Rare.*
[1979 Clark *Oral Coll*]

kitty, *n.* **1.** Also called the POT. In poker, the pool of money bet by the players.
[1953 Crawford *Consistent Winner* 348]
[1891 *OEDS*]
2. In poker, a percentage of each pot taken for the operator of the game or to buy refreshments for the players.
1887 Keller *Poker* 12. Widow, or *Kitty.*—A percentage taken out of the pool to defray the expenses of the game or the cost of refreshments.
[n.d. *Cent. Dict;* 1887 *DAE, OEDS;* 1892 *OED*]
3. Also called the WIDOW. In various card games, a small packet of cards set aside at the beginning of a hand. The packet may perhaps be purchased or made available for use by a designated player.
[1949 Coffin *Secrets* 180]

kn, *n.* Abbreviation for the KNAVE in playing cards; the JACK.
[1950 Morehead *Culbertson* 623]

knap, *n.* The cast of a die so it does not roll over but lands with the same face on top as at the beginning of the cast. Compare CONTROLLED SHOT.
[1658 *OED*]

knapping, *n.* The art of throwing the dice so that one die does not roll or turn, while the other die is allowed to roll freely.
1680 Cotton *Compleat Gamester* 11. . . . by *Knapping,* that is, when you strike a Dye dead that it shall not stir.
1714 Lucas *Memoirs* 27. He was not ignorant in *Knapping,* which is, striking one die dead and let the other *run a Milstone,* as the Gamester's Phrase is, either at Tables or Hazard.
[1680 *OED*]

knave, *n.* A jack in a deck of playing cards; the lowest court card of each suit, bearing a picture of a soldier or servant. *Abbreviation:* KN
[1568 *OED*]

knave noddy, *n.* Same as HIS KNOB.
1680 Cotton *Compleat Gamester* 76. If you have a Knave of that suit which is turned up, it is *Knave Noddy.*
[1680 *OED*]

knock, *n.* In poker, a rap on the table with the knuckles to indicate a player wishes to check, pass, or have the cards dealt without a cut.
[1949 Coffin *Secrets* 180]
[Compare 1377 *OED,* meaning "a sounding blow"]

knock, *v.* In poker, to rap the table with the knuckles, indicating a wish to continue the game without betting or without cutting the cards.
[1949 Coffin *Secrets* 180]
[Compare *c*1000 *OED,* meaning "to strike with a sounding blow"]

knotholes, *n. pl.* In roulette, the 0 and 00 on the American wheel and layout. Compare HOUSE PERCENTAGE.
1980 Clark *Oral Coll.* In roulette, the payoff odds are thirty-six to one. But there are thirty-eight chances every time the wheel spins, so the true odds would be thirty-eight to one. The knotholes [0 and 00] make the house percentage.

Kojak, *n.* In hold 'em poker, a king and a jack as the first two cards dealt to a player.
1981 Golad *Oral Coll.* You sit at a game holding those two cards for such a long time that after awhile the combinations get named . . . A *Kojak* is a king and a jack, after the TV series.

komoke, *v.* In panguingue, to hold two value cards and draw another of the same suit.
[1948 Oncken *Review Journal* 3/14: 13]

k.p. *n.* Abbreviation for *closest to the pin.*
In golf, a wager on a par three hole as to which player's ball will be nearest the flagpole after each player has taken a single stroke. Compare PROXIES and GREENIES.
[1983 Clark *Oral Coll*]

ku klux klan, *n.* In poker, three kings held in the same hand. See also TRIPS.
[1949 Coffin *Secrets* 180]
[From the repetition of the abbreviation *K* for *king* and the similarity to the popular abbreviation *KKK* (1872 *OEDS*) for *Ku Klux Klan* (1867 *OEDS*)]

L

label it, *v. phr.* In bank craps, a call by the dealer when chips are thrown to him for a bet and he either does not know what bet has been requested or he does not know who threw the chips.
1984 Martinet *Oral Coll.* The dealer yells "label it" when he didn't hear what bet was called or if he didn't see who threw the checks. So *label it* can mean either identify the bet or identify yourself [as the owner of the chips].

ladderman, *n.* In baccarat, the employee watching over the progress of the game from an elevated chair near the table, who is responsible for supervising the play, evaluating the dealers, watching for cheating, and settling any disputes.
[(1950) 1981 Maurer *Lang. of the Underworld* 188]

lady, *n.* A queen in a deck of playing cards.
[1949 Coffin *Secrets* 180]
[Compare c1489 *OED,* meaning "The queen in chess"]

Lady Luck, *n.* Same as LUCK.
[1932 *OEDS*]

la grande, *n. French.* In baccarat, a point count of nine on the first two cards dealt.
[1968 Thackrey *Nick the Greek* 140]

lalapalooza, *n.* In poker, an odd or unusual hand, as an ALTERNATE STRAIGHT in one suit, e.g., 2, 4, 6, 8, 10 in diamonds. Usually, a hand declared a *lalapalooza* wins the pot the first time it occurs in a session.
[1949 Coffin *Secrets* 180]
[Compare 1904 *OEDS,* meaning "something outstandingly good of its kind"]

lamb, *n.* A victim of professional cheaters. Used especially in such phrases as **fleece the lamb, shear the lamb, the lamb is bitten.** Also COLL or SUCKER or MARK.

lammer button, *n.* Often shortened to **lammer.** In a casino, a numbered chip used by the floorman to indicate the amount of money represented by chips taken from a table.
[1977 Nevada Gaming Control *Internal Control* 14]

langret, *n.* A die loaded so heavily or shaved that it nearly always lands with the number 3 or the number 4 face upward.
[1550 *OED*]

lap, *n.* **1.** A single turn around a track, as in a race. [1861 *OED*]
2. In euchre, the scoring of extra points which can be applied to the next game.
1887 Keller *Euchre* 24. *Lap* is a term used to describe that variation of the regular game wherein any excess of points over the number necessary to win a game, is counted on the next game.
[1864 *DA, DAE*; 1886 *OED*]

lap, *v.* **1.** To leave a game temporarily to get more money to wager.
[1974 Scarne *Dice* 472]
2. In euchre, to credit extra points in winning to the next game.
[1890 *OED*]
3. In racing, to get one or more laps ahead of a competitor. [1847 *OEDS*]

la petite, *n. French.* In baccarat, a point count of eight on the first two cards dealt.
[1968 Thackrey *Nick the Greek* 140]

larry, *n.* The player in a game who has the last turn to act. See also A and BLIND and FIRST BASE and UNDER THE GUN.
[1950 Morehead *Culbertson* 624]

last, *n.* In cribbage, a point scored for playing the final card before exceeding a count of thirty-one.
[1953 Crawford *Consistent Winner* 349]

last call, *n.* In faro, the act of predicting the order in which the last three cards will appear. If correct, the player receives four times the amount wagered. See also CALL THE TURN.
1868 Trumps *Pocket Hoyle* 207. When three cards only remain in the box, and player has the privilege of calling the order in which they will be dealt—this is termed the *last call.*

last turn, *n.* In faro, the final three cards left in the dealing box. Two of the cards may be bet on, the third and last card is the HOC.
[1943 Maurer *Argot*]

Las Vegas riffle, *n. phr.* A fast, concealed shuffle of a deck of cards, done in such a fashion as to maintain the original sequence of the cards before the shuffle. The concealed shuffle is not allowed in Nevada casinos.
[1968 Wallace *Poker* 218]

Las Vegas Strip, *n.* A section of U.S. Highway 91 extending from the city limits of Las Vegas southward toward Los Angeles. The large resort hotels and casinos built along this section are situated in Clark County, not in Las Vegas.
[1968 Thackrey *Nick the Greek* 77]

late bet, *n.* In bank craps, a wager placed on the layout after the dice have been thrown. See also LATE BETTOR.
[1983 Martinet *Oral Coll*]

late bettor, *n.* In bank craps, a player who interrupts the flow of the game by making wagers after the dice have been thrown. See also NO BET.
1983 Martinet *Oral Coll.* Nobody likes *late bettors.* They screw up the action and everything slows down when the dealer has to yell "no bet." The dealer has to yell "no bet," otherwise the player can claim the bet was down if it's a winner, or claim he's laying on the next roll if it's a loser.

late line, *n.* In horse racing, the odds given for horses in a race shortly before the race. Compare MORNING LINE.
[1961 Scarne *Complete Guide* 682]

late position, *n. phr.* In poker games with seven or eight players, the two positions prior to the dealer. A *late position* is desirable because a player can evaluate the range of betting before having to act on his own hand.
[1978 Brunson *How I Made* 530]

lay, *n.* A wager; a bet.
[1584 *OED*]

lay, *v.* **1.** To make a wager.
[1300 *OED*]
2. To bet a greater amount of money against a lesser amount; to give odds in a wager: **lay a wager, lay a bet.**
[ca. 1961 *Hotel Coll*]
3. To bet on a horse.
[1877 *OEDS*]
4. In the phrases:
lay and pay, In dealing twenty-one, to turn the cards face upward at the conclusion of a hand, pay the winners, take the chips from the losers, then gather all the cards from the layout. See also PICK AND PAY and TAKE AND PAY.
[1977 Anness *Dummy Up*]
lay away, a. In pinochle, to discard after looking at the cards in the widow.
[1953 Crawford *Consistent Winner* 349]
b. In cribbage, to place a card or cards in the crib.
[1953 Crawford *Consistent Winner* 349]
lay odds, To offer a larger amount of money as a wager against a smaller amount. See also GIVE ODDS. [1597 *OED*]
lay off a bet, Of a bookmaker, to place a wager with another bookmaker. Commonly done when a bookmaker has accepted too many bets on one entry in a contest. See quotation at LAYOFF BET.
[1953 Crawford *Consistent Winner* 349]
[n.d. *DAS*]
lay paint, To mark a deck of cards for cheating purposes by using india ink, aniline pencil, or some other substance. See also DAUB or PAINT, *v.* Compare COSMETICS.
[1973 Clark *Oral Coll*]
lay the odds, In bank craps, to bet a larger amount of money against a smaller amount of money that the shooter will not make the point [roll the number required to win].
[(1950) 1981 Maurer *Lang. of the Underworld* 186]

lay bet, *n.* In bank craps, a wager against a specific number that a seven will be rolled before that number is rolled. Most casinos charge a five percent commission on the amount of the wager for a *lay bet.* See also BUY BET and WRONG BETTOR.
[1973 Friedman *Casino Games* 82]

lay card, *n.* A playing card with no value in the game being played.
[1950 Morehead *Culbertson* 624]

laydown, *n.* **1.** Also called the SHOWDOWN. In poker, the showing of cards at the end of all betting so a winner can be determined.
2. In bridge, a winning hand that can be placed face up on the table instead of played out, card by card. [1906 *OEDS*]

layoff bet, *n.* A wager made by one bookmaker with another, to reduce the amount of risk involved in having too much money wagered on one entry in an event.
1985 *Las Vegas Sun* 2/7, 1B. The affidavit alleges that [someone] has instructed [someone] to place *layoff bets* for the group. Legal sports books layoff bets to other books to balance the wagering on games to soften a potential loss.
[(1951) 1981 Maurer *Lang. of the Underworld* 217]

layout, *n.* Also written **lay-out.** The design on a gaming table, showing different wagers available and providing spaces to place wagers so the dealers and players can keep track of them. Compare GREEN CLOTH.
1868 Trumps *Pocket Hoyle* 203. Upon the centre of the table is a suit of cards arranged in order, upon which the players place their money or stakes, and which is called the *lay-out.*
[1864 *DA, DAE;* 1889 *OED*]

Layout. Bettors at most TABLE GAMES place their BEANS or CHIPS on the GREEN CLOTH which has been imprinted with a design designating various kinds of bets.

A ROULETTE-TABLE layout is rectangular and features sections ruled off into three COLUMNS (including DAMNATION ALLEY) and twelve numbered rows with additional boxes for 0 and 00 (as on the AMERICAN WHEEL but not the EUROPEAN WHEEL) as well as boxes for ODD and EVEN. The boxes are for selecting which number and/or color will identify the CANOE into which the ROULETTE BALL will drop. A player may choose a STRAIGHT BET (on one number), or a SPLIT BET (on two neighboring numbers), a LINE BET (on a group of neighboring numbers), a SQUARE BET (on four neighboring numbers), a STREET BET (on a row of numbers), or a COLUMN BET (on one of the three columns). The selection of these bets is determined by the lines straddled by the chips representing the wager.

A CRAP LAYOUT on a large CRAPS table is frequently the same at each end of the table. The individual designs may differ from table to table. They may also identify some variation in play as with the PHILADELPHIA LAYOUT. The portion of the layout in the middle is usually set aside for HARDWAY BETS. The end portions are ruled with variously shaped sections labeled for the PASS LINE, the DON'T PASS LINE, the FIELD, the COME, the DON'T COME BAR, and one each for the 4, 5, 6, 8, 9, 10, and, of course, 7. Some TABLES also label sections for CRAPS and ELEVEN with the abbreviation C AND E. Some layouts will also display the ODDS.

BACCARAT, CHEMIN DE FER, BLACKJACK and FARO are card games with layouts organized as SPOTS. Baccarat and chemin de fer tables tend to resemble the CRAP LAYOUT in that they are double-ended with sections upon which to FADE the BANK or the PLAYER or specific cards.

In FARO actual cards may be dealt in a pattern to constitute the LAYOUT. BLACKJACK (also called TWENTY-ONE) is played with a fan-shaped layout—one SPOT for each player's cards, a FIRST BASE, a THIRD BASE, a place for INSURANCE, and, often, a spot for CHIPS. The rule of play for dealers is frequently printed as part of the GREEN CLOTH: "Dealer must stand on 17, and must draw to 16."

lay suit, *n.* **1.** In trump games, a suit other than trump.
[1950 Morehead *Culbertson* 624]
2. A suit in playing cards with no value in counting points.
[1950 Morehead *Culbertson* 624]

lead, *n.* **1.** In games like bridge, the first card placed face upward on the table after the bidding is finished. [1742 *OED*]
2. In poker, the first wager made in a betting round.
[1968 Wallace *Poker* 218]

lead, *v.* **1.** In games like bridge, to place the first card face upward on the table after the bidding is finished. [1677 *OED*]
2. Also **lead out.** As the first player, to play (a specified card).
[1731 *OED*]
3. In poker, to wager first in a betting round.
[1968 Wallace *Poker* 218]
4. In the phrases:
lead up to, Also **lead to.** In bridge, to play a series of cards on successive tricks in such a fashion as to be able to play what might have been a worthless card and win a trick with it.
[1863 *OED*]
lead through, In games like bridge, to play a card that one's opponent on the left cannot win, but which one's partner can.
[1950 Morehead *Culbertson* 624]

leadout boy, *n.* In greyhound racing, the groom who escorts a dog to its proper position in the starting gate.
[1968 Buchele *Greyhound Racing* 96]

lead pad, *n.* In horse racing, the leather pocket attached to a saddle into which are placed the weights assigned by the handicapper.
[1978 Ainslie *Complete Guide* 292]

lead pony, *n.* In horse racing, the horse used to guide a racehorse to its appropriate position in the starting gate.
[1971 McQuaid *Gambler's Digest* 309]

leakage, *n.* The amount of money lost to cheaters and thieves by a gambling establishment.
[1963 Taylor *Las Vegas* 99]

leaner, *n.* A die that does not land flat on the table but is tilted against the backboard of the table or against a chip; a COCKED DIE.
[1983 Martinet *Oral Coll*]

leather, *n.* **1.** Also called a BAT. In horse racing, the whip carried by a jockey.
[(1951) 1981 Maurer *Lang. of the Underworld* 217]
2. Especially **leathers.** In horse racing, the reins.
[1838 *DAE*]

leather ass, *n.* Among poker players, the quality of patience.
1981 Golad *Oral Coll.* In [playing] hold 'em, you'll sit there for hour after hour, looking at those two cards and then folding. All the time you are waiting for the one good hand to play. That's why people say that to be a good professional player, you have to have a *leather ass,* that means patience.

left, *adj.* In the phrases: **left behind, left at the post, left in the box, left at the gate.** In racing, pertaining to a horse or dog that does not leave the starting gate at the same time as the rest of the entries.
[1968 Buchele *Greyhound Racing* 96]

left bower, *n.* In euchre, the jack of the same color suit as trump. If clubs are trump, then the jack of spades is the *left bower.* Compare BOWER (def. 2) and RIGHT BOWER.
1876 Heather *Cards* 131. *Left Bower.*—The knave of the suit of the same colour as the trump suit, second best card.
[1839 *DA;* 1844 *DAE;* 1871 *OED*]

left pedro, *n.* In cinch, the 5 of the suit of the same color as the trump suit.
[1950 Morehead *Culbertson* 624]

leg, *n.* **1.** Short for BLACKLEG, a professional gambler.
[1815 *OED*]
→*Blackleg* is obsolete. While the clipped form *leg* is still used, it is considered pejorative.
2. One hand, game, or race in a series of similar events, as in bridge, horse racing, and so on.
[1961 Scarne *Complete Guide* 682]
[1938 *OEDS*]

leg a hand, *v. phr.* In poker, to slow the play of the hand by constantly checking the pot to be sure that the appropriate amount of money is in it.
[1973 Preston *Play Poker* 168]

lemon, A picture of the fruit on the reel of a slot machine, indicating a loss.
[1909 *DA, OEDS*]

length, *n.* **1.** The measurement of a horse from nose to tail, used as a measurement in judging distance on a racetrack.
[1812 *OED*]
2. In bridge, the holding of four or more cards of the same suit.
[1927 *OEDS*]

let, *v.* In the phrases:
let it ride, A comment made by a player to a dealer that the original bet and the winnings will be wagered on the next hand or event.
[(1950) 1981 Maurer *Lang. of the Underworld* 188]
let him out, In racing to allow a horse to run at full speed.
[(1951) 1981 Maurer *Lang. of the Underworld* 217]
let them run, Said to a dealer by a player who declines to cut the pack of cards before the deal.
[1980 Quinn *Fools of Fortune* 277]

levant, *n. Especially* **run** (or **throw**) **a levant.** A bet made with the intention of absconding if it is lost. [1714 *OED*]

levant, *v.* To fail to pay for lost bets on horse races.
1829 Brown *Turf* 81. I am inclined to think all honourable well wishers to the turf would very willingly sanction such a system, while those who had manifested inclinations to *levant,* would be under the necessity of acquiescing in a measure which presents so equitable an aspect, and which would so effectually remedy the evil in question.
[1809, 1700 *OED* at *gammon*]

levanter, *n.* A horse race bettor who does not pay his debts.
1829 Brown *Turf* 78. *Levanter* is a word very well understood on the turf, and means a person who does not pay his debts.
[1781 *OED*]

levels, *n. pl.* Dice that have not been altered; honest dice; SQUARE DICE.
[(1951) 1981 Maurer *Lang. of the Underworld* 218]

lever movement box, *n. phr.* Also shortened to **lever box.** In faro, a dealing box, or shoe, altered in such a fashion that the dealer is able to select a specific card by pushing a small projection on the side of the box. See also NEEDLE SQUEEZE.
[1890 Quinn *Fools of Fortune* 199]

LHO, *n.* Also written **l.h.o.** In games like bridge and whist, an initialism for *left-hand opponent.* The *LHO* is more important than the opponent on the right hand because the sequence of play is to the left and any barrier will be found on that side.
[1950 Morehead *Culbertson* 624]

liar dice, *n.* A dice game popular in bars and normally played for small stakes or drinks, in which five or six dice are thrown from a cup and covered by the thrower who announces the results of the throw. The opponent may then throw the dice in an attempt to make a better hand, or call the player a liar. If the player has lied, the game is won by the opponent.
[1946 *OEDS*]

liar's poker, *n.* A game popular in bars and normally played for small stakes or drinks, in which each player holds a dollar bill or bills of the same denomination. The first player claims a poker hand such as a pair of threes. The second player declares a higher poker hand. The first player responds with a higher claim, and the counterclaims continue until one player declares the other a liar. If the accused is lying, he loses the game; if he actually holds the numbers he claims, he wins the game.
[1971 McQuaid *Gambler's Digest* 309]

lid, *n.* **1.** In poker, the top card on the pack.
[1949 Coffin *Secrets* 180]
2. On a gaming table, a plastic or metal cover placed over the rack holding the dealer's chips, indicating the table is temporarily closed. See also CLOSED TABLE.
[ca. 1961 *Hotel Coll*]

light, *adj,* **1.** In poker, noting that the pot has less money than it should have. See also SHY.
[1949 Coffin *Secrets* 180]
2. In dice, noting LOADED DICE which give the shooter a slight percentage.
[(1950) 1981 Maurer *Lang. of the Underworld* 188]

lighter, *adj.* In dominoes, noting a set of tiles held by a player that has a smaller total of pips than an opponent's tiles.
[1950 Morehead *Culbertson* 625]

light Texas corner, *n.* A playing card with a slightly bent corner that serves as an indicator card to a cheater.
[1974 Scarne *Dice* 322]

light work, *n.* Playing cards marked on the back with fine lines.
[1961 Scarne *Complete Guide* 682]

lilies, *n. pl. Plural in form, but singular in use.* In bridge, the suit of spades, when declared trump with an increased value. *Rare.* See ROYALS.
1950 Morehead *Culbertson* 177. The 2-point spade suit became almost meaningless and was used only for artificial bids. To overcome this, spades were given a double valuation: one could bid spades, or *royal spades* (called royals, or, colloquially, "*lilies*"); and whichever won the contract, the same suit would be trump but royal spades counted 9 points per odd-trick.

limit, *n.* **1.** The highest amount one is allowed to wager on a given event. See also MINIMUM.

1866 *American Card Player* 134. *Limit.*—A condition made at the beginning of the game, as to the amount that may be bet on a hand. The *limit* of a game may be one dime, or the trifling sum of one thousand dollars.
[1892 *OEDS*]
2. In bridge, a call that shows the strength of a hand without exceeding a certain value placed on the call by the partners.
[1959 *OEDS*]

limit stakes, *n.* In poker, the maximum amount of money allowed for bets and raises.
[1968 Wallace *Poker* 218]

limp in, *v. phr.* Also shortened to **limp.** In poker, to match the amount of the previous bet, but not increase the size of the wager, especially while holding a strong hand.
[1978 Brunson *How I Made* 536]

line, *n.* **1.** In racebooks and sports books, the odds or points assigned to a team for betting purposes. See also SPREAD.
[1953 Lewis *Sagebrush Casinos* 100]
2. In bank craps, the space on the table layout for placing bets at the beginning of a hand, or series of rolls. See also BACK LINE and COME LINE and FRONT LINE and PASS LINE.
[1953 Lewis *Sagebrush Casinos* 100]
3. Same as BOX. In gin rummy, a point bonus for winning a hand.
1950 Morehead *Culbertson* 33. Each player then adds to his score 25 points for each hand he has won (called a *line* or box).
4. In horse racing, short for MORNING LINE. The early odds declared for a horserace. Compare LATE LINE.
[1978 Ainslie *Complete Guide* 292]
5. In a casino, short for CREDIT LINE. The amount of money a player may temporarily borrow from a gambling establishment.
[1973 Clark *Oral Coll*]
6. In bridge, a line drawn across a score card separating points scored for honors, sets (failure of the opponent to fulfil a contract), overtricks, game and rubber (ABOVE THE LINE) from points scored for tricks bid and won, and counting toward game (BELOW THE LINE).
[1905 *OEDS*]

line bet, *n.* **1.** In roulette, a wager on six numbers simultaneously, made by placing the chips on the juncture of two lines with three numbers on each line.
[ca. 1961 *Hotel Coll*]
2. In bank craps, short for PASS LINE BET.
[1974 Scarne *Dice* 110]

linemaker, *n.* In a sports book, a person who determines the odds for a sporting event or assigns points to be added to a team's score for betting purposes.
[1976 Fisk *Gambler's Bible* 210]

line pass, *n.* In a casino, a note from a pit boss to a maitre d' requesting immediate seating for a valued player, especially a HIGHROLLER.
[ca. 1961 *Hotel Coll*]

lines, *n. pl.* In horse racing, the reins used to guide the horse. See also LEATHERS.
[1852 *OED*]

lineup, *n.* The list of players invited to participate in an illegal poker game.
[1978 Brunson *How I Made* 536]
[Compare 1889 *OEDS,* meaning "list of players"]

line work, *n.* Playing cards marked on the back with lines and dots made to appear part of the design. Compare COSMETICS.
[1961 Scarne *Complete Guide* 682]

linked dice, *n.* Also called CHAIN DICE. A pair of cheating dice connected to one another in such a fashion as to roll one set of numbers more often than another. *Obsolete.*
1726 Wilson *Art and Mystery* 33. Chain or *Link'd Dice* [are] so called from their being made fast together so nicely, with a Horse-hair or Wire stain'd to the Colour of the Ivory, that it is difficult to discover it at any little distance from you, more especially by Candlelight.

list-betting, *n.* The wagering on horse races posted in a list shop.
[1874 *OEDS*]

list-house, *n.* Same as LIST SHOP.
[1902 *OEDS*]

List of Excluded Persons, *n.* Same as the BLACK BOOK.
[1977 Nevada Gaming Control *Internal* 841]

list shop, *n.* An illegal betting room where odds on horse races were displayed. *Obsolete.*
[1902 *OEDS*]

little blind, *n.* In poker, the first, and smallest, bet made by the first player to the left of the dealer before looking at his cards. See also BLIND.
[1978 Brunson *How I Made* 536]

little bobtail, *n.* In poker, a three card straight flush. Among some poker players, the *little bobtail* ranks higher in value than two pair, but lower than three of a kind. Compare BOBTAIL.
[1964 Reese and Watkins *Secrets* 142]

little cassino, *n.* In the card game cassino, the two of spades, which counts one point. Compare CASSINO.
1824 Anon *Hoyle's* 23. Little Cassino . . . the two of spades, which reckons for one point.
[1811 *OED*]

little cat, *n.* Same as LITTLE TIGER. See also BIG CAT.
[1949 Coffin *Secrets* 181]

little Dick Fisher, *n.* Also shortened to **little Dick.** In craps and hazard, the number 4.
1714 Lucas *Memoirs* 203. This game is play'd but with two Dice . . . Four and five to seven is judg'd to have the worst on't because four

(called by the Nickers and Sharpers, *little Dick Fisher*) and five have but two Chances, Trey-Ace, and two Deuces, or Trey-Duce and Quater-Ace.
1726 Wilson *Art and Mystery* 30. This gives me occasion to say something of *little Dick Fisher* so often called upon by the Caster, when his change is Four or Five; what must be done then? Why you must put in a low Die (called a Doctor).

little dog, *n.* In poker, a hand of five unpaired cards of various suits ranging in value from 7 to 2. See also LITTLE TIGER.
[1949 Coffin *Secrets* 181]

little figure, *n.* In faro, the section on the table layout marked ace, 2, 3.
1868 Trumps *Pocket Hoyle* 203. The Ace, Two, and Three [are called] "the *Little Figure.*"
[1864 *DA,* under "figure"]

little joe, *n.* In craps, a roll of 4 on the dice, often as two 2s. The phrase is sometimes expanded to **little joe from (Baltimore, Chicago,** or **Kokomo**). See also LITTLE DICK FISHER.
[1890 *OEDS*]

little joker, *n.* An object used in cheating, as the pea in THIMBLERIG or a shaved card in poker games.
[1849 *DA*]

little Minnie, *n.* In poker, an uninterrupted sequence of five cards, from ace to five; a STRAIGHT. See also WHEEL and A.B.C. STRAIGHT.
[1971 Livingston *Poker Strategy* 220]

little natural, *n.* In craps, a roll of 7 on the first cast of the dice. Compare NATURAL (def. 5).
[1968 Adams *Western Words*]

little Phoebe, *n.* In craps, a total of 5 on two dice.
[1949 Blanche *You Can't Win* 23]

little slam, *n.* In bridge, the winning of twelve tricks by one team. Compare SLAM.
[1897 *OED*]

little tiger, *n.* Also called LITTLE CAT. In poker, a hand of five unpaired cards of various suits ranging in value from 8 to 3. See also BIG TIGER.
[1938 *DA,* under "tiger"]

little wheel, *n.* Also called a BICYCLE or MINNIE WHEEL. In lowball poker, a straight, or sequence of cards, from the ace to the 5.
[1973 Clark *Oral Coll*]

live blind, *n.* In poker, a bet required of the first player to the left of the dealer, which may be raised by that bettor after all the other players have acted in the betting round.
[1976 Sklansky *Hold 'em Poker*]

live card, *n.* A playing card that has not yet been exposed to all the players in a game. See also ALIVE CARD.

live hand, *n.* In poker, a hand held by a player still contending for the pot.
[1953 Crawford *Consistent Winner* 349]

live one, *n.* A gambler with money, usually considered an easy victim by other players.
[(1950) 1981 Maurer *Lang. of the Underworld* 188]

live weight, *n.* In horse racing, the weight of the jockey, especially as contrasted with DEAD WEIGHT, the extra weight assigned to a horse by the track handicapper.
[1968 Ainslie *Complete Guide* 450]

livret, *n.* In faro, a packet of thirteen cards of one suit. Compare FIGURE (def. 2).
1843 Green *Exposure* 165. It [a variant betting system in faro] may be played by any number of persons; and each player, or punter, as he is termed, is furnished with a suit of cards denominated a *livret,* and four other cards which are called figures.
[Compare *c*1450 *OED,* meaning "small book"]

load, *v.* To drill a hole in a die and fill it with a weight, so as to ensure the rolling of a particular number.
1714 Lucas *Memoirs* 84. Indeed Monsieur Shevalier could tell how to *load* Dye with Quicksilver, as well as a Fuzee with Powder and Ball; but having been sometimes detected in his sharping Tricks, he hath been obliged to look on the Point of the Sword, with which being often wounded, latterly he would decline fighting.
[Compare 1578 *OED,* meaning "to add a weight to," see especially 1802 "a bat loaded with lead"]

load, *n.* **1.** A weight placed inside a die to cause one face to land upward more often than other faces.
[(1950) 1981 Maurer *Lang. of the Underworld* 188]
[Compare 1593 *OED,* meaning "a weight"]
2. loads *pl.* Dice that have been altered to roll specific numbers by means of weights placed in them.
[(1950) 1981 Maurer *Lang. of the Underworld* 188]
3. In dice, a percentage which is favorable to the players betting the field, but is unfavorable to the house.
[(1950) 1981 Maurer *Lang. of the Underworld* 188]

loaded dice, *n.* Dice that have been altered by placing weight inside them to cause certain numbers to be rolled more often than others. See also DOCTOR and SCOOPED DICE. Compare BARR DICE.
1726 Wilson *Art and Mystery* 29. And first, *Loaded* or Scooped Dice are either high or low, and changed as often as the Main and Chance, or Occasion requires.
[1781, 1726 *OED,* under *main*]

loan shark, *n.* Also written **loan-shark.** A person who lends money, especially to gamblers, at excessively high interest rates.
[1913 *DA,* 1928 *OEDS*]

loan-sharking, *n.* The lending of money at excessively high interest rates, especially to gamblers.
[1970 *OEDS,* but presumed to be much earlier]

lobster, *n.* A victim of cheaters and swindlers, especially a naive card player. See also JOHN or SUCKER.
[Compare 1896 *OEDS,* meaning "a slow-witted, awkward, or gullible person"]

lock, *n.* Also called CINCH HAND. In poker, a hand considered very strong by the person holding it, strong enough to claim a share of the pot or even the entire pot. See also IMMORTALS and MORTAL CINCH.
[1949 Coffin *Secrets* 181]

lock, *v.* In the particle construction:
lock up, 1. In a casino, to tell a dealer to place chips or cash in the CHIP RACK or the DROP BOX.
[1977 Anness *Dummy Up*]
2. To put chips into the pocket with the intention of keeping them out of a current game.
[1973 Preston *Play Poker* 168]

lock grip, *n.* A method for holding dice tightly in the hand when preparing for a CONTROLLED THROW.
[1974 Scarne *Dice* 258]

locking, *n.* In horse racing, the placement of a group of bets pairing one horse in a race with each of the horses in the following race. See also WHEELING.
[1964 Wykes *Illustrated Guide* 329]

long, *adj.* **1.** Pertaining to overpayment on a bet.
[1983 Martinet *Oral Coll*]
2. On a casino gaming table, pertaining to a larger number of chips held by the bank than was imprest to the table.
[1983 Martinet *Oral Coll*]
3. Pertaining to a large number of chips of one denomination held by a player.
[1983 Martinet *Oral Coll*]

long card, *n.* Often **long cards,** *pl.* One card of a suit still held in the hand after the opponent has played all his cards of that suit.
[1862 *OED*]

long deal, *n.* A dishonest move by a dealer to give a player a card that neither wins nor loses.
[1898 *OEDS*]

long deck, *n.* A dishonest pack of cards that has more than four 10s or cards that count for ten points, as in twenty-one.
[ca. 1961 *Hotel Coll*]

long hand, *n.* In craps, a number of PASSES, or wins, by a single shooter.
[ca. 1961 *Hotel Coll*]

long odds, *n. pl.* A remote chance of winning a bet. Compare SHORT PRICE.
[1818 *OED*]

long roll, *n.* **1.** In craps, same as LONG HAND.
[ca. 1961 *Hotel Coll*]
2. Among slot machine players, ten dollars in quarters or two dollars in nickels, wrapped in a paper tube. See SHORT ROLL.
[1973 Clark *Oral Coll*]

longshot, *n.* **1.** In horse racing, an entry with little chance of winning. See also DARK HORSE and OUTSIDER.
[1867 *OEDS*]
2. A bet with a remote chance of winning but, if it does win, paying many times the amount of the original wager.
[1968 Thackrey *Nick the Greek* 241]
[1869 *DSUE*]

long string, *n.* In backgammon, several pieces on the same point.
1860 Crawley *Backgammon* 79. Eschew many men on one point—five or more (perhaps four) are called a *long string.*

long suit, *n.* In games like bridge or whist, a suit with several cards, usually five or more, held in one hand.
[1876 *OED*]

long trump, *n.* In card games such as bridge or whist, the holding of one or more trump cards in a single hand after the rest have been played.
1746 Hoyle *Short Treatise* 68. *Long Trump* Means the having one or more Trumps in your Hand when all the rest are out.
[1746 *OED*]

loo, *v.* In lanterloo, to win all the money on the board with a particular hand, usually a flush. See also ELDEST HAND and PAM.
1714 Lucas *Memoirs* 223. . . . Lanterloo, in which Game you must note, that he who hath 5 Cards of a Suit in his Hand, *Loos* all the Gamesters then playing, be they never so many, and sweeps the Board; if there be two *Loos,* he that is the eldest Hand hath the Advantage; but if there be a *Loo* of Trumps, that takes the advantage from all, except any one hath Pamm, that is the Knave of Clubs, who saves his *Loo,* and is pair for one Trick out of his Stock.
[1680 *OED,* with spelling variants: 1675 *Lu;* 1680 *loo'd;* 1710 *Liew;* 1731 *lue;* from 1796 *loo* as *n.* and *v.*]

loo, *n.* In lanterloo, a winning combination of cards, usually a flush. See quotation at LOO,*v.*
[1675 *OED,* 1773 *DAE*]

looker out, *n.* In faro, the assistant to the dealer who watches the betting and logs the cards as they are drawn.
1868 Trumps *Pocket Hoyle* 203. The dealer sits at a table prepared for the purpose, with an assistant or "*looker out*" at his right hand.
[1864 *DAE*]

lookout, *n.* **1.** In a casino, an employee who watches the progress of the game, the dealer, the players, the chips on the table. The *lookout* settles disputes about the play and looks for cheaters.
[1888 *DAE,* 1893 *OEDS*]
2. In faro, same as LOOKER OUT.
[1851 *DA*]

looloo, *n.* In poker, an unusual or odd hand, such as a 2, 4, 6, 8, and 10 of various suits, which can be declared a winner the first time it occurs in a poker session, but only one time during a session. See also LOLLAPALOOZA.
[1896 *DA;* probably a variant of earlier 1889 *DAE, DA* and 1886 *OEDS* spelling: *lulu;* compare 1857 *DA* spelling: *looly*]

loose card, *n.* In cards games such as bridge or whist, a card that has no value.
1746 Hoyle *Short Treatise* 68. *Loose Card* Means a Card in a Hand that is of no Value, and consequently the properest to throw away.
[1763 *OED*]

loose coin, *n.* Often shortened to **loose.** In a casino, unwrapped coins from slot machines or in the casino cage. [1978 Alexander *Glossary* 9]

loose horse, *n.* In horse racing, a mount that continues to run after losing its jockey.
[1978 Ainslie *Complete Guide* 293]

loose player, *n.* In poker, a player who tends to stay in every betting round, regardless of the value of his hand. See also TIGHT PLAYER.
[1973 Clark *Oral Coll*]

loose slot, *n.* A slot machine set to pay off at a higher rate than normal. Slot machines are usually set to pay out about eighty-five percent of the coins put into them, so a *loose slot* may be set to pay out ninety-five to one hundred and five percent of the coins played.
[ca. 1961 *Hotel Coll*]

loose table, *n.* **1.** In a casino, a gaming table with few players.
[(1950) 1981 Maurer *Lang. of the Underworld* 188]
2. A table at which all the players are winning.
[1983 Martinet *Oral Coll*]

lose, *v.* **1.** To fail to win a wager on a gambling event.
[1710 *OED*; compare *a*1533 *OED,* with a more general meaning of "to be deprived of (something) in a contest or game"]
2. In the phrase:
lose out, In faro, to fail to win a wager on a card of a particular rank four times during the deal of the entire pack.
[1943 Maurer *Argot*]

lose bet, *n.* In bank craps, a bet that the shooter will throw craps or will not make a pass.
[1964 *OEDS*]

loser, *n.* **1.** A gambler who regularly fails to win.
[ca. 1961 *Hotel Coll*]
2. In faro, the first card dealt from the pack, which wins for the dealer.
3. In bridge, a losing card.
[1938 Asbury *Sucker's Progress* 8]
[1917 *OEDS*]
4. a horse that loses in a race.
[1902 *OED*]

loser-on-loser, *adj.* In bridge, pertaining to putting a losing card on a losing trick.
[1929 *OEDS*]

lottery, *n.* **1.** A scheme for raising money by selling lots, or chances, to share in the distribution of prizes, now usually money, through numbered tickets selected as winners from a LOTTERY WHEEL or KENO GOOSE at a predetermined time and place.
Compare KENO and NUMBERS.
[1567 *OED;* (1612) 1719 *DAE*]
→Many citations in the *DAE* refer to the illegality of or the advisability of a law prohibiting lotteries. Several states of the United States now conduct legal lotteries for the raising of funds for public projects. Compare LOTTO (def. 2).
2. In cards, a game in which prices are obtained by the holders of certain cards.
[1830 *OED*]

Lottery. There are many variations in purchasing chances to win prizes or a share in a money POOL. POOL GAMBLING usually requires the selling of numbered TICKETS such as a KENO TICKET or LOTTERY TICKET. The NUMBERS GAME (also called POLICY) is an illegal betting scheme similar to lottery (sometimes called CHINESE LOTTERY) or SWEEPSTAKES.

KENO WRITERS use a KENO GOOSE (formerly a WOODEN GOOSE) or RABBIT EARS. They rely upon a KENO CALLER to coordinate the KENO RUNNERS' activity in the rooms adjacent to the KENO LOUNGE where KENOISTS may be dining or gambling. INSIDE TICKETS and OUTSIDE TICKETS record the wager. Some KENO TICKETS are dispensed from WRITER MACHINES. HOUSE TICKETS and WAY TICKETS (also called COMBINATION TICKETS) are based upon groups of numbers in contrast to a STRAIGHT TICKET. In either case, one hopes for a WALL TICKET.

Many governments operate LOTTO from a LOTTERY OFFICE which supervises the selling of LOTTERY TICKETS through LOTTERY DEALERS and the drawing of winning tickets from a LOTTERY WHEEL.

At a NUMBERS DROP or POLICY SHOP a bettor may PLAY THE NUMBERS with a STRAIGHT-NUMBER BET (or a STRAIGHT-POLICY PLAY) or may choose a WASHERWOMAN'S GIG, a MAGIC GIG, or a SINGLE-ACTION BET. The bettor gets a POLICY SLIP or, perhaps, a SHORT SLIP. Only some players resort to a DREAM BOOK.

lottery dealer, *n.* A person who sells LOTTERY TICKETS or conducts a LOTTERY.
[1856 *DAE*]

lottery office, *n.* A central clearing-house for carrying out the business of a lottery game.
[1722 *OED*]

lottery ticket, *n.* A ticket sold to a bettor in a lottery, usually by a LOTTERY DEALER.
[1697 *OED*]

lottery wheel, *n.* A wheel-shaped container for mixing LOTTERY TICKETS before the winning tickets are drawn.
[1819 *OED,* 1799 *DAE*]

lotto, *n.* **1.** Sometimes written **loto.** An obsolete game considered to be the forerunner of bingo. The game was played with a caller drawing numbered cards or balls. The pasteboard cards sold to patrons had various random numbers printed on them, and the first person to cover a row of numbers as called by the announcer won the game.
[1778 *OED*]
2. Lotto. The name of a state-run lottery in the United States.
[1973 Clark *Oral Coll*]

love, *n.* In games like bridge or gin, a score of zero.
[1742 *OED*]

lover's leap, *n.* In backgammon, a movement of a single STONE from the one point in the adversary's table to the twelve point, after rolling a number 11 on the dice.
[1950 Morehead *Culbertson* 625]
[Compare 1711 *OED,* meaning "a precipice popularly connected with some legend of a lover's suicide," the connection to backgammon being rather obscure]

low, *n.* **1.** In games using three dice, such as chuck-a-luck, a wager that the throw of the dice will result in a total number of pips facing upward of 4 to 10 inclusive.
[1976 Figgis *Gambler's Handbook* 57]
2. In all fours (high low, jack and the game), the deuce of trumps, or the lowest trump dealt.
1836 Eidrah *Hoyle Famil* 63. *Low,* the deuce of trumps, or the next lowest out, and it is reckoned by the person to whom it is dealt.
[1818 *OED*]

lowball, *n.* A variation in poker in which the lowest hand wins rather than the highest hand. Compare HIGHBALL.
[ca. 1961 *Hotel Coll*]

low-belly strippers, *n. pl.* A deck of cards in which some of the cards have been shaved or trimmed along the long sides to make them narrower than the rest of the pack. Compare HIGH-BELLY STRIPPERS.
[ca. 1961 *Hotel Coll*]

low den, *n.* A gambling establishment in which cheating is tolerated.
[1981 *Nevada Magazine* 6]

low dice, *n.* Dice that have been altered to roll only low numbers. Compare BARR DICE and LOADED DICE.
[1890 Quinn *Fools of Fortune* 283]

low-fullam, *n.* Also spelled **low-fullum** or **low-fulham.** A die that has been altered so that the faces with one, two, or three pips will be turned up after a roll more often than the faces with four, five, or six pips. Compare HIGH-FULLAM. See quotation at FULLAM: 1714 Lucas Memoirs 26.
1680 Cotton *Compleat Gamester* 9. This they do by false Dice, as High-Fullams 4, 5, 6. *low-Fullams* 1, 2, 3.

low-number bet, *n. phr.* In roulette, a wager on the layout section numbered 1 to 18.
[ca. 1961 *Hotel Coll*]
→ *Low-number bet* is the characteristic U.S. use, being replaced elsewhere by the French term MANQUE.

low poker, *n.* A variation of poker in which the lowest ranking hand wins rather than the highest ranking hand; LOWBALL.
[1968 Wallace *Poker* 218]

low roller, *n.* A gambler who wagers for small stakes. See also HIGH ROLLER.
[1981 *Nevada Magazine* 12]

low-stake game, *n.* Also spelled **low-stakes game.** A gambling game played for small amounts of money. See also HIGH-STAKES GAME.
[1953 Lewis *Sagebrush Casinos* 136]

luck, *n.* Also called LADY LUCK. Good or ill-fortune in wagering on games of chance.
[(1481) 1856 *OED*]

luck out, *v.phr.* In poker, to draw a final card that wins the pot for the player drawing it.
[1949 Coffin *Secrets* 181]
[1954 *OEDS,* meaning "to achieve success"]

lucky buck, *n.* In a casino, a premium or coupon that allows a player to wager a certain amount without risking his own money. The coupon is intended to entice the player into continuing gambling after he has lost the *lucky buck.* Compare COMP.
[1974 Powell *Verbal Dexterity* 15]

lucky streak, *n.* A series of wins in gambling events where one would not expect the odds to favor a high percentage of wins. See also WINNING STREAK.
[1961 Smith and Nobel *Quit Winners* 267]

lug, *v.* In the phrases:
lug in, 1. Of a racehorse on an oval track, to angle to the left, toward the inside rail, while running.
[(1951) 1981 Maurer *Lang. of the Underworld* 218]
[n.d. *DAS*]
2. To bring gamblers to a gambling establishment. See also LUGGER.
[(1951) 1981 Maurer *Lang. of the Underworld* 218]
lug out, Of a racehorse on an oval track, to angle to the right, toward the outside rail, while running.
[(1951) 1981 Maurer *Lang. of the Underworld* 218]
[n.d. *DAS*]

lugger, *n.* **1.** An employee of a gambling establishment who brings gamblers to the establishment. See also GREETER and STEERER

and ROPER and JUNKETEER.
[(1950) 1981 Maurer *Lang. of the Underworld* 188]
2. In horse racing, a horse that LUGS IN or LUGS OUT. [n.d. *DAS*]

lumber, *n.* Also called KIBITZER or WOOD. A spectator at a gambling event, usually at card games.
[ca. 1961 *Hotel Coll*]

luminous readers, *n.* Cards marked on the back with an ink that can be seen only through tinted glasses. Compare COSMETICS.
[ca. 1961 *Hotel Coll*]

l'une pour l'autre, *n. phr. French.* In faro, a tie; a draw.
1843 Green *Exposure* 167. *L'une pour L'autre,* means a drawn game, and is said when two of the punter's cards are drawn in the same coup.
→This French expression is now generally obsolete in the United States.

lurch, *n.* **1.** A cheater; swindler. *Obsolete.*
[(1533) 1604 *OED*]
2. Any of several games won before the opponent scores a designated number of points.
1824 Anon *Hoyle's* 28. *Lurched* is when your adversary has won the game before you have gained six points.
[*OED* lists a number of such games: 1653 a cribbage game won before the opponent scores 31 points; 1678 a backgammon game won before the opponent bears off; 1742 a treble win at whist; and cassino, the loss of a game before acquiring six points.]

lurch, *v.* To beat in various games before one's opponent scores a designated number of points. See LURCH, *n.* (def. 2).
1860 Pardon *Handbook* 24. The players who made the double point are said to have *lurched* their adversaries.
[1678 *OED*]

lurching, *n.* In games like piquet and whist, the gaining of a *lurch,* or double point.
[1350 *OED*]

lure, *n.* In dog racing, the artificial rabbit that moves around the track ahead of the dogs.
[1968 Buchele *Greyhound Racing* 96]
[Compare *a*1700 *OED,* meaning "a means of alluring animals"]

M

machine, *n.* In horse racing: **1.** a battery-driven contraption used illegally by a jockey to electrically shock a horse.
[1978 Ainslie *Complete Guide* 293]
2. The TOTALISATOR, a large lighted board that displays the winners of a race and the amounts of money won on a two dollar bet.
[1889 *OEDS*]

machine man, *n.* A cheater who uses mechanical devices to cheat at cards, dice, or roulette.
[1962 Garcia *Marked Cards* 38]
[Compare 1876 *OED,* meaning "one who works a machine"]

machine payout, *n.* The coins delivered to a slot machine player by the slot machine itself rather than by an employee of the gambling establishment.
[1978 Alexander *Glossary* 9]

magic gig, *n.* Also called a WASHERWOMAN'S GIG. In playing numbers, a selection of the grouped numbers 4, 11, and 44.
[1938 Asbury *Sucker's Progress* 92]

magic number, *n.* **1.** In craps, an initial roll of number 7 on the dice.
[ca. 1961 *Hotel coll*]
2. In poker, the number 5.
[1949 Coffin *Secrets* 181]

magnetic spindle, *n. phr.* A wheel of fortune controlled with magnets. See also SQUEEZE SPINDLE.
[1890 Quinn *Fools of Fortune* 293]

mah jong, *n.* A game played with 136-144 tiles resembling a deck of cards, in which players seek to assemble hands consisting of sets of tiles.
[1922 *OEDS,* from Chinese *ma-ch'iao* or *ma-tsiang* (Pinyin: *majiang*), meaning hemp and small birds, from the design on the tiles]

mah jong, *v.* To win at MAH JONG.
[1923 *OEDS*]

maiden, *n.* **1.** A horse or greyhound of either sex, that has not won a race.
[1898 *OED*]
2. A maiden race.
[1807 *OED*]

maiden claiming event, *n. phr.* A race in which none of the entrants has won a race and all entrants are for sale. Compare CLAIMING RACE and MAIDEN RACE.
[1971 McQuaid *Gambler's Digest* 310]

maiden horse, *n.* Also shortened to MAIDEN. A horse that never won a race.
[1760 *OED*]

maiden race, *n.* A horse or dog race in which none of the entrants has ever won a race. [1968 Thackrey *Nick the Greek* 210] [Compare 1886 *OED,* as *maiden bicycle handicap* and 1896 *OED*, as *maiden class*]

main, *n.* Also spelled **mayne, maine.** In hazard, the number, usually 7, on which the shooter loses if it appears before his own number. See also POINT. See quotation at *hazard:* 1680 Cotton *Complete Gamester.*
[1580 *OED*]

main bank, *n. phr.* In a casino or poker room, the primary repository for currency in the gambling establishment. Compare CAGE.
[1979 Hilton Hotel *Procedures* 22]

main game, *n.* In craps, the PASS LINE.
1983 Martinet *Oral Coll.* There are a lot of side bets in craps like hop bets and hardways. When the stick says, "pay the *main game,*" he means that the bets on the pass line won.

main pot, *n.* In poker, the primary pool of money the players are vying for, as opposed to side bets on particular events that may be made between individual players.
[ca. 1961 *Hotel Coll*]

major, *n.* The non-dealer in two-handed card games. Compare MINOR.
[1950 Morehead *Culbertson* 626]

major hand, *n.* In poker, a straight or hand of higher rank. Compare MINOR HAND.
[1949 Coffin *Secrets* 181]

major suit, *n.* Also shortened to **major.** In bridge, the suits of spades or hearts.
[1916 *OEDS*]

major tenace, *n.* In bridge, an ace and a queen of one suit held in the hand; the highest and third-highest ranking cards of a suit held in the hand of the fourth player to act on a trick. See also TENACE.
[1950 Morehead *Culbertson* 626]
[1870 *OED*]

make, *n.* In bridge, a declaration or contract of the number of tricks the highest bidder will take. See also DECLARATION (def. 1).
[1902 *OEDS*]

make, *v.* **1.** In trump games, to win or take a trick; to play a certain card to advantage.
[1608 *OED*]
2. Especially in the phrase: **make a contract.** In bridge, to succeed in winning the number of tricks contracted.
[1953 Crawford *Consistent Winner* 349]
3. To shuffle a pack of cards in preparation for the next deal. [1876 *OED*]
4. In the phrases:
make a book, To accept a series of bets on a single event, as a horse race, with odds on the various bets so as to make a profit from the transactions. See also BOOKMAKING.
1868 Laing-Meason *Turf Frauds* 116. But the bookmaker makes betting his profession, and the very term of *"making a book"* means to have such a combination of bets in his book that he not only cannot lose, but, that no matter what horse comes in first, he must win.
[1828 *OED*]
make a brush, To build a small bet into a large sum by winning and making progressively larger bets.
[1943 Maurer *Argot*]
make a hit, To win a large amount of money betting.
[1983 Martinez *Gambling Scene* 210]
make a move, In horse racing, to break from the pack in the stretch and run ahead of the other horses. See also DRIVE and EXTEND.
[1971 McQuaid *Gambler's Digest* 310]
[Compare *make a move* 1827 *OED,* in a more general sense]
make a pass, 1. In craps, to throw a winning roll of the dice.
[ca. 1961 *Hotel Coll*]
2. In cards, to restore the deck to its original order after a cut by using a cheating move. See also MAKING THE PASS.
[1968 Adams *Western Words*]
make a point, 1. In backgammon, to block a position by putting two stones, or pieces, on the space.
[1974 Scarne *Dice* 320]
2. In craps, to establish a number (4, 5, 6, 8, 9, or 10) that must be rolled before the number 7; to throw a winning roll of the dice, other than the numbers 7 or 11.
[1950 Morehead *Culbertson* 626]
make a run, To move from an inferior position very rapidly so as to nearly catch the leader in a race or game.
[1978 Ainslie *Complete Guide* 293]
make book, To accept a variety of bets on an event offering odds on various possibilities; to manage a bookmaking operation. See also BOOKMAKING.
[ca. 1961 *Hotel Coll*]
make good, In poker, to place the appropriate amount of chips in the pot.
[1890 Quinn *Fools of Fortune* 215]
make up the pack, Also shortened to **make up.** In card games, to gather the cards up after a hand and shuffle them in preparation for the next hand.
[1949 Coffin *Secrets* 181]

maker, *n.* **1.** In bridge, the player who names the trump suit and is required to win enough tricks to meet the terms of the contract.
2. The jack in those poker games in which jacks are wild or count any value declared by the holder. *Obsolete.*
[1753 *OED*]

making the pass, *n. phr.* A method for cutting cards whereby a prepared packet of stacked cards is placed atop the deck. See also MAKE A PASS (def. 2).

1859 Green *Gam Tricks* 11. . . . draw off the lower cards, confined by the little finger and the other parts of the right hand, and place them, with an imperceptible motion, on the top of the pack. But before you attempt any of the tricks that depend on *making the pass,* you must have great practice, and be able to perform it so dextrously and expeditiously, that the eye cannot detect the movement of the hand, or you may expose yourself.

mallillio, *n. Spanish.* In ombre or quadrille, a black deuce or a red seven. See quotation at *spadillo:* 1680 Cotton *Compleat Gamester.*

man, *n.* In board games such as backgammon, the PIECE used as a counter or moved around the board. See also STONE.
[1562 *OED;* meaning "chessman," therefore probably from 1205 *OED,* meaning "a member of a fighting force"]

man in the box, *n. phr.* A variation of backgammon in which one person plays against a team of other players.
[1971 McQuaid *Gambler's Digest* 310]

manque, *n. French.* In roulette, a wager on the table layout for the numbers 1 to 18, inclusive. See also LOW-NUMBER BET.
[1850 *OEDS*]

map, *n.* In a casino twenty-one pit with several tables, the record of dealers' table assignments, time spent dealing during a shift, and relief breaks. The management can trace any sudden shifts in patterns of house losses to a particular dealer by comparing the *map* with the PIT REPORT or MASTER GAME REPORT.
[ca. 1961 *Hotel Coll*]

marbles, *n. pl.* Another word for DICE.
[1983 Martinez *Gambling Scene* 210]

march, *n.* In the card game of euchre, the scoring of two points by taking all five tricks by the partnership which named the trump suit.
1887 Keller *Euchre* 20. If the side which adopts or makes the trump, takes all five tricks, it scores two. This is called a *march.*
[1857 *DAE,* 1886 *OED*]

Maria, *n.* Also called the **black maria.** The queen of spades.
[1950 Morehead *Culbertson* 626]
[Compare *black maria:* 1847 *OEDS,* meaning "a paddy wagon." The direct connection is obscure.]

mark, *n.* **1.** The victim of a swindler or cheater.
[1889 *DA;* 1896 *DAE:* 1897 *OED;* compare 1549 *OED,* figurative uses]
2. A design, smudge, or identifying mark placed on the back of a playing card so that its face value can be dishonestly ascertained. See also COSMETICS.
3. In the card game of quadrille, the ante placed in the pot by the dealer.
1876 Crawley *Card Plyr* 196. *Mark* means the fish [chips or counters] put down by the dealer.
[1876 *OED*]
4. In bowls, the jack. *Obsolete.*
[1630 *OED*]

mark, *v.* **1.** To disfigure the back of a playing card with ink, scratches, or some identifying feature so as to be able to recognize its face value.
1714 Lucas *Memoirs* 109. . . . at this game the Cheat lies in securing an Ace in the Sleeve, or Bosom, or on the Hat, or any other sure winning Card; or if you *mark* the Cards aforehand, so as to know them by the Backside, you know accordingly how to make your Advantage.
2. In bank craps, to place the PUCK, or marker, on the layout number corresponding to the number the shooter must roll in order to win.
[1983 Martinet *Oral Coll*]
3. In a casino, to signify a temporary loan to a player by placing the equivalent amount in chips near the dealer rather than on the player's betting spot on the layout. See also MARKER DOWN.
[1973 Clark *Oral Coll.*]
4. In card games like bridge or whist, to record on paper the points scored by the players.
[1816 *OED*]
5. In the phrases:
mark off, 1. In a casino, to break a tall stack of chips into smaller stacks for ease of counting.
[ca. 1961 *Hotel Coll*]
2. Of a casino dealer, to place a chip of lower denomination between every twenty chips of a larger denomination in a chip rack, for ease in handling stacks of chips and counting the value of the rack.
[1977 Anness *Dummy Up*]
mark card, In horse racing, to give someone information about a horse on which to bet; a tip; dope.
[1961 *OEDS,* ca. 1945 *DSUE*]

marker, *n.* **1.** In a casino, a credit slip signed by a patron, stating the amount of money advanced to the patron; an IOU.
[1887 *OEDS*]
2. On a craps table or faro layout, a small round disk usually made of copper or composition that is placed atop a player's stack of chips that the player temporarily wishes not to bet.
[1983 Martinet *Oral Coll*]
3. In poker games dealt by one person who does not play, the plastic disk that designates the position of the dealer. The *marker* is used to determine the player who must act first in a betting round. See also BUCK and PUCK.
[1968 Wallace *Poker* 219]
4. In keno, a crayon or ink brush used to mark numbers selected on a KENO TICKET.
[ca. 1961 *Hotel Coll*]
5. The person who records scores in bridge or such competitions as billiards and tennis.
[1754 *OED*]

6. In bridge, a scoreboard or card used for recording scores.
[1907 *OEDS*]
7. A point scored in a game.
[n.d. *DAS*]
8. *Usually plural.* Identifying characteristics on the backs of playing cards. See also COSMETICS.
[1870 *OED*]

marker button, *n.* In a casino, a small disk with a number printed on it, indicating the value of the chips removed from the table by a pit boss or floorman. See also LAMMER.
[1974 Friedman *Casino Management* 91]

marker card, *n.* In games with a SHOE, or dealing box, a rectangular piece of plastic the size of a playing card that is placed toward the end of the stack of cards. When the dealer pulls the *marker card* from the shoe, he finishes the hand he is dealing, then reshuffles all the cards and refills the shoe.
[1976 Figgis *Gambler's Handbook* 236]

marker down, *n. phr.* Also called MARKER PAID. In a casino, a call from a dealer to the pit boss or floorman that a player's marker has been paid or removed by use of a credit slip.
[ca. 1961 *Hotel Coll*]

marker inventory, *n* .Same as MARKER LOG.
[1977 Nevada Gaming Control *Internal* 12]

marker log, *n.* A ledger kept in the casino pit or cage that is used to record all credit advances to players and all amounts returned to the casino.
[1978 Alexander *Glossary* 10]

marker paid, *n. phr.* Same as MARKER DOWN.
[ca. 1961 *Hotel Coll*]

marker stub, *n.* In a casino, a portion of a credit slip torn along a perforated edge and deposited in the DROP BOX at the player's table, after the player has signed the slip, acknowledging the loan.
[1978 Alexander *Glossary* 10]

market, *n.* In horse racing, the business of making and accepting bets.
[1886 *OEDS*]

marking board, *n.* A board constructed to register the score in games; a large scoreboard that can be easily read by crowds or galleries, as at golf tournaments.
[1856 *OED*]

markings, *n. pl.* The identifying characteristics of a racehorse. Compare COLORS (def. 2).
[1981 Passer *Winning Big* 232]

Marquis of Queensberry rules, *n. pl.* Also shortened to **Queensberry rules.** The codified rules regulating boxing or prizefighting, first presented in 1865.
[1971 McQuaid *Gambler's Digest* 310]
[(1895) *OEDS,* named for Sir John Sholto Douglas (1844-1900), 8th *Marquis of Queensberry,* responsible for the drawing up of new rules governing boxing matches]
→Sometimes the modern spelling of *Marquess* is substituted for the 19th Century form, *Marquis.* Dictionaries uniformly enter this term in the *Q's;* however the sampling in Nexis® shows more evidence for the longer form. The spelling of *Queensberry* as *Queensbury* while "incorrect" is sufficiently common to justify mentioning.

marriage, *n.* A king and queen of one suit in playing cards, especially as a meld in pinochle.
[1861 *OED*]

martingale, *n.* A betting system in which the player increases the size of a bet after a loss, hoping thereby to make up the loss and perhaps a small amount more. See also DOUBLE PROGRESSION and NEOPOLITAN MARTINGALE SYSTEM. Compare DOUBLE UP.
[1815 *OED;* compare earlier 1589 *OED,* meaning "a strap to prevent a horse from rearing and throwing the rider."]

martingale, *v.* To double a bet after a loss, usually adding one more chip to the doubled bet. Compare DOUBLE UP.
1823 Persius *Rouge et Noir* 164. To *Martingale* is to play one coup at least more than the stake previously lost. This is the boldest manner of playing at any of the games of chance.
[1823 *OED*]

masque, *v. French.* In faro, to place a bet on a card turned facedown.
1843 Green *Exposure* 167. *Masque* signifies turning a card, or placing another face downwards, during any number of coups, on that whereon the punter has staked, and which he may afterwards display at pleasure.

masse, *v. French.* To repeat the same wager after a win. Compare DOUBLE UP and MARTINGALE, *v.*
1714 Lucas *Memoirs* 230. *Masse* is when you have won the Couch, or first Stake, and will venture more Money upon the same Card.
[Compare 1727 *OED,* obsolete meaning: "to set the stake" which cites a French dictionary *Dictionnaire Francois-Anglois 1699.*]

master card, *n.* **1.** In a casino, a serialized recording of all transfers of chips between the table and the cage. See also RIM CARD and TABLE CARD.
[1957 *Nevada Gaming Regulations* 33]
2. In poker, the highest ranking card in play of one particular suit.
[1949 Coffin *Secrets* 181]

master game report, *n.* Also called **master game sheet.** In a casino, an accounting form for recording the drop, or amount of cash taken in by each table. See also PIT REPORT.
[1977 Nevada Gaming Control *Internal* 12]

master rim card, *n.* In a casino, an accounting form recording all credit activity in a specific pit. Compare RIM CARD.
[1978 Alexander *Glossary* 10]

matador, *n. Spanish.* **1.** In the card game ombre or quadrille, the ace of spades, the ace of clubs,

and a black deuce, the holding of which requires all players to pay a specified amount to the person holding a *matador*. See also BASTO and MALLILLIO and SPADILLO.
1680 Cotton *Compleat Gamester* 70. The *Matadors* (or killing Cards) which are the Spadillo, Mallillio, and Basto are the chief Cards, and when they are all in a hand the others pay for them three of the greater Counters apiece.
[1674 *OED*]
2. In several games that have trump cards, any high trump card, such as a queen, king, or ace.
3. In dominos, a variant that requires players to connect dominoes so the total number of pips on the ends touching equals seven.
[1865 *OED*]

match, *v.* In the phrase:
match the pot, *v. phr.* In poker, to bet an amount equal to the pool in the middle of the table.
[1963 Steig *Common Sense* 185]

matchbook shiner, *n.* One of a variety of cheating devices used by dishonest card players, especially a small mirror attached to the inside of a matchbook cover, small matchbox, or cigarette lighter, which allows a player or dealer to see the faces of the cards reflected while dealing. Compare SHINER.
[1981 Jenkins *Johnny Moss*]

matched set, *n.* In games like rummy and pinochle, three or more cards from one hand that can be used together in a valid meld.
[1950 Morehead *Culbertson* 627]

match game, *n.* **1.** In any of a variety of games that are played in a series, the final game of the series determining the winner. A series of games is usually three, five, or seven. The *match game* for each series could be the second, third, or fourth, respectively, if one team or side is undefeated.
2. Generally, any contest or competition between two teams or sides. Compare MATCH RACE.
[1857 *DA,* 1868 *DAE*]

matching card, *n.* A card of the same rank or suit as another held in the hand. Compare MATE.
[1963 Steig *Common Sense* 185]

match-point scoring, *n. phr.* In duplicate bridge, a system for recording the performance of players through the contest.
[1950 Morehead *Culbertson* 627]

match race, *n.* In racing, a contest between two horses or two, three, or four greyhounds.
[1804 *DA,* 1836 *DAE*]

mate, *n.* In card games, a card that matches another in rank, making a pair. Compare MATCHING CARD.
[1949 Coffin *Secrets* 181]
[Compare 1578 *OED,* meaning "a counterpart or parallel"]

matrix player, *n.* In twenty-one, a proficient card counter; a player who remembers cards already played and modifies his betting accordingly.
[1983 Martinet *Oral Coll*]

maw, *n.* A fast-paced card game played with a pack of 32 cards, with from two to six players, and in which the jack and five of trumps count as the strongest.
[1548 *OED*]

maximum bet, *n.* The largest wager allowed on a betting event. Compare MINIMUM BET.
[ca. 1961 *Hotel Coll*]

mechanic, *n.* An adept cheater, especially at dealing cards (CARD MECHANIC) or, less often, manipulating dice (DICE MECHANIC).
[1909 *OEDS;* from *Century Dict.* Supplement]

mechanical game, *n.* In a casino, a game such as craps or roulette that requires no skill to play because each cast of the dice or spin of the wheel is random.
[ca. 1961 *Hotel Coll*]

mechanic's grip, *n.* A method for holding a deck of cards to facilitate cheating by dealing bottom cards or cards beneath the top card, with three fingers along the long side of the deck, the index finger being curled over the front and to the top of the deck, or two fingers along the long side and two over the front.
[ca. 1961 *Hotel Coll*]

medicine turn, *n.* In faro, a combination of a queen and nine on the same turn.
[1943 Maurer *Argot*]
[From a play on the word *quinine.*]

meet, *n.* The period, lasting from one day to several months, for a series of races conducted at a single track.
[1971 McQuaid *Gambler's Digest* 310]

meet a bet, *v. phr.* In poker, to place an amount in the pot that equals the wager of the previous bettor.
[1949 Coffin *Secrets* 181]

meld, *n.* In games like gin rummy and pinochle, a combination of cards that have value and can be placed face up on the table for scoring points.
[1897 *OED,* 1898 *DA*]

meld, *v.* To place a scoring combination of cards face upward on the table to verify a claim for points.
[1950 Morehead *Culbertson* 627]
[from German *melden* to announce]

Memphis dominoes, *n. pl.* Another term for DICE.
[1963 Scarne *Complete Guide* 682]

menel, *n.* In klabberjass and clob, the 9 of trump, which is the second highest ranking card. See also NELL.
1950 Morehead *Culbertson* 278. In the trump suit the cards rank: J (high), 9, A, 10, K, Q, 8,

7. The jack is called jass or *jasz,* and the nine is called *menel.*

meter, *n.* In a slot machine, a counting device that records the number of coins played and the number of coins payed out during a specific period of time.
[1982 Martin *Introduction* 22]
[Compare 1860 *OED,* meaning "a self-actuating measure of the fluctuations of something."]

meter reading summary, *n. phr.* In a casino, a form recording the number of coins played and the number of coins payed out for all the slot machines during a specific period of time, usually eight or twenty-four hours.
[1978 Alexander *Glossary* 10]

Mexican standoff, *n.* **1.** In poker, a condition in which two hands have the same value.
[ca. 1961 *Hotel Coll*]
[Compare 1891 *OEDS,* under *stand-off,* describing a situation with "no chance to benefit"]
2. A condition in which a player leaves a gambling game without having won or lost much money.
[1961 Scarne *Complete Guide* 682]

Michigan bank roll, *n.* Also shortened to **Michigan roll.** A bill of a large denomination wrapped around a large roll of one-dollar bills, usually held together with a rubber band. See also FLASH MONEY.
[1939 MacDougall *Gambler's Don't* 68]

mic the dice, /maik/, *v. phr.* In bank craps, to measure dice with a micrometer to determine whether or not the dice have been shaved or otherwise altered in size. See also SQUARE THE DICE.
[ca. 1961 *Hotel Coll*]
[*mic,* probably a clipping of *micrometer*]

middle dealer, *n.* A card dealer with the expertise to deal cards dishonestly from the middle of the pack. Compare BOTTOM DEALER.
[1968 Wallace *Poker* 219]

middle distance, *n.* In horse racing, a race longer than one mile but less than one mile and a quarter.
[1978 Ainslie *Complete Guide* 293]

middle dozen, *n.* In roulette, the numbers 13 to 24 inclusive, especially when bet as a group.
[ca. 1961 *Hotel Coll*]

middle man, *n.* In poker, a player between two other players who are raising and re-raising each other's bets. Compare WHIPSAW (def. 2).
[1968 Wallace *Poker* 219]
[Compare 1870 *OEDS,* meaning "the man who sits in the middle of a minstrel troupe, between the men on the ends"]

middle position, *n.* In an eight-handed poker game, the fourth, fifth, or sixth position at the table to the left of the dealer.
[1978 Brunson *How I Made* 530]

middle straight, *n.* In poker, a straight of four cards with the middle card missing, as 7, 8, 10, jack, the 9 being required to make the straight. See also INSIDE STRAIGHT.
[1950 Morhead *Culbertson* 627]

mid-game, *n.* In board games such as backgammon, the period of the game after the opening moves by both players, before either player has a decided advantage.
[1950 Morehead *Culbertson* 627]
[Compare *middle game* 1894 *OEDS,* in chess]

midget hand, *n.* A hand of cards in any game that requires fewer than five cards, such as cribbage or monte.
[1949 Coffin *Secrets* 181]

mile pole, *n.* In horse racing, the post placed one mile from the finish line.
[1978 Ainslie *Complete Guide* 293]
[Compare *mile post* 1768 *OEDS,* meaning "a post serving as a mile-mark"]

milk, *v.* **1.** In poker, to derive the most benefit from a mediocre hand.
[1983 Martinez *Gambling Scene* 210]
2. In horse racing, to keep a horse as favorite that has no chance to win.
1889 Ellangowan *Sporting Anecdotes* 63. *Milking* is a word which in the slang of the turf implies that the owner of the horse is obtaining money on the certainty of its not ultimately being allowed to run in the race, or, if it runs, on the certainty of its not winning. Winning a race cannot be made an absolute certainty, but losing a race can.
[1862 *OED*]
3. To withdraw part of the winnings from a gambling venture while continuing to gamble.
[1923 *OEDS*]
4. In the phrase:
milk the pack, In poker, to deal certain cards from the deck dishonestly.
[1938 Asbury *Sucker's Progress* 35]

milker, *n.* In poker, a person who plays very conservatively, even when winning.
[1968 Wallace *Poker* 219]

milking, *adj.* Pertaining to pulling a packet of cards from the middle of the deck while shuffling, and placing the packet on top of the deck.
[1950 Morehead *Culbertson* 627]

milking the cards, *n. phr.* In card games, the act of a player rapidly pulling the cards, one at a time, from the top of his hand and placing them on the bottom of his hand before looking at the hand.
[1968 Wallace *Poker* 219]

milking the game, *n. phr.* In poker, the act of drawing money out of the game by playing conservatively, winning small amounts, and keeping the winnings.
[1968 Wallace *Poker* 219]

mimic the dealer, *v. phr.* In twenty-one, to use the same rules that govern the dealer, such as taking a card while holding sixteen points or less,

never splitting pairs, taking a card if holding a 6 and ace, and so on.
[ca. 1961 *Hotel Coll*]

minimum bet, *n.* Also shortened to **minimum.** The smallest amount of money one is allowed to bet on a gambling proposition.
[ca. 1961 *Hotel Coll*]

minnie, *n.* Also called a BICYCLE or LITTLE WHEEL or WHEEL. In lowball poker, a straight, or sequence of cards from the ace to the 5. Considered a perfect hand.
[1968 Wallace *Poker* 219]

minnow, *n.* In poker, a player who overextends himself by joining a no-limit game with inadequate funds.
[1978 Brunson *How I Made* 538]

minor, *n. French.* Any two-handed card game, such as cribbage or gin.
[1950 Morehead *Culbertson* 628]
[from French *mineur* dealer]

minor hand, *n.* In poker, a hand with three aces or less in rank; a hand with a value lower than a straight. Compare MAJOR HAND.
[1949 Coffin *Secrets* 181]

minor meld, *n.* In games like canasta and samba, a packet of cards worth fewer points than a canasta that can be placed face upward on the table.
[1953 Crawford *Consistent Winner* 349]

minor suit, *n.* In games like bridge, the suits of diamonds or clubs. Compare MAJOR SUIT.
[1967 *OEDS*]

minor tenace, *n.* In games like bridge, a king and jack of the same suit held in the hand of the fourth player to act on a trick, after some cards of that suit have been played. See also TENACE.
[1950 Morehead *Culbertson* 628]

minus pool, *n.* In horse racing, a condition whereby one horse is so heavily favored (at 1 to 10 or more) that the operator of the track must pay part of the winnings because not enough money was wagered on the rest of the field to cover the amount in the mutual fund.
[1955 Hillis *Pari-Mutuel Betting* 115]

mirliro, *n. Spanish.* In ombre, a hazard created by holding in the hand two black aces without a matador, or two red aces with a basto.
[1950 Morehead *Culbertson* 628]

misdeal, *n.* The act of giving any player more or fewer cards than required.
1836 Eidrah *Hoyle Famil* 69. *Misdeal* is when the dealer gives any of the party more or less than the proper number of cards, or deals out of regular order, or shews a card in dealing.
1860 Pardon *Handbook* 22. A *misdeal* is made by giving a card too many or too few to either player.
[1850 *OED*]

misdeal, *v.* To give a player an inappropriate number of cards.
[(1746) 1850 *OED*]

misery, *n.* In card games like misere, a declaration that one will take no tricks.
[1830 *OED,* under *misere*]
[Spelling altered by folk etymology of French *miser* low]

mismarked dice, *n. phr.* Also called MIS-SPOTS. Dice with pips added or removed from certain faces. See also DOOR POPS.
1980 Clark *Oral Coll.* The most common *mismarked dice* are dice with two fives or two twos on the same die.

miss, *n.* In games like cribbage and loo, the extra hand of cards created to be used by one of the players. See also WIDOW.
1836 Eidrah *Hoyle Famil* 69. *Miss* is the spare hand (when there is a pool), and must be dealt in the regular order of the other hands, either first, or last but one, and not according to the dealer's whim. [1767 *OED*]
2. In bank craps, the DON'T PASS bet.

miss, *v.* **1.** In bank craps, to roll a craps or lose on a point.
[1974 Scarne *Dice* 473]
2. In the phrases:
miss a pass, In craps, to cast the number 7 before throwing the point number required to win.
[ca. 1961 *Hotel Coll*]
miss the flop, In hold 'em poker, to have two cards that have no value after the first three community cards have been dealt face upward on the table.
[1978 Brunson *How I Made* 538]

misses, *n. pl.* Dice that have been altered so as to roll the number 7 more often than normal. Compare BARR DICE and LOADED DICE.
[ca. 1961 *Hotel Coll*]

Mississippi marbles, *n. pl.* Another name for DICE.
[ca. 1961 *Hotel Coll*]
[n.d. *DAS*]

Missouri marbles, *n. pl.* Another name for DICE.
[1983 Martinez *Gambling Scene* 210]

missout, *n.* **1.** A loaded die.
[1928 *OEDS*]
2. A losing number in craps.
[1936 *OEDS*]

mis-spots, *n. pl.* Dice with pips added or removed from certain faces; MISMARKED DICE. The most common *mis-spots* are dice with two fives or two twos on the same die.
[1977 Carroll *Playboy's Illustrated* 125]

mistigri, *n.* In games like poker or loo, a joker that has the value of any card, as assigned by the holder; a wild card, specifically, in pam, a jack of clubs, in bouillotte and brelan, the jack of spades.
[1822 *OED,* under *mistigris*]

mites and lice, *n. phr.* In such poker variants as seven card stud or hold 'em, a pair of threes face upward on the board, with a small pair held

face down by a player.
[1949 Coffin *Secrets* 181]
[Probably a variant of MITS AND MICE.]

mits and mice, *n. phr.* In hold 'em poker, a pair of twos and a pair of threes.
1981 Golad *Oral Coll.* There's a name for holding a pair of deuces while a pair of treys is on deck. That's called *mits and mice* . . . It can also be treys in the hand and deuces on deck [face up on the table]. I don't know which are the mits and which are the mice, but it just means the two lowest pair.
[Probably a variant of MITES and LICE.]

mitt, *n.* In poker, a hand of cards; the cards held by one player in a game. See also BIG MITT.
[ca. 1961 *Hotel Coll*]

mitt joint, *n.* A gambling establishment in which marked cards are used to cheat the unwary player. See also BIG MITT.
[1914 *OEDS*]

mixed canasta, *n.* In canasta, a meld of seven cards or more of the same rank, using wild cards as part of the meld.
[1953 Crawford *Consistent Winner* 349]

mixed pair, *n.* In tournament bridge, a team composed of a woman and a man.
[1950 Morehead *Culbertson* 628]

mog or **mogg,** *v.* In the card game costly colours, to call for another card, an option open only to the first player.
1680 Cotton *Compleat Gamester* 89. . . . then the Eldest is to take his choice whether he will *Mogg* (that is chance a Card or no).
[1674 *OED*]

money, *n.* In the prep. phrase:
in the money, In racing, said of a horse or greyhound that finishes first, second or third in a race. [1928 *OEDS*]

money management, *n.* The effective control of betting by a gambler so that lower amounts are bet on less promising propositions, and higher amounts are bet in situations where the player has a better than even chance to win.
[ca. 1961 *Hotel Coll*]

money player, *n.* A gambler, especially one who plays for high stakes; a HIGH ROLLER.
[1935 *OEDS,* labeled "U.S."]

money plays, *n. clause.* In a casino, a call by a dealer to a pit boss or floorman when a player insists on betting cash rather than chips. If the player wins, he is paid with chips.
[ca. 1961 *Hotel Coll*]

money rider, *n.* In horse racing, a jockey who is well-known for riding winning horses.
[ca. 1961 *Hotel Coll*]

money wheel, *n.* A wheel of fortune that uses denominations of bills in place of numbers.
[ca. 1961 *Hotel Coll*]

monkey, *n.* **1.** A victim of card or dice cheaters; a sucker. See also JOHN.
[n.d. *DAS*]
2. In bets, five hundred pounds in Britain, five hundred dollars in the U.S. *Especially British in use.* [1832 *OED*]

monkey flush, *n.* In poker, three cards of the same suit that are not in a sequence. See also BOBTAIL FLUSH.
[1949 Coffin *Secrets* 181]

monte, *n.* **1.** Short for THREE-CARD MONTE. A form of a swindling game practiced late in the eighteenth century. A BROAD TOSSER, or monte dealer, showed two cards of a low denomination and one card of a high rank (usually a queen) to the victim, then mixed the cards face down on a table and took bets as to which was the high card. All three cards would be of a low rank because the dealer PALMED, or held out, the card with the high rank.
[1841 *DAE,* 1850 *OED*]
2. A Mexican card game popular in the Southwest in the latter part of the eighteenth century. The game featured a pack of forty-five (sometimes forty) cards, and the play was similar to faro.
[1824 *OEDS;* 1841 *DA;* 1844 *DAE*]

monte bank, *n.* **1.** The table on which monte is played. [1845 *DAE*]
2. The pile of money placed in front of the MONTE DEALER, used for paying the winners.
[1890 *DAE*]

monte banker, *n.* The person who runs a monte bank. [1855 *OEDS*]

Monte Carlo wheel, *n.* Also called a EUROPEAN WHEEL. A roulette wheel with one zero, as opposed to the AMERICAN WHEEL, which features a zero and a double-zero, in addition to thirty-six numbers.
[1953 Lewis *Sagebrush Casinos* 104]

monte dealer, *n.* Same as MONTE BANKER.
[1844 *DAE, DA*]

monte layout, *n.* In the game of monte, the arrangement of cards.
[1889 *DAE, DA*]

monte mob, *n.* Also called a BROAD-TOSSING MOB. A team of swindlers who cheat victims by playing THREE-CARD MONTE, a game in which three cards are placed face down on a table and bets are taken on which card has the highest rank.
[1961 Scarne *Complete Guide* 682]

monte sharp, *n.* Same as MONTE TOSSER.
[1851 *DA*]

monte table, *n.* **1.** A gaming establishment at which monte is played.
[1847 *DAE,* 1873 *OEDS*]
2. The MONTE LAYOUT itself.
[1948 *DAE*]

monte thrower, *n.* Same as a MONTE TOSSER.
[1961 Scarne *Complete Guide* 682]

monte tosser, *n.* Also called a BROAD TOSSER or BROAD PITCHER. A cheater who swindles victims by playing THREE-CARD MONTE, a game in

which three cards are placed face down on a table and bets are taken on which card has the highest rank.
[1968 Adams *Western Words*]

moon, *n.* In the phrase:
shoot the moon. In high-low poker, to declare an intention to win the entire pot by having the highest ranking hand and the lowest ranking hand at the same time.
[1968 Wallace *Poker* 219]

mop-squeezer, *n.* A queen in a pack of cards.
[1949 Coffin *Secrets* 182]

morning glory, *n.* A racehorse that performs well in morning workouts but runs poorly in races.
[(1904) 1935 *OEDS*]

morning line, *n.* In horse racing, the initial estimate of odds on each horse in a race. The *morning line* is announced early enough to be printed in the program and in racing forms and is considered a general guide to the actual odds at the time of the race in the afternoon. Compare LATE LINE.
[1955 Hillis *Pari-Mutuel Betting* 115]

mortal cinch, *n.* Also called MORTAL LOCK or MORTAL NUTS. A wager that a bettor feels absolutely cannot be lost. See also IMMORTALS.
[1973 Preston *Play Poker* 168]

mortal lock, *n.* Same as MORTAL CINCH.
[n.d. *DAS*]

mortal nuts, *n.* Same as MORTAL CINCH.
[1978 Brunson *How I Made* 538]

mournival, *n.* In the card game gleek, the holding of four face cards of the same denomination. 1680 Cotton *Compleat Gamester* 68. A *mournival* is either all the Aces, the four Kings, Queens, or Knaves, and a gleek is three of any of the aforesaid.
[1530 *OED,* where many spelling variants are listed: *mornyfele, mournaval, mornevall, mournivall, murnivall, mornivall, mournifal, murrinall, mourneval, murnival*]

mouth bet, *n.* An oral wager; a bet made without putting up money or chips. A mouth bet carries the implicit agreement that the loser will pay the bet immediately. *Mouth bets* are accepted by casino floormen or pit bosses who know the patron well, or by bookmakers who take bets by telephone from players they know. See also CALL BET.
[1949 Coffin *Secrets* 182]

move, *n.* **1.** A sleight of hand used to cheat at cards or dice.
[1961 Scarne *Complete Guide* 682]
2. The action of a dealer paying a winning bet at craps or twenty-one.
[1983 Martinet *Oral Coll*]
3. A sudden burst of speed by a racehorse in the stretch. Compare DRIVE and EXTEND.
[1978 Ainslie *Complete Guide* 293]

move-in, *n.* In no-limit poker, the act of placing all of one's chips in the pot for a final, large bet. 1980 Clark *Oral Coll.* Texas Dolly was sitting there [in a championship hold 'em game] with a queen-ten and just figured the time was ripe. He made the *move-in* and that forced all the money into the pot. He has a sense about when to make the *move-in* . . . that means you put everything in the pot.

mover, *n.* **1.** In craps, a player who puts chips on the layout after the shooter has started the roll.
[1983 Martinez *Gambling Scene* 211]
2. A cheater at cards or dice. Compare SHARP.
[ca. 1961 *Hotel Coll*]

muck, *v.* **1.** To gather cards or chips into a pile.
[ca. 1961 *Hotel Coll*]
2. To palm a card for use later in a game.
[1982 Martin *Introduction* 24]

mucker, *n.* **1.** In panguingue, the dealer.
[1973 Clark *Oral Coll*]
2. In roulette, an assistant to the dealer who collects chips and stacks them according to color. Compare STICKMAN.
[1979 Newman *Dealer's Special* 68]

mud, *v.* In horse racing, to run well on a muddy track.
[1978 Ainslie *Complete Guide* 293]

mud calk, *n.* A shoe for a racehorse designed to grip better on a muddy track.
[1981 Passer *Winning Big* 228]

mudder, *n.* A racehorse that performs well on a muddy track.
[1903 *OEDS,* 1905 *DA*]

muddy track, *n.* A racetrack condition officially listed as between "sloppy" and "heavy." Compare HEAVY TRACK and SLOPPY TRACK.
[1955 Hillis *Pari-Mutuel Betting* 118]

mudlark, *n.* A racehorse that performs well on a muddy track.
[1909 *OEDS, Century Dict.* Supplement]

mud runner, *n.* A racehorse that performs well on a muddy track.
[1905 *OEDS*]

mud sire, *n.* A racehorse that performs well on a muddy track and fathers other horses that run well on a muddy track.
[1955 Hillis *Pari-Mutuel Betting* 116]

muggins, *n.* **1.** In card games like cribbage, the right to take any points the opponent has missed in counting his hand.
[1953 Crawford *Consistent Winner* 349]
2. In dominos, a call made when an opponent notes that a player has miscounted. The player making the call adds the points to his own score. 1950 Morehead *Culbertson* 427. Every fives score must be claimed orally to be recorded. If a player overlooks that he is entitled to a score, any other player may call "*muggins*" and take the score himself.
[1881 *OED,* 1884 *DAE*]

multiple deck, *adj. phr.* In twenty-one, pertaining to a table on which several decks are used at one time, usually with a SHOE, or container for several decks of cards.
[ca. 1961 *Hotel Coll*]

multiplier, *n.* **1.** A slot machine that can receive more than one coin per play, usually 3 or 5, but in some cases up to 15. The payout for additional coins is correspondingly higher than for one coin, but a bonus payout is often offered for playing the maximum number of coins.
[1973 Clark *Oral Coll*]
2. In skat, a card or combination of cards that multiplies the score.
[1950 Morehead *Culbertson* 629]

muscle craps, *n.* A betting variant in craps in which a shooter, after making a point [rolling a 4, 5, 6, 8, 9, or 10], makes an additional bet as to whether he will win or lose the first bet.
[1981 Jenkins *Johnny Moss* 143]

mutuel, *n.* In horse racing, the collective wagering made at a track. See also PARI-MUTUEL.
[1908 *OEDS*]

mutuel handle, *n.* In horse racing, the total amount of money wagered in one day at one track.
[1981 Passer *Winning Big* 239]

mutuel pool, *n.* In horse racing, the total amount of money wagered at the track for one race.
[1971 McQuaid *Gambler's Digest* 311]

mystery payoff, *n.* In slot machines, a combination of aligned symbols that pays coins to a player. The player knows only that some such payment is possible, but the combination of symbols is not posted on the machine.
[1973 Clark *Oral Coll*]

N

N, *n.* **1.** In games like bridge and whist, an abbreviation for the position labeled *North.* See N-S, E-W.
[1950 Morehead *Culbertson* 629]
2. In horse racing, an abbreviation for NOSE, as a measurement of length.
[1955 Hillis *Pari-Mutuel Betting* 89]

nab, *v.* To turn a die with a finger after it has been cast. See also COG (def. 2) and NAP.
[1706 *OED*]

nag, *n.* **1.** An inferior race horse.
[1951 *DAS;* compare c1400 *OED,* meaning "a small riding horse or pony"]
2. In cards, a queen.
[1983 Martinet *Oral Coll*]

nail, *v.* **1.** To mark a playing card with a thumbnail or pin so that it can be recognized from the back. Compare BEND.
[1890 Quinn *Fools of Fortune* 237]
2. In poker, to draw the specific card required to win the pot.
[1978 Brunson *How I Made* 538]

Names. The most colorful names are those used in rhyming slang, such as these from dice: ADA ROSS THE STABLE HOSS which relies upon a personal name; EIGHTER FROM DECATUR and NINA FROM CAROLINA rely upon geograpical names; BIG DICK FROM BATTLE CREEK relies upon a pronounciation variation in which *creek* is to be pronounced /krik/ and the choice of *dick* is influenced by French *dix,* for "ten."

A metaphorical connection is behind most of the formations such as: AMERICAN AIRLINES (two red aces), KU KLUX KLAN (three kings), BARBARA HUTTON (for the dimestore heiress), JACK BENNY (his aging stopped at 39), WASHINGTON MONUMENT (it is 555 feet high). WHERE'S BUSTER BROWN is more complicated because the reference to BUSTERS, as a nickname for gaffed dice, is partially obscured by the popular association with Buster Brown Shoes for which the logo is a boy named Buster Brown and his dog who live in the shoes—their picture is on the label in the heel of the shoe.

Other company names appropriated to gambling contexts include: OLDSMOBILE (98 is a model moniker), HART, SCHAFFNER AND MARX (three jacks, for the haberdasher), WOOLWORTH (same as BARBARA HUTTON), and AJAX, also called FOAMY CLEANSER, (for an ace and a jack).

Personal given names appear in the expressions: GEORGE and the feminine counterpart GEORGETTE (for male and female tippers) which contrast with TOMS (non-tippers); JOHN (for a mark), and LARRY (for the last bettor). TONI and OLD BILL are code words among cheaters, especially in the presence of a SQUARE JOHN.

Family names yield such entries as HEMINGWAY (for a gambler). The nickname STONEWALL JACKSON (for a poor tipper or conservative player) is a similar process. JONAH is a biblical reference to proverbial bad luck, ROBIN-HOOD

CHEATER is from English legend. BRODERICK CRAWFORD comes from the motion picture industry. GARY COOPER, also shortened to COOP, is a reference to two 6s because of his association with the movie "High Noon." Indeed, HIGH NOON is also used to refer to the same phenomenon. KOJACK (for king and a jack) is drawn from the television character's name. DOLLY PARTON (for snake eyes) comes from the entertainment industry.

Ethnic connotations arise in AFRICAN GOLFER (a DICER), CHINESE LOTTERY, MEXICAN STANDOFF, and SCOTCH STRAIGHT.

Geographical names contribute these entries: ALAMEDA STRAIGHT (from California), ARKANSAS FLUSH, BIG JOE FROM BOSTON, BROADWAY, CALIFORNIA FOURTEENS, CALIFORNIA PRAYERBOOK, CALIFORNIA C-NOTE, GARDENA MIRACLE (from California), ELK RIVER, CURSE OF SCOTLAND, LAS VEGAS RIFFLE, KENTUCKY SETUP, MARQUIS OF QUEENSBERRY RULES, PHILADELPHIA LAYOUT, and TEXAS SUNFLOWER. A KING CRAB, in cards, consists of a king and a 3. Because a 3 can also be called a CRAB (especially in dice) the variant term ALASKA HAND developed because Alaskan waters are noted for KING CRABS.

For a different point of view on names in gambling see Clark, Thomas, "Noms de Felt: Names in Gambling," *Names,* 34 (1986), pp. 11-29.

nap, *v.* **1.** In dice games, to turn a die with a finger after the roll. See also COG (def. 2) and NAB.
[1673 *OED;* compare quote 1688]
2. To recommend a horse or greyhound as the probable winner in a race; to TIP. Compare NAP SELECTION.
[1927 *OEDS*]

nap, *n.* **1.** In napoleon, a bid to win all the tricks in one hand.
[1899 *OED*]
2. In tresette, a variant of napolitano, an ace, deuce, and trey of the same suit.
[1950 Morehead *Culbertson* 629]

nap selection, *n.* Also shortened to **nap.** A tip that a horse or greyhound is likely to win a particular race.
[1895 *OEDS,* as *nap;* 1927 *OEDS,* for *nap selection*]

natural, *n.* **1.** Generally, an unbeatable combination in gambling at cards or dice that is realized at the first deal of the cards or the first roll of the dice.
[1949 Blanche *You Can't Win* 23]
[1762 *OEDS*]
2. In twenty-one, an ace and any card worth ten points dealt as the first two cards.
[1830 *OED*]
3. In baccarat, a point count of eight or nine on the first two cards dealt to player or bank.
[ca. 1961 *Hotel Coll*]
4. In poker, a high ranking hand without benefit of a wild card.
[1949 Coffin *Secrets* 182]
5. In craps, the number 7 or 11 on the first roll. See also nick.
[1897 *OED,* 1935 *DA*]

natural canasta, *n.* In canasta, a meld of seven or more cards, none of which are wild. Compare NATURAL (def. 4).
[1953 Crawford *Consistent Winner* 350]

natural card, *n.* In poker, a card that is not designated as wild, or allowed to serve at a different value than its index or suit. Compare NATURAL (def. 4).
[1950 Morehead *Culbertson* 629]

natural eight, *n.* In craps, a roll of two 4s on the dice; a hardway eight. Compare NATURAL (def. 4).
[ca. 1961 *Hotel Coll*]

natural jacks, *n.* A variant of draw poker in which no ante is made by the dealer or the players.
[1949 Coffin *Secrets* 182]

natural point, *n.* In games like canasta or cribbage, a point that is scored automatically by circumstances of the deal, such as turning up a jack in cribbage.
[1950 Morehead *Culbertson* 629]

Neapolitan martingale *n.* A method for wagering in which the player alters the sizes of the stakes for each hand, usually in cycles of every four bets. See also MARTINGALE.
[1976 Figgis *Gambler's Handbook* 32]

near, *adj.* Left.
[1559 *OED*]

near side, *n.* In horse racing, the left side of the horse; the side of the horse closest to the inside rail. [1610 *OED*]

neck, *n.* In horse racing. **1.** a unit of measurement, about one-quarter of a length. Compare LENGTH and NOSE.
[1823 *OEDS,* 1851 *DA*]
2. In the phrase:
by a neck, with a margin of about one quarter of a length.
[1823 *OEDS*]

neck and neck, *n. phr.* Also written **neck-and-neck,** especially adjectivally and adverbially. In horse racing, two or more horses running nearly parallel to one another.
[1799 *OEDS*]

needle, *n.* **1.** A card set slightly askew by a cheating dealer so that a confederate knows where to cut a deck of stacked cards.
1891 Hoffman *Baccarat* 78. Some cardsharpers, in lieu of the bridge, employ what is known as the "*needle,*" a card so placed that its edge shall project to an infinitesimal extent beyond the rest of the pack. This card just precedes the arranged series, so that the confederate, cutting next

below it, at once brings such series into operation.
2. A cheat.
[*a*1790 *OED*]
3. needles, *pl.* In poker, a pair of aces.
1983 Martinet *Oral Coll.* There are different names for aces because they are so important to a hand: eyes of Texas, *needles,* and some special ones like American Airlines, two red aces.

needle movement, *n.* Same as a NEEDLE SQUEEZE.
[1890 Quinn *Fools of Fortune* 200]

needle squeeze, *n.* In faro, a dishonest DEALING BOX with a small lever, or *needle,* that the dealer can push, or *squeeze,* to deal a selected card rather than the top card. See also NEEDLE MOVEMENT.
[1983 Asbury *Sucker's Progress* 12]

needle wheel, *n.* **1.** A dishonest wheel of fortune once common at fairgrounds, which stood perpendicular to the ground and was controlled by the operator applying pressure to a brake on the back of the wheel.
[1890 Quinn *Fools of Fortune* 286]
2. A rigged roulette wheel modeled after the fairground *needle wheel.*
[1890 Quinn *Fools of Fortune* 250]

negative, *n.* In craps, the DON'T PASS line.
1983 Martinet *Oral Coll.* Then he said, "I feel a little guilty because I shot from the *negative* and cleaned up, while everybody else was getting dumped [losing] on the pass line."
[So called because the player is betting that the dice will not pass.]

negative double, *n.* Same as TAKEOUT DOUBLE.
1950 Morehead *Culbertson* 148. The principle conventions in general use are: takeout double (or informatory double, or *negative double*). A double of an opponent's suit-bid of one, two, or three requests partner to bid his longest and strongest suit.

negative progression system, *n.* Any of a variety of betting strategies in which a player doubles the stakes after a loss. Compare MARTINGALE and PROGRESSIVE SYSTEM.
1983 Martinet *Oral Coll.* I've never seen a *negative progression system* do what it's supposed to do. Figure it out. If you are on a bad streak at craps or twenty-one, you keep doubling your losses. The only time you make money is when you're on a hot streak and double your winnings. When you're losing, drop back to minimum bets.
[Compare *progression c*1430 *OED,* in the mathematical sense]

neighbors, *n. pl.* On a roulette layout, the numbers adjacent to the winning number.
[ca. 1961 *Hotel Coll*]

nell, *n.* In jass or klaberjass, the nine of trumps.
[1950 Morehead *Culbertson* 629]
[Shortened and altered from MENEL.]

Nevada Gaming Control Act, *n.* The law passed by the Nevada state legislature and made effective by the governor on March 19, 1931, legalizing gambling in Nevada.
[1931 *Nevada Revised Statutes* 4]

Nevada lettuce, *n.* A one-thousand dollar bill.
[ca. 1961 *Hotel Coll*]
[Compare *lettuce,* 1929 *OEDS,* meaning "money"]

Nevada nickle, *n.* A five-dollar chip. *Rare.* See also NICKLE and RED.
[1979 Newman *Dealer's Special* 32]

New York craps, *n.* In bank craps, the practice of charging five percent of a wager to the player wishing to bet on the number 4, 5, 6, 8, 9, or 10 before the shooter has established a point from among those numbers. Compare FLAT and PLACE BET.
1985 Martinet *Oral Coll. New York craps* is charging five percent vig for placing. In Nevada, that became a place bet, in which the first unit bet is paid flat [at even money] and the rest of the bet at true odds.

nick, *n.* **1.** In hazard, a roll of the dice that wins automatically. The winning number is usually 11. See quotation at HAZARD: 1680 Cotton *Compleat Gamester.*
[*a*1635 *OED*]
2. In craps, a roll of 7 or 11 on the COME OUT, or first roll of the dice; a NATURAL.
[1938 Asbury *Sucker's Progress* 40]
3. Short for NICKLE. In a casino, a five-dollar chip; a RED.
[ca. 1961 *Hotel Coll*]

nick, *v.* **1.** In hazard, to win by casting a NICK (def. 1). [*a*1553 *OED*]
2. To gamble. [1676 *OED*]

nick joint, *n.* A gambling establishment devoted to cheating victims.
[1978 Nelson *Gaming* 78]

nickle, *n.* **1.** Also called a RED. In a casino, a five-dollar chip.
[1978 Brunson *How I Made* 538]
2. nickles, *pl.* In craps, a roll of two 5s on the dice; a HARDWAY 10.
[1983 Martinet *Oral Coll*]
[Compare 1883 OED, 1881 *DA, DAE,* meaning "a five cent piece"; compare *five-cent nickel* 1875 *DAE*]

nickle-dime-quarter, *n.* Also shortened to **nickle-dime.** In poker, a game played for small stakes.
[1968 Wallace *Poker* 219]

nickles and dimes, *n. pl. Plural in form, but singular in use.* Also called a BARBARA HUTTON or WOOLWORTH. In hold 'em, a 5 and a 10 as the first two cards dealt.
1981 Golad *Oral Coll.* You sit there holding those two cards for such a long time that after awhile they get names . . . A Barbara Hutton is nickles and dimes or a *Woolworth,* from the dime store heiress.

nigger bet, *n.* An unusual or unlikely amount wagered, such as nine or thirteen dollars in a game where the common wager is ten dollars. *Now usually considered offensive.*
[1968 Wallace *Poker* 219]

nigger-luck, *n.* Unexpected good fortune; an unusual turn of events that results in winning a bet thought lost, such as the first horse being disqualified after a race in which the player had bet on the horse that ran second. *Now usually considered offensive.*
[1851 *DA, DAE, OEDS*]

nightcap, *n.* **1.** In horse racing, the final race of the day at a particular track.
[1939 *OEDS*, in *Webster's NID* 2nd ed.]
2. In sports books, the final race of the day from among all the tracks carried by a betting establishment.
[1973 Clark *Oral Coll*]

nina, *n.* In craps, the first element in a number of rhyming expressions referring to a roll of 9 on the dice: *nina from Argentina, nina from Carolina, nina ross (the stable hoss),* and *nina, nina, ocean liner.* Compare EIGHTER FROM DECATUR.
[1950 Morehead *Culbertson* 630]

nine of hearts, *n.* In horse racing, a horse with little or no chance to win.
[1983 Martinez *Gambling Scene* 211]

nine square, *n.* On a faro layout, the betting section enclosing the numbers 9, 8, 6, and 5.
[1938 Asbury *Sucker's Progress* 8]

nineteen hand, *n.* Also shortened to **nineteen.** In cribbage, a hand, usually the crib worth no points. A score of nineteen points in the hand is impossible.

ninety days, *n. Plural in form, but singular in use.* In craps, the number nine rolled on the dice, especially as the first, or point, roll.
1978 Clark *Oral Coll.* You can hear any oldtimer use *ninety days* for the point nine. Back in Steubenville [Ohio] and Covington [Kentucky], that was a standard sentence for getting caught running a game.

nits and lice, *n. phr.* In poker, two small pairs of cards, especially a pair of twos and a pair of threes. See also MITES AND LICE.
[1949 Coffin *Secrets* 182]

nob, *n.* Same as HIS KNOB.
[1821 *OED,* see HIS NOB]

no bet, *n. phr.* In bank craps, a call by the stickman or dealer to a player who makes an unclear bet or puts chips on the layout after the shooter has started his throw.
[1949 Coffin *Secrets* 182]

noddy, *n.* **1.** Same as HIS KNOB.
1824 Anon *Hoyle's* 32. If the hand at cribbage reveals the knave or *noddy,* of the same suit as was turned up, 1 point.
[1611 *OED*]
2. Also called **cribbage noddy.** A card game similar to cribbage.
[1589 *OED;* perhaps related to *noddy a*1530 *OED*, meaning "a fool," possibly related to *nod* (1386 *OED),* meaning "to make a quick inclination of the head"]

no dice, *n. phr.* Also called NO ROLL. In craps, a call by the operator of the game, indicating the roll of the dice is unacceptable. For example, a die may bounce off the playing surface or lean against a chip.
[(1950) 1981 Maurer *Lang. of the Underworld* 189]
[n.d. *DSUE*]

no limit, *adj.* In poker, pertaining to a game that has no maximum bet size. See also UNLIMITED POKER. [1915 *OEDS*]

non-commoquer, *n.* In panguingue, an ace or a king. In forming a meld group with *non-commoquers,* suits are unimportant. Compare COMMOQUER.
[1950 Morehead *Culbertson* 630]

nonproducer, *n.* In a casino, a player, usually a professional gambler, who wins consistently.
[1953 Fairfield *Las Vegas* 15]

no roll, *n.* Same as NO DICE.
[ca. 1961 *Hotel Coll*]

nose, *n.* In horse racing, **1.** a unit of length ranging from centimeters to several inches; generally, a very short distance of three feet or less; the smallest margin for winning a race. See also NECK. [1908 *OEDS*]
2. In the phrases:
by a nose, Pertaining to winning a race by a very small margin. [1908 *OEDS*]
on the nose, To make a bet on an entry to win, as opposed to betting PLACE (among the first two to finish) or SHOW (among the first three to finish). [1951 *OEDS*]

nose out, *v. phr.* In horse racing, to win by a very short distance. [n.d. *DAS*]

no trump, *n.* Also **no trumps.** In bridge, a hand played without a specific suit as trump.
[1899 *OEDS*, as "no trumps"]

N-S, E-W, *n.* In bridge and whist, an abbreviation for the compass points *N*orth, *S*outh, *E*ast, and *W*est, used to designate partners at a table. North and South positions constitute one team of players; East and West positions constitute the other.
[1953 Crawford *Consistent Winner* 350]

number, *n.* **1.** In craps, a POINT; any roll of the dice in craps [4, 5, 6, 8, 9, 10] which must be repeated before casting a 7.
[(1950) 1981 Maurer *Lang. of the Underworld* 189]
2. numbers, *pl. Plural in form, but singular in use.* Also called BUTTER AND EGGS or THE BUG or CLEARING HOUSE or **numbers game.** Any of a variety of illegal lottery games that use numbers

to determine winners. See also PLAY THE NUMBERS and POLICY. Compare LOTTERY and LOTTO.
[1897 *DA, OEDS,* as *numbers game*; 1949 *OEDS,* as *numbers racket; DA* reports: "The 'numbers' racket is known by different names in various sections of the country—*the numbers, policy, clearing house, butter and eggs,* and *the bug.*]

number count, *n.* In twenty-one, a memory system used to note all cards as they are played, used by gamblers to change betting strategy when certain cards are yet undealt, to improve their odds against the house.
[1973 Friedman *Casino Games* 31]

numbers bet, *n.* In hazard and chuck-a-luck, a wager on a specific number to be thrown on the next roll of the dice.
[1964 Wykes *Illustrated Guide* 328]

numbers drop, *n.* A session of betting in a NUMBERS game.
[1968 *OEDS*]

numbers man, *n.* Also clipped to **number man.** Same as NUMBERS RUNNER.
[1950 *OEDS,* as *number man*]

numbers player, *n.* In racing, keno and numbers, a bettor who uses certain numbers in wagering, such as birthdates, lucky numbers, or numbers occurring in dreams.
[1979 Clark *Oral Coll.* You can find all sorts of *dream books* around here . . . Those are little pamphlets that interpret dreams for the *numbers player.* Say you dream of a white horse or flying. You can look it up and the dream book might tell you to play a washerwoman's gig or something like that.

numbers racket, *n.* An illegally operated policy enterprise. [1949 *OEDS*]

numbers runner, *n.* Also **number runner.** A person who collects bets of people playing a NUMBERS game and who delivers payments to the winners.
[1958 *OEDS,* for *numbers runner;* 1950 for *number runner*]

number two man, *n. phr.* **1.** A dealer adept at dealing the second card from the top of the deck.
[1961 Scarne *Complete Guide* 682]
2. In a casino, the second highest employee, usually responsible for one of the three shifts in the casino.
[1973 Clark *Oral Coll*]

nut, *n.* The daily operating expenses of a casino or a professional gambler; generally, the amount of money an enterprise is required to raise before realizing a profit.
[(1912) 1955 *OEDS*]

nut flush, *n.* In poker, an ace-high flush.
[1973 Preston *Play Poker* 168]

nut hand, *n.* In poker, an unbeatable hand.
[ca. 1961 *Hotel Coll*]

nutman, *n.* A professional gambler. *Often derogatory in use.*
[ca. 1961 *Hotel Coll*]
[(1950) 1981 Maurer *Lang. of the Underworld* 189]

nut player, *n.* In poker, a very conservative player who makes large bets warily and often only when holding a strong hand.
[1979 Brunson *How I Made* 539]

nuts, *n. pl. Plural in form, but singular in use.* Same as IMMORTALS.
[1961 Smith and Noble *Quit Winners* 211]
[Compare 1932 *OEDS,* meaning "any person or thing of superior quality"]

O

objection, *n.* In horse racing, a claim of a foul committed by a jockey, which must be lodged within five minutes of the post-race weigh-in by a jockey, a horse's owner, or the track steward.
[1898 *OEDS*]

odd, *n.* **1.** In faro, a dishonest deck with one extra card inserted by the dealer.
[1968 Adams *Western Words*]
2. In roulette, an area on the table layout for placing a bet that the next number spun on the wheel will be odd rather than even.
[ca. 1961 *Hotel Coll*]

odd-even, *n.* In faro, a betting system that requires a player to alternate wagers on an even-numbered card or an odd-numbered card at each turn. [1943 Maurer *Argot*]

odds, *n. pl.* **1.** The advantage in a wagering situation acknowledged by one party in proportion to the disadvantage of the other party, hence the bettor with the advantage must offer a higher stake on the outcome than the bettor with the disadvantage.
[1597 *OED*]

2. The probability of a particular event's occurrence, stated in terms of a ratio, which in gambling refers to the amount of return on a wager that is negotiated between the betting parties, not to statistical probability. For example, a casino may offer to pay thirty units for each unit bet that the next roll on a pair of dice will result in the number 12. Statistically, the probability of such an event is one in thirty-six. [ca. 1961 *Hotel Coll*]
3. In compounds and phrases: BACK LINE ODDS and DOUBLE ODDS.

odds bet, *n.* In bank craps, a wager made in addition to the original line wager after the shooter has established a point [rolled the number 4, 5, 6, 8, 9, or 10]. The amount of the *odds bet* is determined by the size of the original wager and the POINT.
[1982 Martin *Introduction* 15]

odds board, *n.* In racing and jai alai, the lighted display that carries information about wagering propositions offered for each entry. See also TOTALISATOR.
[ca. 1961 *Hotel Coll*]

odds maker, *n.* The employee of a bookmaking establishment who determines the amount that shall be offered to players who win specific bets.
[ca. 1961 *Hotel Coll*]

odds-on, *adj.* Pertaining to a wagering event in which the probability of a particular outcome is so high that the amount a player wins will be less than he was required to stake.
[1917 *OEDS*]

odds-on, *n.* The state of betting when odds are laid. [1928 *OEDS*]

odds-on favorite, *n.* In horse racing, a horse so highly favored to win that a player will win less than even money if the bet is made and won.
[1898 *OED,* 1941 *OEDS,* as *odds-on favourite*]

odd trick, *n.* In games like whist, the seventh trick; each trick taken by either side beyond the sixth trick.
[1950 Morehead *Culbertson* 630]

off, *adj.* **1.** Pertaining to bets or parts of bets that are declared invalid or "not working." In bank craps, for example, the dealer will announce that certain wagers on the table are inactive during a specific event. On the COME-OUT, or first roll by a shooter, the dealer will announce that HARDWAY bets, odds bets on previously established points, place bets, and buy bets are *off,* or inactive for that roll of the dice.
2. Of or pertaining to gambling equipment such as cards, dice, a roulette wheel, and so on, altered for purposes of cheating.
1983 Martinet *Oral Coll.* Different statements mean different things to people, depending on whether they are casual players or actually working in the business. Usually, if a player says the dice are *off,* nobody thinks anything about it because the player probably means they are cold. But if a dealer says it, watch the boxman jump for the dice. That means somebody slipped a gaff [put a false die into the game].
3. Of or pertaining to racetracks that are muddy or slippery. Compare HEAVY TRACK and MUDDY TRACK.
[1978 Ainslie *Complete Guide* 294]
4. Righthand side. Compare NEAR.
[1675 *OED*]
5. Of or pertaining to poor performance of dice or an entry in a race.
[1846 *DA, DAE*]

off, *n.* The start of a race.
[(1951) 1981 Maurer *Lang. of the Underworld* 220]

off, *adv.* **1.** In bank craps, a common confusion with the term DOWN.
1983 Martinet *Oral Coll.* You'll hear players who want a placed number down after it wins say to the dealer, "Take if off." What they should say is, "Take it down," which means the place bet won and they don't want to leave the original bet on the number after they've taken the winnings.
2. In racing, away from the start, especially: "*They're off* !"
[1833 *OEDS*]

off, *prep.* In the phrases:
off pace, In racing, pertaining to an entry running behind the leaders. Compare OFF, *adj.* (def. 5).
[ca. 1961 *Hotel Coll*]
off the board, 1. In racing, pertaining to an entry that finishes in fifth position or later.
[1978 Ainslie *Complete Guide* 294]
2. In sports books, pertaining to a sporting event on which bookmakers will accept no bets.
[ca. 1961 *Hotel Coll*]
3. In pari-mutuel betting, pertaining to an entry against which the odds are 99 to 1, or higher.
[1978 Ainslie *Complete Guide* 294]
off-the-street, In a casino, of or pertaining to players or dealers not sought after by the management. Thus, *off-the-street trade* refers to players who come into an establishment because they are passing by rather than because of any advertising or coaxing by representatives of the casino; *off-the-street dealer* refers to a card or dice dealer who applies for a job without knowing anyone in a management position.
[1977 Anness *Dummy Up*]
[Compare 1930 *OEDS,* meaning "the ordinary people"]
off the top, In wagering events, pertaining to money removed from the gross before anything else is done with it. For example, in racing, a percentage of the total amount wagered is deducted "off the top" by the management before the rest is distributed to the winners. See also SKIM.
[1960 Cook *Gambling, Inc.* 301]

off card, *n.* In rummy, a playing card that is not part of a meld or a useful combination of cards. [1950 Morehead *Culbertson* 630]

offensive bet, *n.* In poker, a bet made by a player with a strong hand who wishes to make a larger pot.
[1968 Wallace *Poker* 220]

offensive strength, *n.* In bridge, cards held in the hand that can be expected to win tricks.
[1950 Morehead *Culbertson* 630]

office, *n.* In the phrase: **the office.** A sign or gesture to a confederate, especially that a cheating move is about to take place.
[1803 *OED,* as *give the office*]
2. In the phrases:
give the office or **tip the office,** In horse racing, to pass on supposedly private information about a horse or a race.
1889 Ellangowan *Sporting Anecdotes* 336. *Office, to give the,* or sometimes to *tip the office,* is not necessarily a dishonest proceeding, but is simply to give private and exclusive information; and we often hear men assure their friends they "have it straight" from owner, trainer, or jockey.
[19th Century *DSUE*]

office hours, *n. pl. Plural in form, but singular in use.* **1.** In poker, a straight with the cards numbered 4 through 8 or 5 through 9.
[Compare 1802 *OEDS,* meaning "the normal working time in an office or other business"]
2. In poker, two pairs, 9s and 5s or 8s and 4s.
[1949 Coffin *Secrets* 182]

office pool, *n.* An informal mutuel wagering system, usually for special sporting events such as football or baseball playoffs, in which several persons in an office, bar, or place of business put an agreed-upon amount of money into a pot, or *pool,* then select or are assigned a potential score, the winner or winners taking the amount in the *pool.*
[1971 McQuaid *Gambler's Digest* 312]

official, *adj.* Of or pertaining to the results of a race, indicating that the initial posting of the results are final and all winners can be paid.
[1950 Morehead *Culbertson* 630]
[Compare 1854 *OED,* meaning "authorized; authoritative"]

off-number, *n.* In craps, a number rolled that is not a CRAP (2, 3, 12), a NATURAL (7,11), or the POINT. The point can be 4, 5, 6, 8, 9, or 10. Whichever of these is the point of the shooter, the others are *off numbers.*
[1950 Morehead *Culbertson* 630]

offset, *v.* In craps, to cock chips atop a bet, indicating that the player has taken odds on the bet.
[1973 Clark *Oral Coll*]

off side, *n.* In horse racing, the right side of the horse; the side of the horse to the outside of the rail. [1675 *OED*]

offsuit, *adj.* In seven-card stud and hold 'em poker, pertaining to HOLE CARDS that are of different suits.
[1976 Sklansky *Hold 'em Poker*]

off-suit, *n.* A playing card not of the same suit as earlier or other cards.
[1978 Brunson *How I Made* 539]

off-track betting, *n.* Abbreviated OTB. Wagering conducted at a legal gambling establishment located away from the racetrack. Compare ON-TRACK BETTING.
[1960 Cook *Gambling, Inc.* 283]
[1964 *OEDS*]

old bill, *n.* A code phrase used among professional gamblers that, when said with an open palm, asks another player, "Are you a cheater?"
[1961 Scarne *Complete Guide* 683]

old sledge, *n.* Another name for the card game of SEVEN UP.
1843 Green *Exposure* 239. According to Mr. Hoyle, the points to be made before the game is concluded are ten; they are now universally reduced to seven; and the game is most commonly called "seven up" or "*old sledge.*"
[1834 *DAE;* 1837 *OED*]

Oldsmobile, *n.* In hold 'em poker, an 9 and 8 as the first two cards dealt to the same hand.
1981 Golad *Oral Coll.* You sit there for such a long time with just those two cards that after awhile they get names . . . *Oldsmobile* is an 8 and a 9. Its from the model of the car, the ninety-eight.

old thing, *n.* Another name for FARO.
[1943 Maurer *Argot*]
[The reference can also be to syphilis, and implies that the game is crooked, or braced.]

ombre, *n.* **1.** A card game of Spanish origin, popular in the 17th–18th centuries, played by three persons using a deck with forty cards in which ranks 8, 9, and 10 are removed from a standard 52-card pack. *Rare.*
[1660 *OED,* as *hombre,* ultimately from Spanish *hombre* man, because the player who declares he will win says: "I am the man."]
2. The player in ombre who undertakes to win the contract. [1727 *OED*]

on, *adj.* In craps, pertaining to a bet in operation on a specific number during any specific roll, such as the come-out (first) roll.
1983 Martinet *Oral Coll.* On the come-out, you put a button on a come bet, that is a wager made originally on the come line but [is then moved to] a specific number, to signify the bet is *on.* That means the bet is working, along with the odds on it.

on, *prep.* **1.** At stake.
1979 Clark *Oral Coll.* There are a lot of big games this weekend. Do you have any bets *on*?
2. In the following prepositional phrases:
on a roll, having a streak of success, victories, or

intense activity. Compare ROLL (def. 2. a., b.)
[1980 *BDC*, II: 4, 117]
→ Used as a particle in conjunction with a verb.
on board, In hold 'em poker, pertaining to the community cards placed face up in the middle of the table during the betting rounds.
[1976 Sklansky *Hold 'em Poker* 7]
on deck, Same as ON BOARD.
[1981 Golad *Oral Coll*]
on edge, In horse racing, pertaining to a horse that is in good condition for a race and can be expected to run at its best.
[1981 Passer *Winning Big* 232]
on the bank, 1. In baccarat, pertaining to the spot on the table layout where a bet can be made on the side of the bank rather than the side of the player.
[1968 Thackrey *Nick the Greek* 140]
2. In poker, pertaining to having no stake in the pot.
[1978 Brunson *How I Made* 539]
on the bar, 1. In backgammon, pertaining to a STONE, or piece, that has been HIT by an opponent and is awaiting reentry to the board.
[1974 Scarne *Dice* 320]
2. In craps, pertaining to a wager on the DON'T PASS LINE.
[1950 Morehead *Culbertson* 631]
on the Bill Daly, In horse racing, pertaining to a jockey in the leading position during a race.
[1983 Martinez *Gambling Scene* 212]
[1941 *DAS*, named "after 'Father' *Bill Daly*, the famous jockey instructor, who always advised his pupils to take the lead and keep it"]
on the bit, In horse racing, pertaining to a horse that is eagerly straining against the bit, but is prevented from running freely by the jockey.
[1974 Ewart *Flatracing* 150]
on the chin strap, In horse racing, pertaining to winning a race by a long distance.
[1978 Ainslie *Complete Guide* 294]
on the come, 1. In poker, pertaining to wagering on an unfilled flush or straight before all the cards have been dealt.
[ca. 1961 *Hotel Coll*]
2. In bank craps, said of a wager placed in the COME area of the layout.
[1973 Clark *Oral Coll*]
on the cuff bet, 1. A wager allowed to a player without presenting money. See also FINGER BET.
2. In poker, pertaining to a betting round in which all the players CHECK, i.e. do not bet.
[ca. 1961 *Hotel Coll*]
on the finger, Pertaining to a wager made without money changing hands before the event bet on is finished.
[1978 Larson *Vocabulary* 98]
on the floor, hit the door, In craps, pertaining to a die bouncing off the table. See also DIE ON THE FLOOR, SEVEN AT THE DOOR.
1983 Martinet *Oral Coll. On the floor, hit the door* is a piece of folk wisdom. It has to do with the supersitition that if a die goes down, a 7 will be rolled next. So it says if a die goes down, pull your bets. Another form of that is "die on the floor, seven at the door."
on the gamble, Engaged in a gambling game or in a spell of gambling.
[1887 *OED*]
on the hop, In craps, same as ON THE TURN. (def. 2).
[1973 Clark *Oral Coll*]
on the nose, See NOSE.
[1955 Hillis *Pari-Mutuel Betting* 117]
on the outs, See OUT, *n.*
on the piece, In poker, pertaining to chips placed atop currency.
[ca. 1961 *Hotel Coll*]
on the rail, 1. Also **on the rails.** In horse racing, pertaining to a horse running close to the inside rail.
[1971 McQuaid *Gambler's Digest* 312]
[1928 *OEDS*, as *on the rails*]
2. In craps, pertaining to a die that bounces from the layout to the top of the table edge and lands in the grooves where players keep their chips. Compare RAIL (def. 2).
[1983 Martinet *Oral Coll*]
on the square, 1. In card games, pertaining to a deck that is smooth on all four edges, indicating that no cards have been trimmed and the game is presumably honest. Compare CORNER BEND and STRIPPERS.
[ca. 1961 *Hotel Coll*]
2. In dice games, pertaining to dice that are true to within one ten-thousandth of an inch and therefore the game in which they are used can be presumed honest. Compare BARR DICE and CALIPERS and CANDY STORE DICE.
[ca. 1961 *Hotel Coll*]
on the take, Receiving bribes to ignore duties. For example, a law official may be *on the take* to ignore an illegal game, or a sports participant *on the take* may insure that an opponent wins.
[1977 Carroll *Playboy's Illustrated* 44]
[1930 *OEDS*]
on the turn, 1. In hold 'em poker, the card that completes a flush or straight for a hand, usually said of the sixth or seventh card dealt.
2. In craps, the next roll of the dice. See also ON THE HOP.
1984 Martinet *Oral Coll.* When a player wants to make a bet that will win or lose on the next roll of the dice, he throws a check to the stick and says "on the hop" or "*on the turn*," or "bullfrog it."
on the up-and-up, Pertaining to an honest game.
[1863 *DA, OEDS,* under "up"]
on tilt, In an inept fashion; badly. Especially said of a poker player who becomes angry or frustrated and begins playing without caution.
[1978 Brunson *How I Made* 539]
on top, Pertaining to a winner or a potential winner, as a favorite in a horse race.
[1978 Ainslie *Complete Guide* 294]

on bet, *n.* In the phrase:
the on bet. In poker, the first wager made in a betting round.
[1949 Coffin *Secrets* 182]

on-track betting, *n.* The pari-mutuel at a race track, as opposed to OFF-TRACK BETTING, which has no effect on the odds determined at the race track.
[1960 Cook *Gambling, Inc.* 283]

once around, *adj. phr.* In cribbage, a game played to 61 points rather than the normal 121 points.
[1953 Crawford *Consistent Winner* 350]

once-only book, *n.* In a casino pit, a record of regular patrons who have lost all their money and have been assisted with a small amount of money to leave or return home.
[1953 Lewis *Sagebrush Casinos* 152]

one-armed bandit, *n.* Also **one-arm bandit.** A slot machine.
[1940 *DA,* 1938 *OEDS;* So called because a single lever is usually mounted on the machine to be pulled by the right hand of the player, and because the odds of winning are poor.]

one-armed banditry, *adj. phr.* Pertaining to gambling machines generally. *Pejorative.*
[1949 *DA*]

one big one, *n.* A one-thousand dollar bill.
[ca. 1961 *Hotel Coll*]

one down, *adv.* In craps, an oral call by the stickman, made when a die bounces off the table. See also DICE ON THE FLOOR, SEVEN AT THE DOOR.
[1974 Scarne *Dice*]

one down inside, *adv.* In craps, an oral call by the stickman, made when a die bounces off the table and lands on the pit side of the table rather than the players' side.
[1983 Martinet *Oral Coll*]

one-ended straight, *n.* Also called **one-end straight** or ONE-WAY STRAIGHT. In poker, a sequence of four cards: either ace, deuce, trey, four or jack, queen, king, ace. The player holding such a hand must receive a card of a specific rank (either 5 or 10) to successfully complete a straight. See also OPEN-ENDED STRAIGHT.
[1949 Coffin *Secrets* 182]

one-eyed jack, *n.* In playing cards, a jack of spades or a jack of hearts, both of which are pictured in profile, sometimes designated as wild in poker.
[1963 Steig *Common Sense* 185]

one-eyed king, *n.* In playing cards, the king of diamonds, portrayed in profile.
[1963 Steig *Common Sense* 186]

one-eyed man in the game, *n. phr.* In poker, an oral code indicating that a cheater is playing in the game.
[1938 Asbury *Sucker's Progress* 350]
[Compare *one-eyed:* 1833 *OEDS,* meaning "dishonest"]

one-half game, *n.* In Nevada casinos, a designation of certain games for taxing purposes. A *one-half game* is any game with a table layout other than craps, roulette, or twenty-one, such as faro, the wheel of fortune, big six, chuck-a-luck and other side games.
[1957 *Nevada Gaming Regulations* 6]

one hand on the dice, *n. phr.* In bank craps, a command from the stickman or boxman to a player to pick up and throw the dice with a single hand. Compare NO DICE and NO ROLL.
1984 Martinet *Oral Coll.* The house doesn't want a shooter to use two hands in handling the dice. It's too easy to pull a switch. If somebody uses two hands, like cupping the hands and blowing on the dice, the stick or somebody will yell, "*one hand on the dice,* shooter." If there's anything suspicious about the move, the stick will kill the dice [stop the dice while they are rolling] and shove them to the boxman. He has to say "no roll" quickly so there won't be a beef.

one high, *adj.* Said of an overpayment on a table layout, when a player is given one or more additional chips than were won.
[1983 Martinet *Oral Coll*]

one hundred aces, *n. pl. Plural in form, but singular in use.* In pinochle, a meld of four aces, one from each suit.
[1950 Morehead *Culbertson* 631]

one mile from home, *adj. phr.* In craps, one number away from a winning roll.
[ca. 1961 *Hotel Coll*]

one-number bet, *n.* In craps, a wager that a particular number will be rolled before the number 7 is rolled.
[1961 Scarne *Complete Guide* 683]

one-on-one, *adj.* In poker, involving two players still in contention for the pot. See also HEAD-TO-HEAD.
[1976 Sklansky *Hold 'em Poker*]

one on the floor, seven at the door, *n. phr.* In craps, iteration of a superstition that after a die bounces off the table, the number 7 will appear on the next roll of the dice. See also DIE ON THE FLOOR, SEVEN AT THE DOOR.
[1981 *Nevada Magazine* 14]

one-roll bet, *n.* In craps, a proposition wager that is won or lost on the next roll of the dice. See also HOP BET.
[ca. 1961 *Hotel Coll*]

one-run horse, *n.* In horse racing, a horse that can produce only a single burst of speed during a race.
[1971 McQuaid *Gambler's Digest* 312]

one side against the other, *n.* In faro, a betting system that features wagers on the low cards to win and high cards to lose, or vice-versa, in which ace through 6 are low, 8 through king are high and the player does not bet on the 7.
[1968 Adams *Western Words*]

one-to-five game, *n.* In poker, a game with LIMIT STAKES in which the minimum wager is one dollar and the maximum wager is five dollars. See quotation at ONE-TO-THREE GAME.
[1981 Golad *Oral Coll*]

one-to-three game, *n.* In poker, a game with LIMIT STAKES in which the minimum wager is one dollar, and the maximum wager is three dollars. 1981 Golad *Oral Coll.* A *one-to-three game* sounds pretty tame, but remember how quickly it can add up. In hold 'em, say, three players stay in and start bumping [raising bets] each other. On the first round you might have to put in three, if you called the two raises. Then the flop comes and you're sitting third. The two ahead of you bump, and suddenly you're fifteen or twenty dollars in the pot. If you stay with that kind of action, you'll have sixty to seventy-five dollars in before the showdown. You'd better have good cards and guts. The one-to-five game runs even higher. And you start approaching the big time in a five-ten game.

one-two-five blind, *n.* In poker, a game in which the first, second, and third players to the left of the dealer are required to make a wager before looking at their cards. The first player bets one dollar, the second bets two dollars, the third bets five dollars.
[1981 Golad *Oral Coll*]

one-twoing, *adj.* Involving a cheating method, usually in a card game, in which two or more cheaters conspire against a victim. See also THREE PLUCK ONE.
[1931 *Las Vegas Review-Journal* 6/31: 3]

one-way action, *n.* A card game, usually poker, with two players left contending for the pot. See also ONE-ON-ONE.
[1978 Brunson *How I Made* 539]

one-way cards, *n. pl.* A pack of playing cards, usually marked, whose backs feature asymmetrical designs. Compare COSMETICS.
[1961 Scarne *Complete Guide* 683]

one-way straight, *n.* Same as ONE-ENDED STRAIGHT.
[1968 Wallace *Poker* 220]

one-way tops and bottoms, *n. pl.* Also shortened to **one-way tops.** Dice with the same number of pips on opposite faces, usually two 5s or two 2s. Compare CALIFORNIA FOURTEENS.
[1974 Scarne *Dice* 250]

open, *n.* In card games, the first action taken after the deal. In poker, for example, the first wager in a hand; in bridge, the first bid in a hand. Compare OPENING BID.
[1968 Wallace *Poker* 220]

open, *v.* **1.** In card games, to begin the play of the hand after the cards have been dealt by making the first bet, the first bid, etc.
[1880 *DAE, DA,* for poker, as OPEN THE POT. 1958 *OEDS,* for bridge; compare OPENING BID]
2. In the phrases and particle constructions:
open a snap, To begin the operation of an illegal game, especially one in which cheating takes place. Compare SNAP
[1968 Adams *Western Words*]
open blind, In poker, to bet without looking at the cards while sitting in the first position to act in the betting round. See also BLIND BET.
[1963 Steig *Common Sense* 186]
open blind and straddle, In poker, to require a bet by the first player to the left of the dealer and a raise by the second player to the left of the dealer before the two players are allowed to look at the cards dealt to them, as an adopted provision or rule.
[1968 Wallace *Poker* 220]
open the pot, In poker, to begin the first round of betting. Compare OPENER.
[1880 *DAE, DA*]
open up, In a casino, to begin a game on a table that was closed earlier in the day.
[1961 Scarne *Complete Guide* 683]
open up at, In horse racing, to announce the initial odds on a horse before betting on the race begins. See also MORNING LINE.
[1983 Martinez *Gambling Scene* 212]

open, *prep.* In the prepositional phrases:
open at both ends, Also called OPEN ON BOTH ENDS. In poker, pertaining to a four-card sequence that the player has two chances to fill for a straight. For example, with the sequence 8-9-10-jack, the player may make a straight by drawing either a 7 or a queen. See also OPEN-ENDED STRAIGHT.
[1968 Wallace *Poker* 220]
open on both ends, Same as OPEN AT BOTH ENDS.
[1978 Larson *Vocabulary* 100]

open, *adj.* Pertaining to legalized gambling or, if gambling is illegal, operation of a gambling enterprise without police interference. See also WIDE-OPEN.
[1938 Asbury *Sucker's Progress* 9]

open bet, *n.* In faro, a wager on a card to win; specifically, an UNCOPPERED BET.
[1913 *OEDS*]

open card, *n.* A card dealt face upwards, common in stud poker.
[1968 Wallace *Poker* 220]
[Compare *open:* 1390 *OED,* meaning "exposed"]

open craps, *n. pl. Plural in form, but singular in use.* A craps game in which players are allowed to make bets with one another as well as with the house or operator of the game. See also BANK CRAPS and CRAPS. Compare SIDE BET.
[1950 Morehead *Culbertson* 631]

open end, *n.* In dominos, the end of a string of tiles already played, at which a player may place another tile.
[1950 Morehead *Culbertson* 631]
[Compare *open end:* 1908 *OEDS*]

open-ended straight, *n.* Also clipped to **open-end straight.** In poker, a sequence of four cards, to which a player may draw one more card one rank higher or one rank lower in order to make a straight. For example, with the sequence 8-9-10-jack, the player may fill a straight by drawing a 7 or a queen. See also ONE-ENDED STRAIGHT. [ca. 1961 *Hotel Coll*]

opener, *n.* **1.** In poker, the player who starts the betting round.
[1880 *DA, DAE*]
2. In a casino, the amount of chips assigned to a table at the beginning of a shift or the beginning of a game.
[ca. 1961 *Hotel Coll*]
3. openers, *pl.* In draw poker, the rank of a hand, usually one containing at least a pair of jacks required to initiate a betting round.
[1880 *DA, DAE,* under *opener;* 1902 *OEDS*]

open gambling, *n.* Legal gambling or unopposed illegal gambling. Compare WIDE OPEN.
[1931 *Las Vegas Review-Journal* 1/29: 3]

open game, *n.* A gambling game, usually poker, that anyone is welcome to join. Compare CLOSED GAME. [1949 Coffin *Secrets* 182]

open hand, *n.* In card games, a hand that is played with cards placed face upward on the table, such as stud or the dummy in bridge.
[1978 Larson *Vocabulary* 100]

opening bid, *n.* In auction games such as bridge, the initial bid of the game. The first player to the left of the dealer is allowed to make the *opening bid* or to pass the opportunity on to the next player. Compare OPENERS
[1953 Crawford *Consistent Winner* 350]

opening lead, *n.* In games like bridge or cribbage, the first card placed face up on the table by a player that begins the play of the hand.
[1950 Morehead *Culbertson* 631]

open on anything, *n. phr.* In draw poker, a provision that allows any player, beginning with the first player to the left of the dealer, to initiate the betting round. See also OPENERS.
[1971 Livingston *Poker Strategy* 221]

open pair, *n.* In stud poker, two cards of the same rank face upward in one hand.
[1949 Coffin *Secrets* 182]

open play, *n.* In games like contract bridge, a provision allowing extra points to be scored if the person holding the contract shows his cards before playing out the hand and making the contract.
[1950 Morehead *Culbertson* 631]

open point, *n.* In backgammon, a space on the layout without two STONES occupying the space. See CLOSED POINT.
[1950 Morehead *Culbertson* 631]

open poker, *n.* Another term for *stud poker.*
[1968 Wallace *Poker* 220]

open race, *n.* A horse race in which any thoroughbred may be entered.
[1978 Ainslie *Complete Guide* 294]

open seat, *n.* In games like baccarat, poker, or twenty-one, an unoccupied place at the table.
[1949 Coffin *Secrets* 182]

opera, *n.* In comet, a bonus scored for playing the entire hand in one turn.
[1950 Morehead *Culbertson* 631]

operator, *n.* **1.** A person who conducts a gambling game or place for gambling.
[1731 *OED*]
2. A cheat or swindler.
[1956 *DAS;* compare 1895 *OEDS,* meaning "one who acts in an underhand manner"]

opponent, *n.* An adversary in a game.
[1899 *OED,* under *order, v.*]

oppose, *v.* In faro, to reverse the layout of the game, making the cards dealt to the right stand for the bettors, and those dealt to the left stand for the dealer.
1843 Green *Exposure* 166. *Oppose* is reversing the game, and having the cards on the right for the punter and those on the left for the dealer.

option, *n.* A provision, usually in poker, to play another variant of a game if the conditions are not met for playing the announced game. For example, if no player can begin the betting round in draw poker that requires OPENERS to play for the high hand, the game may revert to LOWBALL.
[1968 Wallace *Poker* 220]

optional card, *n.* In certain variations of poker, an extra card that a player may request if particular conditions are met. For example, in a variant of stud, a player dealt a black three may request another card and place an extra chip in the pot. See also TWIST.
[1968 Wallace *Poker* 220]

optional claimer, *n.* In horse racing, a race in which horses may be entered whether or not they are offered for sale. Compare CLAIMING RACE.
[1955 Hillis *Pari-Mutuel Betting* 113]

optional double, *n.* In backgammon, a condition allowing one player to choose whether or not to double the amount being wagered on the outcome of the game.
[1971 McQuaid *Gambler's Digest* 312]

order, *v.* In the phrases and particle constructions:
order it up, In euchre, to be willing to accept the card turned up by the dealer as trump for that hand.
[1950 Morehead *Culbertson* 631]
order up, In euchre, to ask the opponent, who is the dealer, to take up the trump and discard.
[1847 *DA, DAE, OEDS*]

order horse, *n.* In horse racing, an entry that is not expected or intended to win.
[ca. 1961 *Hotel Coll.*]

ordinary, *n.* **1.** In the seventeenth century, a house where gamesters met for dinner and an evening of gambling at cards and dice.
1680 Cotton *Compleat Gamester* 3. Where note,

an *Ordinary* is a handsome house, where every day, about the hour of twelve, a good Dinner is prepared . . . whereby many Gentlemen of great Estates and good repute, make this place their resort, who after dinner play a while for recreation, both moderately and commonly.
[(1590) 1631 *OED*]
2. A gambling game carried on at an *ordinary.*
[1684 *OED*]

original bid, *n.* In games like bridge, the first or opening bid of a bidding round. See also OPENING BID.
[1950 Morehead *Culbertson* 631]

original hand, *n.* In draw poker, the first five cards dealt to a player before the discard and draw takes place.
[1890 Quinn *Fools of Fortune* 215]

OTB, *n.* Abbreviation for OFF-TRACK BETTING.
[ca. 1961 *Hotel Coll*]

out, *adj.* **1.** In poker, noting a retiring from the hand by refusing to bet or to call a previous bet.
[ca. 1961 *Hotel Coll*]
2. In the phrases:
out in front, Ahead, in terms of winning at gambling or leading in a race.
[ca. 1961 *Hotel Coll*]
out of the money, In racing, pertaining to an entry finishing fifth or later in a race. Compare IN THE MONEY
[ca. 1961 *Hotel Coll*]
out of turn, In card games, pertaining to playing a card or making a bet outside of the regular sequence, moving to the left around the table.
[ca. 1961 *Hotel Coll*]

out, *n.* In the phrase:
on the outs, 1. Pertaining to losing money in gambling.
[1983 Martinet *Oral Coll*]
2. In poker, noting a poor hand unlikely to win the pot without drawing several specific cards.
[1974 Scarne *Dice* 38]

outer table, *n.* In backgammon, the area of the board to the player's right, from which the player attempts to move all his pieces. Compare INNER TABLE.
1860 Crawley *Backgammon* 52. It must be understood that the points are named alike—ace, deux, &c.—in each table, and that the left-hand division is called the inner table, and the right-hand the *outer table.*

outfinished, *adj.* In greyhound racing, noting a dog that is passed in the final stretch after leading the race.
[1968 Buchele *Greyhound Racing* 6]

outrider, *n.* In horse racing, a mounted rider who leads the horses to the starting gate and pursues runaway mounts.
[1947 *OEDS*]

outside, *n.* **1.** The portion of the racetrack to the right side of a horse or dog and away from the inside rail. [1978 Ainslie *Complete Guide* 294]
2. In roulette, the layout area for placing bets on red or black, odd or even, high or low, and so on.
[ca. 1961 *Hotel Coll*]
3. In craps, the numbers on the layout to the right or left of the 6 and 8, determined by the POINT, or number, of the shooter. For example, if the shooter's point is 9, the *outside* numbers would be 10 at one end of the layout and 4, and usually 5, at the other end of the layout.
[1983 Martinet *Oral Coll*]

outside, *adj.* **1.** Noting a player cheating the gambling establishment.
[1968 Adams *Western Words*]
[1943 Maurer *Argot*]
2. In a casino, noting a pit boss, floorman, or spotter who circles the outside perimeter of the tables watching for irregularities.
[1983 Martinet *Oral Coll*]

outside bet, *n.* **1.** In bank craps, a wager placed on the numbers at the left and right edges of the layout, usually 4 and 10, and 5 and 9.
2. In roulette, a wager placed on the edges of the table layout, such as red or black, odd or even, high or low.
[ca. 1961 *Hotel Coll*]

outside blocks *n. pl.* In bank craps, the numbers 4, 5, 9 and 10 on the layout. The numbers 4 and 10 constitute one block, the 5 and 9 the other.
[1983 Martinet *Oral Coll*]

outside copy, *n.* Same as OUTSIDE TICKET.
[ca. 1961 *Hotel Coll*]

outside gambler, *n.* A patron of a gambling establishment known for his honesty and large bets. Compare OUTSIDE, *adj.* (def. 1).
[1968 Thackrey *Nick the Greek* 33]

outside hand, *n.* On a craps table large enough to have two dealers and a stickman, the dealer's hand closest to the players at the end of the table.

outside man, *n.* **1.** An employee in a gambling establishment whose duties take him outside of the establishment to bring players to the establishment, to redeem chips from other establishments, and so on. See also ROPER and STEERER.
[1961 Scarne *Complete Guide* 683]
2. An employee in a gambling establishment who acts as a player at a table until enough players have joined the table to keep the game going. See also SHILL.
[1973 Clark *Oral Coll*]
3. In a casino, a spotter; a lookout.
[1983 Martinet *Oral Coll*]

outside original ticket, *n.* In keno, the player's copy of the ticket turned over to the keno writer, who issues a copy of the ticket to the player as a receipt. The original ticket filled out by the player is kept behind the counter. See also OUTSIDE TICKET.
[1978 Alexander *Glossary* 10]

outside post position, *n. phr.* In horse racing, a

starting position far from the inside rail.
[1982 *Today's Racing* 14]

outsider, *n.* **1.** A person who is not a professional gambler or is not employed in the gaming business.
[1979 Newman *Dealer's Special* 7]
2. In horse racing, an entry with little chance to win. See also LONGSHOT.
[ca. 1961 *Hotel Coll*]

outside ticket, *n.* Also called OUTSIDE COPY. In keno, a copy of the original ticket filled out by a player, given to the player as a receipt. The original ticket is retained behind the counter. See also OUTSIDE ORIGINAL TICKET.
[1977 Nevada Gaming Control *Internal* 30]

outside work, *n.* Any of a variety of changes to the surface of a die, such as shaving part of the die or changing the number of pips on a face. See also BARR DICE and MISMARKED DICE.
[1961 Scarne *Complete Guide* 683]

over, *prep.* **1.** In poker, higher in value or rank, such as in a full house, three jacks *over* a pair of kings; or in a hand with two pair, a pair of kings *over* a pair of jacks.
[1949 Coffin *Secrets* 182]
2. In twenty-one, used to indicate a BUST.
[1973 Clark *Oral Coll*]
3. In the phrase:
over the hump, Pertaining to having won enough money to be able to continue to play without risking one's original bankroll.
[ca. 1961 *Hotel Coll*]

over, *n.* **1.** In casino, one point awarded for each spade garnered after eight have been collected.
[1950 Morehead *Culbertson* 632]
2. In dice, same as SLEEPER.
[(1950) 1981 Maurer *Lang. of the Underworld* 189]

overbet, *n.* In poker, a wager higher than allowed by the table limit; a large bet out of proportion to the size of the pot. [1949 Coffin *Secrets* 182]

overbet, *v.* To wager an amount much larger than would be normal for the size of the pot.
[1978 Brunson *How I Made* 540]

overbid, *n.* In games like bridge, a bid that is higher than the value of the hand.
[1917 *OEDS*]

overbid, *v.* In games like bridge, to make an OVERBID. [1908 *OEDS*]

overbidder, *n.* In games like bridge, one who OVERBIDS. [1936 OEDS]

overblind, *n.* In poker, a bet required by the second player to the left of the dealer before looking at the cards dealt. See also BLIND.
[1981 Golad *Oral Coll*]

overboard, *adv.* Pertaining to a player who cannot pay gambling debts or repay loans made to him in a gambling session.
[1961 Scarne *Complete Guide* 683]
[Compare *overboard, adv.* 1931 *OEDS,* meaning "beyond one's means"]

overcall, *n.* **1.** In bridge, a bid that supercedes an earlier bid. [1916 *OEDS*]
2. In poker, a bet matching an earlier wager that has already been matched by a previous player.
[1950 Morehead *Culbertson* 632]

overcall, *v.* **1.** In bridge, **a.** Also written **over-call.** To make a bid much higher than a previous bid.
[1950 Morehead *Culbertson* 632]
[1908 *OEDS*]
b. Also written **over call.** To OVERBID.
[1927 *OEDS*]
2. In poker, to match a wager and say "I call," after a previous bettor has already matched (called) the bet.
[1978 Brunson *How I Made* 540]

overcard, *n.* In hold 'em and stud poker, a faced card higher in rank than a pair held in one's hand.
[1949 Coffin *Secrets* 182]

overflow game, *n.* A casino game, such as the wheel of fortune or chuck-a-luck, usually played by patrons only because the tables they favor, such as craps or twenty-one, are filled with players.
[1948 Oncken *Review Journal* 2/29: 15]

overhand cut, *n.* A method for cutting cards which restores the pack to its original order. Compare DOUBLE CUT.
1865 Evans *Gamblers Win* 38. To execute the *overhand cut,* the player will seize about one-third of the deck in his right hand, and half the remainder in his left, bringing them toward him; he will then drop those in his right hand on that portion of the deck remaining on the table, still keeping his hand on them; throw those in his left hand over and beyond the others, and then throw those in his right hand on the top.

overhand shuffle, *n.* A method for mixing a pack of playing cards by sliding a few cards from one hand to the other, then repeating the motion, continually sliding a few more cards atop the earlier ones.
[1968 Wallace *Poker* 220]

overhand stack, *n.* A method for shuffling a pack of cards so their original order is retained for the cheater. See also OVERHAND CUT.
[1968 Wallace *Poker* 220]

overland, *adj.* Pertaining to a racehorse that runs wide around a turn on an oval track, thereby losing seconds by covering more ground than horses close to the rail.
[1978 Ainslie *Complete Guide* 294]

overlay, *adj.* In horse racing, pertaining to a horse that begins a race at higher odds than offered in the MORNING LINE.
1975 Clark *Oral Coll.* An *overlay* bet indicates the bettor is receiving better odds than could be expected. A horse going off like that could make you nervous. Something's wrong with him or someone's manipulating the odds. You know one thing—you're going to win or lose.

overlays, *n. pl.* In hold 'em and stud poker, a pair of cards ranking higher in value than a pair already face up on the table. Compare OVERCARD.
[1964 Reese and Watkins *Secrets* 143]

overload, *n.* In horse racing, an excessive amount of money wagered on one particular horse in a race. Compare OVERWEIGHT.
[1968 Thackrey *Nick the Greek* 224]

overmatched, *adj.* Pertaining to an entry in a contest that is scheduled to vie against superior competition.
[ca. 1961 *Hotel Coll*]
[Compare 1591 *OED,* meaning "to be more than a match for"]

overnight race, *n.* In horse racing, a race for which entries are accepted within three days before the race is to take place.
[1978 Ainslie *Complete Guide* 295]

overnights, *n. pl.* In horse racing, the list of entries published or mimeographed one day before a race.
[1978 Ainslie *Complete Guide* 295]

overpair, *n.* In poker, a PAIR, two cards of the same rank, higher in value than a pair showing on the table.
[1976 Sklansky *Hold 'em Poker*]

overpay, *v.* Of a dealer, to misdeal or to cheat a gambling establishment by paying a player, usually a confederate, more than he has wagered, or paying a losing wager.
[ca. 1961 *Hotel Coll*]
[Compare *overpay:* 1601 *OED,* meaning "to pay (someone) beyond what is due"]

overplay, *adj.* In horse racing, pertaining to odds considered higher than justified.
[1983 Martinez *Gambling Scene* 213]
[Alternate form of OVERLAY]

overreach, *n.* Also written **over-reach. 1.** Of a racehorse, a step in which the shoe on the hind foot touches the foreleg.
[1607 *OED*]
2. In cards, an act of cheating at dealing, especially by an excessive reach.
[1615 *OED*]

overreach, *v.* Also written **over-reach. 1.** Of a racehorse, to bring a hind foot against a corresponding forefoot in walking or running.
[1523 *OED,* as *overreaching*]
2. In cards, to cheat at dealing.
[1596? *OED*]

overruff, *v.* Also written **over-ruff.** In bridge, to play a second, higher trump on a trick.
[1813 *OEDS*]

overruff, *n.* An act of overruffing.
[1906 *OEDS*]

overtrick, *n.* Also written **over-trick.** In bridge, a trick won in addition to the number required for the contract.
[1921 *OEDS*]

overtrump, *v.* Also written **over-trump.** In bridge, to play a second, higher trump on a trick.
[1746 *OED*]

overweight, *adj.* In horse racing, pertaining to weight carried by a horse in excess of the amount assigned by the track handicapper. Compare OVERLOAD.
[1971 McQuaid *Gambler's Digest* 312]

P

pace, *n.* Rhythm and speed, as of a racehorse or the betting in a card game.
[1955 Hillis *Pari-Mutuel Betting* 117]

pacer, *n.* In harness racing, a horse that is laterally gaited, both legs on the same side move in tandem. See also TROTTER.
[1971 McQuaid *Gambler's Digest* 312]
[*a*1661 *OED*]

pace rating, *n.* In horse racing, the amount of time required by a horse to run from the starting gate to the midpoint of the race.
[1981 Passer *Winning Big* 229]

pacesetter, *n.* In horse racing, the horse that leads early in the race.
[1946 *OEDS*]

pack, *n.* **1.** A deck of playing cards, normally consisting of fifty-two cards and an optional additional card named the joker. The *pack* is composed of four suits, clubs, diamonds, hearts and spades, with thirteen ranks in each suit, 2, 3, 4, and so on to 10, then jack, queen, king, and ace. In different games, the ace may count as the highest or lowest ranking card.
[1597 *OED*]
2. In games like canasta or samba, the discard pile.
[1953 Crawford *Consistent Winner* 350]
3. In racing, the group of horses or dogs bunched together during the race.
[1983 Martinez *Gambling Scene* 213]

pack, *v.* **1.** To arrange or shuffle playing cards in order to cheat. [1599 *OED*]
2. In the phrases:
pack it in, Also called PACK IT UP. To withdraw from a game or contest; to stop playing a game, as for the duration of that session or evening.
[n.d. *DAS*]
pack it up, Same as PACK IT IN.
[1950 Morehead *Culbertson* 632]

package tourist, *n.* One of a group of people brought to a gambling resort for a predetermined number of days and given special premiums, such as a reduced fee rate on the cost of transportation and a room.
[1963 Taylor *City of Sin* 16]

packet, *n.* A portion of a deck of cards; several playing cards together.
[1887 *OED*]

pad, *n.* **1.** The payroll for employees of a gambling establishment.
2. Also in the phrases:
the pad. Graft which is received by and shared among various members of a police precinct or department for ignoring illegal activities.
1971 *Time* 11/1: 23. When a cop was transferred to a new post, *the pad* from his old station kept up for another two months.
1971 *The New York Times* 10/19: 47. Mr. Armstrong said the testimony would show how the gamblers of the city paid off the policemen on a regular monthly basis after they had been placed on what is called *the pad.*" Narcotic bribes, the counsel said, usually "are made on an individual score basis."
[1970 *OEDS*]
on the pad. Sharing in the graft collected by policemen of a precinct or department for ignoring illegal activities.
1971 Peter Hamill *The New York Post* 10/20: 47. "I never knew a plainclothesman," said Phillips, "who wasn't *on the pad.*" And yet for years it went further than that: it was as if the whole town was on the pad, as if a sidewalk couldn't be cleaned without grease, as if the garbage could not be carted without paying grease.
1971 *The New York Times* 10/21: 46. The Knapp Commission investigating police corruption in New York City has added a new phrase to the public lexicon: "*On the pad.*" It refers to lists of policemen paid to ignore illegal activities. As the Commission begins two weeks of public hearings, it has also underscored an old truth: The public plays a role in setting public policies, even those unofficial policies followed by policemen *on the pad.*
[1971 *BDNE I, OEDS*]

paddle, *n.* In a casino, the wooden or plastic spatula used to push bills through the slot on a gaming table into the DROP BOX, fastened to the underside of the table.
[1961 Scarne *Complete Guide* 684]

paddle wheel, *n.* Another term for the WHEEL OF FORTUNE or RAFFLE WHEEL.
[1926 *OEDS*]

paddock, *n.* The area at a racetrack where horses or dogs are gathered for last minute preparations before a race.
[1862 *OED*]

pad roll, *n.* A controlled cast of a pair of dice, held so that the faces with six pips face in the same direction, thereby reducing the chance that a 7 can be rolled. See also WHIP SHOT.
[1981 Demaris *Last Mafioso* 15]

pagot, *n.* In tarot, the lowest valued trump card, worth one point.
[1950 Morehead *Culbertson* 632]

paid outs, *n. pl. Plural in form, but singular in use.* In a casino, the record of amounts paid to winners at keno, bingo, slot machines, and in sports books.
[1978 Alexander *Glossary* 11]

paint, *n.* **1.** Short for PAINT-SKIN. In playing cards, a jack, queen, or king.
[1961 Scarne *Complete Guide* 684]
2. The DAUB, or stain, used to mark the backs of playing cards by a cheater. See also COSMETICS.
[1982 Martin *Introduction* 24]

paint, *v.* **1.** In hearts, to play a card from the heart suit on a trick taken by an opponent.
[1953 Crawford *Consistent Winner* 350]
2. In the phrase:
paint me, In twenty-one, to deal one card, or hit, with a value of ten points.
[1983 Martinet *Oral Coll*]

painted, *adj.* In hearts, pertaining to a player forced to take a trick with a card from the heart suit in it.
[1950 Morehead *Culbertson* 632]

painter, *n.* A cheater who marks the backs of playing cards with india ink, aniline pencil, or some other substance, so they may be read from the backs. Compare COSMETICS.
[1965 Fraiken *Inside Nevada* 75]

paint-skin, *n.* Also called a COURT-SKIN. In playing cards, a jack, queen, or king. See also WHITESKIN.
[1943 Maurer *Argot*]

pair, *n.* **1.** Two playing cards of the same rank or denomination held by one player.
1843 Green *Exposure* 269. *Pairs* are two similar cards, as two aces, or two kings. They reckon for two points [in cribbage], whether in the hand, or in playing.
[1680 *OED*]
2. In roulette, a wager placed on the section of the layout labeled "even."
[1964 Wykes *Illustrated Guide* 328]
[French *pair,* meaning "even"]
3. A pack of cards, not limited to two. *Obsolete.*
[1656 *OED*]

pair royal, *n. pl.* Also **pairs royal.** Also written **pair-royal. 1.** In cribbage, three cards of the same denomination held in one hand or played consecutively on the table. See also PRIAL and PRILE and PROIL.
1824 Anon *Hoyle's* 28. *Pairs royal* are three similar cards, and reckon for six points, whether in hand or playing.
[*OED* lists variant spellings: 1608 *perryall;* 1749 *pairoyal;* 1801 *pairials;* also *perryall, parriall, paroyal, parreiall, parial*]
2. A cast of three dice in which each turns upward the same number of pips.
[1656 *OED*]

pair splitting, *n.* In twenty-one, a condition of the game that allows a player to make two hands when dealt a pair of cards. The player supplies another wager equal to the first, then each card of the pair forms the base for a new hand.
[1973 Friedman *Casino Games* 24]

paix, *n. French.* Also called PONT. In faro, the condition of making the same bet after a win.
1843 Green *Exposure* 167. *Paix,* equivalent of double or quits; is when the punter having won, does not choose to parolet and risk his stake, but bends or makes a bridge of his cards, signifying that he ventures his gains only. A double *paix* is, when the punter having won twice, bends two cards one over the other, Treble *paix,* thrice, &c., or quinze, &c.

paix parolet, *n. French.* In faro, the act of betting both the original wager and the winnings on a new hand.
1843 Green *Exposure* 167. *Paix-Parolet* is when a punter has gained a parolet, wishes then to play double or quits, and save his original stakes; double *paix-parolet* succeeds to winning a *paix-parolet.*

palette, *n.* In chemin-de-fer, a thin, rectangular plate with a handle, used by the operator of the game to move chips and cards around the table. Compare STICK.
[1949 *OEDS*]
[French, diminutive of "shovel"]

palm, *v.* To conceal a card or die in the hand until an opportunity to cheat presents itself.
1680 Cotton *Compleat Gamester* 10. Another way the Rook hath to cheat, is first by *Palming,* that is, he puts one Dye into the Box and keeps the other in the hallow of his little finger.
1714 Lucas *Memoirs* 27. But if he had none of these artificial Helps about him, why then his Hand supply'd whose Wants by *palming* the Die; that is, having the Box in his Hand, he nimbly takes up both the Dice as they are thrown, within the Hollow of his Hand, and puts but one into the Box, reserving the other in the Palm, and observing with a quick Eye what side was upward, he accordingly conforms the next Throw to his Purpose by delivering that in the Box and the other in his Hand smoothly together.
[1664 *OED,* as *palming*]

palmed card, *n.* A playing card held out of a game by a cheater for later use.
[1968 Wallace *Poker* 220]
[Compare *palmed:* 1896 *OED*]

palm holdout, *n.* A pair of altered dice secreted in the hand of a cheater and exchanged on occasion with the true dice being used in the game.
[1977 Carroll *Playbody's Illustrated* 125]

palm stock, *n.* A packet of playing cards, arranged in a specific sequence, held by a cheater until he wishes to use them in a game.
[1890 Quinn *Fools of Fortune* 224]

palm switch, *n.* A cheating action by a dice player who holds a pair of altered dice in the hand until he wishes to exchange them for the dice being used in a game.
[1974 Scarne *Dice* 274]

palooka, *n.* An inferior racehorse.
1948 Mencken *American Language* 768. *Palooka* [in boxing was] Probably borrowed from the racetrack, where it signifies a sorry nag. It may be related to the synonymous *palouser,* which may be derived from the name of the *Palouse* Indians of the Northwest. Holt . . . suggests that it may come from the Spanish *peluca,* a term of reproof.
1963 Mencken *American Langauge,* 4th ed., 210. During the 1920's *baloney* was also used to designate a clumsy prize fighter, but it has given way to *palooka,* which Conway introduced in 1925.
[1948 *DA;* probably originally a boxing term (1925 *OEDS*)]

pam, *n.* Also spelled **pamm.** In the card games lanterloo and pam-loo, the jack of clubs, which has precedence over every other card. Compare ELDEST HAND and LOO.
1714 Lucas *Memoirs* 223. . . . Lanterloo, in which Game you must note, that he who hath 5 Cards of a Suit in his Hand, Loos all the Gamesters then playing, be they never so many, and sweeps the Board; if there be two Loos, he that is the eldest Hand hath the Advantage; but if there be a Loo of Trumps, that takes the advantage from all, except any one hath *Pamm,* that is the Knave of Clubs, who saves his Loo, and is pair for one Trick out of his Stock.
1830 Anon *Hoyle's Improved* 138. *Pam* is the knave of clubs, and ranks above every other card in the pack. It is subject to no laws, but may be played on any suit, at any time, even though you have in your hand the suit which is led.
[1685 *OED*]

pam-blaze, *n.* In loo, a hand with five face cards, including the jack of clubs.
[1950 Morehead *Culbertson* 632]

pam-flush, *n.* In loo, a hand with four cards of the same suit and the jack of clubs.
[1950 Morehead *Culbertson* 632]

panguingui, /pæn'gi: n: or pæn'gwi: n:/, *n.* Also spelled **panguingue, pangingue.** Also shortened to **pan.** A game similar to rummy played with six decks of cards.
1953 Woon *The Why* 75. *Panguingue* was played by Scandinavian sailors hundreds of years ago and they are said to have developed it from a Chinese game. It was played first in this country by hard-rock miners. My personal opinion is that rummy is a variation of *pan* and that it was first played in the West in the latter half of the 19th century. Scarne thinks it derived from Whiskey Poker. We're both guessing.

paper, *n.* **1.** Any playing cards.
[1842 *OEDS, DAE*]
2. Playing cards marked on the backs so they can be identified while face down. Also called SPOTTED PAPERS.
1865 Evans *Gamblers Win* 41. Marked cards, or *paper,* as they are technically termed, are a very great advantage where they can be got in on a party.
[1894 *OED, DA*]

paper game, *n.* A craps game, usually illegal, in which currency is used rather than chips.
[1983 Martinet *Oral Coll*]

paperwork, *n.* Playing cards marked on the back or otherwise given an identity by bending or creasing. See also PAPER (def. 2).
[1968 Wallace *Poker* 220]

parallel-time chart, *n.* In horse racing, a rating system employed by a handicapper that indicates the expected time required for a particular horse to cover a specified distance. Compare PAR TIME.
[1981 Passer *Winning Big* 229]

pari-mutuel, *n.* Also written **parimutuel. 1.** A pool for an event in which those betting on the first three finishers share in the pool, less the percentage kept by the manager of the pool.
[1888 *OEDS*]
2. A machine for recording the amounts wagered and the amounts due to winners of such a betting pool.
[1934 *OEDS*]

pari-mutuel, *adj.* Also written **parimutuel.** Of or having to do with this system of betting: *parimutuel betting, pari-mutuel outlet.*
[1891 *OEDS*]

parked out, *adj. phr.* In horse racing, denoting an entry that runs wide on the turns of an oval track. Compare to RUN WIDE.
[1977 Carroll *Playboy's Illustrated* 191]

parlay, *v. French.* Also spelled **parlee, parley, paroli, parolet.** To increase the amount of a bet by wagering the original bet and its winnings on the next event. See COCKING.
1714 Lucas *Memoirs* 230. *Paroli* is, when having won the Couch or first Stake, and having a mind to go on to get a Sept-et-le-va [seven times the wager], you crook the corner of your Card, letting your Money lie without being paid the Value of it by the Talliere [banker].
[1828 *DA;* 1892 *DAE;* 1895 *OED;* 1890 *OEDS;* ultimately a corruption of PAROLI, from French *paroli,* n., from Italian, meaning "a grand part, set, or cast, at dice"]

parlay, *n.* Also spelled **parley.** A bet equal to the amount of an original bet together with its winnings wagered on the next event, especially in

a series of horse races or card games.
[1904 *OED,* as *parley;* 1956 *DAS;* see PARLEY, *v.*]

parlay card, *n.* In sports books, a printed form listing a number of teams playing a sporting event such as football, with the lists of proposition wagers on several contests from which the bettor may select three or more contests. The money won from each contest is placed automatically on the next contest selected The player must pick the winner of each contest to win the parlay.
[1971 McQuaid *Gambler's Digest* 312]

parlor, *n.* Short for BINGO PARLOR. A room or establishment devoted to bingo playing.
[1953 Lewis *Sagebrush Casinos* 94]

parolet, *n.* Same as PARLAY. The act of betting both the original stake and the winnings of one hand on the next hand.
1843 Green *Exposure* 167. *Parolet,* sometimes called cocking, is when a punter, being fortunate, chooses to venture both his stake and gains, which he intimates by bending a corner of his card upwards [in playing faro].

paroli, *n.* Same as PARLAY. The act of wagering the original bet and the winnings on the next gambling event. *Obsolete.*
1823 Persius *Rouge et Noir* 164. *Paroli* is doubling the stake you have won the preceding coup. [1701 *OED*]

paroli, *v.* To stake one's money over again, plus that gained by it. *Obsolete.*
[1835 *OED;* compare ety. at PARLAY]

partial, *n.* In trump games, the total number of tricks short of winning the game.
[1950 Morehead *Culbertson* 633]

partie carree, *n. French.* In ombre, a hazard created by the holding of three kings and one queen in the same hand.
[1950 Morehead *Culbertson* 633]
[Compare *partie carrée,* 1890 *OED,* meaning "a party of four," at *partie*]

par time, *n.* In horse racing, the average time for a particular horse to cover a specified distance. Compare PARALLEL-TIME CHART.
[1981 Passer *Winning Big* 229]

partner, *n.* **1.** In team games like bridge, a member of the team who shares a common score, bid, and play with another player.
[1680 *OED*]
2. In games requiring that individuals play for their own interests, such as poker, a confederate to a cheater.
[1968 Wallace *Poker* 220]
3. Two or more players who share a common bankroll.
[1978 Brunson *How I Made* 541]

part-score, *n.* Also called PARTIAL. In trump games, the total number of tricks short of winning the game.
[1953 Crawford *Consistent Winner* 350]

party, n. A gambling session with a number of like events, as a bingo *party.*
[1950 Morehead *Culbertson* 633]
[French *partie,* meaning "share"]

party bridge, *n.* A session of bridge playing at which partners are frequently changed and the stakes are low.
[1971 McQuaid *Gambler's Digest* 312]

pass, *n.* **1.** In craps, a winning cast of the dice on the do side.
[1964 Wykes *Illustrated Guide* 328]
2. a. In poker, a refusal to remain eligible for the pot, which entails surrendering the cards held for that hand.
1866 *American Card Player* 135. *Pass.*—The privilege of declining to enter for the pool. This is called *passing* your hand.
[1599 *OED*]
b. In games like bridge, a declination to continue bidding.
[1923 *OEDS*]

pass, *v.* **1.** In craps, to roll a winning number on the dice on the do side.
[1964 Wykes *Illustrated Guide* 328]
2. In craps, to relinquish a turn to be the dice thrower, or shooter.
[1983 Martinet *Oral Coll*]
3. To refrain from betting a poker hand and surrendering the cards dealt for that hand.
[1949 Coffin *Secrets* 183]
4. In bridge, to decline the opportunity to make a bid.
[1869 *OEDS,* 1884 *OED*]
5. To shuffle and cut a pack of cards while maintaining the original order. Compare PULL THROUGH. [1884 *OED*]
6. In the phrases and particle constructions:
pass in one's checks, To redeem chips for cash and retire from a gambling session.
[1865 *DA;* By metaphoric extension, to die.]
pass in one's chips, Same as PASS IN ONE'S CHECKS. [1884 *DA*]
→See CHIP for a usage note contrasting *check* and *chip.*
pass out, Also, FOLD. In draw poker, to refuse to open or bet and relinquish any claim to the pot by throwing in the hand of cards.
[1964 Reese and Watkins *Secrets* 143]
pass the buck, In poker, to relinquish a turn to deal.
[1865 *DA;* The buck is a marker, at one time a buck knife, placed in front of the player acting as the dealer when the game has a single person dealing all hands and not participating in the play.]

pass and back in, *n. phr.* In poker, a provision whereby a player may check during the betting round, then re-enter the betting competition when his turn comes again.
[1950 Morehead *Culbertson* 633]

pass and out, *n. phr.* In poker, a provision whereby a player, having passed, must relinquish

his cards and remain out of competition for the current pot.
[1968 Wallace *Poker* 220]

passe, *v. French.* In roulette, to place a wager on the area of the layout for betting the numbers 19 through 36. See also high-number bet.
[1850 *OEDS*]

passed pot, *n.* In draw poker, a hand in which all the players fold before beginning the betting. The amount in the pot, usually the ANTE, is carried over to the next hand.
[1968 Wallace *Poker* 220]

passers, *n. pl.* In craps, altered dice on which the number 7 is rarely rolled, thus allowing the shooter to make many PASSES.
[1961 Scarne *Complete Guide* 684]

passing, *adj.* In craps, pertaining to a pair of dice or a player rolling many winning numbers in sequence.
[1964 Lemmel *Gambling* 189]

pass line, *n.* In craps, a space on the LAYOUT for making the initial bet in a hand.
[1968 Thackrey *Nick the Greek* 94]

pass line bet, *n.* In craps, a wager that the current shooter will roll a 7 or 11 initially, or will make a POINT (4, 5, 6, 8, 9, or 10), then roll that number again before rolling a 7.
[1973 Friedman *Casino Games* 35]

pass monte, *n.* Another name for THREE-CARD MONTE. [1866 *DA*]

pass-out, *n.* Also spelled **passout.** In poker, the act of retiring from a hand.
[1963 Steig *Common Sense* 186]

pasteboard, *n.* A playing card. *Obsolete.*
[1859 *OED*]

pasteboard track, *n.* In horse racing, a fast track with a thin covering of loose dirt for padding.
[1978 Ainslie *Complete Guide* 295]

past performance, *n.* In racing, an entry's record of earlier races, including times for portions of the races, the order of finish, and so on.
[1971 McQuaid *Gambler's Digest* 313]

past post, *v. phr.* **1.** To place a wager or increase the size of a wager after the outcome of an event, especially after the completion of a keno game, hand of twenty-one, or roll of the dice in craps.
[1973 Clark *Oral Coll*]
2. To place a bet on a horse that has just won a race by obtaining the race results before the bookmaker does.
[n.d. *DAS,* (1951) 1981 Maurer *Lang.* of the Underworld 222]

past poster, *n.* A cheater who PAST POSTS or, generally, bets only on an event he is sure to win.
[1983 Martinet *Oral Coll*]

pat, *adj.* In draw poker, pertaining to a hand so strong that no part of it is discarded and redrawn.
[1963 Steig *Common Sense* 186]
[Compare 1638 *OED,* meaning "ready, prompt," used predicatively]

pat hand, *n.* In draw poker, a hand that cannot be improved by discarding and redrawing any part of it.
1877 Meehan *Laws* 140. When a hand is complete, so that the holder of it can play without drawing to better it, that is called a "*pat*" hand. A bold player will sometimes decline to draw any cards, and pretend to have a *pat hand,* and play it as such, when he has none.
[1868 *DAE, OEDS;* 1889 *OED*]

patter, *n.* In poker, the oral and physical behavior affected by an experienced player designed to mislead opponents; the behavior of a poker player used to hide TELLS, or reactions to cards or situations that may disclose information to another player.
[1981 Golad *Oral Coll*]
[1780? *OED, DSUE*]

pay, *n.* The act of removing the winnings of a wager, then making the same bet again. Compare COCKING and PARLAY.
1714 Lucas *Memoirs* 231. *Pay* is when the Punter has won the Couch or first Stake, whether a Schilling, Crown, Guinea, or whatever he lays down upon his Card; and being fearful to make the Paroli, leaves off; for by going the *Pay,* if the Card turns up wrong he loses nothing, having won the Couch before.

pay, *v.* In the phrase:
pay the ragman, In an establishment catering to dominoes players, to pay the fee for use of a table and tiles. Usually, the winner of the game is expected to put aside an amount that will go to *pay the ragman* when the operator of the establishment comes around to collect the table fee.
[1981 Jenkins *Johnny Moss* 23]

payback, *n.* In a casino, money or chips turned over to an employee by a player to settle a debt or MARKER.
[1983 Martinet *Oral Coll*]
[Compare 1959 *OEDS,* meaning "action of paying back"]

payday game, *n.* A poker game with higher stakes than normal to most of the players.
[1981 Jenkins *Johnny Moss*]

pay line, *n.* In slot machines, the line on the face of the machine on which the appropriate symbols must stop to result in a win or a JACKPOT.
[1961 Scarne *Complete Guide* 684]

payment slip, *n.* In a casino, a form used to record the amount of money or chips a player pays against the amount he owes on his credit. One part is kept by the player, one part is retained in the pit, and one part is kept in the casino cage.
[1977 Nevada Gaming Control *Internal* 5]

payoff, *n.* The total amount of money paid for any winning wager.
[1905 *OEDS;* compare: *pay off,* v. 1710 *OED,* meaning "to pay in full and discharge and 1951 *OEDS,* meaning "to be profitable"]

payoff limit, *n.* In sports books, the highest amount paid to a winner.
[1968 Thackrey *Nick the Greek* 25]

payoff odds, *n. pl. Plural in form, but singular in use.* The total amount paid to a winner who has taken odds on a bet so the amount paid is more than the amount wagered. *Payoff odds* are less than TRUE ODDS in betting propositions where odds on the occurrence of an event can be clearly set, as in bank craps.
[1961 Scarne *Complete Guide* 684]
[1964 *OEDS*]

payoff schedule, *n.* A listing of the amounts to be paid for specific wagers, as in a keno operation.
[1957 *Nevada Gaming Regulations* 155]

payoff slip, *n.* In casino slot machines, a record of the amount paid for a jackpot in addition to the money paid out by the machine.
[1977 Nevada Gaming Control *Internal* 19]

payoff ticket, *n.* In keno, the copy of a KENO TICKET kept by the player and presented for collection when it is a winning ticket. See also INSIDE TICKET.
[1978 Alexander *Glossary* 11]

payout reserve container, *n.* In slot machines, the hopper or tubes containing the coins that drop out of the machine when a winning combination occurs.
[1978 Alexander *Glossary* 7]

payout schedule, *n.* Also called the AWARD SCHEDULE. In a casino, a posted announcement of the amounts to be paid on wagers made at various games in the casino.
[1978 Alexander *Glossary* 1]

PC, *n.* Also spelled **p.c.** or **P-C** or **P.C.** Abbreviation for PERCENTAGE. **1.** Same as HOUSE ADVANTAGE.
[1968 Thackrey *Nick the Greek* 142]
2. Same as POINTS, the percentage of a casino or gambling operation owned by one person.
[1973 Clark *Oral Coll*]

pea, *n.* **1.** In keno, a small round ball with a number between 1 and 80 painted on it. Twenty of the balls, or *peas* are drawn for a game.
2. In racing, a favorite; a horse likely to win.
[1888 *OEDS*]

pecker, *v.* In panguingue, to play a hand without being able to lay down winning cards.
[1948 Oncken *Review Journal* 3/14: 13]

pedro, *n.* **1.** In pedro, the 5 of trump.
[1874 *OEDS,* 1880 *DAE,* 1890 *DA*]
2. A variant of sancho pedro in which the sancho, or nine of trumps, does not count.
[1874 *OEDS,* 1876 *DA,* 1880 *DAE*]

peek, *v.* In card-cheating, to sneak a look at the face of the card atop the undealt portion of the pack, or show it to a confederate. Compare GLEAMER.
[1961 Scarne *Complete Guide* 684]

peekay shot, *n.* Variant spelling of PIQUE SHOT. Also called a PEEK SHOT or WHIP SHOT.
[1950 Morehead *Culbertson* 635]

peeker, *n.* **1.** A dishonest card dealer who looks at undealt cards or shows the faces of undealt cards to a confederate.
[1973 Clark *Oral Coll*]
2. In poker, a person who looks at the cards in the hand of a player still in contention for the pot.
[1968 Wallace *Poker* 221]

peek shot, *n.* Also spelled PIQUE SHOT or PEEKAY SHOT. *French.* Also called a WHIP SHOT. A controlled cast of a pair of dice made so that particular numbers will be rolled more often than others.
[1974 Scarne *Dice* 255]

peek store, *n.* An illegal gambling operation or establishment, especially at a carnival.
[1961 Scarne *Complete Guide* 684]

peeties, *n. pl.* Dice that have been altered, usually with weights placed inside; LOADED DICE.
[1983 Martinez *Gambling Scene* 214]
[*c*1890 *DAS,* probably a shortening and suffix substitution of REPEATERS]

peg, *v.* **1.** In poker, to signify the position of the dealer by placing a button or marker in front of the player who is to deal next.
[1974 Scarne *Dice* 475]
2. To mark cards with a pin or other sharp instrument so they may be recognized from the back.
[1983 Martinez *Gambling Scene* 214]
3. a. In cribbage, to move the point marker along the scoreboard (usually a board with rows of holes drilled in it).
[1821 *OED,* as *pegging*]
b. Sometimes, **peg out.** To win the game at cribbage by reaching the last hole before the showdown of hands.
[1870 *OED*]

pelota, *n.* **1.** Another name for *jai alai.*
[1891 *OED,* Spanish, meaning "ball"]
2. The ball used in jai alai.
[1971 McQuaid *Gambler's Digest* 313]

pelter, *n.* **1.** In poker, a hand consisting of cards with the ranks of 2, 5, and 9, plus two other cards between the 2 and 9. See also KILTER.
[1949 Coffin *Secrets* 183]
2. A worthless racehorse.
[1856 *DA, OEDS*]

penalty, *n.* In bridge, a number of points added to the opponents' score when the declarer fails to make the contract, or to the declarer's score

when his bid is doubled and he makes the contract.
[1908 *OEDS*]

penalty card, *n.* In bridge, an exposed card, which must be played at the first opportunity.
[1958 *OEDS*]

penalty double, *n.* A challenge to an opponent's bid, made in the expectation of defeating the contract.
[1959 *OEDS*]

pencil, *n.* Especially in the phrase: **the power of the pencil.** In a casino, the authority to sign for complimentary rooms, meals, show tickets and so on.
[1961 Scarne *Complete Guide* 684]

pencil, *v.* To enter a horse's name in a betting book. [1871 *OED*]

penciller, *n.* A bookmaker's clerk.
[1879 *OED*]

peneech, *n.* In peneech, an obsolete card game the 7 of diamonds.
[1950 Morehead *Culbertson* 634]

pennant, *n.* In backgammon, one of the twenty-four triangular slots or positions on the layout. See also POINT (def. 5)
[1973 Clark *Oral Coll*]

penny ante; or **penny-ante,** *n.* Also called PENNY POKER. In poker, a small-stakes game.
[1855 *DA, DAE, OEDS;* from the practice of needing only a *penny* to *ante* up]

penny poker, *n.* Same as PENNY ANTE.
[1849 *DA*]

penultimate card, *n.* Also shortened to **penultimate. 1.** In poker, the next-to-last card in the pack.
[1949 Coffin *Secrets* 183]
2. In whist, the next-to-lowest card of a suit.
[1876 *OED*]

percentage, *n.* **1.** Also abbreviated: P.C. In a gambling establishment, the proportion or share of money gambled that the operator of the establishment keeps as a profit.
[1949 Coffin *Secrets* 183]
2. Also abbreviated: P.C. The advantage gained over an opponent by using dishonest equipment or deception in gambling games.
[1983 Martinez *Gambling Scene* 214]
3. An advantage gained by offering bets at less than TRUE ODDS as, for example, the payoffs on certain proposition bets in bank craps.
[1983 Martinet *Oral Coll*]

percentage dice, *n.* Dice that have been altered to roll certain numbers more often than should be possible. Compare BARR DICE and LOADED DICE.
[1953 Fairfield *Las Vegas* 15]

percentage game, *n.* A banking game, such as craps, designed by the operator to give the establishment a significant advantage over the player.
[1961 Scarne *Complete Guide* 684]

percentage player, *n.* A house employee, usually in poker rooms, allowed to play in a game, using money that belongs to him rather than the establishment.
[1982 Martin *Introduction* 20]

percentage tops and bottom, *n. pl.* Also shortened to PERCENTAGE TOPS. *Plural in form, but singular in use.* MISSPOTTED DICE, usually with two fives on opposite faces of one die and two twos on opposite faces of the other.
[1961 Scarne *Complete Guide* 684]

perfecta, *n.* In racing, a wager in which the bettor picks the winning entry and the second place finisher in order.
[1971 McQuaid *Gambler's Digest* 313]
[1971 *BDNE I, OEDS;* from American Spanish, short for *quiniela perfecta* perfect quinella]

perfect dice, *n.* Also called TRUE DICE or SQUARE DICE or PERFECTS. Dice that are unaltered and measure uniformly to within one ten-thousandths of an inch. See also CALIPERS.
[1974 Scarne *Dice* 23]

perfect low, *n.* Also called a WHEEL. In lowball poker, a five-card hand consisting of ace, 2, 3, 4 and 5.
[1968 Wallace *Poker* 221]

perfect pack, *n.* A Complete deck of fifty-two cards, unmarked and untrimmed.
[1949 Coffin *Secrets* 183]

perfects, *n. pl.* Short for PERFECT DICE.
[1961 Scarne *Complete Guide* 684]

perfect seven, *n.* In California lowball poker, a hand of five cards consisting of ace, 2, 3, 4, and 7.
[1971 Livingston *Poker Strategy* 222]

perfect tenace, *n.* In games like bridge and whist, the two highest cards in alternate sequence when held in the hand of the fourth player to act on a trick, such as the ace-queen of trump at the beginning of the hand, or the equivalent during later play of the hand. Compare TENACE.
[1973 Clark *Oral Coll*]

peter, *n.* In whist and bridge, the play of a high card followed by a low one. See also BLUE PETER and ECHO.
[1885 *OED*]

peter, *v.* In whist and bridge, to play a high card and follow with a low one. See also ECHO.
[1887 *OEDS*]

Peter Funk, *n.* A fraud who uses any of a variety of schemes, often with cards, to dupe a victim. *Obsolete.*
1859 Green *Gam Tricks* 61. *Peter Funks*—The tricks of these scoundrels are such in many cases as are calculated to deceive, as sometimes happens, the most cautious "bargain hunter" . . . A trick often practiced by the New York Funks is to knock off to a stranger a genuine watch for much less than its real value . . . a

buyer, upon paying for a dearly bought prize is told by the *funk,* should he offer a small bill, that it is not good [enough] . . . Thus, trick upon trick is hourly practiced by those thieves, and in a way that renders it unsafe to enter their shops, which may be easily distinguished from all others by the impudence of the inmates, and the constant jabbering of the mock auctioneers of these dens during the time of *funk* sales.
[1867 *DA;* compare 1834 *DAE, DA,* meaning "a swindler"]

peter funkism *n.* Trickery; the practice of swindling, often at cards or on table games. *Obsolete.*
[(1849) *DA*]

petit misere ouvert, *n. French.* Also shortened to **petit misere.** In boston (similar to bridge), the act of losing twelve tricks after discarding the first.
[1950 Morehead *Culbertson* 634]

pharao, pharaoh, pharo, *n.* Variant spellings of FARO.
[1717 *OED* for *pharao;* 1721 *OED* for *pharoah;* 1792 *OED* for *pharo*]

Philadelphia bankroll, *n.* Also shortened to **Philadelphia roll.** A roll of one-dollar bills, with a bill of larger denomination wrapped around the outside. See also MICHIGAN BACKROLL.
[1983 Martinet *Oral Coll*]
[n.d. *DAS*]

Philadelphia layout, *n.* A bank craps table with areas on the layout for betting DON'T PASS and DON'T COME.
[1961 Scarne *Complete Guide* 684]
[The opportunity to bet against the shooter in bank craps was first offered in Philadelphia gambling establishments.]

philosopher, *n.* A cardsharp.
[1950 Morehead *Culbertson* 634]
→*Philosopher* is the usual British term for what Americans call PROFESSOR.

phoebe, *n.* In craps, a roll of the dice totalling 5 pips.
[1968 Adams *Western Words*]

phony, *n.* Also spelled **phoney.** A die altered on either the inside or the outside.
[1961 Scarne *Complete Guide* 684]

photo finish *n.* In racing, the end of a race that features two or more entries crossing the finish line so closely together that only a photograph can determine which entry crossed the finish line first.
[1936 *OEDS,* 1944 *DA*]

piano hand, *n.* In whist, a packet of cards that has few advantages or disadvantages for the player holding it.
[1950 Morehead *Culbertson* 634]

pianola hand, *n.* Also shortened to **pianola.** In bridge, a hand of cards held by one player and so straightforward as to make the play of the hand very easy.
[1913 *OEDS;* figurative use of the trademark (1901 *OED*) for the mechanism which drives a player-piano.]

pic, *n.* In piquet, a bonus score of thirty points awarded when a player wins thirty points and the adversary wins nothing.
[1950 Morehead *Culbertson* 634]

pick, *n.* **1.** In gambling generally, a selection by a bettor of a number, entry, or choice on which to wager money.
[1973 Clark *Oral Coll*]
2. Among handicappers, the selection chosen as having the best chance to win a race or other sporting event.
[1973 Clark *Oral Coll*]
3. Among bookmakers, the offering of a choice between two entries so closely matched that neither side can be handicapped, as by having points added to the score of one football team for betting purposes.
[1975 Clark *Oral Coll*]
4. Each of the spots on a die; a PIP. *Obsolete.*
[1610 *OED*]
5. a. The diamond in playing cards.
[1598 *OED*]
b. The spade in playing cards.
[1787 *OED*]
→The designation *pick* for diamonds and spades but not hearts and clubs is perhaps accounted for by the angular top of a diamond or spade.

pick, *v.* **1.** In gambling generally, to select a number, entry, or choice on which to wager money.
[1973 Clark *Oral Coll*]
2. In sports books, to offer a wager on either of evenly matched teams or entries in a sporting event, without odds or handicap.
[1975 Clark *Oral Coll*]
3. In dice, to CACKLE.
[(1950) 1981 Maurer *Lang. of the Underworld* 190]
4. In the phrases:
pick and pay, In casino twenty-one, to turn up the cards of each player, settle the wager, then put that player's cards on the discard pile before moving to the next player to repeat the process. See also LAY AND PAY and TAKE AND PAY.
[1977 Anness *Dummy Up*]
pick off, In poker, to catch bluffing and consequently cause loss of a pot.
[1978 Brunson *How I Made* 541]
pick 'em, In sports books, to declare to the bettor that two opponents, such as sports teams or boxers, are evenly matched and there will be no incentive offered for increasing the number or size of wagers on one entry or the other.
[1981 Miller *Jargon* 293]

pickle, *n.* In heinz, a penalty card, designated by

the dealer before the deal, that requires the recipient to add a specified amount to the pot.
[1949 Coffin *Secrets* 179]

pickpocket turn, *n.* In faro, the appearance of two 5s on the same turn.
[1943 Maurer *Argot*]

picture card, *n.* Also called a FACE CARD. A jack, queen, or king in playing cards.
[1786 *OED*]

pictures, *n. pl.* Playing cards, regardless of rank.
[1853 *DAE*]

piece, *n.* A man, checker, stone, etc., used in playing board games such as chess, backgammon, and so on.
[1497 *OED*]

piece of the action, *n.* Also shortened to **piece.**
1. A share or percentage of profits, as of a gambling establishment.
[(1950) 1981 Maurer *Lang. of the Underworld* 190; Compare 1929 *OEDS.*]
2. A portion of a wager or participation in a wager or scheme.
[1961 Scarne *Complete Guide* 684]

pig, *n.* **1.** An altered die. See also LOADED DICE and TAT. Compare CALIPERS and PERFECTS.
[1974 Scarne *Dice* 362]
2. In certain variations of poker, such as spit-in-the-ocean, a card turned face up that serves as a WILD CARD.
[1968 Wallace *Poker* 221]
3. In high-low poker, a hand that wins both ways for a single player.
[1983 Martinez *Gambling Scene* 214]
4. An inferior race horse.
[1983 Martinez *Gambling Scene* 214]
[1944 *DAS*]

pigeon, *n.* **1.** The victim of a cheater, especially of a cardsharp.
[1593 *OED*]
2. In poker, a drawn card that greatly improves the hand.
[1949 Coffin *Secrets* 183]
3. A member of a lottery cheating ring. *Mainly British use. Rare.*
[1801 *OED,* alluding to *carrier pigeon*]
4. A professional gambler.
[1886 *DAS*]
5. In racing, a horse that quits.
[(1951) 1981 Maurer *Lang. of the Underworld* 223]

pigeon drop, *n.* Any of a variety of schemes in which a swindler befriends a victim, then finds a wallet or case [the *pigeon*] which a confederate has placed on the ground [the *drop*] ahead of the swindler and the victim. The swindler seems to remove the contents from the wallet or case. When the confederate approaches to claim the wallet, the swindler offers to bet there is nothing in the container, and entices the victim to bet with him. The confederate finds the contents intact, and takes the money from the swindler and the victim, who is consoled by the swindler until the confederate is safely away. The verb form, to *drop the pigeon* refers to enacting the fraud.
[1937 *OEDS*]

pigpen, *n.* An illegal gambling establishment.
[1982 Martin *Introduction* 25]

pig's eye, *n.* In playing cards, the ace of diamonds.
[1864 *DSUE;* So called because of the rhomboid shape of the iris of the eye of a pig and the figure for diamonds, a suit in cards]

pike, *v.* To make small and frequent bets, especially at faro.
[1938 Asbury *Sucker's Progress* 16]
[1889 *OEDS,* in Farmer *Americanisms Old & New* 419-420]

piker, *n.* a cautious gambler who makes small and frequent bets, especially at faro.
[1872 *DA, OEDS;* 1898 *DAE*]

pile, *n.* A quantity of money or chips, especially one's table stakes at poker, in disarray. Compare STACK (def. 1).
[1839 *DA,* 1844 *DAE*]

pile, *v.* In the phrase:
pile up the rocks, To accumulate money. Compare ROCKS.
[1897 *OED*]

pilot, *n.* In horse racing, another term for a jockey.
[1983 Martinez *Gambling Scene* 214]
[(1951) 1981 Maurer *Lang. of the Underworld* 223]
[n.d. *DAS,* 1976 *OEDS*]

pimple, *n.* A pip on a die. *Facetious use.*
[1983 Martinet *Oral Coll*]

pinch, *n.* An arrest made during a raid on an illegal game or illegal gambling establishment.
[1961 Scarne *Complete Guide* 684]
[Compare 1900 *OEDS,* meaning "an arrest"]

pinch, *v.* **1.** To arrest a gambler during a raid on an illegal game or establishment.
[1961 Scarne *Complete Guide* 684]
[Compare 1860 *OED*]
2. a. In racing, to urge on a horse.
[1737 *OED*]
b. Of a horse, to cut in front of another horse, especially without sufficient room to spare.
[(1951) 1981 Maurer *Lang. of the Underworld* 223]
4. In the phrase:
pinch back, In racing, to slow down an entry by trapping it behind a group of slower horses, dogs, etc.
[1968 Buchele *Greyhound Racing* 6]

pin gaff, *n.* A die with a small bristle or pin set into the center pip on the face showing five pips.

The bristle retards the roll of the die on a felt or blanketed surface, causing the side with two pips to land face up more often than normal.
[1974 Scarne *Dice* 33]

pink, *adj.* In poker, pertaining to a diamond or heart flush.
[1963 Steig *Common Sense* 186]

pink eye, *n.* Also called RED EYE. Among card sharps, a tinted contact lens worn to read the backs of specially marked cards.
[1968 Wallace *Poker* 221]

pinochle, *n.* Also spelled **pinocle. 1.** A card game played with a double deck of 48 cards comprised of the 9, 10, jack, queen, king, and ace, points being scored for certain combinations.
[1864 *OEDS, DA,* as *peanukle*]
2. In pinochle, a meld of the queen of spades and the jack of diamonds. See also DOUBLE PINOCHLE.
[1864 *DA,* 1897 *OED*]

pinochler, *n.* One who plays pinochle.
[1894 *DA*]

pin work, *n.* Scratches put on the backs of playing cards by a cheater so the cards can be read from the back.
[1968 Adams *Western Words*]

pip, *n.* A dot or spot on dice, dominoes, playing cards, etc. See also PICK (def. 4).
[1604 *OED,* as *peep*]

pipe salesman, *n.* Also called a SQUARE JOHN. An honest player in a cardroom, usually a person who is somewhat knowledgeable about a game and is thought to be honest.
[1982 *Review Journal* 12/5: 1]
[Compare *pipe:* (1935) 1981 Maurer *Lang. of the Underworld* 78, meaning "a victim who is easy to rob," related to 1902 *OEDS,* meaning something easy to do," itself perhaps a contraction of *lead pipe cinch:* 1898 *OEDS* "'J. Kerr' *Cherry Blr.* 71, I never had a 'lead pipe cinch'; I never had a 'pull'; I never had a 'straight' that was not beaten by a 'full'."]

piping, *n.* A cheating method in which an observer of the game signals a confederate as to the value of cards held by an opponent.
1726 Wilson *Art and Mystery* 102. By *Piping* I mean, when one of the Company that does not play (which frequently happens) sits down in a convenient Place to smoke a Pipe and so look on, pretending to amuse himself that Way. Now the disposing of his Fingers on the Pipe, whilst smoking, discovers the principal Cards that are in the Person's Hand he overlooks, which was always esteem'd a sufficient Advantage to win a Game by another Way.
[Compare *pipe:* 1846 *OEDS,* 1848 *DAS,* meaning "to watch"]

pippage, *n.* In backgammon, the collective count of pips on one player's turn.
[1976 Figgis *Gambler's Handbook* 70]

pique shot, *n.* Also spelled PEEK or PEEKAY. *French.* Also called a WHIP SHOT. A controlled cast of the dice made in such a fashion as to cause certain numbers to be rolled more often than would be normally by chance.
[1974 Scarne *Dice* 263]

piquet, *n.* Also spelled **picquet.** A card game popular in the seventeenth and eighteenth centuries, played by two persons using a deck with thirty-two cards comprised of 7, 8, 9, 10, jack, queen, king, and ace, in which points are scored for combinations of cards and for tricks. *Rare.*
[1646 *OED;* ultimately from French, perhaps from PIC]

pit, *n.* In a casino, the area surrounded by a group of gaming tables.
[1963 Taylor *City of Sin* 11]
[Compare 1886 *DAE,* 1903 *OEDS,* meaning "a part of the floor of an exchange appropriated to a special branch of business"]

pit bank, *n.* In a casino, a secured booth or podium in the pit used to keep such things as credit records and inventories of amounts of chips on the tables surrounding the pit.
[1982 Martin *Introduction* 24]

pit boss, *n.* In a casino, the representative of the management who watches over several games.
1983 Martinet *Oral Coll.* Working from the bottom up in the pecking order, you have the dealer, then the boxman in craps, then the floorman in craps or twenty-one. If you have a big dice pit with several games, then you might have a *pit boss* in craps. In twenty-one the *pit boss* has several tables and his floormen report to him. He reports to the shift boss. The shift boss may or may not be the casino manager. And the casino manager usually has some points [owns a percentage of the casino] but probably reports to the owner, or the guy fronting for the owners.
[Compare 1956 *DAS,* meaning "a foreman"]

pit clerk, *n.* In a casino, an employee charged with keeping the records in a pit, such as CREDIT PLAY MEMORANDA, FILL SLIPS, RIM CARDS and STIFF SHEETS.
[1978 Clark *Oral Coll*]

pit credit report, *n.* In a casino, a form used to record the credit limits of players and the amounts due either the casino or the player. Compare CREDIT PLAY MEMORANDA.
[1982 Martin *Introduction* 8]

pit drop, *n.* In a casino, the amount of money wagered by gamblers in one pit, such as a DICE PIT, during a specified period of time, such as a shift.
[1987 *Review Journal* 10/25:1a]

pit fill record, *n.* In a casino, a form used to record the amount of chips on each table at the

beginning of a shift. Compare FILL SLIP.
[1979 Hilton Hotel *Procedures* 31]

pit floorman, *n.* Often shortened to FLOORMAN. A casino employee who supervises one or more tables in a PIT.
[1978 Alexander *Glossary* 12]

pit marker custodian, *n.* Same as a PIT CLERK. A casino employee who keeps on a PIT CREDIT REPORT the records of amounts of money owed to the casino by the players who have credit. Compare MARKER.
[1978 Alexander *Glossary* 12]

pit repayment, *n.* In a casino, the act of a player redeeming credit slips, or MARKERS, from the PIT CLERK, by turning chips over to the pit clerk in exchange for a receipt and a notation on the PIT CREDIT REPORT that payment on an account has been made.
[1978 Alexander *Glossary* 12]

pit report, *n.* Also called the MASTER GAME REPORT. In a casino, a form used to record all money and chip transfers to and from a pit during a designated period of time, such as one shift or one day. See also STIFF REPORT.
[1978 Alexander *Glossary* 12]

pitch, *v.* **1.** To deal playing cards, especially as a professional dealer. See also BROAD TOSSER.
1980 Clark *Oral Coll.* He stayed with us for awhile, maybe a couple of months, then he moved up to the Stardust to *pitch* poker. He was what we call a good man, very dextrous with cards and able to cover it well by appearing to be sloppy while shuffling and dealing.
2. In games like nap, to determine a particular suit as trump by leading a card of that suit.
[1938 Asbury *Sucker's Progress* 51]
[1890 *OED,* in *Century Dict.*]

pitcher, *n.* **1.** A professional card dealer.
[1973 Clark *Oral Coll*]
2. In auction pitch, the highest bidder.
[1971 McQuaid *Gambler's Digest* 313]

place, *n.* **1.** In horse racing, a position among the first four competitors to cross the finish line.
[1885 *OED*]
2. In American racing, second place. Compare SHOW and WIN.
[1836 *OEDS*]

place, *v.* **1.** To announce the position of a horse among the competitors in a race as they cross the finish line. [1831 *OED*]
2. In American racing, to finish a race second, or sometimes first.
[1924 *OEDS,* but compare *v.* 1836 *OEDS*]
3. In British racing, to finish a race fourth or better. [1831 *OED*]
4. In racing, to finish high enough in the field to win a share of the purse, usually fourth or better.
[1976 Figgis *Gambler's Handbook* 237]
[1849 *OED*, n.d. *DAS*]

place bet, *n.* **1.** In bank craps, a wager made on a particular number without waiting for that number to be established as a point by the shooter. Compare POINT BET.
[(1950) 1982 Maurer *Lang. of the Underworld* 190]
2. In racing: **a.** In the U.S., a wager that an entry will finish a race second or better.
b. In Britain, a wager that an entry will finish fourth or better.
[1885 *OED,* as *place betting*]

place number, *n.* Also called a BOX NUMBER. In bank craps, any of the boxes toward the top of the LAYOUT marked with the numbers 4, 5, 6, 8, 9, and 10. Compare POINT NUMBER.
[1974 Scarne *Dice* 115]

place tickets, *n. pl.* In poker, the cards comprising the second best hand at the showdown.
[1968 Wallace *Poker* 221]
[Compare PLACE, *n.* and TICKET (def. 2)]

plain, *adj.* **1.** In playing cards, noting the numbered cards, as opposed to the FACE CARDS.
[1844 *OED:* Dickens *Martin Chuzzlewit* xvii, "Court cards and plain cards of every denomination."]
2. In games like bridge, cards other than TRUMPS. Compare PLAIN SUIT.
[1862 *OED*]

plain limit, *n.* In poker, the highest amount allowed as a bet by the operator of the game.
[1890 Quinn *Fools of Fortune* 193]

plain suit, *n.* In such games as bridge or whist, any card that is not of the trump suit. Compare PLAIN (def. 2).
[1953 Crawford *Consistent Winner* 351]

plaque, *n. French.* A flat, rectangular board, usually measuring about three inches by six inches, used as a substitute for money in some casinos outside the U.S.
1979 Clark *Oral Coll. Plaques* are used in foreign casinos the way we use chips in this country. Of course, there don't seem to be as many demoninations as we have for checks [chips].
[1904 *OEDS*]

plate, *n.* **1.** In horse racing, a horseshoe, especially a lightweight shoe designed for efficiency under specific track conditions or characteristics of a horse's behavior. Also called RACING PLATE.
[1840 *OED*]
2. A silver plate or a silver plated flat trophy awarded to the winners of CLAIMING RACES in place of prize money.
[1675 *OED*]
3. A device for trimming cards to a slightly smaller size. Compare STRIPPERS.
1843 Green *Exposure* 17. Besides this, the players often have a small machine called a *plate,* the use of which is to make such of the cards as they

may wish, a little smaller than the others, by trimming very little from the edges. When this is done, a man can cut so as to have almost any card turned up that he may wish.

plater, *n.* **1.** An inferior racehorse.
[1955 Hillis *Pari-Mutuel Betting* 117]
[(1951) 1981 Maurer *Lang. of the Underworld* 228]
→From the early eighteenth century practice of providing silver plates as trophies to the owners of winning horses. As time went by, the silver plates increasingly became silverplated trophies. The purses in such races were small so the term came to refer to horses that ran in low-stakes races, and then, by extension, inferior horses generally.
2. A racehorse which does not do as well as expected.
[(1951) 1981 Maurer *Lang. of the Underworld* 223]

play, *n.* **1.** The action of risking stakes on the outcome of an event; gambling.
[*a*1300 *OED*]
2. The amount of activity in a gambling establishment, especially in reference to profits. Compare ACTION.
1978 Clark *Oral Coll.* We had pretty good *play* in here [a casino] last night because of the fight [boxing match at a nearby resort]. You always get action [gambling activity] with fight and race fans. They lose happily, we get the *play*. That pleases everybody.
[(1950) 1981 Maurer *Lang. of the Underworld* 190]
3. a. In poker, an action especially dramatic or creative during a betting round.
[1978 Brunson *How I* 541]
b. The general conduct of a hand at games like bridge, such as the bidding and the sequence of leads. [1531 *OED*]
4. A point in a game; a special device used in a game. *Obsolete.*
[1778 *OED*]

play, *v.* **1.** To participate in gambling activity; to wager stakes at a game or on the outcome of an event.
[1511 *OED*; 1858 *DA, DAE, OEDS*]
2. To stake or wager (something) in a game.
[1483 *OED*]
3. To take a card from the hand and place it face up on the table at the appropriate time during the course of a card game.
[1680 *OED*]
4. In the phrases and particle constructions:
play a bet open, In faro, to wager that a particular card will win, as opposed to COPPERING A BET, wagering that a particular card will lose.
1868 Trumps *Pocket Hoyle* 208. *Playing a bet open* is to bet a card will win, not lose.
[1864 *DAE*]
play a designated limit, To bet the maximum allowed in a card game.
[1916 *DAE*]
play a shoestring, In faro, to make a series of wagers of the same size or type.
[1943 Maurer *Argot*]
play at (cards, dice, a game), To engage or take part in a specified game.
[(1297) 1560 *OED*]
play away, To lose (money) by gambling.
[1562 *OED*]
play back, In poker: **1.** To raise a bet that has already been raised by an earlier player.
[1973 Clark *Oral Coll*]
2. To declare there is a greater amount in one's stake than actually exists, especially in table stakes poker.
[1949 Coffin *Secrets* 183]
3. To increase the amount of a previous player's wager; to raise.
[1973 Preston *Play Poker* 168]
4. To wager more than one has on the table; to be LIGHT OR PLAY BEHIND.
[1971 Livingston *Poker Strategy* 222]
play ball, To participate in a scheme to cheat the casino in which one is employed. See also BALL TEAM and BASEBALL TEAM.
[1983 Martinet *Oral Coll*]
[Compare 1867 *DA,* 1880 *DAE*]
play behind, In poker: **1.** To declare a bet larger than the amount of money one has on the table.
[1971 Livingston *Poker Strategy* 222]
2. To declare, before a hand is dealt, an intention to wager more money than one has on the table.
[1978 Brunson *How I Made* 541]
play blind, In poker, to call or raise the bet of a previous bettor before looking at the cards.
[1978 Larson *Vocabulary* 100]
play cases, In faro, a system for betting higher amounts on the last card of a suit still undealt, especially the final card on the last turn (of twenty-five).
[1943 Maurer *Argot*]
play high, 1. To gamble for large stakes.
[1796 *OED*]
2. To place a card of upper rank, usually a king or queen, on the table in trump games.
[1885 *OED*]
play it alone, To play a game of cards without one's partner.
[1864 *DAE*]
play off, In cribbage, to play a card of a rank at least three numbers different from a previously played card to prevent a run, or count of three cards of consecutive rank, as 3, 4, 5. See also PLAY ON.
[1953 Crawford *Consistent Winner* 351]
play on, In cribbage, to play a card near the rank of a previously played card, to make possible a run, or a play of consecutive ranks, as 3, 4, 5, 6. See also PLAY OFF.
[1953 Crawford *Consistent Winner* 351]
play on velvet, To gamble with money already won in a game; to play without risking one's

capital, or original stake.
[1943 Maurer *Argot*]

play or pay, To fail to "play" or engage in a match, so that one's backers have to pay as if he had lost. See also PLAY-OR-PAY BET.
[1877 *OED*]

play over, 1. In bridge, to play a higher card on a trick than any played by an opponent. See also COVER.
[1950 Morehead *Culbertson* 385]
2. In poker, to sit down at a place temporarily vacated by a player and participate in the game until the player returns.
[1981 Golad *Oral Coll*]

play pat, In draw poker, to use only the cards dealt at the beginning of the hand; to refuse to discard. See also PAT HAND.
[1887 *DA*]

play percentages, Also **play the percentages.** To risk money on a wager only when the chance for winning is particularly great. See also PLAY THE FAVORITES.
[1971 Livingston *Poker Strategy* 222]

play the advantage over, Also shortened to **play the advantages.** To cheat, especially in gambling games. [1839 *DA, DAE*]

play the bank, To play FARO.
[1943 Maurer *Argot*]

play the evens, In faro, to use a betting system that requires wagering on the even-numbered cards to win.
[1943 Maurer *Argot*]

play the favorites, Same as PLAY PERCENTAGES. To bet on most probable outcome.
[(1951) 1981 Maurer *Lang. of the Underworld* 223]

play the field, In craps, to place a bet on an area of the layout declaring the next roll to be 2, 3, 4, 9, 10, 11, or 12. In some craps games, a winner in the field receives an extra payoff if the number rolled is 2, 3, or 12.
[1968 Thackrey *Nick the Greek* 91]

play the horses, or **play the ponies** or **play the races,** To bet on the outcome of horse races, especially habitually or frequently.
[1902 *DAE,* for *play the races;* 1916 *DA,* for *play the ponies;* 1948 *DA,* for *play the horses;* compare PLAY, *v.* (def.1)]

play the muts or **play the mutes,** To bet on horse racing using a pari-mutuel machine.
[(1951) 1981 Maurer *Lang. of the Underworld* 223]

play the numbers, To gamble on an illegal lottery game that uses numbers to determine winners.
1976 *U.S. News & World Report* (Nexis) 2/9:50. Why crime succeeds. The numbers racket illustrates one reason criminals are so successful: Many people accept or even willingly participate in criminal operations. One study estimated that 2 out of 3 inner-city adults play the numbers. Millions of people smoke marijuana. For every hijacked load of goods or every piece of stolen property, a buyer stands ready—eager to get the goods at less than wholesale price.

play the nuts, To wager on an event that will almost surely win.
[1983 Martinez *Gambling Scene* 215]
[(1951) 1981 Maurer *Lang. of the Underworld* 223]

play the papers, To gamble. *Obsolete.*
[1858 *OEDS, DAE, DA*]

play the velvet, To wager with money won from the house or bank.
[(1943) 1951 Maurer *Lang. of the Underworld* 139]

play to the score, 1. In bridge, to modify one's bidding system when the score is close to constituting a game.
[1950 Morehead *Culbertson* 635]
2. In cribbage, to modify discarding and playing practices when the score with one's opponent is close and the end of the game is near.
[1973 Clark *Oral Coll*]

playboy, *n.* In spoil five, the jack of the trump suit.
[1950 Morehead *Culbertson* 635]

play-debt, *n.* A gambling debt; the owing of money or stakes to an opponent.
[1712 *OED*]

player, *n.* **1.** A bettor who risks stacks on the outcome of an event.
[1483 *OED*]
2. In baccarat, one of the two positions on the table layout to which cards are dealt. The other position is the BANKER.
[1970 *Baccarat, The Facts*]

player hand, *n.* In baccarat, the position on the layout farthest from the DEALING BOX. It is one of two positions on which participants may place wagers. Compare BANKER HAND.
[1970 *Baccarat, The Facts]*

player's card, *n.* In faro, every second card dealt in a turn and designated as a winner for the players who wagered on that card to win. See also DEAL CARD and FIGURE and SODA.
1868 Trumps *Pocket Hoyle* 205. . . . the Ten, like the Ace, is removed, revealing a King, which is the *player's card,* the bank losing all the stakes found upon it.
1978 Clark *Oral Coll.* The first card is soda, or deal card, and wins for nobody. The second card is dealer's card and wins for everybody who bet that way, not just the dealer. The third card is the *player's card,* and wins for everybody who bet that way, that is, for everybody who had an uncoppered bet on the layout for that card or that figure. It continues that way, the first card is the dealer's, the second is the player's.

playing card, *n.* Each card of a set, pack, or deck used for playing a card game.
[1543 *OED*]

play-money, *n.* Cash or stakes won in gaming

that the player can then use instead of his own capital.
[1705 *OED*]

playoff, *n.* Also written **play-off.** A contest or a series of contests to determine a final winner from among the winners of preliminary games, as in a poker or bridge tournament.
[1895 *OEDS*]

play of the hand, *n. phr.* In poker, the development of the betting pattern during the course of a hand.
1981 Golad *Oral Coll.* You learn a lot while sitting out with rags [poor cards], just watching the *play of the hand.* You learn about the way others bet under certain conditions, and that helps your own play later.

play-or-pay bet, *n.* A bet made on a contest or game which will be paid by a contestant's backers if he fails to participate, as if he had played and lost.
[1821 *OED*]

play-table, *n.* A gaming table; a table designed for a specific gambling game.
[1848 *OED*]

pli, *n.* A method used in betting at faro, whereby the bettor bends a card in such a fashion as to indicate a desire to bet half the stake.
1843 Green *Exposure* 168. *Pli* is when a punter, having lost half his stake by a doublet, bends his card in the middle, and setting it up with the points and foot towards the dealer, signifies thereby a desire either of recovering the moiety, or of losing all.

ploy, *n.* A tactic or stratagem used to confuse or disconcert an opponent, especially at card or board games.
[1971 McQuaid *Gambler's Digest* 313]
[Compare (1722) *OED*, meaning "an action which one pursues; also a trick" 1950 *OEDS*, meaning "a gambit"]

pluck, *v.* **1.** To cheat, especially at cards. Compare PIGEON.
[Compare (*c*1400) *OED*, meaning "to rob; swindle"]
2. To draw cards from the pack. *Obsolete.*
[1606 *OED*]

plug, *n.* A poker player who plays slowly, studying every player and every action on every bet.
[1949 Coffin *Secrets* 183]

plug, *v.* Among casino dealers, to solicit tips.
[1965 Fraiken *Inside Nevada* 61]

plugger, *n.* An employee of a gambling establishment, usually in poker, paid to play small amounts at a table until enough players are present to constitute a game; a SHILL. The *plugger* uses house money, bets minimal amounts, and drops from the hand before the showdown. The *shill* may be allowed to use personal stakes and play to win.
[1890 Quinn *Fools of Fortune* 239]

plumb the bones, *v. phr.* To place weights in dice to make certain numbers appear more often than others. See also BONES and LOAD and DOCTORS.
[1938 Asbury *Sucker's Progress* 42]
[Compare (*a*1450 *OED*, meaning "to weight with lead"]

plunge, *v.* To wager heavily, especially in an attempt to win quickly or to recover large losses.
[1886 *OED*]

plunger, *n.* A player who bets heavily in an attempt to win a large amount quickly or to recover losses.
1889 Ellangowan *Sporting Anecdotes* 281. A "punter" means a person who speculates for small amounts. At baccarat or on the turf he operates generally for shillings, half-crowns, or crown, or the smallest amount the banker or bookmaker will accept. In this way he is distinguished from the "*plunger*," who operates for large amounts.
[1877 *OED*]

plus game, *n.* Also called a SIDE GAME. In a casino, a game that adds variety to the games offered by the casino, such as a BIG SIX WHEEL.
[1953 Lewis *Sagebrush Casinos* 98]

plus value, *n.* In bridge, a card that adds strength to the hand, but is not counted for bidding purposes.
[1950 Morehead *Culbertson* 635]

P.M. line, *n.* Also shortened to P.M. Also written **PM** or **pm.** In racing, the odds listed at the track prior to a race. The distinction is with the MORNING LINE, or the first-posted odds, which may change as the time of the race draws near.
[1955 Hillis *Pari-Mutuel Betting* 89]

pocket, *n.* Especially in the prepositional phrase: **in the pocket. 1.** In horse racing, designating a position in which an entry is prevented from moving out in front because of other entries in front and to the outside; an entry BOXED in and unable to go ahead of other, slower entries.
[1890 *OED,* in *Century Dict.*]
2. In hold 'em and stud poker, designating cards dealt face down, or HOLE CARDS.
[1959 *OEDS*]

pocket, *v.* In racing, to hem in (a competitor) in front and at the sides, so as to prevent him from winning.
[1890 *OED,* in *Century Dict.*]

point, *n.* **1.** A unit of score in a game.
[1746 *OED*]
2. The unit stating the fluctuation of odds in a betting proposition. [1814 *OED*]
3. A pip on a card, die, or domino. *British use.*
[1905 *OED*]
4. In craps, the number rolled, from among 4, 5, 6, 8, 9, 10, which must be repeated before rolling a 7.
[1974 Scarne *Dice* 76]
5. In backgammon, one of the twenty-four

triangles, or fletches, on the table layout. See also PENNANT.
[1588 *OED*]
6. In piquet, the number of cards of the most numerous suit in the hand after the discard.
[1719 *OED*]
7. In bridge, a unit by which a hand is evaluated before the bidding.
[1959 *OEDS*]
8. points, *pl.* The percentage of a casino or gambling operation owned by one person. Compare PERCENTAGE (def. 1).
1983 Martinet *Oral Coll.* And the casino manager usually has some *points* [owns a percentage of the casino] but probably reports to the owner, or the guy fronting for the owners.

point, *v.* In backgammon, to place a *stone* on a pennant. *Rare.*
[1680 *OED*]

point bet, *n.* In craps, a bet that the shooter will or will not roll the established point, 4, 5, 6, 8, 9, or 10. Compare PLACE BET.
[1961 Scarne *Complete Guide* 684]
[(1950) 1981 Maurer *Lang of the Underworld* 190]

point box, *n.* On a craps layout, the numbered box on which the puck is placed when the shooter establishes a point.
[1973 Friedman *Casino Games* 35]

point count, *n.* **1.** The total numeric value of a hand of cards, a roll of dice, a play at dominoes, etc. [1959 *OEDS*]
2. In bridge, the total worth of designated cards used to determine bidding strategy.
[1953 Crawford *Consistent Winner* 351]
3. In twenty-one, a card-counting system.
[1973 Clark *Oral Coll*]

point marker, *n.* In craps, the button or puck placed on the box number corresponding to the point established by the shooter.
[1973 Friedman *Casino Games* 35]

point number, *n.* Same as the POINT. In craps, the number, from 4, 5, 6, 8, 9, or 10 that a shooter rolls and must roll again before rolling a number 7. Compare PLACE NUMBER.
[1974 Scarne *Dice* 80]

point shaving, *n. phr.* The act by a player of keeping the score of a sporting event within a certain number of points so that someone wagering a large amount of money will win his bet.
[1971 McQuaid *Gambler's Digest* 313]

point spread, *n.* Also called THE SPREAD. In sports books, the points assigned to a particular team, usually in football or basketball games, to make a wager more attractive to a bettor.
[1973 Clark *Oral Coll*]

point value, *n.* The number of points assigned to specific playing cards or markers in various games, or for specific moves in a game.
[1950 Morehead *Culbertson* 636]

poker, *n.* Any of a family of card games used for gambling featuring the dealing of at least three cards, a pool or POT, rounds of betting, often with bluffing, and a SHOWDOWN to determine a winner.
[1834 (1836) *DA,* 1836 *DAE, OEDS;* 1855 *OED;* American English, compare German *pochen,* meaning "to brag" and French *poque,* designating a similar game]

poker, *v.* **1.** To play poker.
[1844 *DA*]
2. To beat at poker.
[1949 *DA*]

Poker. Most POKER PLAYERS play a SOCIAL GAME (such as PENNY-ANTE or PENNY POKER) in a PRIVATE GAME. CASINOS may provide a POKER ROOM for CLUB POKER with HOUSE RULES prominently displayed. Gambling establishments providing PUBLIC POKER may be called POKER JOINTS which are frequented by the POKER CLERGY, also refered to as members of the POKER SCHOOL. POKERISTS must be vigilant against the POKER SHARPS with a PINK EYE, GLEAMER, STACKED DECK, or a SCAM such as a SNATCH GAME. If not, they may be given BROKE MONEY or WALKING MONEY.

The variations in play are too numerous to be easily listed. The more bizarre styles are dubbed ENGLISH POKER. Most players deal a version of DRAW POKER, also called CLOSED POKER, in which all the cards dealt are undisclosed to one's opponents, or STUD POKER, called OPEN POKER, in which some of the cards dealt are face upward. STRAIGHT POKER is DRAW POKER with no special variations. Other variations focus mostly on LIMIT STAKES which may range from NO LIMIT, also called UNLIMITED POKER, to TABLE STAKES, to a RESTRICTED POT. Versions like WHISKEY POKER (played for drinks), SINGLE-HANDED POKER (only one deal of the cards), a TEN AND TWENTY GAME (stating betting amounts) exhibit some of the types of variation. LOWBALL (lowest hand wins) contrasts with HIGHBALL (highest hand wins). SEVENS RULE (in lowball) contrasts with JACKS OR BETTER (in highball). FINGER POKER is played on credit.

A WILD GAME designates either a game with WILD CARDS, frequently ONE-EYED JACKS, or a fast-paced game with high stakes and many raises in the betting rounds.

The combinations of cards vary usually as PAIRS, STRAIGHTS, and FLUSHES to determine the strength of a hand which enables a player to vye for the KITTY, sometimes called the JACKPOT. A player without IMMORTALS or an IRON DUKE may choose to BLUFF, as a FOURFLUSHER, or hope for a GARDENA MIRACLE such as to DRAW TO an INSIDE STRAIGHT. An ALTERNATE STRAIGHT, DUTCH STRAIGHT, SKIP STRAIGHT, SCOTCH STRAIGHT, or some other LALAPALOOZA may be allowed to beat THREE OF A KIND.

The frequency of specific card combinations has given rise to monikers. A simple straight may be referred to with " FROM HERE TO THERE WITHOUT A PAIR." Simpler names include AMERICAN AIRLINES (for the aces of hearts and diamonds), KU KLUX KLAN (for any three kings), MITES AND LICE (three of a kind face upward and a pair face downward), JESSIE JAMES (a four and a five as the first cards dealt, in reference to a .45 caliber revolver). JUDGE DUFFY refers to three 10s, in reference to "thirty dollars or thirty days" upon conviction for gambling.

Some hands are associated with specific events or places: DEAD MAN'S HAND (for a pair of aces and a pair of 8s, from the hand dealt to Wild Bill Hickock just before he was shot in the back); SANTA BARBARA, also called a BIG SLICK, (for an ace and a king as the first cards dealt, in reference to a oil spill there); WASHINGTON MONUMENT (for three 5s, because the monument is 555 feet high).

People at a POKER TABLE may be nicknamed for their characteristic pattern of activity or responsibility. A SENATE DEALER is not a BETTOR or a PLAYER. An ASSIGNED BETTOR may be a LOOSE PLAYER with POKER PATIENCE, sometimes called LEATHER ASS, and may become a FREE WHEELER if, as a BULL, he FOURBLUFFS with a SUPER-BLUFF searching for a PIGEON. A RIBBON CLERK, however, may become a TELEPHONE BOOTH unless he chooses to RAT-HOLE and thus become a RAT HOLER. A ROBIN-HOOD CHEATER picks his MARK, hoping to find a FREE WHEELER in a PAYDAY GAME who may attempt a POST OAK BLUFF.

poker chip, *n.* A counter representing money used in playing poker. See also CHIP or CHECK.
[1879 *DA, DAE, OEDS*]

poker clergy, *n.* Poker players.
[1907 *DA*]

poker dice, *n. pl.* **1. a.** A set of five dice featuring a playing card on each face, 9, 10, jack, queen, king, or ace, used to play a variety of games, often for drinks in a bar.
[1874 *DA, OEDS;* 1879 *DAE*]
b. A set of five dice with regular pips thrown for highest score.
[(1950) 1981 Maurer *Lang. of the Underworld,* 190]
2. A game resembling poker played with a set of these dice.
[1901 *OEDS*]

poker face, *n.* **1.** Also written **poker-face**. Card player's face which shows no emotion. Poker players are especially wary of TELLS, facial expressions or movements that may give opponents information about the cards they hold or draw.
[1855 *DA, DAE, OEDS*]
2. A card player who controls his facial expressions so as not to reveal emotion. *Rare.*
[n.d. *DAS*]

poker-face, *v.* To look at someone with a changeless facial expression. *Rare.*
[1925 *DA*]

poker-faced, *adj.* Having a POKER FACE; without change of facial expression.
[1923 *OEDS*]

poker flat, *n.* Same as POKER ROOM.
[1869 *DA,* as *Poker Flat,* a place name, but being used generically and in lower case by 1938]

pokerino, *n.* A poker game in which the stakes played for are very low. Compare PENNY ANTE and PENNY POKER.
[n.d. *DAS*]
→Especially popular in retirement homes and convalescent homes as having recreational and social value.

pokerist, *n.* A person who plays poker; a POKER PLAYER. *Rare.*
1887 Proctor *Chance* 230. For instance, with few players a *pokerist* might safely decide that he would not go in on less than a high pair, as kings or aces, and adhering to that rule throughout the play would be likely to come out without heavy loss.
[1873 *DA*]

poker joint, *n.* Same as POKER ROOM.
[1911 *DA*]

poker machine, *n.* A type of slot machine bearing card symbols.
[1964 *OEDS*]

poker patience, *n.* A form of competitive solitaire, the object of which is to form winning poker combinations in each row and column.
[1912 *OEDS; patience* is another name for solitaire]

poker player, *n.* One who plays poker. See also POKERIST.
[1844 *DA, OEDS*]

poker room, *n.* A place where card players gather to play poker.
[1872 *OED*]

poker school, *n.* A group of people gathered together to play poker. See also POKER CLERGY.
[1944 *OEDS*]

poker sharp, *n.* One who is dextrous at playing poker, especially a cheater at poker. Compare CARD SHARP and SHARPER.
[1861 *DA*]

poker table, *n.* Also written *pokertable.* A specially designed table, usually seven- or eight-sided, for playing poker.
[1861 *OEDS*]

pole, *n.* **1.** In horse racing, one of several posts placed at various points around an oval track, marking distances from the finish line. See also POST (def. 2).
[1836 *DA, DAE;* 1851 *OEDS*]
2. Especially **the pole.** Also called POLE POSITION. In racing, the starting position closest to the

inside rail on an oval track. See also POST (def. 1).
[1851 *OEDS,* 1852 *DA*]
3. Also called the STICK. In bank craps, the position of the dealer who controls the dice and the rhythm of the game.
[1983 Martinet *Oral Coll*]

policy, *n.* Also called NUMBERS. An illegal lottery based on choosing three or more numbers, as of the last three digits of a publicly published tabulation of stocks, scores, etc. *Often used attributively.*
[1830 *DA, OEDS,* 1877 *DAE;* 1890 *OED*]

policy, *v.* To bet on certain numbers coming out in lottery drawings.
[1877 *DAE,* 1889 *OED,* Farmer *Americanisms Old & New*]

policy dealer, *n.* Also called **policy writer.** A person who operates a numbers game.
[1865 *DA,* 1875 *DAE,* as *policy dealer;* 1949 *OEDS,* for *policy writer*]

policy drop, *n.* A centrally located room or office for collecting money and betting slips for a NUMBERS game, or policy.
[1960 Cook *Gambling, Inc.* 273]

policy game, *n.* A NUMBERS game, usually illegal.
[1885 *OEDS*]

policy runner, *n.* Also called NUMBERS RUNNER. A person who carries wagers and betting slips between the players and operators of a numbers game.
[1726 *OED*]

policy shop, *n.* Also called **policy office.** An illegal gambling establishment that specializes in accepting policy, or NUMBERS BETS.
[1858 *DA, OED,* as *policy shop;* 1843 *OEDS,* as *policy office*]

policy slip, *n.* A ticket or receipt given on a stake of money in a NUMBERS game.
[1890 *DA, DAE*]

policy wheel, *n.* A revolving drum from which the winning numbers of a POLICY GAME are drawn.
[1906 *OEDS*]

pone, *n.* **1.** In two-handed card games such as cribbage, the non-dealer.
[1950 Morehead *Culbertson* 636]
2. In card games with several players, such as poker or twenty-one, the player to the right of the dealer.
1843 Green *Exposure* 285. The cards are all dealt out in succession, unless a natural vingt-un occurs; and in the meantime the *pone,* or youngest hand, should collect those that have been played, and shuffle them together, in order that they may be ready for the dealer against the period when he shall have distributed the whole pack.
[1890 *OED,* in *Century Dict*; from Latin *pone,* the imperative of *pōnere* "to place"]

pont, *n. French.* Same as PAIX.
1843 Green *Exposure* 168. *Pont* is the same as paix. It means a repeated wager.

pony, *n.* **1.** Often **ponies,** *pl.* A race horse. *Especially U.S. use.* See also PLAY THE PONIES (a variant of *play the horses*).
[1907 *OEDS*]
2. A LEAD PONY or similar horse stabled at a racetrack but not kept for competition.
[(1951) 1981 Maurer *Lang. of the Underworld* 223]

pool, *n.* **1.** The POT or stakes played for, especially in poker. Compare ANTE and KITTY and WIDOW.
1836 Eidrah *Hoyle Famil* 69. *Pool* is the stake to be played for, usually put into a small salver, which lies in the middle of the table.
1866 *American Card Player* 131. An "ante" or stake is deposited in the centre of the table by the dealer; this is called the *Pool* or Pot.
[1711-12 *OED*]
2. The combined wagers of all bettors on a horse race, lottery, etc., from which winners share the collected funds and the losers receive nothing. The operator of the *pool* often retains a percentage of the amount wagered to cover expenses for maintaining the *pool.* Compare PARIMUTUEL.
[1868 *DA, DAE, OEDS*]

pool bet, *n.* **1.** In golf, a lottery in which all players contribute a specific amount of money to a pot, which is won by the person with the best score.
[1971 McQuaid *Gambler's Digest* 313]
2. Also called an OFFICE POOL. A lottery based on a sporting event, such as a football game, in which each participant contributes a specific amount of money to a pot and receives a randomly drawn score. The winner of the pot is the person whose randomly drawn score matches the final score of the game.
[1955 *OEDS* as "pool-betting"]

pool box, *n.* In horse racing, a box into which the wagers on a certain horse are placed.
[1878 *OEDS;* 1887 *DA, DAE*]

pools coupon, *n.* Also shortened to **pool coupon.** The ticket or receipt recording a wager, usually on a horse race or a series of football matches.
[1951 *OEDS,* as *pools coupon*]

pool dish, *n.* Also shortened to **pool.** A platter or bowl placed in the center of a card table for holding the wagers.
[1878 *OED,* as *pool dish;* 1770 *OED* as *pool*]

pool gambling, *n.* An act of gambling in which the wagers are pooled, or collected together, with those participating sharing proportionately in the gains and losses. Compare PARIMUTUEL.
[1882 *DA, DAE*]

pool game, *n.* **1.** A dominoes game in which each of several players puts a specified amount of money into a pot, which is won by the first person to use all of his tiles.
[1950 Morehead *Culbertson* 636]

2. Any of a variety of domino games in which the tiles are placed together so that the number of pips on one-half the tile matches the number of pips on the half-tile adjacent.
[1865 *OED*]

pool room, *n.* Also written **poolroom.** An establishment in which bets on races, prize fights, and so on can be placed; a BOOKMAKER'S shop. [1875 *DA, DAE*]

pool seller, *n.* One who sells chances in a betting pool. [1887 *DA, DAE, OEDS*]

pool selling, *n.* Wagering by placing money in a communal pot, then choosing or accepting a possible outcome for an event, such as the possible final score of a baseball or football game.
[1869 *DA, DAE, OEDS*]

pools entry, *n.* A wager in a collective bet, as on a group of football matches.
[1972 *OEDS*]

pools win, *n.* A win, especially in a collective bet, as a group of football matches.
[1963 *OEDS*]

pools winner, *n.* A person who wins in a collective bet, as on a group of football matches.
[1960 *OEDS*]

poor man's roulette, *n. phr.* Another term for CRAPS. *Facetious use.*
[1953 Lewis *Sagebrush Casinos* 99]
[Compare *poor man's remedy:* 1657 *OEDS; poor man's sauce:* 1723 *OEDS*]

pop, *n.* A sudden or quick action, as a rapidly placed bet or one in which the outcome is quickly determined.
1983 Martinet *Oral Coll.* [Player to dealer at a craps table] Give me five bucks a *pop* on the 6, ace, and the 4, trey . . . Maybe it's from hop, meaning the next roll of the dice, because I hear "give me five bucks hopping" interchangeably with "give me five bucks popping."
1984 Clark *Oral Coll.* "Five bucks a *pop*" would have reference to some kind of bet that is settled immediately, like the next roll of the dice or a single hand at twenty-one, or one pull on a slot. Something bet and settled quick, like that. Of course, you have the drug connection too, but no gambler would think of that. Money's too precious to waste it on drugs. Dealers and casino workers get into that, but not most of the pro gamblers I know. They stay pretty clean when they're working.

pope, *n.* In Pope Joan, the 9 of diamonds.
[1950 Morehead *Culbertson* 636]

Pope Joan, *n.* A card game played with a deck of cards (from which the 8 of diamonds has been removed), and a tray with eight compartments for the stakes which are won with certain combinations of cards.
[1732 *OED*]

position, *n.* **1.** In poker, the location of a specific seat in relation to the dealer. Compare A, B, C, D, E, F, G, H.
[1949 Coffin *Secrets* 183]
2. On a craps layout, the placement of a bet in relation to where the player stands.
1983 Martinet *Oral Coll.* The dealer moves the player's come bet up to the number on the back line and puts it on the *position* relative to the player. If the player is to his left, he puts it on the left side of the number. If the player is in front of him, he puts it on the front of the box.
3. In racing, The place a horse, dog, etc., has at a particular time in a race.
[(1951) 1981 Maurer *Lang. of the Underworld* 224]

positive double, *n.* In bridge, a challenge to an opponent to play for double the amount of points. Compare DOUBLE and REDOUBLE.
[1950 Morehead *Culbertson* 636]

possible, *n.* In poker, a hand that can be completed, such as a flush or a straight, with one additional card.
[1978 Larson *Vocabulary* 100]

post, *n.* **1.** In racing, the first position next to the inside rail on an oval track.
2. In racing: **a.** the pillar that marks the starting or finishing point of a race.
[1642 *OED*]
b. One of several poles placed at various points around an oval track, marking distances from the finish line.
[(1951) 1981 Maurer *Lang. of the Underworld* 224]

post action, *n.* In racing, the number of the stall in the starting gate from which an entry begins a race.
[1983 Martinez *Gambling Scene* 215]

post manners, *n. pl.* The behavior of a race entrant at the starting gate.
[1983 Martinez *Gambling Scene* 215]

post oak bluff, *n. phr.* In poker, a minimal wager contributed to a large pot in the hope that a mediocre hand can win the pot.
[1978 Brunson *How I Made* 532]
[Compare *post oak:* 1764 *DAE,* probably because this tree typically grows in poor soil]

post odds, *n. pl.* The betting odds of a horse race at the starting time. Compare MORNING LINE and P.M. LINE.
[1887 *DAE*]

post parade, *n.* In horse racing, the organized procession of entrants in front of the stand before a race.
[1977 Carroll *Playboy's Illustrated* 191]

post position, *n.* Abbreviated: P.P. In racing, the first, second, third, etc., positions from the inner rail on an oval track. Compare POLE POSITION.
[(1951) 1981 Maurer *Lang. of the Underworld* 224]

post time, *n.* The time of day at which all the

entrants are assembled at the starting line for the beginning of a race. *Especially U.S. use.* [1941 *OEDS*]

pot, *n.* **1.** Especially in poker: **a:** The area in the center of the table where all bets are placed. [1951 *OEDS*]
b. The POOL which includes the ANTE and BETS wagered.
1866 *American Card Player* 131. An "ante" or stake is deposited in the centre of the table by the dealer; this is called the Pool or *Pot.*
[1847 *OEDS;* 1856 *DA, DAE*]
c. Short for JACKPOT.
[1856 *DAE*]
2. In faro, the section of the layout comprised of the 6, 7, and 8 cards.
1868 Trumps *Pocket Hoyle* 203. The Six, Seven, and Eight [are called] "the *Pot.*"
[1890 *OEDS,* in *Century Dict;* 1891 *DA*]
3. In keno, the entire amount of money wagered by all players on a single game.
[1890 Quinn *Fools of Fortune* 251]
4. The total amount of money handled by one operator or establishment that has been wagered on a specific gaming event, as a horse race.
1889 Ellangowan *Sporting Anecdotes* 336. *Pot.*— The sum of money for which a favourite is backed, and sometimes the favourite himself. When the favourite wins, his backers are said to "land the pot," or "to pull it off."
5. A large amount bet, specifically in horse racing, on the favorite.
[1823 *OED*]

pot hooks, *n. pl.* Also spelled **pothooks.** In poker, a pair of 9s.
[1968 Wallace *Poker* 221]

pot limit, *n.* In poker, a wager that is equal to the amount of money already in the POOL, or POT. [1949 Coffin *Secrets* 183]

pot-limit dig, *n. phr.* In poker, a provision that a player is not restricted to wagering only the money he has on the table in a game where the maximum bet can equal the amount already in the pot. The player is allowed to pull additional money from his pocket to call a bet.
[1949 Coffin *Secrets* 183]

pot odds, *n. pl.* In poker, the relationship between how much a player must wager and the total amount of possible return if the pot is won.
[1978 Brunson *How I Made* 542]

pound, *n.* A five-dollar note or chip. *Rare.*
[1935 *OEDS*]

power, *n.* In stud poker, the strongest hand visible on the table; the hand with the highest cards turned face upward.
[1978 Larson *Vocabulary* 100]

power of the pencil, *n. phr.* Also **power of the pen.** In a casino, the authorization to sign for complementary meals, rooms, and other favors to patrons.
1986 *Las Vegas Review Journal* 1/19, 1B. In Las Vegas, the *power of the pen* has nothing to do with newspapers, magazines or books. Instead, it's the phrase used describing the authority to sign a chit for rooms, food or beverages so the customer's bill is "comped."

P.P., *n.* Also spelled **PP** or **p.p.** Abbreviation for POST POSITION.
[1875 *DAE*]

preempt, *v.* Also written **pre-empt.** In bridge, to make a high opening bid designed to prevent the opposition from responding.
[1914 *OEDS*]

pre-empt, *n.* In bridge, a high opening bid designed to prevent bidding by the opposition.
[1939 *OEDS*]

pre-emption, *n.* Also written **preemption.** The action of making a PRE EMPTIVE BID.
[1961 *OEDS*]

preemptive or pre-emptive, *adj.* **1.** Of or having to do with such bidding.
2. Especially in the phrase:
pre-emptive bid, In bridge, a high opening bid designed to prevent bidding by the opposition.
[1913 *OEDS*]

preferred customer, *n.* A visitor to a casino who regularly makes large bets over a period of time. See also HIGH ROLLER.
1985 Hopkins *Suite Life* 32. The term "high roller" is commonly used to describe anyone who bets large amounts of money. However, people in the gambling business give it a narrower meaning, says Tony "Toby" DiCesare, casino manager at the Tropicana Hotel. DiCesare, one of the few executives who will speak openly about the care and feeding of *high rollers,* explains, "A high roller might come around only once a year, but he will always bet the limit, whatever the limit is." Most big bettors would more properly be described as "*preferred customers,*" he says. "A *preferred customer* is a good, steady customer who comes about once a month, gives you perhaps $20,000 worth of action, and will always bet black chips"—the $100 kind—"but not necessarily the limit. Some *preferred customers* will be high rollers also, but you treat either type the same."

premium, *n.* **1.** In poker, a special bonus awarded for certain rare hands, such as a royal flush.
[1949 Coffin *Secrets* 184]
2. Usually **premiums,** *pl.* In bridge, a point scored other than by winning an odd trick.
[1950 Morehead *Culbertson* 636]

premium customer, *n.* In a casino, a desired patron; a patron who receives special considerations such as complimentary rooms, meals, and so on. See also GRIND CUSTOMER. Compare COMP.
[1974 Friedman *Casino Management* 21]

premium hand, *n.* In poker, a best hand in a particular game, such as a royal flush in highball

poker, or a WHEEL, ace, 2, 3, 4, 5, in razz (another name for lowball).
[1978 Brunson *How I Made* 542]

premium operation, *n.* A casino or gambling establishment in which large amounts of money change hands.
1974 Friedman *Casino Management* 21. The difference between a *premium operation* and a grind store is the high action.

press, *v.* **1.** To increase the size of a previously won wager by betting the original amount plus all or part of the winnings. Compare PARLAY.
[1974 Friedman *Casino Management* 38]
2. To add money to a wager already in place. Compare RAISE.
1868 Trumps *Pocket Hoyle* 208. *Pressing a bet* is to add to the original stake.
3. To surreptitiously add to the size of a bet after an event, as to add chips after cards are dealt in twenty-one or after the dice are rolled in craps.
[1974 Powell *Verbal Dexterity* 9]
4. In the phrase:
press it all the way up, Also shortened to **press it up.** In craps, to increase the size of a wager after a win to the maximum odds allowed under terms of the original wager.
[1983 Martinet *Oral Coll*]

press bet, *n.* In golf, a wager in which the player or team that is losing renews and doubles the amount of the original bet.
[1971 McQuaid *Gambler's Digest* 313]

prial, *n.* Also spelled PRILE or **proil.** In cribbage, another name for PAIR-ROYAL, triplets counting ten points each.
1866 *American Card Player* 90. Pair-Royal or *Prial.*—This consists of three cards of a similar sort, held either in the hand or crib, or occurring in the course of the game, as three Kings, &c.
[1803 *OED,* contraction of *pair royal*]

price, *n.* The odds offered on a wager for any sporting event, such as a horse race.
[1882 *OED*]

pricemaker, *n.* In horse racing, a HANDICAPPER, the track official who declares the initial odds for horses in the race.
[1968 Thackrey *Nick the Greek* 215]

prick, *v.* Among card cheats, to mark the backs of playing cards with a sharp instrument or a thumbnail. Compare PUNCH.
[1968 Wallace *Poker* 221]

prile, *n.* **1.** Same as PRIAL.
[1950 Morehead *Culbertson* 637]
2. In chuck-a-luck, a roll of three dice of the same number, as three 2s, 3s, etc. A wager on *any prile* usually pays 30 to 1, while a wager won on a specific prile usually pays 180 to 1.
[1976 Figgis *Gambler's Handbook* 57]
3. Three cards of equal value.
[1976 Figgis *Gambler's Handbook* 57]

prime, *n.* In backgammon, a block of six consecutive points held by one player, especially on the player's inner table. Each point is blocked by having two or more pieces, or STONES, on it, thereby preventing the opponent from landing on it. [1974 Scarne *Dice* 321]

prison, *n.* Especially in the prepositional phrase: **in prison. 1.** In roulette, noting a wager that does not win or lose, but is held for the next round of betting. Commonly, when a zero is the winner, bets made on the even portion of the layout are frozen until the next turn.
[1867 *OEDS*]
2. In horse racing, noting a horse that cannot be sold within thirty days after running in a CLAIMING RACE.
[1975 Clark *Oral Coll*]

private craps, *n. pl. Plural in form, but singular in use.* A craps game, usually illegal, featuring SIDE BETS, or private bets among the players.
[1974 Scarne *Dice* 102]

private game, *n.* **1. a.** A card or dice game, usually restricted to specific players, without a bank or any charge to players for participating.
[1961 Scarne *Complete Guide* 685]
b. A poker game restricted to certain players in which a fee is collected by the operator of the game.
[1978 Brunson *How I Made* 542]
2. In a casino, a table, usually at twenty-one, sometimes at craps, reserved for one player or a few specific players.
[1973 Clark *Oral Coll*]

prize pile, *n.* In canasta, the discard pile, when FROZEN, or unplayable.
[1953 Crawford *Consistent Winner* 351]

prod, *n.* In horse racing, a battery-charged conductor used to shock a horse illegally during a race.
[1978 Ainslie *Complete Guide* 295]
[Compare 1855 *OED,* meaning a "goad"]

producer, *n.* **1.** A player whose primary source of income is not from gambling.
[1953 Fairfield *Las Vegas* 15]
2. A player who loses steadily. See also NONPRODUCER.
[1983 Martinez *Gambling Scene* 215]

profession, *n.* In the phrase:
the profession, Illegal gambling; cardsharping, cheating, and so on.
[1890 Quinn *Fools of Fortune* 267]

professional gambler, *n.* A person whose primary source of income is from gambling. Compare PRODUCER (def. 1).
[1941 Fair *Spill the Jackpot* 32]

professor, *n.* A gambler who can calculate odds for events in card games and so on. Compare COUNTER and PROFESSION and SHARPER.
1891 *Monte Carlo* 178. The generally-spread knowledge that systems, although conceived and

applied by men versed in all the intricacies of mathematical probabilities, have always proved in the end disastrous for them, does not prevent the great capitals of Europe, as well as the shore of the Mediterranean Sea, to be crowded with so-called *professors* of Roulette, and Trente-et-Quarante. These worthy gentlemen, the majority of them swindlers or confidence-men out of employment, manage to eke a pretty fair living out of the credulity of the newcomers, or the senility of the old frequenters. You can not be in Monte Carlo two hours before being interviewed by one or more of these seedy individuals, ready to supply you, with the greatest generosity, the means of acquiring untold wealth, if you only pay them say four or five dollars down, with a little *douceur* when the big results come in.

profile, *n.* In playing cards, a king of diamonds, a jack of spades, or a jack of hearts.
[1963 Steig *Common Sense* 186]
[because these face cards display profiles of the figure pictured]

programmed slot, *n.* A slot machine set to pay out a specific percentage of the money taken in over a large number of plays.
[1971 McQuaid Gambler's Digest 314]

progression, *n.* **1.** In tournament play, the sequence for moving to the next step of a series of contests, ultimately resulting in a final contest.
[1950 Morehead *Culbertson* 637]
2. Same as PROGRESSIVE SYSTEM.
[1974 Scarne *Dice* 57]

progressive, *adj.* **1.** Noting a betting system requiring increased bets as the game develops.
[1974 Scarne *Dice* 57]
2. In card games, denoting a system of play in which sets of players play simultaneously against others who move from game to game with change in rounds.
[1885 *OEDS,* as *progressive euchre* and 1903, as *progressive whist*]

progressive jackpot, *n.* **1.** In slot machines, a payout amount that increases with each coin played until the total amount is won.
[1979 Hilton Hotel *Procedures* 32]
2. progressive jackpots, *pl. Plural in form, but singular in use.* Also called PROGRESSIVE POKER. A variant of draw poker which requires the opener to have a pair of jacks or better. If no player can open, the pack is reshuffled and redealt and the opener must have a pair of queens or better. If no player can open, the reshuffling and redealing continues on, through kings, then back to jacks.
[1949 Coffin *Secrets* 184]

progressive poker, *n.* Same as PROGRESSIVE JACKPOTS.
[1968 Wallace *Poker* 222]

progressive progressive, *n.* A variant of PROGRESSIVE JACKPOTS in which the ante is increased on each round that no player can open the betting round.
[1949 Coffin *Secrets* 184]

progressive slot machine, *n.* Also shortened to **progressive slot.** A slot machine on which the possible jackpot payout increases with each coin played. Compare PROGRESSIVE JACKPOT (def. 1).
[1982 Martin *Introduction* 22]

progressive system, *n.* Also called PROGRESSION. (def. 2). A betting system in which the player increases the size of a bet after a win and decreases the size of a bet after a loss.
[1974 Scarne *Dice* 57]

proil, *n.* Same as PRIAL.
[1950 Morehead *Culbertson* 637]

prop, *n.* **1.** Also called a SHILL or STARTER or HOUSE PLAYER or PUFF. In a gambling establishment, a person employed to play at a table until enough players are participating so the game can continue without assistance.
[1830 *OED*]
2. a. A name given to cowrie shells used in a gambling game resembling dice.
b. the game itself, characterized by the use of shells thrown in the manner of dice, money being wagered upon the anticipated disposition after the throw. It flourished in New England in the 1830s, 1840s, and 1850s.
[1833 *OED, DA, DAE*]

prop, *v.* In horse and dog racing, to stiffen the legs and refuse to run.
[1870 *OED*]

prop bet, *n.* Short for PROPOSITION BET.
[1983 Martinet *Oral Coll*]

proposition, *n.* Short for PROPOSITION BET.
[1950 Morehead *Culbertson* 637]

proposition bet, *n.* **1.** In craps, a wager that is settled on the next roll of the dice, such as a bet that the next number rolled will be a seven.
[1973 Friedman *Casino Games* 33]
[(1950) 1981 Maurer *Lang. of the Underworld* 190]
2. In twenty-one, a special or unusual bet such as a DOUBLE DOWN, double the amount bet for one additional card.
[1961 Scarne *Complete Guide* 685]
3. In baccarat, a wager that the two hands, bank and player, will score an equal number of points.
[1970 *Baccarat, The Facts*]
4. Any COMBINATION BET, as those popular among hustlers. Compare PROPOSITION HUSTLER.

proposition cheat, *n.* A cheater at cards or dice who wins every bet, who gives the victim absolutely no possible chance to win.
[1961 Scarne *Complete Guide* 685]

proposition hustler, *n.* A schemer who offers a victim a bet that appears fair, but is not. Compare PROPOSITION BET (def. 4).
[1961 Scarne *Complete Guide* 685]

proposition player, *n.* A person who plays in a gambling establishment with his own money, and is additionally paid by the operator to play there.
[1982 Martin *Introduction* 20]

protection, *n.* **1. a.** Also shortened to **pro.** Immunity from prosecution or publicity for an illegal gambling operation, purchased through bribery.
[(1860) 1938 *OEDS,* (ca.1955) 1981 Maurer *Lang. of the Underworld* 249]
b. The money thus paid.
[n.d. *DAS*]
2. In bridge, a reopening of the bidding or a double when the opponent's bidding has stopped at a low level.
[1952 *OEDS*]

proxies, *n. pl.* In golf, a wager as to who will be closest to the pin after two strokes on a par 4 hole, or three strokes on a par 5 hole. Compare BINGLE, BANGLE, BUNGO. and GREENIES.
[1971 McQuaid *Gambler's Digest* 314]
[Altered from *approximate* by clipping and suffixation]

public choice, *n.* In racing, the favorite entry in the betting; the entry with the lowest odds at post time. Compare POST ODDS.
[1983 Martinez *Gambling Scene* 215]

public game, *n.* In poker, a game open to anyone who wishes to join. Compare PRIVATE GAME.
[1978 Brunson *How I Made* 543]

public poker, *n.* A game in a poker room in which a percentage of each pot is kept for the establishment, or in which each player is charged a fee for a period of playing time. Compare PRIVATE GAME.
[1968 Wallace *Poker* 222]

public stable, *n.* In horse racing, a stable in which the horses belonging to various owners are boarded, managed, and trained.
[1978 Ainslie *Complete Guide* 295]

puck, *n.* Also called the BUTTON or BUCK. In bank craps, the marker used to indicate the shooter's point. The *puck* is placed on the appropriate number on the line behind the box numbers 4, 5, 6, 8, 9, or 10.
[1983 Martinet *Oral Coll*]

puff, *n.* A person employed to play at a gaming table in order to attract others to the game. See also SHILL and AGENT.
1726 Wilson *Art and Mystery* 60. It is necessary, before I proceed, to tell you what a Creature a *Puff* is. A *Puff* to a Faro Bank is as a Brace-bird to a Bird-catcher, always upon the Spot, in order to tempt you to sit down to play. For as the Brace-bird is frequently hoisted up upon a Twig, to decoy the harmless Birds, that fly carelessly by, to light upon the Nets: Just so is a *Puff* to a Faro Bank.
[1731 *OED*]

pull, *n.* **1.** The act of checking, or braking, a horse during a race to prevent his winning.
[1737 *OED*]
2. The act of drawing a card from the deck during a game.
[1715 *OED*]

pull, *v.* **1.** Also PULL FOR PRIME. To draw a card from a pack.
[1593 *OED,* as *pull prime;* 1619 *OED*]
2. a. In horse racing, to hold a horse in check to cause him to lose the race.
[*c*1800 *OED*]
b. To prearrange the winner of a horse race; to FIX a race.
[1902 *DAE*]
3. To make or cause to happen, especially as a raid on an illegal gambling house.
[1811 *OED*]
4. In the phrases:
pull down, To remove part of a bet or winnings from the table.
[1950 Morehead *Culbertson* 637]
pull for prime, Also shortened to **pull prime.** To draw a card before beginning a game to determine the player who will begin with first advantage, as being first to deal the cards.
[1593 *OED,* as *pull prime*]
pull out, To stop gambling; to quit a game; to refuse to bet for a time.
[1974 Scarne *Dice* 97]
pull up, In horse racing, to slow down a horse during a race. Compare *pull, v.* (def. 5).
[1844 *OED*]

pulleys, *n. pl.* A contraption for signalling the value of an opponent's cards to a confederate.
1843 Green *Exposure* 119. There is another cheat, commonly called the *pulleys* . . . A man takes his stand overhead, and has a string that passes down the wall and under the floor immediately under the player's foot where a spring is fastened to the floor in which is a small peg which passes through a hole and comes in contact with the foot. The string is made fast to this spring on the under side, and when pulled, the peg protrudes and strikes the bottom of his foot whenever the string is pulled.

pull of the table, *n. phr.* The advantage held by the banker or dealer in gambling games.
[1584 *OED*]

pull through, *n.* In playing cards, a false shuffle in which the dealer pulls half of the pack through the other half without changing the sequence of the cards. Compare PASS (def. 5).
[1961 Scarne *Complete Guide* 685]

pump, *v.* **1.** In poker, to raise a bet made by an earlier player.
[1983 Martinez *Gambling Scene* 216]
2. In the particle construction:
pump up, To win a large amount of money; to feel elated after winning a large amount.
[1978 Brunson *How I Made* 543]
[Compare 1844 *OED,* meaning "to excite"]

punch, *v.* To mark playing cards with a sharp instrument so as to read them from the backs. Compare PRICK.
[1983 Martinez *Gambling Scene* 216]

punch board, *n.* Also written **punch-board** or **punchboard.** A lottery game featuring a board containing holes with slips of paper or disks used for raffles and games of chance, some of which slips list winning numbers or prize designations, the player purchasing opportunities to push out a disk or slip.
[1912 *OEDS,* 1931 *DA*]

puncher, *n.* Also called a BANGER. In keno, the paper punch used for making holes in tickets corresponding to the numbers randomly selected for that game.
[1978 Alexander *Glossary* 12]

pung, *n.* **1.** In mah jongg, a set of three identical tiles held by one player.
[1932 *OEDS*]
2. Said by a mah jongg player when he collects and plays a set of three identical tiles.
[1923 *OEDS*]

pung, *v.* In mah jongg, to take a discarded tile in order to complete a triplet of the same suit.
[1922 *OEDS*]

pung chow, *n.* An alternate name for MAH JONGG.
[1950 Morehead *Culbertson* 637]

punt, *v.* **1.** To wager; to bet, as upon a horse. *Mainly British use.*
[1873 *OED*]
2. To make a wager at faro.
1843 Green *Exposure* 165. The game [faro] may be played without these figures, as every punter has a suit of cards; but they are convenient for those who wish to *punt,* or stake upon seven cards at a time.
[1706 *OED*]

punt, *n.* **1.** A wager, as on a race or sporting event. *Mainly British use.*
2. Same as a PUNTER, a bettor.
[1704 *OED*]
3. A point in faro.
[1850 *OED*]

punter, *n.* **1.** A bettor; one who wagers money on the outcome of an event. *Mainly British use.*
1714 Lucas *Memoirs* 230. *Punter,* a Term for every one of the Gamesters that play.
[1706 *OED*]
2. A person who wagers small amounts on any speculative venture as opposed to a PLUNGER, who bets large amounts. *Old fashioned.*
1889 Ellangowan *Sporting Anecdotes* 281. A "*punter*" means a person who speculates for small amounts. At baccarat or on the turf he operates generally for shillings, half-crowns, or crown, or the smallest amount the banker or bookmaker will accept. In this way he is distinguished from the "plunger," who operates for large amounts.

punting, *n.* The act of wagering or betting on the outcome of an event. *Mainly British use.*
1726 Wilson *Art and Mystery* 62. And as Gentlemen differ much in their manner of Play, it has been thought worth the Banker's while to find out several ways to be provided for those different ways of *Punting.*
[1797 *OED,* 1951 *OEDS*]

punte, *n. Spanish.* In the card game OMBRE or QUADRILLE, a red ace when it is trump.
See quotation at SPADILLO: 1680 Cotton *Compleat Gamester.*
[1728 *OED*]

puppy feet, *n. pl. Plural in form, but singular in use.* **1.** In playing cards, the suit of clubs.
2. In craps, two 5s turned upward on the dice.
1981 Golad *Oral Coll.* You hardly ever hear regular, serious players say *puppy feet* for clubs or fives. You hear it from novices or people who don't get out much beyond their own neighborhoods. I hear *puppy feet* from blue-haired women in California poker rooms.
→Not generally used in either sense by professional gamblers, but compare PUPPYFOOT.

puppyfoot, *n.* Also written **puppy foot.** In playing cards, the ace of clubs.
[1907 *OEDS,* listed as "U.S."]

purse, *n.* **1.** The prize money supplied by promoters for a contest, as a horse race, boxing match, tennis match, golf match, and so on. Compare STAKES.
[(1688) 1804 *DAE,* 1724 *OED*]
2. A contest with such a prize for the winner. Compare STAKES RACE.
[1786 *DAE*]

push, *n.* A tie; a standoff; a draw.
[1973 Friedman *Casino Games* 15]

push, *v.* **1.** In poker, to raise a bet, usually to the maximum allowed.
[1968 Wallace *Poker* 222]
2. In bridge, to entice an opponent to bid a difficult contract by OVERCALLing.
[1927 *OED*]
3. In the phrases and particle constructions:
push the pencil, In a casino, to surreptitiously add amounts due the casino to markers (credit slips) signed by patrons.
[1974 Scarne *Dice* 356]

put, *v.* In the phrases and particle constructions:
put one's money on, To bet a sum of money that a contestant will win, place, or show.
[1855 *OED*]
put on the jacket, In a casino, to move from being a dealer to being a boxman or floorman.
[1983 Martinet *Oral Coll*]
[Because dealers do not wear jackets; boxmen and floormen are considered members of the management and wear jackets. Nor do boxmen or floormen share in tips given to the dealers.]

put the ears on, In craps, to make a controlled shot with fair dice.
[1974 Scarne *Dice* 476]
[(1950) 1981 Maurer *Lang. of the Underworld* 190: "perhaps transferred from cards, where a crimp may be called an ear"]
put the finger on In craps, to make a controlled shot with fair dice.
[1974 Scarne *Dice* 254]
put to his trumps or **trump,** Also **put upon his trumps** or **trump.** In card games like bridge and whist, to force an opponent to play his trumps.
[1559 *OED;* for *put to . . .*; 1681 *OED,* for *put upon . . .*]
put up 1. a. To make a wager; to bet.
[1857 *DA,* 1865 *OEDS*]
b. In poker, to place the appropriate amount of money in the pot.
[1968 Wallace *Poker* 222]
2. In a casino, to make a bet on behalf of the dealer, especially as one method for giving the dealer a tip.
[1977 Anness *Dummy Up*]
put up a deck, To stack a deck of playing cards; to arrange playing cards in a specific sequence for cheating purposes.
[1890 Quinn *Fools of Fortune* 267]

put-and-take top, *n.* **1.** An altered die that is put into a dice game and removed at will. Compare BARR DICE and LOADED DICE.
[1974 Scarne *Dice* 364]
2. A six-sided top used in a gambling game.
[1922 *OEDS*]

Q

Q, *n.* Abbreviation for QUARTER. A twenty-five dollar chip.
[1983 Martinet *Oral Coll*]

quadruple, *v.* In faro, to bet the same rank card four consecutive times.
[1938 Asbury *Sucker's Progress* 9]

quadruple, *n.* **1.** In faro, four consecutive wagers on a single card.
[1938 Asbury *Sucker's Progress* 9]
2. In bridge, a score of four times the normal points when a doubled bid is redoubled. Compare DOUBLE and REDOUBLE.
[1971 McQuaid *Gambler's Digest* 314]

quadruplets, *n. pl.* Four playing cards of the same rank; FOUR OF A KIND.
[1873 *OEDS*]

quail, *n.* Also called a BIRD. In casino craps, a twenty-five cent chip.
[1983 Martinet *Oral Coll*]

qualifier, *n.* Also called OPENERS. In draw poker, the minimal hand required to begin the first betting round.
[1968 Wallace *Poker* 222]

quart, *n.* Also called a BOBTAIL. In card games such as poker or piquet or whist, a sequence of four cards of the same suit. Compare QUART MAJOR and QUART MINOR.
1746 Hoyle *Short Treatise* 69. *Quart* in general is a Sequence of any four Cards immediately following one another, in the same suit.
[1727 *OED*]

quarter, *n.* **1.** A twenty-five dollar chip. See also Q. [1973 Clark *Oral Coll*]
[1704 *DA,* 1783 *DAE,* 1856 *OED*]
2. In horse racing: **a.** Two furlongs; one-quarter mile. *U.S. use.* [1868 *OEDS*]
b. The initial portion of a race, usually the first quarter of the course.
[(1951) 1981 Maurer *Lang. of the Underworld* 224]
c. A quarter-mile race. Compare QUARTER RACING. [1899 *OED*]

quarter action, *adj. phr.* Noting a gaming table at which a minimum wager of twenty-five dollars is required. Compare QUARTER.
[1979 Newman *Dealer's Special* 12]

quarter check, *n.* Also called **quarter chip.** A check or chip worth twenty-five dollars. See also Q. [1978 Brunson *How I Made* 543]

quarter game, *n.* **1.** A craps game at which chips worth twenty-five cents are used.
[1983 Martinet *Oral Coll*]
2. In a casino, a gaming table at which the minimum bet is twenty-five dollars.
[1973 Clark *Oral Coll*]
3. A small stakes poker game.
[1983 Martinet *Oral Coll*]

quarter horse, *n.* A racehorse that performs well only in short races.
[(1951) 1981 Maurer *Lang. of the Underworld* 224]
[1839 *OEDS*]

quarter player, *n.* Also called a TWO-BIT PLAYER. A person who loses regularly and makes small wagers in order to play longer.
[1983 Martinent *Oral Coll*]

quarter pole, *n.* In horse racing: **1.** A pole marking a track into quarter-mile segments.
[(1951) 1981 Maurer *Lang. of the Underworld* 224]
2. The last of four poles placed at quarter-mile intervals around an oval track, one-fourth of a mile from the finish line. The *quarter pole* is usually painted red and white, to distinguish it from the other three poles.
[1982 *Today's Racing*]
[1857 *OEDS*]

quarter race, *n.* A horserace of one-quarter mile.
[1792 *OED*]

quarter racing, *n.* Horse racing on a quarter-mile course. [1857 *OEDS*]

quart major, *n.* In card games such as piquet or whist, a sequence of jack, queen, king, and ace of one suit.
1746 Hoyle *Short Treatise* 69. *Quart-Major* is therefore a Sequence of Ace, King, Queen, and Knave, in any suit.
[1746 *OED*, as *quart-major*]

quart minor, *n.* In card games such as piquet or whist, a sequence of 10, jack, queen, and king of the same suit.
[1950 Morehead *Culbertson* 638]

quatorze, *n.* In piquet, four cards of the same rank from 10 through ace for which a bonus of fourteen points is awarded to the person holding such a hand.
[1950 Morehead *Culbertson* 638]

queen, *n.* In a deck of playing cards, the face card in each suit, ranked between a jack and a king.
[1575 *OED*]

queen nazarene, *n.* In queen nazarene, the queen of diamonds.
[1950 Morehead *Culbertson* 638]

queer, *n.* Any of a variety of devices used to cheat at cards or dice, such as a BUG or HOLDOUT, both devices for hiding a playing card.
[1963 Taylor *City of Sin* 7]

quick tricks, *n. pl.* In bridge, a system for evaluating a hand by counting the number of aces, kings, and queens held by one player.
[1950 Morehead *Culbertson* 638]

quinella, *n.* Also spelled **quiniela** or **quiniella.** In sports like horse racing and jai alai, a wager made on two entries to finish first and second, in either order, and paying higher odds than a ticket to win.
[1942 *OED;* from American Spanish *quiniela*]

quino, *n.* A spelling variant for KENO.
[1843 *OEDS*]

quinola, *n.* In reversis, a privileged card from the suit of hearts. The jack of hearts is the **great quinola,** the queen of hearts is the **little quinola.**
[1950 Morehead *Culbertson* 638]

quint, *n.* **1.** Also called a STRAIGHT FLUSH. In card games such as poker or piquet or whist, a sequence of five cards in one suit. Compare QUINT-MAJOR and QUINT-MINOR.
1746 Hoyle *Short Treatise* 69. *Quint* in general is a Sequence of any five Cards immediately following one another in the same Suit.
[1680 *OED*]
2. In mah jongg, five like titles, especially of wildflowers.
[1950 Morehead *Culbertson* 638]

quint-major, *n.* Also called a ROYAL STRAIGHT FLUSH. In card games such as poker, piquet, or whist, a sequence of ten through ace of one suit.
1746 Hoyle *Short Treatise* 69. *Quint-Major* is therefore a Sequence of Ace, King, Queen, Knave, and Ten, in any [one] suit.
[1663 *OED*]

quint-minor, *n.* In games like piquet or whist, a sequence of 9 through queen of one suit.
[1659 *OED*]

quinze, *n.* **1.** A forerunner of twenty-one, a card game of chance in which players compete with each other to acquire a hand of 15 points or as close to 15 points as they can.
1843 Green *Exposure* 285. The game of vingt-un, or twenty-one, resembles the game of *quinze.*
[1716 *OED*]
2. In the phrase:
et la va quinze. A wager in faro in which the bettor allows wins to ride, or continue on the same bet, success at which pays fifteen times the wager.
1843 Green *Exposure* 108. *Quinze, et la va,* is when the punter having won a sept, &c., bends the third corner of the card, and ventures for fifteen times his stake.

quit, *v.* **1.** In a gambling game, to convert chips to currency and stop playing.
[1949 Coffin *Secrets* 184]
2. Of a racehorse, to slow down or cease trying to win.
[1955 Hillis *Pari-Mutuel Betting* 117]
3. In the phrases:
quit losers, To stop gambling after having lost all or part of one's stake.
[1974 Friedman *Casino Management* 15]
quit winners, To stop gambling while holding more money than one began with.
[1974 Friedman *Casino Management* 15]

quitted trick, *n. phr.* In games like whist, a trick that is turned face down by the player who won the trick. Done to prevent players from referring to cards that have been played.
[1953 Crawford *Consistent Winner* 351]

quitter, *n.* **1.** In racing, an entry that lacks sufficent desire to win a contest.
[1968 Buchele *Greyhound Racing* 97]
2. In horse racing: **a.** An entry with insufficient stamina to finish well.
b. An entry that performs poorly in the lead.
[(1951) 1981 Maurer *Lang. of the Underworld* 224]

quitting time, *n.* In poker, an agreed-upon time to stop a game.
[1968 Wallace *Poker* 222]
[Compare 1835 *OEDS,* meaning "the end of the work day"]

quong, *n.* Same as a KONG. In mah jongg, four tiles of the same kind; a PUNG (three of a kind), plus one.
[1950 Morehead *Culbertson* 638]

quorum, *n.* The number of players required to begin a standard gambling game, such as four for bridge, two for cribbage, six for poker, and so on.
[1968 Wallace *Poker* 222]

R

rabbit, *n.* **1.** An inexperienced gambler.
[1949 Coffin *Secrets* 184]
2. In golf, a point or hole held by one player or team over another.
[1949 Coffin *Secrets* 184]

rabbit ears, *n. pl.* In keno, two clear plastic tubes, about eighteen inches long, fastened atop one style of blower, into which the twenty balls drawn for the game are blown. Compare KENO GOOSE.
[1973 Friedman *Casino Games* 99]
[Compare 1967 *OEDS,* meaning "an indoor television antenna resembling the erect ears of a rabbit"]

rabbit hunting, *n. phr.* In poker, looking through the discards to see what has been dealt.
[1949 Coffin *Secrets* 184]

race, *n.* **1.** A single keno game.
[1973 Clark *Oral Coll*]
[From the early Western practice of using the names of horses on the eighty spaces of a keno ticket.]
2. a. A contest, usually of speed, between entries such as horses, dogs, cars, and so on.
[1513 *OED;* 1674 *DAE*]
b. races, *pl.* A series of such events, especially horseraces. [1641 *OED*]
3. A wager on a horse race.
[1894 *OED*]

race, *v.* In the phrases:
race forwardly, To perform well, especially at the beginning of a horse race.
[(1951) 1981 Maurer *Lang. of the Underworld* 224]
race wide, Of an entry in a race, to avoid the inside rail on an oval track, thereby increasing the distance and time required to complete the race, but often avoiding congestion of the entrants.
[1955 Hillis *Pari-Mutuel Betting* 117]

raceable, *adj.* **1.** Said of a racehorse ready for a specific race. [1965 *OEDS*]
2. Said of a racetrack that is in good shape for a race. [1975 *OEDS*]

race bird, *n.* Also called a RAILBIRD. A person who frequents racetracks or is addicted to gambling on horse races.
[1971 McQuaid *Gambler's Digest* 314]

racebook, *n.* A gambling establishment devoted to accepting wagers on horse races. See also SPORTS BOOK.
[1982 Martin *Introduction* 9]

race card, *n.* Also written **race-card** or **racecard.** A list containing the names of all the horses scheduled for a particular race. See also RACING FORM. [1851 *OED*]

racecaster, *n.* A radio or television announcer who provides the spoken report of a horse race.
[1938 *OEDS;* from *race* + (broad)*caster*]

racecourse, *n.* Also written **race course.** Also called a RACETRACK. A place for racing horses, dogs, cars, and so on.
[1764 *OED,* 1809 *DAE*]

racecup, *n.* A trophy, often silver-plated, awarded the winner of a race.
[1777 *OED*]

race-day, *n.* Also written **race day.** A specific day set aside for the running of horse races.
[1620 *OED,* as *raice day*]

race game, *n.* A board game popular in the late nineteenth century in which a simulated race took place by advancing counters with casts of dice. [1895 *OEDS*]

race-glasses, *n. pl.* Also **race-glass,** *sing.* A pair of binoculars or field-glasses for use at races.
[1865 *OEDS,* as *race-glass*]

racegoer, *n.* Also written **race-goer.** A frequenter of races, especially horse races. See also RACE BIRD and RAILBIRD.
[1880 *OEDS*]

race ground, *n.* Also written **race-ground.** A RACETRACK. *Rare.*
[1802 *OED*]

racehorse, *n.* Also written **race horse,** and

formerly as **race-horse. 1.** A horse bred and raised for racing.
[1626 *OED,* 1753 *DAE*]
2. A gambling game with wagers placed on the performance of toy horses the movements of which are governed by dice, wheel of fortune, or similarly determined random numbers.
[1853 *OED*]

racehorse keno, *n.* Another name for KENO.
[1971 McQuaid *Gambler's Digest* 314]
[Because, at one time, the eighty squares of a keno ticket carried the names of horses]

race-horsing, *adj.* Pertaining to the activities surrounding the racing of horses.
[1745 *OED*]

race list, *n.* The program at a racetrack providing information about the entries. See also RACING FORM. [1833 *OED*]

race-manager, *n.* A trainer of racehorses.
[1812 *OED*]

race meeting, *n.* A designated time period for thoroughbred racing.
[1809 *OED*]

race-nags, *n. pl.* Racehorses, especially of inferior quality. See also NAG. Compare QUITTER.
[1634 *OED*]

race path, *n.* A RACETRACK. *Obsolete.*
[1737 *DA*]

racer, *n.* A RACEHORSE.
[1670 *OED*]

race-reader, *n.* **1.** Also written **race reader.** A person who forecasts the performance of horses in a forthcoming race.
[1951 *OEDS*]
2. A commentator who describes races and entries; a race analyst. Compare RACECASTER.
[1953 *OEDS*]

race rider, *n.* Same as a JOCKEY. *Obsolete.*
[*a*1700 *OED*]

race-riding, *n.* The riding of a horse in a race. *Rare.* [1840 *OED*]

race-runner, *n.* Same as a JOCKEY. *Rare.*
[1647 *OED*]

race-stand, *n.* An elevated platform from which spectators watch horse races.
[1860 *OED*]

racetrack, *n.* Also called a RACECOURSE. A place, usually oval in shape, for conducting speed competitions among horses, dogs, cars, and so on.
[1859 *DAE,* 1862 *OEDS*]

racetracker, *n.* **1.** A professional handler for racehorses.
2. One who works at tracks, moving from place to place with changes in the racing calendar.
[(1951) 1981 Maurer *Lang. of the Underworld* 224]
3. Same as a RACEGOER.

racetrack odds, *n. pl.* In craps, pertaining to the payoffs for such proposition or HOP, "one roll", bets as 2, 3, or 12.
[1983 Martinet *Oral Coll*]

race week, *n.* Also written **race-week.** A designated period of time devoted to thoroughbred racing.
[1716 *OED*]

race-winner, *n.* The winner, especially of a horserace. [1823 *OED*]

racing, *n.* **1.** The action of participating in a race, especially a horse race.
[1680 *OED*]
2. The business of horse racing.

racing-calendar, *n.* A yearly publication providing information about horse races run or to be run. [1709 *OED*]

racing colors, *n.* The color or colors which identify the owners of a racehose and which adorn the SILKS worn by the jockey.
[1908 *OEDS*]

racing colt, *n.* A racehorse, especially a young one. [1828 *OED*]

racing establishment, *n.* The people, equipment, and animals involved in the running of races, especially horse races.
[1828 *OED*]

racing form, *n.* Also shortened to FORM. A newspaper-like publication listing all the entries at several racetracks, along with information on odds, past performance, and recommendations. Sometimes called **Daily Racing Form.**
[(1951) 1981 Maurer *Lang. of the Underworld* 224]

racing jacket, *n.* See also SILKS. Compare RACING COLORS. [1833 *OED*]

racing-like, *adj.* Pertaining to a fast horse; hence, pertaining to any rapid animal or machine.
[1852 *OED*]

racing-loser, *n.* One who loses in or by horse racing. *Obsolete.*
[1680 *OED*]

racing man, *n.* Any person involved in horse racing, as owner, trainer, bettor, and so on.
[1828 *OED*]

racing pace, *n.* A rapid rate of movement, especially of a horse.
[1828 *OED*]

racing-path, *n.* Same as RACETRACK.
[1884 *OED*, compare earlier RACE PATH]

racing plate, *n.* In horse racing, a special shoe worn by a horse during a race. See also PLATE (def. 1).
[1978 Ainslie *Complete Guide* 296]
[1958 *OEDS*]

racing saddle, *n.* A lightweight saddle used for racing horses, as opposed to a *riding saddle.*
[1828 *OED*]

racing season, *n.* A portion of the year, usually

several weeks, set aside for racing meetings, especially for horses.
[1840 *OED*]

racing secretary, *n.* A racetrack official responsible for arranging races, collecting money for purses, and establishing odds on the entries.
[1968 Buchele *Greyhound Racing* 97]
[(1951) 1981 Maurer *Lang. of the Underworld* 224]

racing stable, *n.* A building near a racetrack designed with stalls for keeping the horses participating in a race meet.
[1828 *OED*]

racing stud, *n.* A male horse particularly fit to sire racehorses.
[1828 *OEDS*]

racing-tail, *n.* A tail of natural length worn by a racehorse.
[1843 *OED*, as *racing-tailed*]

racing-whip, *n.* A short leather crop carried by a jockey, used to strike the horse during a race.
[1864 *OED*]

racing wire service, *n.* Also shortened to **racing wire.** A telephone or telegraph service devoted to broadcasting racing events.
[1950 *Review Journal* 1/11: 1]

racing world, *n.* Same as RACING ESTABLISHMENT.
[1841 *OED*]

rack, *n.* Also called a TABLE CHIP TRAY. A box or case with open grooves used to keep chips stacked in an orderly fashion at a gaming table.
[1961 Scarne *Complete Guide* 685]

rack, *v.* **1.** To separate gaming chips by denomination and place them in a tray for orderly storage.
[1961 Scarne *Complete Guide* 685]
[Compare 1855 *OEDS,* meaning "to place in a rack"]
2. In the phrases:
rack out, To redeem chips for currency and stop gambling.
[1983 Martinez *Gambling Scene* 216]
rack up, 1. To win a large amount at gambling.
[1983 Martinez *Gambling Scene* 216]
2. In a casino, to remove chips from a table with a wooden or plastic case constructed for that purpose.
[1983 Martinet *Oral Coll*]
3. In horse racing, to impede other entries, usually by bumping them.
[1978 Ainslie *Complete Guide* 296]

racket, *n.* An illegal or dishonest scheme designed to defraud or cheat people.
[1812 *OED*]

racketeer, *n.* A person who obtains money dishonestly by means of deceit, fraud, or some cheating scheme. When used of a cardsharp, the term carries no connotation of violence.
[1928 *OEDS*]

raffle, *n.* **1.** A form of LOTTERY in which numbered tickets are sold for a drawing on a specific prize.
[1766 *OED*]
2. In chuck-a-luck and raffle and hazard, a wager that the three dice thrown will all have the same number of pips on the upward face.
[1386 *OED*]

raffle, *v.* **1.** To buy or sell tickets for a drawing for a specific prize, or to cast dice or draw lots for such a prize.
[1680 *OED*]
2. In chuck-a-luck and hazard, to wager that the next roll of three dice will result in the same number of pips showing face upward on each die.
[1974 Scarne *Dice* 343]

raffler, *n.* One who operates a raffle game.
[1798 *OED*]

raffle wheel, *n.* Also called a PADDLE WHEEL. A WHEEL-OF-FORTUNE with numbers around the rim of the wheel. Pieces of stiff board, each with a number corresponding to a number on the wheel, are sold before the operator spins the wheel. The person wins who holds the board, or paddle, with the number corresponding to the number against a pointer when the wheel stops.
[1961 Scarne *Complete Guide* 685]

raffling, *adj.* Pertaining to the operation of a raffle: **raffling day,** 1780 *OED;* **raffling dice,** 1732 *OED;* **raffling lottery,** 1682 *OED;* **raffling shop,** 1706 *OED.*

rag, *n.* In poker, a card that has no value in the hand. See also TRASH.
[1978 Brunson *How I Made* 543]

rail, *n.* **1.** On a racecourse, the fence along both sides of an oval track.
[1928 *OEDS;* compare 1541 *OED,* meaning "a fence or railing"]
2. On a craps table, the raised side of the table, often grooved with troughs for holding chips. See also BOARD and CUSHION.
[(1950) 1981 Maurer *Lang. of the Underworld* 190]
3. In a casino, the velvet-covered chain or rope separating players from observers, usually a section devoted to poker or baccarat.
[1950 Morehead *Culbertson* 638]
[Probably influenced more by def. 1 than def. 2; compare RAILBIRD (defs. 1, 2)]

railbird, *n.* **1.** Also written **rail bird.** An ardent fan of racing who keeps records of entries, carries gossip, stands close to the outside rail, and so on. [1892 *DA*]
2. In a casino or cardroom, a spectator who watches the progress of games like poker or baccarat from a position outside the barrier surrounding the gaming tables. Compare RAIL (def. 3).
[1978 Brunson *How I Made* 544]

rail hawker, *n.* A sneak thief who lurks about

craps tables and takes players' chips from the racks built atop the rail.
[1979 Newman *Dealer's Special* 43]

railroad bible, *n.* Another term for a deck of playing cards. Compare CALIFORNIA BIBLE.
1976 Clark *Oral Coll.* I would tell that judge I was not in possession of those cards simply for the purposes of gambling. Rather, I would tell him that these are my tickets for riding the train to glory. My *railroad bible* reminds me of everything I need to remember. The four suits are for the four gospel makers, and each card has a special biblical significance.

rail roll, *n.* On a bank craps table, a cast of the dice in which one or both bounce up onto the rail, invalidating the cast.
[1983 Martinet *Oral Coll*]

rail runner, *n.* In racing, an entrant that performs well when racing next to the inside rail on an oval track. Compare RUN WIDE.
[1968 Buchele *Greyhound Racing* 96]
[(1951) 1981 Maurer *Lang. of the Underworld* 225]

rainbow, *n.* Also called a DIRTY STACK or BARBER POLE. In a casino, a stack of chips that includes different denominations.
[1983 Martinet *Oral Coll*]

rainbow hand, *n.* In poker, a hand with cards from all four suits. Compare PINK.
[1950 Morehead *Culbertson* 638]

raise, *n.* **1.** In poker, an increase of the amount already bet.
[1821 *OEDS,* 1887 *DAE,* 1894 *OED*]
2. In bridge, a higher bid in the same suit as a previous bid by the partner.
[1923 *OEDS*]

raise, *v.* **1.** In poker, to increase the wager made by a previous bettor. Compare CALL (def. 3) and SEE.
1866 *American Card Player* 135. *Raising a Bet.*—The same as going better.
[1821 *OEDS,* 1864 *DAE*]
2. In bridge, to increase the bid in the same suit as a previous bid by the partner.
[1951 *OEDS*; but presumed to be earlier, compare RAISE, *n.* and RAISING]
3. In the phrases:
raise back, In poker, to increase the size of a wager after an opponent has already increased the wager.
[1949 Coffin *Secrets* 184]
raise blind, In poker, to increase the size of a wager before looking at the cards. See also BLIND RAISE.
[1968 Wallace *Poker* 222]
raise out, To cause a player to withdraw from a gambling game by making the stakes higher than his bankroll.
[1872 *DAE, OEDS,* 1894 *OED*]

raised edge work, *n. phr.* A die heated along one edge to alter the size of the die slightly, thereby changing the characteristics of the roll.
[1974 Scarne *Dice* 240]

raised spot work, *n. phr.* A die heated so that one face is slightly rounded, decreasing the likelihood that the die will come to rest on that face.
[1974 Scarne *Dice* 242]

raising, *n.* **1.** In poker, the increasing of a bet made by an opponent.
[1978 *OEDS,* but presumed to be made earlier, compare RAISE, *v.* (def. 1)]
2. In bridge, the act of increasing a bid.
[1929 *OEDS*]

rake, *n.* **1.** Short for RAKE-OFF.
2. A long-handled tool with a blade rather than teeth, used by a dealer or banker to gather money or chips on a gaming table. Compare CROUPIER (def. 2) and STICK.
[1865 *OEDS*]
3. rakes, *pl.* Playing cards that have been shaved or trimmed to a size different from the rest of the pack. Compare CONCAVE CARDS and CONVEX CARDS and STRIPPERS.
[1938 Asbury *Sucker's Progress* 13]

rake, *v.* In the phrases and particle constructions:
rake down, To win money at gambling and put some of the winnings away while continuing to gamble.
[1839 *OEDS,* 1845 *DA,* 1891 *DAE*]
rake off, In a poker room, to take a percentage of the winnings for the expenses and profit of the operator of the establishment.
[1949 Coffin *Secrets* 184]

rake-off, *n.* Also written **rakeoff** or **rake off.** In a poker room, a percentage of each pot taken by the house dealer for expenses and profit for the establishment. [1888 *OEDS*]

rangdoodles, *n. pl.* Same as ROODLES and WHANGDOODLES. Also called PROGRESSIVE PROGRESSIVE. A poker game featuring increased stakes under certain conditions, as when no player can begin the betting process in a game of jacks or better.
[1968 Wallace *Poker* 222]

rank, *n.* The relative value of one item in relation to other like items, as the relative order of cards: 2, 3, 4, etc.; poker hands: one pair, two pair, three of a kind, etc.
[1968 Wallace *Poker* 222]
[Compare 1605 *OED,* meaning "relative position"]

rank, *adj.* In horse racing, pertaining to a fractious or unmanageable horse; noting a horse that is hard to control before or during a race.
[1971 McQuaid *Gambler's Digest* 314]
[(1951) 1981 Maurer *Lang. of the Underworld* 225]

rank card, *n.* In playing cards, a card valued at the number of pips showing on the face; the 2,

3, 4, 5, 6, 7, 8, 9, and 10. Compare COURT CARD and FACE CARD.
[1981 Silverstone *Player's Guide* 142]

rap pat, *v. phr.* In draw poker, to play the original five cards dealt without discarding, and to signify that intention by knocking or rapping on the table when the dealer offers to replace any cards. See also STAND PAT.
[1978 Brunson *How I Made* 544]

rat, *n.* **rats,** *pl.* Also called **rats and mice.** Among craps players, another term for DICE.
[1977 Carroll *Playboy's Illustrated* 125]
[(1950) 1981 Maurer *Lang. of the Underworld* 190]
[Rhyming slang]

rate, *v.* In horse racing, to restrain a horse during a race until the stretch. See also ROPER. Compare DRIVE and EXTEND.
[1920 *OEDS*]

rathole, *v.* Also written **rat-hole.** To put money or chips into the pocket while still gambling, especially at poker.
[1949 Coffin *Secrets* 184]
[Compare 1948 *OEDS,* meaning "To hide or store, not to invest or spend"]

rat holer, *n.* A player, especially at poker, who pockets chips or money while playing.
[1949 Coffin *Secrets* 184]

rattle, *n.* **1.** In craps, a single cast of the dice.
1983 Martinet *Oral Coll.* When a player wants to make a one-shot bet [one determined by the next roll of the dice], he will toss the check to the stick and say something like, "I'll bet five bucks a pop," or "a nickle a *rattle.*"
[From the sound the dice make while shaking them for a roll.]
2. A DICE BOX used in games of chance. *Obsolete.*
[1732 *OED*]
3. In the prepositional phrase:
with a rattle, In horse racing, with sudden or unexpected rapidity.
[1888 *OEDS*]

rattle, *v.* **1.** In snake eyes, to roll the dice and score no points, at which time the game is ended and the player throwing the dice pays double the amount wagered.
[1983 Martinet *Oral Coll*]
2. In the phrase:
rattle away, To lose by gambling at dice.
[1808 *OED*]

read, *v.* In the phrase:
read the players, In poker, especially hold 'em and stud, to make an informed guess about the hands held by other players by observing the cards dealt upward, the reactions of other players, the betting pattern, and so on.
[1978 Brunson *How I Made* 544]
[Compare 1624 *OED,* meaning "to interpret"]

reader, *n.* **readers** *pl.* **1.** Playing cards marked on the back, allowing a cheater to know what cards other players are holding. Compare COSMETICS.
1902 Andrews *Artifice* 16. Marked cards, generally known as "*readers,*" can be distinguished by the backs as readily as by the faces when the key is known.
[1894 *OED*]
2. Tinted glasses or contact lenses worn to read cards marked on the back with a special dye visible only through an optic filter.
[1971 Livingston *Poker Strategy* 223]

ready, *adj.* In the phrase:
ready for patting. Prepared for a race; fit.
[(1951) 1981 Maurer *Lang. of the Underworld* 225]

ready up, *v.* To prepare to make a cheating move, especially while playing cards or dice.
[1961 Scarne *Complete Guide* 685]
[Compare *ready:* 1864 *OEDS,* as *ready up,* meaning, "to make ready"]

ready-up, *n. clause.* Oral statement to a confederate signaling that a cheating move is soon to be made.
[1974 Scarne *Dice* 477]
[Compare 1924 *OEDS,* meaning "a fake; swindle"]

rebid, *n.* In bridge, a bid made by a player who has previously made a bid.
[1953 Crawford *Consistent Winner* 352]
[1927 *OEDS*]

rebid, *v.* In bridge, to bid again. Compare REDOUBLE.
[1923 *OEDS*]

recency, *adj.* In horse racing, pertaining to the elapsed time since a horse has last raced.
[1982 *Today's Racing*]
[Compare 1612 *OED,* meaning "state of being recent"]

red, *n.* **1.** Also called a NICKEL. A chip or check worth five dollars.
[1973 Clark *Oral Coll*]
2. Hearts and diamonds in a pack of cards. See also PINK.
[1764 *OED,* as *red suit*]

redeal, *n.* A fresh shuffle and redistribution of playing cards by the same dealer, usually after a FOUL or MISDEAL.
[1950 Morehead *Culbertson* 639]
[1959 *OEDS*]

redeal, *v.* To reshuffle and redistribute the cards after a foul, or misdeal.
[1935 *OEDS*]

red board, *n.* In horse racing: **1.** The designation employed by the judges to signal a tie.
2. A signal, on the board where race results are posted, that a entry has been disqualified.
[(1951) 1981 Maurer *Lang. of the Underworld* 225]

red game, *n.* In a casino, a table game with a

minimal bet requirement of five dollars. Compare GREEN GAME.
[1983 Martinet *Oral Coll*]
[From the fact that chips worth five dollars are usually red]

red hot, *adj.* **1.** Pertaining to a player winning several times in a row; noting unusual winning patterns.
[1974 Scarne *Dice* 471]
[(1950) 1981 Maurer *Lang. of the Underworld* 190]
2. Pertaining to a horse highly favored to win a race. [1882 *OED*]

red line, *n.* In Las Vegas, an imaginary line circumscribing several blocks in the downtown area in which gambling establishments may be operated.
[1974 Friedman *Casino Management* 22]

redouble, *n.* In bridge, a challenge to an opponent's call for doubling the score.
[1906 *OEDS*]

redouble, *v.* In bridge, to challenge an opponent's call to double the score, in effect quadrupling the potential points for the hand.
[1894 *OEDS*]

redskin, *n.* Also called a PAINTSKIN. In card games, especially faro and poker, any face card; a jack, queen, or king of any suit. Compare WHITESKIN.
[1943 Maurer *Argot*]

red three, *n.* In canasta, a three of hearts or diamonds, worth 100 points when played face up.
[1971 McQuaid *Gambler's Digest* 314]

reduce, *v.* In gin rummy, to discard high cards in order to avoid losing points if an opponent goes out. Compare GO OUT.
[1953 Crawford *Consistent Winner* 352]

reel, *n.* On a mechanical slot machine, one of three or more wheels containing symbols such as cherries, oranges, bars, lemons, and so on.
[1973 Clark *Oral Coll*]

reel clock, *n.* On a mechanical slot machine, a weighted wheel that spins in a random fashion, insuring that the reels lock into place in an irregularly timed fashion. Compare REEL TIMING.
[1973 Clark *Oral Coll*]

reel setting, *n.* On a slot machine, the horizontal, sometimes diagonal, configuration of symbols along the reels that control payouts and jackpots.
[1978 Alexander *Glossary* 12]

reel timing, *n.* On a mechanical slot machine, a system for pulling the handle in a specific rhythm to confound the REEL CLOCK and allow the player to align symbols for payouts.
1982 Clark *Oral Coll.* Since the late 1960s, manufacturers and operators have added counterweights on the clocks to prevent *reel timing.* A cheater could set up a rhythm on the reels and jiggle them into free wheeling. Then he could snap the handle and the reels would lock on a payoff.
[1964 Wykes *Illustrated Guide* 328]

re-entry, *n.* Also called **re-entry card** or **card of re-entry.** In whist or bridge, a card a player can use to take a trick and recapture the lead.
[1884 *OED*]

reflector, *n.* **1.** Same as GLEAMER and SHINER. A brightly polished coin or small mirror placed on the table which allows the dealer to see the undersides of the cards being dealt.
1865 Evans *Gamblers Win* 40. *Reflectors* are on a somewhat similar principle as the convex, but are flat, and generally magnifiers. They are merely looking glasses which magnify.
2. A playing card with an indentation pressed into the back, usually with the thumbnail, detectable by holding the card at an angle toward the light.
[1968 Adams *Western Words*]

refusal, *n.* In games like ecarte and all-fours, the act of the dealer in refusing to allow a discard.
[1877 *OED*]

refuse, *v.* **1.** In horse and dog racing, to fail to break quickly from the starting gate.
[1968 Buchele *Greyhound Racing* 97]
[Compare 1840 and 1525 *OED,* meaning "to fail to take a jump"]
2. In all-fours, to prevent the eldest hand from scoring additional points by the dealer's accepting a BEG, a request for additional cards.
[1950 Morehead *Culbertson* 639]

relief dealer, *n.* In a casino, a dealer with no regular station who spends his shift replacing other dealers so they make take their breaks.
[1983 Martinet *Oral Coll*]

renege, *v.* Also spelled **renegue** or **reneg. 1.** In bridge, to play a card of another suit while holding a card of the suit led.
[1680 *OED,* as *reneg*]
2. To fail to pay a gambling debt. See also WELSH.
[1961 Scarne *Complete Guide* 685]
[Compare (1784) 1962 *OEDS,* meaning "recant"]

renege, *n.* An instance of reneging at cards.
[1654 *OED,* as *reneg*]

renounce, *v.* **1.** In games like whist and bridge, to play a card different from the suit led, though such a card is available.
1836 Eidrah *Hoyle Famil* 4. *Renouncing* is playing a card of a different suit from that led. If a trump card is played, it is called Trumping Suit. Very severe penalties are annexed to *renouncing* or trumping suit, if the player holds a card of suit led, and it is in this case termed Revoking.
[1747 *OED*]
2. In games like whist and bridge, to play a card

which is not trump, when one has no cards of the suit led.
1860 Pardon *Handbook* 24. *Renounce*—Possessing no card of the suit led, and playing another which is not a trump.
[1656 *OED*]

rentrant, *n.* In two-handed card games, the challenger who plays the winner of the previous game.
[1950 Morehead *Culbertson* 639]

rep, *n.* Short for **represent.** A notation printed on the most frequently rolled numbers on a bagatelle layout, requiring that a person wagering on one of those numbers must, if that number is rolled, double his bet for the next roll of the dice or forfeit the money already bet. In effect, the player must win on the same number twice and be willing to bet twice the amount of the original stake. Compare REPRESENT, *v.*
[1890 Quinn *Fools of Fortune* 297]

repeat, *v.* In poker, to bet the same amount as in the previous betting round.
[1949 Coffin *Secrets* 184]

repeat, *n.* In horse racing, a second (or third) heat of a race.
[1856 *DA,* where the citation notes: *repeat* is American usage, *heat* is British usage)
→In other sports such as track or canoeing, *heat* is the customary term in the U.S.

repeat and reverse, *v. phr.* In faro, to win or lose in the same order during the following deal.
1868 Trumps *Pocket Hoyle* 208. *Repeating and Reversing.*—A card is said to *repeat,* when it plays as it did upon the previous deal, and to *reverse* when it plays directly opposite; that is, if it won four times, it reverses if it loses four times.

repeater, *n.* **1.** In horse racing, a horse that wins two consecutive races.
[1971 McQuaid *Gambler's Digest* 314]
2. In craps, a number rolled twice in succession.
[1983 Martinet *Oral Coll*]
3. repeaters, *pl.* Dice loaded in such a fashion that only one number can be rolled, usually the number 7. [n.d. *DAS*]

repic, *n.* In piquet, a bonus of sixty points for scoring sixty points before the opponent has scored any points.
[1950 Morehead *Culbertson* 639]

represent, *v.* In multiple dice games such as bagatelle, to require the player to double his bet for the next roll of the dice or forfeit any money placed on that number. The letters REP are printed on the most frequently rolled numbers on the layout. In effect, the player must double his bet and the same number must be rolled twice in order to win.
[1890 Quinn *Fools of Fortune* 297]

representing, *n.* The forcing of a player to double his wager or forfeit the amount already bet.
[1890 Quinn *Fools of Fortune* 287]

repuesto, *n. Spanish.* In the card game ombre, a tie. The person designated as Player must then double the amount in the pot.
1680 Cotton *Compleat Gamester* 72. Here note, although the other two always combine to make him lose, yet they all do their best (for the common good) to hinder any one from winning, only striving to make it *Repuesto,* which is when the Player wins no more Tricks than another, in which case the Player doubles the Stake without any ones winning it, and remains so for the advantage of the next Player.

requirement, *n.* In bridge, the minimal number of count cards necessary to make a bid. Compare OPENERS.
[1950 Morehead *Culbertson* 639]

reraise, *v.* In poker, to increase the amount wagered in the same bettting round after an opponent has raised a bet. Compare REBID and REDOUBLE.
[1949 Coffin *Secrets* 184]

reraise, *n.* Also called BACKRAISE. In poker, the increasing of the amount wagered in the same betting round after an opponent has raised a bet. Compare REBID and REDOUBLE.
[1949 Coffin *Secrets* 184]

responder, *n.* In bridge, the partner of the person who has taken command in the bidding process. The *responder* gives relevant information about the cards in his hand by answering questions put by the partner in the form of bids.
[1932 *OEDS*]

response, *n.* In bridge, an answer given to a partner who has taken command of the bidding process and requested information put in the form of a bid.
[1939 *OEDS*]

restraddle, *n.* In poker, a wager required of the third player to the left of the dealer, amounting to twice the bet of the second player to the left of the dealer, made before the players look at their cards. See also BLIND and STRADDLE.
[1964 Reese and Watkins *Secrets* 143]

restricted license, *n.* A license issued by a municipality, county, etc. for specific gambling games to be operated legally.
[1957 *Nevada Gaming Regulations* 5]

restricted pot, *n.* In draw poker, a pot amounting to only the ante, won by the player holding OPENERS, the minimal qualifying hand.
[1968 Wallace *Poker* 222]

result chart, *n.* In handicapping, the performance record of entries in previous contests, such as horse racing, football, baseball, jai alai, and so on.
[1981 Passer *Winning Big* 229]

result player, *n.* A gambler who analyzes losses after a game and declares to have an understanding of what went wrong.
[1961 Scarne *Complete Guide* 685]

result writer, *n.* Also called a SHEETWRITER. In sports books, an employee who posts the results of horse races, games, and so on.
[1983 Martinet *Oral Coll*]

return rate, *n.* In slot machines, the percentage of money played into a slot machine that is returned in payouts and jackpots.
[1977 Puzo *Inside Las Vegas* 168]

reverse, *n.* **1.** In the card game whist, the playing of a hand in a different manner than normally expected.
1746 Hoyle *Short Treatise* 69. Playing at any time the *Reverse,* means only the playing of your Hand in a different manner; that is to say, if you are strong in Trumps you play one way, but if weak in Trumps you play the *Reverse,* viz. another.
[1742 *OED*]
2. Also called **reverse bid.** In bridge, a REBID in a suit of higher rank than that which one has previously bid.
[1936 *OEDS*]

reverse, *v.* In bridge, to rebid in a suit of higher rank than that which one has previously bid.
[1939 *OEDS*]

revoke, *v.* In trump games, to play a card of another suit while holding a card of the suit which has been played.
1836 Eidrah *Hoyle Famil* 8. *Revoke* is trumping, by mistake or otherwise, when you happen to hold a card of the suit led.
[1952 *OED*]

revoke, *n.* In trump games, a failure to follow suit when the proper card can be played.
[1709 *OED*]

RFB comp, *n.* Also shortened to **RFB.**
In a casino, complimentary room, food, and beverages provided to valued patrons.
1985 Hopkins *Suite Life* 35. How a player is treated, of course, is directly related to how much he or she bets. For instance, to get complimentary room, food, and beverage—known as *RFB*—a player often must use the black chips. "Betting $100 at a time, four hours a day, is pretty much an industry standard," says Bedich, referring to *RFB.*
[Abbreviated from "Room, Food, and Beverages Compliment"]

rhythm player, *n.* In slot machines, a player who sets up a rhythmic pattern in a mechanical slot machine, puts the reels into a free-wheeling mode, then snaps the handle to lock the reels in place with a payout configuration lined up on the machine. Compare CHEATER'S BAR.
[1953 Lewis *Sagebrush Casinos* 74]

rhythm system, *n.* In slot machines, a method for cheating mechanical slot machines by setting up a rhythmic pattern, putting the reels into a free-wheeling mode, then snapping the handle to lock the reels in place when a payout configuration is lined up on the machine.
[1961 Scarne *Complete Guide* 685]
→Since the late 1960s, manufacturers and operators have added counterweights to the timing clocks in such machines to foil the practice.

ribbon clerk, *n.* A poker player noted for making small wagers and playing in a niggardly fashion. See also DEGENERATE.
[1968 Wallace *Poker* 222]

rib-roaster, *n. Also written* **rib roaster.** In horse racing, a strong hit with the whip by the jockey.
1889 Ellangowan *Sporting Anecdotes* 336. Sidebinder.—Nearly equivalent to a "*rib roaster*"—a heavy cut with the whip to get a horse to make another effort.
[Compare 1854 *OED,* meaning "a severe blow to the ribs"]

rich, *adj.* Pertaining to a pack of playing cards with the majority of cards above 9 still undealt.
[1973 Preston *Play Poker* 169]

rickets, *n. pl.* Three playing cards used in a variety of cheating schemes such as THREE CARD MONTE.
[1968 Adams *Western Words*]

ridden out, *adj. phr.* In horse racing, pertaining to a horse that has made a driving finish in a race without becoming exhausted.
[1971 McQuaid *Gambler's Digest* 314]

ride, *n.* **1.** A wager that includes the original bet plus winnings from a previous bet. Compare PARLAY.
[1973 Clark *Oral Coll*]
2. In poker, a betting round in which no player bets, thereby allowing all players to receive an additional card or cards without risking money.
[1973 Clark *Oral Coll*]
3. The cheating of a victim.
1979 Clark *Oral Coll.* We took him for a *ride* in that game. We could whipsaw [cross bet, with the victim in the middle] him because we had good readers [marked cards] and a good man [dishonest dealer] dealing.
4. A race, especially a horse race.
[Compare 1759 *OEDS,* meaning "an excursion or journey"]

ride, *v.* **1.** To wager the amount won, along with the original bet, on an ensuing event, such as after a win in twenty-one roulette, or craps.
[1974 Scarne *Dice* 80]
2. Also called FREE RIDE. In poker, to CHECK, refuse to wager, during a betting round and receive a card or cards.
[1978 Larson *Vocabulary* 100]
3. To urge a horse to top speed in a race.
[1863 *OED*]
4. In the phrases:
ride along, In poker, to remain in contention for the pot without having to risk much money, as when all players CHECK, or decline to bet during a betting round.
[1968 Wallace *Poker* 222]

ride short, In horse racing, to raise the stirrups higher than normal.
[1978 Ainslie *Complete Guide* 296]

ride the pot, Also, to GO LIGHT. In poker, to borrow chips from the pot to track the amount a player is short during a betting round. The player is expected to draw money from his pocket after the showdown if he loses the hand.
[1949 Coffin *Secrets* 184]

ride with (a horse), In racing, to wager on (a horse).
[(1951) 1981 Maurer *Lang. of the Underworld* 225]

ride with the shooter, 1. In casino craps, to allow a bet made for the dealers to remain on the table while the same shooter continues.
2. Generally, to parlay a bet.
[(1950) 1981 Maurer *Lang. of the Underworld* 190]

ride work, To exercise a racehorse.
[1950 *OEDS*]

rider, n. **1.** In horse racing, a jockey.
[1805 *OED*]
2. In a casino, a player brought to the casino on a junket who does not gamble. Compare COMP.
[1974 Friedman *Casino Management* 136]

ridgeling, *n.* Also spelled RIGLING or RISLING. A partially castrated horse. Compare GELDING.
[1555 *OED:* variants with dates; 1555 *ridgeling, redgelinges;* 1559 *riggot, rygett;* 1597 *ridgell;* 1641 *riggon;* 1662 *riglen*; 1724 *rigling*]

riffle cull, *n.* A method for pulling a few cards from a pack, arranging them in a specific sequence, then shuffling the deck while keeping the arranged packet intact.
[1968 Wallace *Poker* 222]

riffle stack, *v. phr.* To arrange playing cards in a specific sequence, then appear to mix the cards while maintaining the predetermined sequence.
[1968 Wallace *Poker* 222]

riffle shuffle, *n.* Also shortened to **riffle.** A method for mixing a deck of playing cards by parting the deck in half, then using the thumbs to fan the two packets while pushing the halves together.
[1894 *OED,* as *riffle;* 1970 *OEDS,* as *riffle shuffle*]

rig, *v.* To prearrange the outcome of an event, as by altering cards or dice, stacking cards, bribing participants. and so on.
[1851 *OED, DSUE*]

rig, *n.* **1.** A trick, scheme or method for cheating or swindling a person.
[1755 *OED;* compare RIG, *n.,* meaning "a trick or swindle"]
2. Any of a variety of cheating devices, such as a BUG, card holdout, altered roulette wheel, electromagnet arrangement, and so on.
[1961 Scarne *Complete Guide* 685]

rigged game, *n.* A game in which cheating occurs by deception on the part of the operator, use of cheating devices, or some other means.
[1978 Harrah *Recollections* 11]

rigging, *n.* A cheating device, usually more complicated than altered cards or dice, such as a body harness for holding out cards, or an arrangement of electromagnets and switches on a dice or roulette table.
[1968 Adams *Western Words*]

right, *adj.* Same as READY FOR PATTING.
[(1951) 1981 Maurer *Lang. of the Underworld* 225]

right bet, *n.* **1.** In craps, a wager on the PASS LINE, a bet indicating a belief that the dice will pass. See also RIGHT POINT BET.
[1974 Scarne *Dice*]
2. In craps, a wager made in the correct amount to take advantage of the odds offered to the player.
1983 Martinet *Oral Coll.* A *right bet* is one that is made in the correct amount, so the player gets the full odds. For example, a $24 6 [place bet on the number 6 at odds of 7 to 6] takes the right odds, but a $25 6 doesn't get full odds. See also wrong bet.

right bettor, *n.* In craps, a player who wagers that the dice will pass; a pass bettor. See also RIGHT PLAYER. Compare WRONG BETTOR.
[(1950) 1981 Maurer *Lang. of the Underworld* 191]

right bower, *n.* In euchre, the jack of the suit named trump; the knave of trumps generally. Compare BOWER (def. 2) and LEFT BOWER.
1876 Heather *Cards* 131. *Right Bower.*—The knave of the trump suit—best card.
[1839 *DA, OEDS*]

right joint, *n.* A fair and reliable gambling establishment where cheaters are quickly and harshly dealt with.
1979 Clark *Oral Coll.* All of these places [in Las Vegas] are straight joints, but that particular one is known as a *right joint.* A cheater caught in there is almost certain to wind up in the hospital, or just disappear, you know, go away.

right money, *n.* **1.** In craps, a bet placed on the PASS LINE or the COME LINE; a bet indicating a belief that the dice will pass. See also RIGHT BET.
[1974 Scarne *Dice* 249]
[n.d. *DAS*]
2. Also called SMART MONEY. Denoting players who win large amounts, who are deemed worthy of being copied in their betting patterns.
[1941 *DAS*]
[1973 Clark *Oral Coll*]

right numbers, *n. pl.* Same as RIGHT PRICE.
[(1951) 1981 Maurer *Lang. of the Underworld* 225]

right pedro, *n.* In pedro, the five of trump.
[1950 Morehead *Culbertson* 640]

right player, *n.* Same as RIGHT BETTOR. In craps,

a person who places a wager on the PASS LINE or COME LINE.
[(1950) 1981 Maurer *Lang. of the Underworld* 191]

right point bet, *n. phr.* In craps, a wager indicating a belief that the dice will pass.
[1974 Scarne *Dice* 78]

right price, *n.* Also called RIGHT NUMBERS. In horse racing, higher than normal mutual odds on a horse, thereby warranting a bet.
[1968 Ainslie *Complete Guide* 453]

rigling, *n.* Same as RIDGELING.
[1978 Ainslie *Complete Guide* 296]

rim, *n.* In horse racing, a special type of shoe for a horse with a tendon problem. Compare PLATE and RACING PLATE.
[1978 Ainslie *Complete Guide* 296]

rim card, *n.* Also called a TABLE CARD or CREDIT PLAY MEMORANDUM. In a casino, a record of amounts of credit extended to and returned by players.
[1957 *Nevada Gaming Regulations* 33]
[From the practice of keeping a light sheet of cardboard under the rim of a table in a casino, on which a pit boss could note transactions with a specific player at a particular table.]

rim credit, *n.* In a casino, credit extended to a player at the table, eliminating the necessity of the player's going to the casino cage for additional chips. The player's account must be settled at the end of his gambling session at that table.
[1974 Friedman *Casino Management* 55]

rim customer, *n.* In a casino, a patron known well enough by the management to be extended credit for the player's gambling session at that table.
[1974 Friedman *Casino Management* 54]

ring, *v.* **1.** Also spelled WRING. To exchange one item or person for another for purposes of cheating, as substituting one horse, deck of cards, pair of dice, dog, dealer, or some such, for another.
[Compare 1812 *OED, OEDS,* meaning "to change, especially fraudulently"]
2. In the phrases:
ring in, To substitute surreptitiously one item or person for another of the same type, for purposes of cheating; to introduce dishonest dice, cards, players, or a dealer into a game; to exchange a pair of honest dice for a pair of loaded dice, an honest dealer for a dishonest one, and so on. See also RIP IN.
[1890 Quinn *Fools of Fortune* 229]
ring in a cold deck, Also spelled WRING. To slip a stacked deck of cards into a game.
1859 Green *Gam Tricks* 19. Changing packs, or *wringing in "cold decks,"* is practiced in this game to a great extent, and of course any kind of a hand the person wished is got by this trick. Frequently a player will supply himself with a pack of cards such as he knows are in general use where he is, and then, when playing, "*wring*" this pack in for the purpose of having cards that are marked all through by himself.
[1857 *DA, OEDS,* under *cold deck.*]

ring, *n.* **1.** A confederacy of cheaters.
[1973 Clark *Oral Coll*]
[Compare 1862 *DA,* meaning "a group that seeks to control *affairs* for their own advantage."]
2. In the phrase:
have a ring in (one's) nose, Pertaining to a player who is losing heavily and trying to recoup by betting larger amounts of money.
[1974 Scarne *Dice* 477]

ringer, *n.* **1.** In horse racing, a horse substituted for another, slower animal in order to improve the odds on a good horse.
[(1951) 1981 Maurer *Lang. of the Underworld* 225]
2. In card playing, especially poker, a player who is supposedly a novice, but actually is an expert player.
[1982 Martin *Introduction* 25]
3. Also called RIGGING. A device for holding out a card or cards.
[1968 Adams *Western Words*]
[Originally a finger ring with a small flange used for palming cards, but now any clip used to hide a card for later use.]

ring game, *n.* In poker, a table with every seat occupied; a full table; a table with the maximum number of players for that type of game.
[1978 Brunson *How I Made* 544]

ringing up, *n.* The preparation of a three-card monte dealer, including his patter to potential players, the setting up of his collapsible table, arrangement of equipment and costume.
[1890 Quinn *Fools of Fortune* 335]

ripe, *adj.* **1.** Pertaining to a potential victim of a cheater.
[1974 Scarne *Dice* 477]
[1967 *OEDS*]
2. In the phrase:
ripe for the take, Primed for being victimized.
[(1950) 1981 Maurer *Lang. of the Underworld* 191]

rip in, *v.* Also shortened to **rip.** To switch altered dice for honest dice during a game. See also RING IN.
[(1950) 1981 Maurer *Lang. of the Underworld* 191]

ripped, *adj.* Pertaining to a deck of cards separated into two packets, or CUT, then replaced in the original sequence.
[1890 Quinn *Fools of Fortune* 224]

risling, *n.* Same as RIDGELING.
[1978 Ainslie *Complete Guide* 296]

river, *n.* In the prepositional phrase:
down the river. In poker, especially seven card

stud and hold 'em, a period of play late in the hand.
1981 Golad *Oral Coll.* You might catch something good on the flop [in hold 'em, the first three community cards turned up in the middle of the table] and then get snapped off *down the river* if somebody fills a flush on sixth street [fourth card dealt face up in the middle of the table].

river card, *n.* In hold 'em poker, the last card dealt face up in the middle of the table before the final betting round.
[1978 Brunson *How I Made* 544]

river gambler, *n.* Originally a gambler who worked up and down the Mississippi River, but later a pejorative term for any professional gambler who could be expected to cheat.
[1898 *DA*]

river gambling, *n.* The professional gambling that occurred up and down the Mississippi River around 1840–1870, considered a nefarious occupation.
[1866 *DA*]

roadmap, *n.* **1.** In a casino twenty-one pit, the schedule kept by the floorman or pit boss recording the table each dealer is assigned to and the time spent at that table.
2. In bank craps, said of the dice when placed before the shooter with the number of pips required to win turned face upward.
[1983 Martinet *Oral Coll*]

rob, *v.* **1.** In all fours, to exchange a card in the hand for the one turned up on the table.
[1950 Morehead *Culbertson* 640]
2. In the phrases:
rob a kong, In mah jongg, to claim the fourth tile of a set by exhibiting a PUNG, or three tiles of the same suit.
[1950 Morehead *Culbertson* 640]
rob the pack, In cinch, to select cards from the stock of undealt cards and replace them with cards from the hand.
[1950 Morehead *Culbertson* 640]

robin-hood cheater, *n.* A cheater, especially in card games, who causes another player, usually a non-cheater, to win certain pots, games, or points, in order to divert attention from himself.
[1968 Wallace *Poker* 223]

rock, *n.* **1.** In poker, a very conservative player who plays well. Compare STONEWALL JACKSON.
[1961 Scarne *Complete Guide* 686]
2. rocks, *pl.* Money. Compare PILE.
[1840 *DA, OEDS*]
3. Also called a BONE. In dominos, a playing tile.
[1950 Morehead *Culbertson* 640]

rogue, *n.* In horse racing, a chronically fractious and ill-tempered horse.
[1881 *OED*]

rogues's badge, *n.* In horse racing, a pair of blinders or blinkers worn by a nervous or ill-tempered horse.
[1891 *OED*]

roll, *n.* **1.** Short for BANKROLL. An amount of currency; a gambler's stake, especially as a number of bills or notes rolled together. Compare MICHIGAN ROLL.
[1904 *OEDS*]
2. a. A continuing series of passes at craps; a continuing process of winning.
[1983 Martinet *Oral Coll*]
b. Any continuing, intense activity, especially in gambling. Compare ON A ROLL.
[1983 Martinet *Oral Coll*]
[1980 *BDC*, II: 4, 117]
3. In games like craps and backgammon, a cast of the dice.
[1961 Scarne *Complete Guide* 686]
[1926 *OEDS*]
4. The number of pips face upward after a pair of dice have been cast.
[1983 Martinet *Oral Coll*]
5. The turn of a card or die.
[1968 Wallace *Poker* 223]
6. A packet of coins of similar denomination, wrapped in paper tubing. Slot machine players buy nickels in one or two dollar rolls, quarters in five or ten dollar rolls, and so on.
[1973 Clark *Oral Coll*]

roll, *v.* **1. a.** To cast a pair of dice; to play a dice game.
[1929 *OEDS*, as ROLL THE BONES]
b. To play at a craps game.
[1961 Scarne *Complete Guide* 686]
2. To turn a playing card face upward.
[1968 Wallace *Poker* 223]
3. To win a series of bets, as at craps or twenty-one. [1983 Martinet *Oral Coll*]
4. In the phrases and particle constructions:
roll a hand, In craps, to cast the dice a series of times until a 7 is cast instead of a required point number.
[1983 Martinet *Oral Coll*]
roll the bones, To play at a game of craps.
[1953 Lewis *Sagebrush Casinos* 99]
[1929 *OEDS*]
roll the deck, In poker, to slip discards atop of the pack for cheating purposes.
[1982 Martin *Introduction* 27]
roll up, In seven-card stud, to deal the first face-upward card of the same rank as the first two cards dealt face downward, resulting in three of a kind.
[1978 Brunson *How I Made* 545]

roller, *n.* **1.** In keno, the person who draws the twenty balls that constitute a game. Compare KENO CALLER and KENO DEALER.
[1890 Quinn *Fools of Fortune* 251]
2. In craps, the shooter or caster; the person who throws the dice.
[1950 Morehead *Culbertson* 640]

3. rollers, *pl.* Dice, whether crooked or honest. [(1950) 1981 Maurer *Lang. of the Underworld* 191]

rollered, *adj.* Pertaining to a slot machine with an obstruction placed in front of the payout chute to prevent coins from dropping out.
[1953 Woon *The Way, How, and Where* 86]

rolling bones, *n.* **1.** Dice. Compare BONES.
[(1950) 1981 Maurer *Lang. of the Underworld* 191]
2. Gambling using dice.
[(1950) 1981 Maurer *Lang. of the Underworld* 191]

rolling faro, *n.* A wheel similar to a WHEEL OF FORTUNE which uses cards in the place of numbers.
1843 Green *Exposure* 83. *Rolling faro* seems to be a branch of faro: the machine is placed upon a wheel like the roulette, and has cards painted on its face, and other cards painted on a cloth, which is spread on the table for the players to bet on.

rolling full bloom, *n. phr.* **1.** In dice games, continuing, intense activity. Compare ROLL, *n.* (def. 2. a., b.).
[(1950) 1981 Maurer *Lang. of the Underworld* 191]
2. Designating an illegal gambling place operating with PROTECTION.
[(1950) 1981 Maurer *Lang. of the Underworld* 191]

rolling mustang, *n.* Same as ROLLING FARO.
[1931 *DA*]

roll up, *n.* In seven-card stud, the dealing of the first three cards of the same rank to one hand, two face-downward, and one face-upward.
[1978 Brunson *How I Made* 545]

roll your own, *n.* **1.** In any of several variations of poker, a process requiring players to arrange their cards in a desired fashion, then turn them face upward, one at a time, with betting based on each round of face-up cards.
[1978 Silberstang *Winning Poker* 103]
2. In bank craps, said to a new shooter coming out.
[1983 Martinet *Oral Coll*]
[Influenced by the instructions for variants of poker.]

rome, *n.* In romestecq, a pair, ranked at jacks or lower.
[1950 Morehead *Culbertson* 640]

romp, *n.* In horse racing, an easy win by a horse.
[1971 McQuaid *Gambler's Digest* 315]

romp, *v.* In horse racing: **1.**To win a race easily.
[1888 *OED*]
2. To cover ground easily.
[1891 *OED*]

roodles, *n. pl.* Same as RANGDOODLES and WHANGDOODLES. A poker game featuring increased stakes under certain conditions, as when no player can begin the betting process in a game of jacks or better. See also PROGRESSIVE PROGRESSIVE.
[1949 Coffin *Secrets* 184]

rook, *n.* A cheater; one who victimizes inexperienced players; a HUSTLER, a SHARPER. See quotation at LAMB: 1680 Cotton *Compleat Gamester.*
[1577 *OED*]

rook, *v.* To cheat or defraud, originally in gambling. [1590 *OED*]

rookie clerk, *n.* In a casino, a novice dealer.
[1979 Newman *Dealer's Special* 7]
[*Rookie* meaning "a novice" is probably related to *recruit* and perhaps influenced by *rook* (1598 *OED*) meaning "simpleton" or (1508 *OED*) a term of abuse.]

rope, *n.* In games like pan or gin rummy, a meld of three or more cards in a sequenced ranking, as 10, jack, queen, king.
[1950 Morehead *Culbertson* 640]

rope, *v.* **1.** To direct a player to an illegal gambling game.
[(1848) 1859 *OED*, 1877 *DA*]
2. To cheat a victim in a gambling game.
[(1950) 1981 Maurer *Lang. of the Underworld* 191]
3. In racing, to lose a race intentionally by pulling. See also ROPER.
[1887 *OED*]
4. In the phrase:
rope in, In racing, to PULL (def. 2.a.).
[1857 *OED*]

roper, *n.* A jockey who causes his mount to lose by holding him back. See also PULL, *n.* (def. 1) and *v.* (def. 2.a.) and RATE.
[1870 *OED*]

roper in, *n.* Also shortened to **roper.** Also called a STEERER. A person who guides players to an illegal gambling game, often one in which cheating takes place.
[1840 *DA, OEDS*]

rope racing, *n.* The act of holding back a horse during a race to prevent it from winning.
[1857 *OED*]

rotation, *n.* In playing cards or craps, the clockwise order of playing, such as dealing or bidding.
[1950 Morehead *Culbertson* 640]
[Compare 1656 *OED,* meaning "regular succession of a number of persons"]

rouge, *n.* **1.** Also called DAUB or SMEAR. A pastel-colored substance used for marking the backs of playing cards for purposes of cheating.
[1978 Larson *Vocabulary* 100]
2. The red color in the card game rouge et noir.
[1827 *OED*]
3. The red numbers in roulette.
[1850 *OED*]

rouge et noir, *n. French.* Also written **Rouge et**

Noir. **1.** A game at cards the table for which is characterized by two large red diamonds and two large black diamonds upon which players place their wagers according to the color they are betting upon.
[1791–8 *OED*]
2. The table for this game.
[1850 *OED*]

rough, *adj.* **1.** In lowball, pertaining to a mediocre hand in which the two highest cards are 8, 7 or 7, 6. [1968 Wallace *Poker* 223]
2. In racing, pertaining to a race in which an entry encounters interference, such as slower animals in front.
[1983 Martinez *Gambling Scene* 217]

rough gambler, *n.* A ne'er do-well accustomed to supporting himself by cheating at gambling or participating in a variety of illegal activities. *Regional use.*
[1865 *DA*]
→*Rough gambler* was used in the late 19th century in Montana, Idaho, Nevada, and Wyoming, referring especially to thieves, cattle rustlers, and highwaymen.

rough gambling, *n.* The activity of a ROUGH GAMBLER. [1865 *DA*]

rough hustle, *n.* In a casino, the activity of an aggressive dealer who cajoles tips from patrons. [1971 McQuaid *Gambler's Digest* 308]

rough it up, *v. phr.* In poker, to change the tempo or spirit of the progress of the game by betting larger stakes than normal.
[(1950) 1981 Maurer *Lang. of the Underworld* 191]

rough seven, *n.* In lowball poker, a hand in which the two highest-ranked cards are 7 and 6. See also SMOOTH SEVEN and SLICK SEVEN.
[1971 Livingston *Poker Strategy* 223]

roulette, *n.* **1.** A gambling game played at a ROULETTE TABLE with a ROULETTE WHEEL which spins in one direction while a ROULETTE BALL rolls in the opposite direction until it drops into a CANOE, a numbered slot, corresponding to designated figures on a ROULETTE LAYOUT.
[1745 *OED*]
2. The wheel, or center part on a roulette table.
[1850 *OED*]

Roulette. A ROULETTE TABLE is operated by a ROULETTE DEALER (also called a WHEEL ROLLER or WHEELMAN) who spins the ROULETTE WHEEL. His assistant is called a CROUPIER or HAND MUCKER. The KEEPER (or DEALER) spins the WHEEL in one direction and throws the ROULETTE BALL in a groove in the opposite direction while the ROULETTERS place their BETS with ROULETTE CHIPS on a ROULETTE LAYOUT. In this CRANK GAME the wheel is fitted with CANOES separated by FRETS and each is assigned a number from 1 to 36 with one canoe labeled ZERO (0) on the EUROPEAN WHEEL (also called the MONTE CARLO WHEEL); the AMERICAN WHEEL also has a slot labeled 00.

WHEEL CHECKS are dispensed to PLAYERS from the CHIP RACK by color—one color for each player with their value declared by the player and not determined by the color, as in other casino games.

Many regular ROULETTERS are SYSTEMS BETTORS, placing wagers in an effort to BEAT THE HOUSE, such as by BUNCHING. Under certain conditions a dealer may IMPRISON a PUNTER'S a Among the many SYSTEMS used are the MARTINGALE (or its variation the NEOPOLITAN MARTIGALE), THE ALEMBERT, and the PROGRESSIVE SYSTEM; they all require a pattern of increasing wagers based upon recouping ones losses.

A ROULETTE-TABLE layout is rectangular and features sections ruled off into three COLUMNS (including DAMNATION ALLEY) and twelve numbered rows as well as boxes for ODD and EVEN. The squares are for selecting which number and/or color will identify the CANOE into which the ROULETTE BALL will drop. A player may choose a STRAIGHT BET (on one number), or a SPLIT BET (on two neighboring numbers), a LINE BET (on a group of neighboring numbers), a SQUARE BET (on four neighboring numbers), a STREET BET (on a row of numbers), or a COLUMN BET (on one of the three columns). The selection of these bets is determined by the lines straddled by the CHECKS representing the wager.

SNEAK GAMES, unlike honest MECHANICAL GAMES, frequently rely upon a JUICE DEALER, NEEDLE WHEEL or a SQUEEZE WHEEL to manipulate the outcome of the spin.

WHEEL OF FORTUNE and ROLLING FARO are TABLE GAMES similar to roulette.

roulette ball, *n.* A ball which travels in the opposite direction to a rotating ROULETTE WHEEL, and which comes to rest in a numbered slot, CANOE, designating the winner of a betting round. [1844 *OEDS*]

roulette box, *n.* A portable roulette set-up. [1851 *OED*]

roulette chip, *n.* A colored chip without a denomination printed on it.
[1953 Ralli *Viva Vegas* 8]
→Each player is assigned to one set of chips of the same color and declares the value of all chips of that color. The dealer keeps track of the value of each color by placing one chip on the rail around the wheel with its cash value noted by a coin or chip with the appropriate denomination printed on it.

roulette crane, *n.* Same as ROULETTE CRANK. [1975 Clark *Oral Coll*]

roulette crank, *n.* Also called a ROULETTE CRANE. A non-existent tool for adjusting a roulette wheel. New dealers are often sent on extensive

searches to find the imaginary tool.
[1973 Clark *Oral Coll*]

roulette dealer, *n.* In a casino, an employee who conducts a roulette game.
[1979 Newman *Dealer's Special* 5]

rouletter, *n.* One who plays roulette.
[1891 *OED*]

roulette table, *n.* A specially designed table featuring a roulette layout and a frame for a roulette wheel.
[1827 *OED*]

roulette wheel, *n.* A circular hub set in a depression on a roulette table, featuring numbered slots, or CANOES, into one of which a ball drops as the WHEEL spins.
[1863 *OED*]

round, *n.* **1.** One complete cycle of play or wagering, as an opportunity for each poker player to bet before the next card is dealt, or each craps player to settle bets before the dice are rolled again.
[1735 *OED*]
2. rounds, *pl. Usually plural, in form, but singular in use.* **a.** Playing cards marked on the back for ease of recognition by a cheater. See also DENT.
[1890 Quinn *Fools of Fortune* 197]
b. Dice with rounded corners, used by cheaters. See also ROLLERS.
[(1950) 1981 Maurer *Lang. of the Underworld* 191]

rounder, *n.* **1.** A gambler who bets mainly with borrowed money, STAKE MONEY.
[(1943) 1981 Maurer *Lang. of the Underworld* 191]
[Compare 1854 *OEDS,* meaning "one who makes the rounds of saloons"]
2. rounders, *n. pl.* Same as ROUNDS (def. a. and b.).
[(1950) 1981 Maurer *Lang. of the Underworld* 191]

roundhouse, *n.* Also called a ROUND TRIP. In pinochle, a meld of a queen and king of each suit.
[1950 Morehead *Culbertson* 641]

rounding, *n.* The act of marking cards by making various dents in the edges with the thumbnail or some other sharp object. See also DENT.
[1968 Wallace *Poker* 223]

round table game, *n. phr.* Any game where bettors wager among themselves.
[(1950) 1981 Maurer *Lang. of the Underworld* 191]
[Compare *round table:* 1826 *OED,* meaning "a number of people seated around a circular table."]

round-the-corner straight, *n.* In poker, a sequence of cards that cycles from the highest rank to the lowest rank, as queen, king, ace, deuce, trey.
[1963 Steig *Common Sense* 186]

round trip, *n.* Same as a ROUNDHOUSE.
[1950 Morehead *Culbertson* 641]
[Compare 1945 *OEDS,* meaning "something outstanding"]

rouse, *v.* Same as PUT TO THE PUNISHMENT.
[(1951) 1981 Maurer *Lang. of the Underworld* 191]
[Compare c1586 *OED,* meaning "excite to vigorous action"]

route, *n.* Also called ROUT RACE. In horse racing, a relatively long race, usually seven furlongs or more.
[1968 Ainslie *Complete Guide* 453]

router, *n.* A horse or dog that is especially good in longer races. For horses, usually seven furlongs or more.
[1968 Buchele *Greyhound Racing* 97]
[(1951) 1981 Maurer *Lang. of the Underworld* 191]

routine, *n.* In poker, a STRAIGHT FLUSH.
[1949 Coffin *Secrets* 185]

rout race, *n.* Same as ROUTE.
[(1951) 1981 Maurer *Lang. of the Underworld* 191]

rover, *n.* A player who wanders from game to game, playing for a few minutes and then moving on.
[1968 Wallace *Poker* 223]
[Compare c1690 *OED,* meaning "an inconstant lover" and 1611 *OED,* meaning "one who wanders"]

royal, *n.* In poker: **1.** A perfect lowball hand, such as A, 2, 3, 4, 5 [a wheel], or 7, 5, 4, 3, 2 [in razz]; [1968 Wallace *Poker* 223]
2. short for ROYAL FLUSH, or 10 through ace of one suit.
[1971 Livingston *Poker Strategy* 223]
3. royals, *pl.* In a deck of cards featuring sixty-five cards in five suits, the fifth suit, after clubs, diamonds, hearts and spades. See also CROWNS and EAGLES.
[1950 Morehead *Culbertson* 641]

royal casino, *n.* In casino, a jack, queen and king worth eleven, twelve, and thirteen points respectively.
[1971 McQuaid *Gambler's Digest* 315]

royal marriage, *n.* In pinochle, the king and queen of trump held in one hand.
[1950 Morehead *Culbertson* 641]

royal sequence, *n.* In pinochle, the 10, jack, queen, king, and ace of trump, held in one hand.
[1950 Morehead *Culbertson* 641]

royal six, *n.* In lowball, a hand with 6, 4 as the highest cards.
[1971 Livingston *Poker Strategy* 224]

royal straight flush, *n.* Also shortened to **royal flush.** In poker, a hand consisting of 10, jack, queen, king, and ace of the same suit, the highest-ranking hand in highball poker.

[1889 *DA,* 1865 *OEDS,* as *royal flush;* 1895 *OEDS,* as *royal straight;* 1907 *OEDS,* as *royal straight flush*]

royalty, *n.* In poker, a premium or prize awarded for certain hands, such as a straight flush.
[1949 Coffin *Secrets* 185]
[Compare 1880 *OED,* meaning "payment to an author"]

rub, *v.* In the phrase:
rub the board, To bet one's own odds, as a bookmaker seeking an excuse to redesign the prices offered.
[(1951) 1981 Maurer *Lang. of the Underworld* 191]

rubber, *n.* In card games like bridge or whist or boston, the winning of two out of three games. 1836 Eidrah *Hoyle Famil* 7. A *Rubber* is the best of three, or two out of three games.
[1744 *OEDS,* in bridge, 1749 *OED,* in other games]

rubber bridge, *n.* A variant of bridge in which the hands are not replayed, and settlement is made after each hand.
[1936 *OEDS*]

rubber game, *n.* Also called **rubber match.** In bridge, a hand played to determine the winner of a series.
[1908 *OEDS,* as *rubber games;* 1946 *OEDS;* as *rubber match*]

rubicon, *n.* In games like piquet, a lurch, or failure by an opponent to win a minimal number of points.
[1882 *OEDS*]

rubicon, *v.* In games like piquet, to fail to reach a minimum number of points before the opponent wins the game.
[1890 *OED*]

ruff, *v.* **1.** To play a trump card on a trick when unable to follow suit.
1860 Pardon *Handbook* 24. *Ruffing*—Another term for trumping a suit other than trumps.
[1760 *OED*]
2. In bridge, to win a trick by trumping a trick from one hand while discarding a loser from the partner's hand.
[1927 *OEDS*]
3. In an early trump game, to play the ace of trump, take four cards from the table and replace them with four from the hand. *Obsolete.*
[1589 *OED*]

ruff, *n.* **1.** In games like whist, the act of playing trump when one cannot follow suit.
[1856 *OED*]
2. In bridge, an action by the declarer to win a trick by trumping from one hand and discarding a loser from the other hand under his control.
[1939 *OEDS*]

rug joint, *n.* Also called a CARPET JOINT. A well-appointed casino featuring a variety of games, entertainment, and elegant rooms.
[1961 Scarne *Complete Guide* 686]

rule, *v.* In the particle construction:
rule off, To rescind racing privileges at a track.
[(1951) 1981 Maurer *Lang. of the Underworld* 191]

rule rap, *n.* In a casino, the patter of a dealer, explaining the method of play to a novice.
[1979 Newman *Dealer's Special* 61]

rumble, *n.* Any of a variety of systems for cheating at dice games.
[1961 Scarne *Complete Guide* 686]

rumble, *v.* **1.** To catch a player making a cheating move, such as switching dice or manipulating cards.
[1961 Scarne *Complete Guide* 686]
2. To cause (a MARK) to suspect he's about to be cheated. Compare TUMBLE.
[(1950) 1981 Maurer *Lang. of the Underworld* 191]

run, *n.* **1.** A sequence of cards in consecutive order. [1870 *OED*]
2. In backgammon, a strategy to move all one's pieces into the home board before the opponent can hit a blot [send a piece to the rail].
3. A series of winning or losing wagers.
[1697 *OED*]
4. A race, as among horses, dogs, and so on.
[1821 *OED*]
5. In faro, a PARLAY BET.

run, *v.* **1.** To operate a gambling game or casino.
[1885 *DA*]
2. To compete in a race, especially in gambling contexts among horses, dogs, and so on.
[1205 *OED*]
3. In backgammon, to attempt to move all one's pieces into the home board without intereference from the opponent.
[1950 Morehead *Culbertson* 641]
4. To make a series of winning or losing wagers.
[1973 Clark *Oral Coll*]
[Compare 1592 *OED,* meaning "to expose oneself to (a danger)"]
5. To leave a game soon after winning a large amount of money. Compare PULL OUT.
[1983 Martinet *Oral Coll*]
[Compare 1824 *OED,* meaning "to draw back from a pledge"]
6. In faro, to make a PARLAY BET.
[1938 Asbury *Sucker's Progress* 9]
7. In games like bridge and whist, to play successively a number of cards from the same suit. [1929 *OEDS*]
8. Of dice, to roll forward on the surface of the table or board.
[*c*1386 *OED*]
9. To enter a horse or dog in a race.
[1750 *OED*]
10. In the phrases and particle constructions:
run a book, To act as a bookmaker.
[1931 *OEDS*]
run a game, 1. To operate a gambling venture. Compare RUN, *v.* (def. 1).

[1983 Martinet *Oral Coll*]
2. To use trickery or deception to cheat a victim.
[1973 Clark *Oral Coll*]
[1967 *OEDS*]
run a pot, In poker, to win a game by bluffing the opponents.
[1949 Coffin *Secrets* 185]
run barefoot, In craps, to make a flat wager without taking odds.
[1983 Martinet *Oral Coll*]
run down, In a casino, to estimate the amount of chips in a table's rack by looking at it but not touching it. See also CASE THE RACK.
[1977 Anness *Dummy Up*]
run down a stack, In a casino, to break a tall stack of chips into smaller stacks of equal size. See also BREAK DOWN A BET and COUNT DOWN (def. 2).
[1983 Martinet *Oral Coll*]
run flat, To operate a dishonest gambling game or establishment. See also RUN STRONG.
[1973 Clark *Oral Coll*]
run for trumps, In games like seven-up or old sledge, to request that the cards be redealt and a new trump named.
[1890 Quinn *Fools of Fortune* 257]
run in, 1. In shuffling playing cards, to maintain the original order of the deck.
[1890 Quinn *Fools of Fortune* 197]
2. In horse racing, to win a race unexpectedly.
[1978 Ainslie *Complete Guide* 297]
run out of the money, In horse racing, to finish fourth or worse for bettors, fifth or worse for owners. See also OUT OF THE MONEY.
[1971 McQuaid *Gambler's Digest* 315]
run strong, To operate a crooked game or gaming establishment. See also RUN FLAT.
[1961 Scarne *Complete Guide* 686]
run the cards, 1. In all fours, to accept a beg and redeal the cards.
[1950 Morehead *Culbertson* 642]
2. In games like seven-up and old sledge, to deal six cards and turn up the seventh as trump.
[1890 Quinn *Fools of Fortune* 257]
3. Generally, to deal cards in a game.
[1884 *DA*]
run up a hand, To make up a winning hand from cards that have been played and discarded.
1902 Andrews *Artifice* 20. As the reader obtains an understanding of the art of "advantage playing" it will be seen that the old-fashioned or hand shuffle gives the greater possibilities for *running up hands,* selecting desirable cards and palming.
run wide, In horse or dog racing, to be away from the inside rail on an oval track.
[1971 McQuaid *Gambler's Digest* 315]

rundown, *n.* In racebooks and sports books, the list of wagers available to bettors, along with odds offered, point spreads, and the like.
[1935 *OEDS*]

run in, *n.* **1.** In shuffling playing cards, a move that restores the deck to its original order.
[1890 Quinn *Fools of Fortune* 197]
2. In horse racing, an unexpected win by a horse.
[1978 Ainslie *Complete Guide* 297]

runner, *n.* **1.** A person who carries wagers or other materials from the bettor to the person accepting the bet.
[1961 Scarne *Complete Guide* 686]
2. In backgammon, a STONE, or piece, still in the opponent's HOME TABLE.
[1950 Morehead *Culbertson* 641]
3. In horse racing, a fast horse with ability to win in its class.
[1582 *OED*]
4. The term is used in combinations: KENO RUNNER, a casino employee who transports money and tickets between the players and the keno lounge; CHIP RUNNER, a person who carries chips or checks between the tables and the casino cage, or who transports FOREIGN CHECKS from one casino to another; NUMBERS RUNNER (or POLICY RUNNER) a person who transports money and betting slips between the players and the operator of the numbers game.
[1726 *OED,* as POLICY RUNNER]

running game, *n.* In backgammon, a strategy for moving all one's pieces from an opponent's home board. The strategy is used after rolling several high numbers initially.
[1950 Morehead *Culbertson* 642]

running horse, *n.* A racehorse.
[1771 *DAE*]

running mate, *n.* **1.** The number of pips on the opposite face of a die, which always add up to seven pips.
1983 Martinet *Oral Coll.* To check for a misspotted die, hold the diagonal corners between your thumb and forefinger. Then you can check a face and its *running mate.* The two [faces] should add up to seven.
2. A horse entered in a race in order to set the pace for another horse intended to win.
[1868 *OEDS*]

running pair, *n.* In poker: **1.** Two consecutive cards of the same rank. **2.** In hold 'em, two consecutive cards of the same rank are the final two cards dealt.
[1973 Preston *Play Poker* 169]

running race, *n.* A race in which horses run, as opposed to TROTTING or *pacing. Rare.*
[1868 *DAE*]

run plate, *n.* A lightweight shoe used on a racehorse. Compare PLATE.
[1877 *DA*]

runt, *n.* In poker, a hand with mixed suits and low cards or no pair.
[1949 Coffin *Secrets* 185]

S

s, *n.* **1.** Abbreviation for *swing shift,* in a casino.
[ca. 1961 *Hotel Coll*]
2. Abbreviation for *south,* in four-handed card games like bridge.
[1950 Morehead *Culbertson* 642]
3. Abbreviation for *show,* in horse and dog racing, and in jai-alai.
[1955 Hillis *Pari-Mutuel Betting* 89]

sacrifice bid, *n.* Also shortened to **sacrifice.** In bridge, a bid made without hope of winning the hand, but with the strategy that a loss of the game might be avoided.
[1932 *OEDS,* as *sacrifice bid* and *sacrifice*]

sacrifice bidding, *n.* Also shortened to **sacrifice.** The act or process of using sacrifice bids.
[1959 *OEDS,* as *sacrifice bidding;* 1964 *OEDS,* as *sacrifice*]

saddle, *n.* In numbers or policy, a bet on two numbers, both of which must be drawn in order to win.
[1882 *DA*]

saddle-blanket gambler, *n.* A person who plays for low stakes.
[1968 Adams *Western Words*]

saddling, *n.* Bending cards to favor certain ones during the cut.
1888 Kunard *Card Tricks* 175. *Saddling* the cards is another form of the Bridge, but is a term used for another cribbage trick. The sixes, sevens, eights and nines, are bent longways, sides downwards, so by cutting above one of these bent cards, the sharper secures one good card to begin with.

safe card, *n.* In games like gin and canasta, a discard that the following player cannot use.
[1953 Crawford *Consistent Winner* 352]

saliva test, *n.* In horse racing, a test administered to the first four horses to finish a race to determine traces of chemicals in the body of the animal.
[1939 *OEDS*]

salt, *v.* In the phrase and particle construction:
salt away, Also, to RATHOLE. To put money or chips in the pocket for future use while continuing play in a game.
[1902 *OED*]
salt the pack, In rummy, to discard certain cards while intending to retrieve them later in the game.
[1950 Morehead *Culbertson* 642]

salute, *v.* Of a jockey, to request permission to dismount after a horse race.
[1978 Ainslie *Complete Guide* 297]

samba, *n.* In canasta, seven cards of the same suit, in sequence.
[1953 Crawford *Consistent Winner* 352]

same bet, *n. phr.* In bank craps, a request by a player to make the same place bet after winning on that number.
[1983 Martinet *Oral Coll*]

same dice, *n. phr.* In bank craps, a shooter's request to have a die returned after bouncing it off the table rather than taking another die offered by the dealer.
[1983 Martinet *Oral Coll*]

sancho, *n.* **1.** In pedro, the nine of trumps, which has no value.
[1874 *OEDS;* 1880 *DA, DAE*]
2. In sancho pedro, the five of trumps.
[1890 *DA, DAE*]

sand, *v.* To mark the edge of a playing card with sandpaper.
[1961 Scarne *Complete Guide* 686]

sandbag, *v.* In poker, to check, decline to bet, while holding a strong hand, then raise on the following betting round. Compare CHECK and SLOW PLAY.
[1940 *OEDS;* compare 1887 *OEDS*, meaning "bully or coerce"]

sandbagger, *n.* In poker, a player who checks, then raises a later bet.
[1940 *OEDs*]

sandpaper, *n.* A playing card or cards marked by roughing the edges with sandpaper.
[1971 Livingston *Poker Strategy* 224]

sand tell box, *n.* Also shortened to **sand-tell.** In faro, a dishonest dealing box, or shoe that allows the dealer to read marked cards before they are dealt.
[1890 Quinn *Fools of Fortune* 198]

sand-tell liquid, *n.* In faro, a liquid dressing used to mark cards. The liquid affects the sheen on the back of a playing card much as the use of sandpaper.
[1943 Maurer *Argot*]

sandwich, *v.* In poker, to enclose a player between two other players who are raising and re-raising bets. The player who is *sandwiched* rarely wins by calling the bets of the other two players. See also SQUEEZE and WHIPSAW.
[1973 Preston *Play Poker* 169]

sanitary ride, *n.* **1.** In horse racing, a race in which the jockey steers the horse toward the outside rail to avoid flying mud or a pack of slower horses in front.
[1978 Ainslie *Complete Guide* 297]
2. In horse racing, a horse that does not extend itself during a race.
[1978 Ainslie *Complete Guide* 297]

Santa Barbara, *n.* Also called BIG SLICK. In hold 'em poker, an ace and king, when dealt to a player as the first two cards.
1981 Golad *Oral Coll.* A player sits there hour after hour with only two cards to look at, so the different combinations get names . . . an ace and a king are a *Santa Barbara.* The older term for that is big slick, but a few years ago there was an oil spill off the coast and the California players started calling it Santa Barbara. You hear that in Vegas and Texas, too.

sauter la coupe, *n. French.* A cheating method in which the dealer palms a card, places it on the bottom of the deck, and deals it at will.
1888 Kunard *Card Tricks* 172. *Sauter la Coupe.*—This is a trick very frequently practised, and a fair player has no chance of coming out a winner if his opponents make use of this sleight. There are many ways of ascertaining the position of a certain card, which being done (sometimes by having actually palmed it, say such a card as an ace), the cards are cut, and the dealer in taking them up places the ace on the top or middle, and "slips" it from the position to the bottom, so that it is the trump card when the deal is complete. This move is always accompanied by the ruffling of the cards, which makes considerable noise, and covers the action famously.

Savannah, *n.* In craps, another name for the number 7.
[1983 Martinez *Gambling Scene* 218]

save, *v.* In the phrases:
save ground, In horse racing, to move to the inside rail immediately after leaving the starting gate.
[1955 Hillis *Pari-Mutuel Betting* 117]

save inside, In horse or dog racing, to run the race close to the inside rail on an oval track. Compare RUN WIDE.
[1968 Buchele *Greyhound Racing* 6]
save the lurch, In whist, to prevent the adversary from scoring a treble.
[1742 *OED,* under *lurch*]

sawbuck, *n.* **1.** A ten dollar bill.
[1852 *OEDS, DA*]
2. A ten-dollar bet, placed away from the track with a bookmaker. *Obsolete.*
[(1951) 1981 Maurer *Lang. of the Underworld* 226]

sawdust game, *n.* An illegal gambling game that is moved from place to place. See also FLOATING CRAPS GAME.
[1974 Powell *Verbal Dexterity* 10]

sawdust joint, *n.* A small or unpretentious gambling establishment; a gambling establishment patronized by players who bet small amounts. Compare CARPET JOINT and RUG JOINT.
[1964 Wykes Illustrated Guide 329]

saw-tooth edge work, *n. phr.* Serrated cuts made on the edge of a die to control its roll on a padded or felt surface.
[1974 Scarne *Dice* 242]

say, *n.* One's turn to act in a card game; the opportunity to bet or pass in playing a hand of poker.
1866 *American Card Player* 135. *Say.*—When it is the turn of any player to declare what he will do, whether he will bet, or pass his hand, it is said to be his *say.*
[1857 *DA;* 1864 *DAE*]

say, *v.* To bet or pass when one's turn to wager comes. [1887 *DA*]

scale, *n.* In the phrase:
go to scale or **ride to scale**. Of a jockey, to ride his horse to the weighing room before or after a race.
[1837 *OED*]

scale of weights, *n. phr.* In horse racing, the table listing the weight a horse must carry, based on past performance and age.
[1971 McQuaid *Gambler's Digest* 315]

scalper, *n.* A person who places opposing bets with different bookmakers, depending on the difference in odds offered who hopes to lose nothing but perhaps to win something.
[1961 Scarne *Complete Guide* 686]

scam, *n.* A fraudulent or dishonest scheme; a plan to cheat a victim.
[1963 *OEDS, BDNE I*]

scam, *v.* To cheat a victim.
[1963 *OEDS, BDNE I*]

scare card, *n.* In games like poker and twenty-one, a card inadvertently turned face upward during the deal. Supposedly, such a card might frighten an opponent. *Facetious use.*
[1973 Clark *Oral Coll*]

scared money, *n.* An insufficient bankroll for participating in a gambling game. A person holding such a bankroll may not have the courage to bet and raise effectively.
[1978 Silberstang *Winning Poker* 11]

scenic route, *n.* In horse racing, a path taken by a jockey away from the inside rail on an oval track. The horse loses time and must run a longer distance. *Facetious use.*
[1978 Ainslie *Complete Guide* 297]

schneider, *v.* **1.** In games like gin rummy and

skat, to win a game before the opponent has scored any points.
[1950 Morehead *Culbertson* 649]
2. a. To win any game before one's opponent has scored any points.
b. To win all the games in a match before one's opponent has won any games.
[1945 *DAS*]
3. To defeat competition by a substantial margin. [n.d. *DAS*]

schneider, *n.* Also called TAILOR. In games like gin rummy and skat, a shutout; a win achieved before the opponent has scored any points.
[1886 *OEDS*]

schoolboy draw, *n.* In draw poker, an unwise or unsound decision to draw to a particular hand, such as a three card flush or straight.
[1968 Wallace *Poker* 223]

schwarz, *n.* In gin, a bid to win every trick and hence all the points for a hand.
[1880 *OEDS*]

schwarz, *v.* To bid to win every trick and hence all the points for a hand of gin.
[1880 *OEDS*]

scoop, *v.* **1.** In high-low poker, to declare an intention to vie for both the highest hand and the lowest hand with the same cards, or to SHOOT THE MOON. Among many players, the person who *scoops* must win both ways in order to win the pot. If the player wins one way, all claim to the pot is forfeit.
2. To win at draw poker.
[1866 *OEDS*]
3. In the phrases:
scoop the kitty or **scoop the pool,** To win all the money staked at a card game.
[1903 *OEDS*]

scooped dice, *n.* Dice that have been drilled and altered with weights so as to roll a particular number more often than other numbers See also DOCTOR and LOADED DICE.
1726 Wilson *Art and Mystery* 29. And first, Loaded or *Scooped Dice* are either high or low, and changed as often as the Main and Chance, or Occasion requires.
[1726 *OED*]

score, *n.* **1.** A number that expresses accomplishment in a game or contest relative to a standard, as points in a card game.
[1680 *OED*]
2. An amount of money won or obtained by honest or dishonest means, as a large amount in tips, a single gambling venture, or a cheating scheme.
[(1950) 1981 Maurer *Lang. of the Underworld* 191]

score, *v.* **1.** To gain points in a game or contest.
[1742 *OED*]
2. To win or gain a large amount of money by honest or dishonest means.
[(1950) 1981 Maurer *Lang. of the Underworld* 191]
3. In the phrases:
score a big touch, To acquire a large amount of money, usually by questionable or dishonest means, as cheating in a card game or betting scheme.
[(1950) 1981 Maurer *Lang. of the Underworld* 191]
score a double, 1. To ride two winning horses on the same day.
[(1957) 1981 Maurer *Lang. of the Underworld* 226]
2. To enter two winning horses on the same day of racing.
[(1951) 1981 Maurer *Lang. of the Underworld* 226]

score bid, *n.* In bridge, a bid by a player whose side has a part-score sufficient to win a game if the current contract is successful.
[1928 *OEDS*]

scoreboard, *n.* A masterboard used for displaying the score in a contest.
[1936 *OEDS*]

scorebook, *n.* Also written **score-book.** A sports performance ledger. *Mainly British use.*
[1851 *OEDS*]

scorecard, *n.* Also written **score card** or **score-card.** A sheet of paper or lightweight cardboard, often divided into lined sections or grids, on which a person may record numbers or points gained in a game or contest.
[1877 *OEDS*]

scored pair, *n.* In seven card stud or hold 'em poker, two cards of the same rank when they are the first two cards dealt to a hand.
[1973 Preston *Play Poker* 169]

score draw, *n.* A tied game in which goals have been scored, which is normally counted for three points on the coupon of a football betting pool. *British use.* [1970 *OEDS*]

scorekeeper, *n.* **1.** Also a CASE-KEEPER. In faro, an assistant who records the cards as they are drawn.
[1983 Martinet *Oral Coll*]
2. In craps and roulette, a player who records each event in the game, looking for patterns of numbers on which to bet.
[1973 Clark *Oral Coll*]

scoreless, *adj.* Lacking any scoring in a contest or a part of a contest.
[1885 *OED*]

scoreline, *n.* Also written **score line.** A notice, usually in a newspaper, giving the score in a sports contest. Compare LINE. *Mainly British use.*
[1969 *OEDS*]

scorer, *n.* **1.** The person who keeps a record of the score in a game or contest.
[1732 *OEDS*]

2. The person who makes a point or score in a game or contest.
[1884 *OED*]
3. A winner, especially in horse racing.
[1974 *OEDS*]

scoring block, *n.* Scoring sheets used in card games. [1907 *OEDS*]

Scotch straight, *n.* In poker, five even-numbered cards in sequence, as 2, 4, 6, 8, and 10. See also DUTCH STRAIGHT.
[1973 Clark *Oral Coll*]

scratch, *n.* **1.** An entry withdrawn from a race.
[1938 *OEDS*]
2. a. Available, usually paper, money.
[1914 *OEDS*]
b. A loan. [1935 *DAS*]
3. In billiards and pool, any shot that results in a penalty. [1913 *OEDS*]

scratch, *v.* **1.** In horse racing, to eliminate a horse from the race before the race is run.
1889 Ellangowan *Sporting Anecdotes* 63. A stiff one is a dead 'un, or a horse which is in the cart in other words, an animal which will not compete, but will probably be *scratched* (that is, struck out of the race) or made safe before the day appointed for its decision.
[1859 *OED*]
2. In twenty-one, to request another card, or hit, from the dealer by brushing the surface of the table with a finger or with cards.
3. In billiards or pool, to make any shot that results in a penalty.
[1909 *OEDS*]

scratch paper, *n.* Playing cards marked on the backs by using sandpaper or some sharp instrument.
[1938 Asbury *Sucker's Progress* 37]

scratch sheet, *n.* **1.** In racing, the printed list of all the entries in the races for a day along with information on odds and such changes as SCRATCHES. Compare MORNING LINE and RACING FORM. [1939 *OEDS*]
2. In a casino, the list of dealers required for various games on one shift. See also ROAD MAP.
[1979 Newman *Dealer's Special* 10]

scratch time, *n.* The deadline for withdrawing an entry from a race, usually 3:30 a.m. on the day of the race in horse racing.
[(1951) 1981 Maurer *Lang. of the Underworld* 226]

screen, *v.* Especially as the particle construction:
screen out. To divert attention from a player who is making a cheating move during a card or dice game.
[ca. 1961 *Hotel Coll*]

screen out, *n.* Also shortened to **screen.** A distraction designed to divert attention from a cheating move made by a player in a card or dice game.
[1961 Scarne *Complete Guide* 686]

screw, *v.* **1.** Especially in the phrases:
screw through or **screw in**. In horse racing, to force to the front of the pack at the finish line.
[1840 *OED*]
2. To impart a twisting motion to (a ball); causing it to swerve. Compare ENGLISH.
[1839 *OED*]

screw box, *n.* In faro, a DEALING BOX altered for cheating purposes.
[1938 Asbury *Sucker's Progress* 12]

season, *n.* **1.** In mah jongg, one of four tiles, each corresponding to a different period of the year.
[1950 Morehead *Culbertson* 643]
2. The portion of year regularly devoted to horse racing or other competition.
[(1951) 1981 Maurer *Lang. of the Underworld* 226]
[1856 *OED*]
3. In horse racing, a period of time that a mare is in estrus, in heat.
[1978 Ainslie *Complete Guide* 297]

seat-man, *n.* **1.** A professional card dealer.
[*DAS*]
2. A person employed by the operator of a game to sit and play minimal stakes until enough players join the game; a SHILL.
[*c*1930 *DAS*]

seat number, *n.* In twenty-one and baccarat, the number on the LAYOUT indicating a betting space for each player.
[ca. 1961 *Hotel Coll*]

seat position, *n.* In poker, the position of a player relative to the dealer. See also: A, B, C, D, E, F, G.
[1968 Wallace *Poker* 223]

seat shot, *n.* In poker, a bet or a raise by the player at the dealer's right hand, considered the most advantageous position for betting.
[1968 Wallace *Poker* 223]

second, *n.* In cards, the act of dealing the second card from the top of the pack or any other card than the top card. Compare BOTTOM DEALER.
1843 Green *Exposure* 31. He will then try to overrun him, and if the card on the top of the pack, which he knows by the back, will not do it, he will deal the *second* from the top, which probably will. This he will do by elevating the end of the pack next to you, and letting the top card slide a little down, so that his thumb can reach to the end of the *second,* which he will deal off to you.
1865 Evans *Gamblers Win* 68. The only advantage to be obtained in the deal is with a "*second.*" If the player deals a good *second,* he ought to be able to make the game every time he deals.

second base, *n.* **1.** In twenty-one, a position near the middle of the table layout.
[ca. 1961 *Hotel Coll*]
2. On a craps table that requires a stickman and

two dealers, the dealer to the left of the stickman.
[1983 Martinet *Oral Coll*]

second best, *n.* In poker, a hand that loses at the showdown.
[1949 Coffin *Secrets* 185]

second break, *n.* At a bank craps table, the dealer who begins the shift at the stickman's right. Compare THIRD BASE.
1983 Martinet *Oral Coll.* Four dealers are assigned to a table. The shift begins with one dealer on break, so the dealer who starts at third base [to the right of the stickman] gets second break. So he's called *second break.* We don't do that with any other break, like third break, or anything like that.

second button, *n.* **1.** Also called SECOND PAIR. In hold 'em poker, a card that pairs the second highest card exposed on the table.
[1978 Brunson *How I Made* 546]
2. In faro, a wager that the fourth, or CASE, card of a specific rank will win in the same way that the second card of the rank did, either for the dealer or the player.
[1943 Maurer *Argot*]

second card, *v.* In playing cards, to deal the second card from the top as a cheating move.
[1977 Cahill *Recollections* 316]

second deal, *n.* The dealing of the second card from the top of the pack, or any card other than the top card, as a cheating move.
[1968 Wallace *Poker* 223]

second dealer, *n.* A person accomplished at dealing cards other than the top card on a pack.
[1968 Wallace *Poker* 223]

second dealing, *n.* The act of dealing a card other than the top card on a pack.
1891 Hoffman *Baccarat.* There is, however, an expedient familiar to conjurers as "changing a card," which, with a little modification, is extensively used by the cardsharping fraternity under the name of "*second dealing.*" The result of the sleight is that the dealer, while apparently giving the top card in the usual way, actually gives the second card instead of it.

second hand, *n.* In poker, the second player to act during a betting round.
[1953 Crawford *Consistent Winner* 352]

second nuts, *n.* In poker, a good hand that loses to a better hand. See also NUTS.
[1976 Sklansky *Hold 'em Poker* 8]

second pair, *n.* Also called SECOND BUTTON. In hold 'em poker, a card that pairs the second highest card exposed on the table.
[1976 Sklansky *Hold 'em Poker* 8]

second position, *n.* In poker, the second player to the left of the dealer.
[1949 Coffin *Secrets* 185]

second square, *n.* In faro, the area of the table LAYOUT comprising the deuce, trey, queen, and jack.
[1890 Quinn *Fools of Fortune* 194]

second story, *n.* In poker, especially in hold 'em, a raise during a betting round. Compare CATBIRD SEAT and NUT.
1981 Golad *Oral Coll.* I was in the catbird seat [last position, left of the dealer] and figured by this time I had the nuts [best hand], so I came in with a *second story* . . . that's a raise, usually after checking the round before. It's called that because you double the size of the stack of checks you are betting.

second turn, *n.* In skat, the second card turned face upward on the table, which determines the trump suit.
[1950 Morehead *Culbertson* 643]

see, *v.* Especially in the phrase:
see a bet or **see** (someone's) **bet.** In poker, to bet an amount equal to the sum wagered by the previous bettor. Compare CALL (def. 3) and RAISE.
1866 *American Card Player* 135. *Seeing a bet.*—To bet as much as an adversary.
1887 Proctor *Chance* 227. Each player may (in his regular turn only) increase his stake, in which case all who wish to stay must *'see'* him—that is, raise their stakes in the same degree, or go better—that is, raise the stakes further.
[(1599) 1804 *OED,* 1842 *DAE*]

seed, *n.* **1.** Also called a BULLET. In playing cards, an ace.
[1968 Wallace *Poker* 223]
2. Also called a BONE. In poker, a one-dollar chip. [*c*1930 *DAS*]

seed, *v.* In tournaments, as for bridge or tennis, to rank players on the basis of past performance, then pit players of dissimilar skills against one another, so the best players usually meet later in the tournament.
[1971 McQuaid *Gambler's Digest* 315]
[1898 *OEDS,* 1909 *DA*]

seesaw, *n.* Same as CROSS-RUFF.
[1746 *OED*]

seesaw, *v.* In the card games bridge or whist, to play a suit to one's partner that the partner can trump, then the partner plays back a suit that the first player can trump. See also RUFF and CROSS-RUFF.
1746 Hoyle *Short Treatise* 69. *See-saw* is when each Partner trumps a Suit, and they play those Suits to one another to trump.

sell, *v.* **1.** Especially in the phrase:
sell a bet. To entice a player to place a wager by offering what appears to be an easy win, excellent odds, or some other inducement.
[1983 Martinet *Oral Coll*]
2. In the phrase:
sell a hand, In poker, to entice an opponent into

calling or even raising a bet by pretending to have a poor hand.
[1978 Brunson *How I Made* 546]

selling race, *n.* A race after which the winner is sold at auction and the losers may be purchased for a specified amount. See also CLAIMING RACE. *British use.*
[ca. 1961 *Hotel Coll*]

semi-bluff, *n.* In poker, a betting strategy used by a player holding a hand with slight potential.
[1976 Sklansky *Hold 'em Poker*]

semi-two-suiter, *n.* In bridge, a hand with four or more cards of one suit, and more than four in another suit.
[1950 Morehead *Culbertson* 643]

senate dealer, *n.* In poker, a professional dealer, one who does not participate in the playing or wagering.
[1973 Preston *Play Poker* 169]

send, *n.* Any of a variety of bunko schemes involving dice in the cheating of victims.
[1890 Quinn *Fools of Fortune* 331]

send, *v.* In the phrases:
send it around, In poker, to check during a betting round while holding a strong hand, in the hope that another player will bet or raise. See also SANDBAG.
[1978 Brunson *How I Made* 546]
send it in, In poker or craps. To make a large bet or to bet often.
[(1950) 1981 Maurer *Lang. of the Underworld* 191]
send out a scout, In craps, to cast the dice in such a fashion that only one die is cast, necessitating a recast of both dice.
[1983 Martinet *Oral Coll*]

send in, *n.* A large wager or series of wagers. Compare SEND IT IN.
[(1950) 1981 Maurer *Lang. of the Underworld* 191]

senior *n.* In bridge, the player who is required to lead the first card after the bidding has been completed. See also ELDEST HAND.
[1950 Morehead *Culbertson* 643]

sept, et le va, *n. clause. French.* In faro, the act of wagering the stake, plus winnings, twice, which if won return seven times the wager.
1843 Green *Exposure* 168. *Sept, et le va,* succeeds the gaining of a parolet, by which the punter being entitled to thrice his stakes, risks the whole again, and bending his card a second time, tries to win sevenfold.

septiet, *n. French.* In piquet, a sequence of seven cards in consecutive order; a seven-card straight.
[1950 Morehead *Culbertson* 643]

sequence, *n.* **1.** Generally, a group of consecutively numbered playing cards.
→A group of three cards, or maybe six in some card games is a RUN. Poker players' hands with three cards is a RUN, with four cards is a FOUR STRAIGHT; but, a regular STRAIGHT is five cards.
2. Also called a STRAIGHT. In poker, a group of five consecutively numbered cards.
[1882 *OED*]
3. In cribbage, a group of three or more cards of continguous denomination, such as ten, jack, queen or queen, ten, jack.
1843 Green *Exposure* 270. *Sequences* are three, four, or more successive cards, and reckon for an equal number of points, either in hand or playing. In playing a *sequence,* it is of no consequence which card is thrown down first; as thus, your adversary playing an ace, you a five, he a three, you a two, then he a four, he counts five for the sequence.
[1575 *OED*]

sequence flush, *n.* Also called a STRAIGHT FLUSH. In poker, a group of five consecutively numbered cards of a single suit. *Rare.*
[1890 Quinn *Fools of Fortune* 216]

sequential declaration, *n.* In high-low poker, a declaration of intent to play the hand as high or low, beginning with the last bettor and moving backward to the first bettor.
[1968 Wallace *Poker* 223]
→*Sequential declaration* is less commonly found than SIMULTANEOUS DECLARATION.

sergeant from K company, *n. phr.* Usually **sergeants from K company,** *pl.* In poker, a king.
[1949 Coffin *Secrets* 185]

serialized record, *n.* In a casino, a numbered form used to record transactions involving money or chips being transported between a table and the casino cage. See also MASTER CARD, and RIM CARD and TABLE CARD.
[1957 *Nevada Gaming Regulations* 33]

serve, *v.* To deal playing cards, especially for a living. [1949 Coffin *Secrets* 185]

session, *n.* A period of play involving several games or hands, as at bingo, poker, bridge, and so on.
[1949 Coffin *Secrets* 185]

set, *n.* **1.** In hold 'em poker, three cards of the same rank. In other forms of poker, three or four cards of the same rank.
[1978 Brunson *How I Made* 546]
2. In games like pan or gin rummy, cards that have a meld value when grouped together.
[1953 Crawford *Consistent Winner* 352]
3. In dominos, the first BONE, or tile, played in a game.
[1950 Morehead *Culbertson* 643]
4. The stake or amount wagered at a dice game.
[1537 *OED*]
5. A game session at cards or dice.
[1594 *OED*]

set, *v.* **1.** In games like bridge or whist, to defeat an opponent's contract.
[1680 *OED*]

2. To make up a side or team for a four-handed card game. [1609 *OED*]
3. To play the first file in a dominoes game. [1897 *OED*]
5. To make a bet.
[1553 *OED*]
6. In the phrases and particle constructions:
set all-in, In no-limit poker, to make a bet so large that an opponent must place his entire stake in the pot in order to call the bet.
[1978 Brunson *How I Made* 547]
set back, To disqualify a horse for running wide on a turn or for otherwise interfering with other horses in the race.
[(1951) 1981 Maurer *Lang. of the Underworld* 226]
→*Setting back* does not always involve *setting down.* Compare SET DOWN.
set down, In horse racing, to suspend a jockey who commits a foul during a race. Compare SET BACK. [(1951) 1981 Maurer *Lang. of the Underworld* 226]
set the combination, To manipulate the dice in one's hand before making a CONTROLLED SHOT.
[(1950) 1981 Maurer *Lang. of the Underworld* 191]
set up, 1. In poker, to entice an opponent into betting with a weaker hand.
[1981 Golad *Oral Coll*]
2. To prepare a victim to be cheated.
[ca. 1961 *Hotel Coll*]
[1956 *OEDS*]

setback, *n.* In games like pitch or bridge, a deduction made from the accumulated score after a failure to make a contract.
[1950 Morehead *Culbertson* 643]

set over set, *n. phr.* In hold 'em poker, a pair held by one player that ranks higher than a pair held by another player.
1981 Golad *Oral Coll.* When players are holding pairs in the hole, that is the only thing that determines the game when the cards on board don't help either hand. Say you hold tens and somebody else holds queens. If no tens come on the flop, then it's just *set over set.*

settanta, *n.* In scopa, a point awarded for winning the high group of four cards.
[1950 Morehead *Culbertson* 643]

setter, *n.* In hazard, the person who covers the bet of the caster, or thrower. Compare CASTER and MAIN and NICK.
1726 Wilson *Art and Mystery* 14. A number of equal stakes supposed to be put down, one half by the Caster, the other by the *Setter,* to be divided betwixt them according to the Nicks, Outs, and different Proportions of the Chances to the respective Mains throughout the whole Course or Changes of the Dies.
[1726 *OED*]

settlement, *n.* The payment of losses and collecting of winnings at the end of a gambling session; the redemption of chips for cash.
[1950 Morehead *Culbertson* 643]

settler, *n.* **1.** The person in a bookmaking operation who determines, from the amounts wagered on all the horses or dogs, the final odds before the running of a race.
[1964 Wykes *Illustrated Guide* 329]
2. settlers, *pl.* Heavily LOADED DICE, detectable by their action when dropped into a bowl of water. See also FIRST FLOP DICE.
[1974 Scarne *Dice* 285]

set-to, *n.* **1.** A contest or game featuring aggressive and large bets.
[1973 Clark *Oral Coll*]
2. In horse racing, a final effort to get in front, usually in the homestretch. Compare DRIVE.
[1840 *OEDS*]
3. In boxing, **a.** a match.
[17.. *OED*]
b. A round. [1789 *OED*]
c. The action of beginning to box.
[1743 *OED*]

set-to, *v.* 1. To begin a game or contest, especially one featuring vigorous and aggressive wagering.
[ca. 1961 *Hotel Coll*]
2. In a horse race, to make a final effort to get in front, usually in the homestretch. Compare DRIVE and EXTEND.
[1856 *OED*]
3. In boxing, to begin boxing.
[1743 *OED*]

setup, *n.* **1.** The equipment required for conducting a game, such as a table, cards, chips and so on.
[1977 Anness *Dummy Up*]
2. The preparation made for cheating a victim.
[ca. 1961 *Hotel Coll*]
[1968 *OEDS*]

seven, *v.* In the phrases and particle constructions:
seven out, In craps, to roll the number 7 and lose after having established a point. Compare CRAP OUT.
[(1950) 1981 Maurer *Lang of the Underworld* 191]
seven out, line away, In bank craps, a call by the stickman indicating that the shooter has rolled a 7 instead of the point, and the bets on the pass line are lost.
[ca. 1961 *Hotel Coll*]

seven-eleven, *n.* **1.** In a casino, a courtesy wager placed by a FLOORMAN on behalf of a regular patron who has lost all his money. The understanding is that the player will take the chips given to him and leave.
[1974 Scarne *Dice* 478]
2. In small stakes or street games, a new stake for a player who has lost all his money, given by the other gamblers.
[(1950) 1981 Maurer *Lang. of the Underworld* 191]

sevens rule, *n.* In lowball poker, a requirement that a player holding cards ranked 7 or lower must make a bet or forfeit any claim to the pot. The rule insures that a person holding a strong hand will not check, then raise a later bettor. [1968 Wallace *Poker* 224]

seven the main, *n. phr.* In hazard, an oral statement that seven is the designated number, which, if thrown first, wins for the person rolling the dice.
[1680 *OED*]

seven up, *n.* Also called OLD SLEDGE. The card game ALL FOURS, which later became known as *high, low, jack and the game.*
1843 Green *Exposure* 239. According to Mr. Hoyle, the points to be made before the game is concluded are ten; they are now universally reduced to seven; and the game is most commonly called "*seven up*" or "old sledge."
[1830 *DA;* 1836 *DAE;* 1845 *OED*]

sex allowance, *n.* In horse racing, a weight concession given by the track handicapper to a female horse racing against male horses.
[1978 Ainslie *Complete Guide* 297]

shade, *v.* To conceal a cheating move. See also SCREEN. [1943 Maurer *Argot*]

shade work, *n.* Markings on the backs of playing cards, made by inking additional parts of the design, such as adding spokes to bicycle wheels. Compare COSMETICS.
[1968 Adams *Western Words*]

shade worker, *n.* A card cheat who marks the backs of cards by altering the design with additional features.
[1983 Martinez *Gambling Scene* 219]

shading, *n.* The marking of backs of playing cards. See also SHADE WORK.
[1961 Scarne *Complete Guide* 686]

shake, *v.* **1.** To rattle dice together, either in the hand or in a dice cup, preparatory to making a cast. [ca. 1961 *Hotel Coll*]
2. In the particle constructions:
shake off, In horse racing, to outdistance a challenger. [1823 *OED*]
shake up, In horse racing, to use a whip or spurs to force a horse to EXTEND itself during a race. Compare GO TO BAT and PUT TO THE PUNISHMENT.
[1971 McQuaid *Gambler's Digest* 316]

shaker, *n.* In a bingo parlor, the container or cage that holds all the numbered balls available for the game.
[1953 Lewis *Sagebrush Casinos* 93]

shaking up, *n.* In horse racing, the use of whip and spurs to force a horse to extend itself during a race. See also SHAKE UP.
[(1951) 1981 Maurer *Lang. of the Underworld* 226]

shapes, *n. pl.* Dice that have been altered in size by shaving, heating, or carving. See also STRONG SHAPES and WEAK SHAPES.
[ca. 1961 *Hotel Coll*]

shark, *n.* **1.** An expert player at specific forms of gambling, such as cards or dice.
[1950 Morehead *Culbertson* 644]
2. A cheater at gambling games.
[*c*1600 *OED*]
3. A person who makes loans to gamblers at exorbitant interest; a LOAN SHARK.
[1599 *OED*]

shark, *v.* **1.** To throw dice with a CONTROL SHOT.
[(1950) 1981 Maurer *Lang. of the Underworld* 191]
2. To swindle another.
[*a*1650 *OED*]

sharp, *n.* **1.** Short for a CARD SHARP. A cheater at card games. [1797 *OED*]
2. An expert player at specific forms of gambling, such as cards or dice.
[1900 *DAS*]

sharp, *v.* To cheat in a card game.
[1700 *OED*]

sharper, *n.* Short for CARD SHARP.
[1681 *OED*]

sharpie, *n.* Short for CARD SHARP.
[1942 *OEDS*, in Berrey and Van den Bark *Amer. Thesaurus of Slang.*]

sharping, *adj.* Pertaining to duping or cheating in games of chance.
1714 Lucas *Memoirs* 84. Indeed Monsieur Shevalier could tell how to load a Dye with Quicksilver, as well as a Fuzee with Powder and Ball; but having been sometimes detected in his *sharping* Tricks, he hath been obliged to look on the Point of the Sword, with which being often wounded, latterly he would decline fighting if there was any way.
[1691 *OED*]

sharp practice, *n.* The dishonorable taking of advantage of an opponent in gambling games.
[1869 *OED*]

sharps and flats, *n. pl.* Punning reference to cheaters and their victims. Compare FLAT.
[1801 *OED*]

sharpshooter, *n.* **1.** An expert at betting on games of chance, horse racing, and so on.
[(1942) 1944 *OEDS*]
2. Same as HUSTLER.
[(1950) 1981 Maurer *Lang. of the Underworld* 191]

shave, *v.* To take advantage of or cheat a player; to fleece. [1606 *OED*]

shears, *n. pl.* **1.** A tool for trimming and resizing playing cards.
[1943 Maurer *Argot*]
2. Playing cards that have been altered in size for cheating purposes. Compare STRIPPERS.
[ca. 1961 *Hotel Coll*]

sheetwriter, *n.* **1.** In a floating crap game, the person who serves as an overlooker, keeps

records of credit to the players, and acts as a banker in the game.
[1983 Martinet *Oral Coll*]
2. A person who writes bets on slips of paper for an illegal bookmaker. See also RUNNER.
[1895 *DA*]

shell game, *n.* **1.** Same as THIMBLERIG; a cheating scheme using sleight of hand, in which a small object such as a pea is placed under one of three walnut shells which then are swiftly moved about followed by an invitation to onlookers to pick the shell concealing the pea. Compare THREE-CARD MONTE.
[1893 *DAE,* 1890 *OEDS*]
2. Any of a variety of cheating schemes involving cards, dice, or other gambling equipment.

sheriff's card, *n.* A certificate issued by the Metropolitan Police Department in Clark County, Nevada, indicating that a person working in gaming casinos has passed a security investigation. See also A CARD.
1983 Clark *Oral Col.* We used to call a work permit an A card, but since Metro was formed, we just call it a *sheriff's card.*

shift, *n.* In poker, a false move in cutting a deck of cards that restores the original order of the cards in the pack. See also SHIFT THE CUT.
[1983 Martinez *Gambling Scene* 219]

shift, *v.* In the phrases:
shift cards, In dealing playing cards, to reverse the sequence in which two cards are dealt. See also SECOND DEALING.
[1890 Quinn *Fools of Fortune* 222]
shift the cut, To make a cheating move while cutting a deck of cards that returns the pack to its original sequence.
See also JUMP THE CUT.
[1890 Quinn *Fools of Fortune* 225]

shift boss, *n.* In a casino, the representative of the management who watches over all games for one eight-hour period. Compare BOXMAN and FLOORMAN.
1983 Martinet *Oral Coll.* Working from the bottom up in the pecking order, you have the dealer, then the boxman in craps, then the floorman in craps or twenty-one. If you have a big dice pit with several games, then you might have a pit boss in craps. In twenty-one the pit boss has several tables and his floormen report to him. He reports to the *shift boss.* The shift boss may or may not be the casino manager. And the casino manager usually has some points [owns a percentage of the casino] but probably reports to the owner, or the guy fronting for the owners.

shift coverage, *n.* In a casino, the condition of having a casino host on duty who is acquainted with moneyed patrons. See also GREETER.
1980 Clark *Oral Coll.* We make sure we have *shift coverage* . . . That means we have greeters [hosts] who know the high rollers so we don't get stuck during a shift without a baby sitter [someone to talk with and do favors for moneyed patrons].

shifting load, *n.* A liquid weight, such as mercury, placed inside a die to alter the way it rolls.
[ca. 1961 *Hotel Coll*]

shill, *n.* **1.** Also called a STARTER or HOUSE PLAYER. An employee in a gambling establishment hired to play minimal stakes at a table until enough players have joined a game to keep it going.
[1968 Wallace *Poker* 224]
[(1916) 1955 *OEDS;* from earlier *shillaber:* 1913 *OEDS,* meaning "a confidence man's accomplice"]
2. An accomplice to a cheater, usually at cards or dice.
[1949 Coffin *Secrets* 186]

shill, *v.* To play at a gaming table as an employee of a gambling establishment or an accomplice of the operator of an illegal game.
[ca. 1961 *Hotel Coll*]

shim, *n.* A length of stiff wire used to control the reels on a slot machine after a hole has been drilled in the side of the machine.
[ca. 1961 *Hotel Coll*]

shimmy, *n.* Another name for CHEMIN DE FER.
[1961 Scarne *Complete Guide* 686]

shiner, *n.* A reflective surface used to view the faces of playing cards as they are dealt. *Shiners* are found as mirrors in pipe bowls, in matchbooks, and the like, or as highly polished coins, cigarette lighters, and so on. See also GLIMMER. [(1812) 1909 *OED*]

shoe, *n.* A dealing box for holding one or more decks of cards used in games such as baccarat, faro, twenty-one, and so on.
[ca. 1961 *Hotel Coll*]
[1923 *OEDS*]

shoestring gambler, One who risks small amounts of money at gambling games.
[1890 *OEDS*]

shoo-in, *n.* A certain or easy winner, as a racehorse, boxer, sports team, and so on.
[ca. 1961 *Hotel Coll*]
[1928 *OEDS;* probably from the verbal phrase]

shoo in, *v.* To permit a slower horse to win.
[1908 *OEDS*]

shoot, *v.* **1.** To roll dice.
[1961 Smith and Noble *Quit Winners* 109]
[1909 *OEDS*]
2. To play craps.
[1983 Martinet *Oral Coll*]
[1903 *OEDS,* as *shoot craps* and 1899 as *shooting craps*]
3. In horse racing, to pass a competitor as he slows down near the finish line.
[1868 *OEDS*]
4. In the phrases:
shoot the moon, In high-low poker, to declare

an intention to win the stakes for both high and low hand. [If the player loses either way, he forfeits all claims.]
[1968 Wallace *Poker* 224]
shoot the pot up, Also shortened to **shoot the pot.** In poker, to make an unusually large bet.
[1973 Preston *Play Poker* 224]
shoot the works, To wager all of a designated amount of money on a single betting proposition.
[ca. 1961 *Hotel Coll*]
[(1928) *DAS*; Compare 1922 *OEDS* "to do to the fullest extent"]

shooter, *n.* A person who casts the dice in games such as craps or backgammon. Compare CASTER.
[1974 Friedman *Casino Management* 29]
[1910 *OEDS*]

shooting from the don't, *n. phr.* In bank craps, an announcement by the stickman that the person shooting the dice is betting that a pass will not be made. The dealer notes this because it is an unusual bet for the shooter to make.
[1983 Martinet *Oral Coll*]

shop, *n.* Also called a CASINO or HOUSE or JOINT or STORE. A gambling establishment.
[ca. 1961 *Hotel Coll*]

shore game, *n.* In golf, a wagering system based on the number of strokes taken by each player while putting on the green.
[1971 McQuaid *Gambler's Digest* 316]

short, *adj.* **1.** Pertaining to a lack of sufficient time, money, strength, honesty, and so on in gambling situations.
[1963 Steig *Common Sense* 181]
2. In bank craps, pertaining to a die that is not rolled the length of the table.
[1983 Martinet *Oral Coll*]

short, *v.* In the phrase:
short the pot, In poker, to place fewer chips into the pot than required for a bet, usually while concealing the move from other players.
[1981 Jenkins *Johnny Moss*]

shortcake, *n.* The shortchanging of a player, especially in craps.
[1961 Scarne *Complete Guide* 686]

shortcake, *v.* To shortchange a player, especially in craps, by paying the player less than is due after the player has taken odds on a bet.
[ca. 1961 *Hotel Coll*]

short-call, *n.* In poker, part of a bet, made when a player calling a bet does not have sufficient funds to match the required amount.
[1949 Coffin *Secrets* 173]
→Usually accompanied by the player's statement, "ALL-IN."

short-call, *v.* In poker, to match part of a previous bet with all one's money.
[1968 Wallace *Poker* 224]

short-cards, *n. pl. Plural in form, but singular in use.* Also written **short-card,** especially when used attributively. An alternative name for poker. *Obsolete.*
[1845 *DAE, OEDS*]

short-change artist, *n.* A person, often a dealer in a craps game, who pays a player less than is due, usually withholding part of the odds bet by the player.
[1983 Martinet *Oral Coll*]

short changer, *n.* A cheater, especially in gambling games or at carnivals.
[1920 *DA, OEDS*]

short deck, *n.* In twenty-one, a pack of cards from which some have been removed, usually those worth ten points each. Compare LONG DECK and LONG SHOE.
[ca. 1961 *Hotel Coll*]

short end, *n.* The giving of odds on a bet. The player giving odds must put up a larger bet than the person taking odds.
[ca. 1961 *Hotel Coll*]

shorten the odds, *v. phr.* In bookmaking, to reduce the odds on a particular entry to increase the amount of betting on other entries.
[1964 Wykes *Illustrated Guide* 329]

short faro, *n.* Any of a number of variations on a faro game that is speeded up by removing certain cards from the deck before dealing. Some names of the variations are ROLLING FARO, JEWISH FARO, or STUSS.
[1890 Quinn *Fools of Fortune* 207]

short game, *n.* **1.** Any of a variety of card games, such as euchre, gin, or faro, that are speeded up by removing certain cards beforehand. Compare SHORT DECK. [1851 *DA*]
2. A game that is played quickly, such as keno or roulette. Compare SHORT CARDS.
[1890 Quinn *Fools of Fortune* 243]

shorthanded game, *n.* In poker or twenty-one, a table with room for an additional player or players.
[1978 Brunson *How I Made* 547]

short head, *n.* In horse racing, the narrowest of margins between the first and second finisher See also NOSE. *British use.*
[1974 Ewart *Flatracing* 152]

short horse, *n.* A race horse that has difficulty running the full distance.
[1890 *DA*]

short money, *n.* Pertaining to a smaller bankroll than a player normally carries into a card or dic game.
[1948 Oncken *Review Journal* 4/25: 13]

short pair, *n.* In draw poker, a pair of tens or les when a pair of jacks or higher is required to initiate the betting round.
[1949 Coffin *Secrets* 185]

short pay, *n.* Pertaining to a slot machine that

pays less than the listed amount, due to a malfunction in the machine.
[1978 Alexander *Glossary* 13]

short price, *n.* In horse racing, very low final odds on a horse just prior to the race. Compare LATE LINE.
[ca. 1961 *Hotel Coll*]

short roll, *n.* **1.** In a slot machine arcade, twenty nickels or quarters bound in a paper wrapper.
[ca. 1961 *Hotel Coll*]
2. In bank craps, a cast of the dice that fails to reach the opposite end of the table.
[1983 Martinet *Oral Coll*]

short-roll, *v.* Also written **short roll.** In bank craps, to cast the dice so they do not hit the backboard at the other end of the table.
[1983 Martinet *Oral Coll*]

shorts, *n. pl.* **1.** An insufficient bankroll. See also SHORT MONEY.
1979 Clark *Oral Coll.* I've got a bad case of the *shorts,* but I need to get in that game, so I'll jump in and hope for the best . . . The *shorts* means I don't have a stake of the right size to get into a game, say a five-ten [five dollar ante, ten dollar first bet, in poker], so I'll go into a one-three and see if I can't build the stake for a game with more action.
2. In poker, a pair of cards in one hand ranked ten or lower. See also SHORT PAIR.
[1971 Livingston *Poker Strategy* 224]

short slip, *n.* **1** In numbers, a wager at less than the normally-required amount.
[1981 Miller *Jargon* 294]
2. In keno, a special ticket sold at a reduced price as part of a promotion or publicity plan.
[1973 Clark *Oral Coll*]

short stack, *n.* In a casino, a stack of fewer than twenty chips.
1983 Martinet *Oral Coll.* You can tell a short stack as soon as you feel it. All the stacks are counted out in groups of twenty checks, so you can feel automatically what twenty is. If you have a *short stack* with a few missing, you usually know just how many are missing, though it takes awhile to distinguish when three checks are missing and when four are missing.

shortstop, *n.* A player who can afford to lose only a small amount of money by gambling.
[(1950) 1981 Maurer *Lang. of the Underworld* 191]

short suit, *n.* In bridge, a hand dealt to a player that has fewer than four cards of a particular suit.
[1950 Morehead *Culbertson* 644]

shot, *n.* **1.** A chance or risk, especially at a gambling proposition.
[1756 *OED*]
2. An illegal or cheating move made by a gambler.
[ca. 1961 *Hotel Coll*]
3. A shooter who can control the roll of the dice.
[(1950) 1981 Maurer *Lang. of the Underworld* 191]
4. A way to control the roll of unaltered dice.
[(1950) 1981 Maurer *Lang. of the Underworld* 191]

shotgun, *n.* Also called FIRST BASE. In twenty-one, the first position to the left of the dealer.
[1979 Newman *Dealer's Special* 56]

shove over some money, *n. phr.* In a casino, the name of a cheating scheme in which a dealer gives chips to a confederate acting as a player. See also BALL TEAM.
[1961 Smith and Noble *Quit Winners*]

show, *n.* **1.** In racing, the third place finish at the end of a race.
[1955 Hillis *Pari-Mutuel Betting* 118]
[1925 *OEDS*]
2. Short for SHOWDOWN. In poker, the exposure of hands at the end of all betting.
[1887 *DAE,* 1889 *OED*]

show, *v.* **1.** In racing, to finish a race in third place. [1903 *OEDS*]
2. In poker, to expose a hand of cards after all betting is finished.
[1893 *DAE,* 1879 *OED*]
3. In card games, to deal a card or cards face upward.
[ca. 1961 *Hotel Coll*]
4. In the phrase:
show down, In poker, to expose one's hand of cards after finishing the betting process.
[1879 *DA,* 1893 *DAE*]

show bet, *n.* In racing, a wager that an entry will finish among the top three of all entries in a race.
[1971 McQuaid *Gambler's Digest* 316]

showdown, *n.* In poker, a comparison of hands after all betting is completed to determine the winner of the pot.
[1884 *DA, DAE;* 1892 *OEDS*]

show ticket, *n.* Same as a SHOW BET.
[ca. 1961 *Hotel Coll*]

shuck, *v.* In draw poker, to discard before requesting replacement cards.
[1971 Livingston *Poker Strategy* 224]
[Compare *shuck:* 1848 *OED,* meaning "get rid of"]

shuffle, *v.* **1.** To mix together in random fashion such things as playing cards or domino tiles before distributing them to players. Compare CUT. [1570 *OED*]
2. In racing, to HAND RIDE a horse while using spurs to urge the horse further.
[(1951) 1981 Maurer *Lang. of the Underworld* 227]
3. In the phrase:
shuffle in, To put a card or cards into the pack while shuffling. [1583 *OED*]

shuffle, *n.* **1.** The act of mixing gaming cards or tiles in a random fashion. Compare CUT.
[1651 *OED*]
2. In racing, the main group, or pack, of entries running more or less together during a race.
[1968 Buchele *Greyhound Racing* 6]

shuffled back, *adj. phr.* Also shortened to **shuffled.** In racing, pertaining to an entry crowded back by other entries so as to make a poorer finish than could be expected.
[1978 Ainslie *Complete Guide* 298]

shuffler, *n.* The person, not always the dealer, who shuffles the pack of cards before a hand is dealt. [1894 *OED*]

shuffling, *n.* The re-arranging of the sequence of cards in a pack.
1836 Eidrah *Hoyle Famil* 3. *Shuffling* is the first thing done in all games, and signifies mixing the cards; it is proper to shuffle before every new deal. [1579 *OED*]

Shuffling and Dealing. The mixing (called SHUFFLING) and distribution (called DEALING) in some CARD GAMES is performed by one of the players while in many CASINO GAMES it is frequently done by an OPERATOR who is an employee, usually called a BANKER or DEALER. In SOCIAL GAMES players may CUT FOR HIGH CARD to pick the first dealer, after which a new dealer is assigned by ROTATION. The dealer in poker may have DEALER'S CHOICE. In blackjack his play may be dictated by the DEALER'S HITTING RULE. Some games such as FARO require a DEALING BOX or SHOE. Dealers are often referred to more jocularly as THROWERS, BROAD TOSSERS or BROAD PITCHERS. They may be identified by the kind of game they SERVE, such as: BLACKJACK DEALER, FARO-DEALER, MONTE THROWER, and the like.

In contrast to the SENATE DEALER, the unscrupulous dealer is more often referred to by identifying his specialty MOVE or SCAM. One must be carful not to confuse a SQUARE DEALER with a SQUARE DEAL, a CARD MUCKER in panguingue and in twenty-one, or a NUMBER TWO MAN who may manage the joint with the NUMBER TWO MAN who is a SECOND DEALER. SECOND DEALERS and SUBWAY DEALERS and PEEKERS often have a CONFEDERATE to whom they BOTTOM DEAL cards from a STACKED DECK. In faro the dealer may depend upon a CRANK BOX, SNAKE BOX or some other TELL BOX to SNAKE THE GAME.

There are many ways to monitor the identity of cards. Some CARDSHARPS rely upon COSMETICS applied by a DAUBER. Such SHADE WORK, LUMINOUS READERS (which require a PINK EYE), LINE WORK, GLAZED CARDS, and CUTOUT WORK, however, may be preferred to a STAMPED DECK.

MECHANICS rely upon a SLEEVE MACHINE for an ACE UP THE SLEEVE or other HOLDOUT, or upon TRIMS (also called STRIPPERS), PIN WORK, EDGE WORK or the like. Others employ a MECHANIC'S GRIP to produce a FALSE CUT, LAS VEGAS RIFFLE, OVERHAND SHUFFLE, FAST SHUFFLE or find some other way to FOIL THE CUT. CELLAR DEALERS depend on the BOTTOM STOCK to SERVE a STACKED DEAL. PEEKERS may resort to a MATCHBOOK SHINER, GLEAMER or other GLASS WORK. Or they may execute a HEEL PEEK, BUBBLE PEEK, or FRONT PEEK.

When a CARD MOB, set up as THREE COUSINS AND A STRANGER, cannot use a SVENGALI DECK, they may resort to WORKING THE TELEGRAPH. Or, they may EAR the cards with a CORNER-BEND or DEBONE them when the MONKEY isn't watching. DILDOCKS may simply RING IN A COLD DECK.

When a DELIVERY is incorrect or none of the players have OPENERS, players will ABANDON THE DEAL and REDEAL.

shut, *v.* In the particle construction:
shut out, 1. In poker, to make a bet larger than an opponent can match.
[1978 Brunson *How I Made* 547]
2. At racetracks or sports books, to close a betting window before all the bettors waiting have placed wagers.
[1968 Ainslie *Complete Guide* 454]
3. To prevent an opponent from scoring any points. [1896 *OED*]

shut off, *adj.* In racing, pertaining to an entry that is blocked by another entry during a race and prevented from moving to the front.
[(1951) 1981 Maurer *Lang. of the Underworld* 227]

shutout, *n.* **1.** Same as a SHUTOUT BID.
[1936 *OEDS*]
2. A game in which a player or team prevents an opponent from scoring any points.
[1889 *OEDS*]

shutout bid, *n.* In bridge, a PRE-EMPTIVE BID to which an opponent cannot respond.
[1953 Crawford *Consistent Winner* 353]
[1921 *OEDS*]

shy, *adj.* Also LIGHT or SHORT. In poker, pertaining to a bet put into the pot that is smaller than it should be.
[1887 *DA, DAE;* 1895 *OED*]

Shylock, *n.* Also written **shylock.** Same as LOAN SHARK.
[1930 *OEDS;* compare earlier *Shylocky: a*1818 *OED,* meaning "money-lender like"]

Shylock, *v.* Also written **shylock.** To submit (someone) to repaying a loan at usery interest rates. Compare LOAN-SHARKING.
[(1930) 1933 *OEDS*]

sice, *n.* In dice: **1.** The number 6 marked upon a die. [*c*1386 *OED*]
2. A throw in which a die shows 6.
[*a*1550 *OED*]
3. In craps, the point and the number 6.
[(1950) 1981 Maurer *Lang. of the Underworld* 191]
[*c*1386 *OED?*]

side, *n.* Also called a TEAM. A person or group of contenders in a competition, as at backgammon or bridge or football.
[1698 *OED*]

side arms, *n. pl.* In poker, a pair of cards of the same rank, but lower in value than another pair of cards in the same hand; a SECOND PAIR.
[1949 Coffin *Secrets* 186]

side bet, *n.* A wager ancillary to the main betting proposition, often between two onlookers or concerning an event not directly relevant to the primary ends of the game in process, such as which team in a football game will first have to punt on the fourth down. Compare MAIN BET.
[1894 *OED*]

sidebinder, *n.* In horse racing, a strong hit with the whip by the jockey. Compare GO TO BAT and RIB ROASTER.
1889 Ellangowan *Sporting Anecdotes* 336. *Sidebinder.*—Nearly equivalent to a "rib roaster"—a heavy cut with the whip to get a horse to make another effort.

side card, *n.* **1.** A card without value to a hand.
[1963 Steig *Common Sense* 187]
2. A card that does not belong to a set, as the deuce in a three card sequence, 2, 5, 5.
[1857 *DA, DAE*]
3. In poker, in the case of a tie at the showdown, the highest ranking card outside of the cards involved in the tie.
[1949 Coffin *Secrets* 186]
4. Also spelled **sidecard.** Also called a KICKER. A card of high rank, usually an ace, retained during the discarding process in draw poker.
[1978 Brunson *How I Made* 548]
5. In trump games, a nontrump card.
[1973 Clark *Oral Coll*]

side game, *n.* **1.** In a casino, a minor banking game such as the BIG SIX, WHEEL OF FORTUNE, or CHUCK-A-LUCK.
[1961 Scarne *Complete*]
2. In a poker parlor, any game that is not considered the main or most important game in the room.
1982 Clark *Oral Coll.* During the World Championship [of Poker, at Binnion's Horseshoe in Las Vegas], the *side games* get more action than the main game. At a couple of tables in the middle are twelve or fifteen people still in contention for the no-limit hold 'em championship, and the guys who have been knocked out of the tournament are at a *side game* ten feet away playing for stakes twice as high.

side money, *n.* In poker, any money or chips set apart from the main pot, usually to indicate money owed by a player, money due to the operator or house, or money to be used for refreshments. Compare KITTY and POT.
[1949 Coffin *Secrets* 186]

side partner, *n.* A confederate to a cheater, usually in card games.
[1890 Quinn *Fools of Fortune* 276]
[Compare 1890 *OED,* meaning "colleague"]

side pot, *n.* In poker, a second POT created by players contending for a pot when some event has taken place to force the beginning of a new pot, such as one player placing his entire stake in the pot before the end of the betting round, but who is still eligible for the portion of the pot on which he did bet. Compare SIDE MONEY.
[1949 Coffin *Secrets* 186]

side strength, *n.* In bridge, the holding of high cards or several cards in a suit not named as trump.
[1953 Crawford *Consistent Winner* 353]

side stripper, *n.* A playing card trimmed on the long side for purposes of cheating.
Compare STRIPPERS.
[1890 Quinn *Fools of Fortune* 197]

side suit, *n.* In bridge, a PLAIN SUIT, one not named as trump.
[1950 Morehead *Culbertson* 645]

sight, *n.* The calling of part of a raise in poker when the player cannot meet the full amount of the raise. The player is then playing only for the part of the pot covered by the insufficient raise.
1866 *American Card Player* 135. *Sight.*—Every player is entitled to a "*sight* for his pile," and when a player makes a bet, and his opponent bets higher, if the player who makes the first bet has not funds sufficient to cover the bet made by his adversary, he can put up all the funds he may have and call a show of hands for that amount.
[1821 *OEDS;* 1823 *DA;* 1857 *DAE*]

sign, *n.* **1.** Also called an OFFICE. A signal given to a partner or an accomplice during a gambling game, usually transmitting information or demanding an action.
[1961 Scarne *Complete Guide* 687]
[Compare 13.. *OED,* meaning "omen"]
2. In the clause:
have a sign on one's back. Said of a player, especially at card games, known widely to be a cheater.
[ca. 1961 *Hotel Coll*]

signal, *n.* A communication passed between or among confederates by means of a gesture, look, or oral statement. Compare SIGN (def. 1).
[1953 Crawford *Consistent Winner* 353]

signing up, *n.* In card playing, especially poker, a method of collusion in which an accomplice signals the value of the cards held in his hand to a confederate cheater. Compare SIGN, *n.* (def. 1).
[1890 Quinn *Fools of Fortune* 222]

sign-off, *n.* In bridge, a bid designed to request a partner to close the bidding by passing.
[1953 Crawford *Consistent Winner* 353]

sign off, *v.* To signal that one is stopping the bidding. [1933 *OEDS*]

silent game, *n.* Especially **the silent game.** Another name for WHIST.
1816 Singer *Researches* 270. Seymour, in the *Complete Gamester,* 1739, says Whist, vulgarly called whisk, is said to be a very ancient game among us; but its original denomination is "Whist or the *silent game.*"

silent partner, *n.* In poker, an innocent player used by a cheater to avert suspicion by receiving several winning hands for small pots while the cheater takes large pots.
[1968 Wallace *Poker* 224]
[Compare 1828 *OEDS,* meaning "a business partner who does not take an active part in the conduct of his business"]

silks, *n. pl.* In horse and harness racing, the colored cap and blouse or jacket worn by a jockey or driver made of the colors registered by the owner of the stable to which the horse belongs.
[(1891) *OED,* singular; 1946 *OEDS*]

simple, *n.* In mah-jongg, any of the tiles of one suit, ranked 2 through 8.
[1950 Morehead *Culbertson* 645]

simple game, *n.* Any of a variety of card or dice games in which each player puts a standard amount of money into a pool and the selection of a winner is by chance.
[1950 Morehead *Culbertson* 645]

simultaneous declaration, *n.* Also called SEQUENTIAL DECLARATION. In high-low poker, the method by which all players contending for the pot signal their intentions to play for the high portion, the low portion, or both the high and low portions of the pot. Each player holds a closed fist over the table. At a signal, all the players open their hands. An agreed convention might be: a hand with nothing signals an intent to vie for the high half of the pot, a hand holding one chip signals an intent to vie for the low half of the pot, and a hand with two chips signals an intent to vie for the entire pot, both high and low. Normally, the person contending for both high and low must win both ways or forfeit any claim to the pot. Compare SEQUENTIAL DECLARATION.
[1968 Wallace *Poker* 224]

single, *v.* In bank craps, to pay EVEN MONEY, or an amount equal to the wager made.
1978 Clark *Oral Coll.* On a roll like that, the stickman says, "3 craps, line away, single the field." He is telling the dealers that the shooter has thrown a point count of three on the dice, that they should remove the bets on the pass line, which lose, and they should pay even money on the bets that were put in the field area of the table.
→*Single* is dealer's patter used to distinguish payments for those layouts that pay 2 to 1 on a roll of 3.

single-action, *n.* In numbers, an hourly game in a neighborhood.
[1971 McQuaid *Gambler's Digest* 316]

single-action bet, *n.* In numbers, a wager on one digit instead of the usual three.
[1961 Scarne *Complete Guide* 687]

single-cat-harp, *n.* In faro, the condition whereby three cards remain undealt, and two are of the same denomination. Compare DOUBLE-CAT-HARP.
1843 Green *Exposure* 210. When there are five cards in the box, one case (odd card) and two doubles (such as two fours and two sevens,) this is called "double-cat-harp;" when these are in, one odd and one doublet, it is called "*single-cat-harp.*"

single deck, *n.* In twenty-one, a game in which one pack of playing cards is used, as distinct from DOUBLE-DECK. Compare SHOE.
[ca. 1961 *Hotel Coll*]

single game, *n.* In backgammon, a game won at minimal stakes without use of the doubling cube.
[1950 Morehead *Culbertson* 645]

single-handed poker, *n.* A variant of poker in which five cards are dealt and no more are drawn before the showdown. Compare DRAW POKER. [1844 *DA*]

single line play, *n. phr.* On slot machines, pertaining to playing one coin on the center line in a machine that features multiple lines available for play by means of dropping more coins into the slot before pulling the handle.
[ca. 1961 *Hotel Coll*]

single-o, *n.* A cheater who works alone.
[1961 Scarne *Complete Guide* 687]

single-o, *adj.* Working without the aid of a confederate.
[(1950) 1981 Maurer *Lang. of the Underworld* 191]

single odds, *n. pl.* In bank craps, an odds bet equal to the amount of the FLAT BET.
[ca. 1961 *Hotel Coll*]

single-out, *n.* In faro, a betting system in which the player wagers that a particular card will win or lose in opposition to the previous time it appeared.
[(1943) 1981 Maurer *Lang. of the Underworld,* 139]

single point, *adj. phr.* In bank craps, pertaining to a player who bets only on the PASS LINE, who never has multiple bets by placing chips on the COME LINE.
[1968 Thackrey *Nick the Greek* 27]

single stakes, *n. pl.* In roulette, wagers that pay even money, such as red, black, odd, or even.
[1890 Quinn *Fools of Fortune* 248]

single throw bet, *n. phr.* In craps, a wager that is resolved on the next roll of the dice; a ONE-ROLL BET. See also HOP BET.
[ca. 1961 *Hotel Coll*]

singleton, *n.* In bridge or whist, a single card of

one suit held in a hand. See also DOUBLETON.
[1876 *OED*]

sink, *v.* In piquet, to omit announcing the holding of a scoring combination of cards, thereby forfeiting the points such a combination offers.
[1950 Morehead *Culbertson* 645]

sister hix, *n.* Also called JIMMY HICKS. In craps, a roll of the number 6.
[1983 Martinet *Oral Coll*]
[Rhyming slang]

sit, *v.* In the phrases and particle constructions:
sit chilly, Same as SIT-STILL. In horse racing, to refrain from using the whip to extend a horse during a race; to lose a race by refusing to force the horse to run as fast as possible.
[1978 Ainslie *Complete Guide* 298]
sit in, 1. To have a place at a game.
[1599 *OED*]
2. In poker, to join a game.
[1868 *DA, DAE, OEDS;* 1954 *DAS,*
3. To substitute for another player for a short time.
[1978 Larson *Vocabulary* 101]

sit-still, *v.* Same as to SIT CHILLY.
[1978 Ainslie *Complete Guide* 298]

sitting, *adj.* In cards, very strong and therefore difficult to lose.
[1932 *OEDS*]

sitting duck, *n.* An easy target for a cheater; a victim of a cheating scheme.
[1973 Clark *Oral Coll*]
[n.d. *DAS*]

six-ace flat, *n.* A die that has been shaved on opposite faces showing one pip and six pips, making those faces land face upward more often than normal.
[(1950) 1981 Maurer *Lang. of the Underworld* 191]

six-card option, *n.* In stud, a variant that allows a player to purchase a sixth card for a specified amount of money to be added to the pot. At the showdown, the player may use only five of the six cards to make up his hand.
[1963 Steig *Common Sense* 187]

six dollar combine, *n. phr.* In racing, a wager on a single entry to win, place, and show. Compare PERFECTA and QUINELLA.
[1964 Wykes *Illustrated Guide* 329]

six-five pick 'em, *n. phr.* In bookmaking, a wager offered in an event with two contestants. The bettor may take either side and pay six dollars to win five.
[1960 Cook *Gambling, Inc.* 268]

sixie from dixie, *n. phr.* In craps, a term for the number 6.
[1968 Adams *Western Words*]
[Rhyming slang]

six-number bet, *n.* In roulette, a single wager covering six numbers.
[1971 McQuaid *Gambler's Digest* 316]

six-number line, *n.* In roulette, the space on the table layout for placing chips on a SIX-NUMBER BET.
[1968 Thackrey *Nick the Greek* 157]

six number wheel, *n. phr.* A wheel of fortune featuring a twelve pointed star with six spaces between each point, totalling seventy-two slots.
[1890 Quinn *Fools of Fortune* 290]

six on the end, *n. phr.* In a poker parlor, a ONE-THREE GAME that allows a player to bet six dollars and raise bets in increments of six dollars during the final betting round.
[ca. 1961 *Hotel Coll*]

sixteenth pole, *n.* In horse racing, a post, usually painted black and white, placed a half-furlong (110 yards) before the finish line. Compare EIGHTH POLE.
[1963 Drazazgo *Wheels* 298]

sixth street, *n.* **1.** In seven-card stud, the sixth card dealt to a player.
[1978 Brunson *How I Made* 548]
2. In hold 'em poker, the fourth card dealt face upward in the center of the table.
[1981 Golad *Oral Coll*]

six tits, *n. pl.* Three queens in poker.
[1983 Martinet *Oral Coll*]

sixty days, *n. pl.* In craps, a term for the number 6.
[(1950) 1981 Maurer *Lang. of the Underworld* 191]

sixty queens, *n. pl.* In pinochle, a meld of four queens, one from each suit. Compare EIGHTY KINGS and FORTY JACKS.
[1953 Crawford *Consistent Winner* 353]

size, *v.* In a casino, to pay a wager by placing a taller stack of chips next to the bet, then removing the excess chips from the taller stack. The method, required by casino operators, prevents arguments about the size of the original wager which could result from placing the winnings atop the player's stack. Compare BANG INTO and BUMP INTO.
[1840 *DA, DAE;* the same quote in *OED* with date of 1836–39]

skate race, *n.* A horserace in which all the entries carry the same amount of weight.
[ca. 1961 *Hotel Coll*]

skeet, *n.* Also called KILTER or PELTER. In poker, a hand containing 9, 5, 2, and two other cards numbered 8 or below, but with no pair or flush. Compare SKEET FLUSH.
[1949 Coffin *Secrets* 186]

skeet flush, *n.* In poker, a hand containing 9, 5, 2, and two other cards numbered 8 or below, all of the same suit, but with no pair.
[1968 Wallace *Poker* 224]

skim *v.* In a casino, to remove money from the profits before it is officially counted.
[ca. 1961 *Hotel Coll*]

skim, *n.* In a casino, the money removed from the

profits before it is officially counted.
[1960 Cook *Gambling, Inc.* 301]

skim money, *n.* Same as SKIM, *n.*
[1973 *OEDS*]

skin, *v.* **1.** In horse racing, to increase track speed by packing down and rolling the surface of the track.
[1978 Anslie *Complete Guide* 298]
2. To cheat a victim in a gambling venture.
[1812 *OED*]
3. In card games, to deal cards by sliding them from the top of the pack rather than lifting each card from the pack as it is dealt.
[1950 Morehead *Culbertson* 646]
4. To look at one's own cards by spreading them slightly. See also SKIN OUT.
[1884 *DA;* 1895 *OED*]
5. In the phrases:
skin out, To spread and display a card hand, especially at the showdown in poker.
Compare SKIN *v.* (def. 4).
[1873 *DAE, OEDS;* c1895 *OED*]
skin the deck, In poker, to secrete a card or cards in the palm of the hand for later use.
Compare SKINNING.
[ca. 1961 *Hotel Coll*]
skin the hand, In poker, to rid a hand of excess cards before the showdown.
[ca. 1961 *Hotel Coll*]
skin the lamb, In horse racing, to have no bets against the winning horse.
1889 Ellangowan *Sporting Anecdotes* 63. *Skinning the lamb* denotes that the bookmakers have a clear book as regards the winner; in other words, have not betted against it, and have, therefore, nothing to pay. The origin of the phrase is not given in the *Slang Dictionary*, and the writer has not been able to trace it.
[(1864) 1883 *OED*]

skin faro, *n.* A dishonest faro game. Compare SKIN GAME.
[1882 *DA, DAE, OED*]

skin gambler, *n.* A person who depends on his main source of income from cheating others, usually at cards or dice.
[1890 Quinn *Fools of Fortune* 197]

skin game, *n.* Any of a variety of games in which confederates work together to cheat a victim.
[1868 *DA, OEDS*]

skinning, *n.* The act of removing cards from a fresh pack and altering them. Compare STACKED DECK and STRIPPERS.
1888 Kunard *Card Tricks* 174. *Skinning.*—A novice would think a pack placed upon the table in its original stamped cover must be genuine, but such is not the case. Sharpers can easily open the cover with the aid of a little warm water, and, after removing certain cards, substituting for them "pricked" or other prepared cards, fasten the cover up again, giving it a most innocent appearance, and very few persons would even suspect that such a pack has been tampered with; yet this is frequently done.

skinning-house, *n.* A gambling establishment devoted to cheating, especially at faro.
[1938 Asbury *Sucker's Progress* 9]

skinny dugan, *n.* In craps, another name for the number 7.
[1983 Martinet *Oral Coll*]

skins, *n. pl. Plural in form, but singular in use.* In golf, a wagering system in which the person winning a hole is paid by all the other players. If there is no winner on the hole, the wagers carry over and are added to the pool for the next hole.
[1973 Clark *Oral Coll*]

skip bid, *n.* In bridge, a bid considerably higher than a partner's previous bid, used as a prearranged signal.
[1950 Morehead *Culbertson* 646]

skipper, *n.* **1.** A person who leaves a gambling establishment without paying money owed. See also welsher.
[ca. 1961 *Hotel Coll*]
2. Same as SKIP STRAIGHT.
[1963 Steig *Common Sense* 187]

skip straight, *n.* Also called SKIPPER. In poker, a hand in which cards are of alternate rank, as 2, 4, 6, 8, 10. See also ALTERNATE STRAIGHT, DUTCH STRAIGHT, SCOTCH STRAIGHT.
[1887 *DAE*]

skunk, *n.* A game won by a wide margin.
[1850 *DA;* 1853 *DAE*]

skunk, *v.* **1.** To defeat someone in a game by a wide margin or with one's opponent not scoring any points.
[1846 *DA;* 1847 *DAE*]
2. To cheat a victim.
[1973 Clark *Oral Coll*]
[1890 *OEDS*]

slam, *n.* **1.** In card games such as bridge and whist, the winning of all the tricks in a game, or all but one trick. See GRAND SLAM and SMALL SLAM.
1816 Singer *Researches* 270. The term *Slamm,* at Whist, we are informed, now signifies one party winning the game before the adverse party have gained a trick.
[1660 *OED*]
2. Short for SLAMBANG.
[1961 Scarne *Complete Guide* 688]
3. Another name for the obsolete game, *ruff and honours.* [1621 *OED*]

slambang, *n.* Cheating moves performed in a rapid or fast-paced fashion.
[ca. 1961 *Hotel Coll*]

slambang, *v.* To cheat a victim in a rapid, almost careless, fashion.
[(1950) 1981 Maurer *Lang. of the Underworld* 191]

sleeper, *n.* **1. a.** An unclaimed bet left on a table layout.
1868 Trumps *Pocket Hoyle* 208. A bet becomes

a *sleeper,* when the owner has forgotten it. It is then public property, any one having a right to take it.
[1856 *OEDS,* 1864 *DA*]
b. In faro, a wager left on a layout card that has already been dealt.
[1938 Asbury *Sucker's Progress* 16]
c. In craps, an unclaimed wager left on the layout after a shooter has finished a hand.
[1983 Martinet *Oral Coll*]
2. A winning keno ticket that is not presented for collection.
[1973 Clark *Oral Coll*]
3. a. A racehorse that finishes a race better than expected. See also LONGSHOT.
[1941 *DA;* compare 1892 *OEDS,* with the meaning of an athelete who performs better than expected]
b. A racehorse which has been trained secretly in preparation for substituting it for another entry giving the owners a LONGSHOT.

sleeve holdout, *n.* In poker, a mechanical contrivance that is strapped to the arm and is designed to hold cards up a cheater's sleeve.
[1890 Quinn *Fools of Fortune* 234]

sleeve machine, *n.* Same as SLEEVE HOLDOUT.
[1938 Asbury *Sucker's Progress* 66]

slick, *n.* The act of making some cards smoother than others so they might slide more easily.

1674 Cotton *Compleat Gamester* 94. The *slick* is when before hand the Gamester takes a Pack of Cards, and with a slickstone smooths all the Putt Cards [i.e. certain cards], that when he comes to cut to his Adversary with his four-finger above and his thumb about the middle, he slides the rest of the Cards off that which was slickt.
[1978 Larson *Vocabulary* 101]
[1674 *OED*]

slick, *v.* To smooth the backs of certain playing cards so they might slide more easily for a card cheater.
[1978 Larson *Vocabulary* 101]

slick, *adj.* In lowball poker, pertaining to a good hand, usually one in which the highest card is 6, 7, or 8, and the next highest card is 4. *Slick eight* is a hand with 8, 4, 3, 2, ace.
[1971 Livingston *Poker Strategy* 233]

slick-ace deck, *n.* A pack of playing cards in which the aces have been made smoother on the back to slide easily against other cards.
[1968 Wallace *Poker* 224]

slick box, *n.* A dice cup that is smooth on the inside so the dice cheat can manipulate the dice to cast a desired number.
[(1950) 1981 Maurer *Lang. of the Underworld* 191]

slick dice, *n.* A die or dice on which one or more faces have been polished so the dice will slide on a surface rather than roll.
[1943 Conboie *Lincoln Slim* 253]

slick dice cup, *n.* Also shortened to **slick cup.** Same as SLICK BOX.
[1961 Scarne *Complete Guide* 687]

slick-dice roll, *n.* Also called a SLIDE SHOT, SLIDE THROW. A cast of a pair of dice in which one die rolls and turns, while the other die slides and keeps the same face upward at the end of the cast as was upward at the beginning. See also WHIP SHOT.
[1983 Martinez *Gambling Scene* 220]

slick seven, *n.* Also called a SMOOTH SEVEN. A lowball poker hand composed of 7, 4, 3, 2, ace. Compare ROUGH SEVEN.
[1971 Livingston *Poker Strategy* 223]
→Occasional reference is made to *slick six* or *slick eight,* in which the highest card is 6 or 8 respectively; but, *slick seven* is more frequently heard.

slide shot, *n.* Same as SLICK-DICE ROLL.
[1974 Scarne *Dice* 268]

slide throw, *n.* Same as SLICK-DICE ROLL.
[ca. 1961 *Hotel Coll*]

slip, *v.* **1.** To palm a card for later use in a card game. [1760 *OED*]
2. In the phrases:
slip the cards, To place a stacked packet of cards atop the deck after the deck has been cut. Compare SNAKE THE CARD.
1859 Green *Gam Tricks* 100. *Slipping the cards* is performed in various ways, all which tend to put the same cards at the top again which have been cut off and ought to be put underneath.
[1807 *OED,* as "slip a card"]
slip the cut, or **slip the deck,** Same as SLIP THE CARDS.
[1879 *OED*, as "slip the cut"]

slip dispenser, *n.* Also called a WHIZ MACHINE. In a casino cage, a machine filled with a continuous roll of numbered forms used in recording transactions between the cage and various pits in the casino. See also fill slip.
[1982 Martin *Introduction* 9]

slippery Anne, *n.* In playing cards, another name for the queen of spades.
[1950 Morehead *Culbertson* 645]

slip-runner, *n.* In policy gambling, a person who carries slips of paper recording wagers to the place where the gambling operation is centered.
[1901 *DA*]

slit bet, *n.* In roulette, a wager placed on two adjacent numbers.
[ca. 1961 *Hotel Coll*]

slobberhannes, *n.* **1.** A card game resembling euchre, but with object of losing tricks rather than winning.
[1877 *OEDS,* perhaps from Dutch *slabberjan,* a card game]
2. A point in the game.
[1877 *OEDS*]

sloppy track, *n.* In horse racing, a track that is wet on the surface, but firm beneath. A *sloppy track* is one stage firmer and consequently faster than a MUDDY TRACK.
[(1951) 1981 Maurer *Lang. of the Underworld* 227]

slot, *n.* **1. a.** Short for SLOT MACHINE.
[ca. 1961 *Hotel Coll*]
b. slots, *pl.* Especially in the phrase: **the slots.** Short for SLOT MACHINES. Coin operated gambling devices, usually with a handle and designed to win or lose for a player at a single pull of the handle.
[1968 Thackrey *Nick the Greek* 165]
[1950 *OEDS*]
2. The opening in a slot machine for the reception of a coin.
[1888 *OED*]
3. In racing, a position at the starting line.
[1961 Scarne *Complete Guide* 687]
4. At a gaming table, a position assigned to a player or dealer.
[1950 Morehead *Culbertson* 646]
5. The narrow aperture on a gaming table into which the dealer places paper money and slips to be deposited in the DROP BOX.
[ca. 1961 *Hotel Coll*]

slot booth, *n.* A small enclosure in a casino or gambling establishment from which an employee makes change and watches over slot machine players.
[1977 Nevada Gaming Control *Internal* 20]

slot booth bank, *n. phr.* A repository of money kept in a slot booth that can be used by an employee to make change for players or pay off large jackpots.
[1982 Martin *Introduction* 1]

slot cheater, *n.* Also called **slot cheat.** A person who steals from slot machines. See also BLOCKER.
[1973 Binion *Recollections* 33]

slot count sheet, *n.* A form used by gambling establishments to record the number of coins dropped into a machine, the amount paid out, and the amounts added to the hopper by an attendant. See also SLOT MACHINE REEL COMBINATION SHEET and SLOT WIN SHEET.
[1978 Alexander *Glossary* 14]

slot drop, *n.* The number of coins put into a slot machine by players during a specific period of time.
[1977 Nevada Gaming Control *Internal* 25]

slot fill, *n.* The coins added to a hopper by an attendant after all the coins in a slot machine have been paid out to players.
[1982 Martin *Introduction* 22]

slot fill slip, *n.* A form used in a gambling establishment to record the time and amount of coins added to a slot machine by an attendant.
[1957 *Nevada Gaming Regulations* 33]

slot joint, *n.* A gambling establishment that is filled with slot machines and which has few or no gaming tables. See also GRIND JOINT.
[1974 Clark *Oral Coll*]

slot machine, *n.* A mechanical or electronic gaming device into which a player may deposit coins and from which certain numbers of coins are paid out when a particular configuration of symbols appears on the machine. See also LEMON and TRADE STIMULATOR.
[1891 *OEDS,* 1892 *OED,* 1896 *DAE*]

Slot Machine. Some gambling establishments are totally devoted to THE SLOTS and are consequently dubbed SLOT JOINTS. The moniker ONE-ARMED BANDIT and the expression FLUSHING THE JOHN are well deserved. Each of these COIN OPERATED GAMING DEVICES is equipped with a CHEATER'S BAR, VARIATION TIMER and a REEL CLOCK which prevent RHYTHM PLAYERS from manipulating the REELS to award JACKPOTS or JACKPOT PAYOUTS. GRIND CUSTOMERS have found LOOSE SLOTS based on observing the RETURN RATE of MACHINE PAYOUTS in the SLOT MIX.

Some casinos group the SLOT MACHINES in CAROUSELS with a CAROUSEL ATTENDANT who, with an APRON GIRL or CHANGE PERSON, keeps the players supplied with coins, and, with the aid of a SLOT MECHANIC (also called a KEY MAN), keeps the machines in operation.

Some machines display SLOT MACHINE FRUIT while others are POKER MACHINES. If a LEMON is displayed the player loses. The PROGRESSIVE SLOT allows the PAYOUT on a JACKPOT to increase with each coin played.

slot machine fruit, *n. phr.* Any of a variety of symbols used on a slot machine, such as a cherry, LEMON, orange, or plum.
[1941 Fair *Spill the Jackpot* 67]
→Other symbols have come to be incorporated under the term, such as a *bell, bar,* or numeral *7.*]

slot machine load, *n. phr.* The number of coins initially placed in an empty slot machine before it is offered to the public for play. Compare SLOT FILL.
[1978 Alexander *Glossary* 14]

slot machine load bank, *n. phr.* In a gambling establishment, a record of the amounts paid out by all slot machines during a specific period of time. Compare SLOT COUNT SHEET.
[1982 Martin *Introduction* 1]

slot machine reel combination sheet, *n. phr.* Also called a SLOT THEORETICAL HOLD CALCULATION SHEET. In a gambling establishment, a record of the reel settings or award schedule for each slot machine that determines the percentage of HOLD, or profit, for that machine.
[1978 Alexander *Glossary* 14]
→The total percentage of profit for a legal gambling establishment is set by law, but the amount of profit for each machine can vary, so

that some machines have a higher percentage of return than others.

slot mechanic, *n.* A person who maintains, repairs, and resets slot machines.
[ca. 1961 *Hotel Coll*]

slot mix, *n.* In a gambling establishment, the distribution of slot machines by denomination, type, traffic patterns, award schedules and so on.
[ca. 1961 *Hotel Coll*]

slot theoretical hold calculation sheet, *n. phr.* Same as a SLOT MACHINE REEL COMBINATION SHEET.
[1978 Alexander *Glossary* 14]

slot win sheet, *n. phr.* In a gambling establishment, a form for recording the total number of coins put into a slot machine, the *drop,* and the total number paid out, based on the readings of meters attached to the inside of the machine.
[1978 Alexander *Glossary* 14]

slough, *v.* **1.** In bridge, to rid the hand of an undesirable card by playing it on a trick won by an opponent.
[1953 Crawford *Consistent Winner* 353]
2. Also in the phrase:
slough up. In a casino, to close a table or discontinue a game on a particular table.
[(1950) 1981 Maurer *Lang. of the Underworld* 192]

slow, *adj.* In horse racing, pertaining to a track that is damp or wet, but not muddy. It is usually slower than a SLOPPY TRACK.
[1978 Ainslie *Complete Guide* 298]

slow crap, *n.* In craps, the point 4 or 10.
1983 Martinet *Oral Coll.* The points 4 and 10 are called *slow crap* because getting either of those as a point is almost as bad as a craps. The chances are much greater that a shooter will seven-out before making one of those points.

slow death, *n.* Another term for BINGO.
1948 Oncken *Review Journal* 3/28: 13. Fast action players say that bingo is called "the *slow death.*"

slow game, *n.* In poker, a session with few large bets or raises.
[1978 Brunson *How I Made* 548]

slow play, *n.* In poker, a strategy for making small bets while holding a strong hand, so as to make large raises in a later betting round. See also CHECK-RAISE and SANDBAGGING.
[1981 Golad *Oral Coll*]

slug, *n.* **1.** A disk or token fashioned in the shape of a coin, to be used in a machine for purposes of cheating; a counterfeit coin.
[1953 Lewis *Sagebrush Casinos* 74]
[1887 *OEDS*]
2. A metal weight placed in a die to alter its roll.
[(1950) 1981 Maurer *Lang. of the Underworld* 192]
3. In cards, a packet of stacked cards slipped into a deck by a cheater.
[1983 Martinez *Gambling Scene* 220]

slugger, *n.* A person who uses counterfeit coins in coin-operated machines, especially slot machines.
[1931 *Review Journal* 2/24: 3]

slur, *n.* A method of cheating at dice in which the dice slide rather than tumble when cast.
[*a*1643 *OED*]

slur, *v.* To throw dice in such a fashion that they do not roll, but the number on top when the dice are thrown remain on top when the dice come to rest. Compare CONTROLLED SHOT and SLICK DICE CUP.
[1594 *OED*]

slurring, *n.* The act of throwing dice so they do not roll, but the number on top when the dice are thrown remains on top when the dice come to rest.
1680 Cotton *Compleat Gamester* 11. . . . by *slurring,* that is by taking up your dice as you will have them advantageously lie in your hand, placing the one a top the other, not caring if the uppermost run a Mill-stone (as they use to say) if the undermost run without turning, and therefore a smooth table is altogether requisite for this purpose.
1714 Lucas *Memoirs* 28. And he was very dexterous at *Slurring,* which is, throwing the Dice so smoothly on a Table, that they turn not; for which, the smoothest Part of the Table must be chose; and some are so expert at this, that they'll *slur* a Die a Yard in length without turning. [1668 *OED*]

small misery, *n.* Also called PETIT MISERE. In the card game boston, the declaration that one will not take a single trick.
1843 Green *Exposure* 22. There are also hands in this game called "*small misery*:" in each of these, the person playing it obligates himself not to take a trick out of the twelve, as the rule is for each man to discard one, and yet he follows suit every time he has it, and if he should have one high card, say clubs, and all the rest spades and hearts, he will, if the lead comes from his partner, give him a sign to lead diamonds, on which he will throw his high club, and is then safe.

small nickel, *n.* A fifty-dollar bill, or fifty dollars worth of chips or cash.
[ca. 1961 *Hotel Coll*]

small one, *n.* A one-hundred dollar bill, or one hundred dollars worth of chips or cash.
[ca. 1961 *Hotel Coll*]

small play, *n.* The act of gambling for low stakes.
[1629 *OED*]

small slam, *n.* In bridge, the taking of twelve out of thirteen tricks in a hand. See also LITTLE SLAM. Compare GRAND SLAM.

[1953 Crawford *Consistent Winner* 353]
[1921 *OEDS*]

small table, *n.* A gaming table at which small wagers are accepted and which has a low limit.
[(1950) 1981 Maurer *Lang. of the Underworld* 192]

smart bettor, *n.* A player who is aware of the the various odds and percentages in gambling propositions and acts accordingly. See also SMART MONEY.
[ca. 1961 *Hotel Coll*]

smart money, *n. pl.* Gamblers who supposedly have inside information on how to win in a particular betting proposition.
[ca. 1961 *Hotel Coll*]
[1926 *OEDS*]
→Although ambiguous in form, usage of *smart money* is usually singular in form and use.

smooth, *adj.* In lowball poker, pertaining to the best hand that can be held in a particular version of lowball, such as ace, 2, 3, 4, 5 in straight lowball.
[1968 Wallace *Poker* 224]

smooth call, *n.* In poker, a successful strategy of calling a previous bettor while planning that a following player will raise the bet, which can then be raised again by the player who called the original bet. Similar in operation to a CHECK-RAISE.
[1978 Brunson *How I Made* 548]

smooth seven, *n.* Same as a SLICK SEVEN. See also ROUGH SEVEN.
[1971 Livingston *Poker Strategy* 223]

smother, *v.* In bridge, to draw a high trump card from an opponent and win the trick by playing a higher trump.
[1950 Morehead *Culbertson* 646]

smother play, *n.* In bridge, the act of taking a high trump card from an opponent with a higher trump card.
[1950 Morehead *Culbertson* 646]

smudge, *v.* In pitch, to announce an intention to win all four points.
[1953 Crawford *Consistent Winner* 353]

snake, *v.* **1.** To wave a playing card or bend it slightly so it can be identified later in the game. Compare CORNER-BEND and WAVE.
[ca. 1961 *Hotel Coll*]
2. To cheat at cards.
[*a*1861 *OEDS*]
3. In the phrases:
snake a game, To create a dishonest card game, usually faro, by marking cards, stacking cards, or modifying the dealing box, or shoe.
[1864 *DAE*]
snake the card, In faro, to sneak a card into the dealer's pack. Compare SLIP THE CARDS.
[1890 Quinn *Fools of Fortune* 202]

snake bet, *n.* In roulette, a wager on twelve contiguous numbers on the layout, usually of the same color, such as starting at red 1 and ending at red 34.
[1983 Martinet *Oral Coll*]

snake eyes, *n. pl. Plural in form, but singular in use.* Also written **snake-eyes. 1.** A cast of the number 2 on a pair of dice, one pip showing on each die.
[1949 Blanche *You Can't Win* 23]
[1929 *OEDS*]
2. The die face showing two pips.
[n.d. *DAS*]

snake tell box, *n.* Also shortened to **snake box.** In faro, a dishonest DEALING BOX, or SHOE. Compare SLICK DICE CUP.
[1891 *DA, DAE,* as *snake box*]

snap, *n.* **1.** A temporary or short lived game, such as a faro bank set up for an hour or a few hours in a saloon by a traveling gambler.
1868 Trumps *Pocket Hoyle* 208. *Snap.*—A temporary bank, not a regular or established game.
[1864 *DAE*, 1845 *OEDS*]
2. A twenty-one game.
[1961 Smith and Noble *Quit Winners* 213]
3. Also called a SNAPPER. The act of receiving an ace and a card worth ten points in a game of twenty-one.
[1973 Clark *Oral Coll*]

snap, *v.* **1.** In twenty-one, to deal an ace and a card worth ten points.
[1979 Hughes *Dealing* 41]
2. In the particle construction:
snap off, 1. In hold 'em poker, to win a hand by having a required card dealt as the fifth, or last card dealt face upward.
[1976 Sklansky *Hold 'em Poker*]
2. In poker, to call the bet of a person who is bluffing.
[1978 Brunson *How I Made* 548]

snap house, *n.* Also called a DEADFALL or WOLF HOUSE. A gambling establishment or low dive devoted to cheating victims in gambling game.
[1938 Asbury *Sucker's Progress* 185]

snapper, *n.* **1.** Also called a NATURAL. In twenty-one, an ace and a card worth ten points, dealt as the first two cards to a player or the dealer.
[ca. 1961 *Hotel Coll*]
2. In dice, an accomplice.
[1532 *OED*]

snatch, *v.* In a poker parlor, to take a higher percentage of a pot for the operator of the game than has been agreed upon. See also SNATCH GAME.
1981 Golad *Oral Coll.* He wants his people to deal a snatch game. Say the house is supposed to rake five percent. Any poker dealer should be able to *snatch* twelve percent from a decent sized pot.

snatch game, *n.* In a poker parlor, a game in which the house dealer retains a higher

percentage of the money gambled than he is entitled to.
1981 Golad *Oral Coll.* He wants his people to deal a *snatch game.* Say the house is supposed to rake five percent. Any poker dealer should be able to snatch twelve percent from a decent sized pot.

sneak, *n.* **1.** In whist, a lead of a singleton from a PLAIN SUIT, suit that is not trump.
[1950 Morehead *Culbertson* 646]
2. A cheating move made by a card player who is adding cards to or removing cards from his hand.
1902 Andrews *Artifice* 15. "Hold outs" that are adjusted to the person are of most ingenious construction and very expensive. A sleeve machine which passes the cards into and from the palm by spreading the knees may be worth from seventy-five dollars to several hundred dollars. Some are worked by arm pressure, some pass the cards through an opening in the vest about the usual height the hands are held. One of the most novel and perfect machines ever constructed makes the "*sneak*" by simply expanding the chest an inch or two, or taking a deeper breath than usual.
[Compare *a*1700 *OED,* meaning "pilfering"]

sneak, *v.* In trump games, to lead a card from a weak suit that is not the trump suit.
[1891 *DA, DAE*]

sneak game, *n.* An illegal gambling game, especially without police PROTECTION.
[(1950) 1981 Maurer *Lang. of the Underworld* 192]

sneak joint, *n.* An illegal gambling establishment.
[1979 Newman *Dealer's Special* 6]

sniff, *n.* In the domino variant of muggins, the first doublet tile played, usually the first bone of the game.
1950 Morehead *Culbertson* 427. The first doublet played, whether or not it is set, is the *sniff.* It is open four ways.

snoozer, *n.* The joker in poker games allowing that card to be used as an ace or in straights or flushes.
[1950 Morehead *Culbertson* 646]
[Compare 1862 *OEDS,* meaning "a thief"]

snow, *v.* **1.** In poker, to make an obvious or outrageous bluff; to try to intimidate an opponent, even before cards are completely dealt.
[1963 Steig *Common Sense* 187]
2. In the phrase:
snow the cards, To shuffle a hand or a deck of playing cards in an overhand fashion, moving one or a few from the top of the pack to the bottom, then repeating the action several times. See also FUZZ and MILK, *v.*
[1949 Coffin *Secrets* 186]

snowball, *n.* **1.** In poker, a worthless or unplayable hand, usually a busted straight or flush.
[1973 Preston *Play Poker* 169]
2. In horse racing, unwon stakes that are carried forward in a kitty or pool to the next race. Illegal bookies may declare a *snowball* because of a tie, and hold the money to be divided among the bettors winning on the next race. Sometimes the players who bet on the entries that tied are allowed to pick a choice for the following race without risking additional money.
[1976 Figgs *Gambler* 238]
3. snowballs, *pl.* Also called CANTALOUPES. In craps, misspotted dice showing only the numbers 4, 5, and 6.
1983 Martinet *Oral Coll. Snowballs* are dice with 4, 5, and 6 spots on each, so you can roll only 8 through 12. People will sneak them in for a field bet. They are called *snowballs* because the spots are white and when they roll down the table you can see a lot of white, very little red. All those white spots just run together.

snowball, *v.* In the phrase:
snowball the layout, In faro, to place many small bets on the table layout.
[1943 Maurer *Argot*]

snow-balling, *n.* A betting practice in which the player, after successful bets, increasingly enlarges the minimum amount of the bet.
Compare PARLAY.
1891 *Monte Carlo* 232. But you ought to have seen him on the days when he had been successful for some time, and had piled up before him the money of the bank. Then he would do what is called *snow-balling*—that is, instead of putting 3 Napoleons to start his system, he would begin with 6, or 12, or even 24.

snug, *v.* To hold back a horse in preparation for a DRIVE later in the race.
[(1951) 1981 Maurer *Lang of the Underworld* 227]

social game, *n.* A gambling game, usually at cards, played for small stakes, such as PENNY-ANTE poker.
[1971 Livingston *Poker Strategy* 225]

soda card, *n.* Also shortened to **soda**. In faro, the card that shows in the top of the dealing box before play commences. Compare DEAL CARD and HOCK CARD.
1843 Green *Exposure* 194. The top card, when the deal is first commenced, is called the deal card; this card neither wins nor loses, and on that account is sometimes called the *soda card.*
[1843 *DA,* 1864 *DAE*]

soda to hock, *adj. phr.* Also **soda card to hock.** In faro, pertaining to one entire game of twenty-five turns, from first card to last.
[1902 *DA, DAE, OEDS,* as *soda card to hock*]

soft, *adj.* **1.** Pertaining to money gained easily

through a sure win or by cheating.
[1974 Scarne *Dice* 84]
2. Pertaining to a racetrack on which the dirt is dry but not packed down. Compare SLOPPY and SLOW.
[1974 Ewart *Flatracing* 150]
3. Pertaining to a twenty-one hand that includes an ace and another card or cards not equalling ten points.
[1953 Crawford *Consistent Winner* 353]
4. In craps, pertaining to the numbers 4, 6, 8, or 10 when the number is rolled without doublets, as 3-1, 4-2, and so on.
[1983 Martinet *Oral Coll*]

soft, *n.* **1.** Paper currency in high-stakes betting such as no-limit poker.
[1821 *OEDS,* n.d. *DAS*]
2. In a casino, the fill and credit slips deposited in the drop boxes at a gaming table.
[ca. 1961 *Hotel Coll*]

soft count, *n.* **1.** In twenty-one, a hand in which the ace counts as one or eleven points, depending on the advantage to the hand.
[1968 Thackrey *Nick the Greek* 115]
2. In a casino cage, the record of credit and fill slips and currency taken from a drop box at the end of a shift.
[ca. 1961 *Hotel Coll*]

soft doubling, *n. phr.* In twenty-one, a wagering strategy in which a player may double his bet and receive one additional card when he holds an ace and a card ranked less than ten points.
[ca. 1961 *Hotel Coll*]

soft drop, *n.* In a casino, the receipts for FILL SLIPS, recording the amount of chips brought to the table from the cage. The receipts are put in the DROP BOX attached to the table on which the transaction takes place.
[ca. 1961 *Hotel Coll*]

soft eighteen, *n.* In twenty-one, a total card count that includes an ace and another card or cards valued at seven points. In legal gambling establishments, a dealer may not take another card while holding *soft eighteen.* See also SOFT SEVENTEEN.
[1973 Friedman *Casino Games* 19]

soft hand, *n.* In twenty-one, a hand containing an ace that can have a value of one or eleven points, as declared by the player.
[1973 Friedman *Casino Games* 18]

soft-pad roll, *n.* Also called a SOFT ROLL. In craps, a controlled cast of the dice in which one or both dice spin but do not turn, keeping the same face upward at the end of the cast as the beginning; a form of BLANKET ROLL. See also CONTROLLED SHOT.
[1974 Scarne *Dice* 257]

soft play, *n.* A system of casual betting without paying attention to odds or opportunities.
[1953 Fairfield *Las Vegas* 15]

soft player, *n.* A naive or inexperienced gambler.
[1961 Scarne *Complete Guide* 688]

soft roll, *n.* Same as a SOFT-PAD ROLL.
[1967 Goffman *Interaction Ritual*]

soft seventeen, *n.* In twenty-one, an ace and one or more cards with a point value of 6. Because an ace can count for 1 or 11 points, some legal gambling establishments rule that a dealer must take another card if his first two cards are an ace and a six. See also SOFT SIXTEEN.
[ca. 1961 *Hotel Coll*]

soixante, et le va, *n. clause. French.* In faro, the act of wagering the original amount plus all winnings, six times. Compare TRENTE, ET LE VA.
1843 Green *Exposure* 168. *Soixante, et le va,* is when the player having obtained a trente, ventures all once more, which is signified by making a fifth parolet, either on another card, if he has paroleted on one only before, or by breaking the side of that one which contains four, to pursue his luck in the next deal.

solid bet, *n.* A wager that a player has a good chance to win.
[1961 Scarne *Complete Guide* 688]

solid horse, *n. phr.* A race horse with a record of performing well in its class.
[(1951) 1981 Maurer *Lang. of the Underworld* 227]

solid six, *n.* In keno, a ticket with six numbers bet as a block, as 1, 2, 3, 11, 12, 13.
[1973 Clark *Oral Coll*]

solid suit, *n.* In trump games, all the winning cards of a particular suit other than trump, when held in one hand.
[1950 Morehead *Culbertson* 646]
[1927 *OEDS*]

sophomore, *n.* In horse racing, a three-year-old horse.
[1981 Passer *Winning Big* 233]

spade over, *n.* In casino, a point for each spade collected beyond eight spades.
[1950 Morehead *Culbertson* 647]

spades, *n. pl.* **1.** *Plural in form, but singular in use.* One of four suits in a pack of cards, the others being HEARTS, DIAMONDS, and CLUBS, characterized by a black figure shaped like a leaf or pointed spade, originally a sword. In some trump games such as bridge, *spades* ranks first among the suits, so that a bid of one spade is higher than a bid of one heart, which is the second ranked suit.
[1651 *OED*]
2. spade, *sing.* The black figure shaped like a leaf or pointed spade.
[1598 *OED*]

spadillo, *n. Spanish.* In card games such as ombre, primero or quadrille, the ace of spades. Compare BASTO and CINQUO PRIMERO and MALLILLIO and PUNTO.
1680 Cotton *Compleat Gamester* 70. There are

two suits, Black and Red; of the Black there is first the *Spadillo,* or Ace of Spades; the Mallillio or black Deuce, the Basto or Ace of Clubs . . . The Red Ace enters into the fourth place when it is Trump, and it is called Punto then, otherwise only called an Ace.

1714 Lucas *Memoirs* 137. . . . and played very well at Primero; in which Game it is to be observ'd, that whoever of the Players has in his hand Cinquo Primero, which is a Sequence of 5 of the best Cards, assisted with *Spadillo,* which is the Ace of Spades, and counted the best Card, or any other valuable Trump, he is sure to be successful over his Adversary.
[1680 *OED*]

spatula, *n.* In games like chemin-de-fer, a thin wooden paddle used by the dealer to move cards about the table. Compare RAKE and STICK.
[1976 Figgis *Gambler's Handbook* 238]

speeding, *n.* In poker, the act of playing in a loose fashion, making large bets and bluffing often. See also SPEEDY.
1983 Clark *Oral Coll.* He was knocked out of the [poker] tournament early. He was caught *speeding* . . . That means he was playing fast and loose, making a lot of bluffs and got caught in them.

speed jam, *n.* In horse racing, an instance of being outdistanced. *Facetious use.*
[(1957) 1981 Maurer *Lang. of the Underworld* 227]

speedy, *n.* A poker player who makes large bets and moves the game along at a rapid pace. See also SPEEDING.
1981 Golad *Oral Coll.* A *speedy* keeps the game moving and lively. He'll make large bets, sometimes right out of the blue, bluff a fair amount, and generally chatter a lot. That doesn't mean he's a bad player or a good player. A *speedy* won't win or lose much more than anybody else, he just has bigger swings in profit and loss.

spell, *n.* A period of time during which a player wins or loses a series of wagers. See also COLD and HOT.
1983 Martinet *Oral Coll.* All *spells* are "hot" or "cold." Once in a while they will be "freezing." But no one seems to have a "medium" or "lukewarm" *spell.*
[(1950) 1981 Maurer *Lang. of the Underworld* 192]
[Compare 1740 *OED,* meaning "a period of specified weather"]

spike, *n.* **1.** In poker, another name for an ACE.
[1978 Brunson *How I Made* 549]
2. In lowball poker, two cards of the same rank; a PAIR.
[1968 Wallace *Poker* 225]

spin, *v.* In dice, to make a CONTROLLED CAST so that the dice rotate with the same faces up as they travel across the playing surface.
[(1950) 1981 Maurer *Lang. of the Underworld* 192]

spindle, *n.* The horizontally mounted arrow or pointer that spins above a stationary circle with numbers or figures representing betting opportunities on a variation of a WHEEL-OF-FORTUNE.
[1961 Scarne *Complete Guide* 688]

spin expert, *n.* In craps, a person who can control dice so that they rotate horizontally during a cast and come to rest with the same faces upward as were up at the beginning of the cast. See also SPIN, *v.*
[ca. 1961 *Hotel Coll*]

spinner, *n.* **1.** In poker, a winning streak; a series of winning hands by the same player.
[1968 Wallace *Poker* 225]
2. In two-up, the person who tosses the coins onto the playing surface.
[1964 Wykes *Illustrated Guide* 329]
[1911 *OEDS*]
3. In dominos, the doublet tile used to start the game.
[1976 Figgis *Gambler's Handbook* 78]
4. A thrown die that spins for a few moments on one corner before coming to rest.
[1983 Martinet *Oral Coll*]

spitballing, *n.* A cheating system used in card games in which two players conspire to cheat a third; FALSE PICKING.
[1961 Scarne *Complete Guide* 688]

spit card, *n.* In variations of draw poker, a card that is dealt face up in the middle of the table and serves, along with the other three of the same rank, as a wild card for each player.
[1968 Wallace *Poker* 225]

splash the pot, *v. phr.* In poker, to throw chips directly into the pot rather than placing a bet next to the pot so other players can determine that the correct amount is being bet.
[ca. 1961 *Hotel Coll*]

split, *n.* **1.** In faro, the loss of half the bet made by a player when two cards of the same denomination appear in the same turn.
1868 Trumps *Pocket Hoyle* 205. Whenever two cards of the same denomination, as, for example, two Sevens or two Fours, appear in the same turn, the dealer takes half the money found upon such card—this is called a "*split,*" and is said to be the bank's greatest percentage.
[1843 *DA,* as *splitting;* 1864 *DAE*]
2. In twenty-one, a hand with two cards of the same rank that the player decides to separate and make into two hands by putting up a wager equal in value to his first wager, then treating each card as the base for a separate hand.
[1977 Anness *Dummy Up*]
3. In highlow poker, one-half of the total amount in the pot.
[1981 Golad *Oral Coll*]

4. In craps, a single chip used to cover two or more bets.
[1983 Martinet *Oral Coll.* Most of the time a *split* is made on C and E [a proposition bet on craps or eleven, resolved on the next roll of the dice]. It just means you are covering two or more bets with a single check.
5. Especially in poker, two hands of equal value.
[1908 *DA, DAE*]

split, *v.* **1.** In twenty-one, to separate a pair, making each card the base for a new hand.
[1953 Crawford *Consistent Winner* 353]
2. In the phrase:
split openers, In draw poker games requiring a pair of jacks or higher to begin betting, to discard one card of the pair after initiating the betting round. The player doing so must announce his intention and place the discard on the table away from the discard pile so that it can be checked after the showdown.
[1963 Steig *Common Sense* 187]

split bet, *n.* Same as SPLIT PLAY. In roulette, a wager on two adjacent numbers of a layout made by placing the chips on the line between the numbers.
[1961 Scarne *Complete Guide* 688]

split choice, *n.* In horse racing, equal odds on the two favorite horses in a race.
[(1951) 1981 Maurer *Lang. of the Underworld* 227]

split-edge work, *n.* Also called SAW-TOOTH EDGE WORK. Jagged cuts made on the edge of a die to affect the roll of the die on a soft surface. Compare BARR DICE and LOADED DICE.
[1974 Scarne *Dice* 242]

split pair, *n.* **1.** In stud poker, a card dealt face downward and one of a matching rank dealt face upward to the same player.
[1963 Steig *Common Sense* 187]
2. In twenty-one, two cards of matching rank that have been separated as base cards for two hands rather than one.
[1973 Friedman *Casino Games* 24]

split play, *n.* Same as a SPLIT BET.
[1964 Lemmel *Gambling* 192]

split pot, *n.* In poker, a pot divided equally for players with winning hands of equal value.
[ca. 1961 *Hotel Coll*]

split race, *n.* In horse racing, a race divided into heats, usually because the track cannot accommodate the number of entries.
[ca. 1961 *Hotel Coll*]

splitter, *n.* A die that has been altered so that some faces appear more often than others. See also BUSTERS.
[(1951) 1981 Maurer *Lang. of the Underworld* 192]

split week, *n.* In poker, four cards of a straight with the middle card missing, as 10, jack, king, ace; the queen is required to make the straight. Compare INSIDE STRAIGHT.
[n.d. *DAS*]

spoon, *v.* To insert a concave or spoon-shaped device into the payout chute of a slot machine so that coins will continue to drop out after a winning combination is paid.
[ca. 1961 *Hotel Coll*]
[Compare 1715 *OED,* meaning "to lift or transfer by means of a spoon"]

sport, *n.* **1.** Gambling activity.
[1856 *DAE, DA*]
2. A gambler, especially one who appears to be carefree and prosperous.
[1859 *DAE*]
3. Among professional gamblers, an inexperienced or naive gambler who is easy prey for cheaters.
[1973 Clark *Oral Coll*]

sporting book, *n.* A record of bets placed with a SPORTS BOOK.
[n.d. *Century Dict.*]

sporting gentleman, *n.* A gambler. *Old-fashioned.* [1835 *DAE*]

sporting house, *n.* A place frequented by gamblers and bettors. *Old-fashioned.*
[1857 *DAE,* 1891 *DA*]

sporting man, *n.* A gambler. *Old-fashioned.*
[1833 *DA,* 1840 *DAE*]

sporting room, *n.* A place frequented by gamblers and bettors. *Old-fashioned.*
[1878 *DA*]

sports bet, *n.* A wager on the outcome of a sporting event, such as a football game or a horse race.
[ca. 1961 *Hotel Coll*]

sports book, *n.* Also written **sportsbook.** A gambling establishment, usually legalized, that receives wagers on the outcome of sporting events such as ball games and horse races. See also RACEBOOK.
[1973 Clark *Oral Coll*]

sports line, *n.* The information provided by a SPORTS BOOK concerning ODDS, POINT SPREADS, and so on for sporting events.
[1971 McQuaid *Gambler's Digest* 317]

sportsman, *n.* A gambler. *Old-fashioned.*
[1740 *DAE, DA*]
→The following quotation found in *OED* under *sporting man* shows an interesting distinction in usage from *sportsman:*

> 1899 *Pall Mall Gazette* 22 Oct. 6/1. Every sporting man is flattered if termed a sportsman, but it would be almost an insult to speak to a sportsman as a sporting man.

sports parlay card, *n. phr.* A two-part betting form provided by SPORTS BOOKS on which a bettor may select a number of teams to win their contests. Normally, all teams selected must win

in order for the bettor to collect. The *sports parlay card* most commonly lists football games.
[1978 Alexander *Glossary* 15]

sports pool, *n.* A common fund among several bettors in which each participant is assigned a score for the outcome of a sporting event. The person whose score corresponds to the outcome of the sporting event wins the fund.
[ca. 1961 *Hotel Coll*]

spot, *n.* **1. a.** A pip on a playing card, die, or domino.
[1578 *OEDS;* 1843 *DA, DAE*]
→Usually characterized by a designating number such as *ten spot, eight spot.* See def. 6.
b. spots, *pl.* A deck of playing cards.
[ca. 1961 *Hotel Coll*]
[*DAS*]
2. A number selected on a keno ticket.
[1973 Clark *Oral Coll*]
3. A betting space on a table layout, as in twenty-one or baccarat.
[ca. 1961 *Hotel Coll*]
4. In playing cards, an ace.
[1968 Wallace *Poker* 225]
5. A favorable betting opportunity. See also SPOT BETTOR.
[1973 Clark *Oral Coll*]
[(1951) 1981 Maurer *Lang. of the Underworld* 227]
6. A banknote of specified amount, as *five spot, ten spot,* etc.
[n.d. *DAS*]

spot, *v.* **1.** To offer ODDS, POINTS, or some other inducement to a bettor in an attempt to arrange a wager.
[1961 Scarne *Complete Guide* 688]
2. To detect an irregularity or a cheating move in a gambling game.
[1974 Scarne *Dice* 249]
3. In horse racing, to concede weight to a horse by adding weights to another.
[1978 Ainslie *Complete Guide* 299]
4. To single out or guess beforehand the winner of a race.
[1857 *OED*]

spot bettor, *n.* Also called a **spot player.** A person who wagers only at the most favorable opportunities.
[(1951) 1981 Maurer *Lang. of the Underworld* 227]

spot card, *n.* A playing card with pips; a card numbered ace through ten. Compare COURT CARD and PAINT-SKIN.
[1949 Coffin *Secrets* 186]

spotted papers, *n. pl.* Also shortened to PAPERS. Playing cards with markings on the back so they can be identified while face down.
[1862 *DAE,* at *paper*]

spotter, *n.* **1.** An employee of a gambling establishment who watches for cheaters or irregular play. See also EYE IN THE SKY.
[1953 Lewis *Sagebrush Casinos* 94]
[Compare 1878 *OED,* meaning "one employed by a company to keep watch on employees"]
2. A cheat's accomplice.
[(1951) 1981 Maurer *Lang. of the Underworld* 228]

spread, *n.* **1.** Also called the POINT SPREAD. In sports books, the points assigned to a particular team, usually in football or basketball games, to make a wager more attractive and challenging to a bettor.
[1973 Clark *Oral Coll*]
2. The use of signals by confederate card cheaters.
[1968 Wallace *Poker* 225]
3. In games like panguingue or pinochle, the melding of CONDITION sets of cards.
[1950 Morehead *Culbertson* 647]
4. a. Also called the SHOWDOWN. In poker, the exposure of all cards by players still contending for the pot after all betting rounds have been completed.
[1949 Coffin *Secrets* 186]
b. In bridge, the cards shown to prove the SLAM claimed.
[1929 *OEDS*]

spread, *v.* **1.** Among card cheats, to exchange information or cards.
[1968 Wallace *Poker* 225]
2. a. In poker, to expose the cards of players still contending for the pot after all betting rounds have been completed.
[1953 Crawford *Consistent Winner* 354]
b. In games like gin rummy or pinochle or bridge, to meld condition sets of cards in order to be credited with claimed points.
[1929 *OEDS*]
3. Of a twenty-one dealer, to fan the cards face downward in a semicircle on the table when relieved by another dealer.
[ca. 1961 *Hotel Coll*]
4. In a casino, to separate chips of different denominations after a player has won a bet, in order to pay the player accurately. Compare BARBER POLE and DIRTY STACK.
1983 Martinet *Oral Coll.* If a dealer gets a barber pole or a dirty stack [a stack of chips of different denominations], a boxman or pit boss will tell him to *spread* it before he pays off. *Spreading* is breaking down a stack by denominations in order to count it or pay it off.
5. In the phrases:
spread the action, In bookmaking, to place bets with other bookmakers when too much has been bet on one side of a proposition and the bookmaker runs the risk of losing heavily. See also LAYOFF.
[1973 Clark *Oral Coll*]
spread the play, Same as SPREAD THE ACTION.
[1960 Cook *Gambling, Inc.* 268]

spring, *v.* In poker, to make an unexpectedly large bet.
[1961 Scarne *Complete Guide* 688]

spring table, *n.* A card table specifically constructed to hide cards, which can be retrieved by means of a spring attached to the underside of the playing surface.
1843 Green *Exposure* 119. In other establishments, I have seen *spring tables* . . . There is in the table a crack or split, which seems to be from a defect in the wood. The whole bottom of the table is boxed up, as if it had a drawer, and the inside is so fixed, that a card let down into this crack will stand upright. The player can at any time push it up by means of a peg, which projects a little from the bottom of the table, using his knee for the purpose.

sprint, *n.* In horse racing, a race of less than a mile, usually seven furlongs or less.
[ca. 1961 *Hotel Coll*]

sprinter, *n.* In horse or dog racing, an animal best suited for short races.
[1971 McQuaid *Gambler's Digest* 317]

spur, *n.* Also spelled **spurr.** A method for marking cards by indenting the edges with the thumbnail or some sharp instrument. Compare CORNER-BEND.
1680 Cotton *Compleat Gamester* 95. In dealing these Rooks have a trick they call the *Spurr,* and that is, as good Cards come into their hand that they may know them again by the outside . . . somewhere on the outside they give them a gentle touch with their nail.
[1674 *OED*]

square, *n.* In the prepositional phrase:
upon the square, In a fair or honest manner. Compare ON THE SQUARE.
1714 Lucas *Memoirs* 67. There was no Game but what he was an absolute Artist at, either *upon the Square* or foul Play.
1726 Wilson *Art and Mystery* 35. It has been observed, that when ever a Sharper plays *upon the Square,* he commonly loses his money.

square, *v.* **1.** To arrange a pack of cards so that all four sides are even and thereby demonstrate that none of the edges of the cards have been trimmed to make some narrower or shorter. Compare STRIPPERS.
[1973 Clark *Oral Coll*]
2. To measure a die with a micrometer to insure that none of the faces or edges have been shaved. Compare CALIPERS.
[1983 Martinet *Oral Coll*]

square, *adj.* **1.** Fair; in an honest fashion.
[1606 *OED*]
2. In harness racing, pertaining to a steady, even gait, especially that of a trotter or pacer.
[(1832) 1868 *DA*]

square bet, *n.* In roulette, a wager on a block of four contiguous numbers. The payoff for a win is usually eight to one.
[1961 Scarne *Complete Guide* 688]

square count, *n.* An honest or fair payoff on a wager, especially one that includes odds.
1983 Martinet *Oral Coll.* When a shooter takes the correct odds on a bet [at craps], say ten bucks on a nickel [five dollar] bet on the 4 or 10 point, then he gets a *square count* of two for one on the back [the odds], and flat on the front [even money on the original bet].

squared cards, *n. pl.* In faro, an honest deck of cards. [1938 *DA*]

square dealing, *n.* Also **square deal. 1.** A fair distribution of cards for players.
[1633 *OED,* as *square dealing*]
2. An honest deal, especially at faro, made so because none of the cards have been trimmed on the edges to allow narrower or shorter cards to be selected by the dealer or with a crooked dealing box such as a NEEDLE SQUEEZE, which allows off-sized cards to be selected from the pack.
[1883 *DA, DAE,* as *square deal*]

square deck, *n.* **1.** An honest deck of cards with no edges trimmed, a condition that is detectable when the deck is squared, or stacked so that all four sides are even.
[1973 Clark *Oral Coll*]
2. In faro, a pack of apparently honest cards that have been prearranged by the dealer or an accomplice. Compare STACKED DECK.
[1943 Maurer *Argot*]

square decker, *n.* A person who prearranges a pack of unmarked or untrimmed cards, especially at faro. Compare STACKED DECK.
[1943 Maurer *Argot*]

square dice, *n.* Dice that have not been altered internally or externally; honest dice. Compare BARR DICE and LOADED DICE and MISMARKED DICE.
[1890 Quinn *Fools of Fortune* 283]

square-gaited, *adj.* In horse racing, pertaining to a trotter or pacer with a steady, even gait.
[1868 *DA*]

square game, *n.* **1.** An honest card game, especially a game that features unmarked and untrimmed cards. Compare SQUARE CARDS and SQUARE DEALING and SQUARE DECK.
[1938 *DA*]
2. Any gambling game that is conducted without guile or cheating.
1891 *Monte Carlo* 185. Sometimes we hear people say that the bank of Monte Carlo keeps a *square game,* and you will find nothing in this book which says that it does not. We mean by that, that there is no special contrivance that may change the regular working of the Roulette, nor is there any well-substantiated accusation that the dealer at the Trente-et-Quarante game does otherwise than act like a machine; i.e. distribute the cards on the table with absolute impartiality.

square john, *n.* A dupe; a victim of cheaters, especially one who appears to be completely honest and naive.
[1962 Garcia *Marked Cards* 163]

square pacer, *n.* A harness racer with a steady gait. [1832 *DA*]

square pair, *n.* In craps, another term for two fours on a pair of dice; a HARD eight.
1983 Martinet *Oral Coll.* A pair of fours on the dice is a hard eight or a *square pair.*

square play, *n.* An honest move in a gambling game. [1591 *OED*]

squares and rounds, *n. phr. Plural in form, but singular in use.* A dishonest deck of playing cards, some of which have been trimmed on the edges, others on the corners.
[1890 Quinn *Fools of Fortune* 198]

square trot, *n.* The steady gait of a horse in harness racing.
[1868 *DA*]

square trotter, *n.* A horse in harness racing with a steady gait.
[1832 *DA*]

squeeze, *n.* **1.** Any of a variety of controls or devices used to operate a piece of gambling equipment, such as an electromagnet on a dice table, a friction handle on a wheel of fortune or roulette wheel, a lever on a faro dealing box or baccarat shoe, and so on.
[1961 Scarne *Complete Guide* 688]
2. squeezes, *pl.* Dice that have been compressed in a vice so as to alter their shape and, consequently, roll a predictable number.
[(1950) 1981 Maurer *Lang. of the Underworld* 192]
3. A tactic in bridge designed to force a player to discard prematurely a game winning card.
[1926 *OEDS*]

squeeze, *v.* **1.** To spread a hand of playing cards slowly to read the faces.
[1968 Wallace *Poker* 225]
2. To hold a pack of cards in the hand and push together the edges of the top card between the thumb and little finger in order to see surreptitiously the face value of the card.
[1973 Clark *Oral Coll*]
3. In poker, to force a following bettor to call a bet he knows will be raised by a still later bettor. See also WHIPSAW.
[1949 Coffin *Secrets* 186]
4. In the phrases:
squeeze in, To slowly peep at a playing card in one's hand.
[1983 Martinez *Gambling Scene* 221]
squeeze out, Same as SQUEEZE IN.
[1971 Livingston *Poker Strategy* 225]

squeeze bet, *n.* In poker, a bet made by a player that is designed to force another player to bet on a weak hand or fold.
[1968 Wallace *Poker* 225]

squeeze play, *n.* **1.** In bridge, the use of a SQUEEZE. [1926 *OEDS*]
2. In baseball, a tactic which calls for the runner on third base attempting to reach home plate as the batter bunts the ball away from the catcher.
[1905 *OEDS*]

squeeze raise, *n.* In poker, an increased bet designed to force another player to bet on a weak hand or fold.
[1968 Wallace *Poker* 225]

squeezers, *n. pl.* A deck of playing cards that have the rank and suit pictured in the upper left-hand corner. *Obsolescent.*
[1871 *DA, DAE,* 1876 *OEDS*]
→Modern decks of playing cards are uniformly marked this way. However, the practice began with poker players using cards produced by Lawrence Brothers and New York Consolidated Card Company.

squeeze spindle, *n.* A hidden paddle on a wheel of fortune or similar device with which the operator of the game may apply pressure to control the wheel.
[1891 *DA*]

squeeze wheel, *n.* A wheel of fortune or roulette wheel that can be controlled by the operator using a SQUEEZE SPINDLE.
[1909 *DA*]

squib, *n.* A decoy or SHILL in a gambling establishment. *Rare.*
[1731 *OED*]

squirt, *v.* In the phrase:
squirt dimes, To work as a dealer on a table that features a ten-cent minimum for wagers.
1985 Martinet *Oral Coll.* I once worked *squirting dimes.* That's a game that has a ten-cent minimum and all transactions are usually in coin, as opposed to a game in which checks [chips] are used.

squirter, *n.* A craps dealer who works at a table that features a ten-cent minimum for wagers.
[1973 Clark *Oral Coll*]

stabbing, *n.* A method for throwing dice from a DICE BOX with a narrow bottom inside, whereby the caster may arrange a predetermined number.
1680 Cotton *Compleat Gamester* 12. . . . by *Stabbing,* that is, by having a Smooth Box, and small in the bottom, you drop in both your Dice in such manner as you would have them sticking therein by reason of its narrowness, the Dice lying one upon the other; so that turning up the Box, the Dice never tumble.
[1680 *OED*]

stable, *n.* A group of horses owned or managed by one person or partnership. Compare RACING STABLE.
[1810 *OED*]

stable boy's favorite, *n. phr.* A method for throwing dice on dirt so a desired number lands face upward. Compare CONTROLLED SHOT.
[1974 Scarne *Dice* 256]

stack, *n.* **1. a.** Gambling chips placed atop one another.
[1949 Coffin Secrets 187]
[Compare 1892 *OEDS,* meaning "pile of money"]

b. In a casino, a column of twenty gambling chips of the same denomination.
[1977 Anness *Dummy Up*]
2. In mah jongg, two superposed tiles in a WALL.
[1950 Morehead *Culbertson* 647]

stack, *v.* **1.** To place a group of gambling chips atop one another in a column.
[1896 *DAE*]
2. To arrange the sequence of a pack of cards before the deal for the purposes of cheating.
[1825 *DA,* 1896 *DAE*]
3. In the clause:
stack it or rack it, In a casino, a directive from a dealer to a player, to pick up the winnings from a previous bet or combine the winnings and the previous bet into a single wager.
[1983 Martinet *Oral Coll*]

stacked deal, *n.* In cards, a deal made with a STACKED DECK.
[ca. 1961 *Hotel Coll*]

stacked deck, *n.* A pack of playing cards with a prearranged sequence.
[1961 Scarne *Complete Guide* 688]

stag craps, *n.* An informal and illegal CRAPS game. See also ALLEY CRAPS and ARMY CRAPS and BLANKET CRAPS.
[1983 Martinet *Oral Coll*]

stake, *n.* **1.** Also called a BANKROLL. The amount of money available to a gambler.
[1968 Wallace *Poker* 225]
2. An amount of money or something else of value bet or wagered on the outcome of a gambling event.
[1540 *OED*]
3. In racing: **a.** The prize money for a race supplied by both the owner and the racetrack officials.
[1696 *OED*]
b. Often **stakes.** Short for STAKES RACE.
[(1951) 1981 Maurer *Lang. of the Underworld* 228]
[1734 *OED*]
4. The commission paid to a winning jockey, trainer, driver, or groom.
[1968 Ainslie *Complete Guide* 454]

stake, *v.* **1.** To make a wager or bet.
[1591 *OED*]
2. To loan money to or otherwise provide financial support to a gambler.
[1973 Clark *Oral Coll*]
[1894 *OEDS*]

stake horse, *n.* In horse racing, an animal with the quality or performance history required to win a STAKES RACE.
[ca. 1961 *Hotel Coll*]

stake money, *n.* An amount of money designated for gambling, especially an amount intended for a loan to a gambler.
[1943 Maurer *Argot*]
[1810 *OED*]

stakes play, *n.* Also called TABLE STAKES. In poker, a requirement that a player can bet only the amount of money on the table in front of him when the hand begins and cannot produce additional amounts after play of the hand begins.
[1968 Thackrey *Nick the Greek* 217]

stakes player, *n.* In poker, a participant in a game at which wagering is restricted to the amount of money in front of a player when the hand begins.
[1982 Martin *Introduction* 20]

stakes race, *n.* Also written **stake race.** A race in which the owners of the entries provide at least part of the prize money, or purse.
[1955 Hillis *Pari-Mutuel Betting* 118]
[1896 *OEDS,* as *stake-race*]

stall gate, *n.* In horse racing, a starting gate made up with a series of partitions to separate each horse from its neighbor.
[1978 Ainslie *Complete Guide* 299]

stallion, *n.* In horse racing, an uncastrated horse. Compare GELDING.
[(*a*1388 *OED,* 1747 *DAE*]

stamped cards, *n. pl.* Dishonest playing cards that have markings placed on the back during the printing process and are sold to cheaters with a key describing how to read the markings. Compare COSMETICS.
[1890 Quinn *Fools of Fortune* 230]

stamping machine, *n.* In keno, a punch-clock used for stamping a game number, date, and time on the back of the original copy of a KENO TICKET.
[1978 Alexander *Glossary* 15]

stand, *n.* In dice, the raised area from which onlookers observe the game.
[(1950) 1951 Maurer *Lang. of the Underworld* 192]

stand, *v.* **1.** In card games such as draw poker and twenty-one, to play a hand with the cards one holds, without requesting other or additional cards. Compare PASS.
[1824 *OED*]
2. In craps, to decline one's turn to cast the dice.
[1983 Martinez *Gambling Scene* 221]
3. In the phrases:
stand dead, Of a casino dealer, to stand at an empty table and wait for players to come and gamble.
[1983 Martinet *Oral Coll*]
stand pat, In games like draw poker and twenty-one, to play a hand without requesting different or additional cards.
[1882 *DA, DAE, OED*]
stand stiff, In twenty-one, to stay, refuse additional cards, when holding a hand worth 12 through 16 points.
[1973 Clark *Oral Coll*]
stand up, 1. In a casino, to become a FLOORMAN in a casino pit after being a BOXMAN. A boxman

sits at one table, while a floorman watches over two or more tables.
[1983 Martinet *Oral Coll*]
2. Of a mediocre poker hand, to win a pot in spite of a player's misgivings.
[1983 Martinez *Gambling Scene* 222]

standoff, *n.* **1.** Also written **stand-off.** Also called a PUSH. A tie; an outcome of an event in which no one wins or loses. Usually, all bets are off or the bettor gets his money back.
[1843 *DA,* 1895 *OED*]
2. A betting system at faro in which a player wagers on a card of a certain rank to win or lose, then, when that card appears, reverses the wager until the next appearance of a card of that rank, at which time, he reverses the wager again. Compare STANDPAT SYSTEM.
[1943 Maurer *Argot*]

standpat system, *n.* Also called **stand pat to stand off, and switch every time you have action.** In faro, a betting strategy in which all bets ride until betting by others develops, at which time the bettor reverses all his other bets. Compare STANDOFF.
[(1943) 1981 Maurer *Lang. of the Underworld* 140]

start, *n.* In the phrase:
the start. In cribbage, the state of the pack after the cards have been shuffled, but before they have been dealt.
1863 Pardon *Hoyle's* 97. *The Start*—The state of the pack after being cut and before the cards are dealt.
→In modern cribbage play, the pack is not cut until after the deal.

starter, *n.* **1.** Also called a SHILL or PROP. A person employed by a gambling establishment to sit at a table and play until more players join the game.
[1977 Puzo *Inside Las Vegas* 152]
2. In cribbage, the card cut by the non-dealer to initiate the play of the hand.
[1953 Crawford *Consistent Winner* 354]
3. a. Any entry in a race or a contest.
[1983 Martinez *Gambling Scene* 222]
[1847 *OED*]
b. A member of a team at the beginning of a competition, such as basketball, football, baseball, etc.
[1967 *OEDS*]
4. A person who gives the signals to begin a race.
[1622 *OED*]

starter handicap, *n.* The handicap assigned to a horse that has not raced before.
[1971 McQuaid *Gambler's Digest* 317]

starting box, *n.* In dog racing, one of a series of boxes placed at the starting line in which the dogs are held until the beginning of a race, when the doors to all the boxes are opened simultaneously.
[1968 Buchele *Greyhound Racing* 95]

starting gate, *n.* In horse racing, the mechanical barrier that restrains the horses until the race begins, when the doors to all the stalls are opened simultaneously. See also STALL GATE.
[1898 *OED*]

starting price, *n.* The final odds on a horse as the race begins, as determined by the total amount of money wagered on each horse at the PARI-MUTUEL WINDOWS. Compare MORNING LINE and LATE LINE.
[1964 Wykes *Illustrated Guide* 329]

star wheel, *n.* In a mechanical slot machine, the large flywheel that controls the reels.
[1973 Clark *Oral Coll*]
[Compare 1848 *OED,* meaning "a wheel with radial projections or teeth, used in winding machines"]

stash, *n.* The portion of a gambler's bankroll kept in reserve for later play.
[1973 Preston *Play Poker* 159]
[Compare 1914 *OEDS,* meaning "a hoard, cache"]

station, *n.* In keno, the designated working area or window assigned to a KENO WRITER.
[ca. 1961 *Hotel Coll*]

station number, *n.* In policy or numbers, a specific position in a group of numbers, such as the third digit of the number listing the total number of stock shares traded in one day.
[1938 Asbury *Sucker's Progress* 92]

station saddle, *n.* In policy or numbers, a bet on numbers in two specific positions in a group of numbers, such as the third and fifth digit of the number listing the total number of stock shares traded in one day.
[1938 Asbury *Sucker's Progress* 92]
[1938 *DA* under *saddle*]

stay, *v.* **1.** In poker, to remain in contention for a pot by meeting the betting requirements.
[1861 *DA,* 1882 *OED*]
2. In twenty-one, to decline additional cards.
[1964 Wykes *Illustrated Guide* 329]
3. In racing, to hold out, exhibit powers of endurance. [1843 *OED*]
4. In the phrase:
stay the line, Same as PLAY THE NUTS.
[(1951) 1981 Maurer *Lang. of the Underworld* 228]

stayer, *n.* **1.** In poker, a hand that is worth betting on, but is not necessarily strong enough to merit raising the bet of another player.
[1949 Coffin *Secrets* 187]
2. A horse without great speed, but one whose ability is strong in longer races.
1889 Ellangowan *Sporting Anecdotes* 336. *Stayer.*—A horse whose forte is endurance rather than speed.
[1862 *OED*]

steal, *v.* In the phrases:
steal a hand, In poker, to win a pot or hand by successfully bluffing the rest of the players while holding a mediocre or poor hand.

[1973 Preston *Play Poker* 169]
steal a pot, Same as STEAL A HAND.
[1968 Adams *Western Words*]

steam, *v.* To increase the size of bets after losing. Compare PARLAY.
[1978 Brunson *How I Made* 549]

steamer, *n.* A person who increases the size of bets after losing in an attempt to recoup losses.
[1968 Thackrey *Nick the Greek*]

stecq, *n.* In romestecq, the last trick of the hand.
[1950 Morehead *Culbertson* 648]

steer, *v.* To direct a potential player to a gambling game or establishment, usually illegal.
[1889 *OED, DA;* in *Century Dict.*]

steerer, *n.* Also called STEER MAN. A representative of the operator of a gambling game or establishment who receives a commission or wages for guiding potential players to the location of the game, usually an illegal game. See also ROPER.
[1873 *OEDS,* 1875 *DAE, DA,* 1883 *OED*]

steer game, *n.* A dishonest gambling game to which victims are brought by STEERERS, or persons who are given a percentage of what the victim loses.
[1961 Scarne *Complete Guide* 688]

steer joint, *n.* An illegal gambling establishment that normally features cheating of players.
[(1950) 1981 Maurer *Lang. of the Underworld* 192]

steer man, *n.* Same as a STEERER.
[1973 Binion *Recollections* 11]

steer money, *n.* Money paid as a commission or wage to individuals who guide potential players to the location of an illegal game.
[1983 Martinet *Oral Coll*]

stenographer, *n.* In poker, another term for a QUEEN.
[1949 Coffin *Secrets* 187]

step, *n.* A playing card which the dealer deliberately allows to extend slightly beyond the rest of the deck so a confederate may cut the pack at that place.
1888 Kunard *Card Tricks* 174. The *Step* is a particular card which is placed by the shuffler in such a position as to project slightly beyond the others, so that when he offers the cards to be cut to his opponent, this is almost sure to be the turn-up.

step, *v.* To cut a stacked deck of cards in such a fashion as to retain the original sequence of cards, especially by using a STEP in cutting the cards.
[1968 Wallace *Poker* 225]

step bet, *n.* In poker rooms, a betting process in which later betting rounds have a higher limit than early betting rounds.
1981 Golad *Oral Coll.* In hold 'em games, there is a *step bet.* In the first betting round, the limit may be five dollars, with an increase to a ten-dollar limit after the flop. You can have a one-three game, a five-ten game, and so on.

steward, *n.* In horse racing, a track official who serves as a judge, oversees races, investigates claims of fouls, and sets fines for infractions.
[1703 *OED*]

stick, *n.* **1.** In craps, the wooden or rattan cane used to move the dice to the shooter. Compare RAKE.
[(1950) 1981 Maurer *Lang. of the Underworld* 192]
2. Short for STICKMAN. In craps, the person who moves the dice to the shooter.
[(1950) 1981 Maurer *Lang. of the Underworld* 192]
[*DAS*]
3. Also called a SHILL. An employee of a gambling establishment who plays at a game as an inducement for others to play.
[ca. 1961 *Hotel Coll*]
[*c*1930 *DAS*]
4. sticks, *pl. a.* In mah jongg, another term for the suit of BAMBOOS.
[1950 Morehead *Culbertson* 648]
b. Local players whom a STICKHANDLER recruits to act as shills.
[(1947) 1981 Maurer *Lang. of the Underworld* 172]
5. In horse racing, same as BAT.
[(1951) 1981 Maurer *Lang. of the Underworld* 192]

stick, *v.* Same as STAND. In poker and twenty-one, to play with the cards one is dealt, without requesting other or additional cards. Compare DRAW, *v.* (def. 2).
[1973 Clark *Oral Coll*]

sticker, *n.* **1.** Same as STICKMAN.
[1983 Martinet *Oral Coll*]
2. stickers, *pl.* Cleated horseshoes designed for specific track conditions. Compare PLATE.
[1978 Ainslie *Complete Guide* 299]

stick horse, *n.* In horse racing, a racehorse that performs best when hit with the whip.
[1978 Ainslie *Complete Guide* 299]

stickman, *n.* In bank craps, the dealer who moves the dice about the table to the various players, calls the numbers as they are rolled, and handles the proposition bets in the center of the table layout.
[(1950) 1981 Maurer *Lang. of the Underworld* 192]

stiff, *n.* **1.** A player in a casino who does not tip the dealers.
[1977 Anness *Dummy Up*]
2. An unlucky player, or one who loses consistently.
[(1950) 1981 Maurer *Lang. of the Underworld* 192]
3. In twenty-one, a hand with a total point count 12 to 16, usually without an ace.
[1964 Lemmel *Gambling* 192]

4. In racing: **a.** a horse that is held in check in order to deliberately lose a race.
[*a*1890 *OEDS*]
b. a horse which is entered with no expectation of winning. [1871 *OED*]
c. any worthless horse.
[(1951) 1981 Maurer *Lang. of the Underworld* 192]
5. In dice, a losing combination.
[(1950) 1981 Maurer *Lang. of the Underworld* 192]

stiff, *adj.* **1.** In sports, not expected to win.
[1890 *OEDS*]
2. In the phrase:
stiff one, a race horse which is entered with no expectation of winning.
[1871 *OEDS*]

stiff, *v.* **1.** To win at a gaming table and leave no tip for the dealer.
[ca. 1961 *Hotel Coll*]
2. In horse racing, to deliberately prevent an entry from having a chance to win.
[1978 Ainslie *Complete Guide* 299]

stiff hand, *n.* **1.** In twenty-one, a point count from 12 through 16. See also PAT HAND.
[ca. 1961 *Hotel Coll*]
2. In poker, a difficult hand to play during the betting rounds, one that requires expertise.
[1968 Thackrey *Nick the Greek* 3]

stiff sheet, *n.* In a casino, a financial report for one shift, recording the amount of money played, won, and lost at each of the games.
[ca. 1961 *Hotel Coll*]
→Originally, *stiff sheets* were pieces of cardboard about 10 × 14 inches that were backing pieces for men's new or laundered shirts.

still pack, *n.* In playing cards, the deck not in play when two decks are being used alternately to play hands.
[1949 Collin *Secrets* 187]

still spot, *n.* A permanent location for an illegal craps game. See also FLOATING CRAP GAME.
[1983 Martinet *Oral Coll*]

sting, *n.* An illegal cheating move or scam.
[1930 *OEDS*]

sting, *v.* To cheat someone, usually through fraud or deception.
[1812 *OED;* compare 1905 *OEDS,* in a general sense applied outside the realm of gambling]

stock, *n.* **1.** Also called the TALON. The undealt portion of a pack of cards.
[1584 *OED*]
2. The set of cards used in a particular game; a deck, or one or more incomplete decks.
[1584 *OED*]

stock, *v.* To stack a deck of cards; to arrange cards in a predetermined sequence.
1853 Green *Gam Tricks* 17. *Stocking* is practiced more, perhaps, in this game [old sledge], than in whist, as it is more easily done. By slipping, they are often *stocked* as follows: while gathering the tricks that have been won, the player who intends to *stock,* will put three low cards on the top of three high cards . . . he keeps them at the top by deceptive shuffling.
[1735 *OED*]

stocking, *n.* The act of prearranging a deck of cards during the shuffle.
1843 Green *Exposure* 27. This game [euchre], like others, is subject to various cheats, such as marking the cards, sometimes *stocking,* playing by signs, playing two and three, secret partners against one, stealing out and retaining cards from one deal to another.
[1887 *OED*]

stone, *n.* **1.** In backgammon, one of fifteen pieces or men used by one player in the game as his markers.
[1950 Morehead *Culbertson* 648]
2. In dominoes, a playing tile.
[1865 *OED*]
→The use of *stone* to designate a piece in dominoes is generally obsolete, being replaced by BONE.

stonewall jackson, *n.* Also shortened to STONEWALL. **1.** A player who never tips the dealer.
[(1950) 1981 Maurer *Lang. of the Underworld* 192]
2. In poker, a conservative player, one who bets small amounts and rarely raises the previous wager.
[1971 Livingston *Poker Strategy* 225]

stool pigeon, *n.* A person employed by illegal gamblers as a decoy.
[1836 *OEDS,* 1859 *OED*]
→Among modern gamblers the use of *stool pigeon* has become obsolete, but remains frequent in the more general sense.

stooper, *n.* A person who scavenges through used betting tickets at a race track or in a keno lounge, looking for discarded winning tickets.
[(1951) 1981 Maurer *Lang. of the Underworld* 228]

stop, *n.* A specific position on a slot-machine reel.
[1973 Clark *Oral Coll*]

stop, *v.* **1.** In racing: **a:** To slow down from weariness before the end of the race.
[(1951) 1981 Maurer *Lang. of the Underworld* 228]
b. To cause a race horse to lose a race. See also STIFF, *v.* (def. 2).
[(1951) 1981 Maurer *Lang. of the Underworld* 228]
c. To be boxed in during a race.
[(1951) 1981 Maurer *Lang. of the Underworld* 228]
2. In the phrase:
stop in, In bridge, to discontinue increasing one's bids at a specific point.
[1959 *OEDS*]

stop card, *n.* In canasta, a black 3 or a wild card placed on the discard pile.
[1953 Crawford *Consistent Winner* 354]
[Compare 1808 *OED: stop,* meaning "the card which stops the run of a sequence"]

stopper, *n.* In bridge, a card that can keep an adversary from winning a trick.
[1953 Crawford *Consistent Winner* 354]
[1901 *OEDS*]

store, *n.* **1.** Also called a CASINO or HOUSE or JOINT or SHOP. A gambling establishment ranging in size from a small, illegal operation to a large resort with a legalized casino.
[ca. 1961 *Hotel Coll*]
2. a. A sports book away from the racetrack.
[(1951) 1981 Maurer *Lang. of the Underworld* 228]
→The implication of this seemingly innocuous term is that it is an illegal operation.
b. A record of bets which has been fraudulently altered to give the bettor less than is due him.
[(1951) 1981 Maurer *Lang. of the Underworld* 228]

store dice, *n.* Also called CANDYSTORE DICE or DRUGSTORE DICE. Mass-produced, inexpensive dice that may not be precisely weighted and sized.
[(1950) 1981 Maurer *Lang. of the Underworld* 192]

storm, *n.* A sudden and apparent change in the law of averages; a series of wins or losses that seems unusual.
[1961 Scarne *Complete Guide* 688]

straddle, *n.* In poker, a doubled bet, usually by the second or third bettor to act in the hand.
1864 Trumps *American Hoyle* 158. Another feature that may be introduced when betting upon the original hand [in draw poker] is the *straddle.* The straddle is nothing more than a double blind. For example: A, B, C, D, and E play. A deals. B, the player holding the Age, antes one chip. C can straddle B's ante by putting in the pool two chips, provided he does so before the cards are cut for the deal. D may double the straddle, i.e., straddle C, and so on up to the Age, provided the bets do not exceed the agreed limit. In the above instance, supposing C only to straddle, it would cost D, E, and A each four chips to *go in,* and it would cost B three and C two chips. Each straddle costs double the preceding one. The straddle does not give a player the Age, it only gives him the brief advantage of betting last, and raising—before the draw. *After* the draw, the Age resumes his privilege of the last bet, provided he remains in. The best players very seldom straddle.
[1864 *DA, DAE,* OEDS]

straddle, *v.* In poker, to make the second or third required bet. See quotation at STRADDLE, *n.*
1866 *American Card Player* 133. A is the dealer, B, who is eldest hand, goes a dime blind, and deposits that sum in the pool, C doubles the blind, and places two dimes in the pool, D *straddles* C, and puts four dimes in the pool, and A doubles the straddle, and deposits eight dimes in the pool.
[1864 *DAE, DA, OEDS*]

straddler, *n.* In poker, the second player to the left of the dealer in games that require an automatic, or blind bet by the first player to the left of the dealer. The *straddler* is required to double the amount of the BLIND BET.
1949 Coffin *Fortune* 169. Before the deal, the nearest player to the left of the dealer, known as the age, puts up a partial bet of one chip, the blind, and the second player to the left of the dealer, known as the *straddler,* puts up a partial bet of two chips, the *straddle.*
[1882 *OED*]

straight, *n.* **1.** In poker, five consecutively ranked cards in more than one suit. See also STRAIGHT FLUSH.
[1841 *OEDS,* 1857 *DA,* 1864 *DAE,* 1882 *OED*]
2. a. The portion of an oval race course without a curve. See also STRAIGHTAWAY.
[1864 *OED*]

straightaway, *n.* **1.** In horse racing, a section of racetrack without a curve or turn.
[[1895 *OED*]
2. Same as CHUTE (def. 2).
[(1951) 1981 Maurer *Lang. of the Underworld* 228]

straight bet, *n.* **1.** In roulette, a wager placed on a single number.
[1968 Thackrey *Nick the Greek* 157]
2. Also called **straight wager.** In horse racing, a wager placed on an entry to win.
[(1951) 1981 Maurer *Lang. of the Underworld* 228]
[1924 *OEDS,* as *straight betting;* 1972 *OEDS,* as *straight wager*]

straight draw, *n.* In draw poker, a game requiring no special cards or hand to begin the betting process. See also JACKPOTS and STRAIGHT POKER.
[1963 Steig *Common Sense* 187]

straighten out, *v.* In horse racing: **1.** Of a horse, Same as EXTEND.
[(1951) 1981 Maurer *Lang. of the Underworld* 228]
2. Of a jockey, same as DRIVE.
[(1951) 1981 Maurer *Lang. of the Underworld* 228]
3. Of a horse, to move next to the rail from a position on the outside.
[(1951) 1981 Maurer *Lang. of the Underworld* 228]

straight five, *n.* Another term for POKER. *Obsolete.* [1895 *OED*]

straight flush, *n.* In poker, five consecutively ranked cards of one suit.
[1864 *DA, DAE*; 1882 *OED*]

straight-number bet, *n.* In policy or numbers, a wager on three digits in a specific order. Compare STRAIGHT-POLICY PLAY.
[1973 Clark *Oral Coll*]

straight poker, *n.* A term for DRAW POKER with no variations.
[1864 *DA, DAE,* OEDS; 1882 *OED*]

straight-policy play, *n.* In policy or numbers, a wager on all possible combinations of three digits. Compare STRAIGHT-NUMBER BET.
[1960 Cook *Gambling, Inc.* 277]

straight ticket, *n.* In keno, a wager made on a single set of numbers.
1979 Clark *Oral Coll.* [In keno] you got your way ticket and you got your *straight ticket.* Your way ticket is made up of different groups of numbers, say groups of two in circles, and you pay for each grouping and combination of groupings. The *straight ticket* is a bet on a single group of numbers, up to fifteen different numbers.

straight tip, *n.* A piece of betting advice on a horse race that comes directly from the owner or trainer. [1871 *OED*]

straight up, *adj. phr.* Pertaining to a wager made that pays even money. See also FLAT BET.
[1968 Adams *Western Words*]

stranger, *n.* In poker, a drawn or dealt card that does not improve the hand.
[1949 Coffin *Secrets* 187]

strap, *n.* Short for STRAPPED MONEY.
[ca. 1961 *Hotel Coll*]

strap game, *n.* A swindling game using a stick and a strap. *Obsolete.*
[1847 *OEDS*]

strapped money, *n.* In a casino cage, bundles of currency encircled with paper bands in groups of specified denomination.
[1983 Martinet *Oral Coll*]

streak, *n.* A series of gambling wins or losses; a run of luck, good or bad.
[1843 *DAE, DA, OEDS*]

street, *n.* **1.** In poker, the dealing of one card to each player; a single round of dealing.
[ca. 1961 *Hotel Coll*]
2. Short for STREET BET in roulette.
[1964 Wykes *Illustrated Guide* 329]

street bet, *n.* Also called a THREE-NUMBER BET. Also shortened to STREET. In roulette, a wager on three adjacent numbers across the table layout. The usual payoff on a win is 11 to 1.
[1964 Lemmel *Gambling* 192]

stretch, *n.* On an oval racetrack, a straight portion of the track, either the section of the track across from the clubhouse, the BACKSTRETCH, or the portion of the track between the last turn and the finish line, the HOMESTRETCH.
[1868 *DAE,* 1895 *OED;* 1839 *OEDS,* as *back stretch*]

stretch call, *n.* In racing, the announcement of the positions of the entries as they enter the HOMESTRETCH during a race.
[1978 Ainslie *Complete Guide* 299]

stretch drive, *n.* In racing, the extra effort exerted by the entries as they near the finish line.
[1968 Buchele *Greyhound Racing* 6]

stretch run, *n.* A burst of speed on a straightaway, especially in the HOMESTRETCH. See also STRETCH DRIVE.
[1934 *OEDS*]

stretch runner, *n.* In horse and dog racing, an animal noted for beginning slowly in a race, but finishing fast.
[1983 Martinez *Gambling Scene* 222]

stretch turn, *n.* On an oval race track, the final curve before the finish line.
[1971 McQuaid *Gambler's Digest* 317]
[1972 *OEDS*]

strike, *v.* To throw dice or a die in a dishonest or fraudulent manner. *Obsolete.*
[1586 *OED*]

string, *n.* **1.** All the race horses of one owner or one trainer. See also STABLE.
[(1951) 1981 Maurer *Lang. of the Underworld* 228]
2. a. One player or a team of athletes of a particular level of skill.
[1893 *OED*]
b. Of a race horse, one of a particular level of performance. [1863 *OED*]

string a bet, *v. phr.* In faro, to wager an amount on two cards widely separated on the layout.
1868 Trumps *Pocket Hoyle* 208. *Stringing a bet* is taking in one or more cards remote from the one upon which the bet is placed.

string bet, *n.* **1.** In poker, a wager made with a slight hesitation, designed to bluff or arouse a reaction from other bettors.
[1968 Wallace *Poker* 225]
2. In faro, a series of wagers made at the same time or on the same card.
[1890 Quinn *Fools of Fortune* 195]
3. In craps, a normally combined bet made as a series of wagers one at a time before the shooter casts the dice.
1983 Martinet *Oral Coll.* Dealers hate to get a player who dawdles over bets because it slows the action and can destroy the pace of the game. That's called a *string bet,* where a player throws in a check and calls one bet, say a craps, then after the stick puts the check there, he throws in another and calls for maybe an eleven, then another and calls a hardway. I've seen stickmen just stop everything and stare at a player like that for maybe thirty seconds, and say, "if you're finished taking up all these nice people's time, they would like to play some craps." Dealers don't like *string bets.*

stringer, *n.* **1.** Same as a STRAIGHT. In poker, five consecutively ranked cards from more than one suit.

[1949 Coffin *Secrets* 187]
2. In panguingue, a meld of a sequence of cards. [1950 Morehead *Culbertson* 648]
3. A horse, player, or team member of a particular level of skill.
1975 Pete Axthel *Newsweek* 3/10: 71. In an age where it is fashionable to be cool and casual, the Bulls play at an emotional boiling point. Second-stringers on other teams routinely pick up six-figure salaries and young stars like Marvin Barnes and Bill Walton earn millions that enable them to buy Rolls-Royces or contemplate their tree houses. But the Bulls scramble as if they were still getting $50 a game in some low-ceilinged old-time ballroom.

stringing along, *n.* In faro, the act of making a series of bets in a specific fashion, such as betting all the odd cards or alternating bets on dealer and player cards. See also HEEL A STRING.
[1938 Asbury *Sucker's Progress* 9]

strip, *n.* **1.** A race course.
[1968 Buchele *Greyhound Racing* 97]
2. a. Strip. In Clark County, Nevada, the section of Las Vegas Boulevard extending southward from the Las Vegas city limits at Sahara Avenue to an indeterminate point near the Tropicana and Hacienda hotels. Formerly part of U. S. Highway 95.
[1968 Thackrey *Nick the Greek* 12]
b. Usually, **Strip.** A section of a street devoted to gambling, night clubs, etc.
[1939 *OEDS*]

strip, *v.* To trim cards in such a fashion as to make some narrower than others. See also STRIPPERS.
1843 Green *Exposure* 179. There is also another kind of strippers called "hollows and rounds;" they are cut in plates made for the purpose; and a portion of the deck is wider across the middle, and taper away a very little towards the ends. The other portion is hollowed out a little, so as to be narrowest across the middle, and strippers of this kind are used for the same purpose as the other kind, and are *stripped* by taking hold on the middle and at one end, and not by catching hold on the two ends, as in the other cases.

stripped deck, *n.* A pack of playing cards from which some cards are removed (usually those ranked 2, 3, and 4) when playing certain games or playing with fewer players than a game normally requires.
[1949 Coffin *Secrets* 187]

stripped pack, *n.* Same as STRIPPED DECK.
[1950 Morehead *Culbertson* 649]

stripper deck, *n.* A pack of playing cards with one or more altered in size by trimming the sides or ends. See also BRIEF and BELLY STRIPPER and LOW BELLY STRIPPERS.
[1968 Wallace *Poker* 225]

strippers, *n. pl.* Playing cards or a packet of cards that have been altered in size by trimming the edges or ends. Compare CONCAVE CARDS and CONVEX CARDS and RAKES.
1865 Evans *Gamblers Win* 30. *Strippers* are made by selecting two "hands" from the pack, and trimming the remainder of the pack down on the sides, leaving the pack narrower than the hands thus selected.
[1887 *OED*]

stripping, *n.* The shuffling of a deck of cards by pulling small packets from the top and placing them at the bottom of the pack, usually with a rapid motion.
[1979 Hughes *dealing*]

strong, *adj.* Of a die or dice, altered to produce an unfair advantage over proper dice.
[(1950) 1981 Maurer *Lang. of the Underworld* 192]

stronger than the nuts, *adj. phr.* Also shortened to **stronger than nuts.** Describing a card game so blatantly dishonest that it is considered more dishonest than a shell game, a notorious cheating scam.
[1943 Maurer *Argot*]
[*Nuts* is a reference to the nut shells used in the shell game, not THE NUTS, meaning an unbeatable hand]

strong hand, *n.* In poker, a hand that has a high probability of winning the pot for the player holding it.
[1864 *OED*]

strong shape, *n.* A die that has been crudely and obviously shaved or altered in size. See also SHAPES and WEAK SHAPE.
[1974 Scarne *Dice* 235]

strong suit, *n.* In card games like rummy and bridge, a hand with several cards of a particular suit. [1879 *OED*]

strong work, *n.* A dishonest deck of cards with heavy or obvious lines marked on the backs.
[ca. 1961 *Hotel Coll*]

strychnine, *n.* In craps, the point nine.
[(1950) 1981 Maurer *Lang. of the Underworld* 192]

stuck, *part. adj.* Especially **be stuck.** Having lost all one's money, originally especially in faro, but now in any gambling venture. Compare BUCK THE TIGER.
[1938 Asbury *Sucker's Progress* 18]

stud, *n.* Short for STUD POKER.
[1902 *DAE,* 1891 *DA,* 1890 *OEDS*]

stud-horse poker, *n. phr.* A variety of poker in which some of the cards are dealt face upward.
[1891 *OED*]

stud poker, *n.* See article a POKER.
[1864 *DAE, DA, OEDS*]

sub, *n.* Short for SUBMARINE.
[1974 Friedman *Casino Management* 38]

sub-echo, *n.* In whist, a signal to a partner given by leading a card from a PLAIN SUIT (nontrump) in a manner prearranged by the team.
[1950 Morehead *Culbertson* 649]

submarine, *n.* Usually shortened to SUB. In a casino, a secret pocket under the belt or apron of a dishonest dealer into which chips stolen from the casino are placed while the dealer is working at a table.
[1977 Puzo *Inside Las Vegas*]

sub-sneak, *n.* In whist, a lead card by a player holding a DOUBLETON, or two cards, of a PLAIN, or non-trump, suit.
[1950 Morehead *Culbertson* 649]

subway dealer, *n.* A card dealer who cheats by distributing cards from the middle or bottom of the pack. See also BASE DEALER and CELLAR DEALER.
[ca. 1961 *Hotel Coll*]

suck, *v.* **1.** In poker, to call a small wager made by a previous bettor while the caller is holding a weak hand.
[1949 Coffin *Secrets* 187]
2. In the phrase:
suck out on, In stud or hold 'em poker, to receive, at the final dealing round, a card that improves a weak hand enough to win.
1981 Golad *Oral Coll.* I had the best hand at the river card but then [he] *sucked out on* me . . . Someone *sucks out on* you when he catches the winning card at the end, that is, when an opponent hits an unlikely card at the backdoor.

sucker, *n.* A person who is easily swindled or cheated.
1843 Green *Exposure* 192. And to avoid this, he locks it with a secret spring, to prevent Mr. *Sucker* (so the gamblers call those they can cheat,) from detecting his box.
1859 Green *Gam Tricks* 79. They continued to practice their wicked artifice in this room for some time, until they enticed a couple to their room, whom they supposed to be "*suckers*;" (an epithet applied to those who are unacquainted with the tricks of gambling and are consequently easily fleeced).
[1831 *DA,* 1836 *DAE,* 1838 *OEDS,* 1857 *OED*]

sucker, *v.* To cheat; trick.
[1939 *OEDS;* 1951 *DAS*]

sucker bet, *n.* A wager in which the player's chance to win is very low; a poor-percentage proposition bet.
[(1950) 1981 Maurer *Lang. of the Underworld* 192]
[1920 *OEDS*]

sucker dice, *n. pl.* Also called SUCTION DICE. Dishonest dice that have been made slightly concave on one face to give them a slight suction on a rubberized surface.
[1983 Martinez *Gambling Scene* 223]

sucker holdout, *n.* In dice, a die held by the shooter between his little finger and palm while the other die is cast.
[(1950) 1981 Maurer *Lang. of the Underworld* 192]

suction dice, *n. pl.* Same as SUCKER DICE.
[(1950) 1981 Maurer *Lang. of the Underworld* 192]

suicide king, *n.* In playing cards, another term for the king of hearts.
[1968 Wallace *Poker* 226]
[So called because this card depicts a king with a sword to his head.]

suit, *n.* **1.** The symbol used to designate one grouping of cards. Usually, playing cards have four suits: SPADES, HEARTS, DIAMONDS, and CLUBS.
1836 Eidrah *Hoyle Famil* 4. There are four *suits* in a complete pack of cards, viz. Spades and Clubs (black), and Hearts and Diamonds (red), each consisting of 13 cards, viz. Ace, King, Queen, Knave, ten, nine, and so on down to two. [1529 *OED*]
2. In mah jongg, one of the groups of tiles depicted with a common symbol, such as BAMBOOS or CHARACTERS.
[1950 Morehead *Culbertson* 649]
3. In dominos, one of seven sets of bones with the same number of pips at one end.
[1976 Figgis *Gambler's Handbook* 79]
4. In bridge, a game played with one suit designated as trump. Compare NO TRUMP,
[1910 *OEDS*]

suit call, *n.* In trump games, a call for lead from a particular suit, usually accomplished by means of a prearranged signal.
[1907 *OED*]

suited, *adj.* Pertaining to two or more playing cards in a hand that belong to the same suit.
[1976 Sklansky *Hold 'em Poker*]

suit-mark, *n.* Any of the marks, such as a club, heart, diamond, or spade use to distinguish the suit of a playing card.
[1905 *OED*]

suit system, *n.* A method for cheating at cards by marking the suit of each card on the back. Compare COSMETICS.
[ca. 1961 *Hotel Coll*]

sulky, *n.* A light, two-wheeled carriage without a body, used in trotting races to carry the driver. Also called TROTTING SULKY.
[1903 *DAE*]

summertime hand, *n.* In poker, a hand that can be expected to win the pot but loses to an unusually strong hand. See also STRONG HAND.
[1949 Coffin *Secrets* 187]

super-bluff, *n.* In poker, a successful bluff against a player holding a STRONG HAND.
[1949 Coffin *Secrets* 187]

superfecta, *n.* In racing or jai-alai, a wager on the exact order of the first four entries to finish a contest.
[ca. 1961 *Hotel Coll*]
[Blend of (su)*per* + (per)*fecta*]

super-full, *n.* In poker, four cards of the same rank held in one hand.
[1949 Coffin *Secrets* 187]

[So called because a FULL HOUSE at one time designated four-of-a-kind.]

super george, *n.* In a casino, a player who tips dealers extravagantly. Compare GEORGE.
[ca. 1961 *Hotel Coll*]

support, *n.* In bidding games like bridge, an indication of the value of the cards in one's hand, signaled by appropriately responding to a partner's bids.
[1950 Morehead *Culbertson* 649]

sure pops, *n. pl.* Dice which have been heavily loaded.
[(1950) 1981 Maurer *Lang. of the Underworld* 192]

sure thing, *n.* A wager made that a player is certain to win.
[1836 *DA, OEDS*]

sure-thing bet, *n.* A wager that a player expects, but has little chance, to win.
[1947 *DA*]

sure-thing man, *n.* Also called a **sure thing gambler** or **surething boy.** A person who offers enticing, but losing, odds to a bettor.
[(1950) 1981 Maurer *Lang. of the Underworld* 192]
[1903 *DA,* as *sure-thing man;* 1908 *OEDS,* as *sure thing gambler*]

sure-thing operator, *n.* Same as SURE-THING MAN.
[1931 *Review Journal* 3/20: 1]

surrender, *n.* In casino twenty-one, a provision that allows a player to retire from a hand after the first two cards are dealt. In giving up his hand, the player normally surrenders half of his wager.
[ca. 1961 *Hotel Coll*]

svengali deck, *n.* An altered pack of playing cards used for performing sleight-of-hand maneuvers or for cheating players.
[1939 MacDougall and Furnas *Gambler's Don't* 15]
[Named for the fictional character in George D. Maurier's novel *Trilby* (1894), who was a hypnotist.]

sweat, *n.* **1.** A run given in training to a horse, often while wearing a coat.
[1705 *OED*]
2. Short for SWEAT-CLOTH. Another name for CHUCK-A-LUCK.
[1843 *DA,* 1894 *OED*]

sweat, *v.* **1.** In cards, to win a game by careful and watchful play and by avoiding risks.
[1907 *OED,* 1938 *DA*]
2. In poker, to spread the cards in one's hand slowly apart to read the faces.
[1968 Wallace *Poker* 225]
3. In horse racing, to give a horse a run in his training schedule.
[1589 *OED*]
4. In the phrases:
sweat out, 1. In bidding games, to refuse to bid when nearly out, so as to go out by winning a few points at a time.
[1907 *DA*]
2. to gamble very cautiously, taking few risks.
[1938 *DA*]
sweat the brass, To run a horse over a long period with very little rest.
[(1951) 1981 Maurer *Lang. of the Underworld* 192]

sweat card, *n.* In casino twenty-one, the joker or plastic rectangle used to cut the deck before the deal.
[1977 Anness *Dummy Up*]

sweat-cloth, *n.* Also spelled **sweatcloth.** Another name for CHUCK-A-LUCK.
1843 Green *Exposure* 90. This game is sometimes called *sweat-cloth,* and is mostly played by the lowest class of gamblers; though sometimes played by the men who have the hardness of face to call themselves gentlemen.
[1843 *DA,* 1850 *DAE,* 1872 *OED*]

sweater, *n.* **1.** A bystander who watches the progress of a card game; a KIBITZER.
[1968 Adams *Western*]
2. Also called a BLEEDER. In a casino, a FLOORMAN or PIT BOSS who becomes angry with his dealers when the players win too much or too often.
[1974 Friedman *Casino Management* 46]
3. A dealer or casino executive who cheats a customer.
[1977 Puzo *Inside Las Vegas* 144]

sweep, *v.* In the phrase:
sweep the layout, In games such as craps or roulette, to clear all losing bets from a table layout with a sweeping motion of the hands.
1983 Martinet *Oral Coll.* In craps, the stickman will tell the dealers to *sweep the layout* when a shooter sevens out and most of the bets are on the front and back, which all lose. In roulette, you really see the sweeping action because the dealer puts the marker on the winning number and scoops all the rest of the chips from the layout, sometimes even bending forward and using his forearms. In twenty-one, the dealer will *sweep the layout* if she has a ten showing and turns up an ace. Nobody has a chance to take insurance in that case.

sweep, *n.* **1.** In casino, the taking of all cards in a hand, which is worth one point for the player.
[1814 *OED*]
2. In whist, the winning of all the tricks in a hand; a SLAM.
[1879 *OED*]

sweepstake, *n.* Also **sweepstakes,** *pl. Plural in form, but singular in use.* **1.** A race in which the owner of the winning horse receives the entire amount of the entry fees. Compare STAKE, *n.* (def. 3 a.)
1843 Green *Exposure* 43. He replied, "I do not understand the meaning of the term *sweep-stake.*" "Oh, that is, when they make a race they will, as many as wish, put up perhaps

one hundred dollars each; and each man that has a horse, which he thinks can win, enters him, and they run, and the fastest horse takes the whole of the money."
[1773 *OED*]
2. Any of a variety of LOTTERIES, especially a betting situation in which each bettor's contribution, stake, is won by one or more players according to the conditions of the transaction.
[1862 *OED*]
3. A person who wins or takes the entire stakes wagered at a game. *Obsolete.*
[1593 *OED*]

sweet deedee, *n.* In racing, another term for the DAILY DOUBLE. A combination wager in which the winner must pick the first entry to finish in two separate races or events. Compare QUINELLA and EXACTA and PERFECTA.
[1968 Thackrey *Nick the Greek* 228]

sweeten, *v.* **1.** Especially in the phrase:
sweeten the pot, In cards or dominos, to increase the stakes. [1903 *OED*]
2. In poker, to increase the stakes in a pot that has not been opened.
[1896 *OED,* as *sweetening*]

sweetener, *n.* A decoy for a cheater or sharper. *Obsolete.* [1700 *OED*]

swing, *v.* **1.** Also, to SHOOT THE MOON. In highlow poker, to contend for both halves of a pot by declaring an intention to win with the highest hand and the lowest hand simultaneously.
[1981 Golad *Oral Coll*]
2. Of a dealer, to steal from the establishment or casino.
[1983 Martinet *Oral Coll*]

swing hand, *n.* In highlow poker, a hand that has potential for winning both halves of the pot by being the highest hand and the lowest hand simultaneously.
[1978 Brunson *How I Made* 550]

switch, *n.* A lead from a different suit.
[1921 *OEDS*]

switch, *v.* **1.** To substitute dishonest cards, dice, chips, and so on, for honest ones.
[(1950) 1981 Maurer *Lang. of the Underworld* 192]
2. In games like bridge and whist, to lead from a different suit. [1906 *OED*]

switch man, *n.* A person who puts dishonest cards, dice, and so one, into a game.
[ca. 1961 *Hotel Coll*]

system, *n.* A strategy for placing wagers over a period of time.
1891 *Monte Carlo* 223. *Systems* at Roulette and Trente-et-Quarante, or in other words, the calculation of "probabilities" in those famous games of chance, have not only been conceived and minutely studied by people addicted to that fatal vice—gambling, but have formed the subject of interested and interesting investigations on the part of mathematicians of not mean reputation, whose very last thought would have been to stake one pound, dollar or franc upon the green cloth.
[1850 *OEDS*]

system horse, *n.* A horse picked to win using a SYSTEM.
[(1951) 1981 Maurer *Lang. of the Underworld* 230]

system player, *n.* Same as SYSTEMS BETTOR.
[ca. 1961 *Hotel Coll*]

systems bettor, *n.* Also **system bettor.** A person who relies on a predetermined order for placing wagers in an attempt to avoid being governed by emotions.
[1983 Martinet *Oral Coll*]

system tally, *n.* The recording of a series of events such as rolls of dice at a craps table, numbers rolled in roulette, numbers called in consecutive keno or bingo games, cards played in faro or baccarat. Printed forms are sometimes furnished to the players for recording their observations. The results often are used in determining a bettor's pattern of wagering.
[1968 Thackrey *Nick the Greek* 185]

T

tab, *n.* **1.** In faro, a score sheet used to record the cards as they are drawn. Sometimes, printed forms are produced for the players who wish to keep a running tally, or who wish to double-check the casekeeper, who also records the cards drawn and displays the running tally for all players. Compare KEEP CASE.
[1943 Maurer *Argot*]
2. A credit allowance given to a player by a gambling establishment. See also CREDIT SLIP.
[(1890) 1926 *OEDS*]

tab, *v.* In racing: **1.** To watch the record of a race horse.
[(1951) 1981 Maurer *Lang. of the Underworld* 230]
2. To win a horse race.
[(1951) 1981 Maurer *Lang. of the Underworld* 230]

table, *n.* **1.** A board or layout on which a game takes place, such as for chess, checkers, backgammon, etc.
[1470 *OED*]
2. A playing surface, often covered with felt or other cloth on which a LAYOUT or design is painted to assist the placing of wagers in a gambling game. See also GREEN CLOTH.
[1770 *OED*]
3. The company of players at a gaming table.
[1750 *OED*]
4. the tables, *pl.* General gambling activity.
[1972 Kofoed *Meanderings* 204]
5. In backgammon, one of four quadrants on the layout for playing the game, divided into the INNER TABLE and OUTER TABLE for both players.
[1483 *OED*]
6. tables, *pl.* The game of backgammon.
[1950 Morehead *Culbertson* 649]
7. In the prepositional phrase:
from the table, 1. In mah jongg, pertaining to a set that is filled by using the tile just discarded by the previous player.
2. In games such as bridge that feature a dummy hand, pertaining to a card played from those laid face upward on the table.
[1950 Morehead *Culbertson* 649]

table, *v.* To put down money or a playing card on a gaming table. [1827 *OED*]

tableau, *n.* **1.** In dominos, the configuration made by playing the tiles during the course of a game.
[1950 Morehead *Culbertson* 649]
2. In cards, the configuration of cards in playing solitaire. [1875 *OEDS*]

table bank, *n.* In a casino, the amount of money or its equivalent in chips assigned to a gaming table at the beginning of a game or shift as imprest funds.
[1978 Alexander *Glossary* 15]

table bankroll, *n.* In a casino, the amount of cash, chips, and credit markers on a gaming table and in the DROP BOX attached to the table.
[1979 Hilton Hotel *Procedures* 29]

tableboard, *n.* A board for playing backgammon, etc. [1483 *OED*]

table card, *n.* **1.** In a casino, any of a variety of forms used to record fund transfers or transactions made at a gaming table between the player and PIT CLERK or credit manager, the dealer and the casino cage, the pit boss and a player, and so on. See also CREDIT PLAY MEMO and MASTER CARD and RIM CARD.
[1957 *Nevada Gaming Regulations* 33]
2. Same as COMMUNITY CARD. In games like hold 'em poker, a playing card placed face upward in the middle of the table and available for use by all players. See also FLOP.
[1968 Wallace *Poker* 226]

table chip tray, *n. phr.* Also called a RACK. A box or case with open grooves used to keep chips stacked in an orderly fashion at a gaming table; a wooden, metal, or plastic platform, usually ranging twelve to fourteen inches high and up to three feet long and two or three inches deep, with grooves designed to store gaming chips in an orderly fashion.
[1978 Alexander *Glossary* 15]

table count, *n.* In a casino, the recording of the amount of chips in the TABLE CHIP RACK at the time the drop box is replaced on a table at the end of a shift.
[1979 Hilton Hotel *Procedures* 29]

table down, *n. clause.* In a casino, an announcement made by a twenty-one dealer to a pit boss after being told to close a game, and after all players have left the table. The pit boss then secures the TABLE CHIP TRAY.
[ca. 1961 *Hotel Coll*]

table fee, *n.* In a state licensed casino, a charge made for the operation of a gaming table, often in the form of a sliding scale tax, such as two percent of the gross revenue from the table.
[1953 Woon *The Why, How and Where* 7]

table game, *n.* A gambling venture that takes place on a table, usually with a layout designed

for the table, such as craps, twenty-one, roulette, baccarat, and so forth, as opposed to gambling ventures such as slot machines, keno, bingo, lotteries, and so forth.
[1957 *Nevada Gaming Regulations* 33]
[(1864) 1905 *OEDS*]

table holdout, *n.* A spring or clip attached to the underside of a table that a cheater may use to hold a playing card until the opportunity for using it arises.
[1890 Quinn *Fools of Fortune* 234]

table hopper, *n.* A gambler who moves from table to table in a casino, making one or two wagers at each, then moving on. See also HIT AND RUN.
[ca. 1961 *Hotel Coll*]
[Compare *table-hop:* 1958 *OEDS,* meaning "to make brief visits while moving among the tables of a restaurant"]

table inventory form, *n. phr.* In a casino, a record of the imprest, or advancement of chips, for each gaming table at the beginning of a shift.
[1977 Nevada Gaming Control *Internal* 12]

table inventory load, *n.* Also called the **table inventory** OR TABLE LOAD. In a casino, the amount of chips in the TABLE CHIP RACK at the beginning of a shift or the opening of a table.
[1978 Alexander *Glossary* 15]

table load, *n.* Same as a TABLE INVENTORY LOAD.
[1982 Martin *Introduction* 4]

table lock box, *n.* Also called the DROP BOX. In a casino, a box attached to the underside of a gaming table, into which chips and cash are dropped through a slot in the table.
[1979 Hilton Hotel *Procedures* 31]

table manners, *n.* **1.** In poker, the deportment of a gambler while playing; the telltale signs in a player's mannerisms that betray information about the cards he holds. See also TELL.
[1981 Golad *Oral Coll*]
2. In a casino, the appearance, mien, and adroitness of a DEALER, including his individual habits, shrugs, tics and so on.
1979 Clark *Oral Coll.* The pit boss watches the play of the game and the players closely, but he also knows the dealer's *table manners.* If a dealer shrugs a shoulder while shuffling, or shifts his weight regularly from one foot to another—any of a thousand things—the pit boss knows them. And if a dealer suddenly shifts his *table manners,* the pit boss knows something is up.

table money, *n.* **1.** The amount of capital that a professional gambler sets aside for use in gaming.
[ca. 1961 *Hotel Coll*]
2. In a casino, the amount of chips in a dealer's rack at a gaming table.
[1974 Scarne *Dice* 190]

table-play, *n.* The act of playing backgammon.
[1550 *OED*]

table rack, *n.* Also called a RACK. A box, case, or platform with open grooves used to keep chips stacked in an orderly fashion at a gaming table.
[1978 Alexander *Glossary* 15]

table stake, *n.* **1.** In poker, a method of play in which each player can use only the money in front of him during a given hand. Between hands, the player may increase the size of the stake from his pocket.
1880 Blackbridge *Complete Poker* 135. A *table stake* simply means that each player places his stake where it may be seen, and that a player cannot be raised more than he has upon the table; but, at any time between deals, he may increase his stake from his pocket, or he may put up any article for convenience sake, say a knife, and state that that makes his stake as large as any other player's, and he is then liable to be raised to any amount equal to the stake of any other player, and must make good with cash.
2. table stakes, *pl.* Same as STAKES PLAY.
[1949 Coffin *Secrets* 187]

table tax, *n.* In a state-licensed casino, the (usually) sliding scale tax charged by the state for the operation of a gaming table.
[1953 Lewis *Sagebrush Casinos* 61]

tailleur, *n. French.* Also spelled **talliere.** An individual who serves as the banker for a card game, meeting all wagers, paying winners, and collecting lost bets.
See BASSET: 1714 Lucas *Memoirs* 229.
1843 Green *Exposure* 108. *Tailleur* is the dealer; generally the banker.
[1709 *OED,* as *talliere*]

tailor, *v.* Also called SCHNEIDER. In games like gin rummy and skat, to win a game before the opponent has scored any points.
[ca. 1961 *Hotel Coll*]

tailor, *n.* Also called SCHNEIDER. In games like gin rummy and skat, a shutout; a win achieved before the opponent has scored any points.
[1950 Morehead *Culbertson* 649]

taint bet, *n.* Money or chips placed on a wager that is still unresolved.
1984 Martinet *Oral Coll.* Chips in action [on the table layout] are a *taint bet:* 'taint [cont. of "it ain't"] yours and taint mine.

take, *n.* **1.** The proceeds or profits from a gambling operation. The *take* can refer to either gross earnings or net profit.
[(1950) 1981 Maurer *Lang. of the Underworld* 192]
2. Money gained by fraud or deception in a cheating scheme.
[1888 *OEDS*]
3. In racing, the percentage of a mutuel pool retained by the track or turned over to the state in the form of a tax.
[1935 *OEDS*]
4. Also called the RAKE. In a public cardroom, the percentage of each pot retained as a profit for the house.
[1968 Buchele *Greyhound Racing* 15]

5. In games such as backgammon, the taking of a piece. [1870 *OED*]

take, *v.* **1.** To cheat a victim, usually by fraud or deception in a gambling scheme.
[ca. 1961 *Hotel Coll*]
[1927 *OEDS,* 1932 *DAS*]
2. To accept a bribe.
[(1950) 1981 Maurer *Lang. of the Underworld* 192]
3. In various games such as backgammon or trump card games, to capture an adversary's piece, man, or card.
[1812 *OED*]
4. To accept a wager.
[1602 *OED*]
5. In the phrases:
take a bath, To lose heavily in a gambling venture.
[(1950) 1981 Maurer *Lang. of the Underworld* 192]
take and pay, In casino twenty-one, to turn up the cards of the players at the conclusion of a hand, remove the wagers of the losers, then pay the winners. See also LAY AND PAY and PICK AND PAY.
[ca. 1961 *Hotel Coll*]
take a run-out powder, Of a bookmaker, to leave without paying the winners what they are due; welsh.
[(1951) 1981 Maurer *Lang. of the Underworld* 230]

take a shot, 1. To make a wager or place a bet.
[1983 Martinet *Oral Coll*]
2. To make a cheating move, usually at dice or cards.
[1983 Martinet *Oral Coll*]
3. To take advantage of or cheat a person in a gambling venture.
[1973 Clark *Oral Coll*]
take back, In horse racing, to restrain a horse during a race to change the position of the finish. A horse finishing poorly in a race may have higher odds next time.
[(1951) 1981 Maurer *Lang. of the Underworld* 230]

take care of, In saddle racing, to prevent other entries from winning by blocking them with one's own horse.
[1978 Ainslie *Complete Guide* 300]

take command, In horse racing, to move into the lead and begin to draw away.
[(1951) 1981 Maurer *Lang. of the Underworld* 230]
take down, In bank craps, to remove a wager from the layout before the dice are cast.
[ca. 1961 *Hotel Coll*]

take down the number or **take the number down,** In horse racing, to disqualify a horse that finished a race in the first, second, third, or fourth position.
[(1951) 1981 Maurer *Lang. of the Underworld* 230]

take in, 1. In casino, to capture cards face upward on the table with a specific card from the hand.
[1950 Morehead *Culbertson* 650]
2. To cheat or defraud a victim in a gambling scheme.
[1973 Clark *Oral Coll*]
take it, In dice, to wager that the shooter will win by making the odds.
[(1951) 1981 Maurer *Lang. of the Underworld* 192]
take it off the top, To remove money from the gross income before calculating and distributing profits.
[(1950) 1981 Maurer *Lang. of the Underworld* 193]
take it or lay it, In bank craps, an announcement made by a dealer urging a player to take odds on a pass-line bet or to lay odds on a don't pass bet.
1983 Martinet *Oral Coll.* Part of the dealer's patter is designed to make players take additional bets, to get more money in action. For example, if no one is taking or laying odds on pass and don't, he will likely say, "take it or lay it," trying to get the player to put up additional money.

take odds, or **take the odds,** To wager that an event will transpire even though the chances of its happening are low. In return, the payoff is greater than the original bet if the player wins. See also LAY ODDS.
[1845 *OED*]
take out, In a casino, to take the place of another dealer at a gaming table.
[1983 Martinet *Oral Coll*]

take someone, To win from someone in gambling.
[(1951) 1981 Maurer *Lang. of the Underworld* 230]

take the chill out of a game, In three-card monte, to allay suspicion of a game being crooked.
[(1947) 1981 Maurer *Lang. of the Underworld* 172]

take the free odds, In bank craps, to make a pass-line bet of the correct denomination so as to take full advantage of the odds offered by the house.
[1974 Scarne *Dice* 113]

take the load, 1. In poker, to make a large bet of raise the previous bettor.
[1968 Wallace *Poker* 226]

2. In trump games like bridge, to win a trick and thereby be the player allowed to choose the next card to be led.
[1973 Clark *Oral Coll*]
take up, 1. In horse racing, to slow a horse during a race to prevent a collision or avoid some other problem.
[1942 *OEDS*]

2. In rummy, to take a card from the discard pile.
[1950 Morehead *Culbertson* 650]
3. In euchre, to accept the card turned face upward after the deal as trump.
[1950 Morehead *Culbertson* 650]
take your best shot, In craps, a statement made by the operator of a game to a player who specializes in whip shots or other special means of casting the dice.
[(1950) 1981 Maurer *Lang. of the Underworld* 193]

take-all, *n.* In hearts, the act of capturing all the count-cards, thereby winning the entire amount of a wager or pool from each of the other players.
[1950 Morehead *Culbertson* 650]

take off, *n.* In the phrase:
the take off, In a poker room, the money, removed from each pot, that is kept by the operator of the establishment.
[1890 Quinn *Fools of Fortune* 219]

take-off craps, *n. phr.* Also called **take-off game.** A craps game, usually illegal, in which the operator of the game takes a small portion, or RAKE, of each wager made by the players.
[1974 Scarne *Dice* 40, for *craps;* (1950) 1981 Maurer *Lang. of the Underworld* 193, for *game*]

takeout, *n.* **1.** In a poker game, the amount of chips that a player has when he begins playing. See also BUY-IN.
[1978 Brunson *How I Made* 551]
2. In racing, same as TAKE, n. (def. 3).
[(1951) 1981 Maurer *Lang. of the Underworld* 230]

takeout double, *n.* Also called a NEGATIVE DOUBLE or INFORMATORY DOUBLE. In bridge, a CONVENTION, or request, made early in the bidding round, asking a partner what his longest and strongest suit is.
1950 Morehead *Culbertson* 148. The principle conventions in general use are: *takeout double* (or informatory double, or negative double). A double of an opponent's suit-bid of one, two, or three requests partner to bid his longest and strongest suit.

talliere, *n. French.* In basset, the operator of the game and the person who controls the wagering. See quotation at BASSET.
[1645 *OED*]

tall pot, *n.* In poker, a large amount of money in the center of the table; a pot that will make a high stack of chips for the winner.
[1968 Thackrey *Nick the Greek* 194]

tally, *n.* **1.** Also called **tally card.** A scoresheet, especially a scoresheet used in a PROGRESSIVE SYSTEM in bridge.
[1909 *DA, OEDS,* in the *Century Dict. Supplement*]
2. In baccarat, slips of paper provided by the house on which players may record the denominations of cards that have been played.
3. In games like faro and basset, a complete deal of the cards. [1706 *OED*]

tally, *v.* **1.** To keep score in a card game, especially bridge.
[1950 Morehead *Culbertson* 650]
2. In games like faro and basset, to be the banker of a game; to deal a game.
[1701 *OED*]

talon, *n.* The packet of cards remaining after a hand has been dealt.
1836 Eidrah *Hoyle Famil* 44. *Talon,* or stock, is the eight remaining cards, after twelve are dealt to each person.
[1830 *OED*, under *stock*]

tank fight, *n.* Also called TANK JOB. A boxing match in which the outcome has been agreed upon in advance.
[n.d. *DAS*]

tank job, *n.* A crooked or fixed sporting event, especially a prizefight or boxing match.
[1961 Scarne *Complete Guide* 689]

tap, *v.* **1.** In table stakes poker, to wager the entire amount of a player's chips.
[1949 Coffin *Secrets* 188]
2. In the phrases:
tap out, 1. In poker, to lose the entire stake.
[1949 Coffin *Secrets* 188]
2. In dice: **a.** To loose all one's money.
[(1950) 1981 Maurer *Lang. of the Underworld* 193]
b. To wager just as much money as one's opponent has to bet.
[(1950) 1981 Maurer *Lang. of the Underworld* 193]
c. To win all of one's opponents money, thus forcing the end of play.
[(1950) 1981 Maurer *Lang. of the Underworld* 193]
3. In a casino, to relieve another dealer for a break. Compare TAKE OUT.
[ca. 1961 *Hotel Coll*]
[From the act of touching the dealer being replaced on the shoulder]
tap the bank, In house-operated table games, such as casino twenty-one or baccarat, to win all the money assigned to a particular table. See also BREAK THE BANK.
1868 Trumps *Pocket Hoyle* 212. In this game, the limit is the bank, the player having the right, at any time, to bet the whole amount, which is called "*tapping the bank,*" which the player indicates by turning over the card upon which he bets, and placing his money thereupon.
[1864 *DA*]

taper box, *n.* A dice cup designed to hold back a die until a specific number is required by the caster.
1714 Lucas *Memoirs* 130. If those Instruments [loaded dice] are not be had, a *Taper Box* will not be amiss, that as the Dice are thrown in, they may stick by the way, and be so thrown to Advantage.

tappers, *n. pl.* Also called **tap dice.** Altered dice that contain a shifting weight, usually mercury. As a result, certain numbers are rolled with higher frequency than could be expected. Compare LOADED DICE.
[(1950) 1981 Maurer *Lang. of the Underworld* 193]

tat, *n.* Also **tats,** *pl. Plural in form, but singular in use.* A MISMARKED die or dice, usually with duplicated numbers of pips, especially 4, 5, and 6. See also MIS-SPOTS.
[1688 *OED*]

tat box, *n.* Same as a DICE BOX.
[1812 *OED,* as *tatt box*]

tat-monger, *n.* A sharper who uses false dice. Compare DICE MECHANIC.
[1688 *OED*]

tea, *n.* Any of a variety of drugs, such as cocaine or strychnine, given illegally to a horse as a stimulant before a race.
[(1951) 1981 Maurer *Lang. of the Underworld* 193]

team, *n.* **1.** A group of partners or players acting as a unit in a sporting or gaming event such as bridge, jai alai, football, and so on.
[1846 *OEDS,* 1868 *DAE,* for "baseball"]
2. In bank craps, a group of four dealers assigned to a specific table for one shift. Three dealers work while a fourth is on a twenty-minute work break.
[1974 Powell *Verbal Dexterity* 23]

team player, *n.* A member of a cheating ring made up of employees of a casino who steal from the casino.
[1983 Martinet *Oral Coll*]

teaser, *n.* In a sports book, a special parlay card offered to bettors that offers additional points for any team bet, in particular a wager comprised of a minimum number of games and the winning combination for each contest.
[1981 Passer *Winning Big* 223]

tees, *n. pl.* Same as MIS-SPOTTED DICE.
[(1950) 1981 Maurer *Lang. of the Underworld* 194]

tee-totum, *n.* A die with eight sides.
1865 Evans *Gamblers Win* 76. Dice tops, or "*tee-totums,*" as they are sometimes called, are small, octagon, or eight-sided ivory tops, on each side of which is a number, ranging from one to eight.
"Compare 1720 *OED,* meaning "a four-sided disk or die with letters, on a spindle"]

telebet, *n.* A wager made by telephone. Compare HAND-BETTING TERMINAL and OFF-TRACK BETTING.
1987 *New Scientist* 8/20: 27. The gadget, the first of its kind in the world, is to be tested next April among 200 customers that currently have telephone (*telebet*) accounts with the club.
[from *tele*(phone) + bet]

telebet, *adj.* Noting a wager made by telephone.
1987 *New Scientist* 8/20: 27. The club presently has 365,000 *telebet* accounts.

telegraph, *n.* In card cheating, a wire or string used by confederates to signal one another.
[1890 Quinn *Fools of Fortune* 237]

telegraph, *v.* **1.** To use a cheating move ineptly, one detectable by the victim.
[(1950) 1981 Maurer *Lang. of the Underworld* 193]
2. In card-playing, to cheat by means of prearranged signals.
1888 Kunard *Card Tricks* 172. *Telegraphing.*—This is done either by means of preconcerted signals with the fingers, or by conversation. Suppose the rogue has a confederate, he (the confederate) places himself in such a position that he can see all the cards held by the opponent, and communicates the result of his inspection to the player, who, of course, plays to suit his own hand.

telephone booth, *n.* Also called a CALLING STATION. In poker, a player who will call nearly every bet and is therefore difficult to bluff. Such a player is unwelcome in most games.
[1968 Wallace *Poker* 226]

telephone numbers, Large amounts of money won in gambling, especially money won at long odds.
[ca. 1961 *Hotel Coll*]

teletimer, *n.* In horse racing, a device for measuring the elapsed time of a race and flashing the results on the tote board just after the winner crosses the finish line.
[1978 Ainslie *Complete Guide* 300]

tell, *n.* **1.** A repeated gesture, tic, or habitual nervous movement by a card player from which an opponent can learn something about the player's cards.
1976 Wallace *Poker* 57. All players have repeating habits and nervous patterns that give away their hands. The task of the good player is to find and interpret these patterns. Most poker players offer readable patterns (*tells*) in their initial reaction to looking at cards.
1979 Clark *Oral Coll.* Every player, no matter how good he is, has *tells,* those unconscious mannerisms that give away the bluff, the good hand, or even rags.
2. A device in a faro DEALING BOX whereby the dealer can select a card other than the top card. See also TELL BOX.
1843 Green *Exposure* 197. This box generally has a "*tell*" that protrudes its head out of the opposite screw that has the lever attached to it. This tell is set differently from the other *tells.* It tells either the third or fifth card, and the screw is made hollow, so that it may come through, and very close observation will be requisite to see it.

tell box, *n.* In faro, a dishonest DEALING BOX with which a dealer can select a card to be dealt other than the top card. See also TELL, n. (def. 2).
[1894 *OED*]

tell card, *n.* a card dealt from a TELL BOX.
[1894 *OED*]

tenace, *n.* In card games such as bridge and whist, the combination of the highest and third highest cards in the hand, especially of the fourth player at any given point during the game. See also DOUBLE TENACE and MAJOR TENACE and MINOR TENACE, and PERFECT TENACE.
1746 Hoyle *Short Treatise* 70. Having the *Tenace* in any Suit supposes the having the first and third best Cards, and being the last Player, and consequently you catch the Adversary when that Suit is play'd; As for Instance, in case you have the Ace and Queen of any Suit, and that your Adversary leads that Suit, you must win those two Tricks; and so of any other Tenace in inferior Cards.
[1655 *OED*]

ten and twenty game, *n. phr.* In hold 'em poker, a game in which bets are made in multiples of ten dollars before the flop and in multiples of twenty dollars thereafter. See also TEN-TWENTY.
[1981 Golad *Oral Coll*]

ten cent line, *n. phr.* **1.** In bookmaking, the one-half point between laying odds and taking odds on an even bet.
[ca. 1961 *Hotel Coll*]
2. In bookmaking, the ten percent charge for making a bet; VIGORISH.
[1973 Clark *Oral Coll*]

tenderfoot, *n.* In racing, a horse that performs well on a track that is MUDDY or SOFT.
[(1951) 1981 Maurer *Lang. of the Underworld* 230]

tender hand, *n.* In poker, a hand that a player feels doubtful about playing, such as two middle pairs after the draw in draw poker.
[1949 Coffin *Secrets* 188]

ten percent house, *n. phr.* A gambling establishment that condoned cheating and charged all cheaters ten percent of the winnings taken from victims. *Obsolete.* See also BRACE HOUSE and WOLF TRAP.
[1938 Asbury *Sucker's Progress* 185]

ten-point card, *n.* In canasta, any king, queen, jack, 10, 9, or 8. Each of these cards counts for ten points. Compare TENTH CARD.
[1950 Morehead *Culbertson* 650]

ten-stop machine, *n.* A crooked slot machine with twenty symbols on each reel, only ten of which operate correctly to form a winning combination.
[ca. 1961 *Hotel Coll*]

tenth card, *n.* In cribbage, any card worth ten points; the 10, jack, queen, or king. Compare TEN-POINT CARD.
[1950 Morehead *Culbertson* 650]

ten-twenty, *n.* In poker, a betting rule in which bets and raises are initially in multiples of ten dollars, and later (after a draw in draw poker, the flop in hold 'em, the first faced card in stud, and so on) in multiples of twenty dollars.
[1976 Sklansky *Hold 'em Poker* 3]

terce, *n.* Also spelled TIERCE. In card games such as piquet or whist, the sequence of three cards in a single suit.
1746 Hoyle *Short Treatise* 70. *Terce* in general is a Sequence of any three Cards immediately following one another in the same Suit.
[(1659) 1765 *OED,* labeled "Obsolete, archaic, or variant form"]

terce major, *n.* Also spelled TIERCE MAJOR. In card games such as piquet or whist, the sequence of queen, king, and ace in a single suit.
1746 Hoyle *Short Treatise* 70. *Terce Major* is therefore a Sequence of Ace, King, and Queen, in any suit.
[1688 *OED,* as *tierce major*]

terminal, *n.* In mah jongg, any of the suit tiles of the first or ninth rank.
[1950 Morehead *Culbertson* 650]

Texas sunflowers, *n. phr.* In craps, another term for HARD TEN, a cast resulting in two fives face upward on the dice.
[1983 Martinet *Oral Coll*]

theoretical hold, *n. phr.* The percentage of money played into a slot machine that is retained by the operator as profit. In state-licensed establishments, the percentage is computed by reel set and the payout schedule. Because the percentage is determined over a great number of plays (allowing for large jackpots, malfunctions, and so on), the actual hold and the *theoretical hold* often seem to be different amounts.
[1978 Alexander *Glossary* 15]

there is work down, *n. clause.* This statement is used between confederate cheaters to indicate that crooked cards or dice are being used in a game.
[(1950) 1981 Maurer *Lang. of the Underworld* 193]

they hit, *n. clause.* In dice, the exclamation of the RIGHT BETTOR upon winning the bet.
[(1950) 1981 Maurer *Lang. of the Underworld* 193]

they miss, *n. clause.* In dice, the exclamation of the WRONG BETTOR upon winning the bet.
[(1950) 1981 Maurer *Lang. of the Underworld* 193]

they're off, *n. clause.* In horse racing, the expression used to announce that the gate has opened and the race begun.
[ca. 1961 *Hotel Coll*]
→When used by someone other than a track announcer, the phrase is often extended to **"They're off and running."**

thief, *n.* **1.** A card cheat.
[1973 Preston *Play Poker* 169]
2. In horse racing, an unreliable horse, one that runs poorly when expected to run well.
[1896 *OED*]

thimblerig, *n.* Also **thimble rig** or **thimble-rig** or SHELL GAME. **1.** A cheating scheme in which three thimbles [or walnut shells] are inverted on a table, and a pea is placed under one. After some movement of the thimbles, onlookers are invited to wager on which thimble contains the pea.
1829 Brown *Turf* 88. . . . but of all the kinds of swindling, none is equal in fraud to the *Thimble Rig.* A fellow, in this case, lounges about with a small table, followed at a short distance by a confederate or two; when he perceives a likely customer, down goes the table, upon which he places three large thimbles and a pea; he covers the pea with one of the thimbles (or seems to cover it;) moves the thimbles to and fro, and offers to bet from "one to ten sovereigns," that the bystander cannot tell which thimble covers the pea: his confederates advance and play: they win, and thus it is endeavoured to draw the bystander into the snare. If we consider this infamous robbery of the unwary, it will be immediately perceived that there are two to one in favour of the table at the first glance; but the fact is, there is no chance for the player: these fellows have a dexterous method of either removing the pea altogether, or placing it under one of the thimbles, as it may happen to suit their purpose, and thus to make sure of their prey.
[1825 *OED*]
2. Now, any cheating scheme.
[1938 Asbury *Sucker's Progress* 59]
[n.d. *OED*]

thimblerig, *v.* **1.** To cheat at a THIMBLERIG.
[1840 *OED*]
2. to cheat anyone in an obvious way and for small amounts of money.
[n.d. *OED*]

thimblerigged, *adj.* **1.** Cheated at the thimblerig scam. [1840 *OED*]
2. cheated in any obvious manner.
[n.d. *OED*]

thimblerigger, *n.* **1.** A person who runs a thimblerig scam.
[1831 *OED*]
2. any small-time cheater.
[n.d. *OED*]

thimbleriggery, *n.* An instance or condition of cheating, originally at thimblerig.
[1841 *OED*]
2. Any obvious scam.
[n.d. *OED*]

third base, *n.* In twenty-one, the table position for the player at the dealer's right side.
[1973 Clark *Oral Coll*]

third card, *n.* In baccarat, the final card dealt to any set of hands.
[1982 Martin *Introduction* 17]

third card rule, *n. phr.* In baccarat, the conditions under which a third card must be dealt to a hand.
[ca. 1961 *Hotel Coll*]

third dozen, *n.* In roulette, the numbers 25 through 36.
[ca. 1961 *Hotel Coll*]

third hand, *n.* In poker, the player in the third position to the left of the dealer, important because this player is the first bettor after a BLIND or DOUBLE BLIND or STRADDLE.
[1953 Crawford *Consistent Winner* 355]

third nuts, *n. pl.* In poker, the third best possible hand. Compare NUTS.
[1978 Brunson *How I Made* 546]

third pair, *n.* In hold 'em poker, a pair consisting of one card held in the hand with the third-highest card face upward on the table.
[1976 Sklansky *Hold 'em Poker*]

third street, *n.* In seven-card stud, the first card dealt face upward to each player; the third card dealt.
[1978 Brunson *How I Made* 551]

thirty days, *n. phr.* In poker, a hand with three 10s.
[1949 Coffin *Secrets* 188]

thirty dirty miles, *n. phr.* Also shortened to **thirty miles.** In poker, a hand with three 10s.
[1963 Steig *Common Sense* 188]

three-card monte, *n.* **1.** A swindling scheme in which a game operator shows a particular card, such as a queen or ace, to a victim, then, after palming the card, places three cards face downward on the table and offers to bet that the victim cannot pick the card he was shown.
[1854 *DA, DAE, OED*]
2. A version of brag, or three-card poker.
[1890 Quinn *Fools of Fortune* 334]

three-card trick, *n.* Same as THREE-CARD MONTE.
[1887 *DAE, OED*]

three cousins and a stranger, *n. phr.* Any of a variety of cheating schemes at cards in which three confederates cheat the fourth player, the victim.
[1973 Clark *Oral Coll*]

three eighths pole, *n. phr.* In racing, a post positioned six furlongs before the finish line on a race course.
[1978 Ainslie *Complete Guide* 300]

three fates, *n. pl.* In poker, another term for three queens.
[1949 Coffin *Secrets* 188]

three for the last, *n. phr.* In cribbage, the scoring of three points by the person who loses the deal before beginning play.
1843 Green *Exposure* 272. The person cutting the lowest cribbage card is the dealer, and the non-dealer scores three points, which is called *three for the last,* and may be marked at any period of the game.

three-for-two coupon, *n. phr.* In a casino, a slip of paper given to potential players as a

promotional premium, with which a player may collect three dollars if he wins a two-dollar flat bet, usually at craps, twenty-one, or the wheel of fortune.
[ca. 1961 *Hotel Coll*]

three line play, *n. phr.* Pertaining to a slot machine into which a player may insert three coins and play for a winning combination on any or all of three horizontal lines of symbols across the reels. See also MULTIPLIER.
[ca. 1961 *Hotel Coll*]

three-number bet, *n. phr.* Also called a STREET BET. In roulette, a wager on three numbers across the layout. The payoff for a win is usually 11 to 1.
[ca. 1961 *Hotel Coll*]

three of a kind, *n. phr.* Also called TRIPS or TRIPLETS. In Poker, three playing cards of equal rank.
[1949 Coffin *Secrets* 188]

three-one, *n.* In faro, a betting system in which a player bets a card of a particular rank to win or lose three times, then reverses the bet on the CASE CARD, the last one.
[1943 Maurer *Argot*]

three pluck one, *n. phr.* A cheating scheme, often in poker games, in which three confederates conspire to cheat a victim by preventing him from winning large amounts.
[1973 Clark *Oral Coll*]

three-quarter pole, *n. phr.* In racing, a post standing two furlongs from the finish line on a race course.
[1978 Ainslie *Complete Guide* 300]

three-roll bet, *n. phr.* In craps, a SIDE BET made between players that a specific number will or will not appear within three casts of the dice. See also TWO-NUMBER ROLL.
[1974 Scarne *Dice* 79]

three spindle machine, *n. phr.* A WHEEL of FORTUNE constructed so the operator can control the spin of the wheel by friction. See also SQUEEZE SPINDLE.
[1890 Quinn *Fools of Fortune* 294]

three-way craps, *n. phr.* In craps, a wager that the numbers 2, 3, or 12 will be rolled on the next cast of the dice.
[ca. 1961 *Hotel Coll*]

throw, *n.* A cast of the dice by a shooter.
[1692 *OED*]

throw, *v.* **1.** To cast dice, originally from a DICE-BOX; to play at dice.
[1587 *OED*]
2. To play a card from one's hand; to discard.
[1879 *OED,* but 1748 as THROW AWAY]
3. In the phrases and particle constructions:
throw a fight, To compete in a boxing or wrestling match so that the outcome is predetermined by a contestant.
[1940 *OEDS*]
throw a game, To play a game in such a fashion as to alter the outcome, determining a winner by other than honest means.
[1951 *OEDS*]
throw a race, To compete in a race so that the outcome is predetermined by a contestant.
[1868 *OEDS*]
throw away, To play a losing card on a trick when one cannot follow suit or trump.
[1748 *OED*]
throw in, In hazard, to throw the same number as the MAIN; to win at hazard.
[1880 *OED*]
throw off, 1. In card games, to discard, either placing a card out of play, or placing it face upward on a discard pile.
2. In faro, to deal the cards in such a fashion as to allow a confederate to win.
[1864 *DAE*]
throw off a sucker, In cheating schemes, to distract a victim after he has been cheated. A confederate usually accompanies the victim until he is sure the victim will not cause trouble by alerting authorities or otherwise creating problems for the cheater.
[1890 Quinn *Fools of Fortune* 238]
throw on, To win a MAIN at hazard. *Obsolete.*
[1801 *OED*]
throw up a hand, In poker, to fold a hand; to decline to bet and thereby remove oneself from contention for the pot.
[1968 Wallace *Poker* 226]

thrower, *n.* **1.** Also called a BROAD-TOSSER. The operator of a three-card monte scheme.
[1968 Adams *Western Words*]
2. In dice games, the person whose turn it is to roll or cast the dice. See also CASTER.
[1983 Martinet *Oral Coll*]

thumb-cut, *n.* A method for separating stacks of chips, especially by dealers in casinos, by using the thumb. See also DROP CUT.
[ca. 1961 *Hotel Coll*]

tib, *n.* In the card game gleek, the name of the ace, especially the ace of trumps. *Obsolete.*
See quotation at GLEEK: 1680 Cottom *Compleat Gamester.* [1655 *OED*]

tickerman, *n.* The person who announces the results of a race at a bookmaker's establishment from a ticker-tape machine. See also BOARDMAN.
[(1951) 1981 Maurer *Lang. of the Underworld* 230]

ticket, *n.* **1.** A receipt for a wager made with a bookmaker or keno writer.
[(1951) 1981 Maurer *Lang. of the Underworld* 231]
2. A playing card.
[1870 *DA, DAE*]

ticketer, *n.* A person who produces counterfeit receipts for a bookmaker or keno writer.
[1964 Wykes *Illustrated Guide* 329]

tick-tack, *n.* Also written **tic-tac.** Among British bookmakers, a system of hand signals for relaying information about changes in betting odds. [1905 *OED*]

tiddy, *n.* In the card game gleek, the name for the 4 of trumps. Compare TIB.
See quotation at GLEEK: 1680 Cotton *Compleat Gamester.* [1655 *OED*]

tie, *n.* **1.** An equal score in a game between two or more contestants, and therefore a contest in which there is no winner.
[1680 *OED*]
2. A game played after a draw; the match played by victors in previous matches or heats. *Obsolete.* [1895 *OED*]

tie, *v.* To equal the score of an opponent, resulting in no winner.
[1680 *OED*]

tie game, *n.* A game or match in which each teams score the same number of points, resulting in no winner.
[1928 *OEDS* (1933 ed.)]

tierce, *n. French.* In games like poker and piquet and whist, a three-card straight flush. See also TERCE.
[1659 *OED,* as *tearse;* other spelling variants are *terse, teyrse, teers, tearce, tearse, teirce, teirse, ters*]

tierce major, *n.* In games like piquet or whist, the three highest cards of a suit. See also TERCE MAJOR. [1688 *OED*]

tierce minor, *n.* In games like piquet and whist, the three lowest cards of a suit.
[n.d. *OED*]

tierce to a (king, queen, etc.), *n. phr.* In games like piquet and whist, three consecutive cards in a suit in which the highest is the king, queen, etc.
[*OED* traces structure (*n.*, 7) to 1765: "tierce to a nine."]

tiger, *n.* **1.** Another name for the game of FARO. Compare BUCK THE TIGER.
[1845 *DA, DAE;* 1851 *OED;* because, often a tiger is pictured on the cards, chips or layout used in faro.]
2. In poker, an unusual hand composed of cards ranking from 2 to 7 with no pairs, especially when all of the same suit.
[1889 *OED,* 1938 *DA*]

tight play, *adj. phr.* Especially in poker, pertaining to a card player who bets only when holding a very strong hand.
[1976 Sklansky *Hold 'em Poker*]

tight player, *n.* In poker, a player who bets only when holding a very strong hand; a conservative card player who wagers only on hands in which he has a high percentage of favorable odds.
[1949 Coffin *Secrets* 188]
[Compare *tight:* 1828 *OED,* and 1805 *OEDS,* meaning "unwilling to part with money"]

tile, *n.* In dominos and mah jongg, a playing piece with pips or other markings on one side. See also BONE. [1923 *OEDS*]

timber, *n.* Also called DEADWOOD. In poker, cards in the discard pile; used cards that are out of play.
[1978 Larson *Vocabulary* 102]

time, *n.* In the phrase: **the time.** In poker rooms, the money collectd by the house dealer or another employee from each player at regular intervals to pay for the use of the room and equipment.
[1978 Brunson *How I Made* 552]

time-and-a-half, *n. phr.* In twenty-one, the 3 to 2 payoff to a player who gets an ace and a ten as the first two cards.
[1977 Anness *Dummy Up*]

time buy-in, *n. phr.* Also called TIME CUT or TIME GAME. In a cardroom, a fee required of each player for participating in a game. Cardrooms using the *time buy-in* do not normally employ professional dealers. Rather, each player deals in turn.
[1977 Nevada Gaming Control *Internal* 35]

time cut, or **time game,** *n.* Same as TIME BUY-IN.
[1968 Wallace *Poker* 227]

time order, *n.* In a casino, a request, usually by a dealer or pit boss, to have the restaurant prepare a specific food order at a specific time, normally the time of the next rest period.
[1977 Anness *Dummy Up*]

timer, *n.* In racing, the track official charged with recording the exact time of the racers. Compare STEWARD.
[(1951) 1981 Maurer *Lang. of the Underworld* 193]

tin, *n.* **1.** A security guard in a casino who carries a sidearm but is not officially a law-enforcement officer.
[ca. 1961 *Hotel Coll*]
2. A police officer.
[(1950) 1981 Maurer *Lang. of the Underworld* 193]
[Perhaps shortened from *tin-star.*]

tinhorn gambler, *n.* Also shortened to **tinhorn.** Sometimes written **tin-horn.** A gambler who plays for small stakes, especially a noisy or boistrous one.
[1885 *DA, DAE, OEDS*]

tip, *n.* **1.** Also called a TOKE. A gift of money given to a dealer, cocktail waitress, or other employee of an establishment for efficient or well-performed service.
[1755 *OED*]
2. Privileged information given to an individual about circumstances that may alter the outcome of a certain event, such as a horse race.
1887 Proctor *Chance* 97. All that answers my present purpose is to indicate the nature of the 'book' which the gentlemenaly Dallison succeeds in making for himself and his equally gentlemanly friend on the strength of the '*tip*' given by the latter.
[1845 *OED*]

3. In three-card monte or shell game, the crowd or a small group being worked by an operator.
[(1947) 1981 Maurer *Lang. of the Underworld* 172]

tip, *v.* **1.** To give money as a gratuity for services well-performed.
[1706 *OED*]
2. To give privileged information to an individual about circumstances that may alter the outcome of an event such as a horse race.
[1889 *OEDS*]
3. In the phrases:
tip the hand, In card playing, to cheat by signaling a confederate the value of a card that is face downward.
[1890 Quinn *Fools of Fortune* 2263]
tip the office, In horse racing, to pass on supposedly private information about a horse or a race.
1889 Ellangowan *Sporting Anecdotes* 336. *Office, to give the,* or sometimes to *tip the office,* is not necessarily a dishonest proceeding, but is simply to give private and exclusive information; and we often hear men assure their friends they "have it straight" from owner, trainer, or jockey.
[Among criminals, *tipping the office* is a signal to begin a pickpocket operation or a scam.]

tip run, *n.* Among bookmakers, the bets grouped on one horse on the basis of reliable information from a trainer, jockey, etc., which if heavy enough may bankrupt smaller bookmakers.
[(1951) 1981 Maurer *Lang. of the Underworld* 230]

tip sheet, *n.* Also called a DOPE SHEET or TOUT SHEET. In horse and dog racing, a publication that lists information about the past performances of the entries, often with suggestions for making wagers. Compare RACING FORM. [1955 *OEDS*]

tipster, *n.* Also called a TOUT. A person who sells gambling information and advice, usually around race tracks.
[1862 *OED*]

tipster sheet, *n.* Same as a TIP SHEET.
[1933 *OEDS*]

to, *prep.* Expressing a relationship between two numbers or quantities compared to each other in terms the value, especially as the odds in a wager. Compare FOR.
1969 Clark *Oral Coll.* The only admonition I have to offer is to beware of the distinction between *to* and for when you are taking or placing a bet. *To* means you are placing one wager against that of another person, at whatever odds, and the winner will take both bets. For example, if you take either side of a bet at 5 to 1 odds and win, you end up with the six units placed at stake. On the other hand, for means that the wager of one person offering odds replaces that of the person taking the bet. Say you put up 1 unit for 5, that is, you take odds of 5 for 1. If you win, the person offering the odds replaces your one unit with his five. So when you win at 5 *to* 1, you end up with six units, and when you win at 5 for 1 you end up with five units.
[1530 *OED*]

toed plate, *n.* In racing, a horseshoe with a sharp projection on the front.
[1951) 1981 Maurer *Lang. of the Underworld* 193]

toilet, *n.* A shabby, run-down, or seedy gambling establishment, lounge, or bar. *Derogatory.* Compare JOINT.
[1977 Anness *Dummy Up*]

toke, *n.* A gratuity; a TIP given to a casino dealer or other employee for services rendered, especially services perceived as bringing luck or good fortune to the person giving the tip. See also ZUKE.
[ca. 1961 *Hotel Coll*]

toke, *v.* To give a tip or gratuity to a dealer, cocktail waitress, etc. for services rendered or perceived assistance in winning at gambling.
1983 Martinet *Oral Coll.* The notion behind toking dealers is that they are somehow responsible for a person winning a number of bets in a row. It's ridiculous, of course, because dealers in our joint deal automatically. But dealers live on tokes. They are paid the minimum wage, so toking is an important factor in how well somebody can live. The competition is to get into a joint where gamblers *toke* well, then get on a shift with the best action. That's where the tokes are made.

toke-box, *n.* A receptacle in a casino pit where dealers place their tips or gratuities as they come off a table. At the end of a shift, a person or persons designated by the dealers divides the tips into shares and distributes the money to participating dealers.
[1977 Anness *Dummy Up*]

token, *n.* A metal disk used in place of money for operating slot machines or similar coin-operated gaming devices.
[ca. 1961 *Hotel Coll*]
[Compare 1598-1604 *OED,* meaning "a stamped piece of metal resembling a coin . . ."]

toker, *n.* A person who gives money in the form of gratuities to casino dealers while gambling. See also GEORGE. Compare TOM.
[1979 Newman *Dealer's Special* 4]

tom, *n.* **1.** Also called a STIFF. A gambler who offers no gratuities or tips to dealers in gambling establishments.
[1977 *Gambling Times* 21]
2. In the card game gleek, the name for the knave.
See quotation at GLEEK: 1680 Cotton *Compleat Gamester.*
[1655 *OED*]

Tom Bray's Bilk, *n. phr.* In cribbage, the playing of the ace and deuce by the same player. *Obsolete.*
[1812 *OED:* J.H. Vaux *Flash Dict.* "Tom Bray's Bilk, laying out the ace and deuce at cribbage."]

tongue-tell, *n.* In faro, a dealing box with a cheating device in the shape of a small flat paddle which the dealer can manipulate to select a specific card. See also TELL BOX.
[1938 Asbury *Sucker's Progress* 12]

toni, *n.* Also spelled **tony. 1.** In craps, a code word used by a cheater to tell confederates that loaded dice have been put into the game.
[ca. 1961 *Hotel Coll*]
[(1950) 1981 Maurer *Lang. of the Underworld* 193]
2. tonys, *pl.* Same as TOPS.
[(1950) 1981 Maurer *Lang. of the Underworld* 193]

too tall to call, *n. phr.* Also shortened to **too tall.** In bank craps, dealer's patter indicating that a die has bounced from the layout onto the rail surrounding the table. Compare DICE ON THE FLOOR, SEVEN AT THE DOOR.
[1983 Martinet *Oral Coll*]
→A variety of terms are used for the same occurrence, most of them in a similar rhyming pattern: "too high to qualify (specify, verify, identify); no good, in the wood; a perch in the birch; one is loose in the spruce; and so on.

tool, *n.* **1.** Generally, any cheating device or gadget used for cheating, such as a marked card, altered dice, a TELL BOX, HOLDOUT, BUG, GLIM, and so on.
[1938 Asbury *Sucker's Progress* 63]
[Compare 1938 *OEDS,* meaning "anything used as a weapon"]
2. In bank craps, the stick or wand used by the dealer to move the dice around the layout. See also STICK and RAKE.
[1983 Martinet *Oral Coll*]
3. A person who is easily deceived or victimized; an easy MARK.
[Compare 1663 *OED,* meaning "a person used by another"]

toots, *n. pl. Plural in form, but singular in use.* In a variation of backgammon, the act of filling the home table with all one's pieces.
1680 Cotton *Compleat Gamester* 114. *Toots* is, when you fill up your Table at home, and then there is required small throws [small numbers on the dice].

top, *v.* **1.** To win a contest or wager.
[1949 Coffin *Secrets* 188]
2. In dice games, to PALM a die or hold it against the side of a DICE BOX in a cheating move.
[1663 *OED*]
3. In the phrases:
top in, In dice, to introduce TOPS into a game.
[(1950) 1981 Maurer *Lang. of the Underworld* 193]
top the deck, To palm cards from the top of the deck. [1894 *OED*]

top, *n.* **1.** The gross amount of money gained by a gambling establishment before deductions are made for salaries, operating expenses, and other overhead.
[1961 Scarne *Complete Guide* 689]
2. A public official who shields an illegal gambling operation in exchange for bribes.
[1974 Scarne *Dice* 181]
3. A trick in which a die is palmed or held against the side of a DICE box so that a particular number will be cast.
[1709 *OED*]
4. tops, *pl.* Short for TOPS AND BOTTOMS, dice on which the number of pips on each face has been altered.
[(1950) 1981 Maurer *Lang. of the Underworld* 193]
5. tops, *pl.* In panguingue, the initial ante to begin a pot.
[1981 Silverstone *Player's Guide* 143]

top and bottom, *n. phr.* **1.** As **the top and bottom.** In craps, a cheating scam in which confederates switch an altered die into the game, usually a die with the same number of pips on two faces, such as 5s or 2s. See also TOPS AND BOTTOMS.
[1890 Quinn *Fools of Fortune* 281]
2. tops and bottoms, a. Altered dice used for cheating. One die usually has two sets of the numbers 4, 5, and 6, while the other die has two sets of the numbers 1, 2, and 3.
[1949 Blanche *You Can't Win* 23]
b. In poker, a hand with a pair of aces, a pair of deuces, and one other card.
[1978 Larson *Vocabulary* 102]

top and bottom boxes, *n. phr.* False bottomed boxes in which a small object can be hidden after taking bets on which box the object might be in, similar to the SHELL GAME, usually practiced at fairgrounds and similar places.
[1890 Quinn *Fools of Fortune* 309]

top card, *n.* The first card on a pack of cards.
[ca. 1961 *Hotel Coll*]

top-card draw, *n.* A form of showdown in which each contestant draws a card from the pack and the highest card wins. Often used at the beginning of games to determine the first dealer.
[1949 Coffin *Secrets* 188]

top horse, *n.* **1.** In horse racing, the favorite, according to the amount bet by the spectators.
[(1951) 1981 Maurer *Lang. of the Underworld* 231]
2. In racing, the horse assigned to the first, or POLE POSITION.
[ca. 1961 *Hotel Coll*]

top kicker, *n.* In poker, the highest ranking side card used to determine the winner in two otherwise identical winning hands.
[1978 Brunson *How I Made* 552]

top layout, *n.* In three-card monte, the first two cards drawn from the top of the deck, used to initiate the game.
[1938 Asbury *Sucker's Progress* 53]

top of the class, *n. phr.* In bank craps, said of the first player to the left of the third-base dealer's position. The third-base dealer stands at the left of the boxman, and the dice are passed from player to player in clockwise fashion.
[1983 Martinet *Oral Coll*]

top pair, *n.* In hold 'em poker, a HOLE-CARD paired with the highest ranking COMMON CARD placed face upward in the center of the table.
[1976 Sklansky *Hold 'em Poker*]

topped out, *past part.* In poker, to be beaten by a person holding a slightly better hand.
[ca. 1961 *Hotel Coll*]

topper, *n.* **1.** A dice cheat who holds a die against the side of a dice box or otherwise manipulates a die to yield a specific number. Compare TOP, *v.* (def. 2.) [1671 *OED*]
2. toppers, *pl.* Altered dice designed to land with a specific number of pips facing face upward.
[*ca.* 1961 *Hotel Coll*]

topping, *n.* A method for holding one die in the hand to prevent its rolling during a cast of the dice.
1680 Cotton *Compleat Gamester* 11. . . . by *Topping,* and that is when they take up both Dice and seem to put them in the Box, and shaking the Box you would think them both there, by reason of the ratling occasioned with the screwing of the Box, whereas one of them is at the top of the Box between his two forefingers, or secur'd by thrusting a forefinger into the Box.
1714 Lucas *Memoirs* 27. He sometimes us'd *Topping;* which is, by pretending to put both Dice into the Box, but still holding one of 'em betwixt his Fingers, which he would turn to his Advantage.
1726 Wilson *Art and Mystery* 40. [Topping] is justly called so, because it is securing a Die on the Top or Rim of the Box with your Forefinger.
[1663 *OED*]

top-sight tell, *n.* In faro, a DEALING BOX designed for cheating with which the dealer knows the value of the next card to be dealt and can select an alternate card. See also TELL BOX.
[1938 Asbury *Sucker's Progress* 12]

top stock, *n.* A small packet of cards arranged in a predetermined order, then placed atop the pack before the deal.
1865 Evans *Gamblers Win* 20. *Top Stock*—The reader can do this on his own deal, by placing as many cards between the pair he wishes to put up as there are players besides himself. [The player then deals two cards, the pair, to himself.]

top weight, *n.* Also written **topweight**. In horse racing, the horse carrying the most weight in a race, and thus the horse most favored as a winner by the track handicapper.
[1892 *OED*]

toss, *v.* To throw dice. Compare CAST and THROW.
[1570 *OED*]

toss, *n.* In games like craps and backgammon, a single throw of the dice.
[1660 *OED*]

toss-up, *n.* An even chance to win or lose a contest or wager. [1809 *OED*]

total handle, *n.* Also called HANDLE. In a gambling enterprise, the total amount of money exchanging hands in a given time period.
[1983 Martinez *Gambling Scene* 224]

totalizator, *n.* Also spelled **totalisator.** At a race course, the machine used to keep track of changes in odds and amounts wagered on each entry, which information is usually displayed on a large lighted board for all in attendance to see; the TOTE BOARD.
[1879 *OED*]

Totalizator Agency Board, *n. phr.* An officially recognized, off-track betting organization throughout Australia and New Zealand.
[1950 *OEDS*]

tote, *n.* **1.** Short for TOTALIZATOR.
[1891 *OED*]
2. In Australia and New Zealand a lottery.
[1926 *OEDS*]

tote, *adj.* Of or having to do with a TOTALIZATOR.
[1891 *OED*]

tote board, *n.* Same as TOTALIZATOR.
[1950 *OEDS*]

touch, *n.* Money obtained by cheating or borrowing. [1846 *OEDS*]

touch, *v.* To obtain money by cheating or by asking a person for a loan.
[1760 *OED*]

touching cards, *n. phr.* In card games like canasta or poker, cards in a sequence, such as a straight or run.
[1953 Crawford *Consistent Winner* 355]

toughie, *n.* Sometimes **tough guys.** In craps, a number that has a low order of frequency, such as 4 or 10, or the HARDWAYS, such as doublets of 2, 3, 4, or 5.
[1983 Martinet *Oral Coll*]
[Compare 1945 *OEDS,* meaning "a difficult problem, enterprise, or contest"]

tough money, *n.* Among professional gamblers, the reserve funds that are to be used for living expenses, not for gambling. See also NUT.
[1981 Miller *Jargon* 294]

tough player, *n.* A superior or very successful card player, usually a professional poker player.
[1968 Wallace *Poker* 227]

tough spot, *n.* **1.** In poker, a game with fixed betting limits so that bluffing is difficult or impossible.
[1949 Coffin *Secrets* 188]

2. In poker: **a.** a game in which betting patterns by the different players are difficult to discern, so that any player is uncertain about possible bluffing patterns by other players.
[1981 Golad *Oral Coll*]
b. a position in the betting sequence in which a player has difficulty evaluating the power of his hand in relation to the hands of other players and therefore is uncertain about whether or how much to bet.
[ca. 1961 *Hotel Coll*]

tout, *n.* Also called a TIPSTER. Especially in racing, A person who sells gambling information and advice, frequently unreliable, and usually gathered by spying on a horse's training.
1889 Ellangowan *Sporting Anecdotes* 238. The *tout,* or horse watcher (to use the term orginated, I believe, by Admiral Rous) should have some knowledge of a horse.
[1865 *OED,* 1887 *DAE*]

tout, *v.* **1.** To spy on the training of a race horse with the intention of selling information for betting purposes.
[1812 *OED*]
2. To give or sell a tip or information about a race or a horse entered in a race.
[1909 *DAE, DA*]

touter, *n.* A person who spies on race horses during their training periods and sells information about the horse for betting purposes. *Obsolete.* See also TOUT, *n.*
[1812 *OED*]

tout sheet, *n.* Also called a DOPE SHEET or TIP SHEET. In horse and dog racing, a publication that lists information about the past performances of the entries, often with suggestions for making wagers. Compare RACING FORM.
[ca. 1961 *Hotel Coll*]

town dollars, *n.* Money wagered at an off-track betting parlor or with a bookie rather than at a track.
[(1951) 1981 Maurer *Lang. of the Underworld* 231]

towser, *n.* In the card game gleek, the 5 of trumps.
See quotation at GLEEK: 1680 Cotton *Compleat Gamester.*
[1680 *OED*]

track, *n.* Short for RACETRACK.
[1852 *DAE,* 1887 *OED*]

track line, *n.* In racing, the odds for each entry announced the day before a race by the track handicapper. See also LATE LINE and MORNING LINE.
[1968 Thackrey *Nick the Greek* 218]

track odds, *n.* In racing, the odds offered and paid on at a race track, as opposed to those offered by a bookmaker with his own handicapper. *Obsolescent.*
[(1951) 1981 Maurer *Lang. of the Underworld* 231]

track record, *n.* **1.** *As a phrase.* The best performance of a horse, dog, etc., in a specified race at a designated track.
[(1951) 1981 Maurer *Lang. of the Underworld* 231]
2. The record of performance by a horse or dog in racing.
[1965 *OEDS*]
→Often used figuratively outside of racing contexts.

track take, *n.* In racing, the percentage of money withheld from each parimutuel betting fund to pay local or state taxes on wagering, and overhead for operating the parimutuel.
[1981 Passer *Winning Big* 239]

track variant, *n.* A number expressing the relative value of the speed of a track, used by handicappers in assessing the odds for a horse that has run on different tracks.
[1981 Passer *Winning Big* 230]

trail a hand around, *v. phr.* In poker, to refrain from betting heavily at the first opportunity when holding a strong hand and sitting in a position near the left hand of the dealer, an early betting position. The intention is to see how other players bet before plotting a plan for betting and raising.
[1978 Brunson *How I Made* 552]

trailer, *n.* **1.** A confederate for a cheater who distracts the victim during a cheating move or who leads the victim away from the scene after cheating has taken place.
[1890 Quinn *Fools of Fortune* 315]
2. In racing, a horse which will usually RUN OUT OF THE MONEY.
[(1951) 1981 Maurer *Lang. of the Underworld* 231]

trainer, *n.* In racing, boxing, football, etc., the person charged with the physical conditioning of a competitor.
[1659, 1812 *OED*]

trap, *n.* **1.** A gambling game in which the operator serves as a banker, covering all bets rather than allowing patrons to bet against one another. Compare SIDE BET.
[1961 Scarne *Complete Guide* 689]
2. A gambling establishment in which cheating is common.
[1977 Cahill *Recollections* 315]
3. In dog racing, same as GATE *n.* (def. 2).
[1928 *OEDS*]

trap, *v.* In poker, to check during the first betting round while holding a strong hand. The action is designed to catch unwary players on the next betting round by significantly raising any bet.
[1978 Brunson *How I Made* 552]

trapper, *n.* A cheater; one who attempts to talk people into bets they will almost certainly lose.
[1981 Jenkins *Johnny Moss*]

trash, *n.* In poker, any useless or worthless cards. See also RAG.
[1949 Coffin *Secrets* 188]

treble, *n.* In short whist, a game in which one side scores five and the other side scores none, resulting in three points to the winner.
[1870 *OED*]

treble-header, *n.* The pot in poker when two successive hands have not been played.
1888 *American Card Player* 135. *Treble-Header.* →When all the players have passes for two games in succession, or when two misdeals have been made in succession.

trente, et la va, *n.* In faro, the fourth attempt to let the original wager and all winnings from the first three wagers win once more. Compare SOIXANTE, ET LE VA.
1843 Green *Exposure* 168. *Trente, et le va* follows a quinze, &c. when the punter makes a fourth parolet.
[1706 *OED:* "I have lost a trente and leva"]

trente et quarente, *n. French.* Another name for the card game of ROUGE ET NOIR, from the fact that 30 and 40 points are winning and losing numbers in that game.
[1671 *OED*]

trey, *n.* **1.** In playing cards, a card ranked 3 of any suit.
[1680 *OED;* from French]
2. In dice, a face with three pips.
[1386 *OED*]

trey, *v.* To divide or deal a deck of cards into three piles before shuffling. *Obsolescent.*
[1888 *OED*]

trey-ace, *n.* A cast of two dice in which the top faces show three pips and one pip, respectively.
[(1390) 1553 *OED*]

trey-deuce, *n.* A cast of two dice in which the top faces show three pips and two pips, respectively.
[1680 *OED*]

treydeucer, *n.* Also spelled **traydeucer.** In faro, a card with the rank of 2 and a card with the rank of 3 drawn on a single turn.
[1943 Maurer *Argot*]

trey-point, *n.* Pertaining to three pips on the upward face of a die.
[1657 *OED*]

trey-table, *n.* A table on which dice games are played. *Obsolete.*
[1646 *OED*]

trey-trip, *n.* A game of dice in which success depended upon casting a three. *Obsolete.*
[1564-78 *OED*]

triche, *n.* In romestecq, three cards of the same rank held in the hand or played on the same trick.
[1950 Morehead *Culbertson* 651]

trick, *n.* **1.** A packet of cards, one played from each hand, in trump games.
1836 Eidrah *Hoyle Famil* 4. *Trick*—Each person having played one card in succession after the elder hand, the cards played in that round are called a *trick,* which thus consists of as many cards as there are individuals in the party playing. The card which ranks highest in value of those played takes the *trick,* provided it be of the suit led; but it must be observed, that the cards rank differently in value at different games.
1859 Green *Gam Tricks* 14 When each player has played a card, they constitute a *trick,* and the person who plays the best card wins the *trick.*
[1607 *OED*]
2. A job, especially regular employment in an illegal or unsavory activity.
[1973 Clark *Oral Coll*]

trick score, *n.* In bridge, the points earned by the declarer for odd tricks taken.
[1950 Morehead *Culbertson* 651]

tricon, *n.* Also called a TRIPLET or TRIPS. In poker, three cards of the same rank.
[1798 *OED*]

trifecta, *n.* Also called TRIPLE, *n.* (def. 2). In racing, a wager in which the bettor picks the first three entries to finish the race, in the correct sequence. Compare EXACTA and PERFECTA.
[ca. 1961 *Hotel Coll*]
[1974 *BDNE II, OEDS*]

trim, *v.* **1.** To cheat a victim.
[1974 Scarne *Dice* 236]
2. To shave the edge of a playing card for purposes of cheating.
[1890 Quinn *Fools of Fortune* 197]

trimming shears, *n. pl.* Heavy scissors used to cut the edges of playing cards in various ways for purposes of cheating.
[1890 Quinn *Fools of Fortune* 197]

trims, *n. pl.* Playing cards that have been shaved or cut along the edges or ends in various ways. See also strippers, belly strippers.
[1961 Scarne *Complete Guide* 689]

trio, *n.* **1.** Also called TRIPLETS or TRIPS. In playing cards, three cards of the same rank.
[1968 Wallace *Poker* 227]
2. In piquet, three aces, kings, queens, or jacks in one hand.
[1983 Martinez *Gambling Scene* 225]

trip, *n.* In bank craps, the movement made by the dealer who pays out chips or takes chips from the betting areas on the layout.
1983 Martinet *Oral Coll.* After he collects the losing checks from the layout, the dealer makes the *trip* from the working stack of checks in front of him to the payouts. He'll usually have two denominations [of chips], one in each hand, for the *trip.* Three denominations or more in play requires additional *trips.*

trip box, *n.* In dice, a DICE BOX with a rim that causes the dice to tumble as they are cast in order to prevent a CONTROLLED SHOT by a cheat.

trip cup, *n.* A DICE BOX lined with rubber so the other players cannot detect by the sound of the rattle whether the dice are being freely shaken or held against the inside of the cup in a cheating move. Compare TRIP BOX.
[1974 Scarne *Dice* 282]

[(1950) 1981 Maurer *Lang. of the Underworld* 193]

trip dice, *n. pl.* Dice with the edges altered by shaving so that certain points will be rolled more often than others.
[(1950) 1981 Maurer *Lang. of the Underworld* 193]

triple, *n.* **1.** In faro, a wager on the same denomination card to win or lose three times in a game.
[1938 Asbury *Sucker's Progress* 9]
2. Also called a TRIFECTA. In racing, a wager in which the bettor selects the first three entries to finish a race, in the correct sequence.
[1976 Fisk *Gambler's Bible* 9]
[1972 *BDNE I, OEDS*]

triplet, *n.* **1.** Usually **triplets,** *pl.* In poker, three cards of the same rank.
[1864 *DAE, OEDS*]
2. In bank craps, a roll of 12 on the dice.
1983 Martinet *Oral Coll.* A 12-roll is called a *triplet* because the player who has a field bet gets triple the amount of the bet.
[With a play on the words *triple it* (the field bet)]

triple threat, *n.* In a casino, a dealer who is adept at dealing craps, twenty-one, and roulette.
[1979 Newman *Dealer's Special* 19]

triple-through, *v. phr.* In poker, to triple the number of one's chips by winning a pot from two other players who stay in the hand until the showdown.
[1978 Brunson *How I Made* 529]

triple time, *n.* In bank craps, the payout at three to one of a wager made in the FIELD area of the table layout when the number 12 is rolled on the dice.
[1983 Martinet *Oral Coll*]

tripleton, *n.* In a variety of card games, three cards of the same rank. See also DOUBLETON and SINGLETON.
[1950 Morehead *Culbertson* 651]

triple trouble in the bubble, *n. phr.* In bank craps, dealer patter indicating that the number 12 has been rolled on the dice and bets placed in the field, or *bubble,* are to be paid at three to one.
[1983 Martinet *Oral Coll*]

trips, *n. pl.* Short for TRIPLETS.
[1949 Coffin *Secrets* 188]

trot, *n.* **1.** In racing, a gait of a horse in which the feet of the right-front and left-back legs reach forward simultaneously, followed by the left-front and right-back legs.
[*a* 1300 *OED*]
2. a. A trotting race.
[1856 *OEDS*]
b. trots, *pl. Plural in form, but singular in use.* a program of trotting races.
[1899 *OEDS*]

trotter, *n.* In harness racing, a standardbred horse that is diagonally gaited, in which the left front leg and right back leg reach forward simultaneously, followed by the right front leg and the left back leg. See also PACER.
[1391-2 *OED*]

trotting, *n.* A race for trotters.
[1846 *DAE,* 1883 *OED*]

trotting, *adj.* Pertaining to a harness race in which horses must have two hooves on the ground at all times.
[1882 *OEDS,* as *trotting match*]

trotting buggy, *n.* Same as TROTTING SULKY.
[1866 *DAE*]

trotting course, *n.* Same as TROTTING TRACK.
[1860 *DAE*]

trotting cross, *n.* A mixing of breeds for producing TROTTERS.
[1883 *DAE*]

trotting horse, *n.* Same as TROTTER.
[1856 *DAE*]

trotting match, *n. phr.* Same as TROTTING RACE.
[1822 *OEDS,* 1834 *DAE*]

trotting meeting, *n.* Same as TROTTING RACE.
[1893 *DAE*]

trotting-men, *n.* The people participating in harness racing. [1868 *DAE*]

trotting race, *n. phr.* A race for TROTTERS.
[1840 *OED,* 1858 *DAE*]

trotting record, *n.* A record performance made by a TROTTER. [1893 *DAE*]

trotting register, *n.* A roll of TROTTERS.
[1883 *DAE*]

trotting sulky, *n. phr.* Usually shortend to SULKY.
[1846 *DAE,* 1884 *OED*]

trotting track, *n. phr.* Also called **trotting park** and TROTTING TURF (def. 1). A race track for TROTTING RACES.
[1893 *DAE,* for *track;* 1856, for *park*]

trotting turf, *n. phr.* **1.** Same as TROTTING TRACK.
[1868 *DAE*]
2. Harness racing as an institution.
[1856 *DAE*]

trouble line, *n.* Brief comment or comments about racehorses published in some editions of a RACING FORM
[1978 Ainslie *Complete Guide* 301]

trough, *n.* In bank craps, the rail around the raised wall of a craps table into which players can set chips.
[1983 Martinet *Oral Coll*]

true dice, *n. pl.* Also called CALIPERS or PERFECT DICE or PERFECTS or SQUARE DICE. Unaltered dice uniform in size to within one ten-thousandth of an inch.
[ca. 1961 *Hotel Coll*]

true odds, *n. pl. Plural in form, but singular in use.* The mathematical probability for the outcome of an event such as the throw of a die. See also PAYOFF ODDS.
1887 Proctor *Chance* 107. Suppose that the newspapers inform us that the betting is 2 to 1 against a certain horse for such and such a race,

what inferences are we to deduce? To learn this, let us conceive a case in which the *true odds* against a certain event are as 2 to 1.
→In a casino, the term usually refers to the possibility of a particular number being rolled with a pair of dice, as opposed to payoff odds, the amount paid at the occurrence of a wagered event. For example, the *true odds* for rolling a twelve in craps is one in thirty-six, but the *payoff odds* are usually thirty to one on such a bet.

trump, *n.* **1. a.** Often **trumps,** *pl.* In cards such as bridge, pinochle, etc, a single suit designated as ranking higher than any card in the other suits.
1836 Eidrah *Hoyle Famil* 4. *Trump* is the card turned up after all the players have got their portions, and in games where all the cards are dealt out, it belongs to the dealer. All the cards of the suit to which the trump card belongs are called *trumps,* and the smallest card of the suit ranks higher in value than the best card of any other suit.
b. A card of this suit.
[1529 *OED*]
2. The act of taking a trick with a card designated as trump.
[1853 *OED*]

trump, *v.* **1.** In games like bridge and whist, to play a TRUMP on a trick after a card from another suit has been led.
[1598 *OED*]
2. In the phrase:
trump out, To play all the trumps in one's hand by leading them one after another.
[1746 *OED*]

trump card, *n.* Any card from the suit declared to dominate all cards of the other suits.
[1876 *OED*]

trumpet, *n.* In bank craps, another term for HORN BET, a wager that the next roll will be a 2, 3, 11, or 12. The bettor is normally required to place at least four times the minimum wager on the bet.
[1983 Martinet *Oral Coll*]

trump lead, *n.* In games like bridge and whist, the act of placing, as first player, a card from the trump suit on the table to begin a trick.
[1870 *OED*]

trumpless, *n.* In games like bridge and whist, the condition of having no trump cards in a hand.
[1899 *OED*]

trump-like, *adj.* In games like bridge and whist, pertaining to a high ranking card, one that has nearly the power of a trump card.
[1836-39 *OED*]

trump signal, *n.* In card games like bridge and pinochle, an agreed-upon sign between partners indicating which card is to be played next.
[1895 *OED*]

trump suit, *n.* The suit declared to have power greater than any other suit. Any card from the *trump suit* is ranked higher than the highest card from any other suit.
[1861 *OED*]

tsiter, *n.* A card cheat's confederate who stands behind an opponent and sends signals by sucking his teeth.
[ca. 1961 *Hotel Coll*]

tub, *n.* A small crap table that can be operated by one person.
[1983 Martinet *Oral Coll*]

tube, *n.* **1.** The groove in a CHIP RACK in which chips are stacked to provide easy access to a dealer.
[ca. 1961 *Hotel Coll*]
2. One of a series of cylinders formerly used in slot machines to contain stacked coins. When the appropriate configuration appeared on the reels, the bottom of one or more *tubes* would release, allowing the coins to drop as a JACKPOT.
[1941 Fair *Spill the Jackpot!* 47]
3. In casino slot machine departments, a clear plastic cylinder in which coins are stacked, often in multiples of ten, fifty, or one hundred dollar amounts, and used to refill slot machine hoppers.
[1974 Clark *Oral Coll*]

tumble, *v.* Especially in the particle construction: **tumble to,** To perceive a scheme or trickery.
[1846 *OEDS,* 1859 *DAE,* 1877 *DA*]

tumbler, *n.* **1.** In the card game gleek, the 6 of trumps.
See quote at GLEEK: 1680 Cotton *Compleat Gamester.* [1680 *OED*]
2. tumblers, *pl.* Same as ROLLERS. Dice whether crooked or honest.
[(1950) 1981 Maurer *Lang. of the Underworld* 193]

turf, *n.* **1.** Often in the phrase **the turf.** The grassy track or surface on which thoroughbred racing often takes place.
[1803-5 *OED,* 1840 *DAE*]
2. The realm of racing generally with all its accoutrements.
[1755 *OED,* 1798 *DAE*]

turf accountant, *n.* A bookmaker at a racetrack. *Facetious use, primarily in Britain.*
[1915 *OED*]

turf consultant, *n.* Same as TOUT a racetrack habitue who peddles information about entries, track conditions, etc. *Facetious use.*
[ca. 1961 *Hotel Coll*]

turf course, *n.* A grass racetrack.
[(1951) 1981 Maurer *Lang. of the Underworld* 231]

turf-man, *n.* A devotee of the racetrack and horse racing. [1818 *OED*]

turf race, *n.* A race, usually of horses, run on a grass track rather than a dirt track.
[(1951) 1981 Maurer *Lang. of the Underworld* 231]

turkey, *n.* Also called a STIFF. In a casino, a gambler who refuses to tip the dealers and is difficult to deal with during the course of a game. See also TOM. Compare GEORGE.

Twenty-one

1975 Clark *Oral Coll.* The term [*turkey*] is used by the general public as a simple name-calling device, but we [in the gaming industry] have always used it to refer to a tom, somebody who doesn't toke or gives dealers a hard time. Maybe there is word play or a shortening from *tom turkey.* That seems most likely.
[Compare 1951 *OEDS,* meaning "a stupid person"]

turn, *n.* **1.** The curved ends of an oval racetrack.
[(1951) 1981 Maurer *Lang. of the Underworld* 231]
[Compare 1412-20 *OED*]
2. In poker generally, the opportunity given to a player to bet or pass.
[1949 Coffin *Secrets* 188]
3. In faro, one betting round, consisting of two drawn cards, one for the dealer, one for the player. The entire game of faro consists of 25 *turns.* See also CALL THE TURN. Compare SODA and HOCK.
1868 Trumps *Pocket Hoyle* 205. The drawing of these two cards is called "a *turn,*" which being made, the dealer takes and pays all the money won and lost, and then proceeds as before, drawing out two more cards—the first for the bank and the second for the player, and thus he continues until the whole pack is dealt out.
[1864 *OEDS*]
4. In hold 'em poker, the three cards turned face upward in the center of the table (the flop) after all players have received two cards face downward.
[1973 Preson *Play Poker* 169]
5. In hold 'em, the fourth card, dealt face upward in the center of the table. See also FOURTH STREET.
[1978 Sklansky *Hold 'em Poker*]
6. In bank craps, the change of direction for throwing dice when the dice pass to a player on the other side of a dealer.
[1983 Martinet *Oral Coll*]
7. A change of position by a rotary movement of something inanimate, specifically a die when thrown. [1801 *OED*]

turn, *v.* In the phrases:
turn a draw, In hold 'em poker, to get a complete hand, as a flush or straight, when the fourth card to be placed face upward on the table, called FOURTH STREET, is dealt. For the player, the card counts as the sixth card dealt, since the player already holds two cards face downward.
1980 Golad *Oral Coll.* I was in good betting position when I *turned a draw.* I had my flush with still one card to be dealt.
turn a pair, In hold 'em poker, to hold a card in the hand that matches the rank of the TURN CARD, or fourth community card to be dealt face upward on the table.
1980 Golad *Oral Coll.* Your [betting] strategy has to be flexible. Say you have four cards to a straight after the flop, then *turn a pair.* There's only one card coming [the seventh] so you have to weigh the odds against how much you have in the pot and how much you can gain before you decide to continue or to fold.
turn on, In faro, to begin one turn of the deck by displaying a card from the pack.
[1846 *OED*]
turn up, To turn (a card) face upwards, especially in determining trumps in dealing.
[1611 *OED*]

turn card, *n.* In hold 'em poker, the fourth community card dealt face upward, bringing to six the number available for each player. See also TURN A PAIR. [1981 Golad *Oral Coll*]

turned loose, *adj.* Said of a horse which is required to carry only a light weight.
1889 Ellangowan *Sporting Anecdotes* 336. *Turned loose.*—Handicapped at a very light, ridiculous, or unfair weight.

turn-ins, *n. pl.* In a casino, the chips or money returned to the casino cage at the end of a shift by shills working at various games in the casino. Compare HOUSE CHIPS.
[1978 Alexander *Glossary* 16]

turn-up, *n.* **1.** In games like canasta or cribbage, a card turned up after the hands have been dealt, especially to determine the trump suit.
[1810 *OED*]
2. Also in the phrase **turn-up for the books.** In racing, an unexpected streak of luck.
[1873 *OED*]
3. In boxing, a match. [1810 *OED*]

twenty-one, *n.* Same as BLACKJACK.
[1790 *OEDS,* 1843 *DA,* 1852 *DAE*]

Twenty-one. This CARD GAME is frequently called BLACKJACK and, sometimes VINGT-ET-UN. It is a TABLE GAME with six or seven HOLES and a BLACKJACK DEALER playing for the HOUSE BANK. On the GREEN BAIZE is a simple LAYOUT upon which each PLAYER bets AGAINST THE HOUSE to reach 21 points, or to be closest to 21 and not GO BUST.

The PLAYERS and the DEALER each receive two cards. The players may elect to have one or more additional cards depending upon the value of the HOLE-CARD or they may STAND PAT. The player may express his desire with the words "PAINT ME" in looking for a high card. Or, he may use a HAND SIGNAL. If the CARD COUNT is HARD SEVENTEEN or HARD EIGHTEEN he may STAND STIFF or SCRATCH; if it is a SOFT COUNT he will probably say "HIT ME" and hope not to GO OVER.

A HUNCH PLAYER or a CARD COUNTER may CALL FOR INSURANCE if the dealer has an ace showing, which often contributes to a CALIFORNIA BLACKJACK. Others may DOUBLE DOWN, while PAIR-SPLITTING gives a player two HANDS to play simultaneously.

CARD COUNTING cuts into the DEALER'S ADVANTAGE. CARD COUNTERS may be excluded from the casino but not be entered on the LIST OF EXCLUDED PERSON, also called the BLACK

BOOK. To make this strategy less inviting a BLACKJACK DEALER may employ a MULTIPLE DECK with a CUT CARD or an INDICATOR CARD in a SHOE.

twice around, *n.* In cribbage, the act of moving pegs around the board twice. The standard cribbage game is played to 121 points, while the normal cribbage board has sixty holes for each player to peg.
[1953 Crawford *Consistent Winner* 355]

twig, *n.* Same as HOOK (def. 2). See also SPREAD.
1984 Clark *Oral Coll.* Around here, everyone refers to the half point on a spread as the hook. I've seen the term *twig* used only in sports betting publications.

twin fins, *n. pl.* In craps, another term for HARD TEN, a roll of two fives on the dice.
[1983 Martinet *Oral Coll*]
[Rhyming slang]

twist, *n.* In poker, a variant in which an additional card or cards may be drawn by a player when certain conditions are met or when a player is allowed to contribute a specified amount of money to the pot for the privilege of receiving another card. See also GIANT TWIST. See also OPTIONAL CARD.
[1968 Wallace *Poker* 227]

twist shot, *n.* In craps, a cast of the dice in which the thrower grips the dice and throws them so the dice rotate horizontally but not vertically, increasing the likelihood that the number of pips showing atop the dice at the beginning of the cast will still be upward at the end of the cast. See also SLIDE SHOT.
[1974 Scarne *Dice* 270]

twist the tiger's tail, *v. phr.* To play faro.
[1943 Maurer *Argot*]
[From the fact that faro layouts often feature a picture of a tiger.]

two, *n.* A card of any suit with two pips. Compare DEUCE. [*a*1500 *OED*]
→In card games in which the ace is high card, the two is the low card. Two's are often wild cards in some games.

two-bit, *adj.* Sometimes **two-bits.** Worth TWO-BITS, or twenty-five cents.
[1802 *DAE: OEDS;* compare 1856 *DA*]

two bits, *n. pl.* **1.** Twenty-five dollars.
[1983 Martinez *Gambling Scene* 225]
2. One quarter of a dollar.
[1730 *DA, DAE,* or *two bitts;* 1802 *OEDS*]

two-bit craps, *n.* Also called QUARTER CRAPS. A crap game in which the minimum bet allowed is twenty-five cents; any small stakes crap game. *Often derogatory.*
[1983 Martinet *Oral Coll*]

two-bit player, *n.* A person who makes small wagers regularly. *Derogatory.*
[1973 Clark *Oral Coll*]

two-dollar bet, *n. phr.* In racing, A bet of two dollars, the smallest wager accepted at most racetracks.
Compare SIX DOLLAR COMBINE.
1980 Denis Collins *The Washington Post* 9/15: C1 "We're not gamblers," confided Bob Sparkman, a television salesman at Springfield Mall, escaping for a day of boardwalking with his wife Elsie, "I might put down a two-dollar bet somewhere before the day is over, but mostly we'll just watch."

two-dollar bettor, *n.,* Often **two-dollar bettors,** *pl.* A person who makes small bets, but often bets frequently, as in lotteries, at racetracks, on small denomination slot-machines.
1975 Clark *Oral Coll.* Grind joints cater to the *two-dollar bettors,* the people who will drop a quarter here and there, sometimes a lot of nickels, but by no stretch of the imagination would any expect to become high rollers, though they might harbor idle thoughts.
[From the TWO-DOLLAR BET at racetracks, the smallest wager accepted at most racetracks and the most common.]

two-for-a-dime place, *n. phr.* A bingo parlor considered fancy because cards cost more, payouts are higher, and the surroundings more pleasant than ordinary bingo rooms. See also TWO-FOR-A-NICKEL JOINT.
[1978 Harrah *Recollections* 134]

two-for-a-dimers, *n. phr.* **1.** Bingo parlors considered fancier than normal. Cards cost more, payoffs are higher, and surroundings are more pleasant than usually found in bingo rooms.
[1978 Harrah *Recollections* 94]
2. People who play bingo in such establishments.
[ca. 1961 *Hotel Coll*]

two-for-a-nickel joint, *n. phr.* Also shortened to **two-for-a-nickle.** A bingo room in which cards are cheap to buy and payouts are generally low.
[1978 Harrah *Recolletions* 119]

two-forty, *n.* **1.** A reference to two minutes and forty seconds, at one time the trotting record in racing for one mile. *Obsolete.*
[1855 *DAE, DA;* 1889 *OED*]
2. A horse that had attained such a time. *Obsolete.*
[1856 *DAE,* DA]

two-handed, *adj.* Engaged in or played by two persons, especially in card games such as whist or poker. [1680 *OED*]

two-horse parlay, *n. phr.* A wager made on two horses in separate races. The winnings from the first race are applied to the second, therefore both horses must win for the bettor to collect. The percentage of the amount won is higher than if the same size bet were made on each race independently.
[ca. 1961 *Hotel Coll*]

two-horse race, *n. phr.* A horse race with only two strong contestants.
[1976 *OEDS,* presumed to be much earlier]

two-jump, *n.* In bridge, a raise of a partner's bid by two ranks rather than one rank, in order to demonstrate a particularly strong hand. [1928 *OEDS,* (1933 ed.)]

two-number bet, *n. phr.* In private crap games, a wager that either of two specified numbers will be rolled before the number seven is rolled. [(1950) 1981 Maurer *Lang. of the Underworld* 193]

two-roll bet, *n. phr.* In craps, a wager that is decided in the next two casts of the dice. [ca. 1961 *Hotel Coll*]

two rolls and no coffee, *n. phr.* In craps, referring to rolling the number seven, and thereby losing, on the cast following the establishment of a point. [1949 Blanche *You Can't Win* 28]

two-spot, *n.* A playing card of any suit with two pips. [1885 *DAE, OEDS*]

two-suit, *n.* In whist and bridge, a suit in which the player has only two cards. [1868 *OEDS* (1933 ed.)]

two-suiter, *n.* In bridge, a hand with five or more cards in each of two suits. [1923 *OEDS*]

two way bet, *n. phr.* Also shortened to **two way.**
1. In bank craps, a wager made by a player which, if won, is shared with the dealers. [1983 Martinet *Oral Coll*]
2. In bank craps, a wager that the next roll of the dice will yield a combination of 6-3 or 5-4. [1983 Martinet *Oral Coll*]

two-way flats, *n. pl.* Dice that have been shaved on opposite faces so that specific numbers, usually combinations of 7, are rolled more frequently than normal. See also BARR DICE and SHAPES. [ca. 1961 *Hotel Coll*]

two-way hand, *n. phr.* **1.** In high-low poker, a hand that can be played as both the highest ranking and the lowest ranking hand. [1968 Wallace *Poker* 227]
2. In twenty-one, any hand with an ace and another card lower than a ten-count card, often A-6 or A-7, that can be counted in two ways. [1968 Thackrey *Nick the Greek* 115]

two-way joint, *n. phr.* A gambling establishment in which cheating takes place. [1961 Scarne *Complete Guide* 689]

two-way work, *n. phr.* A pair of dice, one of which is true and the other is altered with weights, mis-spots, by shaving, or in some other fashion. [1974 Scarne *Dice* 237]

two-year old, *n.* In horse racing, a horse that is two years old or is in his second year, all birthdays for racing colts being January 1 regardless of their actual foaling date. Horses born on January 2 or later, e.g. in June and December, will all become one-year olds on January 1st of the next year, two-year olds on their second New Year's Day, etc. [(1951) 1981 Maurer *Lang. of the Underworld* 231]

U

uhu, *n.* In alsos, an expression indicating an intention to win the penultimate trick with the ace of diamonds. [1950 Morehead *Culbertson* 652]

ultimo, *n. Spanish.* In games like tarok and alsos, a spoken word announcing the winning of of the final trick by playing a low trump card. [1950 Morehead *Culbertson* 652]

unbalanced hand, *n. phr.* In games like bridge, a hand held by a player that contains a singleton of one suit or is void in one suit. Compare BALANCED HAND. [1953 Crawford *Consistent Winner* 355]

unblock, *v.* **1.** In games like bridge, to rid a hand of cards that may stop the leader from playing cards of a particular suit. [1950 Morehead *Culbertson* 652]
2. In games like whist or bridge, to give a partner free rein by playing an unnecessarily high card as a signal. [1885 *OED*]

uncalled bet, *n. phr.* In poker, a wager by a player that is not matched by any other player, thereby giving the pot to the player who made the bet. [1981 Jenkins *Johnny Moss*]

uncap the birds, *n. clause.* In bank craps, an order given by a pit boss, telling a boxman or dealer to allow chips worth twenty-five cents to be put into play. [1983 Martinet *Oral Coll*]

under, *prep.* In the phrases:
under the gun, In poker, said of the first player to the left of the dealer or the player who must be the first to act (bet or pass) in a betting round. [1949 Coffin *Secrets* 188]

under the wire, In horse racing, referring to a horse crossing the finish line.
[ca. 1961 *Hotel Coll*]
under restraint, Of a horse in horse racing, running to conserve energy. Compare PULL.
[(1951) 1981 Maurer *Lang. of the Underworld* 232]
under wraps, Of a horse in horse racing: **1.** Running smoothly without having to EXTEND.
[(1951) 1981 Maurer *Lang. of the Underworld* 232]
2. In a race with the expectation of running OUT OF THE MONEY but with the plan of gaining experience.
[(1951) 1981 Maurer *Lang. of the Underworld* 232]

underbet, *v.* In poker, to make a smaller wager than one normally would as part of a betting strategy to keep other players in the game.
[1978 Brunson *How I Made* 553]

underbid, *n.* Also written **under-bid.** In bridge: **1. a.** bid that is too low relative to the strength of the player's hand.
[1945 *OEDS*]
2. A weaker bid than those preceding. *Rare.*
[1923 *OEDS*]

underbid, *v.* In bridge, to make a lower bid on a hand than the strength of the hand warrants.
[1908 *OEDS*]

underbidder, *n.* A bridge player who makes a lower bid on a hand than the strength of the hand warrants. [1923 *OEDS*]

undercut, *v.* In poker, to move a preset packet of cards from the bottom of the deck to the top.
[1968 Wallace *Poker* 227]

undercut, *n.* **1.** In poker, a prepared packet of cards placed in the deck for purposes of cheating.
[ca. 1961 *Hotel Coll*]
2. In lowball stud poker, the lowest card in a hand, when dealt as the final, face-down card to a hand.
[1968 Wallace *Poker* 227]

underdog, *n.* Also shortened to DOG. In a gambling game or in football, boxing or sporting contest, an entry thought to have little chance to win. See also DARK HORSE.
[1879 *DAE, DA,* 1887 *OED*]

underfull, *n.* In poker, a FULL HOUSE, three cards of one rank and two of another, that is not three aces and two kings, known as a BIG FULL.
[1978 Brunson *How I Made* 553]

underlay, *n.* In horse racing, odds on an entry, usually lower than the MORNING LINE, that are consequently lower than circumstances would otherwise predict and that are unfavorable for the bettor.
[(1951) 1981 Maurer *Lang. of the Underworld* 232]

underlead, *v.* In bridge, Same as UNDERPLAY (def. 1). [1934 *OEDS*]

underpay, *v.* **1.** In a casino, to cheat a player by paying off a wager with fewer than the correct number of chips.
[ca. 1961 *Hotel Coll*]
2. Of a dealer, to mistakenly pay less to a player than owed.
[1983 Martinet *Oral Coll*]

underplay, *v.* **1.** In bridge, to lead a lower card in a suit while retaining a higher card of the same suit for later play.
[1863 *OED*]
2. In poker, to make small bets while holding a strong hand so that more players will stay in the game. [1850 *OED*]
3. To play below one's ability.
[1733 *OED*]

undertrick, *n.* In bridge, a trick won by an opponent that the declarer needed to fulfill his contract. [1908 *OEDS*]

undertrump, *v.* In bridge or whist, to play after one's partner with a trump card lower than one's partner played.
[1863 *OED*]

unit, *n.* In betting, a fixed quantity of money or chip denomination.
[1970 *Baccarat, The Facts*]

unit progression, *n. phr.* In betting systems, an increase of a fixed amount wagered in certain betting situations.
[1949 Blanche *You Can't Win* 23]

unlimited poker, *n. phr.* Same as NO LIMIT.
[1949 Coffin *Secrets* 188]

unload, *v.* **1.** In card cheating, to drop unwanted cards in the lap or dispose of them in some other fashion.
[ca. 1961 *Hotel Coll*]
2. In rummy, to reduce the card count held in the hand by discarding the higher ranked cards.
[1950 Morehead *Culbertson* 652]

unmarked cards, *n. pl.* A deck of playing cards free from markings on the backs for purposes of cheating.
[1973 Clark *Oral Coll*]

unmatched card, *n. phr.* In games like gin rummy, a worthless card; a card that does not form part of a set, as multiple cards of the same rank or cards in sequence that form a run.
[1953 Crawford *Consistent Winner* 355]

unpaid shill, *n. phr.* In a casino, a player who makes small bets and plays for a long time. See also FLEA.
[1961 Scarne *Complete Guide* 690]

unplaced, *adj.* In horse racing, pertaining to an entry that finishes OUT OF THE MONEY.
[(1951) 1981 Maurer *Lang. of the Underworld* 232]

untrack, *v.* Of a horse, in horse racing, to make a DRIVE, especially as a response to the urging of a jockey or driver.
Usually humorous use.
[(1951) 1981 Maurer *Lang. of the Underworld* 232]

→The use of *untrack* is accompanied by a reflexive pronoun, as "he untracked himself."

up, *prep.* **1.** In poker, referring to the higher ranked of two pair.
[1949 Coffin *Secrets* 188]
2. In poker, referring to the three cards of the same rank in the case of a full house.
[1981 Golad *Oral Coll*]
3. In the phrase:
up to (you, me, etc.), being one's turn to bet.
[1896 *DAE, DA*]

up, *adv.* **1.** Of a horse-racing jockey, under contract to ride a horse.
[(1951) 1981 Maurer *Lang. of the Underworld* 232]
[1856 *OED*]
2. In poker: **a:** in the position of having put the ante in the pot. [1844 *DA, DAE*]
b. Said of the money, at stake.
[1867 *DAE*]
3. In poker, being the highest card in a flush hand. [1882 *OEDS* (1933 ed.)]

up, *v.* **1.** In poker, to raise.
[1915 *OEDS*]
2. In horse racing, as a command to jockeys to mount their horses.
[1978 Ainslie *Complete Guide* 301]

up-card, *n.* Any card dealt face upward, as in stud, hold 'em, twenty-one, cribbage, and so on.
[1938 *OEDS*]

uphills, *n. pl.* Dice that have been altered so that only high numbers will land face upward. Compare HIGH-FULLUM.
[(*a* 1700) 1785 *OED*]

up jumped the devil, *v. clause.* In craps, an expression used when the shooter rolls seven rather than the point.
[(1950) 1981 Maurer *Lang. of the Underworld* 193]

urge, *v.* Of a jockey in horse racing, to encourage a horse to move up in the pack or farther ahead. See also GO TO BAT and BOOT (def. 1).
[(1951) 1981 Maurer *Lang. of the Underworld* 232]

V

vacant spot, *n.* In bank craps, referring to a proposition betting area on the LAYOUT that has no chips on it.
[1983 Martinet *Oral Coll*]

valet, *n.* In poker, another term for the jack, or knave.
[1950 Morehead *Culbertson* 654]

valle, *n.* In panguingue, a card with the rank of 3, 4, or 7, each of which are cards requiring that other players pay the person holding them.
[1948 Oncken *Review Journal* 3/14: 13]

Van John, *n.* Also written **van John.** A corrupted form of the French name for twenty-one, *vingt-et-un. Obsolete.*
[1853 *OED*]

van-tu-ann, *n.* Also spelled **vantoon.**
Another name for VINGT UN, twenty-one. *Obsolete.*
1843 Green *Exposure* 285. It is better known by the name of twenty-one or *van-tu-ann.*
[1839 *DA, DAE,* as *vantoon*]
[from French]

variation timer, *n.* In a mechanical slot machine, a mechanism, usually driven by a spring, that varies the rhythm of reel settings, thereby preventing players from setting a rhythm to fix a payoff configuration on the machine.
[1968 Thackrey *Nick the Greek* 173]

variety pack, *n.* Also called a FUN PACK. In bank craps, referring to the different denominations of chips requested by a regular player, usually a small-stakes player, consisting of a large number of chips of low denomination. Compare BIRD and BONE.
1983 Martinet *Oral Coll.* We get these fleas [regular patrons who bet small amounts, lose slowly but inexorably, and play for long periods of time] who stop by [the casino] everyday for what we call a *variety pack* or fun pack. Usually they break a ten and ask for birds [quarters] and bones [one dollar chips], then settle down to lose slowly and noisily. The fun pack term comes from the fact that a lot of casinos have these little come-on booklets offering a few nickels, a free drink, and such. They're called fun books or packs.

velvet, *n.* Money won by gambling, usually a large amount of money won in some illegal game.
[1901 *DA,* 1912 *OED*]

verbal bet, *n.* Also called a MOUTH BET. A wager made orally, without either party producing the amount wagered until the outcome of the bet is known.
[1963 Steig *Common Sense* 188]

vest holdout, *n.* Also called a BREASTWORKS. A

mechanical device worn under a coat used by a cheater to withhold playing cards.
[1890 Quinn *Fools of Fortune* 235]

vice-president, *n.* In poker, a term for the player holding the second-best hand at the showdown.
[1949 Coffin *Secrets* 188]

vig, *n.* Short for VIGORISH.
[1973 Clark *Oral Coll*]

vigorish or **viggerish,** *n.* Also called JUICE. **1.** In bookmaking, the percentage of a wager kept by the bookmaker for handling the bet.
[1960 Cook *Gambling, Inc.* 267]
2. A percentage of any wager, pot, or bet kept by the cardroom, game banker, craps dealer, and so on for handling a bet by a player.
[1943 Maurer *Argot*]
[1912 *OEDS*]
3. Same as BROKE MONEY.
[(1950) 1981 Maurer *Lang. of the Underworld* 193]
[The word *vigorish* is probably of Yiddish origin from Russian *vyigrysh* meaning "winnings".]

village, *n.* In romesteq, a hand with two combinations of the two cards ranked queen/jack or ten/nine.
[1950 Morehead *Culbertson* 654]

vingt-et-un, *n.* Also called **vingt un.** *French.* The French name for twenty-one, or blackjack; a card game in which the object is to take cards totalling twenty-one points without exceeding that number. [1772 *OEDS*]
→The form *vingt un* is now obsolete.

virlicque, *n.* In romesteq, four cards of the same rank.
[1950 Morehead *Culbertson* 654]

void, *n. Also used attributively.* **1.** In bridge, a hand without a card or cards of a particular suit.
[1933 *OEDS*]
2. In skat, cards, with a rank of 7, 8, or 9, which have no value in counting the score.
[1891 *OED*]
3. In twenty-one, a hand that is declared finished.
[1983 Martinet *Oral Coll*]

volat, *n.* In alsos, an oral declaration signifying an intention to win nine tricks with one hand.
[1950 Morehead *Culbertson* 654]

voll, *n. Spanish.* In the card game ombre, the act of winning all the tricks in one's hand.
1680 Cotton *Compleat Gamester* 73. . . . if you win all the Tricks in your hand or the *Voll,* they likewise are to give you one Counter apiece.

vowel, *v.* To pay off a lost wager with an IOU. *Obsolete.*
[1709 *OED,* from the letters IOU, indicating money owed.]

vulnerable, *adj.* In bridge, pertaining to the team that has won one hand of a rubber. In case of a loss, the penalty to that team is more severe than it would be if the opponent lost.
[1927 *OEDS*]

vye, *n.* Also spelled **vie.** A wager. *Obsolete.*
[1950 Morehead *Culbertson* 654]

W

W, *n.* **1.** In bridge or whist, an abbreviation for WEST.
[1950 Morehead *Culbertson* 654]
2. On racing forms, an abbreviation for WON.
[1955 Hillis *Pari-Mutuel Betting* 89]
3. In a casino, the abbreviation on a DROP BOX for a wheel game.
[1982 Martinet *Oral Coll*]

wager, *n.* Also called a BET. A stake placed on the outcome of an event, such as a horse race or hand of a card game or the roll of the dice.
[1303 *OED*]

wager, *v.* **1.** To stake or hazard (money, chips, etc.) on the outcome of an event such as a horse race or hand of cards or roll of the dice.
[1611 *OED*]
2. To make a bet.
[1602 *OED*]

wagering excise tax, *n. phr.* A charge made to bookmakers in the state of Nevada for handling bets.
[1957 *Nevada Gaming Regulations* 3]

walk, *adj.* Of a jockey, pertaining to his weight
[1856 *OED*]

walk, *v.* **1.** To leave a gambling game or a casino, usually with winnings.
[1977 Anness *Dummy Up*]
2. In the phrases:

walk over, To cheat, especially at cards or dice.
[1852 *DA*]

walk round, Same as WALK OVER.
[1844 *DA*]

walk away *n.* A horse race in which the winner easily defeats the other entrants.
[1888 *OED*]

walking money, *n.* Cash provided to a patron who has lost his stake. The money so given is intended to assist the player to leave the area.
[ca. 1961 *Hotel Coll*]

walking the pegs, *v. phr.* In cribbage, to move the scoring pegs surreptitiously.
1859 Green *Gam Tricks* 100 *Walking the pegs* means either putting your own pegs forward [in cribbage], or those of your adversary back, as they may best suit your purpose; and it is always executed while you are laying out your cards for the crib.
[1803 *OED*]

walk over, To cheat, especially at cards or dice. [1852 *DA*]

walk-up start, *n.* In horse racing, the beginning of a race in which the horses approach the starting line or wire, and break at the command of the starter. Compare GATE, *n.* (def. 2).
[1938 *OEDS*]

wall, *n.* In mah jongg, the array of tiles on the board after all have been shuffled together.
[1922 *OEDS*]

wall game, *n.* In mah jongg, a voided game, accomplished when the WALL, or supply of tiles, has been depleted without anyone winning the game.
[1950 Morehead *Culbertson* 654]

wall sheet, *n.* In a bookmaking establishment, the results of races posted on large printed sheets of paper and tacked to the wall.
[1983 Martinet *Oral Coll*]

wall ticket, *n.* In keno, a ticket representing a large win [said to be worthy of posting on a wall as an inspiration to other players].
[ca. 1961 *Hotel Coll*]

wand, *n.* Also called the STICK or ROD or WHIP or POLE or TOOL. In bank craps, the wooden or rattan cane with which the dealer moves the dice around the layout.
[1983 Martinet *Oral Coll*]

warm, *adj.* **1.** In horse racing, pertaining to a larger amount of money than expected wagered on a particular entry. Compare HOT.
[1899 Ellangowan *Sporting Anecdotes* 336]
2. Pertaining to dice in a craps game that is more favorable to the players than the house.
[1983 Martinet *Oral Coll*]

wash, *v.* **1.** To shuffle a pack of playing cards.
[1963 Steig *Common Sense* 188]
[From the motion of moving the hands together and over one another.]
2. In the phrase:
wash cards, In a casino, to clean reusable plastic cards with club soda water.
[ca. 1961 *Hotel Coll*]

washerwoman's gig, *n.* Also called a MAGIC GIG. In playing numbers or policy, a selection of the grouped numbers 4, 11, and 44.
[1938 Asbury *Sucker's Progress* 92]

Washington Monument, *n.* In poker, a term for three cards ranked 5.
[1971 Livingston *Poker Strategy* 226]
[The Washington Monument is 555 feet high.]

washy, *adj.* In horse racing, referring to excessive perspiration on a horse.
[1639 *OED*]

watcher, *n.* Same as EYE-IN-THE-SKY.
[1978 Harrah *Recollections* 141]

watcher system, *n.* In bank craps, a betting system in which the player bets the *don't pass* line on the layout.
[ca. 1961 *Hotel Coll*]
[From the notion that such a player does not take an active role in the game, but "watches" for other players to lose.]

wave, *n.* A slight bend made in a playing card by a cheater so he knows the value of the card and can identify it while cutting the pack or dealing the cards. See also CRIMP.
[1961 Scarne *Complete Guide* 690]

wave, *v.* To slightly bend a playing card so a cheater knows the value of the card and can identify it while cutting the pack or dealing the cards. See also CRIMP.
[1983 Martinet *Oral Coll*]

way, *n.* One or more alternatives in placing a multiple wager.
1979 Clark *Oral Coll.* I watched him take win, place, and show with a hundred each *way.*
1983 Martinet *Oral Coll.* He threw a couple of checks on the [craps] table and said, "Give me C & E [crap and eleven, proposition bets], a buck a *way.*"

way ticket, *n.* Also called a COMBINATION TICKET. In keno, a betting slip with groups of numbers circled, each group bet in combination with the others.
1979 Clark *Oral Coll.* [In keno] you got your *way ticket* and you got your straight ticket. Your *way ticket* is made up of different groups of numbers, say groups of two in circles, and you pay for each grouping and combination of groupings. The straight ticket is a bet on a single group of numbers, up to fifteen different numbers.

weak, *adj.* In card games: **1.** Pertaining to a hand without commanding cards.
[1680 *OED*]
2. Pertaining to a player without commanding cards. [1746 *OED*]

weak hand, *n. phr.* In poker or whist, a hand that has a low probability of winning the game.
[1864 *OED*]

weak roll, *n. phr.* In bank craps, a cast of the dice that fails to get both dice to the opposite end of the layout. Compare WHIP SHOT.
1983 Martinet *Oral Coll.* The boxman watches for a person who makes more than one *weak roll.* Everyone has a *weak roll* once in awhile. But someone who does it consistently may be using a whip shot [controlled throw of the dice] and doesn't want the dice to bounce off the backboard.

weak suit, *n.* In card games, a hand with few cards of a particular suit.
[1742 *OED*]

wedges, *n. pl.* Playing cards that have been trimmed or shaved along the edges so a cheater can recognize high ranking cards without seeing the faces. Compare STRIPPERS.
[1943 Maurer *Argot*]

weed, *v.* **1.** To stake a shill with money or chips. Compare HOUSE CHIPS.
[(1947) 1981 Maurer *Lang. of the Underworld* 172]
2. To reclaim money from a shill who is winning.
[(1947) 1981 Maurer *Lang. of the Underworld* 172]

weigh, *n.* In a casino, an amount of money comprised of coins, usually of the same denomination, the value of which is determined by weight.
[1977 Nevada Gaming Control *Internal* 22]

weigh, *v.* **1.** Of a jockey, to take his place on the scales so his declared weight can be confirmed before and after a race.
[1805 *OED*]
2. In the phrases:
weigh in, a: Of a jockey, to WEIGH before a race
[1868 *OED*]
b. Of a fighter, to weigh before a boxing match.
[1909 *OEDS*]
weigh out, Of a jockey, to weigh following a race. [1877 *OED*]

weigh count, *n.* In a casino, the value of bagged coins of the same denomination as determined by their weight.
[1978 Alexander *Glossary* 16]

weigh-in, *n.* Also called **weighing in.** An official recording of the weight of a jockey before and after a race.
[1971 McQuaid *Gambler's* 320]
2. An official recording of the weight of a fighter before a boxing match.
[1939 *OEDS*]

weigh-out, *n.* An official recording of a jockey and his tack before and after a horse race.
[1886 *OED*]

weight, *n.* **1.** The total poundage carried by a racehorse, including the jockey, equipment, and lead assigned by the track handicapper.
[1692 *OED*]
2. In dice, the tempo of the game.
[(1950) 1981 Maurer *Lang of the Underworld* 193]
3. In boxing, a match between boxers of a particular range in weight.
[1914 *OED*]

weight, *v.* **1.** Of a horse, to be assigned the weight to be carried in a handicap race.
[1846 *OED*]
2. In the phrase:
weight in or **out,** Same as WEIGH IN and WEIGH OUT. [1877 *OED*]

weight for age race, *n. phr.* A horse race in which the weight assigned to a horse depends on the age of the horse, the distance of the race, and the season of the year.
[(1951) 1981 Maurer *Lang. of the Underworld* 232]

welsh, *v.* Also spelled **welch.** Sometimes as the phrases **welsh out** or **welsh out on.** To refuse to pay a gambling debt.
[1857 *OED,* as *welch*]
→The spelling *welch* and, in the following entry, *welcher* are obsolescent, or at least significantly less common than the spellings with *-sh*

welsher, *n.* Also spelled **welcher.** A person who fails to pay gambling debts.
1868 Laing-Meason *Turf Frauds* 112. To the honour of this new calling, the former class predominate greatly, and if any person wishing to bet finds himself in the hands of a "*welcher*"—the name given to scamps who take everything and pay nothing—it must be his own fault.
[1860 *OED,* as *welcher*]

west, *n.* Abbreviated as W. One of four positions at a bridge or whist table, the others being east, north, and south.
[1950 Morehead *Culbertson* 654]

whangdoodle, *n. pl.* Also written **wang-doodle.** Also called PROGRESSIVE PROGRESSIVE or RANDOODLES or ROODLES. A poker game featuring increased stakes under certain conditions, as when no player can begin the betting process in a game of JACKS OR BETTER.
[1949 Coffin *Secrets* 188]
[1904 *OEDS*]

wheel, *n.* **1.** Also called a BICYCLE or MINNIE or LITTLE WHEEL. In lowball poker, a straight or sequence of cards from ace to 5, considered a perfect hand.
[1949 Coffin *Secrets* 188]
2. Short for ROULETTE WHEEL.
[ca. 1961 *Hotel Coll*]
3. Short for BIG SIX WHEEL.
[1982 Martin *Introduction* 11]
4. A circular device or wheel with stops marked by numbers used for gambling.
[1750 *DAE*]
5. In racing, a wager, usually on the DAILY DOUBLE in which the bettor pairs a horse from one race with each horse in the other race in a COMBINATION BET.
[1968 Buchele *Greyhound Racing* 98]

wheel, *v.* **1.** Of a race horse, to change direction toward or away from the rail upon leaving the gate.
[(1951) 1981 Maurer *Lang. of the Underworld* 232]
2. In the phrase:
wheel off, Of a race horse, to run a distance, especially in a stated time or condition.
[(1951) 1981 Maurer *Lang. of the Underworld* 232]

→The use of *wheel off* is usually in reference to a training session with a favorable performance.

wheel checks, *n. pl.* In a casino, specially designed chips, without a denomination printed on them, used at the roulette wheel, each player having a different color of chips and the denomination of the chips being declared by the player.
[1981 Silverstone *Player's Guide* 143]

wheel dealer, *n.* In a casino, an employee who conducts the game at a ROULETTE TABLE. See also WHEELMAN.
[ca. 1961 *Hotel Coll*]

wheelhead, *n.* Also written **wheel head.** On a roulette table, the frame featuring an upward-projecting series of ball bearings or roller bearings atop which the wheel is balanced for spinning. Compare WHEEL WELL.
[ca. 1961 *Hotel Coll*]

wheelman, *n.* Also called WHEEL ROLLER. Another name for a ROULETTE TABLE operator. See also WHEEL DEALER.
[1979 Newman *Dealer's Special* 12]

wheel of fortune, *n.* **1. a.** Also called a BIG SIX WHEEL. A circular board or wheel, usually vertically standing with fifty-four spaces divided by pegs. Players may bet on any of six designated spaces on the table layout, with the assurance that one of those spaces will correspond with a space similarly marked on the wheel. Payoffs for the different spaces vary according to the number of spaces on the wheel and are so marked.
[1760 *DAE*]
b. A game of chance with such a wheel and layout. [1763 *DAE*]
2. Another name for a ROULETTE WHEEL.
[1950 Morehead *Culbertson* 655]

wheel roller, *n.* Also called a WHEEL DEALER and WHEELMAN. Another name for a ROULETTE TABLE operator.
[1961 Scarne *Complete Guide* 690]

wheel well, *n.* Also called BOWL. The concave impression on a roulette table that accommodates the roulette wheel. Compare WHEELHEAD.
[1983 Martinet *Oral Coll*]

where's Buster Brown, *n. clause.* An oral statement made by a cheater to a confederate, indicating that crooked dice are being put into a craps game. Compare BUSTER BROWN.
[ca. 1961 *Hotel Coll*]
→Used especially as a signal to a stickman in the presence of a mark.

whip, *n.* **1.** Also called the WAND or ROD or POLE or TOOL. In bank craps, the STICK, about three feet long, curved at one end, and used by the dealer to move the dice around the table layout.
[1983 Martinet *Oral Coll*]
2. Also called the BAT or STICK. In horse racing, a leather-wrapped lash carried by a jockey and used to strike the flanks of a horse in urging it to greater speed.
[Compare 1535 *OED*]

whiplashed, *adj.* In poker, referring to being caught between two players who raise each bet.
[1978 Silberstang *Winning Poker Strategy* 54]
[From a misunderstanding of WHIPSAW (def. 2)]

whipsaw, *v.* **1.** In faro, to lose two bets in a single turn.
[1938 Asbury *Sucker's Progress* 17]
2. In poker, to victimize a player from two directions at the same time, such as the raising of a bet by one player, then, when the victim calls the raise, to have the bet raised again by another player on the other side of the victim.
[1949 Coffin *Secrets* 188]
[From the reciprocal action of a two-man, crosscut saw wielded by two men felling a tree.]

whipsaw bet, *n.* In dice, a bet that the shooter will or will not throw seven before rolling the point.
[(1950) 1981 Maurer *Lang. of the Underworld* 193]

whip shot, *n.* In dice games, any of several controlled casts, such as a DROP, PEEKAY, or HUDSON SHOT, in which the person throwing the dice holds them in a grip with the desired number of pips showing on top, then casts the dice so they rotate horizontally and land with the same number of pips upward at the end of the toss as at the beginning. Compare SPIN.
[1961 Scarne *Complete Guide* 690]

whirl bet, *n.* Often called a WORLD BET. In bank craps, a wager that the next roll of the dice will yield 2, 3, 7, 11, or 12.
[ca. 1961 *Hotel Coll*]

whisk, *n.* A variant name for WHIST.
1816 Singer *Researches* 270. Seymour, in the *Complete Gamester,* 1739, says Whist, vulgarly called *whisk,* is said to be a very ancient game among us; but its original denomination is "Whist or the silent game."
[1621 *OED*]

whisker, *n.* A player at whist.
[1723 *OED;* probably a pun.]

whiskey hole, *n.* In cribbage, the hole before the last hole that marks the end of the game.
[1950 Morehead *Culbertson* 655]

whiskey poker, *n.* Also spelled **whisky poker.**
1. A poker game in which the loser buys drinks.
[1856 *DA,* 1878 *OED*]
2. A variation of poker for which the strongest hand one can draw is a straight flush.
[1864 *DAE*]

whiskey pool, *n.* A game of pool in which the loser buys drinks.
[1860 *DA*]

whist, *n.* Also called WHISK. A trump game resembling its later cousin, bridge.
[1663 *OED*]

white, *n.* In many casinos, a white-colored chip worth five hundred dollars.
[ca. 1961 *Hotel Coll*]

whiteskin, *n.* Also written **white-skin.** In poker, a card ranked 10 or below; any card other than a face card. See also REDSKIN and PAINTSKIN.
[1943 Maurer *Argot*]

whiz machine, *n.* Also spelled WHIZZ MACHINE. In a casino cage, a mechanism for feeding continuously numbered, perforated, multiple-copy forms used to record FILL SLIPS and CREDIT SLIPS for various pits in the casino.
[1982 Martin *Introduction* 9]

whore, *n.* In poker, another term for a QUEEN of any suit.
[1968 Wallace *Poker* 227]

whorehouse cut, *n.* In poker, an irregular method for cutting a deck of cards before the deal, usually by pulling a packet from the middle of the deck and placing it on top of the rest of the pack.
[1971 Livingston *Poker Strategy* 226]

wide cards, *n. phr.* In cribbage, cards with ranks too far apart to form runs, or sequences.
[1953 Crawford *Consistent Winner* 356]

wide-open, *adj.* **1. a.** Pertaining to illegal gambling without concealment.
[1896 *DA,* 1923 *OEDS* (1933 ed.)]
b. Pertaining to a place or activity regarded as notable and unusual.
2. In boxing, unprotected from attack.
[1915 *OEDS*]

widow, *n.* Also called the KITTY. **1.** In various card games, a small packet of cards set aside at the beginning of a hand. The packet may sometimes be purchased or used by a designated participant in the game.
[1864 *DAE, DA*]
2. An amount of money drawn from the pot at poker games used for refreshments for the players.
1887 Keller *Poker* 12. *Widow,* or Kitty.—A percentage taken out of the pool to defray the expenses of the game or the cost of refreshments.
[1887 *DAE, DA*]

wild, *adj.* In various card games, pertaining to a specified card or cards that have a value declared by the player, such as deuces or one-eyed jacks.
[1976 Figgis *Gambler's Handbook* 236]
[1927 *OEDS*]

wild bone, *n.* Also called a WILD FLOWER. In gin rummy, a discard considered unsafe, because discards may be used by the opponent.
[1950 Morehead *Culbertson* 655]

wild card, *n.* In various card games, a card assigned specific values that might vary during the course of a game, and take on any value assigned by the holder, within prescribed limits.
[1949 Coffin *Secrets* 188]
[1940 *OEDS*]

wild flower, *n.* Same as a WILD BONE.
[1950 Morehead *Culbertson* 655]

wild game, *n.* **1.** A card game that features wild cards.
[1949 Coffin *Secrets* 188]
2. A fast-moving poker game, usually featuring high stakes and many raises of the bets.
[1968 Wallace *Poker* 228]

will, *n.* In bank craps, an oral statement indicating a desire to place a bet on the PASS area of the layout. See also WON'T.
1983 Martinet *Oral Coll.* A player can throw a check onto the the table and yell, "bet ten" or whatever [denomination] "he will" or "he won't." That means the player is betting the pass line for *will,* the don't pass for won't.

william, *n.* Also written **william.** Also called **willy.** Any banknote.
1983 Martinet *Oral Coll.* A willy is a bill of any denomination. I regularly hear people refer to, say, a twenty dollar *william* or willy.
[1865 *DA, OEDS; DAS,* labeled "obsolete;" a pun on the nickname *Bill*]

win, *n.* **1.** Usually, **the win.** In a casino, the amount of money generated in a specified period of time, such as one shift.
[ca. 1961 *Hotel Coll*]
2. A victory, especially in a horse race, at dice, cards, roulette, etc.
[1862 *OED*]
3. wins, *pl.* Also **gains.** Winnings, as in a gambling proposition.
[1891 *OED*]

win, *v.* **1.** To achieve a victory in horse racing, at dice, cards, roulette, etc.
[*c*1400 *OED*]
2. To gain in gaming or betting, as a wager.
[1320 *OED*]
3. In cards, to be of higher value and beat another card; to take a trick.
[1680 *OED*]
4. In the phrase:
win out, 1. In faro, to win a bet on the CASE CARD, last card of a rank to be dealt, especially after winning on the first three cards of that rank. Compare LOSE OUT.
[1943 Maurer *Argot*]
2. To achieve victory in a contest at horse racing, at dice, cards, roulette, etc.
[1902 *DAE,* 1898 *OEDS*]

window, *n.* **1.** At race tracks and jai-alai frontons, the counter space at which designated amounts of wagers can be placed and winnings collected, often designated by a system that expedites wagering as two-dollar window, ten-dollar window, etc.
[ca. 1961 *Hotel Coll*]
2. Short for WINDOW CARD.
[1968 Wallace *Poker* 228]

window card, *n.* In poker, a card seen by other players at the table, often intentionally flashed by the player holding the card.
[1978 Brunson *How I Made* 554]

window dressing, *n.* In poker, a card intentionally flashed by a player during a hand for strategic purposes in betting.
[1968 Wallace *Poker* 228]

window's open, *v. clause.* An expression announcing that crooked dice are being switched in and out of the game in an obvious or inept fashion. Compare WHERE'S CHARLIE BROWN.
[(1950) 1981 Maurer *Lang. of the Underworld* 194]

winds, *n. pl.* In mah jongg, sixteen tiles comprising one suit.
[1950 Morehead *Culbertson* 655]

win line, *n.* In bank craps, another term for the pass line, the betting area on the table layout reserved for placing an initial bet at the beginning of a hand.
[1974 Scarne *Dice* 145]

winner, *n.* **1.** One who is victorious in a horse race, at dice, in cards, roulette, etc.
[1611 *OED*]
2. One who gains at gambling.
[1596 *OED*]
3. In faro, the second card exposed in one turn, or set of two cards.
[1938 Asbury *Sucker's Progress* 8]
4. winners, *pl.* In dice games, dice that have been altered and which win more often than chance should allow.
[(1950) 1981 Maurer *Lang. of the Underworld* 194]

winner take all, *n. phr.* Also **winner-takes-all.** An event or contest in which the victor claims the entire prize, there being no award for second place or any other entries.
[ca. 1961 *Hotel Coll*]
[1969 *OEDS*]

winning hand, *n. phr.* In poker, the best hand at the showdown, or end of the game.
[ca. 1961 *Hotel Coll*]

winning out, *n. phr.* In faro, betting on a card rank that wins all four times in one game. See also WIN OUT.
[1938 *DA*]

winning post, *n. phr.* In racing, the pillar that marks the finish line on a race track.
[1820 *OED*]

winnings, *n. pl.* *Usually plural in form, but singular in use.* The amount of money accumulated from gambling propositions or contests in which monetary rewards are offered to the victor. [*c*1380 *OED*]

winning streak, *n. phr.* The achieving of victory in several consecutive contests or gambling propositions.
[1978 Brunson *How I Made* 545]
[1968 *OEDS*]

winning team, *n. phr.* In horse racing, an entry comprised of a horse and jockey that has won before while paired together.
[1955 Hillis *Pari-Mutuel Betting* 119]

winning ticket, *n. phr.* In keno, an OUTSIDE ORIGINAL TICKET, or player's copy of a purchased keno slip, with a winning combination of numbers marked on it.
[1982 Martin *Introduction* 11]

win ticket, *n.* In racing, a slip recording a wager that an entry will win, as opposed to *place* or *show,* that is, finish second or third.
[ca. 1961 *Hotel Coll*]

wire, *n.* **1.** On a race course, the finish line, as marked with an imaginary line crossing the track.
[1887 *DAE, DA, OEDS*]
2. A signal sent between cheaters in a card or dice game.
[(1950) 1981 Maurer *Lang. of the Underworld* 194]

wired, *adj.* **1.** In poker games like stud and hold 'em, referring to the first two cards of the same rank being dealt to one player.
[1949 Coffin *Secrets* 172]
2. In twenty-one, referring to an unbeatable hand, that is, an ace and a card counting for ten points.
[1983 Martinet *Oral Coll*]

wire joint, *n.* Same as JUICE JOINT.
[(1950) 1981 Maurer *Lang. of the Underworld* 194]

wire to wire, *adj. phr.* Also written **wire-to-wire.** From start to finish; on a race track, from the beginning line for a race to the finish line.
[1982 *Today's Racing Digest*]
[1974 *OEDS*]

with the house, *prep. phr.* Especially in the expression: **bet with the house.** In bank craps, to place a wager on the don't pass area of the layout.
[1972 Kofoed *Meanderings* 204]

wolf trap, *n.* Also called a BRACE HOUSE or DEADFALL or SNAP HOUSE. A gambling establishment devoted to cheating victims. *Obsolete.* Compare TRAP.
[1938 Asbury *Sucker's Progress* 185]

won, *n.* Abbreviated as W. On a racing form, an indication of any previous victory by a horse.
[1955 Hillis *Pari-Mutuel Betting* 89]

won't, *n.* In bank craps, an oral statement indicating a desire to place a bet on the DON'T PASS area of the layout. See also WILL.
1983 Martinet *Oral Coll.* A player can throw a check onto the table and yell, "bet ten" or whatever [denomination] "he will" or "he won't." That means the player is betting the pass line for will, the don't pass for *won't.*

woo, *v.* In mah jongg, to declare a completed hand and the end of play. Compare BINGO.
[1922 *OEDS*]

wood, *n.* **1.** Also called KIBITZER or LUMBER. An observer of a game of cards, chess, etc., who

makes comments about the playing of the game, but does not participate.
[(1950) 1981 Maurer *Lang. of the Underworld* 194]
2. In casino craps, the grooved railing around the top of the craps table where players stack their chips.
[1983 Martinet *Oral Coll*]

wooden goose, *n. phr.* In keno, a sphere, usually eight to ten inches in diameter, that contains the small numbered balls drawn for the game. Compare KENO GOOSE.
[1978 Nelson *Gaming* 34]

wooden hand, *n. phr.* In poker, a hand that has no possibility for being improved or being competitive. Discards or useless cards are referred to as DEADWOOD.
[1978 Larson *Vocabulary* 102]

Woolworth, *n.* Also written **woolworth.** In hold 'em poker. Same as BARBARA HUTTON.
1981 Golad *Oral Coll.* A player sits there hour after hour with only two cards to look at [in hold 'em poker], so the different combinations get names . . . for example, a 5 and a 10 is a barbara hutton or a *woolworth.* That's after the five-and-dime stores. She was the Woolworth heiress.
[1949 Coffin *Secrets* 188]
[For (F.W.) *Woolworth,* a retail store chain, often called a "5 & 10¢ store"]

woppitzer, *n.* A person with halitosis or body odor who hangs around card games, usually offering advice and making comments, and otherwise making a nuisance of himself.
[1961 Scarne *Complete Guide* 690]

work, *n.* **1.** Also **works,** *pl.* A cheating device or tool, usually an altered die or playing card.
[(1950) 1981 Maurer *Lang. of the Underworld* 194]
2. Any of a variety of methods for altering cards or dice for purposes of cheating.
[(1950) 1981 Maurer *Lang. of the Underworld* 194]

work, *v.* **1.** To operate a cheating scheme; to exploit or swindle persons while gambling.
[1882 *DAE*, 1892 *OED*, 1884 *OEDS*]
2. Of a wager on the layout in craps, to be operational as a bet on the next roll of the dice. See WORKING COMING OUT.
1983 Martinet *Oral Coll.* On the come out, a dealer will ask those who have hardway bets whether those bets *work*, that is, are eligible to win or lose. Some bets don't *work* on the come out roll, but are left on the layout for the next roll.
3. In the phrases:
work the broads or **fake the broads.** To cheat at cards, especially at three-card monte. See also BROAD TOSSER.
[*DSUE:* ca 1840]
work the juice, To operate an electromagnet on a crooked dice table, roulette wheel, wheel of fortune, etc. Compare JUICE (def. 2).
[1981 Jenkins *Johnny Moss* 127]

worker, *n.* **1.** A cheater or a hustler; one who finds opportunities to cheat others, often on a small scale.
[ca. 1961 *Hotel Coll*]
2. In bank craps, a bet that is in action, or on the table layout.
[1983 Martinet *Oral Coll*]

working, *adj.* In bank craps, referring to a wager on the table layout, especially in the case of a bet that is normally withdrawn, such as a HARDWAY bet, during the first, or COMEOUT roll of a hand.
[ca. 1961 *Hotel Coll*]

working a cup, *n. phr.* Cheating on a slot machine by wedging the payout chute open with a tube or some other rounded, cuplike device.
[1941 Fair *Spill the Jackpot!* 37]

working coming out, *n. phr.* In bank craps, an announcement that place bets or odds on bets, which are normally called off during the first roll of a new hand, are active wagers. Oftentimes players will leave certain wagers on the layout rather than removing them and then replacing them. Oral directions to the dealers indicate which bets are *working,* or active, and which are to be considered inactive.
[1983 Martinet *Oral Coll*]

working host, *n.* In a casino, a representative of the owner who greets favorite customers and helps them arrange for rooms, show tickets, and special favors. See also CASINO HOST, GREETER.
[ca. 1961 *Hotel Coll*]

working points, *n. pl.* A percentage of ownership in a casino by a person employed full time in the casino. The arrangement ensures the individual of a job and reassures other owners that the establishment is being carefully watched. Compare POINTS.
[ca. 1961 *Hotel Coll*]

working stack, *n.* In bank craps, the stack of chips directly under the hand of the dealer, used after a roll of the dice to pay players' winnings, and replenished with other players' losses.
[1973 Clark *Oral Coll*]

working the telegraph, *n.* A method of cheating whereby a confederate signals the value of the victim's cards to the victim's opponent. Compare TELEGRAPH, *n.* and *v.*
1859 Green *Gambler's Tricks* 104. Behind the rich player, and in such a position as enables him to have a full view of his hand, is stationed a confederate of the rogue-player, who conveys to his colleague, by preconcerted telegraphic signals, made by the fingers, what is doing, or passed, by the rich opponent. This is called *working the telegraph,* and is as successful as it is dishonorable.

world bet, *n.* Same as a WHIRL BET.
[1973 Clark *Oral Coll*]

wrap, *n.* **1.** In a casino, coins, collectively, rolled by denomination in paper tubes. Nickels are in one-dollar or two-dollar *wrap,* quarters in five-dollar or ten-dollar *wrap,* and so on.
[1977 Nevada Gaming Control *Internal* 22]
2. In a casino weigh room, the process for separating coins and encasing them in paper tubes.
[1982 Martin *Introduction* 23]

wring, *v.* Same as RING, *v.* Compare COLD DECK.
[Compare *a*1300 *OED,* meaning "to extort (money) from"]

write, *n.* In a casino, the total amount collected in a fixed period, usually one shift, from keno, bingo and bookmaking.
[1957 *Nevada Gaming Regulations* 33]

write, *v.* In keno, to copy tickets for customers, collect wagers and pay winners.
[1973 Clark *Oral Coll*]

writer, *n.* In keno, a person who copies tickets for customers, collects wagers, and pays winners.
[1973 Friedman *Casino Games* 103]

writer machine, *n.* In keno, the mechanism that feeds consecutively numbered tickets to the writer and in which the inside original ticket is locked during the drawing of numbers for the game.
[1978 Alexander *Glossary* 17]

wrong bet, *n.* In bank craps, a wager placed on the *don't pass* area of the table layout, indicating the player expects the dice not to pass. Compare RIGHT BET.
[1974 Scarne *Dice* 77]

wrong bettor, *n.* Also called a WRONG PLAYER or WRONGIE. In casino craps, a person who wagers that the dice will lose, that a point will not be established, or if established, that the point will not be rerolled before a 7 is rolled. Compare RIGHT BETTOR
[(1951) 1981 Maurer *Lang. of the Underworld* 194]

wrong horse, *n.* Also shortened to **wrong. 1.** A racehorse held back during the race so that it cannot win. [1889 *OED*]
2. Usually **wrong 'un.** A horse that has run at a flat-race meeting not recognized by the Jockey Club. [1895 *OED*]

wrongie, *n.* Same as a WRONG BETTOR.
[1974 Scarne *Dice* 77]

wrong player, *n.* Same as a WRONG BETTOR.
[(1950) 1981 Maurer *Lang. of the Underworld* 194]

X, Y, Z

X, *n.* **1.** In card playing, a symbol for a low ranking card or one unimportant to the hand.
[1922 *OEDS*]
→Usually *X* appears in printed descriptions of card games.
2. A ten dollar bill.
[1834 *DA,* 1837 *DAE, OED*]
3. the X. The control of gambling in a city, town, neighborhood, etc.
[(1950) 1981 Maurer *Lang. of the Underworld* 194]
4. In the phrase:
have the x or **have the x on, 1.** To control the gambling in a place, especially a town.
[(1950) 1981 Maurer *Lang. of the Underworld* 194]
2. To be good enough to beat consistently another player.
[(1951) 1981 Maurer *Lang. of the Underworld* 194]

yarborough, *n.* Also written **Yarborough.** In games like bridge and whist, a worthless hand, usually one with no cards ranked higher than 9.
[1900 *OED*]

yard, *n.* **1.** A sum of one hundred dollars.
[1926 *OEDS*]
2. A sum of one thousand dollars.
[1932 *OEDS*]

yard and a half, *n. phr.* A sum of one hundred and fifty dollars.
[ca. 1961 *Hotel Coll*]

ye old eleven, *n. phr.* In craps, the number 11 rolled with the dice; mistaken from YOLEVEN. 1983 Martinet *Oral Coll.* Craps dealers learn to call out numbers in a distinctive way so the other dealers can make no mistake in hearing. The number 11 is called "yoleven." There can be no mistaking that for "seven." But players don't hear correctly and start saying "ye old eleven."

yo, *n.* Short for YOLEVEN.
[1973 Clark *Oral Coll*]

yoleven, *n.* In craps, the oral call for the number eleven.
[1983 Martinet *Oral Coll*]

→The pronunciation distinguishes the number from "seven," so there can be no mistake in the noisy environment of most crap games.

younger hand, *n.* Any of the players to the left of the first player, who is called the ELDER HAND. 1860 Pardon *Handbook* 25. *Younger hand*—The player to the right of the dealer.
[1714 *OED*]

zero, *n.* On an American roulette wheel, one of thirty-eight slots on the wheel, with a corresponding betting spot on the table layout.
[1859 *OED*]

z-game, *n.* In a cardroom, the lowest-stake poker game in progress.
[1949 Coffin *Secrets* 188]

zing it in, *v. phr.* Also shortened to **zing.** To bet heavily, especially on a gambling proposition that seems to promise a sure winner.
[(1950) 1981 Maurer *Lang. of the Underworld* 194]

zombie, *n.* In poker, a player without TELLS, one who shows no emotion and has no distinctive habits that allow other players to estimate the worth of his hand.
[ca. 1961 *Hotel Coll*]
[Compare 1819 *OEDS,* meaning "a soulless corpse said to have been revived by witchcraft"]

zoo joint, *n.* An establishment or a group of establishments, as at a carnival, devoted to confidence games and in which cheating regularly takes place.
[1977 Cahill *Recollections* 6]

zuke, *n.* Gratuity; tip given to a casino dealer or other employee for services rendered, especially services perceived as bringing luck or good fortune to the person giving the tip. See also TOKE.
[1973 Clark *Oral Coll*]
→Used almost exclusively by dealers.

SOURCES

Some source materials found with references in the body of the dictionary are not listed here. These sources generally provide one or perhaps two quotations for one or two entries and do not deal in their general scope with gambling.

Adams, Ramon F. *Western Words: A Dictionary of the American West*. Norman; University of Oklahoma Press, 1968.

Ainslie, Tom. *Ainslie's Complete Guide to Thoroughbred Racing*. New York; Simon and Schuster, 1968 (1979).

______. *Ainslie's Encyclopedia of Thoroughbred Handicapping*. New York; William Morrow and Co., Inc., 1978.

Alexander Grant and Company. *A Glossary of Terms Used in the Casino Industry*. Boulder City, Nev.; I & O Publishing Company, 1978.

Andrews, E. S. *Artifice Ruse and Subterfuge at the Card Table; A Treatise on the Science and Art of Manipulating Cards* by S. W. Erdnase [psued.]. Cover title *Card Secrets Exposed*. Chicago; K. C. Card Co., 1902.

Anness, Diane. *Dummy Up and Deal: A Glossary of the Las Vegas 21 Dealers* [sic] *Language*. Las Vegas; University of Nevada unpublished M.A. thesis, Anthropology, 1977.

Anonymous. *The American Card Player: Containing Clear and Comprehensive Directions for Playing the Games of Euchre, Whist, Bezique, All-Fours, Pitch, Commercial Pitch, French Fours, All Fives, Cassino, Cribbage, Straight and Draw Poker, and Whiskey Poker: Together with all the Laws of Those Games*. New York; Dick & Fitzgerald, Publishers, 1866.

Anonymous. *Guide—Monte Carlo. Explanation of Trente et Quarente and Roulette. Various Methods of Staking and Progressing*. [n.p.], 1886.

Anonymous. *Hoyle's Card Games, Complete; With an Appendix, Containing His Guide to the Turf*. Bath, England, 1824.

Anonymous. *Hoyle's Games: Containing Laws on Chess, Draughts, Backgammon, Billiards, Cricket, and Games of Cards*. London, 1857.

Anonymous. *Hoyle's Games Improved: Being Practical Treatises on the Following Fashionable Games, Viz. Whist, Quadrille, Piquet, Chess, Backgammon, Billiards, Cricket, Tennis, Quinze, Hazard, and Lansquenet; In Which are also Conttained the Method of Betting at Those Games Upon Equal or Advantageous Terms; Including the Laws of the Several Games as Settled and Agreed to at White's and Stapleton's Chocolate Houses*. London, 1779.

Anonymous. *Hoyle's Improved Edition of the Rules for Playing Fashionable Games at Cards, &c*. New York, 1830.

Anonymous. *Poker: How to Play It. A Sketch of the Great American Game with its Laws and Rules and Some of its Amusing Incidents*. London: Griffith, Farrar, Okeder, & Welsh, 1887.

"A Professor." See [Meehan, Charles Henry Wharton], 1877.
"A Professor." *The Law and Practice of the Game of Euchre*. Philadelphia; T. B. Peterson & Brothers, 1862.
Asbury, Herbert. *Sucker's Progress: An Informal History of Gambling in America from the Colonies to Canfield*. New York; Dodd, Mead & Company, 1938.
Atti, David Michael. "Dealing on the Las Vegas Strip." Audiotape interview, Special Collections, University of Nevada, Las Vegas, 1978.
Baccarat, The Facts of. Las Vegas; Gambler's Book Club, 1970.
Baxter-Wray. *Round Games with Cards: A Practical Treatise on all the Most Popular Games, with their Different Variations, and Hints for their Practice*. London, 1897.
Betram, James Glass. See Curzon, Louis Henry.
Binion, Lester Ben. *Some Recollections of a Texas and Las Vegas Gaming Operator*. Reno; University of Nevada Oral History Project, 1973.
Blackbridge, John. *The Complete Poker Player: A Practical guide book to the American national game: containing mathematical and experimental analyses of the probabilities of draw poker*. New York; Fitzgerald Publishing Corporation, 1880.
Black, Robert. *Horse-racing in England: A Synoptical Review*. London, 1893.
Blanche, Ernest. *You Can't Win: Facts and Fallacies About Gambling*. Washington, D.C.; Public Affairs Press, 1949.
Bohn, H. G., ed. *The Handbook of Games: Comprising New or Carefully Revised Treatises on Whist, Piquet, Ecarte, Lansquenet, Boston, Quadrille, Cribbage, and other Card Games; Faro, Rouge et Noir, Hazard, Roulette, Backgammon, Draughts, Billiards, Bagatelle, American Bowls, Etc., Etc.* London; Bell & Daldy, 1867.
Brown, C. F. *The Turf Expositor; Containing the Origin of Horse Racing, Breeding for the Turf, Training, Trainers, Jockeys; Cocktails, and the system of Cocktail Racing Illustrated; The Turf and its Abuses; The Science of Betting Money, so as Always to Come off a Winner, Elucidated by a Variety of Examples; The Rules and Laws of Horse Racing; and Every Other Information Connected with the Operations of the Turf.* London, 1829.
Brown, Garret. *How to Beat the Game.* New York, 1903.
Buchele, W(alter) J. *Greyhound Racing Guide.* Bonita Spring, Florida; n.p., 1968.
Cahill, Robbins E. *Recollections of Work in State Politics, Government, Taxation, Gaming Control, Clark County Administration, and the Nevada Resort Association.* Reno; University of Nevada Oral History Project, 1977.
Caroll, David. *Playboy's Illustrated Treasury of Gambling*. New York; Crown Publishers, Inc., 1977.
Cassidy, Frederic G., ed. *Dictionary of American Regional English,* vol. 1. Boston; Harvard University Press, 1985.
"Cavendish". See [Jones, Henry].
Chatto, William Andrew. *Facts and Speculations on the Origin and History of Playing Cards*. London, 1848.
Churchill, Major Seton. *Betting and Gambling*. London, 1894.
Clark, Thomas L. *Oral Collection*. Las Vegas, 1971-1987.
Coffin, George S. *Fortune Poker*. Philadelphia; David McKay Company, 1949.
Coffin, George S. *Secrets of Winning Poker.* North Hollywood, Cal.; Wilshire Book Company, 1949, 1976.
Coggins, Ross. *The Gambling Menace.* Nashville; Broadman Press, 1966.
Conboie, Joseph A. *Lincoln Slim from the Golden West*. San Francisco; by the author, 1943.
Cook, Fred J. *Gambling, Inc.: Treasure Chest of the Underground.* New York; The Nation Company, 1960. Special Issue, *The Nation.*
Cotton, C. *The Compleat Gamester: Or, Instructions how to Play at Billiards, Trucks, Bowls, and Chess: Together with all manner of usual and most Gentile Games either on Cards, or Dice.* Second ed. London, 1680.

Cox, William R. *Murder in Vegas.* New York; Signet Books, 1970.
Courtney, William Prideaux. *English Whist and Whist Players.* London, 1894.
Craigie, William A. and James R. Hulbert, eds. *A Dictionary of American English on Historical Principles.* Chicago; The University of Chicago Press, 1938-44.
Crawford, John R. *How to be a Consistent Winner in the Most Popular Card Games.* New York; Doubleday and Co., Inc., 1953.
Crawley, Captain. *Backgammon: Its Theory and Practice; with Something of its History.* London, 1860.
Curzon, Louis Henry [James Glass Bertram]. *The Blue Ribbon of the Turf.* London, 1893.
Curtis, David A. *The Science of Draw Poker; A Treatise Comprising the Analysis of principles, Calculations of Chances, Codification of Rules, Study of Situations, Glossary of Poker Terms Necessary to a Comprehensive Understanding of the Great American Game.* New York, 1901.
Custer, Robert L. and Lillian F. "Characteristics of the Recovering Compulsive Gambler: A Survey of 150 Members of Gamblers Anonymous." *Proceedings of the Fourth Annual Conference on Gambling.* Reno, Nevada, pp. 20 ft. December, 1978.
Demaris, Ovid. *The Last Mafioso.* New York; Times Books, 1981.
[Dick, William Brisbane] See "Trumps," 1868
Drazazgo, John. *Wheels of Fortune.* Springfield, Ill.; Charles C. Thomas, 1963.
Dunne, Charles. See Persius, Charles.
Eichhorn, J. Charles. *American Skat, or The Game of Skat Defined: A Descriptive and Comprehensive Guide on the Rules and Plays of this Interesting Game, Including Table, Definitions of Phrases, Fitnesses, and a Full Treatise on Skat as Played To-day.* Michigan, 1898.
Eidrah, Trebor [Robert Hardie]. *Hoyle Made Familiar; Being a Companion to the Card Table.* Edinburgh, 1836.
Ellangowan. *Sporting Anecdotes: Being Anecdotal Annals, Descriptions, Tales and Incidents of Horse-Racing, Betting, Card-Playing, Pugilism, Gambling, Cock-Fighting, Pedestrianism, Fox-hunting, Angling, Shooting, and Other Sports.* London, 1889.
Erdnase, S. W. [anagram] See Andrews, E. S.
Evans, Gerritt M. *How Gamblers Win: or, The Advantage Player's Manual; Being a Complete and Scientific Expose of the Manner of Playing All the Various Advantages in the Games of Bluff, or Poker; Seven Up; Euchre; Vingt-un, or Twenty-one; Whist, Etc., Etc. Together with a Thorough and Finished Analysis of the Science of Playing "on the Square," and A General Treatise on Advantage Playing.* New York; Gerritt M. Evans & Co., 1865.
Ewart, Andrew, ed. *Win at Flatracing with the Experts.* London; Stanley Paul, 1974.
Fair, A. A. (Erle Stanley Gardner). *Spill the Jackpot!* Philadelphia; William Morrow and Company, Inc., 1941.
Fairfield, William S. "Las Vegas: The Sucker and the Almost-Even Break." *Reporter,* vol. 8, no. 12, June 9, 1953, pp. 15-21.
Figgis, E. Lenox. *Gambler's Handbook.* Feltham, England; Hamlyn Publishing Group Limited, 1976.
Fisher, Steve. *No House Limit: A Novel of Las Vegas.* New York; E. P. Dutton, 1958.
Fisk, Margaret Cronin. *The Gambler's Bible.* New York; Drake Publications, 1976.
Florence, William James. *The Handbook of Poker.* London and New York, 1982.
Forster, R. F. *Cooncan (Conquian); A Game of Cards Also Called "Rum".* New York, 1913.
______. *Dice and Dominoes.* New York, 1897.
______. *Poker.* New York, 1897.
______. *Practical Poker.* London, 1904.
Fraiken, Glenn L. *Inside Nevada Gambling: Adventures of a Winning System Player.* New York; Exposition Press, 1965.

Frere, Thomas. *Hoyle's Games, Containing all the Modern Methods of Playing the Latest and Most Fashionable Games. With a Brief History of Playing Cards.* Boston; DeWolfe, Fiske and Company, 1875.

Friedman, Bill. *Casino Games.* New York; Golden Press, 1973.

Friedman, William. *Casino Management.* Secaucus, N.J.; Lyle Stuart, Inc., 1974.

Gamblers Anonymous. *Sharing Recovery Through Gamblers Anonymous.* Los Angeles; Gamblers Anonymous Publications, 1983.

Gambling Times. Hollywood, Cal.; S.R.S. Enterprises, 1977-82.

Garcia, Frank. *Marked Cards and Loaded Dice.* Englewood Cliffs, N.J.; Prentice-Hall Publishers, 1962.

______. *How to Detect Crooked Gambling.* New York; Arco Publishing Company, Inc., 1977.

Gard, T. *Guide to the Turf.* London, 1809.

Gardner, Jack. *Gambling: A Guide to Information Sources.* Detroit; Gale Research Co., 1980.

Goffman, Erving. *Interaction Ritual.* Garden City, New York, 1967.

Golad, Brad. *Oral Collection.* Las Vegas, 1981.

Gould, Nat. *On and Off the Turf in Australia.* London, 1895.

Grafstein, Sam. "The Dice Doctor." Oral Collection. Las Vegas, 1984.

Greene, Jonathan H. *An Exposure of the Arts and Miseries of Gambling; Designed Especially as a Warning to the Youthful and Inexperienced, Against the Evils of that Odious and Destructive Vice.* Cincinnati, 1843.

______. *Gambling Exposed. A Full Exposition of all the Various Arts, Mysteries, and Miseries of Gambling.* Philadelphia, 1857. [Same text as Greene, 1843.]

Green, J. H. *Gambler's Tricks with Cards, Exposed and Explained.* New York; Dick & Fitzgerald, Publishers, 1859.

"H." *Roulette: A Treatise on the Game.* London, 1905.

Hardie, Robert. See Eidrah, Trebor.

Harrah, William F. *My Recollections of the Hotel-Casino Industry and as an Auto Collecting Enthusiast.* Reno; University of Nevada Oral History Project, 1978.

Heather, H. E. *Cards and Card Tricks, Containing a Brief History of Playing Cards; Full Instructions, with Illustrated Hands, for Playing Nearly all Known Games of Chance or Skill; And Directions for Performing a Number of Amusing Tricks.* London; L. Upcott Gill, [1876]

Herwitz, Raymond A. *Yes, You Can Win . . . But Don't Bet the Rent Money: The Story of Nevada Gaming.* New York; Vantage Press, 1969.

Hillis, James. *Pari-Mutuel Betting: The Information Needed for Conservative Successful Betting.* Fresno, Calif.; Academy Library Guild, 1955.

Hilton Hotel. *Systems and Procedures Documentation.* Unpublished, 1979.

Hoffman, Professor [Angelo John Lewis]. *Baccarat Fair and Foul; Being an Explanation of the Game, and a Warning Against its Dangers.* London; George Routledge and Sons, Ltd., 1891.

Hopkins, A. D. "The Suite Life", *Nevada,* vol. 45, no. 5 (September/October), 1985, pp. 30 ff.

Hotel College, UNLV. Unpublished Manuscript (Collected from a Variety of sources, 1961-1979 by students of David J. Christianson, Robert Martin, W. Friedman, and others).

Hoyle, Edmond. *A Short Treatise on the Game of Whist.* 6th ed. London, 1746.

______. *A Short Treatise on the Game of Back-gammon.* London, 1745.

______. *The Accurate Gamester's Companion: Containing Infallible Rules for Playing the Game of Whist to Perfection in all its Branches; Treated in an Easy Manner, and*

Illustrated with Variety of Cases; Also the Laws of the Game, Calculations Relative to it, &c. To Which are Added the Games of Quadrille, Piquet, Chess and Back Gammon, Fully Explained; Likewise a Dictionary for Whist, and an Artificial Memory. London, 1748.

Hughes, Thomas F. *Dealing Casino Blackjack.* Las Vegas; by the author, 1979.

Jackdaw, John [Douglas William Jerrold]. *The Hand-book of Swindling. By the Late Captain Barabbas Whitefeather, Late of the Body-Guard of His Majesty, King Carlos; Treasurer of the British Wine and Vinegar Company; Trustee for the Protection of the River Thames from Incendiaries; Principal Inventor of Poyais Stock; Ranger of St. George's Fields; Original Patenter of the Parachute Conveyance Association; Knight or Every Order of the Fleece; Scamp and Cur.* London, 1839.

Jenkins, Don. *Johnny Moss: Champion of Champions.* (n.c.); JM, 1981 (by the author).

Jerrold, Douglas William. See Jackdaw, John.

[Jones, Henry] "Cavendish". *Card Essays, Clay's Decisions, and Card-Table Talk.* London; Thomas De La Rue & Co., 1879.

______. *The Laws of Ecarte; Adopted by the Turf and Portland Clubs with a Treatise on the Game,* Fourth Edition. London; Thomas De La Rue & Co., Ltd., 1897.

______. *The Laws of Piquet; Adopted by the Portland and Turf Clubs with a Treatise on the Game.* London; Thomas De La Rue & Co., Ltd., 1901.

Jones, Jack. *Wilbur Clark's Desert Inn, Las Vegas, Nevada: Souvenir Gaming Guide.* Las Vegas; Silver State Publishing Co., 1951.

K(izzire), Jimmy. *25 Different Ways to Wager at Golf and Win.* [Las Vegas, Nevada] 1985.

Keller, John W. *The Game of Draw Poker.* New York; Frederick A. Stokes Company, 1887.

______. *The Game of Euchre.* New York; Frederick A. Stokes Company, 1887.

Kofoed, Leslie S. *Kofoed's Meanderings in Lovelock Business, Nevada Government, the U.S. Marshal's Office, and the Gaming Industry.* Reno; University of Nevada Oral History Project, 1972.

Kunard, R. S. *The Book of Card Tricks for Drawing Room and Stage Entertainments; with an Exposure of Tricks as Practiced by Card-Sharpers and Swindlers.* London, 1888.

Laing-Meason, M. R. *Turf Frauds and Turf Practices; or Spiders and Flies.* London; George Rutledge and Sons, 1868.

Las Vegas Review Journal, 1960-1987, passim.

Las Vegas Sun, 1950-1987, passim.

Leeds, Josiah W. *Horse-Racing; The Beginnings of Gambling; The Lottery.* Philadelphia, 1895.

Lemmel, Maurice. *Gambling, Nevada Style.* New York; Doubleday and Co., 1964.

Lewis, Angelo John. See Hoffman, Professor.

Lewis, Oscar. *Sagebrush Casinos: The Story of Legal Gambling in Nevada.* Garden City, N.Y.; Doubleday and Company, 1953.

Lillard, Richard G. *Desert Challenge: An Interpretation of Nevada.* Lincoln; University of Nebraska Press, 1942.

Linn, Edward A. *Big Julie.* New York; Walker Press, 1974.

Livingston, A. D. *Poker Strategy and Winning Play.* New York; J.B. Lippincott Co., 1971.

Lucas, Theophilus. *Memoirs of the Lives, Intrigues, and Comical Adventures of the Most Famous Gamesters and Celebrated Sharpers in the Reigns of Charles II, James II, William III, and Queen Anne. Wherein is Contained the Secret History of Gaming, Discovering all the Most Sharping Tricks and Cheats (Us'd by Slight of Hand) at Picquet, Gleek, Lanterloo, Bankasalet, Basset, Primero, Cribbidge, Verquere, Tick-Tack, Grand-Tricktrack; and all the English, Dutch, French, Spanish, and Italian Games, Play'd with Cards, Dice, Tables, or Otherwise. The Whole Calculated for the Meridians of London, Bath, Tunbridge, and the Groom-Quarters: Printed for Jonas*

Brown without Temple-bar, and Ferdinando Burleigh in Amencorner. London, 1714.
Lyall, J. G. *The Merry Gee-Gee; How to Breed, Break, and Ride Him For'ard Away and the Noble Art of Backing Winners on the Turf.* London, 1899.
MacDougall, Michael and Furnas, J.C. *Gambler's Don't Gamble.* New York; Garden City Publishing Co., 1939.
MacDougall, Samuel Davis (Michael). *Danger in the Cards.* Chicago; Ziff-Davis Publishing Co., 1943.
"The Major" [Barnet Phillips]. *The Poker Primer or How to Play Draw Poker.* New York, 1913.
Martin, Robert. "Introduction to Casino Management: General Glossary," College of Hotel Administration, University of Nevada, Las Vegas. Unpublished, 1982.
Martinet, Thomas A. *Oral Collection.* Las Vegas, 1983-1987.
Martinez, Tomas M. *The Gambling Scene (Why People Gamble).* Springfield, Ill.; Charles C. Thomas, 1983.
Maskelyne, John Nevil. *Sharps and Flats, A Complete Revelation of the Secrets of Cheating at Games of Chance and Skill.* London, 1895.
Mathews, Mitford M., ed. *A Dictionary of Americanisms on Historical Principles.* Chicago; The University of Chicago Press, 1951.
Maurer, David W. "The Argot of the Faro Bank," *American Speech,* vol. 18, no. 1, pp. 3-11, 1943.
______. *Language of the Underworld.* Lexington; University Press of Kentucky, 1981. [Dates in parentheses indicate previous date of publication of a monograph.]
Maxim, Sir Hiram S. *Monte Carlo Facts and Fantasies.* London, 1904.
McQuaid, Clement, ed. *Gambler's Digest.* Chicago; Follett Publishing Co., 1971.
[Meehan, Charles Henry Wharton] "A Professor". *The Laws and Practice of the Game of Euchre.* Philadelphia, 1877.
Mencken, H.L. *The American Language: Supplement II.* New York; Alfred A. Knopf, 1948.
Miller, Don Ethan. *The Book of Jargon.* New York; Macmillan Publishing Co. Inc., 1981.
Monte Carlo: Its Sin and Splendor; by one of the victims. New York; Richard K. Fox Publishers, 1893.
Monte Carlo Secret Service Sealed Book ("Don't be a Sucker;" Cheating Exposed; 100 Ways to Win, 100 Ways to Cheat; Protection Information, 200 Illustrations, Price $5.00. [No City or Publisher,] 1925.
Morehead, Albert H., and Mott-Smith, Geoffrey. *Culbertson's Hoyle: The New Encyclopedia of Games with Official Rules.* New York; The Greystone Press, 1950.
Morris, John. *Wanderings of a Vagabond; An Autobiography.* New York; 1873.
Murray, James A. H. *et al,* eds. *A New English Dictionary on Historical Principles,* and Supplements. Oxford; Oxford University Press, 1933 ff.
Nelson, Warren. *Gaming from the Old Days to Computers.* Reno; University of Nevada Oral History Project, 1978.
Nevada Gaming Control Board. *Internal Control Questionnaire 1.* Carson City; State of Nevada, 1977.
Nevada Gaming Regulations. Carson City; Nevada Gaming Commission and State Gaming Control Board, 1935-1982.
Nevada Magazine. (Special Issue: "Fifty Years of Gaming.") Carson City; State of Nevada, vol. 41. Spring, 1981.
Nevada Revised Statutes: Vol. 4, Gambling and Sports. Carson City; Legislative Counsel Bureau, 1963.
Newman, David, ed. *Esquire's Book of Gambling.* New York; Harper and Row, 1935, 1962.
Newman, Mike, *Dealer's Special.* Las Vegas; Gambler's Book Club Press, 1979.
Olsen, Edward A. *My Careers as a Journalist in Oregon, Idaho, and Nevada; in Nevada*

Gaming Control; and at the University of Nevada. Reno; University of Nevada Oral History Project, 1972.

[Payne, William]. *Maxims for Playing the Game of Whist; With all Necessary Calculations and Laws of the Game.* London, 1773.

Pardon, George Frederick. *A Handbook of Whist on the Text of Hoyle.* London; George Routledge and Sons, 1860.

[Pardon, George Frederick]. *Hoyle's Games Modernised. Being Explanations of the Best Modes of Playing the Most Popular Games in Present Use with Rules and Regulations Adopted at the Clubs.* London; George Routledge and Sons, 1863.

Parollini, Jim. *Oral Collection.* Las Vegas, 1982.

Partridge, Eric. *Dictionary of Slang and Unconventional English.* Eighth Edition. New York, 1984.

Passer, Don. *Winning Big at the Track with Money Management.* New York; Playboy Press, 1981.

Persius, Charles [Charles Dunne]. *Rouge et Noir: The Academicians of 1823; or the Greeks of the Palais Royale and the Clubs of St. James's.* London, 1823.

Phillips, Barnet. See "The Major."

Powell, J. V. *Verbal Dexterity and the Gambler's Art: A Socio-Linguistic Study of Language Skills and Strategies in Las Vegas Gambling.* Vancouver, Canada; University of British Columbia Dept. of Anthropology and Sociology, 1974.

Preston, Thomas Austin (Amarillo Slim), with Cox, Bill G. *Play Poker to Win.* New York; Grosset and Dunlap, 1973.

Proctor, Richard A. *Chance and Luck: A Discussion of the Laws of Luck, Coincidences, Wagers, Lotteries, and the Fallacies of Gambling; with Notes on Poker and Martingales.* London, 1887.

Puzo, Mario. *Inside Las Vegas.* New York; Grosset & Dunlap, 1977.

Quinn, John Philip. *Fools of Fortune: Or, Gambling and Gamblers, Comprehending a History of the Vice in Ancient and Modern Times, and in Both Hemispheres, and Exposition of its Alarming Prevalence and Destructive Effects; With an Unreserved and Exhaustive Disclosure of such Frauds, Tricks and Devices as are Practiced by "Professional" Gamblers, "Confidence Men" and "Bunko Steerers."* Chicago; G. L. Howe & Co., 1890.

______. *Gambling and Gambling Devices. Being a Complete Systematic Educational Exposition Designed to Instruct the Youth of the World to Avoid all Forms of Gambling.* Canton, Ohio; by the author, 1912.

Ralli, Paul. *Viva Vegas.* Hollywood, Cal.; House-Warven, 1953.

Regulations of the Nevada Gaming Commission and State Gaming Control Board. Carson City; State of Nevada, 1977.

Reese, Terrence and Watkins, Anthony T. *Secrets of Modern Poker.* New York; Sterling Publishing Co., 1964.

Rice, James. *History of the British Turf, From the Earliest Times to the Present Day.* London; Sampson Low, Marsten, Searle, and Rivington (2 vol), 1879.

Riddle, Major A. and Hyams, Joe. *The Weekend Gambler's Handbook.* New York; Random House Publishers, 1963.

Robert-Houdin. *Memoirs of Robert-Houdin, Ambassador, Author, and Conjuror.* [Title on cover: *Card Sharping Exposed.*] London; Chapman and Hall, 1860.

Robert-Houdin [Jean Eugene]. *Card Sharping Exposed.* Trans. Professor Hoffman. New York; George Routledge and Sons, 1882.

Robert-Houdin, Jean Eugene. *Card-sharpers: Their Tricks Exposed or the Art of Always Winning.* London; Spencer Blackett, 1860 (reprinted 1891).

Romain, James Harold. *Gambling: Or, Fortuna, Her Temple and Shrine. The True Philosophy and Ethics of Gambling.* Chicago: The Craig Press, 1891.

[Royal, H.W.] *Gambling and Confidence Games Exposed; Showing How the Proprietor of Gambling Houses and the Players can be Cheated; Giving the Introduction and Story of all Confidence Games; Exposing all Crooked Tools and Giving the Exact Per Cent. Of ALL Square Games, by Kid Royal—The Only Reformed Confidence-Man and Gambler that Exposes and Executes Confidence and Gambling Tricks.* Chicago, 1896.

Sanford, John. *Printer's Ink in My Blood.* Reno; University of Nevada Oral History Project, 1971.

Sarlat, Noah, ed. *Sintown, U.S.A.* New York; Prime, 1952.

Scarne, John. *Scarne on Dice.* Harrisburg, Pa; Stackpole Books, 1974.

Scarne, John. *Scarne's Complete Guide to Gambling.* New York; Simon and Schuster, 1961.

Schneider, Maxine. *Jackpot: To the Casino by Bus.* Las Vegas; Gambler's Book Club Press, 1977.

Sheinwold, Alfred. *First Book of Bridge.* New York; Barnes and Noble, 1952.

Silberstang, Edwin. *Winning Poker Strategy.* New York, David McKay Company, Inc., 1978.

Silverstone, Sidney M. *A Player's Guide to Casino Games.* New York; Grosset and Dunlap, 1981.

Singer, Samuel Weller. *Researches into the History of Playing Cards; with Illustrations of the Origin of Printing and Engraving on Wood.* London, 1816.

Sklansky, David. *Hold'em Poker.* Las Vegas; Gambler's Book Club, 1976.

Skolnick, Jerome H. *House of Cards: Legalization and Control of Casino Gambling.* Boston; Little, Brown and Co., 1978.

Smith, Harold S. and Noble, John Wesley. *I Want to Quit Winners.* Englewood Cliffs, N.J.; Prentice-Hall, 1961.

Smith, Jester. *Games They Play in San Francisco.* n.p., 1971.

Spencer, Edward. *The Great Game and How it is Played, A Treatise on the Turf, Full of Tales.* London, 1903.

Steig, Irwin. *Common Sense in Poker.* New York; Galahad Books, 1963.

Surveillance System Guidlines. Carson City, Nev.; Gaming Control Board Bulletin; March 20, 1979.

Taylor, Richard Blackburn. *Las Vegas, City of Sin?* San Antonio; Naylor Co., 1963.

Templar. *The Poker Manual: A Practical Course of Instruction in the Game, with Illustrative Hands and Chapters on Bluffing, and Jack-pots; Together with the International Code of Laws.* London, 1895.

Thackrey, Ted, Jr. *Gambling Secrets of Nick the Greek.* New York; Rand McNalley, 1968.

Today's Racing Digest. San Diego; Trade Service Publications, Inc. Thursday, July 29, 1982 (Del Mar Edition).

Toulmin, Alfred H. *Rogues and Vagabonds of the Racecourse; Full Explanations of How They Cheat at Roulette, Three-cards, Thimblerig, &c. And Some Account of the Welsher and Money-Tender in Connection with the Turf.* London, 1872(?).

Trebor, Eidrah. See Eidrah, Trebor.

"Trumps" [William Brisbane Dick]. *The American Hoyle, or Gentleman's Hand-book of Games.* New York; Dick & Fitzgerald, Publishers, (1864) Fifteenth edition [1902, 1868 and 1877 editions used].

______. *The Modern Pocket Hoyle; Containing all the Games of Skill and Chance as Played in this Country at the Present Time.* Ninth ed. New York, 1868.

Ullman, Joe. *What's the Odds? Funny, True and Clean Stories of the Turf.* New York, 1903.

Vainquear. *How to Play Monte Carlo Roulette and Trente et Quarante to Win at Every Seance; Marches, Systems and Improved Methods of Application with Golden Rules to be Observed under all Conditions of Play.* London, [1900]

Van Rensselaer, Mrs. John Ring. *The Devil's Picture Books: A History of Playing Cards.* London, 1892.

V. B. *Ten Days at Monte Carlo at the Bank's Expense; Containing Hints to Visitors and a General Guide to the Neighbourhood.* London, 1898.

______. *Monte Carlo Anecdotes and Systems of Play.* London, 1901.

Wallace, Frank R. *Poker: A Guaranteed Income for Life.* New York; Crown Publishers, Inc., 1968. (Rev. 1977).

Watson, Alfred E. T. *The Racing World and its Inhabitants.* London, 1904.

______. *The Turf.* London, 1898.

Wentworth, Harold and Flexner, Stuart Berg. *Dictionary of American Slang.* New York; Thomas Y. Crowell, Co., 1967.

White, E. *A Practical Treatise on the Game of Billiards; Accurately Exhibiting the Rules and Practice Admitted and Illustrated with a Numerous Collection of Cases Explanatory of Each of the Games, Calculations for Betting, Tables of Odds, &c. &c.* London, 1807.

Whyte, James Christie. *History of the British Turf, From the Earliest Period to the Present Day.* Two Volumes. London, 1840.

Wilson, Allan N. *The Casino Gambler's Guide.* New York; Harper & Row, 1965.

[Wilson, Ralph?]. *The Whole Art and Mystery of Modern Gaming; Fully Expos'd and Detected; Containing an Historical Account of All the Secret Abuses Practised in the Games of Chance.* London, 1726.

Wong, Stanford. *Professional Blackjack.* Las Vegas; Gambler's Book Club, 1975.

Woon, Basil Dillon. *The Why, How and Where of Gambling in Nevada.* Reno; Bonanza Publishing Co., 1953.

Wykes, Alan. *The Complete Illustrated Guide to Gambling.* Garden City, New York; Doubleday & Co., Inc., 1964.

Young, Ralph. *Oral Collection.* Las Vegas, 1982.